Java™ All-in-One Desk Reference For Dummies®

Cheat Sheet

Important Web Addresses

Sun's main Java Web site
java.sun.com

Java documentation
java.sun.com/docs

Java 1.5 API documentation
java.sun.com/j2se/1.5.0/docs/api/index.html

Jakarta Tomcat site
jakarta.apache.org/tomcat

TextPad
www.textpad.com

Eclipse
www.eclipse.org

Java Statements

The break statement
```
break;
```

The continue statement
```
continue;
```

The do statement
```
do
    {statements...}
while (expression);
```

The for statement
```
for (init; test; count)
    {statements...}
```

The enhanced for statement
```
for (type variable : array-or-
    collection)
    {statements...}
```

The if statement
```
if (expression)
    {statements...}
else
    {statements...}
```

The throw statement
```
throw (exception)
```

The switch statement
```
switch (expression)
{
    case constant:
        statements;
        break;
    default:
        statements;
        break;
}
while (expression)
    {statements...}
```

The try statement
```
try
    {statements...}
catch (exception-class e)
    {statements...}...
finally
    {statements...}

try
    {statements...}
finally
    {statements...}
```

Java™ All-in-One Desk Reference For Dummies®

Cheat Sheet

Primitive Data Types

Type	Wrapper Class	Parse Method of Wrapper Class
int	Integer	int parseInt (String s)
short	Short	short parseShort (String s)
long	Long	long parseLong (String s)
byte	Byte	byte parseByte (String s)
float	Float	float parseFloat (String s)
double	Double	double parseDouble (String s)
char	Char	(none)
boolean	Boolean	boolean parseBoolean (String s)

Favorite Classes and Methods

The Math class

num abs(num y);	Absolute value of y (num can be any numeric data type)
num max(num y, num z);	Maximum of y and z
num min(num y, num z);	Minimum of y and z
double = Math. random();	Random number — 0.0 < x <= 1.0

The NumberFormat class

NumberFormat getNumberInstance();	Gets an instance that formats numbers.
NumberFormat getCurrencyInstance();	Gets an instance that formats currency.
String format(x);	Formats the specified number.

Operators

Arithmetic

+	Addition
-	Subtraction
*	Multiplication
/	Division
%	Remainder
++	Increment
—	Decrement
+=	Addition and assignment
-=	Subtraction and assignment
*=	Multiplication and assignment
/=	Division and assignment
%=	Remainder and assignment

Relational

==	Equal
!=	Not equal
<	Less than
<=	Less than or equal
>	Greater than
>=	Greater than or equal

Logical

!	Not
&	And
&&	Conditional and
|	Or
||	Conditional or
^	xor

For Dummies: Bestselling Book Series for Beginners

Java™
ALL-IN-ONE DESK REFERENCE
FOR
DUMMIES®

by Doug Lowe

WILEY

Wiley Publishing, Inc.

Java™ All-in-One Desk Reference For Dummies®

Published by
Wiley Publishing, Inc.
111 River Street
Hoboken, NJ 07030-5774
www.wiley.com

WILEY

About the Author

Doug Lowe has been writing computer programming books since the guys who invented Java were still in high school. He's written books on COBOL, Fortran, Visual Basic, for IBM mainframe computers, mid-range systems, PCs, Web programming, and probably a few he's forgotten about. He's the author of more than 30 *For Dummies* books, such as *Networking For Dummies* (7th Edition), *Networking For Dummies All-in-One Desk Reference, PowerPoint 2003 For Dummies*, and *Internet Explorer 6 For Dummies*. He lives in that sunny All-American City Fresno, California, where the motto is, "It's a sunny, All-American City," with his wife and the youngest of his three daughters. He's also one of those obsessive-compulsive decorating nuts who puts up tens of thousands of lights at Christmas and creates computer-controlled Halloween decorations that rival Disney's Haunted Mansion. Maybe his next book should be *Tacky Holiday Decorations For Dummies*.

Dedication

To Debbie, Rebecca, Sarah, and Bethany.

Author's Acknowledgments

I'd like to thank project editor Kim Darosett, who did a great job of managing all the editorial work that was required to put this book together in spite of a short schedule and oft-missed deadlines, and acquisitions editor Katie Feltman who made the whole project possible. I'd also like to thank John Purdum who gave the entire manuscript a thorough technical review, tested every line of code, and offered many excellent suggestions, as well as copy editor Rebecca Senninger who made sure the i's were crossed and the t's were dotted (oops, reverse that!). And, as always, thanks to all the behind-the-scenes people who chipped in with help I'm not even aware of.

Publisher's Acknowledgments

We're proud of this book; please send us your comments through our online registration form located at www.dummies.com/register/.

Some of the people who helped bring this book to market include the following:

Acquisitions, Editorial, and Media Development

Project Editor: Kim Darosett

Acquisitions Editor: Katie Feltman

Copy Editor: Rebecca Senninger

Technical Editor: John Purdum

Editorial Manager: Leah Cameron

Media Development Manager: Laura VanWinkle

Media Development Supervisor: Richard Graves

Editorial Assistant: Amanda Foxworth

Cartoons: Rich Tennant (www.the5thwave.com)

Composition Services

Project Coordinator: Maridee Ennis

Layout and Graphics: Andrea Dahl, Lauren Goddard, Stephanie D. Jumper, Melanee Prendergast, Heather Ryan, Julie Trippetti

Proofreaders: John Greenough, Leeann Harney, Jessica Kramer, Arielle Mennelle, Carl Pierce

Indexer: Ty Koontz

Publishing and Editorial for Technology Dummies

Richard Swadley, Vice President and Executive Group Publisher

Andy Cummings, Vice President and Publisher

Mary Bednarek, Executive Acquisitions Director

Mary C. Corder, Editorial Director

Publishing for Consumer Dummies

Diane Graves Steele, Vice President and Publisher

Joyce Pepple, Acquisitions Director

Composition Services

Gerry Fahey, Vice President of Production Services

Debbie Stailey, Director of Composition Services

Contents at a Glance

Table of Contents

Book VII: Web Programming 603

Chapter 1: Creating Applets 605

Chapter 2: Creating Servlets 613

Chapter 3: Using Java Server Pages 633

Introduction

Welcome to *Java All-in-One Desk Reference For Dummies,* the one Java book that's designed to replace an entire shelf full of the dull and tedious Java books you'd otherwise have to buy. This book contains all the basic and not-so-basic information you need to know to get going with Java programming, starting with writing statements and using variables and ending with techniques for writing programs that use animation and play games. Along the way, you find information about programming user interfaces, working with classes and objects, creating Web applications, and dealing with files and databases.

You can, and probably should, eventually buy separate books on each of these topics. It won't take long before your bookshelf is bulging with 10,000 or more pages of detailed information about every imaginable nuance of Java programming. But before you're ready to tackle each of those topics in depth, you need to get a birds-eye picture. That's what this book is about.

And if you already own 10,000 pages or more of Java information, you may be overwhelmed by the amount of detail and wonder, do I really need to read 1,200 pages about JSP just to create a simple Web page? And do I really need a six-pound book on Swing? Truth is, most 1,200 page programming books have about 200 pages of really useful information — the kind you use every day — and about 1,000 pages of excruciating details that apply mostly if you're writing guidance control programs for nuclear missiles or trading systems for the New York Stock Exchange.

The basic idea here is that I've tried to wring out the 100 or so most useful pages of information on nine different Java programming topics: setup and configuration, basic programming, object-oriented programming, programming techniques, Swing, file and database programming, Web programming, and animation and game programming. Thus, a nice, trim 900 page book that's really nine 100 page books. (Well, they didn't all come out to 100 pages each. But close!)

So whether you're just getting started with Java programming or you're a seasoned pro, you've found the right book.

About This Book

Java All-in-One Desk Reference For Dummies is intended to be a reference for all the great things (and maybe a few not-so-great things) that you may need to know when you're writing Java programs. You can, of course, buy a huge 1,200-page book on each of the programming topics covered in this book. But then, who would carry them home from the bookstore for you? And where would you find the shelf space to store them? In this book, you get the information you need all conveniently packaged for you in between one set of covers.

This book doesn't pretend to be a comprehensive reference for every detail on these topics. Instead, it shows you how to get up and running fast so that you have more time to do the things you really want to do. Designed using the easy-to-follow *For Dummies* format, this book helps you get the information you need without laboring to find it.

Java All-in-One Desk Reference For Dummies is a big book made up of several smaller books — minibooks, if you will. Each of these minibooks covers the basics of one key element of programming, such as installing Java and compiling and running programs, or using basic Java statements, or using Swing to write GUI applications.

Whenever one big thing is made up of several smaller things, confusion is always a possibility. That's why this book is designed to have multiple access points to help you find what you want. At the beginning of the book is a detailed table of contents that covers the entire book. Then, each minibook begins with a minitable of contents that shows you at a miniglance what chapters are included in that minibook. Useful running heads appear at the top of each page to point out the topic discussed on that page. And handy thumbtabs run down the side of the pages to help you quickly find each minibook. Finally, a comprehensive index lets you find information anywhere in the entire book.

This isn't the kind of book you pick up and read from start to finish, as if it were a cheap novel. If I ever see you reading it at the beach, I'll kick sand in your face. This book is more like a reference, the kind of book you can pick up, turn to just about any page, and start reading. You don't have to memorize anything in this book. It's a "need-to-know" book: You pick it up when you need to know something. Need a reminder on the constructors for the `ArrayList` class? Pick up the book. Can't remember the goofy syntax for anonymous inner classes? Pick up the book. After you find what you need, put the book down and get on with your life.

How to Use This Book

This book works like a reference. Start with the topic you want to find out about. Look for it in the table of contents or in the index to get going. The table of contents is detailed enough that you can find most of the topics you're looking for. If not, turn to the index, where you can find even more detail.

Of course, the book is loaded with information, so if you want to take a brief excursion into your topic, you're more than welcome. If you want to know the big picture on inheritance, read the whole chapter on inheritance. But if you just want to know the rules for calling the superclass constructor, just read the section on inheritance and constructors.

Whenever I describe console output from a program or information that you see on-screen, I present it as follows:

```
A message from not-another-Hello-World program
```

If the program involves an interaction with the user, you see the text entered by the user in **bold type**.

How This Book Is Organized

Each of the nine minibooks contained in *Java All-in-One Desk Reference For Dummies* can stand alone. Here is a brief description of what you find in each minibook.

Book I: Java Basics

This minibook contains the information you need to get started with Java. After a brief introduction to what Java is and why it's so popular, you download Java and install it on your computer and use its command-line tools. Then, you use two popular development tools — TextPad and Eclipse — to create Java programs.

Book II: Programming Basics

This minibook covers all the basic details of programming with the Java language. I start with such basics as data types, variables, and statements, and then move on to expressions, conditional statements, looping statements, and methods. I end with a discussion of how to handle exceptions. You really need to know everything that's in this minibook to do any serious programming, so you'll probably spend a lot of time here if you're new to programming.

Book III: Object-Oriented Programming

This minibook goes deep into the details of object-oriented programming with Java. You create your own classes, as well as work with inheritance and polymorphism. You also get the scoop on abstract classes, interfaces, packages, inner classes, and even anonymous inner classes.

Book IV: Strings, Arrays, and Collections

This minibook focuses on working with strings, arrays, and collections. You find out all about Java's strange immutable strings as well as the `StringBuilder` and `StringBuffer` classes. You also create and work with arrays, and their collection counterparts including array lists and linked lists. Along the way, you find out about a cool new object-oriented programming feature called *generics,* which is designed to simplify the handling of arrays and collections.

Book V: Programming Techniques

In this minibook, you discover a variety of interesting and often useful programming techniques. For example, I include a chapter on working with threads so you can create programs that do more than one thing at a time. There's a chapter on using regular expressions that shows you how to do some amazing string handling. And there's a chapter on a programming technique called *recursion* that every programmer needs to feel comfortable with.

Book VI: Swing

Swing is the part of Java that lets you create graphical user interfaces. In this minibook, you find out all about Swing: how to create windows with controls like buttons, text fields, check boxes, drop-down lists, and so on; how to write programs that respond when the user clicks a button or types text; and how to control the layout of complicated forms.

Book VII: Web Programming

In this minibook, you use various Java features for creating Web applications. First, you turn Swing applications into applets that run in a user's browser. Then, you create full-blown Web applications using servlets and JSP.

Book VIII: File and Database Programming

The chapters in this minibook show you how to work with data stored on disk, whether it's in files, in a database, or in an XML file. You find chapters on working with files and directories, reading and writing data from streams, using Java's database interface (JDBC) to access databases, and using Java's XML features to read and write XML data.

Book IX: Fun and Games

This last minibook gets into some of the more interesting and fun aspects of Java programming. Specifically, you play with fonts and colors, draw pictures, work with images and media, and even create animations and write simple game programs.

This book's Web site

This book has an accompanying Web site (www.dummies.com/go/ javaaiofd) that includes even more goodies. If you're the kind of person who's always looking for a way to save time typing, the Web page includes all the code listings that are used in this book. And for those of you who are yearning for even more Java information, be sure to check out the three bonus chapters on the Web site: "Using the BigDecimal Class," "Twiddling Your Bits," and "Using Menus."

Icons Used in This Book

Like any *For Dummies* book, this book is chock-full of helpful icons that draw your attention to items of particular importance. You find the following icons throughout this book:

Pay special attention to this icon; it lets you know that some particularly useful tidbit is at hand.

Hold it — overly technical stuff is just around the corner. Obviously, because this is a programming book, almost every paragraph of the next 900 or so pages could get this icon. So I reserve it for those paragraphs that go in depth into explaining how something works under the covers — probably deeper than you really need to know to use a feature, but often enlightening.

You also sometimes find this icon when I want to illustrate a point with an example that uses some Java feature that hasn't been covered so far in the book, but that is covered later. In those cases, the icon is just a reminder that you shouldn't get bogged down in the details of the illustration, and instead focus on the larger point.

Danger, Will Robinson! This icon highlights information that may help you avert disaster.

Did I tell you about the memory course I took?

One of the recent hot topics among programming gurus is the notion of *design patterns,* which provide predictable ways to do common things. This icon appears alongside sidebars that describe such patterns.

Where to Go from Here

Yes, you can get there from here. With this book in hand, you're ready to plow right through the rugged Java terrain. Browse through the table of contents and decide where you want to start. Be bold! Be courageous! Be adventurous! And above all, have fun!

Book I

Java Basics

"I'm sure there will be a good job market when I graduate. I created a virus that will go off that year."

Contents at a Glance

Chapter 1: Welcome to Java

This chapter is a gentle introduction to the world of Java. In the next few pages, you find out what Java is, where it came from, and where it's going. You also discover some of the unique strengths of Java, as well as some of its weaknesses. And I also compare Java to the other popular programming languages, including C, C++, C#, and Visual Basic.

By the way, I assume in this chapter that you have at least enough background to know what computer programming is all about. That doesn't mean that I assume you're an expert or professional programmer. It just means that I don't take the time to explain such basics as what a computer program is, what a programming language is, and so on. If you have absolutely no programming experience, I suggest you pick up a copy of *Java 2 For Dummies*.

Throughout this chapter, you find little snippets of Java program code, plus a few snippets of code written in other languages like C, C++, or Basic. If you don't have a clue what this code means or does, don't panic. I just want to give you a feel for what Java programming looks like and how it compares to programming in other languages.

All the code listings that are used in this book are available for download at www.dummies.com/go/javaaiofd.

What Is Java, and Why Is It So Great?

Java is a programming language in the tradition of C and C++. As a result, if you have any experience with C or C++, you'll find yourself in familiar territory often as you learn the various features of Java. (For more information about the similarities and differences between Java and C or C++, see the section "Comparing Java to Other Languages" later in this chapter.)

However, Java differs from other programming languages in a couple of significant ways. The following sections describe the most important differences.

Platform independence

One of the main reasons Java is so popular is its *platform independence,* which means simply that Java programs can be run on many different types of computers. A Java program runs on any computer with a *Java Runtime Environment,* also known as a *JRE,* installed. A JRE is available for almost every type of computer you can think of, from PCs running any version of Windows, Macintosh computers, Unix or Linux computers, huge mainframe computers, and even cell phones.

Before Java, other programming languages promised platform independence by providing compatible compilers for different platforms. (A *compiler* is the program that translates programs written in a programming language into a form that can actually run on a computer.) The idea was that you could compile different versions of the programs for each platform. Unfortunately, this idea never really worked. The compilers were never completely identical on each platform — each had its own little nuances. As a result, you had to maintain a different version of your program for each platform you wanted to support.

Java's platform independence isn't based on providing compatible compilers for different platforms. Instead, Java is based on the concept of a *virtual machine.* You can think of the Java Virtual Machine (sometimes called the *JVM*) as a hypothetical computer platform — a design for a computer that doesn't really exist on any actual computer. Instead, the Java Runtime Environment is an emulator that creates a Java Virtual Machine environment that can execute Java programs.

The Java compiler doesn't translate Java into the machine language of the computer the program is run on. Instead, the compiler translates Java into the machine language of the Java Virtual Machine, which is called *bytecode.* Then the Java Runtime Environment runs the bytecode in the JVM. Because of the JVM, you can execute a Java program on any computer that has a Java Runtime Environment installed, without recompiling the program.

That's how Java provides platform independence, and believe it or not, it works pretty well. The programs you write run just as well on a PC running any version of Windows, a Macintosh, Unix or Linux, or any other computer with a JRE installed.

While you lay awake tonight pondering the significance of Java's platform independence, here are a few additional thoughts to ponder:

✦ The JRE is separate from the Java compiler. As a result, you don't have to install a Java compiler to run compiled Java programs. All you need is the JRE.

✦ When someone asks if your computer "has Java," they usually mean "have you installed the Java Runtime Environment" so that you can run Java programs.

✦ Platform independence only goes so far. If you have some obscure type of computer system, such as an antique Olivetti Programma 101, and a Java JRE isn't available for it, you can't run Java programs on it.

✦ If you're interested, the Java Virtual Machine is completely *stack oriented* — it has no registers for storing local data. I'm not going to explain what that means, so if it didn't make sense, skip it. It's not important. It's just interesting to nerds who know about stacks, registers, and things of that ilk.

✦ Java's platform independence isn't perfect. Although the bytecode runs identically on every computer that has a JRE, some parts of Java use services provided by the underlying operating system. As a result, sometimes minor variations crop up, especially with applications that use graphical interfaces.

✦ Because a runtime system that emulates a Java Virtual Machine executes Java bytecode, some people mistakenly compare Java to interpreted languages, such as Basic or Perl. However, those languages aren't compiled at all. Instead, the interpreter reads and interprets each statement as it is executed. Java is a true compiled language — it's just compiled to the machine language of JVM rather than the machine language of an actual computer platform.

✦ I didn't make up the Olivetti Programma 101. It was a desktop computer made in the early 1960s, and happened to be my introduction to computer programming. (My junior high school math teacher had one in the back of his classroom and let me play with it during lunch.) Do a Google search for "Olivetti Programma 101," and you can find several interesting Web sites about it.

Object orientation

Java is inherently *object-oriented*, which means that Java programs are made up from programming elements called *objects*. Simply put (don't you love it when you read that in a computer book?), an object is a programming entity that represents either some real-world object or an abstract concept.

All objects have two basic characteristics:

✦ Objects have data, also known as *state*. For example, an object that represents a book has data such as the book's title, author, and publisher.

✦ Objects also have *behavior,* which means that they can perform certain tasks. In Java, these tasks are called *methods*. For example, an object that represents a car might have methods such as start, stop, drive, or crash. Some methods simply allow you to access the object's data. For example, a book object might have a `getTitle` method that tells you the book's title.

Classes are closely related to objects. A class is the program code you write to create objects. The class describes the data and methods that define the object's state and behavior. Then, when the program executes, classes are used to create objects.

For example, suppose you're writing a payroll program. This program probably needs objects to represent the company's employees. So, the program includes a class (probably named `Employee`) that defines the data and methods for each `employee` object. Then, when your program runs, it uses this class to create an object for each of your company's employees.

The Java API

The Java language itself is very simple. However, Java comes with a library of classes that provide commonly used utility functions that most Java programs can't do without. This class library, called the *Java API*, is as much a part of Java as the language itself. In fact, the real challenge of learning how to use Java isn't learning the language; it's learning the API. The Java language has only 48 keywords, but the Java API has several thousand classes, with tens of thousands of methods you can use in your programs.

For example, the Java API has classes that let you do trigonometry, write data to files, create windows on-screen, or retrieve information from a database. Many of the classes in the API are general purpose and commonly used. For example, a whole series of classes stores collections of data. But many are obscure, used only in special situations.

Fortunately, you don't have to learn anywhere near all of the Java API. Most programmers are fluent with only a small portion of it — the portion that applies most directly to the types of programs they write. If you find a need to use some class from the API that you aren't yet familiar with, you can look up what the class does in the Java API documentation at `java.sun.com/docs`.

The Internet

Java is often associated with the Internet, and rightfully so. That's because Al Gore invented Java just a few days after he invented the Internet. Okay, Java wasn't really invented by Al Gore. But Java was developed during the time that the Internet's World Wide Web was becoming a phenomenon, and Java was specifically designed to take advantage of the Web. In particular, the whole concept behind the Java Virtual Machine is to allow any computer that's connected to the Internet to be able to run Java programs, regardless of the type of computer or the operating system it runs.

You can find two distinct types of Java programs on the Internet:

✦ **Applets,** which are Java programs that run directly within a Web browser. To run an applet, the browser starts a Java Virtual Machine, and that virtual machine is given a portion of the Web page to work with. Then the virtual machine runs the applet's bytecode.

Applets are a grand idea. However, marketing and legal battles between Microsoft and Sun have left applets in a precarious situation. The problem is that not all Web browsers provide a JVM, and those that do often provide an old version that isn't able to take advantage of the latest and greatest Java features.

✦ **Servlets,** which are Web-based Java programs that run on an Internet server computer rather than in an Internet user's Web browser. Servlets are how many, if not most, commercial Web sites work. Basically, a servlet is a program that generates a page of HTML that is then sent to a user's computer to be displayed in a Web browser. For example, if you request information about a product from an online store, the store's Web server runs a servlet to generate the HTML page that contains the product information you requested.

You find out how to create both types of applications in Book VII.

Comparing Java to Other Languages

Superficially, Java looks a lot like many of the programming languages that preceded it. For example, here's the classic Hello, World! program written in the C programming language:

```
main()
{
    Printf("Hello, world!");
}
```

This program simply displays the text `"Hello, World!"` on the computer's console. Here's the same program (almost) written in Java:

```
public class HelloApp
{
    public static void main(String[] args)
    {
        System.out.println("Hello, World!");
    }
}
```

Although the Java version is a bit more verbose, the two have several similarities:

✦ Both require that each executable statement end with a semicolon.

✦ Both use braces ({}) to mark blocks of code.

✦ Both use a routine called *main* as the main entry point for the program.

There are many other similarities besides these that aren't evident in this simple example.

However, these two trivial examples bring the major difference between C and Java front and center: Java is inherently object-oriented. Object-oriented programming rears its ugly head even in this simple example:

✦ In Java, even the simplest program is a class, so you have to provide a line that declares the name of the class. In this example, the class is named `HelloApp`. `HelloApp` has a method named `main`, which the Java Virtual Machine automatically calls when a program is run.

✦ In the C example, `printf` is a library function you call to print information to the console. In Java, you use the `PrintStream` class to write information to the console. `PrintStream`? There's no `PrintStream` in this program! Yes, there is. Every Java program has available to it a `PrintStream` object that writes information to the console. You can get this `PrintStream` object by calling the `out` method of another class, named `System`. Thus, `System.out` gets the `PrintStream` object that writes to the console. The `PrintStream` class, in turn, has a method named `println` that writes a line to the console. So `System.out.println` really does two things:

  • It uses the `out` field of the `System` class to get a `PrintStream` object.

  • Then it calls the `println` method of that object to write a line to the console.

  Confusing? You bet. It will all make sense when you read about object-oriented programming in Book III, Chapter 1.

✦ `void` looks familiar. Although it isn't shown in the C example, you could have coded `void` on the main function declaration to indicate that the main function doesn't return a value. `void` has the same meaning in Java. But static? What does that mean? That, too, is evidence of Java's object orientation. It's a bit early to explain what it means in this chapter, though, but you can find out in Book II, Chapter 7.

Important Features of the Java Language

If you believe the marketing hype put out by Sun and others, you'd think that Java is the best thing to happen to computers since the invention of memory. Java may not be *that* revolutionary, but Java does have many built-in features that set it apart from other languages (with the possible exception of Microsoft's C#, which is basically a rip-off of Java). The following sections describe just three of the many features that make Java so popular.

Type checking

All programming languages must deal in one way or the other with *type checking*. Type checking refers to how a language handles variables that store different types of data. For example, numbers, strings, and dates are commonly used data types available in most programming languages. Most programming languages also have several different types of numbers, such as integers and real numbers.

All languages must do type checking, so make sure that you don't try to do things that don't make sense, such as multiplying the gross national product by your last name. The question is, does the language require you to declare every variable's type so you can do type checking when it compiles your programs, or does the language do type checking only after it runs your program?

Some languages, such as Basic, do almost no type checking at compile time. For example, in Microsoft's Visual Basic for Applications (VBA), you can assign any type of data to a variable. Thus, the following statements are all allowed:

```
Let A = 5
Let A = "Strategery"
Let A = 3.14159
```

Here, three different types of data — integer, string, and decimal — have been assigned to the same variable. This flexibility is convenient, but comes with a price. For example, the following sequence is perfectly legal in VBA:

```
Let A = 5
Let B = "Strategery"
Let C = A * B
```

Here, an integer is assigned to variable A, and a string is assigned to variable B. Then the third statement attempts to multiply the string by the integer. You can't multiply strings, so the third statement fails.

Java, on the other hand, does complete type checking at run time. As a result, you must declare all variables as a particular type so the compiler can make sure you use the variables correctly. For example, the following bit of Java code won't compile:

```
int a = 5;
String b = "Strategery";
String c = a * b;
```

If you try to compile these lines, you get an error message saying that Java can't multiply an integer and a string.

In Java, every class you define creates a new type of data for the language to work with. Thus, the data types you have available to you in Java aren't just simple predefined types, such as numbers and strings. You can create your own types. For example, if you're writing a payroll system, you might create an `Employee` type. Then you can declare variables of type `Employee` that can only hold `Employee` objects. This prevents a lot of programming errors. For example, consider this code snippet:

```
Employee newHire;
newHire = 21;
```

This code creates a variable (`newHire`) that can hold only `Employee` objects. Then it tries to assign the number 21 to it. The Java compiler won't let you run this program because 21 is a number, not an employee.

An important object-oriented programming feature of Java called *inheritance* adds an interesting and incredibly useful twist to type checking. Inheritance is way too complicated to completely get into just yet, so I'll be brief here. In Java, you can create your own data types that are derived from other data types. For example, Employees are people. Customers are people too. So you might create a `Person` class and then create `Employee` and `Customer` classes that both inherit the `Person` class. Then you can write code like this:

```
Person p;
Employee e;
Customer c;
p = e;    // this is allowed because an Employee is also a Person.
c = e;    // this isn't allowed because an Employee is not a Customer.
```

Confused yet? If so, that's my fault. Inheritance is a pretty heady topic for Chapter 1 of a Java book. Don't panic if it makes no sense. It will all be clear by the time you finish reading Book III, Chapter 4, which covers all the subtle nuances of using inheritance.

Automatic memory management

Memory management is another detail that all programming languages have to deal with. All programming languages let you create variables. When you create a variable, the language assigns a portion of the computer's memory to store the data referred to by the variable. Exactly how this memory is allocated is a detail that you can usually safely ignore, no matter what language you're working with. But a detail that many languages do *not* let you safely ignore is what happens to that memory when you no longer need the data that was stored in it.

In C++ and similar languages, you had to write code that explicitly released that memory so that other programs could access it. If you didn't do this, or if you did it wrong, your program might develop a *memory leak*, which means that your program slowly but surely sucks memory away from other programs, until the operating system runs out of memory and your computer grinds to a halt.

In Java, you don't have to explicitly release memory when you're done with it. Instead, memory is freed up automatically when it is no longer needed. The Java Virtual Machine includes a special process called the *garbage collector* that snoops around the Virtual Machine's memory, determines when data is no longer being used, and automatically deletes that data and frees up the memory it occupied.

A feature related to garbage collection is *bounds checking*, which guarantees that programs can't access memory that doesn't belong to them. Languages such as C or C++ don't have this type of safety. As a result, programming errors in C or C++ can cause one program to trample over memory that's being used by another program. That, in turn, can cause your whole computer to crash.

Exception handling

As Robert Burns said, "The best laid schemes of mice and men gang oft agley, and leave us nought be grief and pain for promised joy." (Well, that's not exactly what he said, but pretty close.) When you tinker with computer programming, you'll quickly discover what he meant. No matter how carefully you plan and test your programs, errors happen. And when they do, they threaten to grind your whole program to a crashing halt.

Java has a unique approach to error handling that's superior to that found in any other language (except, as I've mention a few times, C# that just copies Java's approach). In Java, the Java Runtime Environment intercepts and folds errors of all types into a special type of object called an *exception object*. After all, Java is object-oriented through and through, so why shouldn't its exception handling features be object-oriented?

Java requires that any statements that can potentially cause an exception must be bracketed by code that can catch and handle the exception. In other words, you as the programmer must anticipate errors that can happen while your program is running, and make sure that those errors are properly dealt with. Although this feature can sometimes be annoying, the result is programs that are more reliable.

On the Downside: Java's Weaknesses

So far, I've been tooting Java's horn pretty loudly. Lest you think that learning Java is a walk in the park, the following paragraphs point out some of Java's shortcomings. Note that many of these drawbacks have to do with the API rather than the language itself:

✦ The API is way too big. It includes so many classes and methods, you'll never learn even half of them. And the sheer size of the Java API doesn't allow you to wander through it on your own, hoping to discover that one class that's perfect for the problem you're working on.

✦ The API is overdesigned. In some cases, it seems as if the Java designers go out of their way to make things that should be simple hard to use. For example, the API class that defines a multi-line text input area doesn't have a scroll bar. Instead, a separate class defines a panel that has a scroll bar. To create a multi-line text area with a scroll bar, you have to use both classes. That's fine if you ever want to create a text area that doesn't have a scroll bar, but you never will. Java's designers complicated the design of the text area and scroll panel classes to provide for a case that no one ever uses or would want to use.

✦ Some corners of the API are haphazardly designed. Most of the problems can be traced back to the initial version of Java, which was rushed to market so it could ride the crest of the World Wide Web explosion in the late 1990s. Since then, many parts of the API have been retooled more thoughtfully. But the API is still riddled with remnants of Java's early days.

✦ As long as Microsoft and Sun don't get along, Windows computers with Internet Explorer will have problems running Java applications. These problems are easily solved by going to the Sun Web site and downloading the latest version of the Java Runtime Environment, but that requires extra effort that, in an ideal world, you shouldn't have to deal with. Sigh. Maybe one of these days there will be peace.

✦ In my opinion, the biggest weakness of Java is that it doesn't directly support true decimal data. This issue is a little too complicated to get into right now, but the implication is this: Without special coding (which few Java books explain), Java doesn't know how to add. For example, consider this bit of code:

```
double x = 5.02;
double y = 0.01;
double z = x + y;
System.out.println(z);
```

This little program should print 5.03, right? It doesn't. Instead, it prints 5.029999999999999. This little error may not seem like much, but it can add up. If you ever make a purchase from an online store and notice that the sales tax is a penny off, this is why. The explanation for why these errors happen and how to prevent them is pretty technical, but it's something every Java programmer needs to understand. You can find all the gory details in Bonus Chapter 1 on this book's Web site.

Java Version Insanity

Like most products, Java gets periodic upgrades and enhancements. Since its initial release in 1996, Java has undergone the following version updates:

✦ **Java 1.0:** The original release of Java in 1996. Most of the language itself is still pretty much the same as it was in version 1.0, but the API has changed a lot since this release.

✦ **Java 1.1:** This version was the first upgrade to Java, released in 1997. This release is important because most Internet browsers include built-in support for applets based on Java 1.1. To run applets based on later versions of Java, you must, in most cases, download and install a current JRE.

✦ **Java 1.2:** This version, released in late 1998, was a huge improvement over the previous version. So much so, in fact, that Sun called it "Java 2." It included an entirely new API called Swing for creating graphical user interfaces, as well as other major features.

✦ **Java 1.3:** This version, released in 2000, was mostly about improving performance by changing the way the runtime system works. Interestingly, Java 1.3 is actually called Java 2 version 1.3. Go figure.

✦ **Java 1.4:** Released in 2001, this version offered a slew of improvements. As you might guess, it is called Java 2 version 1.4. Keep figuring. . . .

✦ **Java 1.5:** Released in 2004, this version of Java is the latest and greatest. To add to Sun's apparent unpredictability with its version numbering, this version officially has two version numbers. Sun's official Java Web site explains it like this:

> "Both version numbers "1.5.0" and "5.0" are used to identify this release of the Java 2 Platform Standard Edition. Version "5.0" is the *product version*, while "1.5.0" is the *developer version*."

That clears it right up, doesn't it? Personally, I think someone at Sun has been talking to George Lucas. I fully expect the next version of Java to be a prequel, called Java 2 Episode 1.

Anyway, throughout this book I use the version numbers 1.5 and 5.0 interchangeably to mean the current version. (Of course, Sun isn't finished with Java, so there will probably one day be a version 1.6 or 6.0 or whatever.)

You may need to be aware of version differences if you're writing applications that you want to be able to run on earlier versions of Java. Bear in mind, however, that one of the chief benefits of Java is that the runtime system is free and can be easily downloaded and installed by end users. As a result, you shouldn't hesitate to use the features of Java 1.5 when you need them.

What's in a Name?

The final topic I want to cover in this chapter is the names of the various pieces that make up Java's technology — specifically, the acronyms you constantly come across whenever you read or talk about Java, such as JVM, JRE, JDK, J2EE, and so on. Here they are, in no particular order of importance:

✦ **JDK:** The *Java Development Kit* — that is, the toolkit for developers that includes the Java compiler and the runtime environment. To write Java programs, you need the JDK. This term was used with the original versions of Java (1.0 and 1.1) and abandoned with version 1.2 in favor of *SDK*. But with version 5.0, the term JDK is officially back in vogue.

✦ **SDK:** The *Software Development Kit* — what Sun called the JDK for versions 1.2, 1.3, and 1.4.

✦ **JRE:** The *Java Runtime Environment* — the program that emulates the JVM, so that users can run Java programs. To run Java programs, you need only download and install the JRE.

✦ **JVM:** The *Java Virtual Machine* — the platform-independent machine that is emulated by the JRE. All Java programs run in a JVM.

✦ **J2SE:** *Java 2 Standard Edition* — a term that describes the Java language and the basic set of API libraries that are used to create Windows and applet applications. Most of this book focuses on J2SE.

✦ **J2EE:** *Java 2 Enterprise Edition* — an expanded set of API libraries that provide special functions, such as servlets.

Chapter 2: Installing and Using Java Tools

In This Chapter

↳ **Downloading Java from the Sun Web site**

↳ **Installing Java**

↳ **Using Java's command-line tools**

↳ **Getting help**

*J*ava development environments have two basic approaches. On the one hand, you can use a sophisticated Integrated Development Environment (IDE) such as Sun's Forte for Java or Inprise's JBuilder. These tools combine a full-featured source editor that lets you edit your Java program files with integrated development tools, including visual development tools that let you create applications by dragging and dropping visual components onto a design surface.

At the other extreme, you can use just the basic command-line tools that are available free from Sun's Java Web site (java.sun.com). Then you can use any text editor you wish to create the text files that contain your Java programs (called *source files*), and compile and run your programs by typing commands at a command prompt.

As a compromise, you may want to use a simple development environment, such as TextPad or Eclipse. TextPad is an inexpensive Java tool that provides some nice features for editing Java programs (such as automatic indentation) and shortcuts for compiling and running programs. However, it doesn't generate any code for you or provide any type of visual design aids. TextPad is the tool I used to develop all the examples shown in this book. For information about downloading and using TextPad, refer to Book I, Chapter 3. Eclipse is an open-source free development environment that's gaining popularity. I describe it in Book I, Chapter 4.

Downloading and Installing the Java Development Kit

Before you can start writing Java programs, you have to download and install the correct version of the Java Development Kit (JDK) for the computer system you're using. Sun's Java Web site provides versions for Windows, Solaris, and Unix. The following sections show you how to download and install the JDK.

Downloading the JDK

To get to the download page, point your browser to: `java.sun.com/j2se/1.5.0/download.jsp`. Then follow the appropriate links to download the J2SE 5.0 JDK for your operating system.

At the time I wrote this, a menu of popular downloads is on the right side of Java's home page at `java.sun.com`. At the top of that menu is a link to the download site for the current version of Java. So, if you don't want to type the entire link, you can just go to `java.sun.com` and then use the popular downloads links to get to the download page.

When you get to the Java download page, you find links to download the JDK or the JRE. Follow the JDK link; the JRE link gets you only the Java Runtime Environment, not the complete Java Development Kit.

The JDK download comes in two versions: an online version that requires an active Internet connection to install the JDK, and an offline version that lets you download the JDK installation file to your disk, then install it later. I recommend you use the offload version. That way, you can reinstall the JDK if you need to without downloading it again.

The exact size of the offline version depends on the platform, but they're all between 40MB and 50MB. As a result, the download takes a few hours if you don't have a high-speed Internet connection. With a cable, DSL, or T1 connection, the download takes less than five minutes.

Legal mumbo jumbo

Before you can download the JDK, you have to approve of the Java license agreement, all 2,393 words of it including the thereupons, whereases, and hithertos all finely crafted by Sun's legal department. I'm not a lawyer (and I don't play one on TV), but I'll try to summarize the license agreement for you:

✔ Sun grants you the right to use Java as-is and doesn't promise that it will do anything at all.

✔ The party of the second part (you) in turn promise to use Java only to write programs. You're not allowed to try to figure out how Java works and sell your secrets to Microsoft.

✔ You can't use Java to run a nuclear power plant. (I'm not making that up. It's actually in the license agreement.)

Installing the JDK

After you download the JDK file, you can install it by running the executable file you downloaded. The procedure varies slightly depending on your operating system, but basically you just run the JDK installation program file after you download it:

+ On a Windows system, open the folder you saved the installation program to and double-click the installation program's icon.

+ For a Linux or Solaris system, use console commands to change to the directory you downloaded the file to, and then run the program.

After you start the installation program, it asks any questions it needs to know to properly install the JDK. You're prompted for information such as which features you want to install and what folder you want to install the JDK to. You can safely choose the default answers for each of the options.

Perusing the JDK folders

When the JDK installs, it creates several folders on your hard drive. The location of these folders vary depending on your system, but in most cases the JDK root folder is found under `Program Files\Java` on your boot drive. The name of the JDK root folder also varies, depending on the exact Java version you've installed. For version 1.5, the root folder is named `jdk1.5.0`.

Table 2-1 lists the subfolders created in the JDK root folder. As you work with Java, you'll frequently refer to these folders.

Table 2-1	Folders in the JDK Root Folder
Folder	*Description*
bin	The compiler and other Java development tools.
demo	Demo programs you can study to learn how to use various Java features.
docs	The Java API documentation. (For instructions on how to create this folder, see the section "Using Java Documentation" later in this chapter.)
include	This library contains files needed to integrate Java with programs written in other languages.
jre	The runtime environment files.
lib	Library files, including the Java API class library.
src	The source code for the Java API classes. This folder is only created if you unpack the `src.zip` file (this file may be named `src.jar`). After you get your feet wet with Java, looking at these source files can be a great way to learn more about how the API classes work.

In addition to these folders, the JDK installs several files into the JDK root folder. I list these files in Table 2-2.

Table 2-2	Files in the JDK Root Folder
File	*Description*
README.html	The Java readme file in HTML format.
README.txt	The readme file again, this time in text format.
LICENSE	The Java license that you agreed to when you downloaded the JDK, on the outside chance you enjoyed it so much the first time you want to read it again. (If you work for Microsoft, you probably *should* read it again, at least twice.)
LICENSE.rtf	The license file once again, this time in RTF format. (RTF is a document format that can be understood by most word processing programs.)
COPYRIGHT	Most companies are happy to just say © 2004 Sun Microsystems, Inc. at the bottom of the `readme` file or in the `license` file. But not Sun. It puts the copyright notice in a separate text file, along with information about all the copyright and export laws that apply.

I guess the Java license you have to agree to at least twice — once when you download the JDK, and again when you install it — isn't clear enough about what you're not allowed to use Java for. The license says you can't use it for nuclear power applications. But the copyright notice (in the COPYRIGHT file) also prohibits you from using it in missile systems or chemical or biological weapons systems. If you work for the Defense Department, you'd better read the copyright notice!

Setting the path

After you install the JDK, you need to configure your operating system so that it can find the JDK command-line tools. To do that, you must set the Path environment variable. This variable is a list of folders that the operating system uses to locate executable programs. To do this on Windows XP, follow these steps:

1. **Open the Control Panel and double-click the System icon.**

The System Properties dialog box comes up.

2. **Click the Advanced tab, and then click the Environment Variables button.**

The Environment Variables dialog box, as shown in Figure 2-1, appears.

3. **In the System Variables list, select Path, and then click the Edit button.**

A little dialog box comes up to let you edit the value of the Path variable.

4. **Add the JDK bin folder to the beginning of the path value.**

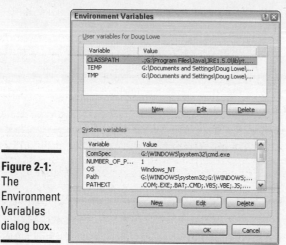

Figure 2-1:
The
Environment
Variables
dialog box.

Use a semicolon to separate the bin folder from the rest of the information that may already be in the path. *Note:* The exact name of the bin
folder may vary on your system. For example:

```
c:\Program Files\Java\jdk1.5.0\bin;other
    directories...
```

5. **Click OK three times to exit.**

The first OK gets you back to the Environment Variables dialog box. The
second OK gets you back to the System Properties dialog box. And the
third OK closes the System Properties dialog box.

For earlier versions of Windows (such as ancient Windows 98 or Me), you set
the path by adding a Path statement to the AutoExec.bat file in the root
directory of your C drive. For example:

```
path c:\Program Files\Java\jdk1.5.0\bin;other
    directories...
```

For Linux or Solaris, the procedure depends on which shell you're using.
Consult the documentation for the shell you're using for more information.

Using Java's Command-Line Tools

Java comes with several command-line tools you can run directly from a command prompt. The two most important are javac, the Java compiler used to
compile a program, and java, the runtime used to run a Java program. These
tools work essentially the same no matter what operating system you're
using. The examples in this section are all for Windows XP.

Compiling a program

You can compile a program from a command prompt by using the `javac` command. Before you can do that, however, you need a program to compile. Using any text editor, type the following text into a file and save it as `HelloApp.java`:

```
public class HelloApp
{
    public static void main(String[] args)
    {
        System.out.println("Hello, World!");
    }
}
```

Save the file in any directory you wish. Pay special attention to capitalization. For example, if you type `Public` instead of `public`, the program won't work. (If you don't want to bother with the typing, you can download the sample programs from this book's Web site.)

Open a command prompt and use a `cd` command to change to the directory you saved the program file in. Then enter the command `javac HelloApp.java`. This command compiles the program (`javac`) and creates a class file named `HelloApp.class`.

Assuming you typed the program exactly right, the `javac` command doesn't display any messages at all. If the program contains any errors, one or more error messages display. For example, if you type `Public` instead of `public`, the compiler displays the following error message:

```
C:\java\samples>javac HelloApp.java
HelloApp.java:1: 'class' or 'interface' expected
Public class HelloApp
^
1 error

C:\java\samples>
```

The compiler error message indicates that an error is in line 1 of the `HelloApp.java` file. If the compiler reports an error message like this one, your program contains a coding mistake. You need to find the mistake, correct it, and then compile the program again.

Compiling more than one file

Normally, the `javac` command compiles just the file that you specify on the command line. However, you can coax `javac` into compiling more than one file at once by using any of the techniques I describe in the following paragraphs:

✦ If the Java file you specify on the command line contains a reference to another Java class that's defined by a `java` file in the same folder, the Java compiler automatically compiles that class too.

For example, suppose you have a `java` program named `TestProgram`, and that program refers to a class called `TestClass`, and the `Test Class.java` file is located in the same folder as the `TestProgram. java` file. Then, when you use the `javac` command to compile the `TestProgram.java` file, the compiler automatically compiles the `TestClass.java` file, too.

✦ You can list more than one filename on the `javac` command. For example, the following command compiles three files:

```
javac TestProgram1.java TestProgram2.java
    TestProgram3.java
```

✦ You can use a wildcard to compile all the files in a folder, like this:

```
javac *.java
```

✦ If you need to compile a lot of files at once, but don't want to use a wild-card (perhaps you want to compile a large number of files, but not all the files in a folder), you can create an *argument file* that lists the files to com-pile. In the argument file, you can type as many filenames as you want. You can use spaces or line breaks to separate the files. For example, here's an argument file named `TestPrograms` that lists three files to compile:

```
TestProgram1.java
TestProgram2.java
TestProgram3.java
```

Then, you can compile all the programs in this file by using an @ charac-ter followed by the name of the argument file on the `javac` command line, like this:

```
javac @TestPrograms
```

Using Java compiler options

The `javac` command has a gaggle of options you can use to influence the way it compiles your programs. For your reference, I list these options in Table 2-3. To use one or more of these options, type the option either before or after the source filename. For example, either of the following commands compile the `HelloApp.java` file with the `-verbose` and `-deprecation` options enabled:

```
javac HelloWorld.java -verbose -deprecation
javac -verbose -deprecation HelloWorld.java
```

Don't get all discombobulated if you don't understand what all these options do. Most of them are useful only in unusual situations. The options you'll use the most are

✦ **-classpath** or **-cp:** Use this option if your program makes use of class files that you've stored in a separate folder.

✦ **-deprecation:** Use this option if you want the compiler to warn you whenever you use API methods that have been *deprecated*. (Deprecated methods are older methods that were once a part of the Java standard API but are now on the road to obsolescence. They still work, but may not in future versions of Java.)

✦ **-source:** Use this option to limit the compiler to previous versions of Java. Note, however, that this option only applies to features of the Java language itself, not to the API class libraries. For example, if you specify -source 1.4, the compiler won't allow you to use new Java language features that were introduced with Java 1.5, such as generics or enhanced for loops. However, you can still use the new API features that were added with version 1.5, such as the Scanner class.

✦ **-help:** Use this option to list the options that are available for the javac command.

Table 2-3	Java Compiler Options
Option	*Description*
-g	Generate all debugging info
-g:none	Generate no debugging info
-g:{lines,vars,source}	Generate only some debugging info
-nowarn	Generate no warnings
-verbose	Output messages about what the compiler is doing
-deprecation	Output source locations where deprecated APIs are used
-classpath <path>	Specify where to find user class files
-cp <path>	Specify where to find user class files
-sourcepath <path>	Specify where to find input source files
-bootclasspath <path>	Override location of bootstrap class files
-extdirs <dirs>	Override location of installed extensions
-endorseddirs <dirs>	Override location of endorsed standards path
-d <directory>	Specify where to place generated class files
-encoding <encoding>	Specify character encoding used by source files
-source <release>	Provide source compatibility with specified release
-target <release>	Generate class files for specific VM version
-version	Version information
-help	Print a synopsis of standard options
-X	Print a synopsis of nonstandard options
-J<flag>	Pass <flag> directly to the runtime system

Running a Java program

When you successfully compile a Java program, you can then run the program by typing the `java` command followed by the name of the class that contains the program's `main` method. The Java Runtime Environment loads, along with the class you specify, and then runs the `main` method in that class. For example, to run the `HelloApp` program, type this command:

```
C:\java\samples>java HelloApp
```

The program responds by displaying the message `"Hello, World!"`.

The class must be contained in a file with the same name as the class and the extension `.class`. You don't usually have to worry about the name of the class file because it's created automatically when you compile the program with the `javac` command. Thus, if you compile a program in a file named `HelloApp.java`, the compiler creates a class named `HelloApp` and saves it in a file named `HelloApp.class`.

If Java can't find a filename that corresponds to the class, you get a simple error message indicating that the class can't be found. For example, here's what you get if you type `JelloApp` instead of `HelloApp`:

```
C:\java\samples>java JelloApp
Exception in thread "main"
    java.lang.NoClassDefFoundError: JelloApp
```

This error message simply means that Java couldn't find a class named `JelloApp`.

However, if you get the class name right but capitalize it incorrectly, you get a slew of error messages. Ponder this example:

```
C:\java\samples>java helloapp
Exception in thread "main" java.lang.
  NoClassDefFoundError: helloapp (wrong name:
  HelloApp)
   at java.lang.ClassLoader.defineClass1(Native Method)
   at java.lang.ClassLoader.defineClass(ClassLoader.
java:620)
   at java.security.SecureClassLoader.defineClass
       (SecureClassLoader.java:124)
   at java.net.URLClassLoader.defineClass
       (URLClassLoader.java:260)
   at java.net.URLClassLoader.access$100
       (URLClassLoader.java:56)
   at java.net.URLClassLoader$1.run
       (URLClassLoader.java:195)
```

```
      at java.security.AccessController.doPrivileged
         (Native Method)
      at java.net.URLClassLoader.findClass
         (URLClassLoader.java:188)
      at java.lang.ClassLoader.loadClass
         (ClassLoader.java:306)
      at sun.misc.Launcher$AppClassLoader.loadClass
         (Launcher.java:268)
      at java.lang.ClassLoader.loadClass
         (ClassLoader.java:251)
      at java.lang.ClassLoader.loadClassInternal
         (ClassLoader.java:319)
```

Wow, that's a pretty serious looking set of error messages considering that
the only problem is that I forgot to capitalize `HelloApp`. Java isn't just case
sensitive, it's *very* case sensitive.

Like the Java compiler, the Java runtime lets you specify options that can
influence its behavior. Table 2-4 lists the most commonly used options.

Table 2-4	Commonly Used Java Command Options
Option	*Description*
`-client`	Runs the client VM.
`-server`	Runs the server VM, which is optimized for server systems.
`-classpath` *directories and archives*	A list of directories or JAR or Zip archive files used to search for class files.
`-cp <search path>`	Same as `-classpath`.
`-D` *name=value*	Sets a system property.
`-verbose`	Enables verbose output.
`-version`	Displays the JRE version number, then stops.
`-showversion`	Displays the JRE version number, then continues.
`-?` or `-help`	Lists the standard options.
`-X`	Lists nonstandard options.
`-ea` or `-enableassertions`	Enables the `assert` command.
`-ea` *classes or packages*	Enables assertions for the specified classes or packages.
`-esa` or `-enablesystemassertions`	Enables system assertions.
`-dsa` or `-disablesystemassertions`	Disables system assertions.

Using the javap command

The `javap` command is called the Java *disassembler* because it takes apart class files and tells you what's inside them. It's not a command you'll use often, but using it to find out how a particular Java statement works is sometimes fun. You can also use it to find out what methods are available for a class if you don't have the source code that was used to create the class.

For example, here's the information you get when you run the `javap` `HelloApp` command:

```
C:\java\samples>javap HelloApp
Compiled from "HelloApp.java"
public class HelloApp extends java.lang.Object{
    public HelloApp();
    public static void main(java.lang.String[]);
}
```

As you can see, the `javap` command indicates that the `HelloApp` class was compiled from the `HelloApp.java` file and that it consists of a `HelloApp` public class and a `main` public method.

You may want to use two options with the `javap` command. If you use the `-c` option, the `javap` command displays the actual Java bytecodes created by the compiler for the class. And if you use the `-verbose` option, the bytecodes plus a ton of other fascinating information about the innards of the class are displayed. For example, here's the `-c` output for the `HelloApp` class:

```
C:\java\samples>javap HelloApp -c
Compiled from "HelloApp.java"
public class HelloApp extends java.lang.Object{
public HelloApp();
  Code:
   0:   aload_0
   1:   invokespecial   #1; //Method
java/lang/Object."<init>":()V
   4:   return

public static void main(java.lang.String[]);
  Code:
   0:   getstatic       #2; //Field
java/lang/System.out:Ljava/io/PrintStream;
   3:   ldc      #3; //String Hello, World!
   5:   invokevirtual   #4; //Method
java/io/PrintStream.println:(Ljava/lang/String;)V
   8:   return

}
```

If you become a big-time Java guru, you can use this type of information to find out exactly how certain Java features work. Until then, you should probably leave the `javap` command alone, except for those rare occasions when you want to impress your friends with your in-depth knowledge of Java. (Just hope that when you do, they don't ask you what the aload or invokevirtual instruction does.)

Other Java command-line tools

Java has many other command-line tools that might come in handy from time to time. You can find a complete list of command-line tools at the following Web site:

`java.sun.com/j2se/1.5.0/docs/tooldocs/index.html#basic`

I describe three of these additional tools elsewhere in this book:

✦ **applet viewer:** Runs a Web applet application. For more information, see Book VII, Chapter 1.

✦ **javadoc:** Automatically creates HTML documentation for your Java classes. For more information, see Book III, Chapter 8.

✦ **jar:** Creates Java archive files, which store classes in a compressed file similar to a Zip file. I cover this command in Book III, Chapter 8.

Using Java Documentation

You won't get very far learning Java before you find yourself wondering if some class has some other method that I don't describe in this book, or if some other class may be more appropriate for an application you're working on. When that time comes, you'll need to consult the Java help pages.

Complete documentation for Java is available from the Sun Java Web site at `java.sun.com/docs`. Although this page contains many links to documentation pages, the two you'll use the most are the JS2E API documentation pages and the Java Language Specification pages. The following sections describe these two links.

If you don't have a reliable high-speed Internet connection, you can download Java's documentation by using the download links on the main `java.sun.com/docs` page. Then, you can access the documentation pages directly from your computer.

JS2E API Docs

The links under the Java 2 SDK, Standard Edition, Documentation heading take you to the complete documentation for all currently supported versions of the Java API, in English as well as Japanese. Figure 2-2 shows the English JS2E API documentation page.

You can use this page to find complete information for any class in the API. By default, all the Java classes are listed in the frame that appears at the bottom left of the page. You can limit this display to just the classes in a particular package by selecting the package from the menu at the upper-left side of the page. (If you don't know what a package is, don't worry. You find out about packages in Book I, Chapter 4.)

Click the class you're looking for in the class list to call up its documentation page. For example, Figure 2-3 shows the documentation page for the `String` class. If you scroll down this page, you find complete information about everything you can do with this class, including an in-depth discussion of what the class does, a list of the various methods it provides, and a detailed description of what each method does. In addition, you also find links to other classes that are similar.

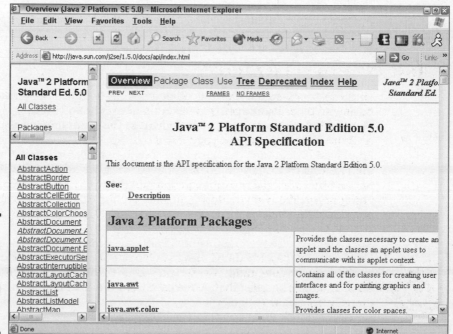

Figure 2-2:
The documentation page for JS2E API 5.0 (English version).

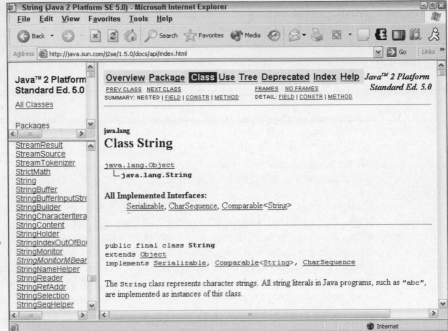

Figure 2-3:
The documentation page for the String class.

Java Language Specification

If you're interested in learning details about some element of the Java language itself rather than the information about a class in the API class library, click the Java Language Specification link near the bottom of the page. That takes you to a set of pages that describe in sometimes excruciating and obscure detail exactly how each element of the Java language works.

Frankly, this documentation isn't that much help for beginning programmers. It was written by computer scientists for computer scientists. You can tell just by looking at the table of contents that it isn't for novices. The first chapter is called Introduction (that's not so bad), but then Chapters 2 and 3 are titled "Grammars" and "Lexical Structure."

That's why you're reading this book, after all. You won't even find a single sentence about Lexical Structure in this book (other than this one, of course). Even so, at some time in your Java journeys you may want to get to the bottom of the rules that govern strange Java features, such as anonymous inner classes. When that day arrives, grab a six pack of Jolt Cola, roll up your sleeves, and open the Java Language Specification pages.

Chapter 3: Working with TextPad

In This Chapter

✓ **Downloading and installing TextPad**

✓ **Using TextPad to edit source files**

✓ **Compiling Java programs**

✓ **Running Java programs**

*T*extPad is an inexpensive ($29) text editor that you can integrate with the Java SDK to simplify the task of coding, compiling, and running Java programs. It isn't a true Integrated Development Environment (IDE), as it lacks features such as integrated debugging, code generators, or drag-and-drop tools for creating graphical user interfaces. If you want to work with an IDE, I suggest you skip this chapter and instead look to Book I, Chapter 4, which covers a free IDE called Eclipse.

TextPad is a popular tool for developing Java programs because of its simplicity and speed. It's ideal for learning Java because it doesn't generate any code for you. Writing every line of code yourself may seem like a bother, but the exercise pays off in the long run because you have a better understanding of how Java works.

Downloading and Installing TextPad

You can download a free evaluation version of TextPad from Helios Software Systems at `www.textpad.com`. You can use the evaluation version free of charge, but if you decide to keep the program, you must pay for it. Helios accepts credit card payment online.

If the Java SDK is already installed on your computer when you install TextPad, TextPad automatically configures itself to compile and run Java programs. If you install the SDK after you install TextPad, you need to configure TextPad for Java. Follow these steps:

1. **Choose Configure⇨Preferences.**

2. **Click Tools in the tree that appears at the left of the Preferences dialog box.**

3. **Click the Add button to reveal a drop-down list of options, and then click Java SDK Commands.**

Figure 3-1 shows how the Preferences dialog box appears when the Java tools are installed. As you can see, the Tools item in the tree at the left of the dialog box includes three Java tools: Compile Java, Run Java Application, and Run Java Applet.

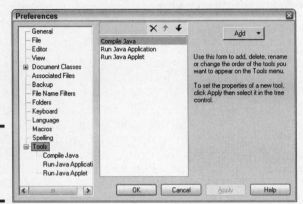

Figure 3-1:
Configuring
tools in
TextPad.

4. **Click OK.**

The commands to compile and run Java programs are added to TextPad's Tools menu.

Editing Source Files

Figure 3-2 shows TextPad editing a Java source file. If you've worked with a Windows text editor before, you'll have no trouble learning the basics of using TextPad. I won't go over such basic procedures as opening and saving files because they're standard. Instead, the following paragraphs describe some of TextPad's features that are useful for editing Java program files.

When you first create a file (by clicking the New button on the toolbar or by choosing File⇨New), TextPad treats the file as a normal text file, not as a Java program file. After you save the file (click the Save button or choose File⇨Save) and assign `java` as the file extension, TextPad's Java editing features kick in.

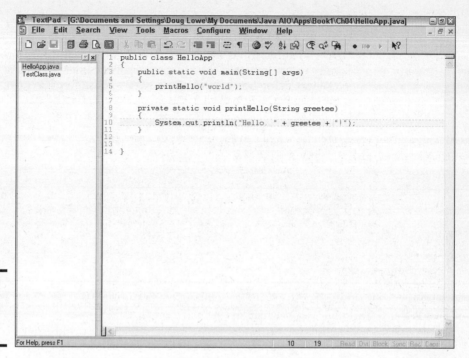

Figure 3-2:
Editing a
Java file in
TextPad.

The following paragraphs describe some of TextPad's more noteworthy features for working with Java files:

✦ You can't really tell from Figure 3-2, but TextPad uses different colors to indicate the function of each word or symbol in the program. Brackets are red so you spot them quickly and make sure they're paired correctly. Keywords are blue. Comments and string literals are green. Other text, such as variable or method names, are black.

✦ TextPad automatically indents whenever you type an opening bracket, and then reverts to the previous indent when you type a closing bracket. Keeping your code lined up is easy.

✦ Line numbers display down the left edge of the editing window. You can turn these line numbers on or off by choosing View➪Line Numbers.

✦ To go to a particular line, press Ctrl+G to bring up the Go To dialog box. Make sure Line is selected in the Go to What box, enter the line number in the text box, and click OK.

✦ If you have more than one file open, you can switch between the files by using the Document Selector, the pane on the left side of the TextPad window. If the Document Selector isn't visible, choose View➪Document Selector to summon it.

Using workspaces

In TextPad, a *workspace* is a collection of files that you work on together. Workspaces are useful for projects that involve more than just one file. When you open a workspace, TextPad opens all the files in the workspace. And you can configure TextPad to automatically open the last workspace you were working on whenever TextPad starts.

To create a workspace, first open all the files that you want to be a part of the workspace. Then, choose File⇨Workspace⇨Save As and give a name to the workspace. (The list of files that make up the workspace is saved in a file with the `tws` extension.)

To open a workspace, choose File⇨Workspace⇨Open. Then, select the workspace file you previously saved and click Open. Or, choose the workspace from the list of recently used workspaces that appears at the bottom of the File⇨Workspace menu.

To configure TextPad to automatically open the most recently used workspace whenever you start TextPad, choose Configure⇨Preferences. Click General in the preferences tree at the left of the dialog box, and then check the Reload Last Workspace at Startup option and click OK to close the Preferences dialog box.

✦ Another way to switch between multiple files is to choose View⇨Document Tabs. The tabs at the bottom of the document window display. You can click these tabs to switch documents.

✦ A handy Match Bracket feature lets you pair up brackets, braces, and parentheses. To use this feature, move the insertion point to a bracket. Then press Ctrl+M. TextPad finds the matching bracket.

✦ To search for text, press F5. In the Find dialog box, enter the text you're looking for and click OK. To repeat the search, press Ctrl+F.

✦ To replace text, press F8.

Compiling a Program

To compile a Java program in TextPad, choose Tools⇨Compile Java or use the keyboard shortcut Ctrl+1. The `javac` command launches in a separate command prompt window and displays the compiler output to a separate Command Results window. If the program compiles successfully, TextPad returns immediately to the source program. But if the compiler finds something wrong with your program, the Command Results window stays open, as shown in Figure 3-3.

In this example, the following three compiler error messages are displayed:

```
J:\Book1\Ch04\HelloApp.java:10: ')' expected
        System.out.println("Hello,  + greetee + "!");
                                                    ^
```

```
J:\Book1\Ch04\HelloApp.java:10: unclosed string literal
        System.out.println("Hello,  + greetee + "!");
                                                     ^

J:\Book1\Ch04\HelloApp.java:11: ';' expected
        }
        ^
3 errors

Tool completed with exit code 1
```

TIP If you double-click the first line of each error message, TextPad takes you to the spot where the error occurred. For example, if you double-click the line with the `unclosed string literal` message, you're taken to line 10, and the insertion point is positioned on the last quotation mark on the line, right where the compiler found the error. Then, you can correct the error and recompile the program.

TIP Often, a single error can cause more than one error message to display. That's the case here. The error is that I left off a closing quotation mark after the word `Hello` in line 10. That one error caused all three error messages.

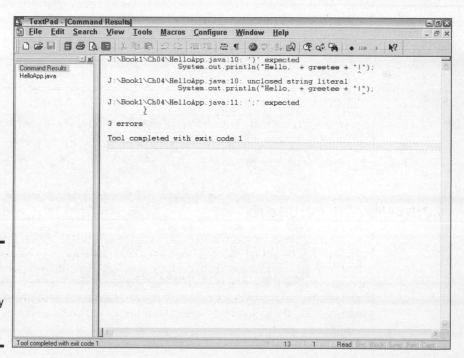

Figure 3-3:
Error
messages
displayed by
the Java
compiler.

Running a Java Program

After you compile a Java program with no errors, you can run it by choosing Tools⇨Run Java Application or pressing Ctrl+2. A command window opens, in which the program runs. For example, Figure 3-4 shows the `HelloApp` program running in a separate window atop the TextPad window.

When the program finishes, the message `Press any key to continue` displays in the command window. When you press a key, the window closes and TextPad comes back to life.

In case you're wondering, TextPad actually runs your program by creating and running a *batch file* — a short text file that contains the commands necessary to run your program. This batch file is given a cryptic name, such as `tp02a11c.BAT`. Here's the batch file generated for the `HelloApp` program:

```
@ECHO OFF
C:
CD \Book1\Ch04
"G:\Program Files\Java\jdk1.5.0\bin\java.exe" HelloApp
PAUSE
```

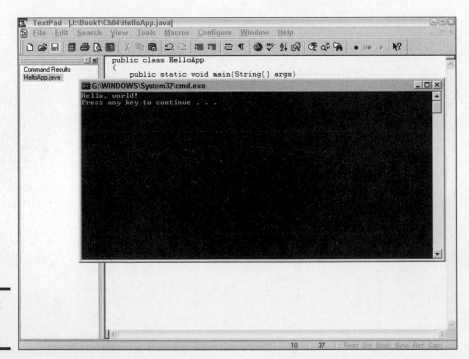

Figure 3-4: Running a program.

Here's a closer look at these commands:

✦ The first command tells MS-DOS not to display the commands in the command window as the batch file executes.

✦ The next two commands switch to the drive and directory that contains the java program.

✦ Next, the `java.exe` program is called to run the `HelloApp` class.

✦ And finally, a `PAUSE` command executes. That's what displays the `Press any key to continue` message when the program finishes.

Running an Applet

You can also run an applet directly from TextPad. First, compile the program. Then, if the program contains no errors, choose Tools⇨Run Java Applet or press Ctrl+3. A command window appears. Then, the Java applet viewer is started. It runs the applet in a separate window, without the need for a Web browser. Figure 3-5 shows an applet in action.

When you quit the applet, the applet viewer window and the DOS command window closes and you return to TextPad.

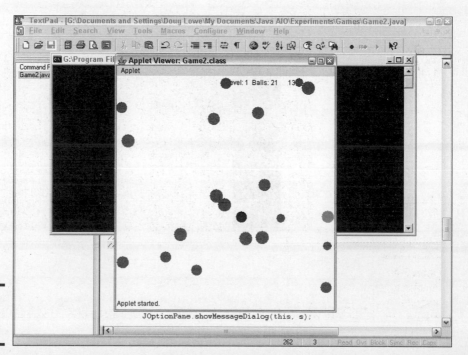

Figure 3-5:
Running an
applet.

Chapter 4: Using Eclipse

In This Chapter

✓ Understanding Eclipse projects and workbenches

✓ Creating a Java project

✓ Compiling, running, and debugging with Eclipse

✓ Refactoring with Eclipse

*E*clipse is a development environment that includes many powerful features for creating Java programs. Because Eclipse is free and very powerful, it has become popular among Java developers. In this chapter, you discover the basics of using Eclipse for simple Java development.

Because Eclipse is such a powerful tool, it has a steep learning curve. If you're brand new to Java, I suggest you start out using a simpler environment, such as TextPad (described in Book I, Chapter 3) and turn to Eclipse only after you have your mind around some of Java's programming fundamentals. That way, you start out by concentrating on Java programming rather than learning Eclipse.

When you're ready to get started with Eclipse, go to the Eclipse Web site (www.eclipse.org), click the downloads link, and download the current version of Eclipse. Unlike most programs, Eclipse doesn't have a complicated setup program. You just download the Eclipse Zip file, extract all of the files, and then run the Eclipse executable file (eclipse.exe) directly from the folder you extracted it to.

If you're using Windows, you may want to add a desktop shortcut for Eclipse to make it more convenient to start. To do that, open the folder that contains the eclipse.exe file. Then, right-click the file and drag it to the desktop. Release the mouse button and choose Create Shortcut from the menu that appears. You can then start Eclipse by double-clicking this desktop shortcut.

Note that many of the techniques I describe in this chapter won't make much sense to you until you learn how to use the Java programming features they apply to. For example, the information about how to create a new Java class file won't make much sense until you learn about creating Java classes in Book III. As you learn about Java programming features in later chapters, you may want to refer back to this chapter to learn about related Eclipse features.

If you plan on using Eclipse, I suggest you pick up a copy of *Eclipse For Dummies* by Barry Burd (Wiley Publishing).

Getting Some Perspective on Eclipse

Eclipse is designed to be a general-purpose development environment, which means that it isn't specifically designed for Java. It's like the *Seinfeld* of IDEs: As its own designers put it, Eclipse is "an IDE for anything and nothing in particular." You can easily customize Eclipse with plug-in components called *features* that make it useful for specific types of development tasks. And because Eclipse is most commonly used for Java program development, it comes pre-configured with features designed for developing Java programs.

Eclipse uses some unusual terminology to describe its basic operation. In particular:

✦ **Workbench:** The *workbench* is the basic Eclipse desktop environment. When you run Eclipse, the workbench opens in a window, as shown in Figure 4-1.

Workbench window   Java perspective

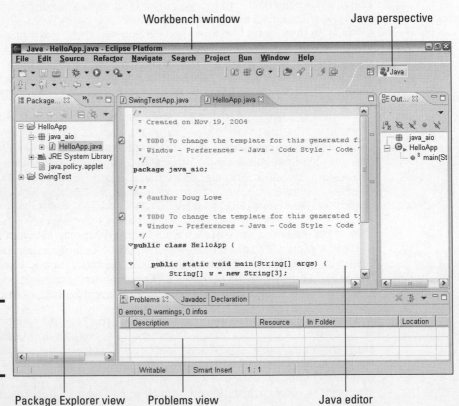

Figure 4-1:
The Eclipse
Workbench
window.

Package Explorer view   Problems view   Java editor

If you can juggle and chew gum at the same time, you may want to open two workbench windows to work on two different projects at once. However, those of us with less than super-hero abilities of concentration can work with just one workbench window at a time.

✦ **Editor:** An *editor* is a workbench window pane that's designed for editing a certain type of file. Eclipse comes with a standard text editor that can edit any kind of text file and a special Java editor that's specifically designed for editing Java programs. In Figure 4-1, the Java editor is in the middle portion of the workbench window.

The Java editor in this figure looks small because I captured this screen image with the computer's monitor set to 800 x 600 pixels. Because Eclipse puts so much information on the screen at once, however, running it on a large monitor (preferably 19" or larger) at a resolution of at least 1,024 x 768 is best. That way, the editor window is large enough to let you comfortably work with your program's text, while leaving ample room for the other elements displayed in the Eclipse workbench window.

✦ **Views:** A *view* is a pane of the workbench window that displays other information that's useful while you're working with Eclipse. Figure 4-1 displays several additional views in addition to the editor. For example, the *Package Explorer view* lets you navigate through the various files that make up an Eclipse project, and the *Problems view* displays error messages.

You can display a view in its own pane, or combine it with other views in a single pane. Then, the views in the pane are indicated with tabbed dividers you can click to call up each view in the pane. For example, the Problems view in Figure 4-1 shares its pane with two other views, called JavaDoc and Declaration.

Strictly speaking, an editor is a type of view.

✦ **Perspective:** A *perspective* is a collection of views that's designed to help you with a specific type of programming task. For example, the workbench window pictured in Figure 4-1 shows the *Java perspective*, designed for working with Java program files. Figure 4-2 shows a different perspective, called the *Debug perspective.* In this perspective, the Java editor is still present, but a different set of views that are useful while testing and debugging Java programs are shown. For example, a Console view appears at the bottom of the window so you can see the output created by the program, and a Variables view lets you monitor the contents of variables as the program executes. (For more information about the Debug perspective, see the section "Debugging a Java Program" later in this chapter.)

Breakpoints view (hidden)

Debug view   Variables view

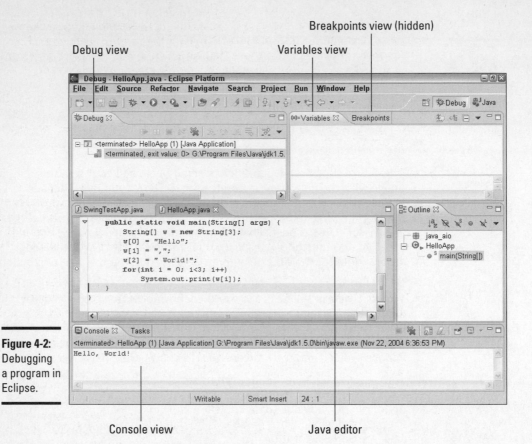

Figure 4-2:
Debugging
a program in
Eclipse.

Console view   Java editor

Understanding Projects

An Eclipse *project* is a set of Java files that together build a single Java program. Although some simple Java programs consist of just one file, most real-world Java programs are made up of more than one Java program file. In fact, a complicated Java program may require hundreds of Java program files. When you work on programs that require more than one file, Eclipse lets you treat those files together as a project.

A project consists not just of Java source files, but also the class files that are created when you compile the project and any other files that the program requires. That might include data files or configuration files, as well as other files such as readme files, program documentation, image files, sound files, and so on.

All the files for a project are stored together in a project folder, which may include subfolders if necessary. In addition to the files required by the program, the project folder also includes files that are created by Eclipse to store information about the project itself. For example, a file named .project stores descriptive information about the project, and a file named .classpath stores the locations of the classes used by the project.

All your project folders are stored in a folder called the *workspace*. Each time you start Eclipse, a dialog box appears asking for the location of the workspace folder. If you want to change to a different workspace, use File⇨Switch Workspace.

Eclipse lets you create two types of projects:

✦ For **simple projects** that have just a few Java source files, you can create a project that stores all the project's Java files in a single folder. Then, when those files are compiled, the resulting class files are stored in this same folder. This type of project is the easiest to work with, and it's ideal for small and medium-sized projects.

✦ For **large projects** — those that involve dozens or even hundreds of Java source files — you can create a project that uses one or more subfolders to store source files. You are then free to create whatever subfolders you want to help you organize your files. For example, you might create one subfolder for user interface classes, another for database access classes, and a third for image files displayed by the application.

Eclipse doesn't have a File⇨Open command that lets you open projects or individual files. Instead, the Package Explorer view (on the left side of the Java perspective; refer to Figure 4-1) displays a list of all the Java projects in your workspace. When you start Eclipse, the project you were last working on is automatically displayed. You can switch to a different project by right-clicking the project in the Package Explorer, and then choosing Open Project. And you can open an individual file in a project by double-clicking the file in the Package Explorer.

Creating a Simple Project

The following procedure takes you step by step through the process of creating a simple project based on a slightly more complicated version of the Hello, World! program from Book I, Chapter 1. Follow these steps to create this application:

1. **Start Eclipse and click OK when the Workspace Launcher dialog box appears.**

The Workspace Launcher dialog box asks for the location of your workspace folder; in most cases, the default location is acceptable. When you click OK, Eclipse opens with the Java perspective, with no projects or files displayed as shown in Figure 4-3.

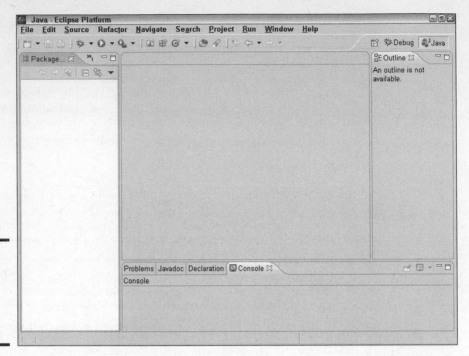

Figure 4-3:
Eclipse
waits for
you to
create a
project.

2. **Choose File⇨New⇨Project.**

   The New Project dialog box comes up, shown in Figure 4-4. This dialog box lists several wizards you can use to create various types of Eclipse projects.

3. **Select Java Project from the list of wizards, and then click Next.**

   The New Java Project dialog box displays, shown in Figure 4-5.

4. **Type** HelloApp **in the text box, and then click Finish.**

   HelloApp is the project name. The other options in this dialog box let you specify whether the project should be stored in the workspace folder or some other folder and whether the project should use the project folder for source files or create separate subfolders for source files. The default settings for both of these options is fine for the HelloApp application.

   When you click Finish, you return to the Java perspective. But now, HelloApp appears in the Package Explorer view to indicate that you've added a project by that name to your workspace.

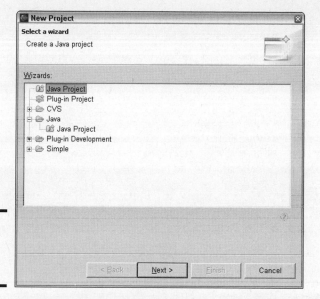

Figure 4-4:
The New
Project
dialog box.

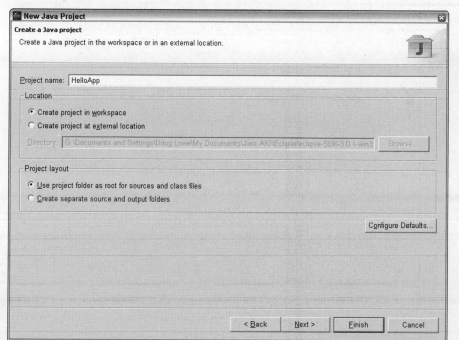

Figure 4-5:
The New
Java Project
dialog box.

5. **Right-click `HelloApp` in the Package Explorer view, and then choose New⇨Class from the shortcut menu that appears.**

   The New Java Class dialog box opens, as shown in Figure 4-6.

6. **Set the options for the new class.**

   In particular:

   - Set the Package text field to `JavaAIO`.
   - Set the Name text field to `HelloApp`.
   - Select the Public Static Void `main(String[] args)` check box.

7. **Click Finish.**

   The `HelloApp.java` file is created and Eclipse displays it in the Java editor, as shown in Figure 4-7.

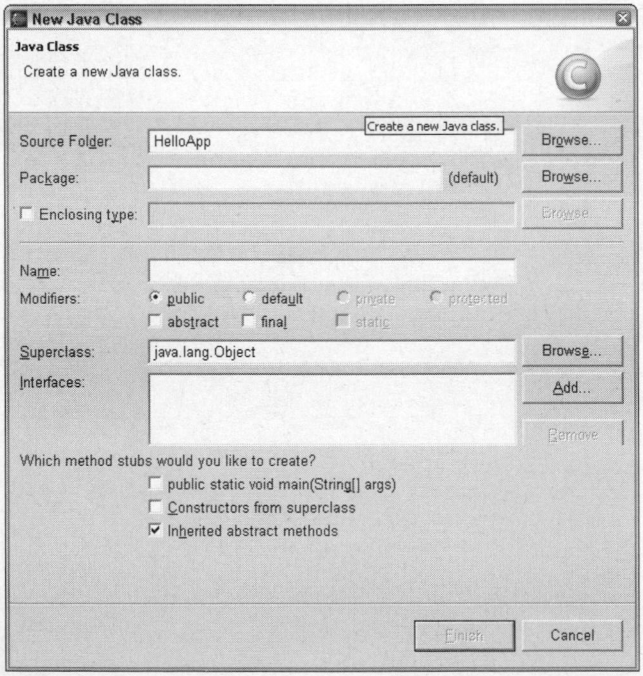

New Java Class

Java Class

Create a new Java class.

Source Folder:	HelloApp	Browse...
Package:	(default)	Browse...
☐ Enclosing type:		Browse...

Name:

Modifiers: ⦿ public ○ default ○ private ○ protected
☐ abstract ☐ final ☐ static

Superclass: java.lang.Object   Browse...

Interfaces: Add...
                                     Remove

Which method stubs would you like to create?
☐ public static void main(String[] args)
☐ Constructors from superclass
☑ Inherited abstract methods

Finish   Cancel

Figure 4-6:
The New
Java Class
dialog box.

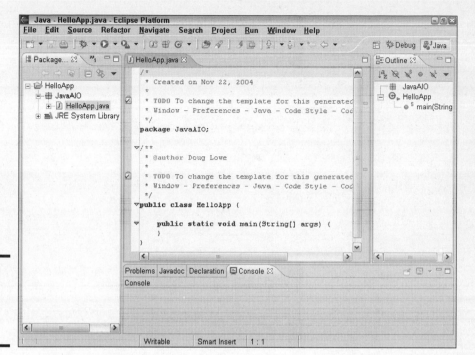

Figure 4-7:
The newly created HelloApp class.

8. Edit the `main` method.

Move the insertion point to the empty block for the `main` method, and then edit it to look exactly like this:

```
public static void main(String[] args) {
    String[] w = new String[3];
    w[0] = "Hello";
    w[1] = ", ";
    w[2] = "world!";
    for (int i = 0; i<3; i++)
        System.out.print(w[i]);
}
```

9. Choose Run⇨Run As⇨Java Application.

The program is compiled and run. A console window with the program's output appears at the bottom of the Eclipse window, as shown in Figure 4-8.

Note: If a Save Resources dialog box appears before the program runs, click OK. The program then runs.

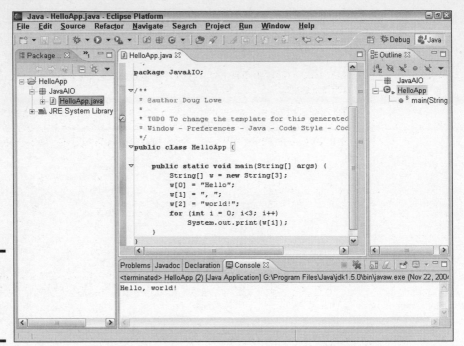

Figure 4-8: The HelloApp program in Eclipse.

Adding a Class File

In this section, I walk you through the process of adding a second class file to the `HelloApp` application to demonstrate some of Eclipse's most useful features for speeding up Java program development by generating code for commonly used class features.

Unless you've already read Book III, you probably won't understand much (if any) of the code that's presented in this procedure. Don't worry; this code will make complete sense once you read about creating your own classes.

So follow these steps to add a second class to the `HelloApp` application:

1. **Right-click `HelloApp` in the Package Explorer and choose Add⇨Class.**

The New Java Class dialog box opens (refer to Figure 4-6).

2. **Set the options for the new class.**

For this class, set the options as follows:

- Leave the Package text field to `JavaAIO`.

- Set the Name text field to `HelloSayer`.

- Uncheck the Public Static Void `main(String[] args)` check box.

3. Click Finish.

A new class file named HelloSayer is created and Ecilpse opens it in a Java editor.

4. Add declarations for two public fields named greeting and addressee.

Add these lines immediately after the line that declares the HelloSayer class. Then, other than the comments and the package statement that appears at the beginning of the class, the class looks like this:

```
public class HelloSayer {

    private String greeting;
    private String addressee;

}
```

5. Use a wizard to add a constructor to the class.

To do that, choose Source⇨Generate Constructor Using Fields. The Generate Contructors Using Fields dialog box appears, shown in Figure 4-9.

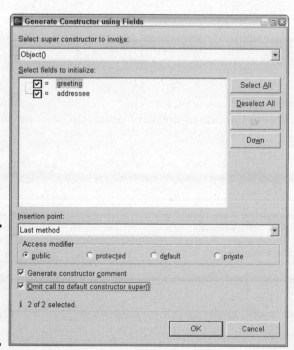

Figure 4-9: Eclipse can automatically create constructors for you.

Check both greeting and addressee in the list of fields to initialize, select First Method in the Insertion Point drop-down list, and check the Omit Call to Default Constructor Super() option. Then click OK. The following code is inserted into the class:

```
/**
 * @param greeting
 * @param addressee
 */
public HelloSayer(String greeting, String
    addressee) {
        this.greeting = greeting;
        this.addressee = addressee;
}
```

6. Add the code for a method named sayHello.

Add the following code after the constructor created in Step 5, immediately before the closing brace (}) in the last line of the program:

```
public void sayHello()
{
    System.out.println(greeting + ", " + addressee
        + "!");
}
```

The entire HelloSayer class file is shown in Listing 4-1.

LISTING 4-1: THE HELLOSAYER CLASS

```
/*
 * Created on Nov 22, 2004
 *
 * TODO To change the template for this generated file go to
 * Window - Preferences - Java - Code Style - Code Templates
 */
package JavaAIO;

/**
 * @author Doug Lowe
 *
 * TODO To change the template for this generated type comment
 * go to Window - Preferences - Java - Code Style - Code Templates
 */
public class HelloSayer {

    private String greeting;
    private String addressee;

    /**
     * @param greeting
     * @param addressee
     */
```

```
public HelloSayer(String greeting, String addressee) {
    this.greeting = greeting;
    this.addressee = addressee;
}

public void sayHello() {
    System.out.println(greeting + ", " + addressee + "!");
}
}
```

7. **Click the HelloApp.java tab at the top of the Java editor pane.**

   The HelloApp.java file comes to the front so you can edit it.

8. **Edit the main method so that it uses the new HelloSayer class.**

   Delete the code that was in the main method and replace it with this code:

   ```
   public static void main(String[] args) {
       HelloSayer h = new HelloSayer("Hello",
       "World!");
       h.sayHello();
   }
   ```

   The entire HelloApp.java class now looks like Listing 4-2. Eclipse generated all the code except the two lines within the main method.

LISTING 4-2: THE HELLOAPP CLASS

```
/*
 * Created on Nov 22, 2004
 *
 * TODO To change the template for this generated file go to
 * Window - Preferences - Java - Code Style - Code Templates
 */
package JavaAIO;

/**
 * @author Doug Lowe
 *
 * TODO To change the template for this generated type comment
 * go to Window - Preferences - Java - Code Style - Code Templates
 */
public class HelloApp {

    public static void main(String[] args) {
        HelloSayer h = new HelloSayer("Hello", "World!");
        h.sayHello();
    }
}
```

Running a Program

After you enter the source code for your Eclipse project, you can run it to see if it works as expected. Eclipse has several ways to run a Java program:

✦ In the Package Explorer, select the source file for the class you want to run. Then, choose Run⇨Run As⇨Java Application.

✦ Right-click the source file for the class you want to run, then choose Run⇨Java Application from the shortcut menu that appears.

✦ Select the source file in the Package Explorer, and then click the Run button (shown in the margin) and choose Run As⇨Java Application from the menu that appears. (If you recently ran the program, you can also choose the program from the list of recently run programs that appears in this menu.)

When the program runs, its console output is displayed in a Console view that appears beneath the Java Editor pane, as shown in Figure 4-10.

Note: If the program uses Swing to create a window, that window is displayed separately, not within the Eclipse workbench window. (See Book VI for more on Swing.)

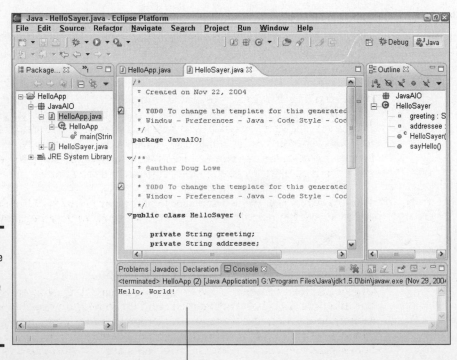

Figure 4-10:
The Console View displays the program's console output.

Console view

Eclipse is designed so that it automatically compiles Java programs as you work on them. Every time you save a Java source file in Eclipse, the file is automatically compiled to create a class file. As a result, you don't usually have to perform a separate compile step before you can run a program. If the project contains large source files, this feature can become annoying. To disable automatic compilation, choose Project⇨Build Automatically. Then, you must manually build the project by choosing Project⇨Build All before you can run it. (To switch back to automatic builds, choose Project⇨Build Automatically again.)

Debugging a Java Program

No matter how carefully you plan your programs, sooner or later you encounter bugs. You need to watch out for basically two kinds of bugs:

✦ **Incorrect results,** such as a program that's supposed to calculate test scores but gives you a C when you score 99 out of 100 or a program that's supposed to calculate sales tax of 5% but that says the sales tax on a $29.95 purchase is $149.75 instead of $1.50.

✦ **Program crashes,** such as when a program that's supposed to divide one number into another and print the answer instead prints out this message:

```
Exception in thread "main" java.lang.ArithmeticException: / by
    zero
    at BugApp.main(BugApp.java:19)
```

Then, the program abruptly stops.

Fortunately, Eclipse has a powerful debugger that can help you find the cause of either type of bug and fix it. To start the debugger, run your program by choosing Project⇨Debug As⇨Java Application instead of Project⇨Run As⇨Java Application. Or, click the Debug button on the Workbench toolbar as shown in the margin. Eclipse switches to the Debug perspective, as shown in Figure 4-11, and runs the program in debug mode.

The following sections describe some of the key features of the Debug perspective that are useful for tracking down and correcting bugs in your Java programs.

Stepping through your programs

One of the most basic skills for debugging is executing program statements one at a time. This is called *stepping*, and it can be a very useful debugging technique. By stepping through your program one statement at a time, you can view the effects of each statement and identify the source of errors. Sometimes, just knowing which statements are being executed is all you need to know to determine why your program isn't working.

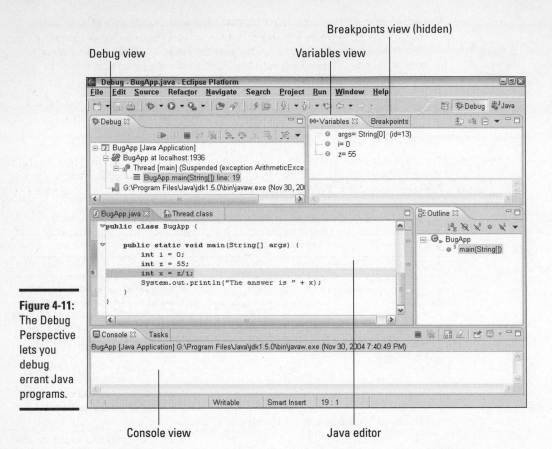

Figure 4-11:
The Debug
Perspective
lets you
debug
errant Java
programs.

In Eclipse, the Debug View section of the Debug perspective is where you control the execution of the program you're debugging. This view displays a tree that indicates each of the *threads* in your program. (If you don't know what threads are, don't worry about it. Most console-based programs, such as the `BugApp` program, shown in Figure 4-11 uses only one thread anyway. You find out how to code programs that use more than one thread in Book V.)

Before you can control the execution of a thread, you must first *suspend* the thread so that its statements stop executing. In general, you can suspend a thread for debugging three ways:

✦ When an unhandled exception occurs, the thread is automatically suspended. In Figure 4-11, the `BugApp` program's `main` method is suspended because a divide-by-zero exception has occurred and the program didn't catch it. If your program is throwing an exception that you don't expect, you can simply debug the program and allow the exception to suspend the thread. Then, you can try to track down the cause of the problem.

✦ Before you debug the program, you can set a *breakpoint* at any statement in the program. Then, when execution reaches that statement, the thread is suspended. To set a breakpoint, simply double-click the left margin of the Java editor next to the statement where you want the thread to be suspended.

 ✦ If a long-running thread is in a loop, you can suspend it by clicking the thread in the Debug View window and clicking the Suspend button (shown in the margin).

When you suspend a thread, the statement that will be executed next is highlighted in the Java editor. Then, you can continue the thread's execution one or more statements at a time by clicking the buttons at the top of the Debug view. Table 4-1 describes the most commonly used buttons.

Table 4-1	Commonly Used Buttons	
Button	*Name*	*Description*
	Resume	Resumes execution with the next statement. The thread continues executing until it is suspended by an uncaught exception or a breakpoint.
	Terminate	Terminates the thread.
	Step Into	Executes the highlighted statement, and then suspends the thread.
	Step Over	Skips the highlighted statement and executes the next statement, and then suspends the thread.
	Run to Return	Executes the highlighted statement and continues executing statements until the end of the current method is reached. Then, the thread is suspended.

Examining variables

When a thread is suspended, you can examine its variables to see if they're set to the values you expect. In many cases, you can discover programming errors. For example, if you think a variable named `customerFirstName` should contain a customer's first name and instead it contains the name of the state in which the customer lives, you can conclude that you didn't assign the variable's value properly. (Of course, this might be ambiguous if the customer happens to be named Indiana Jones.)

The easiest way to examine the value of a variable is to simply point the mouse at the variable in the Java editor. For example, Figure 4-12 shows how the value of the variable i appears when you hover the mouse pointer over it. Here, the pop-up message indicates that the variable i is an int type and has a value of 0. (This message might be a clue as to why the program has thrown a divide by zero exception.)

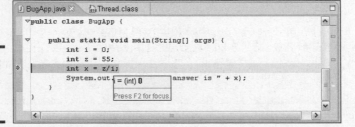

Figure 4-12:
Displaying
a variable
value.

You can also inspect variables by using the Variables view, as shown in Figure 4-13. Each variable is listed on a separate line in the top part of the Variables view. In addition, the bottom part (called the Detail pane) displays the value of the currently selected variable. Note that as you step through the various statements in your program, variables appear in the Variables view as they are declared and they disappear from view when they go out of scope.

Figure 4-13:
The
Variables
view shows
the value
of each
variable.

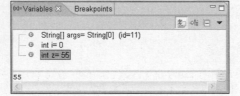

Setting breakpoints

A *breakpoint* is a line in your program where you want the program to be suspended. Setting a breakpoint allows you to efficiently execute the portions of your program that are working properly, while stopping the program when it reaches the lines you believe to be in error.

All the breakpoints in your program are listed in Breakpoints view, as shown in Figure 4-14. The following paragraphs describe some of the ways you can work with breakpoints in this view:

✦ The check box next to each breakpoint indicates whether or not the breakpoint is enabled. Execution is suspended at a breakpoint only if the breakpoint is enabled.

✦ You can delete a checkpoint by clicking the breakpoint to select it, and then pressing the Delete key or clicking the Remove Selected button (shown in the margin).

✦ You can remove all the breakpoints you've set by clicking the Remove All Breakpoints button (shown in the margin).

✦ If you double-click a breakpoint in Breakpoint view, the Java Editor window scrolls to the line at which the breakpoint is set.

✦ If you only want the program to be suspended after it has hit the break-point a certain number of times, right-click the breakpoint and choose Hit Count from the shortcut menu that appears. Then, enter the number of times you want the statement to execute before suspending the program and click OK.

Figure 4-14:
The
Breakpoints
view is
where you
control
breakpoints.

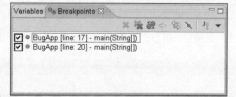

Refactoring Your Code

Refactoring refers to the task of making mass changes to a project. For example, suppose you decide that a class name you created when you started the project doesn't really accurately describe the purpose of the class, so you want to change it. Simple text editors, such as TextPad, include a Replace command that lets you change occurrences of text strings within a file, but changing the name of a class requires that you change the name in all the files in a project.

Eclipse includes a whole menu of refactoring options — called, as you might guess, the Refactor menu. This menu contains 18 different types of refactoring commands. If you're just starting to learn Java, most of these 18 commands won't make any sense to you. For example, the Refactor menu contains commands that let you change an anonymous inner class to a nested class, push members down to a subclass, or introduce a factory.

A few of the Refactor menu commands are useful to you as you work your way through the basics of learning Java. In particular:

✦ **Rename:** Lets you rename a variable, method, or other symbol. First, select the symbol you want to rename. Then, choose Refactor⟹Rename, type the new name, and then click OK.

✦ **Extract Method:** This command lets you create a separate method from one or more statements. Select the statements you want to place in the method, and then choose Refactor⟹Extract Method. In the dialog box that appears, type the name you want to use for the method. Eclipse creates a method with the statements you selected, and then replaces the original selection with a call to the new method.

✦ **Inline:** This command is pretty much the opposite of the Extract Method command. It replaces a call to a method with the statements that are defined in the body of that method. This command is most useful in situations where you thought a method was going to be either more complicated than it turned out to be, or you thought you'd call it from more locations than you ended up calling it from.

✦ **Extract Local Variable:** This one is weird. Sometimes, you discover that you have a whole string of statements in a row that use an expression, such as $x + 1$. Wouldn't it be better if you just created a separate variable to hold the value of $x + 1$, and then used that variable instead of repeatedly recalculating the expression? The Extract Local Variable command can do this for you. Highlight the first occurrence of the expression and choose Refactor⟹Extract Local Variable. Eclipse creates a local variable, adds an assignment statement that assigns the expression to the new local variable, and then replaces all occurrences of the expression with the local variable.

Book II

Programming Basics

The 5th Wave   By Rich Tennant

Okay — you were right, I was wrong. F5 opens the garage door, and F6 backs the car out.

Contents at a Glance

Chapter 1: Java Programming Basics

In This Chapter

✔ **The famous Hello, World! program**

✔ **Basic elements of Java programs such as keywords, statements, and blocks**

✔ **Different ways to add comments to your programs**

✔ **Basic information about object-oriented programming**

✔ **Importing classes**

In this chapter, you find the basics of writing simple Java programs. The programs you see in this chapter don't do anything very interesting; they just display simple information on a *console* (in Windows, that's a command prompt window). You need to cover a few more chapters before you start writing programs that do anything worthwhile. But the simple programs you see in this chapter are sufficient to illustrate the basic structure of Java programs.

Be warned that in this chapter, I introduce you to several Java programming features that are explained in greater detail in later chapters. For example, you see some variable declarations, a method, and even an `if` statement and a `for` loop. The goal of this chapter isn't for you to become proficient with these programming elements, but just to get an introduction to them.

You can find all the code listings used in this book at `www.dummies.com/go/javaaiofd`.

Looking At the Infamous Hello, World! Program

Many programming books begin with a simple example program that displays the text, `"Hello, World!"` on the console. In Book I, Chapter 1, I show you a Java program that does that to compare it with a similar program written in C. Now, take a closer look at each element of this program, shown in Listing 1-1.

LISTING 1-1: THE HELLOAPP PROGRAM

```
public class HelloApp                                    → 1
{                                                        → 2
    public static void main(String[] args)               → 3
    {                                                    → 4
        System.out.println("Hello, World!");             → 5
    }                                                    → 6
}                                                        → 7
```

Later in this chapter, you discover in detail all the elements that make up this program. But first, I want to walk you through it word by word.

Lines 1 and 2 mark the declaration of a public class named HelloApp:

→ **1** **public:** A *keyword* of the Java language that indicates that the element that follows should be made available to other Java elements. In this case, what follows is a class named HelloApp. As a result, this keyword indicates that the HelloApp class is a *public class,* which means other classes can use it. (In Book III, Chapter 2, I cover the most common alternative to public: private. There are also other alternatives, but they're covered in later chapters.)

class: Another Java keyword that indicates that the element being defined here is a class. All Java programs are made up of one or more *classes.* A class definition contains code that defines the behavior of the objects created and used by the program. Although most real-world programs consist of more than one class, the simple programs you see in this minibook have just one class.

HelloApp: An *identifier* that provides the name for the class being defined here. While keywords, such as public and class, are words that are defined by the Java programming language, identifiers are words that you create to provide names for various elements you use in your program. In this case, the identifier HelloApp provides a name for the public class being defined here. (Although *identifier* is the technically correct term, sometimes identifiers are called *symbols* or *names.*)

→ **2** **{:** The opening brace on line 2 marks the beginning of the *body* of the class. The end of the body is marked by the closing brace on line 7. Everything that appears within these braces belongs to the class. As you work with Java, you'll find that it uses these braces a lot. Pretty soon the third and fourth fingers on your right hand will know exactly where they are on the keyboard.

Lines 3 through 6 define a *method* of the `HelloApp` class named `main`:

→ **3** **public:** The `public` keyword is used again, this time to indicate that a method being declared here should have public access. That means classes other than the `HelloApp` class can use it. All Java programs must have at least one class that declares a public method named `main`. The `main` method contains the statements that are executed when you run the program.

static: You find all about the `static` keyword in Book III, Chapter 3. For now, just take my word that the Java language requires that you specify `static` when you declare the `main` method.

void: In Java, a method is a unit of code that can calculate and return a value. For example, you could create a method that calculates a sales total. Then, the sales total would be the return value of the method. If a method doesn't need to return a value, you must use the `void` keyword to indicate that no value is returned. Because Java requires that the `main` method not return a value, you must specify `void` when you declare the `main` method.

main: Finally, the identifier that provides the name for this method. As I've already mentioned, Java requires that this method be named `main`. Besides the `main` method, you can also create additional methods with whatever names you want to use. You discover how to create additional methods in Book II, Chapter 7. Until then, the programs consist of just one method named `main`.

(String[] args): Oh boy. This Java element is too advanced to thoroughly explain just yet. It's called a *parameter list,* and it's used to pass data to a method. Java requires that the `main` method must receive a single parameter that's an array of `String` objects. By convention, this parameter is named `args`. If you don't know what a parameter, a `String`, or an array is, don't worry about it. You can find out what a `String` is in the next chapter, and parameters are in Book II, Chapter 7; arrays in Book IV. In the meantime, realize that you have to code `(String[] args)` on the declaration for the `main` methods in all your programs.

→ **4** **Another {:** Another set of braces begins at line 4 and ends at line 6. These mark the body of the `main` method. Notice that the closing brace in line 6 is paired with the opening brace in line 4, while the closing brace in line 7 is paired with the one in line 2. This type of pairing is commonplace in Java. In short, whenever you come to a closing brace, it is paired with the most recent opening brace that hasn't already been closed — that is, that hasn't already been paired with a closing brace.

→ **5** **System.out.println("Hello, World!");:** This is the only statement in the entire program. It calls a method named `println` that belongs to the `System.out` object. The `println` method displays a line of text on the console. The text to be displayed is passed to the `println` method as a parameter in parentheses following the word `println`. In this case, the text is the string literal `Hello, World!` enclosed in a set of quotation marks. As a result, this statement displays the text `Hello, World!` on the console.

Note that in Java, statements end with a semicolon. Because this is the only statement in the program, this line is the only one that requires a semicolon.

→ **6** **}:** Line 6 contains the closing brace that marks the end of the `main` method body that was begun by the brace on line 4.

→ **7** **Another }:** Line 7 contains the closing brace that marks the end of the `HelloApp` class body that was begun by the brace on line 2. Because this program consists of just one class, this line also marks the end of the program.

To run this program, you must first use a text editor to enter it exactly as it appears in Listing 1-1 into a text file named `HelloApp.java`. Then, you can compile it by running this command at a command prompt:

```
javac HelloApp.java
```

This command creates a class file named `HelloApp.class` that contains the Java bytecodes compiled for the `HelloApp class`.

You can run the program by entering this command:

```
java HelloApp
```

Now that you've seen what a Java program actually looks like, you're in a better position to understand exactly what this command does. First, it loads the Java Virtual Machine into memory. Then, it locates the `HelloApp class`, which must be contained in a file named `HelloApp.class`. Finally, it runs the `HelloApp` class' `main` method. The `main` method, in turn, displays the message `"Hello, World!"` on the console.

The rest of this chapter describes some of the basic elements of the Java programming language in greater detail.

Dealing with Keywords

A *keyword* is a word that has special meaning defined by the Java programming language. The program shown earlier in Listing 1-1 uses four keywords: `public`, `class`, `static`, and `void`. In all, Java has 51 keywords. They're listed in alphabetical order in Table 1-1.

Table 1-1		Java's Keywords		
abstract	do	if	package	synchronized
boolean	double	implements	private	this
break	else	import	protected	throw
byte	extends	instanceof	public	throws
case	false	int	return	transient
catch	final	interface	short	true
char	finally	long	static	try
class	float	native	strictfp	void
const	for	new	super	volatile
continue	goto	null	switch	while
default				

Strangely enough, three keywords listed in Table 1-1 — `true`, `false`, and `null` — aren't technically considered to be keywords. Instead, they're called *literals*. Still, they're reserved for use by the Java language in much the same way that keywords are, so I lumped them in with the keywords.

Stranger still, two keywords — `const` and `goto` — are reserved by Java but don't do anything. Both are carryovers from the C++ programming language. The `const` keyword defines a constant, which is handled in Java by the `final` keyword. As for `goto`, it's a C++ statement that is considered anathema to object-oriented programming purists, so it isn't used in Java. Java reserves it as a keyword solely for the purpose of scolding you if you attempt to use it.

Like everything else in Java, keywords are case sensitive. Thus, if you type `If` instead of `if` or `For` instead of `for`, the compiler complains about your error. Because Visual Basic keywords begin with capital letters, you'll make this mistake frequently if you have programmed in Visual Basic.

Considering the Java community's disdain for Visual Basic, it's surprising that the error messages generated when you capitalize keywords aren't more insulting. Accidentally capitalizing a keyword in Visual Basic style can really throw the Java compiler for a loop. For example, consider this program, which contains the single error of capitalizing the word `For`:

```
public class CaseApp
{
    public static void main(String[] args)
    {
        For (int i = 0; i<5; i++)
            System.out.println("Hi");
    }
}
```

When you try to compile this program, the compiler generates a total of six error messages for this one mistake:

```
C:\Java AIO\CaseApp.java:5: '.class' expected
                  For (int i = 0; i<5; i++)
                         ^
C:\Java AIO\CaseApp.java:5: ')' expected
                  For (int i = 0; i<5; i++)
                                ^
C:\Java AIO\CaseApp.java:5: illegal start of type
                  For (int i = 0; i<5; i++)
                               ^
C:\Java AIO\CaseApp.java:5: > expected
                  For (int i = 0; i<5; i++)
                                    ^
C:\Java AIO\CaseApp.java:5: not a statement
                  For (int i = 0; i<5; i++)
                                   ^
C:\Java AIO\CaseApp.java:5: ';' expected
                  For (int i = 0; i<5; i++)
                                          ^

6 errors
```

Even though this single mistake generates six error messages, none of the messages actually point to the problem. The little arrow beneath the source line indicates what part of the line is in error, and none of these error messages have the arrow pointing anywhere near the word For! The compiler isn't smart enough to realize that you meant for instead of For. So it treats For as a legitimate identifier, and then complains about everything else on the line that follows it. It would be much more helpful if it generated an error message like this:

```
C:\Java AIO\CaseApp.java:5: 'For' is not a keyword
                  For (int i = 0; i<5; i++)
                  ^
```

The moral of the story is that keywords are case sensitive, and if your program won't compile and the error messages don't make any sense, check for keywords that you've mistakenly capitalized.

Working with Statements

Like most programming languages, Java uses statements to build programs. Unlike most programming languages, statements are not the fundamental unit of code in Java. Instead, that honor goes to the class. However, every class must have a body, and the body of a class is made up of one or more statements. In other words, you can't have a meaningful Java program without at least one statement. The following sections describe the ins and outs of working with Java statements.

Types of statements

Java has many different types of statements. Some statements simply create variables that you can use to store data. These types of statements are often called *declaration statements,* and tend to look like this:

```
int i;
String s = "This is a string";
Customer c = new Customer();
```

Another common type of statement is an *expression statement*, which performs calculations. Here are some examples of expression statements:

```
i = a + b;
salesTax = invoiceTotal * taxRate;
System.out.println("Hello, World!");
```

Notice that the last statement in this group is the same as line 5 in Listing 1-1. Thus, the single statement in the HelloApp program is an expression statement.

There are many other kinds of statements besides these two. For example, if-then statements execute other statements only if a particular condition has been met. And statements such as for, while, or do execute a group of statements one or more times.

Book II
Chapter 1

Java Programming
Basics

It is often said that all Java statements must end with a semicolon. Actually, this isn't quite true. Some types of Java statements must end with a semicolon, but others don't. The basic rule is that declaration and expression statements must end with a semicolon, but most other statement types do not. Where this rule gets tricky, however, is that most other types of statements include one or more declaration or expression statements that do use semicolons. For example, here's a typical if statement:

```
if (total > 100)
    discountPercent = 10;
```

Here, the variable named discountPercent is given a value of 10 if the value of the total variable is greater than 100. The expression statement ends with semicolons, but the if statement itself doesn't. (The Java compiler lets you know if you use a semicolon when you shouldn't.)

White space

In Java, the term *white space* refers to one or more consecutive space characters, tab characters, or line breaks. All white space is considered the same. In other words, a single space is treated the same as a tab or line break or any combination of spaces, tabs, or line breaks.

If you've programmed in Visual Basic, white space is different from what you're used to. In Visual Basic, line breaks mark the end of statements unless special continuation characters are used. In Java, you don't have to do anything special to continue a statement onto a second line. Thus, the statement

```
x = (y + 5) / z;
```

is identical to this statement:

```
x =
(y + 5) / z;
```

In fact, you could write the above statement like this if you wanted:

```
x
=
(
y
+
5
)
/
z
;
```

I wouldn't advise it, but the statement does compile and execute properly.

TIP

Using white space liberally in your programs is a good idea. In particular, you should usually use line breaks to place each statement on a separate line and use tabs to line up elements that belong together. The compiler ignores the extra white space, so it doesn't affect the bytecode that's created for your program. As a result, using extra white space in your program doesn't affect your program's performance in any way, but it does make the program's source code easier to read.

Working with Blocks

A *block* is a group of one or more statements that's enclosed in braces. A block begins with an opening brace ({) and ends with a closing brace (}). Between the opening and closing brace, you can code one or more statements. For example, here's a block that consists of three statements:

```
{
    int i, j;
    i = 100;
    j = 200;
}
```

A block is itself a type of statement. As a result, any time the Java language requires a statement, you can substitute a block to execute more than one statement. For example, in Book II, Chapter 4, you discover that the basic syntax of an `if` statement is this:

```
if ( expression ) statement
```

Here, the *statement* can be a single statement or a block. If you find this idea confusing, don't worry. It will make more sense when you turn to Book II, Chapter 4.

You can code the braces that mark a block in two popular ways. One is to place both braces on separate lines, and then indent the statements that make up the block. For example:

```
if ( i > 0)
{
    String s = "The value of i is " + i;
    System.out.print(s);
}
```

The other style is to place the opening brace for the block on the same line as the statement the block is associated with, like this:

```
if ( i > 0) {
    String s = "The value of i is " + i;
    System.out.print(s);
}
```

Which style you use is a matter of personal preference. I prefer the first style, and that's the style I use throughout this book. But either style works, and many programmers prefer the second style because it's more concise.

Creating Identifiers

An *identifier* is a word that you make up to refer to a Java programming element by name. Although you can assign identifiers to many different types of Java elements, they're most commonly used for the following elements:

+ Classes, such as the `HelloApp` class in Listing 1-1
+ Methods, such as the `main` method in Listing 1-1
+ Variables and fields, which hold data used by your program
+ Parameters, which pass data values to methods

Identifiers are also sometimes called *names*. Strictly speaking, a name isn't quite the same thing as an identifier. A name is often made up of two or more identifiers connected with periods (called *dots*). For example, in line 5 of Listing 1-1, System and out are both identifiers. But System.out is a name. In practice, the terms *name* and *identifier* are used interchangeably.

You must follow a few simple rules when you create identifiers:

✦ Identifiers are case sensitive. As a result, SalesTax and salesTax are distinct identifiers.

✦ Identifiers can be made up of upper- or lowercase letters, numerals, underscore characters (_), and dollar signs ($).

✦ All identifiers must begin with a letter. Thus, a15 is a valid identifier, but 13Unlucky isn't because it begins with a numeral.

✦ An identifier can't be the same as any of the Java keywords listed in Table 1-1. Thus, you can't create a variable named for or a class named public.

✦ The Java language specification recommends that you avoid using dollar signs in names you create. Instead, dollar signs are used by code generators to create identifiers. Thus, avoiding dollar signs helps you avoid creating names that conflict with generated names.

Crafting Comments

A *comment* is a bit of text that provides explanations of your code. Comments are completely ignored by the compiler, so you can place any text you wish in a comment. Using plenty of comments in your programs is a good idea to explain what your program does and how it works.

Java has three basic types of comments: *end-of-line comments, traditional comments,* and *JavaDoc comments.*

End-of-line comments

An end-of-line comment begins with the sequence // and ends at the end of the line. You can place an end-of-line comment at the end of any line. Everything you type after the // is ignored by the compiler. For example:

```
total = total * discountPercent; // calculate the discounted total
```

If you want, you can also place end-of-line comments on separate lines, like this:

```
// calculate the discounted total
total = total * discountPercent;
```

You can place end-of-line comments in the middle of statements that span two or more lines. For example:

```
total = (total * discountPercent)   // apply the discount first
    + salesTax;                     // then add the sales tax
```

Traditional comments

A traditional comment begins with the sequence /* and ends with the sequence */ and can span multiple lines. For example:

```
/* HelloApp sample program.
   This program demonstrates the basic structure
   that all Java programs must follow. */
```

A traditional comment can begin and end anywhere on a line. If you want, you can even sandwich a comment between other Java programming elements, like this:

```
x = (y + /* a strange place for a comment */ 5) / z;
```

Usually, traditional comments appear on separate lines. One common use for traditional comments is to place a block of comment lines at the beginning of a class to indicate information about the class such as what the class does, who wrote it, and so on. However, that type of comment is usually better coded as a JavaDoc comment, as described in the next section.

You may be tempted to temporarily comment out a range of lines by placing /* in front of the first line in the range and */ after the last line in the range. However, that can get you in trouble if the range of lines you try to comment out includes a traditional comment. That's because traditional comments can't be *nested*. For example, the following code won't compile:

```
/*
int x, y, z;
y = 10;
z = 5;
x = (y + /* a strange place for a comment */ 5) / z;
*/
```

Here, I tried to comment out a range of lines that already included a traditional comment. Unfortunately, the */ sequence near the end of the fifth line is interpreted as the end of the traditional comment that begins in the first line. Then, when the compiler encounters the */ sequence in line 6, it generates an error message.

JavaDoc comments

JavaDoc comments are actually a special type of traditional comment that you can use to automatically create Web-based documentation for your programs. Because you'll have a better appreciation of JavaDoc comments when you know more about object-oriented programming, I devoted a section in Book III, Chapter 8 to creating and using JavaDoc comments.

Introducing Object-Oriented Programming

Having presented some of the most basic elements of the Java programming language, most Java books would next turn to the important topics of variables and data types. However, because Java is an inherently object-oriented programming language, and classes are the heart of object-oriented programming, I look next at classes to explore the important role they play in creating objects. I get to variables and data types first thing in the next chapter.

Understanding classes and objects

As I've already mentioned, a *class* is code that defines the behavior of a Java programming element called an *object*. An object is an entity that has both *state* and *behavior*. The state of an object consists of any data that the object might be keeping track of, and the behavior consists of actions that the object can perform. The behaviors are represented in the class by one or more methods that can be called upon to perform actions.

The difference between a class and an object is similar to the difference between a blueprint and a house. A blueprint is a plan for a house. A house is an implementation of a blueprint. One set of blueprints can be used to build many houses. Likewise, a class is a plan for an object, and an object is — in Java terms — an *instance* of a class. You can use a single class to create more than one object.

When an object is created, Java sets aside an area of computer memory that's sufficient to hold all the data that's stored by the object. As a result, each instance of a class has its own data, independent of the data used by other instances of the same class.

Understanding static methods

You don't necessarily have to create an instance of a class to use the methods of the class. If a method is declared with the `static` keyword, the method can be called without first creating an instance of the class. That's because static methods are called from classes, not from objects.

The `main` method of a Java application must be declared with the `static` keyword. That's because when you start a Java program by using the `java` command from a command prompt, Java doesn't create an instance of the application class. Instead, it simply calls the program's static `main` method.

The difference between static and non-static methods will become more apparent when you look at object-oriented programming in more depth in Book III. But for now, consider this analogy. The blueprints for a house include the details about systems that actually perform work in a finished house, such as electrical and plumbing systems. In order to use those systems, you have to actually build a house. In other words, you can't turn on the hot water by using the blueprint alone; you have to have an actual house to heat the water.

Book II
Chapter 1

However, the blueprints do include detailed measurements of the dimensions of the house. As a result, you *can* use the blueprints to determine the square footage of the living room. Now imagine that the blueprints actually had a built-in calculator that would display the size of the living room if you pushed the "Living Room" button. That button would be like a static method in a class: You don't actually have to build a house to use it; you can use it from the blueprints alone.

Many Java programs — in fact, many of the programs in the rest of Book II — are entirely made up of static methods. However, most realistic programs require that you create one or more objects that the program uses as it executes. As a result, learning how to create simple classes and how to create objects from those classes is a basic skill in Java programming.

Creating an object from a class

In Java, you can create an object from a class in several ways. But the most straightforward is to create a variable that provides a name you can use to refer to the object, then use the `new` keyword to create an instance of the class, and assign the resulting object to the variable. The general form of a statement that does that is this:

```
ClassName variableName = new ClassName();
```

For example, to create an object instance of a class named `Class1` and assign it to a variable named `myClass1Object`, you would write a statement like this:

```
Class1 myClass1Object = new Class1();
```

Why do you have to list the class name twice? The first time, you're providing a *type* for the variable. In other words, you're saying that the variable you're creating here can be used to hold objects created from the `Class1` class. The second time you list the class name, you're creating an object from the class. The `new` keyword tells Java to create an object, and the class name provides the name of the class to use to create the object.

The equals sign (=) is an *assignment operator*. It simply says to take the object created by the new keyword and assign it to the variable. Thus, this statement actually does *three* things:

✦ It creates a variable named myClass1Object that can be used to hold objects created from the Class1 class. At this point, no object has been created — just a variable that can be used to store objects.

✦ It creates a new object in memory from the Class1 class.

✦ It assigns this newly created object to the myClass1Object variable. That way, you can use the myClassObject variable to refer to the object that was created.

A program that uses an object

To give you an early look at what object-oriented programming really looks like, Listings 1-2 and 1-3 show another version of the HelloApp application, this time using two classes, one of which is actually made into an object when the program is run. The first class, named HelloApp2, is shown in Listing 1-2. This class is similar to the HelloApp class shown in Listing 1-1. However, it uses an object created from the second class, named Greeter, to actually display the "Hello, World!" message on the console. The Greeter class is shown in Listing 1-3. It defines a method named sayHello that displays the message.

Both the HelloApp and the Greeter class are public classes. Java requires that each public class be stored in a separate file, with the same name as the class and the extension .java. As a result, the HelloApp2 class is stored in a file named HelloApp2.java, and the Greeeter class is stored in a file named Greeter.java.

The HelloApp2 class

The HelloApp2 class is shown in Listing 1-2.

```
LISTING 1-2: THE HELLOAPP2 CLASS

// This application displays a hello message on        → 1
// the console by creating an instance of the
// Greeter class, then calling the Greeter
// object's sayHello method.

public class HelloApp2                                 → 6
{
    public static void main(String[] args)             → 8
    {
        Greeter myGreeterObject = new Greeter();       → 10
```

```
        myGreeterObject.sayHello();                →  11
    }
}
```

The following paragraphs describe the key points:

→ **1** This class begins with a series of comment lines that identify the function of the program. For these comments, I used simple end-of-line comments rather than traditional comments. (For more on commenting, see the "Crafting Comments" section, earlier in this chapter.)

→ **6** The `HelloApp2` class begins on line 6 with the public class declaration. Because the `public` keyword is used, a file named `HelloApp2.java` must contain this class.

→ **8** The `main` method is declared using the same form as the `main` method in the first version of this program (Listing 1-1). Get used to this form because *all* Java applications must include a `main` method that's declared in this way.

→**10** The first line in the body of the `main` method creates a variable named `myGreeterObject` that can hold objects created from the `Greeter` class. Then, it creates a new object using the `Greeter` class and assigns this object to the `myGreeterObject` variable.

→**11** The second line in the body of the `main` method calls the `myGreeterObject` object's `sayHello` method. As you'll see in a moment, this method simply displays the message `"Hello, World!"` on the console.

The Greeter class

The `Greeter` class is shown in Listing 1-3.

LISTING 1-3: THE GREETER CLASS

```
// This class creates a Greeter object               →  1
// that displays a hello message on
// the console.

public class Greeter                                  →  5
{
    public void sayHello()                            →  7
    {
        System.out.println("Hello, World!");          →  9
    }
}
```

The following paragraphs describe the key points:

→ **1** This class also begins with a series of comment lines that identify the function of the program.

→ **5** The class declaration begins on this line. The class is declared as public so other classes can use it. This declaration is required so that the `HelloApp2` class can access the `Greeter` class.

→ **7** The `sayHello` method is declared using the `public` keyword so that it's available to other classes that use the `Greeter` class. The `void` keyword indicates that this method doesn't provide any data back to the class that calls it, and `sayHello` simply provides the name of the method.

→ **9** The body of this method consists of just one line of code that displays the `"Hello, World!"` message on the console.

So what's the difference?

You might notice that the only line that actually does any real work in the HelloApp2 program is line 9 in the `Greeter` class (Listing 1-3), and this line happens to be identical to line 5 in the original `HelloApp` class (Listing 1-1). Other than the fact that the second version requires roughly twice as much code as the first version, what really is the difference between these two applications?

Simply put, the first version is procedural, and the second is object-oriented. In the first version of the program, the `main` method of the application class does all the work of the application by itself: It just says hello. The second version defines a class that knows how to say hello to the world, and then creates an object from that class and asks that object to say hello. The application itself doesn't know or even care exactly how the `Greeter` object says hello. It doesn't know exactly what the greeting will be, what language the greeting will be in, or even how the greeting will be displayed.

To illustrate this point, consider what would happen if you used the `Greeter` class shown in Listing 1-4 rather than the one shown in Listing 1-3. This version of the `Greeter` class uses a Java library class called `JOptionPane` to display a message in a dialog box rather than in a console window. (I won't bother explaining how this code works, but you can find out more about it in the next chapter.) If you were to run the `HelloApp2` application using this version of the `Greeter` class, you'd get the dialog box shown in Figure 1-1.

LISTING 1-4: ANOTHER VERSION OF THE GREETER CLASS

```
// This class creates a Greeter object
// that displays a hello message
// in a dialog box.
```

```
import javax.swing.JOptionPane;                      → 5

public class Greeter
{
    public void sayHello()
    {
        JOptionPane.showMessageDialog(null, "Hello,  → 11
            World!","Greeter", JOptionPane.
            INFORMATION_MESSAGE);
    }
}
```

Figure 1-1:
The class in
Listing 1-4
displays this
dialog box.

The important point to realize here is that the HelloApp2 class doesn't
have to be changed to use this new version of the Greeter class. Instead,
all you have to do is replace the old Greeter class with the new one, and
the HelloApp2 class won't know the difference. That's one of the main benefits of object-oriented programming.

Importing Java API Classes

You may have noticed that the Greeter class in Listing 1-4 includes this
statement:

```
import javax.swing.JOptionPane;
```

The purpose of the import statement is to let the compiler know that the
program is using a class that's defined by the Java API called JOptionPane.

Because the Java API contains literally thousands of classes, some form of
organization is needed to make the classes easier to access. Java does this
by grouping classes into manageable groups called *packages*. In the previous
example, the package that contains the JOptionPane class is named
javax.swing.

Strictly speaking, `import` statements are never required. But if you don't use `import` statements to import the API classes your program uses, you must *fully qualify* the names of the classes when you use them by listing the package name in front of the class name. So, if the class in Listing 1-4 didn't include the `import` statement in line 5, you'd have to code line 11 like this:

```
javax.swing.JOptionPane.showMessageDialog(null, "Hello,
    World!","Greeter", JOptionPane.
    INFORMATION_MESSAGE);
```

In other words, you'd have to specify `javax.swing.JOptionPane` instead of just `JOptionPane` whenever you referred to this class.

Here are some additional rules for working with `import` statements:

✦ `import` statements must appear at the beginning of the class file, before any class declarations.

✦ You can include as many `import` statements as are necessary to import all the classes used by your program.

✦ You can import all the classes in a particular package by listing the package name followed by an asterisk wildcard, like this:

```
import javax.swing.*;
```

✦ Because many programs use the classes that are contained in the `java.lang` package, you don't have to import that package. Instead, those classes are automatically available to all programs. The `System` class is defined in the `java.lang` package. As a result, you don't have to provide an `import` statement to use this class.

Chapter 2: Working with Variables and Data Types

In This Chapter

- ✔ Creating proper variable declarations
- ✔ Discovering the difference between primitive and reference types
- ✔ Looking at Java's built-in data types
- ✔ Introducing strings
- ✔ Getting input from the console
- ✔ Getting input if you're using an older version of Java

In this chapter, you find out the basics of working with variables in Java. Variables are the key to making Java programs general purpose. For example, the Hello, World! programs in the previous chapter are pretty specific: The only thing they say are "Hello, World!" But with a variable, you can make this type of program more general. For example, you could vary the greeting, so that sometimes it would say "Hello, World!" and other times it would say "Greetings, Foolish Mortals." Or you could personalize the greeting, so that instead of saying "Hello, World!," it said "Hello, Bob!" or "Hello, Amanda!"

Variables are also the key to creating programs that can perform calculations. For example, suppose you want to create a program that calculates the area of a circle given the circle's radius. Such a program uses two variables: one to represent the radius of the circle, the other to represent the circle's area. The program asks the user to enter a value for the first variable. Then, it calculates the value of the second variable.

Declaring Variables

In Java, you must explicitly declare all variables before using them. This rule is in contrast to some languages — most notably Basic and Visual Basic — which let you use variables that haven't been automatically declared. Allowing you to use variables that you haven't explicitly declared might seem like a good idea at first glance. But it's a common source of bugs that result from misspelled variable names. Java requires that you explicitly declare variables so that if you misspell a variable name, the compiler can detect your mistake and display a compiler error.

The basic form of a variable declaration is this:

```
type name;
```

Here are some examples:

```
int x;
String lastName;
double radius;
```

In these examples, variables named x, lastName, and radius, are declared. The x variable holds integer values, the lastName variable holds String values, and the radius variable holds double values. For more information about what these types mean, see the section "Working with Primitive Data Types" later in this chapter. Until then, just realize that int variables can hold whole numbers (like 5, 1,340, and -34), double variables can hold numbers with fractional parts (like 0.5, 99.97, or 3.1415), and String variables can hold text values (like "Hello, World!" or "Jason P. Finch").

Notice that variable declarations end with a semicolon. That's because the variable declaration is itself a type of statement.

Variable names follow the same rules as other Java identifiers, as I describe in Book II, Chapter 1. In short, a variable name can be any combination of letters and numerals, but must start with a letter. Most programmers prefer to start variable names with lowercase letters, and capitalize the first letter of individual words within the name. For example, firstName and salesTaxRate are typical variable names.

Declaring two or more variables in one statement

You can declare two or more variables of the same type in a single statement, by separating the variable names with commas. For example:

```
int x, y, z;
```

Here, three variables of type int are declared, using the names x, y, and z.

As a rule, I suggest you avoid declaring multiple variables in a single statement. Your code is easier to read and maintain if you give each variable a separate declaration.

Declaring class variables

A *class variable* is a variable that any method in a class can access, including static methods such as main. When declaring a class variable, you have two basic rules to follow:

✦ You must place the declaration within the body of the class, but not within any of the class methods.

✦ You must include the word `static` in the declaration. The word `static` comes before the variable type.

The following program shows the proper way to declare a class variable named `helloMessage`:

```
public class HelloApp
{
    static String helloMessage;

    public static void main(String[] args)
    {
        helloMessage = "Hello, World!";
        System.out.println(helloMessage);
    }
}
```

As you can see, the declaration includes the word `static` and is placed within the `HelloApp` class body, but not within the body of the `main` method.

You don't have to place class variable declarations at the beginning of a class. Some programmers prefer to place them at the end of the class, as in this example:

```
public class HelloApp
{
    public static void main(String[] args)
    {
        helloMessage = "Hello, World!";
        System.out.println(helloMessage);
    }

    static String helloMessage;
}
```

Here, the `helloMessage` variable is declared *after* the `main` method.

I think classes are easier to read if the variables are declared first, so that's where you seem them in this book.

Declaring instance variables

An *instance variable* is similar to a class variable, but doesn't specify the word `static` in its declaration. As its name suggests, instance variables are associated with instances of classes. As a result, you can only use them when you create an instance of a class. Because static methods aren't associated with an instance of the class, you can't use an instance variable in a static method — including the main method.

For example, the following program won't compile:

```
public class HelloApp
{
    String helloMessage;      // error -- should use static keyword

    public static void main(String[] args)
    {
        helloMessage = "Hello, World!";
        System.out.println(helloMessage);   // will not compile
    }
}
```

If you attempt to compile this program, you get the following error messages:

```
C:\Java\HelloApp.java:7: non-static variable helloMessage
        cannot be referenced from a static context
                helloMessage = "Hello, World!";
                ^
C:\Java\HelloApp.java:8: non-static variable helloMessage
        cannot be referenced from a static context
                System.out.println(helloMessage);
                                   ^
```

Both of these errors occur because the main method is static, so it can't access instance variables.

Instance variables are useful whenever you create your own classes. But because I don't cover that until Book III, you won't see many examples of instance methods in the remainder of the chapters in Book II.

Declaring local variables

A *local variable* is a variable that's declared within the body of a method. Then, you can use the variable only within that method. Other methods in the class aren't even aware that the variable exists.

Here's a version of the HelloApp class in which the helloMessage variable is declared as a local variable:

```
public class HelloApp
{
    public static void main(String[] args)
    {
```

```
        String helloMessage;
        helloMessage = "Hello, World!";
        System.out.println(helloMessage);
    }
}
```

Note that you don't specify `static` on a declaration for a local variable. If you do, the compiler generates an error message and refuses to compile your program. Local variables always exist in the context of a method, and they exist only while that method is executing. As a result, whether or not an instance of the class has been created is irrelevant.

Unlike class and instance variables, where you position the declaration for a local variable is important. In particular, you must place the declaration prior to the first statement that actually uses the variable. Thus, the following program won't compile:

```
public class HelloApp
{
    public static void main(String[] args)
    {
        helloMessage = "Hello, World!";   // error -- helloMessage
        System.out.println(helloMessage); // is not yet declared
        String helloMessage;
    }
}
```

When it gets to the first line of the `main` method, the compiler generates an error message complaining that it can't find the symbol `"helloMessage"`. That's because it hasn't yet been declared.

Although most local variables are declared near the beginning of a method's body, you can also declare local variables within smaller blocks of code marked by braces. This will make more sense to you when you read about statements that use blocks, such as `if` and `for` statements. But here's an example:

```
if (taxRate > 0)
{
    double taxAmount;
    taxAmount = subTotal * taxRate;
    total = subTotal + total;
}
```

Here, the variable `taxAmount` exists only within the set of braces that belongs to the `if` statement.

Initializing Variables

In Java, local variables are not given initial default values. The compiler checks to make sure that you have assigned a value before you use a local variable. For example, the following program won't compile:

```
public class testApp
{
    public static void main(String[] args)
    {
        int i;
        System.out.println("The value of i is " + i);
    }
}
```

If you try to compile this program, you get the following error message:

```
C:\Java\testApp.java:6: variable i might not have been
    initialized
        System.out.println("The value of i is " + i);
                                                   ^
```

To avoid this error message, you must initialize local variables before you can use them. You can do that by using an assignment statement or an initializer, as I describe in the following sections.

Unlike local variables, class variables and instance variables are given default values. Numeric types are automatically initialized to zero, and String variables are initialized to empty strings. As a result, you don't have to initialize a class variable or an instance variable, although you can if you want them to have an initial value other than the default.

Initializing variables with assignment statements

One way to initialize a variable is to code an *assignment statement* following the variable declaration. Assignment statements have this general form:

```
variable = expression;
```

Here, the *expression* can be any Java expression that yields a value of the same type as the variable. For example, here's a version of the main method from the previous example that correctly initializes the i variable before using it:

```
    public static void main(String[] args)
    {
        int i;
        i = 0;
        System.out.println("i is " + i);
    }
```

In this example, the variable is initialized to a value of zero before the `println` method is called to print the variable's value.

You find out a lot more about expressions in Book II, Chapter 3. For now, you can just use simple literal values, such as 0 in this example.

Initializing variables with initializers

Java also allows you to initialize a variable on the same statement that declares the variable. To do that, you use an *initializer,* which has the following general form:

```
type name = expression;
```

In effect, the initializer lets you combine a declaration and an assignment statement into one concise statement. Here are some examples:

```
int x = 0;
String lastName = "Lowe";
double radius = 15.4;
```

In each case, the variable is both declared and initialized in a single statement.

When you declare more than one variable in a single statement, each can have its own initializer. For example, the following code declares variables named x and y, and initializes x to 5 and y to 10:

```
int x = 5, y = 10;
```

When you declare two class or instance variables in a single statement but use only one initializer, you can mistakenly think the initializer applies to both variables. For example, consider this statement:

```
static int x, y = 5;
```

Here, you might think that both x and y would initialize to 5. But the initializer only applies to y, so x is initialized to its default value, 0. (If you make this mistake with a local variable, the compiler displays an error message for the first statement that uses the x variable because it isn't properly initialized.)

Using Final Variables (Or Constants)

A *final variable,* also called a *constant,* is a variable whose value you can't change once it's been initialized. To declare a final variable, you add the `final` keyword to the variable declaration, like this:

```
final int WEEKDAYS = 5;
```

Although you can create final local variables, most final variables are class or instance variables. To create a final class variable (sometimes called a *class constant*), add `static final` (not `final static`) to the declaration:

```
static final WEEKDAYS = 5;
```

Although it isn't required, using all capital letters for final variable names is common. You can easily spot the use of final variables in your programs.

Constants are useful for values that are used in several places throughout a program and that don't change during the course of the program. For example, suppose you're writing a game that features bouncing balls and you want the balls to always have a radius of 6 pixels. This program probably needs to use the ball diameter in several different places — for example, to draw the ball on-screen, to determine whether the ball has hit a wall, to determine whether the ball has hit another ball, and so on. Rather than just specify 6 whenever you need the ball's radius, you can set up a class constant named `BALL_RADIUS`, like this:

```
static final BALL_RADIUS = 6;
```

Using a class constant has two advantages:

✦ If you later decide that the radius of the balls should be 7, you make the change in just one place — the initializer for the `BALL_RADIUS` constant.

✦ The constant helps document the inner workings of your program. For example, the operation of a complicated calculation that uses the ball radius is easier to understand if it specifies `BALL_RADIUS` rather than 6.

Working with Primitive Data Types

The term *data type* refers to the type of data that can be stored in a variable. Java is sometimes called a *strongly typed* language because when you declare a variable, you must specify the variable's type. Then, the compiler ensures that you don't try to assign data of the wrong type to the variable. For example, the following code generates a compiler error:

```
int x;
x = 3.1415;
```

Because `x` is declared as a variable of type `int` (which holds whole numbers), you can't assign the value `3.1415` to it.

Java has an important distinction between *primitive types* and *reference types*. Primitive types are the data types that are defined by the language itself. In contrast, reference types are types that are defined by classes in the Java API rather than by the language itself.

A key difference between a primitive type and a reference type is that the memory location associated with a primitive type variable contains the actual value of the variable. As a result, primitive types are sometimes called *value types*. In contrast, the memory location associated with a reference type variable contains an address (called a *pointer*) that indicates the memory location of the actual object. I explain reference types more fully in the section "Using Reference Types" later in this chapter, so don't worry if this explanation doesn't make sense just yet.

It isn't quite true that reference types are defined by the Java API and not by the Java language specification. A few reference types, such as `Object` and `String`, are defined by classes in the API, but those classes are specified in the Java Language API. And a special type of variable called an *array*, which can hold multiple occurrences of primitive or reference type variables, is considered to be a reference type.

Java defines a total of eight primitive types. For your reference, Table 2-1 lists them. Of the eight primitive types, six are for numbers, one is for characters, and one is for true/false values. Of the six number types, four are types of integers and two are types of floating-point numbers. I describe each of the primitive types in the following sections.

Table 2-1	Java's Primitive Types
Type	*Explanation*
`int`	A 32-bit (4-byte) integer value
`short`	A 16-bit (2-byte) integer value
`long`	A 64-bit (8-byte) integer value
`byte`	An 8-bit (1-byte) integer value
`float`	A 32-bit (4-byte) floating-point value
`double`	A 64-bit (8-byte) floating-point value
`char`	A 16-bit character using the Unicode encoding scheme
`boolean`	A true or false value

Integer types

An *integer* is a whole number — that is, a number with no fractional or decimal portion. Java has four different integer types, which you can use to store numbers of varying sizes. The most commonly used integer type is `int`. This type uses four bytes to store an integer value that can range from about negative two billion to positive two billion.

If you're writing the application that counts how many hamburgers McDonald's has sold, an `int` variable might not be big enough. In that case, you can use a `long` integer instead. `long` is a 64-bit integer that can hold numbers ranging from about negative 9,000 trillion to positive 9,000 trillion. That's a big number, even by Federal Deficit standards.

In some cases, you may not need integers as large as the standard `int` type provides. For those cases, Java provides two smaller integer types. The `short` type represents a two-digit integer, which can hold numbers from –32,768 to +32,767. And the `byte` type defines an 8-bit integer that can range from –128 to +127.

Although the `short` and `byte` types require less memory than the `int` or `long` types, there's usually little reason to use them. A few bytes here or there isn't going to make any difference in the performance of most programs, so you should stick to `int` and `long` most of the time. And use `long` only when you know that you're dealing with numbers too large for `int`.

In Java, the size of integer data types is specified by the language and is the same regardless of what computer a program runs on. This is a huge improvement over the C and C++ languages, which let compilers for different platforms determine the optimum size for integer data types. As a result, a C or C++ program written and tested on one type of computer might not execute identically on another computer.

Java allows you to *promote* an integer type to a larger integer type. For example, Java allows the following:

```
int xInt;
long yLong;
xInt = 32;
yLong = xInt;
```

Here, you can assign the value of the `xInt` variable to the `yLong` variable because `yLong` is a larger size than `xInt`. However, Java does not allow the converse:

```
int xInt;
long yLong;
yLong = 32;
xInt = yLong;
```

The value of the `yLong` variable cannot be assigned to the `xInt` because `xInt` is smaller than `yLong`. Because this assigment might result in a loss of data, Java doesn't allow it.

(If you need to assign a `long` to an `int` variable, you must use explicit casting as described in the section "Type casting" later in this chapter.)

Floating-point types

Floating-point numbers are numbers that have fractional parts. You should use a floating-point type whenever you need a number with a decimal, such as 19.95 or 3.1415.

Java has two primitive types for floating-point numbers: `float`, which uses four bytes, and `double`, which uses eight bytes. In almost all cases, you should use the `double` type whenever you need numbers with fractional values.

The *precision* of a floating-point value indicates how many significant digits the value can have. The precision of a `float` type is only about 6 or 7 decimal digits, which isn't sufficient for most types of calculations. For example, if you use Java to write a payroll system, you might get away with using `float` variables to store salaries for employees such as teachers or firefighters, but not for professional baseball players or corporate executives.

In contrast, double variables have a precision of about 15 digits, which is enough for most purposes.

Floating-point numbers actually use *exponential notation* (also called *scientific notation*) to store their values. That means that a floating-point number actually records two numbers: a base value (also called the *mantissa*) and an exponent. The actual value of the floating-point number is calculated by multiplying the mantissa by two raised to the power indicated by the exponent. For `float` types, the exponent can be from –127 to +128. For `double` types, the exponent can be from –1023 to +1024. Thus, both `float` and `double` variables are capable of representing very large and very small numbers.

You can find more information about some of the nuances of working with floating-point values in Book II, Chapter 3.

When you use a floating-point literal, you should always include a decimal point, like this:

```
double period = 99.0;
```

If you omit the decimal point, the Java compiler treats the literal as an integer. Then, when it sees that you're trying to assign the literal to a double variable, it generates a compiler error message.

You can add an F or D suffix to a floating-point literal to indicate whether the literal itself is of type `float` or `double`. For example:

```
float value1 = 199.33F;
double value2 = 200495.995D;
```

Getting scientific with floats and doubles

If you have a scientific mind, you may want to use scientific notation when you write floating-point literals. For example

```
double e = 5.10e+6;
```

This equation is equivalent to

```
double e = 5100000D;
```

The sign is optional if the exponent is positive, so you can also write:

```
double e = 5.10e6;
```

Note that the exponent can be negative to indicate values smaller than 1. For example

```
double impulse = 23e-7;
```

This equation is equivalent to

```
double impulse = 0.0000023;
```

If you omit the suffix, D is assumed. As a result, you can usually omit the D suffix for double literals.

Interestingly, floating-point numbers have two distinct zero values: a negative zero and a positive zero. You don't have to worry about these much, because Java treats them as equal. Still, it would make for a good question on *Jeopardy!*. ("I'll take weird numbers for $200, Alex.")

The char type

The char type represents a single character from the Unicode character set. Keeping in mind that a character is not the same as a string is important. You find out about strings later in this chapter, in the section "Working with Strings." For now, just realize that a char variable can store just one character, not a sequence of characters as a string can.

To assign a value to a char variable, you use a character literal, which is always enclosed in apostrophes rather than quotes. For example:

```
char code = 'X';
```

Here, the character X is assigned to the variable named code.

The following statement won't compile:

```
char code = "X";   // error -- should use apostrophes, not quotes
```

That's because quotation marks are used to mark strings, not character constants.

Unicode is a two-byte character code that can represent the characters used in most languages throughout the world. Currently, about 35,000 codes in the Unicode character set are defined. That leaves another 29,000 codes unused. The first 256 characters in the Unicode character set are the same as the characters of the ASCII character set, which is the most commonly used character set for computers with Western languages.

For more information about the Unicode character set, see the official Unicode Web site at www.unicode.org.

Character literals can also use special *escape sequences* to represent special characters. Table 2-2 lists the allowable escape sequences. These escape sequences let you create literals for characters that can't otherwise be typed within a character constant.

Table 2-2	Escape Sequences for Character Constants
Escape Sequence	*Explanation*
\b	Backspace
\t	Horizontal tab
\n	Linefeed
\f	Form feed
\r	Carriage return
\"	Double quote
\'	Single quote
\\	Backslash

The boolean type

A *boolean* type can have one of two values: true or false. Booleans are used to perform logical operations, most commonly to determine whether some condition is true. For example:

```
boolean enrolled = true;
boolean credited = false;
```

Here, a variable named enrolled of type boolean is declared and initialized to a value of true, and another boolean named credited is declared and initialized to false.

In some languages, such as C or C++, integer values can be treated as booleans, with 0 equal to false and any other value equal to true. Not so in Java. In Java, you can't convert between an integer type and boolean.

Wrapper classes

Every primitive type has a corresponding class defined in the Java API class library. This class is sometimes called a *wrapper class*, because it wraps a primitive value with the object-oriented equivalent of pretty wrapping paper and a bow to make the primitive type look and behave like an object. Table 2-3 lists the wrapper classes for each of the eight primitive types.

As you find out later in this chapter, you can use these wrapper classes to convert primitive values to strings and vice-versa.

Table 2-3	Wrapper Classes for the Primitive Types
Primitive Type	*Wrapper Class*
int	Integer
short	Short
long	Long
byte	Byte
float	Float
double	Double
char	Character
Boolean	Boolean

Using Reference Types

In Book III, Chapter 1, you're introduced to some of the basic concepts of object-oriented programming. In particular, you see how all Java programs are made up of one or more classes, and how to use classes to create objects. In this section, I show how you can create variables that work with objects created from classes.

To start, a *reference type* is a type that's based on a class rather than on one of the primitive types that are built-in to the Java language. The class can either be a class that's provided as part of the Java API class library or a class that you write yourself. Either way, when you create an object from a class, Java allocates however much memory the object requires to store the object. Then, if you assign the object to a variable, the variable is actually assigned a *reference* to the object, not the object itself. This reference is the address of the memory location where the object is stored.

For example, suppose you're writing a game program that involves balls, and you create a class named `Ball` that defines the behavior of a ball. To declare a variable that can refer to a `Ball` object, you use a statement like this:

```
Ball b;
```

Here, the variable b is a variable of type Ball.

To create a new instance of an object from a class, you use the new keyword along with the class name. This second reference to the class name is actually a call to a special routine of the class called a *constructor*. The constructor is responsible for initializing the new object. For example, here's a statement that declares a variable of type Ball, calls the Ball class constructor to create a new Ball object, and assigns a reference to the Ball object to the variable:

```
Ball b = new Ball();
```

Book II
Chapter 2

**Working with
Variables and Data
Types**

One of the key concepts for working with reference types is to remember that a variable of a particular type doesn't actually contain an object of that type. Instead, it contains a reference to an object of the correct type. An important side effect is that two variables can refer to the same object. For example, consider these statements:

```
Ball b1 = new Ball();
Ball b2 = b1;
```

Here, I've declared two Ball variables, named b1 and b2. But I've only created one Ball object. In the first statement, the Ball object is created, and b1 is assigned a reference to it. Then, in the second statement, the variable b2 is assigned a reference to the same object that's referenced by b1. As a result, both b1 and b2 refer to the same Ball object.

If you use one of these variables to change some aspect of the ball, the change is visible to the ball no matter which variable you use. For example, suppose the Ball class has a method called setSpeed that lets you set the speed of the ball to any int value, and a getSpeed method that returns an integer value that reflects the ball's current speed. Now consider these statements:

```
b1.setSpeed(50);
b2.setSpeed(100);
int speed = b1.getSpeed();
```

When these statements complete, is the value of the speed variable 50 or 100? The correct answer is 100. Because both b1 and b2 refer to the same Ball object, changing the speed using b2 affects b1 as well.

This is one of the most confusing aspects of programming with an object-oriented language such as Java, so don't feel bad if you get tripped up from time to time.

Working with Strings

A *string* is a sequence of text characters, such as the message `"Hello, World!"` displayed by the `HelloApp` program illustrated in this chapter and the previous chapter. In Java, strings are an interesting breed. Java doesn't define strings as a primitive type. Instead, strings are a *reference type* that are defined by the Java API String class. The Java language does have some built-in features for working with strings. In some cases, these features make strings appear to be primitive types rather than reference types.

Java's string-handling features are advanced enough to merit an entire chapter to explain them. So, for the full scoop on strings, I refer you to Book IV, Chapter 1. The following sections present just the bare essentials of working with strings so you can incorporate simple strings in your programs.

Declaring and initializing strings

Strings are declared and initialized much like primitive types. In fact, the only difference you may notice at first is that the word `String` is capitalized, unlike the keywords for the primitive types such as `int` and `double`. That's because `String` isn't a keyword. Instead, it's the name of the Java API class that provides for string objects.

The following statements define and initialize a string variable:

```
String s;
s = "Hello, World!";
```

Here, a variable named `s` of type `String` is declared and initialized with the *string literal* `"Hello, World!"` Notice that string literals are enclosed in quotation marks, not apostrophes. Apostrophes are used for character literals, which are different than string literals.

Like any variable declaration, a string declaration can include an initializer. Thus, you can declare and initialize a string variable in one statement, like this:

```
String s = "Hello, World!";
```

Class variables and instance variables are automatically initialized to empty strings, but local variables aren't. To initialize a local string variable to an empty string, use a statement like this:

```
String s = "";
```

Combining strings

Combine two strings by using the plus sign (+) as a *concatenation operator*. (In Java-speak, combining strings is called *concatenation*.) For example, the following statement combines the value of two string variables to create a third string:

```
String hello = "Hello, ";
String world = "World!";
String greeting = hello + world;
```

The final value of the `greeting` variable is `"Hello, World!"`

When Java concatenates strings, it doesn't insert any blank spaces between the strings. As a result, if you want to combine two strings and have a space appear between them, you need to make sure that the first string ends with a space or the second string begins with a space. In the previous example, the first string ends with a space.

Book II
Chapter 2

Working with
Variables and Data
Types

Alternatively, you can concatenate a string literal along with the string variables. For example:

```
String hello = "Hello";
String world = "World!";
String greeting = hello + ", " + world;
```

Here, the comma and the space that appear between the words `Hello` and `World` are inserted as a string literal.

Concatenation is one of the most commonly used string handling techniques, so you see plenty of examples in this book. In fact, I've already used concatenation once in this chapter. Earlier, I showed you a program that included the following line:

```
System.out.println("The value of i is " + i);
```

Here, the `println` method of the `System.out` object prints the string that's created when the literal `"The value of i is "` is concatenated with the value of the `i` variable.

Converting primitives to strings

Because string concatenation lets you combine two or more string values, and primitive types such as `int` and `double` are *not* string types, you might be wondering how the last example in the previous section can work. In other words, how can Java concatenate the string literal `"The value of i is "` with the integer value of `i` in this statement:

```
System.out.println("The value of i is " + i);
```

The answer is that Java automatically converts primitive values to string values whenever you use a primitive value in a concatenation.

You can explicitly convert a primitive value to a string by using the `toString` method of the primitive type's wrapper class. For example, to convert the `int` variable x to a string, you use this statement:

```
String s = Integer.toString(x);
```

In the next chapter, you discover how to use a special class called the `NumberFormat` class to convert primitive types to strings while applying various types of formatting to the value, such as adding commas, dollar signs, or percentage marks.

Converting strings to primitives

Converting a primitive value to a string value is pretty easy. Going the other way — converting a string value to a primitive — is a little more complex, because it doesn't always work. For example, if a string contains the value `10`, you can easily convert it to an integer. But if the string contains `thirty-two`, you can't.

To convert a string to a primitive type, you use a `parse` method of the appropriate wrapper class, as listed in Table 2-4. For example, to convert a string value to an integer, you use statements like this:

```
String s = "10";
int x = Integer.parseInt(s);
```

Of course, you have no real reason to do this. However, as you see later in this chapter, you can use the parse methods to convert string values entered by the user to primitive types. That way, you can write programs that let the user enter numeric data via the console window.

Table 2-4	Methods That Convert Strings to Numeric Primitive Types	
Wrapper Class	Parse Method	Example
Integer	parseInt(String)	`int x = Integer.parseInt("100");`
Short	parseShort(String)	`short x = Short.parseShort("100");`
Long	parseLong(String)	`long x = Long.parseLong("100");`
Byte	parseByte(String)	`byte x = Byte.parseByte("100");`
Float	parseByte(String)	`float x = Float.parseFloat ("19.95");`

Wrapper Class	Parse Method	Example
Double	parseByte(String)	`double x = Double.parseDouble ("19.95");`
Character	(none)	
Boolean	parseBoolean (String)	`boolean x = Boolean.parseBoolean ("true");`

Note that you don't need a `parse` method to convert a `String` to a `Character`. If you need to do that, you can find out how in Book IV, Chapter 1.

Converting and Casting Numeric Data

From time to time, you need to convert numeric data of one type to another. For example, you might need to convert a double value to an integer, or vice versa. Some conversions can be done automatically. Others are done using a technique called *casting*. I describe automatic type conversions and casting in the following sections.

Automatic conversions

Java can automatically convert some primitive types to others and do so whenever necessary. Figure 2-1 shows which conversions Java allows. Note that the conversions shown with dotted arrows in the figure may cause some of the value's precision to be lost. For example, an `int` can be converted to a `float`, but large `int` values won't be converted exactly because `int` values can have more digits than can be represented by the `float` type.

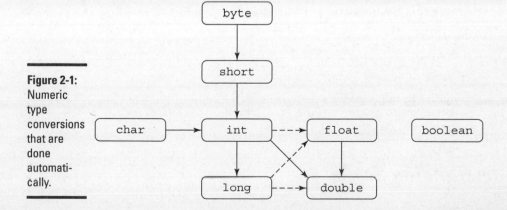

Figure 2-1:
Numeric
type
conversions
that are
done
automati-
cally.

Whenever you perform a mathematical operation on two values that aren't of the same type, Java automatically converts one of them to the type of the other. Here are the rules Java follows when doing this conversion:

✦ If one of the values is a `double`, the other value is converted to a `double`.

✦ If neither is a `double` but one is a `float`, the other is converted to a `float`.

✦ If neither is a `double` nor a `float` but one is a `long`, the other is converted to a `long`.

✦ If all else fails, both values are converted to `int`.

Type casting

Casting is similar to conversion, but isn't done automatically. You use casting to perform a conversion that is *not* shown in Figure 2-1. For example, if you want to convert a `double` to an `int`, you must use casting.

When you use casting, you run the risk of losing information. For example, a `double` can hold larger numbers than an `int`. In addition, an `int` can't hold the fractional part of a `double`. As a result, if you cast a `double` to an `int`, you run the risk of losing data or accuracy. For example, `3.1415` becomes `3`.

To cast a primitive value from one type to another, you use a *cast operator,* which is simply the name of a primitive type in parentheses placed before the value you want to cast. For example:

```
double pi = 3.1314;
int iPi;
iPi = (int) pi;
```

Note that the fractional part of a double is simply discarded when cast to an integer; it isn't rounded. For example:

```
double price = 9.99;
int iPrice = (int) price;
```

Here, `iPrice` is assigned the value 9. If you want to round the double value when you convert it, use the `Round` method of the `Math` class as I show you in the next chapter.

Understanding Scope

The *scope* of a variable refers to which parts of a class the variable exists in. In the simplest terms, every variable exists only within the block in which the variable is declared as well as any blocks that are contained within that block. That's why class and instance variables, which are declared in the class body, can be accessed by any methods defined by the class, but local variables defined within a method can be accessed only by the method in which they are defined.

In Java, a *block* is marked by a matching pair of braces. Java has many different kinds of blocks: class bodies, method bodies, and block statements that belong to statements such as `if` or `for` statements. But in each case, a block marks the scope boundaries for the variables declared within it.

The program in Listing 2-1 can help clarify the scope of class and local variables.

> **LISTING 2-1: A PROGRAM THAT DEMONSTRATES SCOPE FOR CLASS AND**
> **LOCAL VARIABLES**

```
public class ScopeApp
{                                                              → 2

    static int x;

    public static void main(String[] args)
    {
        x = 5;
        System.out.println("main: x = " + x);
        myMethod();
    }

    public static void myMethod()
    {
        int y;
        y = 10;                                                → 16
        if (y == x + 5)                                        → 17
        {
            int z;
            z = 15;                                            → 20
            System.out.println("myMethod: z = " + z);
        }                                                      → 22
        System.out.println("myMethod: x = " + x);
        System.out.println("myMethod: y = " + y);
    }                                                          → 25

}                                                              → 27
```

The following paragraphs explain the scope of each of the variables used in this class:

✦ The variable x is a `class` variable. Its scope begins in line 2 and ends in line 27. As a result, both the `main` method and the `myMethod` method can access it.

✦ The variable y is a local variable that's initialized in line 16. As a result, its scope begins in line 16 and ends in line 25, which marks the end of the body of the `myMethod` method.

✦ The variable z is a local variable that's declared and initialized in the statement block that belongs to the `if` statement in line 17. Its scope begins when the variable is initialized in line 20 and ends when the statement block ends in line 22.

Strictly speaking, the scope of a local variable begins when the variable is initialized and ends when the block that contains the variable's declaration ends. In contrast, the scope for a class or instance variable is the entire class in which the variable is declared. That means that you can use a class or instance variable in a method that physically appears before the variable is declared. But you can't use a local variable before it's declared.

Shadowing Variables

A *shadowed variable* is a variable that would otherwise be accessible, but is temporarily made unavailable because a variable with the same name has been declared in a more immediate scope. That's a mouthful, but the example in Listing 2-2 makes the concept clear. Here, a class variable named x is declared. Then, in the `main` method, a local variable with the same name is declared.

LISTING 2-2: A CLASS THAT DEMONSTRATES SHADOWING

```
public class ShadowApp
{                                                          → 2

    static int x;                                          → 4

    public static void main(String[] args)
    {
        x = 5;                                             → 8
        System.out.println("x = " + x);                    → 9
        int x;                                             → 10
        x = 10;                                            → 11
        System.out.println("x = " + x);                    → 12
        System.out.println("ShadowApp.x = " +
            ShadowApp.x);                                  → 13
    }                                                      → 14

}                                                          → 16
```

The following paragraphs explain the scoping issues in this program:

✦ The class variable x is declared in line 4. Its scope is the entire class body, from line 2 to line 16.

✦ The class variable x is assigned a value of 5 in line 8. Then, this value is printed to the console in line 9.

✦ In line 10, a local variable named x is declared. The local variable shadows the class variable x, so any reference to x through the end of this method in line 14 refers to the local variable rather than the class variable.

✦ The local variable x is initialized in line 11. At that point, the local variable x comes into scope and remains in scope until the end of the method in line 14.

✦ The `System.out.println` statement in line 12 prints the value of the local variable x. Note that this statement is identical to the statement in line 9, which printed the class variable x because the class variable had not yet been shadowed.

✦ While a class variable is shadowed, you can access it by specifying the class name as shown in line 13. Here, `ShadowApp.x` refers to the class variable.

✦ When the `main` method ends in line 14, the class variable x is no longer shadowed.

The scope of a local variable that shadows a class variable doesn't necessarily begin at the same point that the local variable's scope begins. The shadowing begins when the local variable is declared, but the local variable's scope doesn't begin until the variable is initialized. If you attempt to access the variable between the declaration and the initialization, the Java compiler displays an error message.

Because shadowing is a common source of errors, I suggest you avoid it as much as possible.

Printing Data with System.out

You've already seen several programs that use `System.out.println` to display output on the console. In the following sections, I officially show you how this method works, along with a related method called just `print`.

Standard input and output streams

Java applications are designed to work in a terminal I/O environment. Every Java application has at its disposal three *I/O streams* that are designed for terminal-based input and output, which simply sends or receives data one character at a time. The three streams are

✦ **Standard input:** A stream designed to receive input data. This stream is usually connected to the keyboard at the computer where the program is run. That way, the user can type characters directly into the standard input stream. In the section "Getting Input with the Scanner Class" that appears later in this chapter, you connect this input stream to a class called `Scanner` that makes it easy to read primitive data types from the standard input stream.

✦ **Standard output:** A stream designed to display text output on-screen. When you run a Java program under Windows, a special console window is opened, and the standard output stream is connected to it. Then, any text you send to standard output is displayed in that window.

✦ **Standard error:** Another stream designed for output. This stream is also connected to the console window. As a result, text written to the standard output stream is often intermixed with text written to the error stream.

Windows and other operating systems allow you to *redirect* standard output to some other destination — typically a file. When you do that, only the standard output data is redirected. Text written to standard error is still displayed in the console window.

To redirect standard output, you use a greater-than sign on the command that runs the Java class, followed by the name of the file you want to save the standard output text to. For example:

```
C:\Java>java TestApp >output.txt
```

Here, the standard output created by the class `TestApp` is saved in a file named `output.txt`. However, any text sent to the standard error stream still appears in the console window. As a result, the standard error stream is useful for programs that use output redirection to display status messages, error messages, or other information.

All three standard streams are available to every Java program via the fields of the `System` class, as described in Table 2-5.

Table 2-5	Static Fields of the System Object
Field	*Description*
System.in	Standard input
System.out	Standard output
System.err	Standard error

Using System.out and System.err

Both `System.out` and `System.err` represent instances of a class called `PrintWriter`, which defines the `print` and `println` methods used to write data to the console. You can use both methods with either a `String` argument or an argument of any primitive data type.

The only difference between the `print` and the `println` methods is that the `println` method adds a line-feed character to the end of the output, so the output from the next call to `print` or `println` begins on a new line.

Because it doesn't start a new line, the `print` method is useful when you want to print two or more items on the same line. For example:

```
int i = 64;
int j = 23;
System.out.print(i);
System.out.print(" and ");
System.out.println(j);
```

The console output produced by these lines is:

```
64 and 23
```

Note that you could do the same thing with a single call to `println` by using string concatenation, like this:

```
int i = 64;
int j = 23;
System.out.println(i + " and " + j);
```

Getting Input with the Scanner Class

Until recently, getting text input from the user in a console-based Java program wasn't easy. But with Java 1.5, a new class — called `Scanner` — has been introduced to simplify the task of getting input from the user. In the following sections, you use the `Scanner` class to get simple input values from the user. The techniques that I present here are used in many of the programs shown in the rest of this book.

If you're using an older version of Java, you should still read this section, because many of the programs in this book use the `Scanner` class. However, you should also read the next section, "Getting Input with the JOptionPane Class," because that section describes a way of getting user input that works with earlier versions of Java.

Throughout the following sections, I refer to the program shown in Listing 2-3. This simple program uses the Scanner class to read an integer value from the user, and then displays the value back to the console to verify that the program received the value entered by the user. Here's a sample of the console window for this program:

```
Enter an integer: 5
You entered 5.
```

The program begins by displaying the message Enter an integer: on the first line. Then, it waits for you to enter a number. When you press the Enter key, it displays the confirmation message (You entered 5.) on the second line.

LISTING 2-3: A PROGRAM THAT USES THE SCANNER CLASS

```
import java.util.Scanner;                                    → 1

public class ScannerApp
{

    static Scanner sc = new Scanner(System.in);              → 6

    public static void main(String[] args)
    {
        System.out.print("Enter an integer: ");              → 10
        int x = sc.nextInt();                                → 11
        System.out.println("You entered " + x + ".");        → 12
    }

}
```

Importing the Scanner class

Before you can use the Scanner class in a program, you must import it. To do that, you code an import statement at the beginning of the program, before the class declaration as shown in line 1 of Listing 2-3:

```
import java.util.Scanner;
```

Note that java and util are not capitalized, but Scanner is.

If you're using other classes in the java.util package, you can import the entire package by coding the import statement like this:

```
import java.util.*;
```

Declaring and creating a Scanner object

Before you can use the Scanner class to read input from the console, you must declare a Scanner variable and create an instance of the Scanner class. I recommend you create the Scanner variable as a class variable, and create the Scanner object in the class variable initializer, as shown in line 6 of Listing 2-3:

```
static Scanner sc = new Scanner(System.in);
```

That way, you can use the sc variable in any method in the class.

To create a Scanner object, you use the new keyword followed by a call to the Scanner class constructor. Note that the Scanner class requires a parameter that indicates the *input stream* that the input comes from. You can use System.in here to specify standard keyboard console input.

Getting input

To read an input value from the user, you can use one of the methods of the Scanner class that are listed in Table 2-6. As you can see, the primitive data type has a separate method.

Table 2-6	Scanner Class Methods that Get Input Values
Method	*Explanation*
boolean nextBoolean()	Reads a boolean value from the user.
byte nextByte()	Reads a byte value from the user.
double nextDouble()	Reads a double value from the user.
float nextFloat()	Reads a float value from the user.
int nextInt()	Reads an int value from the user.
String nextLine()	Reads a String value from the user.
long nextLong()	Reads a long value from the user.
short nextShort()	Reads a short value from the user.

Notice in the first column of the table that each method listing begins with the type of the value that's returned by the method. For example, the nextInt method returns an int value. Also, notice that each of the methods ends with an empty set of parentheses. That means that none of these methods require parameters. If a method requires parameters, the parameters are listed within these parentheses.

Because these methods read a value from the user and return the value, you most often use them in statements that assign the value to a variable. For example, line 11 in Listing 2-3 reads an int and assigns it to a variable named x.

When the `nextInt` method is executed, the program waits for the user to enter a value in the console window. To let the user know what kind of input the program expects, you should usually call the `System.out.print` method before you call a `Scanner` method to get input. For example, line 10 in Listing 2-3 calls `System.out.print` to display the message `Enter an integer:` on the console. That way, the user knows that the program is waiting for input.

If the user enters a value that can't be converted to the correct type, the program crashes, which means that it abruptly terminates. As the program crashes, it displays a cryptic error message that indicates what caused the failure. For example, if you enter `three` instead of an actual number, the console window looks something like this:

```
Enter an integer: three
    Exception in thread "main" java.util.InputMismatchException
        at java.util.Scanner.throwFor(Scanner.java:819)
        at java.util.Scanner.next(Scanner.java:1431)
        at java.util.Scanner.nextInt(Scanner.java:2040)
        at java.util.Scanner.nextInt(Scanner.java:2000)
        at ScannerApp.main(ScannerApp.java:11)
```

This message indicates that an *exception* called `InputMismatch Exception` has occurred, which means that the program was expecting to see an integer, but got something else instead. In Book II, Chapter 8, you find out how to provide for exceptions like these so that the program can display a friendlier message and give the user another shot at entering a correct value. Until then, you have to put up with the fact that if the user enters incorrect data, your programs crash ungracefully.

You can prevent the `nextInt` and similar methods from crashing with incorrect input data by using one of the methods listed in Table 2-7 to first test the next input to make sure it's valid. I haven't covered the Java statements you need to perform this test yet. Don't worry; in Book II, Chapter 8, I show you the solution.

Table 2-7	Scanner Class Methods That Check for Valid Input Values
Method	*Explanation*
`boolean hasNextBoolean()`	Returns `true` if the next value entered by the user is a valid `boolean` value.
`boolean hasNextByte()`	Returns `true` if the next value entered by the user is a valid `byte` value.
`boolean hasNextDouble()`	Returns `true` if the next value entered by the user is a valid `double` value.

Method	Explanation
`boolean hasNextFloat()`	Returns `true` if the next value entered by the user is a valid `float` value.
`boolean hasNextInt()`	Returns `true` if the next value entered by the user is a valid `int` value.
`boolean hasNextLong()`	Returns `true` if the next value entered by the user is a valid `long` value.
`boolean hasNextShort()`	Returns `true` if the next value entered by the user is a valid `short` value.

Getting Input with the JOptionPane Class

If you're using a version of Java prior to Java 1.5, you don't have the luxury of using the `Scanner` class to read input directly from the user via a console window. However, you can use the `JOptionPane` class to display simple dialog boxes such as the one shown in Figure 2-2 to get text input from the user. Then, you can use the `parse` methods of the primitive type wrapper classes to convert the text entered by the user to the appropriate primitive type.

Figure 2-2:
A dialog box
displayed
by the
JOptionPane
class.

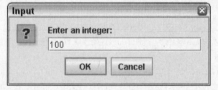

Although the `JOptionPane` class has many methods, the only one you need to get simple text input is the `showInputDialog` method. This method uses a single parameter that specifies the prompting message that's displayed in the dialog box. It returns a string value that you can then parse to the proper type.

The `JOptionPane` class is a part of the `javax.swing` package, so you need to add an `import javax.swing.JOptionPane` statement to the beginning of any program that uses this class.

Listing 2-4 shows a simple program that uses the `JOPtionPane` class to get an integer value and display it on the console.

LISTING 2-4: A PROGRAM THAT USES THE JOPTIONPANE CLASS TO GET USER INPUT

```
import javax.swing.JOptionPane;                          → 1

public class DialogApp
{
    public static void main(String[] args)
    {
        String s;
        s = JOptionPane.showInputDialog("Enter an
            integer:");                                  → 8
        int x = Integer.parseInt(s);                     → 9
        System.out.println("You entered " + x + "."); → 10
    }
}
```

The following paragraphs describe the important lines in this program:

→ **1** This line imports the JOptionPane class.

→ **8** This statement displays an input dialog box with the prompt Enter an integer: and assigns the string entered by the user to the variable named s.

→ **9** This statement uses the parseInt method of the Integer class to convert the string entered by the user to an integer.

→**10** This statement displays the integer value to confirm that the data entered by the user was converted properly to an integer.

This program terminates abruptly if the user enters anything other than an integer in the input dialog box. For example, if the user enters ten, the program terminates, and a cryptic message indicating that a NumberFormat Exception has occurred is displayed. You can provide for this situation in Book II, Chapter 8. Until then, just be careful to enter correct numbers when you use the JOptionPane class.

Chapter 3: Working with Numbers and Expressions

In This Chapter

- Dealing with operators, such as +, -, *, and /
- Creating finely crafted expressions
- Incrementing and decrementing
- Accepting an assignment
- Using the `Math` class
- Formatting your numbers
- Strange things that can happen with numbers

In Book II, Chapter 2, you discover the various primitive numeric types that are supported by Java. In this chapter, you build on that knowledge by doing basic operations with numbers. Much of this chapter focuses on the complex topic of expressions, which combine numbers with operators to perform calculations. But this chapter also covers techniques for formatting numbers when you display them and performing advanced calculations using the `Math` class. In addition, you find out why Java's math operations sometimes produce results you might not expect.

Working with Arithmetic Operators

An *operator* is a special symbol or keyword that's used to designate a mathematical operation or some other type of operation that can be performed on one or more values, called *operands*. In all, Java has about 40 different operators. This chapter focuses on the operators that do arithmetic. These *arithmetic operators* perform basic arithmetic operations, such as addition, subtraction, multiplication, and division. In all, there are 7 of them. Table 3-1 summarizes them.

Table 3-1	Java's Arithmetic Operators
Operator	*Description*
+	Addition
–	Subtraction
*	Multiplication
/	Division
%	Remainder
++	Increment
--	Decrement

The following section of code can help clarify how these operators work for int types:

```
int a = 21, b = 6;
int c = a + b;        // c is 27
int d = a - b;        // d is 15
int e = a * b;        // e is 126
int f = a / b;        // f is 3   (21 / 6 is 3 remainder 3)
int g = a % b;        // g is 3   (20 / 6 is 3 remainder 3)
a++;                  // a is now 22
b--;                  // b is now 5
```

Notice that for division, the result is truncated. Thus, 21 / 6 returns 3, not 3.5. For more information about integer division, see the section "Dividing Integers" later in this chapter.

Here's how the operators work for double values:

```
double x = 5.5, y = 2.0;
double m = x + y;       // m is 7.5
double n = x - y;       // n is 3.5
double o = x * y;       // o is 11.0
double p = x / y;       // p is 2.75
double q = x % y;       // q is 1.5
x++;                    // x is now 6.5
y--;                    // y is now 1.0
```

When you divide two int values, the result is an integer value, even if you assign it to a double variable. For example:

```
int a = 21, b = 6;
double answer = a / b;    // answer = 3.0
```

Categorizing operators by the number of operands

A common way to categorize Java's operators is by the number of operands the operator works on. Categorizing the operators in this way, there are three types:

✔ **Unary operators:** Operators that work on just one operand. Examples of unary operators are negation (–x, which returns the negative of x) and increment (x++, which adds 1 to x).

A unary operator can be a prefix operator or a postfix operator. A *prefix operator* is written before the operand, like this:

```
operator operand
```

A *postfix operator* is written after the operand:

```
operand operator
```

✔ **Binary operators:** Operators that work on two operands. Examples of binary operators are addition (x + y), multiplication (invoiceTotal * taxRate), and comparison operators (x < leftEdge). In Java, all binary operators are *infix operators*, which means they appear between the operands, like this:

```
operand1 operator operand2
```

✔ **Ternary operators:** Operators that work on three operands. Java has only one ternary operator, called the *conditional operator* (?:). The conditional operator is also infix:

```
operand1 ? operand2 : operand3
```

If that's not what you want, you can cast one of the operands to a double before performing the division, like this:

```
int a = 21, b = 6;
double answer = (double)a / b;    // answer = 3.5
```

The moral of the story is that if you want to divide int values and get an accurate double result, you must cast at least one of the int values to a double.

Here are a few additional things to think about tonight as you lay awake pondering the wonder of Java's arithmetic operators:

✦ In algebra, you can write a number right next to a variable to imply multiplication. For example, *4x* means "four times x." Not so in Java. The following statement doesn't compile:

```
int x;
y = 4x;    // error, won't compile
```

✦ The remainder operator (%) is also called a *modulus* operator. It returns the remainder when the first operand is divided by the second operand. The remainder operator is often used to determine if one number is evenly divisible by another, in which case the result is 0. For more information, see the next section, "Dividing Integers."

✦ All operators, including the arithmetic variety, are treated as separators in Java. As a result, any use of white space in an expression is optional. Thus, the following two statements are equivalent:

```
a = ( (x + 4) * 7 ) / (y * x);
a=((x+4)*7)/(y*x);
```

Just remember that a little bit of white space never hurt anyone, and sometimes it helps make Java a little more readable.

Dividing Integers

When you divide one integer into another, the result is always another integer. Any remainder is simply discarded, and the answer is *not* rounded up. For example, 5 / 4 gives the result 1, and 3 / 4 gives the result 0. If you want to know that 5 / 4 is actually 1.25 or that 3 / 4 is actually 0.75, you need to use floats or doubles instead of integers.

If you need to know what the remainder is when you divide two integers, use the remainder operator (%). For example, suppose you have a certain number of marbles to give away and a certain number of children to give them to. The program in Listing 3-1 lets you enter the number of marbles and the number of children. Then, it calculates the number of marbles to give to each child and the number of marbles you have left over.

Here's a sample of the console output for this program, where the number of marbles entered is 93 and the number of children is 5:

```
Welcome to the marble divvy upper.
Number of marbles: 93
Number of children: 5
Give each child 18 marbles.
You will have 3 marbles left over.
```

LISTING 3-1: A PROGRAM THAT DIVIES UP MARBLES

```
import java.util.Scanner;                                        → 1

public class MarblesApp
{
    static Scanner sc = new Scanner(System.in);                  → 5

    public static void main(String[] args)
    {
        // declarations                                          → 9
        int numberOfMarbles;
        int numberOfChildren;
        int marblesPerChild;
        int marblesLeftOver;
```

```
// get the input data                                           → 15
System.out.println("Welcome to the marble divvy upper.");
System.out.print("Number of marbles: ");
numberOfMarbles = sc.nextInt();
System.out.print("Number of children: ");
numberOfChildren = sc.nextInt();

// calculate the results
marblesPerChild = numberOfMarbles / numberOfChildren;          → 23
marblesLeftOver = numberOfMarbles % numberOfChildren;          → 24

// print the results                                           → 26
System.out.println("Give each child " +
    marblesPerChild + " marbles.");
System.out.println("You will have " +
    marblesLeftOver + " marbles left over.");
    }

}
```

The following paragraphs describe the key lines in this program:

→ **1** Imports the `java.util.Scanner` class so the program can use it to get input from the user.

→ **5** Creates the `Scanner` object and assigns it to a class variable so it can be used in any method in the class.

→ **9** The next four lines declare the local variables used by the program.

→**15** The next five lines get the input from the user.

→**23** Calculates the number of marbles to give to each child by using integer division, which discards the remainder.

→**24** Calculates the number of marbles left over.

→**26** The next two statements print the results.

TIP

It's probably obvious if you think about it, but you should realize that if you use integer division to divide a by b, then the result times b plus the remainder equals a. In other words:

```
int a = 29;          // any value will do
int b = 3;           // any value will do
int c = a / b;
int d = a % b;
int e = (c * b) + d;  // e will always equal a
```

Combining Operators

You can combine operators to form complicated expressions. When you do, the order in which the operations are carried out is determined by the *precedence* of each operator in the expression. The order of precedence for the arithmetic operators is:

✦ Increment (++) and decrement (--) operators are evaluated first.

✦ Next, sign operators (+ or -) are applied.

✦ Then, multiplication (*), division (/), and remainder (%) operators are evaluated.

✦ Finally, addition (+) and subtraction (-) operators are applied.

For example, in the expression a + b * c, multiplication has a higher precedence than addition. Thus, b is multiplied by c first. Then, the result of that multiplication is added to a.

If an expression includes two or more operators at the same order of precedence, the operators are evaluated left to right. Thus, in the expression a * b / c, a is first multiplied by b, then the result is divided by c.

If you want, you can use parentheses to change the order in which operations are performed. Operations within parentheses are always performed before operations that aren't in parentheses. Thus, in the expression (a + b) * c, a is added to b first. Then, the result is multiplied by c.

If an expression has two or more sets of parentheses, the operations in the innermost set are performed first. For example, in the expression (a * (b + c)) / d, b is first added to c. Then, the result is multiplied by a. And finally, that result is divided by d.

Apart from the increment and decrement operators, these precedence rules and the use of parentheses are the same as they are for basic algebra. So if you were paying attention in the eighth grade, precedence should make sense.

With double or float values, changing the left to right order for operators with the same precedence doesn't affect the result. However, with integer types, it can make a huge difference if division is involved. For example, consider these statements:

```
int a = 5, b = 6, c = 7;
int d1 = a * b / c;    // d1 is 4
int d2 = a * (b / c);  // d2 is 0
```

This difference occurs because integer division always returns an integer result, which is a truncated version of the actual result. Thus, in the first expression, a is first multiplied by b, giving a result of 30. Then, this result is divided by c. Truncating the answer gives a result of 4. But in the second expression, b is first divided by c, which gives a truncated result of 0. Then, this result is multiplied by a, giving a final answer of 0.

Using the Unary Plus and Minus Operators

The plus and minus unary operators let you change the sign of an operand. Note that the actual operator used for these operations is the same as the binary addition and subtraction operators. The compiler figures out whether you mean to use the binary or the unary version of these operators by examining the expression.

Book II
Chapter 3

Working with Numbers and Expressions

The unary minus operator doesn't necessarily make an operand have a negative value. Instead, it changes whatever sign the operand has to start with. Thus, if the operand starts with a positive value, the unary minus operator changes it to negative. But if the operand starts with a negative value, the unary minus operator makes it positive. The following examples illustrate this point:

```
int a = 5;      // a is 5
int b = -a;     // b is -5
int c = -b;     // c is +5
```

Interestingly enough, the unary plus operator doesn't actually do anything. For example:

```
int a = -5;     // a is -5
int b = +a;     // b is -5
a = 5;          // a is now 5
int c = +a;     // c is 5
```

Notice that if a starts out positive, +a is also positive. But if a starts out negative, +a is still negative. Thus, the unary + operator has no effect. I guess Java provides the unary plus operator out of a need for balance.

You can also use these operators with more complex expressions, like this:

```
int a = 3, b = 4, c = 5;
int d = a * -(b + c);      // d is -27
```

Here, b is added to c, giving a result of 9. Then, the unary minus is applied, giving a result of -9. Finally, -9 is multiplied by a giving a result of -27.

Using Increment and Decrement Operators

One of the most common operations in computer programming is adding or subtracting 1 from a variable. Adding 1 to a variable is called *incrementing* the variable. Subtracting 1 is called *decrementing*. The traditional way to increment a variable is like this:

```
a = a + 1;
```

Here, the expression a + 1 is calculated, and the result is assigned to the variable a.

Java provides an easier way to do this type of calculation: the increment (++) and decrement (--) operators. These are unary operators that apply to a single variable. Thus, to increment the variable a, you can code just this:

```
a++;
```

Note that an expression that uses an increment or decrement operator is a statement by itself. That's because the increment or decrement operator is also a type of assignment operator, as it changes the value of the variable it applies to.

You can only use the increment and decrement operators on variables, not on numeric literals or other expressions. For example, Java doesn't allow the following expressions:

```
a = b * 5++;    // can't increment the number 5
a = (b * 5)++;  // can't increment the expression (b *
     5)
```

Note that you can use an increment or decrement operator in an assignment statement. For example:

```
int a = 5;
int b = a--;   // both a and b are set to 4
```

When the second statement is executed, the expression a-- is evaluated first, so a is set to 4. Then, the new value of a is assigned to b. Thus, both a and b are set to 4.

The increment and decrement operators are unusual because they are unary operators that can be placed either before *(prefix)* or after *(postfix)* the variable they apply to. Whether you place the operator before or after the variable can have a major affect on how an expression is evaluated. If you place an increment or decrement operator before its variable, the operator is applied before the rest of the expression is evaluated. As a result, the incremented value of the variable is used in the expression. In contrast, if you place the operator after the variable, the operator is applied after the expression is evaluated. Thus, the original value of the variable is used in the expression.

Confused yet? A simple example can clear it up. First, consider these statements with an expression that uses a postfix increment:

```
int a = 5;
int b = 3;
int c = a * b++;    // c is set to 15
```

When the expression in the third statement is evaluated, the original value of b — 3 — is used in the multiplication. Thus, c is set to 15. Then, b is incremented to 4.

Now consider this version, with a prefix increment:

```
int a = 5;
int b = 3;
int c = a * ++b;    // c is set to 20
```

This time, b is incremented before the multiplication is performed, so c is set to 20. Either way, b ends up set to 4.

Similarly, consider this example:

```
int a = 5;
int b = --a;    // b is set to 5, a is set to 4.
```

This example is similar to an earlier example, but this time the prefix increment operator is used. When the second statement is executed, the value of a is assigned to b. Then, a is decremented. As a result, b is set to 5, and a is set to 4.

Because the increment and decrement operators can be confusing when used with other operators in an expression, I suggest you use them alone. Whenever you're tempted to incorporate an increment or decrement operator into a larger expression, pull the increment or decrement out of the expression and make it a separate statement either before or after the expression. In other words, code this:

```
b++;
c = a * b;
```

instead of this:

```
c = a * ++b;
```

In the first version, it's crystal clear that b is incremented before the multiplication is done.

Using the Assignment Operator

The standard assignment operator (=) is used to assign the result of an expression to a variable. In its simplest form, you code it like this:

```
variable = expression;
```

For example:

```
int a = (b * c) / 4;
```

You've already seen plenty of examples of assignment statements like this one, so I won't belabor this point any further. However, I do want to point out — just for the record — that you *cannot* code an arithmetic expression on the left side of an equals sign. Thus, the following statement doesn't compile:

```
int a;
a + 3 = (b * c);
```

In the rest of this section, I point out some unusual ways in which you can use the assignment operator. I don't actually recommend that you use any of these techniques, as they are rarely necessary and almost always confusing. However, knowing about them can shed light on how Java expressions work and can sometimes help you find sneaky problems in your code.

The key to understanding the rest of this section is realizing that in Java, assignments are expressions, not statements. In other words, a = 5 is an assignment expression, not an assignment statement. It becomes an assignment statement only when you add a semicolon to the end.

The result of an assignment expression is the value that's assigned to the variable. For example, the result of the expression a = 5 is 5. Likewise, the result of the expression a = (b + c) * d is the result of the expression (b + c) * d.

The implication is that you can use assignment expressions in the middle of other expressions. For example, the following is legal:

```
int a;
int b;
a = (b = 3) * 2;    // a is 6, b is 3
```

As in any expression, the part of the expression inside the parentheses is evaluated first. Thus, b is assigned the value 3. Then, the multiplication is performed, and the result (6) is assigned to the variable a.

Now consider a more complicated case:

```
int a;
int b = 2;
a = (b = 3) * b;     // a is 9, b is 3
```

What's happening here is that the expression in the parentheses is evaluated first, which means that b is set to 3 before the multiplication is performed.

The parentheses are important in the previous example because without parentheses, the assignment operator is the last operator to be evaluated in Java's order of precedence. Thus, consider one more example:

```
int a;
int b = 2;
a = b = 3 * b;     // a is 6, b is 6
```

This time, the multiplication 3 * b is performed first, giving a result of 6. Then, this result is assigned to b. Finally, the result of that assignment expression (6) is assigned to a.

Incidentally, the following expression is also legal:

```
a = b = c = 3;
```

This expression assigns the value 3 to all three variables. Although this code seems pretty harmless, you're better off just writing three assignment statements. (You might guess that clumping the assignments together is more efficient than writing them on three lines, but you'd be wrong. These three assignments require the same number of bytecode instructions either way.)

Using Compound Assignment Operators

A *compound assignment operator* is an operator that performs a calculation and an assignment at the same time. All of Java's binary arithmetic operators (that is, the ones that work on two operands) have equivalent compound assignment operators. Table 3-2 lists them.

Table 3-2	Compound Arithmetic Operators
Operator	*Description*
+=	Addition and assignment
−=	Subtraction and assignment
*=	Multiplication and assignment
/=	Division and assignment
%=	Remainder and assignment

For example, this statement

```
a += 10;
```

is equivalent to

```
a = a + 10;
```

And this statement

```
z *=2;
```

is equivalent to

```
z = z * 2;
```

To avoid confusion, compound assignment expressions are best used by themselves, not in combination with other expressions. For example, consider these statements:

```
int a = 2;
int b = 3;
a *= b + 1;
```

Is a set to 7 or 8?

In other words, is the third statement equivalent to

```
a = a * b + 1;      // This would give 7 as the result
```

or

```
a = a * (b + 1);    // This would give 8 as the result
```

At first glance, you might expect the answer to be 7, because multiplication has a higher precedence than addition. But assignment has the lowest precedence of all, and the multiplication here is performed as part of the assignment. As a result, the addition is performed before the multiplication. Thus, the answer is 8. (Gotcha!)

Using the Math Class

Java's built-in operators are useful, but they don't come anywhere near providing all the mathematical needs of most Java programmers. That's where the Math class comes in. It includes a bevy of built-in methods that perform a wide variety of mathematical calculations, from basic functions such as calculating an absolute value or a square root to trigonometry functions such as sin and cos, to practical functions such as rounding numbers or generating random numbers.

I was going to make a joke here about having to take a Math class to fully appreciate the Math class, or how you'd better stay away from the Math class if you didn't do so well in Math class, or how if you're on the football team, maybe you can get someone to do the Math class for you. But it seemed too easy, so I decided not to.

All the methods of the Math class are declared as static methods, which means you can use them by specifying the class name Math followed by a period and a method name. For example, here's a statement that calculates the square root of a number stored in a variable named y:

```java
double x = Math.sqrt(y);
```

The Math class is contained in the java.lang package, which is automatically available to all Java programs. As a result, you don't have to provide an import statement to use the Math class.

The following sections describe the most useful methods of the Math class.

Constants of the Math class

The Math class defines two constants that are useful for many mathematical calculations. Table 3-3 lists these constants.

Table 3-3	Constants of the Math Class	
Constant	*What It Is*	*Value*
PI	The constant Pi (π), the ratio of a circle's radius and diameter	3.141592653589793
E	The base of natural logarithms	2.718281828459045

Note that these constants are only approximate values, because both π and *e* are irrational numbers.

The program shown in Listing 3-2 illustrates a typical use of the constant PI. Here, the user is asked to enter the radius of a circle. The program then calculates the area of the circle in line 13. (The parentheses aren't really required in the expression in this statement, but they help clarify that the expression is the Java equivalent to the formula for the area of a circle, πr^2.)

**Book II
Chapter 3**

**Working with
Numbers and
Expressions**

Here's the console output for a typical execution of this program, in which the user entered 5 as the radius of the circle:

```
Welcome to the circle area calculator.
Enter the radius of your circle: 5
The area is 78.53981633974483
```

LISTING 3-2: THE CIRCLE AREA CALCULATOR

```
import java.util.Scanner;

public class CircleAreaApp
{
    static Scanner sc = new Scanner(System.in);

    public static void main(String[] args)
    {
        System.out.println(
            "Welcome to the circle area calculator.");
        System.out.print("Enter the radius of your circle: ");
        double r = sc.nextDouble();
        double area = Math.PI * (r * r);                          → 13
        System.out.println("The area is " + area);
    }
}
```

Mathematical functions

Table 3-4 lists the basic mathematical functions that are provided by the Math class. As you can see, you can use these functions to calculate such things as the absolute value of a number, the minimum and maximum of two values, square roots, powers, and logarithms.

Table 3-4	Mathematical Functions Provided by the Math Class
Method	*Explanation*
abs(argument)	Returns the absolute value of the argument. The argument can be an int, long, float, or double. The return value is the same type as the argument.
cbrt(argument)	Returns the cube root of the argument. The argument and return value are doubles.
exp(argument)	Returns e raised to the power of the argument. The argument and the return value are doubles.
hypot(arg1, arg2)	Returns the hypotenuse of a right triangle calculated according to the Pythagorean theorem — $\sqrt{x^2 + y^2}$ The argument and the return values are doubles.

Method	Explanation
log(argument)	Returns the natural logarithm (base *e*) of the argument. The argument and the return value are doubles.
log10(argument)	Returns the base 10 logarithm of the argument. The argument and the return value are doubles.
max(arg1, arg2)	Returns the larger of the two arguments. The arguments can be int, long, float, or double, but both must be of the same type. The return type is the same type as the arguments.
min(arg1, arg2)	Returns the smaller of the two arguments. The arguments can be int, long, float, or double, but both must be of the same type. The return type is the same type as the arguments.
pow(arg1, arg2)	Returns the value of the first argument raised to the power of the second argument. Both arguments and the return value are doubles.
random()	Returns a random number that's greater than or equal to 0.0 but less than 1.0. This method doesn't accept an argument, but the return value is a double.
signum(argument)	Returns a number that represents the sign of the argument: –1.0 if the argument is negative, 0.0 if the argument is zero, and 1.0 if the argument is positive. The argument can be a double or a float. The return value is the same type as the argument.
sqrt(argument)	Returns the square root of the argument. The argument and return value are doubles.

Book II
Chapter 3

Working with
Numbers and
Expressions

The program shown in Listing 3-3 demonstrates each of these methods except random. When run, it produces output similar to this:

```
abs(b)      = 50
cbrt(x)     = 2.924017738212866
exp(y)      = 54.598150033144236
hypot(y,z)  = 5.0
log(y)      = 1.0986122886681096
log10(y)    = 0.47712125471966244
max(a, b)   = 100
min(a, b)   = -50
pow(a, c)   = 1000000.0
random()    = 0.8536014557793756
signum(b)   = -1.0
sqrt(x)     = 1.7320508075688772
```

You can use this output to get an idea of the values returned by these Math class methods. For example, you can see that the expression Math.sqrt(y) returns a value of 5.0 when y is 25.0.

The following paragraphs point out a few interesting tidbits concerning these methods:

✦ You can use the abs and signnum methods to force the sign of one variable to match the sign of another, like this:

```
int a = 27;
int b = -32;
a = Math.abs(a) * Math.signum(b);    // a is
    now -27;
```

✦ You can use the pow method to square a number, like this:

```
double x = 4.0;
double y = Math.pow(x, 2);    // a is now 16;
```

However, simply multiplying the number by itself is often just as easy and just as readable:

```
double x = 4.0;
double y = x * x;    // a is now 16;
```

✦ In the classic movie *The Wizard of Oz*, when the Wizard finally grants the Scarecrow his brains, the Scarecrow suddenly becomes intelligent and quotes the Pythagorean theorem, which is used by the hypot method of the Math class. Unfortunately, he quotes it wrong. What the Scarecrow actually says in the movie is: "The sum of the square roots of any two sides of an isosceles triangle is equal to the square root of the remaining side." Silly scarecrow. What he should have said, of course, is "The square of the hypotenuse of any right triangle is equal to the sum of the squares of the other two sides."

✦ Every time you run the program in Listing 3-3, you get a different result for the random method call. The random method is interesting enough that I describe it separately, in the next section "Creating random numbers."

LISTING 3-3: A PROGRAM THAT USES THE MATHEMATICAL METHODS OF THE MATH CLASS

```
public class MathFunctionsApp
{
    public static void main(String[] args)
    {
        int a = 100;
        int b = -50;
        int c = 3;
        double x = 25.0;
        double y = 3.0;
        double z = 4.0;

        System.out.println("abs(b)    = " + Math.abs(b));
        System.out.println("cbrt(x)   = " + Math.cbrt(x));
```

```
System.out.println("exp(y)     = " + Math.exp(z));
System.out.println("hypot(y,z)= " + Math.hypot(y,z));
System.out.println("log(y)     = " + Math.log(y));
System.out.println("log10(y)  = " + Math.log10(y));
System.out.println("max(a, b) = " + Math.max(a, b));
System.out.println("min(a, b) = " + Math.min(a, b));
System.out.println("pow(a, c) = " + Math.pow(a, c));
System.out.println("random()   = " + Math.random());
System.out.println("signum(b) = " + Math.signum(b));
System.out.println("sqrt(x)    = " + Math.sqrt(y));
    }
}
```

Creating random numbers

Sooner or later, you're going to want to write programs that play simple games. Almost all games have some element of chance built in to them, so you need a way to create computer programs that don't work exactly the same every time you run them. The easiest way to do that is to use the `random` method of the `Math` class, which Table 3-4 lists along with the other basic mathematical functions of the `Math` class.

The `random` method returns a `double` whose value is greater than or equal to 0.0 but less than 1.0. Within this range, the value returned by the `random` method is different every time you call it, and is essentially random.

Strictly speaking, computers are not capable of generating truly random numbers. However, clever computer scientists over the years have developed ways to generate numbers that are random for all practical purposes. These numbers are called *pseudorandom numbers* because although they aren't completely random, they look random to most mortal human beings.

The `random` method generates a random `double` value between 0.0 (inclusive, meaning it could be 0.0) and 1.0 (exclusive, meaning it can't be 1.0). However, most computer applications that need random values need random integers between some arbitrary low value (usually 1, but not always) and some arbitrary high value. For example, a program that plays dice needs random numbers between 1 and 6, while a program that deals cards needs random numbers between 1 and 52 (53 if jokers are used).

As a result, you need a Java expression that converts the `double` value returned by the `random` function into an `int` value within the range your program calls for. The following code shows how to do this, with the values set to 1 and 6 for a dice-playing game:

```
int low = 1;       // the lowest value in the range
int high = 6;      // the highest value in the range
int rnd = (int)(Math.random() * (high - low + 1)) + low;
```

This expression is a little complicated, so I show you how it's evaluated step by step:

1. The `random` method to get a random double value. This value is greater than 0.0 but less than 5.0.

2. The random value is multiplied by the high end of the range minus the low end, plus 1. In this example, the high end is 6, and the low end is 1, so you now have a random number that's greater than or equal to 0.0 but less than 6.0. (It could be 5.99999999999999, but it never is 6.0.)

3. This value is then converted to an integer by the (int) cast. You now have an integer that's either 0, 1, 2, 3, 4, or 5. (Remember that when you cast a double to an int, any fractional part of the value is simply discarded. Because the number is less than 6.0, it never truncates to 6.0 when it is cast to an int.)

4. The low value in the range is now added to the random number. Assuming the low is 1, the random number is now either 1, 2, 3, 4, 5, or 6. That's just what you want: a random number between 1 and 6.

To give you an idea of how this random number calculation works, Listing 3-4 shows a program that places this calculation in a method called `randomInt` and then calls it to simulate 100 dice rolls. The `randomInt` method accepts two parameters representing the low and high ends of the range, and it returns a random integer within the range. In the `main` method of this program, the `randomInt` method is called 100 times, and each random number is printed by a call to `System.out.print`.

The console output for this program looks something like this:

```
Here are 100 random rolls of the dice:
4 1 1 6 1 2 6 6 6 6 5 5 5 4 5 4 4 1 3 6 1 3 1 4 4 3 3 3 5 6 5 6 6 3 5 2
  2 6 3 3
4 1 2 2 4 2 2 4 1 4 3 6 5 5 4 4 2 4 1 3 5 2 1 3 3 5 4 1 6 3 1 6 5 2 6 6
  3 5 4 5
2 5 4 5 3 1 4 2 5 2 1 4 4 4 6 6 4 6 3 3
```

However, every time you run this program, you see a different sequence of 100 numbers.

The program in Listing 3-4 uses several Java features you haven't seen yet.

LISTING 3-4: ROLLING THE DICE

```java
public class DiceApp
{
    public static void main(String[] args)
    {
        int roll;
        String msg = "Here are 100 random rolls of the dice:";
```

```
        System.out.println(msg);
        for (int i=0; i<100; i++)                              → 8
        {
            roll = randomInt(1, 6);                            → 10
            System.out.print(roll + " ");                      → 11
        }
        System.out.println();
    }

    public static int randomInt(int low, int high)            → 16
    {
        int result = (int)(Math.random()                       → 18
            * (high - low + 1)) + low;
        return result;                                         → 20
    }
}
```

The following paragraphs explain how the program works, but don't worry if you don't get all of the elements in this program. The main thing to see is the expression that converts the random `double` value returned by the `Math.double` method to an integer.

→ **8** The `for` statement causes the statements in its body (lines 10 and 11) to be executed 100 times. Don't worry about how this statement works for now; you find out about it in Book II, Chapter 5.

→**10** This statement calls the `randomInt` method, specifying 1 and 6 as the range for the random integer to generate. The resulting random number is assigned to the `roll` variable.

→**11** The `System.out.print` method is used to print the random number followed by a space. Because this statement calls the `print` method rather than the `println` method, the random numbers are printed on the same line rather than on separate lines.

→**16** The declaration for the `randomInt` method indicates that the method returns an `int` value and accepts two `int` arguments, one named `low`, the other named `high`.

→**18** This expression converts the random `double` value to an integer between `low` and `high`.

→**20** The `return` statement sends the random number back to the statement that called the `randomInt` method.

Rounding functions

The `Math` class has four methods that round or truncate `float` or `double` values. Table 3-5 lists these methods. As you can see, each of these methods uses a different technique to calculate an integer value that's near the `double` or `float` value passed as an argument. Note that even though all four of these methods rounds a floating-point value to an integer value, only the round method actually returns an integer type (int or long, depending on whether the argument is a float or a double). The other methods return doubles that happen to be integer values.

Table 3-5	Rounding Functions Provided by the Math Class
Method	*Explanation*
ceil(argument)	Returns the smallest double value that is an integer and is greater than or equal to the value of the argument.
floor(argument)	Returns the largest double value that is an integer and is less than or equal to the value of the argument.
rint(argument)	Returns the double value that is an integer and is closest to the value of the argument. If two integer values are equally close, returns the one that is even. If the argument is already an integer, returns the argument value.
round(argument)	Returns the integer that is closest to the argument. If the argument is a double, returns a long. If the argument is a float, returns an int.

Listing 3-5 shows a program that uses each of the four methods to round three different double values: 29.4, 93.5, and –19.3. Here's the output from this program:

```
round(x) = 29
round(y) = 94
round(z) = -19

ceil(x) = 30.0
ceil(y) = 94.0
ceil(z) = -19.0

floor(x) = 29.0
floor(y) = 93.0
floor(z) = -20.0

rint(x) = 29.0
rint(y) = 94.0
rint(z) = -19.0
```

Note that each of the four methods produces a different result for at least one of the values:

✦ All the methods except ceil return 29.0 (or 29) for the value 29.4. ceil returns 30.0, which is the smallest integer that's greater than 29.4.

✦ All the methods except floor return 94.0 (or 94) for the value 93.5. floor returns 93.0 because that's the largest integer that's less than

93.99. `rint` returns `94.0` because it's an even number, and 93.5 is midway between 93.0 and 94.0.

✦ All the methods except `floor` return `-19.0` (or `-19`) for `-19.3`. `floor` returns 2-20 because –20 is the largest integer that's less than –19.3.

LISTING 3-5: A PROGRAM THAT USES THE ROUNDING METHODS OF THE MATH CLASS

```
public class RoundingApp
{
    public static void main(String[] args)
    {
        double x = 29.4;
        double y = 93.5;
        double z = -19.3;

        System.out.println("round(x) = " + Math.round(x));
        System.out.println("round(y) = " + Math.round(y));
        System.out.println("round(z) = " + Math.round(z));
        System.out.println();
        System.out.println("ceil(x) = " + Math.ceil(x));
        System.out.println("ceil(y) = " + Math.ceil(y));
        System.out.println("ceil(z) = " + Math.ceil(z));
        System.out.println();
        System.out.println("floor(x) = " + Math.floor(x));
        System.out.println("floor(y) = " + Math.floor(y));
        System.out.println("floor(z) = " + Math.floor(z));
        System.out.println();
        System.out.println("rint(x) = " + Math.rint(x));
        System.out.println("rint(y) = " + Math.rint(y));
        System.out.println("rint(z) = " + Math.rint(z));
    }
}
```

Formatting Numbers

Most of the programs you've seen so far have used the `System.out.println` or `System.out.print` method to print the values of variables that contain numbers. When you pass a numeric variable to one of these methods, the variable's value is converted to a string before it's printed. The exact format used to represent the value isn't very pretty. For example, large values are printed without any commas. And all the decimal digits for `double` or `float` values are printed, whether you want them to or not.

In many cases, you want to format your numbers before you print them. For example, you might want to add commas to large values and limit the number of decimal places printed. Or, if a number represents a monetary amount, you might want to add a dollar sign (or whatever currency symbol is appropriate for your locale). To do that, you can use the `NumberFormat` class. Table 3-6 lists the `NumberFormat` class methods.

Like many aspects of Java, the procedure for using the `NumberFormat` class is a little awkward. It's designed to be efficient for applications that need to format a lot of numbers, but it's overkill for most applications.

Table 3-6	Methods of the NumberFormat Class
Method	*Explanation*
`getCurrencyInstance()`	A static method that returns a `NumberFormat` object that formats currency values.
`getPercentInstance()`	A static method that returns a `NumberFormat` object that formats percentages.
`getNumberInstance()`	A static method that returns a `NumberFormat` object that formats basic numbers.
`format(number)`	Returns a string that contains the formatted number.
`setMinimumFractionDigits(int)`	Sets the minimum number of digits to display to the right of the decimal point.
`setMaximumFractionDigits(int)`	Sets the maximum number of digits to display to the right of the decimal point.

The procedure for using the `NumberFormat` class to format numbers takes a little getting used to. First, you must call one of the static get*Xxx*Instance methods to create a `NumberFormat` object that can format numbers in a particular way. Then, if you want, you can call the `setMinimumFractionDigits` or `setMaximumFractionDigits` methods to set the number of decimal digits to be displayed. Finally, you call that object's `format` method to actually format a number.

Note that the `NumberFormat` class is in the `java.text` package, so you must include the following `import` statement at the beginning of any class that uses `NumberFormat`:

```
import java.text.NumberFormat;
```

Here's an example that uses the `NumberFormat` class to format a `double` value as currency:

```
double salesTax = 2.425;
NumberFormat cf = NumberFormat.getCurrencyInstance();
System.out.println(cf.format(salesTax));
```

When you run this code, the following line is printed to the console:

```
$2.43
```

Note that the currency format rounds the value from 2.425 to 2.43.

Here's an example that formats a number using the general number format, with exactly three decimal places:

```
double x = 19923.3288;
NumberFormat nf = NumberFormat.getNumberInstance();
nf.setMinimumFractionDigits(3);
nf.setMaximumFractionDigits(3);
System.out.println(nf.format(x));
```

When you run this code, the following line is printed:

```
19,923.329
```

Here, the number is formatted with a comma, and the value is rounded to three places.

Here's an example that uses the percentage format:

```
double grade = .92;
NumberFormat pf = NumberFormat.getPercentInstance();
System.out.println(pf.format(grade));
```

When you run this code, the following line is printed:

```
92%
```

If your program formats several numbers, consider creating the `NumberFormat` object as a class variable. That way, the `NumberFormat` object is created once when the program starts. Then, you can use the `NumberFormat` object from any method in the program's class. Here's a simple example that shows how this works:

```
import java.text.NumberFormat;

public class NumberFormatClassApp
{

    static NumberFormat cf =
        NumberFormat.getCurrencyInstance();

    public static void main(String[] args)
    {
        printMyAllowance();
        printCostOfPaintBallGun();
    }
```

```
public static void printMyAllowance()
{
    double myAllowance = 5.00;
    cf = NumberFormat.getCurrencyInstance();
    System.out.println("My allowance: "
        + cf.format(myAllowance));
}

public static void printCostOfPaintBallGun()
{
    double costOfPaintBallGun = 69.95;
    cf = NumberFormat.getCurrencyInstance();
    System.out.println("Cost of Paint Ball Gun: "
        + cf.format(costOfPaintBallGun));
}
}
```

Here, the `cf` variable is created as a class variable. Then, both the `printMy Allowance` and `printCostOfPaintBallGun` methods can use it.

Weird Things about Java Math

Believe it or not, computers — even the most powerful ones — have certain limitations when it comes to performing math calculations. These limitations are usually insignificant, but sometimes they sneak up and bite you. The following sections describe the things you need to watch out for when doing math in Java.

Integer overflow

The basic problem with integer types is that they have a fixed size. As a result, the number has a size limit that can be stored in a `short`, `int`, or `long` variable. Although `long` variables can hold numbers that are huge, sooner or later you come across a number that's too big to fit in even a `long` variable.

For example, consider this admittedly contrived example:

```
int a = 1000000000;
System.out.println(a);
a += 1000000000;
System.out.println(a);
a += 1000000000;
System.out.println(a);
a += 1000000000;
System.out.println(a);
```

Here, you expect the value of a to get bigger after each addition. But here's the output that's displayed:

```
1000000000
2000000000
-1294967296
-294967296
```

The first addition seems to work, but after that, the number becomes negative! That's because the value has reached the size limit of the int data type. Unfortunately, Java doesn't tell you that this error has happened. It simply crams the int variable as full of bits as it can, discards whatever bits don't fit, and hopes you don't notice. Because of the way int stores negative values, large positive values suddenly become large negative values.

The moral of the story is that if you're working with large integers, you should use long rather than int because long can store much larger numbers than int. If your programs deal with numbers large enough to be a problem for long, consider using floating-point types instead. As you see in the next section, floating-point types can handle even larger values than long, and they let you know when you exceed their capacity.

Floating-point weirdness

Floating-point numbers have problems of their own. For starters, floating-point numbers are stored using the binary number system (base 2), but humans work with numbers in the decimal number system (base 10). Unfortunately, accurately converting numbers between these two systems is sometimes impossible. That's because in any number base, certain fractions can't be represented exactly. For example, base 10 has no way to exactly represent the fraction ⅓. You can approximate it as 0.3333333, but eventually you reach the limit of how many digits you can store, so you have to stop. In base 2, it happens that one of the fractions you can't accurately represent is the decimal value ⅒. In other words, a float or double variable can't accurately represent 0.1.

Don't believe me? Try running this code:

```
float x = 0.1f;
NumberFormat nf = NumberFormat.getNumberInstance();
nf.setMinimumFractionDigits(10);
System.out.println(nf.format(x));
```

The resulting output is this:

```
0.1000000015
```

Although 0.1000000015 is *close* to 0.1, it isn't exact.

In most cases, Java's floating-point math is close enough not to matter. The margin of error is extremely small. If you're using Java to measure the size of your house, you'd need an electron microscope to notice the error. However, if you're writing applications that deal with financial transactions, normal rounding can sometimes magnify the errors to make them significant. You might charge a penny too much or too little sales tax. And, in extreme cases, your invoices might actually have obvious addition errors.

I'll have much more to say about this floating-point numbers in Bonus Chapter 1 on this book's Web site. For now, just realize that you can't use `float` or `double` to represent money unless you don't care whether or not your books are in balance.

Of course, integer types are stored in binary too. But integers aren't subject to the same errors that floating-point types are because integers don't represent fractions at all. So you don't have to worry about this type of error for integer types.

Dividing by zero

According to the basic rules of mathematics, you can't divide a number by zero. The reason is simple: Division is the inverse of multiplication. That means that if `a * b = c`, then it is also true that `a = c / b`. If you were to allow `b` to be zero, division would be meaningless because any number times zero is zero. Therefore, both `a` and `c` would also have to be zero. In short, mathematicians solved this dilemma centuries ago by saying that division by zero is simply not allowed.

So what happens if you do attempt to divide a number by zero in a Java program? The answer depends on whether you're dividing integers or floating-point numbers. If you're dividing integers, the statement that attempts the division by zero chokes up what is called an *exception*, which is an impolite way of crashing the program. In Book II, Chapter 8, you find out how to intercept this exception to allow your program to continue. But in the meantime, any program you write that attempts an integer division by zero crashes.

If you try to divide a floating-point type by zero, the results are not so abrupt. Instead, Java assigns the floating-point result one of the special values listed in Table 3-7. The following paragraphs explain how these special values are determined:

✦ If you divide a number by zero and the sign of both numbers is the same, the result is positive infinity. For example, `40.0` divided by `0.0` is positive infinity, as is `-34.0` divided by `-0.0`.

✦ If you divide a number by zero and the signs of the numbers are different, the result is negative infinity. For example, `-40.0` divided by `0.0` is negative infinity, as is `34.0` divided by `0.0`.

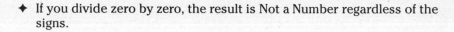

♦ If you divide zero by zero, the result is Not a Number regardless of the signs.

Floating-point zeros can be positive or negative. Java considers positive and negative zeros to be equal numerically.

If you attempt to print a floating-point value that has one of these special values, Java converts the value to an appropriate string. For example, suppose you execute the following statements:

```
double i = 50.0;
double j = 0.0;
double k = i / j;
System.out.println(k);
```

The resulting console output is

```
infinity
```

If `i` were `-50.0`, the console would display `-infinity`. And if `i` were zero, the console would display `NaN`.

Table 3-7	Special Constants of the float and double Classes
Constant	*Meaning*
POSITIVE_INFINITY	Positive infinity
NEGATIVE_INFINITY	Negative infinity
NaN	Not a number

The following paragraphs describe some final bits of weirdness I want to sneak in before closing this chapter:

♦ NaN is not equal to itself, which can have some strange consequences. For example:

```
double x = Math.sqrt(-50);    // Not a number
double y = x;
if (x == y)
    System.out.println("x equals y");
```

Okay, I know I jumped the gun here on the `if` statement, because I don't cover `if` statements until Book II, Chapter 4. So just assume for the sake of argument that the `if` statement tests whether the variable `x` is equal to the variable `y`. Because this test follows immediately after an assignment statement that assigns the value of `x` to `y`, you can safely assume that `x` equals `y`, right?

Wrong. Because x is NaN, y also is NaN. And NaN is never considered to be equal to any other value, including another NaN. Thus, the comparison in the `if` statement fails.

✦ Another strange consequence: You can't assume that a number minus itself is always zero. Consider this statement:

```
double z = x - x;    // not necessarily zero
```

Shouldn't this statement always set z to zero? Not if x is NaN. In that case, not a number minus not a number is still not a number.

✦ One more, and then I'll stop: Any mathematical operation involving infinity results in either another infinity or not a number. For example, infinity + 5 still equals infinity. So Buzz Lightyear's call to "Infinity and beyond" just isn't going to happen. But infinity minus infinity gives not a number.

Chapter 4: Making Choices

In This Chapter

✔ Boolean expressions for fun and profit (or is it, for fun *or* profit?)

✔ Your basic, run-of-the mill `if` statement

✔ `else` **clauses and** `else-if` **statements**

✔ Nested `if` statements

✔ Using logical operators

✔ The weird `?:` operator

✔ The proper way to do string comparisons

So far in this book, all the programs have run straight through from start to finish, without making any decisions along the way. In this chapter, you discover two Java statements that let you create some variety in your programs. The `if` statement lets you execute a statement or a block of statements only if some conditional test turns out to be true. And the `switch` statement lets you execute one of several blocks of statements depending on the value of an integer variable.

The `if` statement relies heavily on the use of *boolean expressions*, which are expressions that yield a simple `true` or `false` result. Because you can't do even the simplest `if` statement without a boolean expression, this chapter begins by showing you how to code simple boolean expressions that test the value of a variable. Later, after looking at the details of how the `if` statement works, I revisit boolean expressions to see how to combine them to make complicated logical decisions. Then, I get to the `switch` statement.

You're going to have to put your thinking cap on for much of this chapter, as most of it plays with logic puzzles. Find yourself a comfortable chair in a quiet part of the house, turn off the TV, and pour yourself a cup of coffee.

Using Simple Boolean Expressions

All `if` statements, as well as several of the other control statements that I describe in Book II, Chapter 5 (`while`, `do`, and `for`) use *boolean expressions* to determine whether to execute or skip a statement (or a block of statements). A boolean expression is a Java expression that, when evaluated, returns a boolean value — either `true` or `false`.

As you discover later in this chapter, boolean expressions can be very compli-cated. However, most of the time, you use simple expressions that compare the value of a variable with the value of some other variable, a literal, or perhaps a simple arithmetic expression. This comparison uses one of the *relational operators* listed in Table 4-1. All these operators are *binary opera-tors,* which means they work on two operands.

Table 4-1	Relational Operators
Operator	*Description*
==	Returns true if the expression on the left evaluates to the same value as the expression on the right.
!=	Returns true if the expression on the left does not evaluate to the same value as the expression on the right.
<	Returns true if the expression on the left evaluates to a value that is less than the value of the expression on the right.
<=	Returns true if the expression on the left evaluates to a value that is less than or equal to the expression on the right.
>	Returns true if the expression on the left evaluates to a value that is greater than the value of the expression on the right.
>=	Returns true if the expression on the left evaluates to a value that is greater than or equal to the expression on the right.

A basic boolean expression has this form:

```
expression relational-operator expression
```

Java evaluates a boolean expression by first evaluating the expression on the left, then evaluating the expression on the right, and finally applying the relational operator to determine if the entire expression evaluates to true or false.

Here are some simple examples of relational expressions. For each example, assume that the following statements were used to declare and initialize the variables:

```
int i = 5;
int j = 10;
int k = 15;
double x = 5.0;
double y = 7.5;
double z = 12.3;
```

Now, here are the sample expressions along with their results based on the values supplied:

Expression	Value	Explanation
i == 5	true	The value of i is 5.
i == 10	false	The value of i is not 10.
i == j	false	i is 5, and j is 10, so they are not equal.
i == j - 5	true	i is 5, and j - 5 is 5.
i > 1	true	i is 5, which is greater than 1.
j == i * 2	true	j is 10, and i is 5, so i * 2 is also 10.
x = i	true	Casting allows the comparison, and 5.0 is equal to 5.
k < z	false	Casting allows the comparison, and 15 is greater than 12.3.
i * 2 < y	false	i * 2 is 10, which is not less than 7.5.

Note that the relational operator that tests for equality is two equal signs in a row (==). A single equal sign is the assignment operator. When you're first learning Java, you may frequently type the assignment operator when you mean the equals operator, like this:

```
if (i = 5)
```

Java won't let you get away with this, so you have to correct your mistake and recompile the program.

At first, doing so seems like a nuisance. The more you work with Java, the more you realize that it really is a nuisance, but one you can get used to.

Another important warning: Do *not* test strings using any of the relational operators listed in Table 4-1, including the equals operator. You're probably tempted to test strings like this:

```
inputString == "Yes"
```

However, this is not the correct way to compare strings in Java. You find out the correct way to compare strings in the section "Comparing Strings" later in this chapter.

Using If Statements

The `if` statement is one of the most important statements in any programming language, and Java is no exception. The following sections describe the ins and outs of using the various forms of Java's powerful `if` statement.

Simple if statements

In its most basic form, an `if` statement lets you execute a single statement or a block of statements only if a boolean expression evaluates to `true`. The basic form of the `if` statement is this:

```
if (boolean-expression)
    statement
```

Note that the boolean expression must be enclosed in parentheses. Also, if you use only a single statement, it must end with a semicolon. But the statement can also be a statement block enclosed by braces. In that case, each statement within the block needs a semicolon, but the block itself doesn't.

Here's an example of a typical `if` statement:

```
double commissionRate = 0.0;
if (salesTotal > 10000.0)
    commissionRate = 0.05;
```

In this example, a variable named `commissionRate` is initialized to `0.0`, and then set to `0.05` if `salesTotal` is greater than 10,000.

Some programmers find it helpful to visualize the operation of an `if` statement in a flowchart, as shown in Figure 4-1. In this flowchart, the diamond symbol represents the condition test. If the sales total is greater than 10,000, the statement in the rectangle is executed. If not, that statement is bypassed.

Indenting the statement under the `if` statement is customary to make the structure of your code more obvious. It isn't necessary, but always a good idea.

Here's an example that uses a block rather than a single statement:

```
double commissionRate = 0.0;
if (salesTotal > 10000.0)
{
    commissionRate = 0.05;
    commission = salesTotal * commissionRate;
}
```

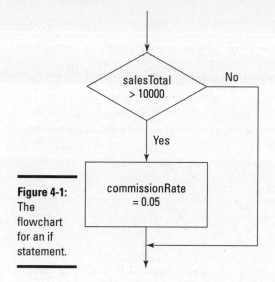

Figure 4-1:
The
flowchart
for an if
statement.

In this example, the two statements within the braces are executed if `salesTotal` is greater than 10000.0. Otherwise, neither statement is executed.

Here are a few additional points about simple `if` statements:

✦ Some programmers prefer to code the opening brace for the statement block on the same line as the `if` statement itself, like this:

```
if (salesTotal > 10000.0) {
    commissionRate = 0.05;
    commission = salesTotal * commissionRate;
}
```

This method is simply a matter of style, so either technique is acceptable.

✦ Indentation by itself doesn't create a block. For example, consider this code:

```
if (salesTotal > 10000.0)
    commissionRate = 0.05;
    commission = salesTotal * commissionRate;
```

Here, I didn't use the braces to mark a block, but indented the last statement as if it were part of the `if` statement. Don't be fooled; the last statement is executed whether or not the expression in the `if` statement evaluates to `true`.

✦ Some programmers like to code a statement block even for `if` statements that conditionally execute just one statement. For example:

```
if (salesTotal > 10000.0)
{
    commissionRate = 0.05;
}
```

That's not a bad idea, because it makes the structure of your code a little more obvious by adding extra white space around the statement. And if you later decide you need to add a few statements to the block, the braces are already there.

✦ If only one statement needs to be conditionally executed, some programmers put it on the same line as the `if` statement, like this:

```
if (salesTotal > 10000.0) commissionRate = 0.05;
```

This method works, but I'd avoid it. Your classes are easier to follow if you use line breaks and indentation to highlight their structure.

if-else statements

An `if-else` statement adds an additional element to a basic `if` statement: a statement or block that's executed if the boolean expression is not `true`. Its basic format is

```
if (boolean-expression)
    statement
else
    statement
```

Here's an example:

```
double commissionRate;
if (salesTotal <= 10000.0)
    commissionRate = 0.02;
else
    commissionRate = 0.05;
```

In this example, the commission rate is set to 2% if the sales total is less than or equal to 10,000. If the sales total is greater than 10,000, the commission rate is set to 5%.

Figure 4-2 shows a flowchart for this `if-else` statement.

In some cases, you can avoid the need for the `else` part of an `if-else` statement by cleverly rearranging your code. For example, this code has the same effect as the previous `if-else` statement:

```
double commissionRate = 0.05;
if (salesTotal <= 10000.0)
    commissionRate = 0.02;
```

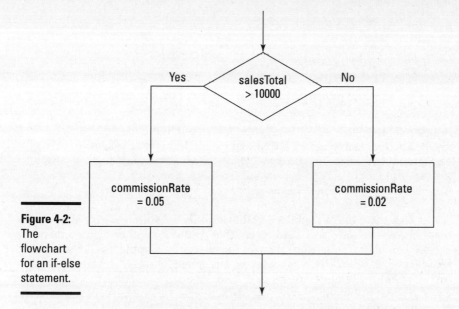

Book II
Chapter 4

Making Choices

Figure 4-2:
The flowchart for an if-else statement.

You can use blocks for either or both of the statements in an `if-else`. For example, here's an `if-else` statement in which both statements are blocks:

```
double commissionRate;
if (salesTotal <= 10000.0)
{
    commissionRate = 0.02;
    level1Count++;
}
else
{
    commissionRate = 0.05;
    level2Count++;
}
```

Nested if statements

The statement that goes in the if or else part of an `if-else` statement can be any kind of Java statement, including another `if` or `if-else` statement. This is called *nesting,* and an `if` or `if-else` statement that includes another `if` or `if-else` statement is called a *nested if statement.*

The general form of a nested `if` statement is this:

```
if (expression-1)
    if (expression-2)
        statement-1
```

```
    else
        statement-2
else
    if (expression-3)
        statement-3
    else
        statement-4
```

In this example, *expression-1* is first evaluated. If it evaluates to true, *expression-2* is evaluated. If that expression is true, *statement-1* is executed; otherwise, *statement-2* is executed. But if *expression-1* was false, then *expression-3* is evaluated. If *expression-3* is true, *statement-3* is executed; otherwise, *statement-4* is executed.

An if statement that's contained within another if statement is called an *inner if statement,* and an if statement that contains another if statement is called an *outer if statement.* Thus, in the previous example, the if statement that tests *expression-1* is an outer if statement, and the if statements that test *expression-2* and *expression-3* are inner if statements.

Nesting can be as complex as you want, but try to keep it as simple as possible. And be sure to use indentation to indicate the structure of the nested statements.

As an example, suppose your company has two classes of sales representatives (class 1 and class 2), and they get a different sales commission for sales below $10,000 and sales above $10,000 according to this table:

Sales	Class 1	Class 2
$0 to $9,999	2%	2.5%
$10,000 and over	4%	5%

You could implement this commission structure with a nested if statement:

```
if (salesClass == 1)
    if (salesTotal < 10000.0)
        commissionRate = 0.02;
    else
        commissionRate = 0.04;
else
    if (salesTotal < 10000.0)
        commissionRate = 0.025;
    else
        commissionRate = 0.05;
```

This example assumes that if the salesClass variable isn't 1, it must be 2. If that's not the case, you have to use an additional if statement for class-2 sales reps:

```
if (salesClass == 1)
    if (salesTotal < 10000.0)
        commissionRate = 0.02;
    else
        commissionRate = 0.04;
else if (salesClass == 2)
    if (salesTotal < 10000.0)
        commissionRate = 0.025;
    else
        commissionRate = 0.05;
```

Notice that I place this extra `if` statement on the same line as the `else` key-word. That's a common practice for a special form of nested `if` statements called `else-if` statements. You find more about this type of nesting in the next section.

You could also just use a pair of separate `if` statements:

```
if (salesClass == 1)
    if (salesTotal < 10000.0)
        commissionRate = 0.02;
    else
        commissionRate = 0.04;

if (salesClass == 2)
    if (salesTotal < 10000.0)
        commissionRate = 0.025;
    else
        commissionRate = 0.05;
```

The result is the same. However, this technique works only if the `if` state-ment itself doesn't change the variable being tested. If the first `if` statement changes the value of the `salesClass` variable, this statement doesn't work.

Note that you could also have implemented the sales commission structure by testing the sales level in the outer `if` statement and the sales representa-tive's class in the inner statements:

```
if (salesTotal < 10000)
    if (salesClass == 1)
        commissionRate = 0.02;
    else
        commissionRate = 0.04;
else
    if (salesClass == 1)
        commissionRate = 0.025;
    else
        commissionRate = 0.05;
```

The trick when using nested `if` statements is knowing how Java pairs `else` keywords with `if` statements. The rule is actually very simple: Each `if` keyword is matched with the most previous `if` statement that hasn't already been paired with an `else` keyword. You can't coax Java into pairing the `if` and `else` keywords differently by using indentation. For example, suppose that class 2 sales reps don't get any commission, so the inner `if` statements in the previous example don't need `else` statements. You might be tempted to calculate the commission rate using this code:

```
if (salesTotal < 10000)
    if (salesClass == 1)
        commissionRate = 0.02;
else
    if (salesClass == 1)
        commissionRate = 0.025;
```

However, it won't work. The indentation creates the impression that the `else` keyword is paired with the first `if` statement, but in reality it's paired with the second `if` statement. As a result, no sales commission rate is set for sales of $10,000 or more.

This problem has two solutions. One is to use braces to clarify the structure:

```
if (salesTotal < 10000)
{
    if (salesClass == 1)
        commissionRate = 0.02;
}
else
{
    if (salesClass == 1)
        commissionRate = 0.025;
}
```

The other is to add an `else` statement that specifies an *empty statement* (a semicolon by itself) to the first inner `if` statement:

```
if (salesTotal < 10000)
    if (salesClass == 1)
        commissionRate = 0.02;
    else ;
else
    if (salesClass == 1)
        commissionRate = 0.025;
```

The empty `else` statement is paired with the inner `if` statement, so the second `else` keyword is properly paired with the outer `if` statement.

else-if statements

A common pattern for nested `if` statements is to have a series of `if-else` statements with another `if-else` statement in each `else` part:

```
if (expression-1)
    statement-1
else if (expression-2)
    statement-2
else if (expression-3)
    statement-3
```

These are sometimes called `else-if` statements, although that's an unofficial term. Officially, all that's going on is that the statement in the `else` part happens to be another `if` statement, so this statement is just a type of a nested `if` statement. However, it's an especially useful form of nesting.

For example, suppose you want to assign four different commission rates based on the sales total, according to this table:

Sales	Commission
Over $10,000	5%
$5,000 to $9,999	3.5%
$1,000 to $4,999	2%
Under $1,000	0%

You can easily implement a series of `else-if` statements:

```
if (salesTotal >= 10000.0)
    commissionRate = 0.05;
else if (salesTotal >= 5000.0)
    commissionRate = 0.035;
else if (salesTotal >= 1000.0)
    commissionRate = 0.02;
else
    commissionRate = 0.0;
```

Figure 4-3 shows a flowchart for this sequence of `else-if` statements.

You have to carefully think through how you set up these `else-if` statements. For example, at first glance, this sequence looks like it might also work:

```
if (salesTotal > 0.0)
    commissionRate = 0.0;
else if (salesTotal >= 1000.0)
    commissionRate = 0.02;
```

```
else if (salesTotal >= 5000.0)
    commissionRate = 0.035;
else if (salesTotal >= 10000.0)
    commissionRate = 0.05;
```

However, this scenario won't work. These `if` statements always set the commission rate to 0% because the boolean expression in the first `if` statement always tests `true` (assuming the `salesTotal` isn't zero or negative — and if it is, none of the other `if` statements matter). As a result, none of the other `if` statements are ever evaluated.

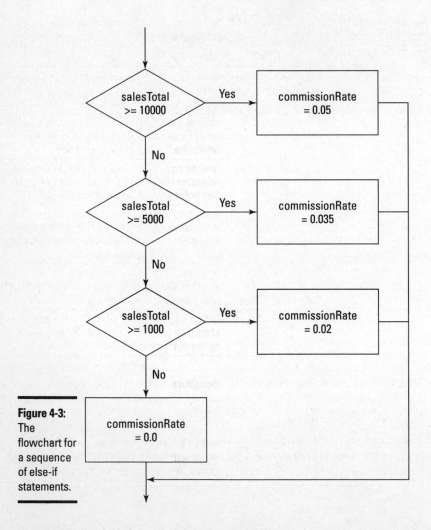

Figure 4-3: The flowchart for a sequence of else-if statements.

Mr. Spock's Favorite Operators (The Logical Ones, of Course)

A *logical operator* (sometimes called a *boolean operator*) is an operator that returns a boolean result that's based on the boolean result of one or two other expressions. Expressions that use logical operators are sometimes called *compound expressions* because the effect of the logical operators is to let you combine two or more condition tests into a single expression. Table 4-2 lists the logical operators.

Table 4-2			Logical Operators
Operator	**Name**	**Type**	**Description**
!	Not	Unary	Returns `true` if the operand to the right evaluates to `false`. Returns `false` If the operand to the right is `true`.
&	And	Binary	Returns `true` if both of the operands evaluate to `true`. Both operands are evaluated before the And operator is applied.
|	Or	Binary	Returns `true` if at least one of the operands evaluates to `true`. Both operands are evaluated before the Or operator is applied.
^	Xor	Binary	Returns `true` if one and only one of the operands evaluates to `true`. If both operands evaluate to `true` or if both operands evaluate to `false`, returns `false`.
&&	Conditional And	Binary	Same as &, but if the operand on the left returns `false`, returns `false` without evaluating the operand on the right.
||	Conditional Or	Binary	Same as |, but if the operand on the left returns `true`, returns `true` without evaluating the operand on the `right`.

The following sections describe these operators in excruciating detail.

Using the ! operator

The simplest of the logical operators is *not* (!). Technically, it's a unary prefix operator, which means that you use it with one operand, and you code it immediately in front of that operand. (Also, this operator is technically called the *complement operator,* not the *not operator.* But in real life, everyone calls it *not.*)

The not operator reverses the value of a boolean expression. Thus, if the expression is `true`, not changes it to `false`. If the expression is `false`, not changes it to `true`.

For example:

```
!(i = 4)
```

This expression evaluates to `true` if i is any value other than 4. If i is 4, it evaluates to `false`. It works by first evaluating the expression (i = 4). Then, it reverses the result of that evaluation.

Don't confuse the not logical operator (`!`) with the not equals relational operator (`!=`). Although they are sometimes used in similar ways, the not operator is more general. For example, I could have written the previous example like this:

```
i != 4
```

The result is the same. However, the not operator can be applied to any expression that returns a `true-false` result, not just an equality test.

Note: You must almost always enclose the expression that the `!` operator is applied to in parentheses. For example, consider this expression:

```
! i == 4
```

Assuming that i is an integer variable, the compiler doesn't allow this expression because it looks like you're trying to apply the `!` operator to the variable, not the result of the comparison. A quick set of parentheses solves the problem:

```
!(i == 4)
```

Using the & and && operators

The `&` and `&&` operators combine two boolean expressions and return `true` only if both expressions are `true`. This is called an *and operation,* because the first expression and the second expression must be `true` for the And operator to return a `true`.

For example, suppose the sales commission rate should be 2.5% if the sales class is 1 and the sales total is $10,000 or more. You could perform this test with two separate `if` statements (as I did earlier in this chapter), or you could combine the tests into one `if` statement:

```
if ( (salesClass == 1) & (salesTotal >= 10000.0) )
    commissionRate = 0.025;
```

Here, the expressions (salesClass == 1) and (salesTotal >= 10000.0) are evaluated separately. Then, the & operator compares the results. If they're both `true`, the & operator returns `true`. If one or both are `false`, the & operator returns `false`.

Notice that I used parentheses liberally to clarify where one expression ends and another begins. Using parentheses isn't always necessary, but when you use logical operators, I suggest you always use parentheses to clearly identify the expressions being compared.

The `&&` operator is similar to the `&` operator but leverages our knowledge of logic. Because both expressions compared by the `&` operator must be `true` for the entire expression to be `true`, there's no reason to evaluate the second expression if the first one returns `false`. The `&` isn't aware of this, so it blindly evaluates both expressions before determining the results. The `&&` operator is smart enough to stop when it knows what the outcome is.

As a result, almost always use `&&` instead of `&`. Here's the previous example, this time coded smartly with `&&`:

```
if ( (salesClass == 1) && (salesTotal >= 10000.0) )
    commissionRate = 0.025;
```

Why do I say you should *almost* always use `&&`? Because sometimes the expressions themselves have side effects that are important. For example, the second expression might involve a method call that updates a database, and you want the database updated whether or not the first expression evaluates to `true` or `false`. In that case, you want to use `&` instead of `&&` to ensure that both expressions get evaluated.

Relying on side effects of expressions can be risky, and you can almost always find a better way to write your code so that the side effects are avoided. In other words, placing an important call to a database update method inside a compound expression buried in an `if` statement probably isn't a good idea.

Using the | and || operators

The `|` and `||` operators are called *or operators* because they return `true` if the first expression is `true` or if the second expression is `true`. They also return `true` if both expressions are `true`. (You find the `|` symbol on your keyboard just above the Enter key.)

Suppose that sales representatives get no commission if the total sales are less than $1,000 or if the sales class is 3. You could do that with two separate `if` statements:

```
if (salesTotal < 1000.0)
    commissionRate = 0.0;
if (salesClass == 3)
    commissionRate = 0.0;
```

But with an or operator, you can do the same thing with a compound condition:

```
if ((salesTotal < 1000.0) | (salesClass == 3))
    commissionRate = 0.0;
```

To evaluate the expression for this `if` statement, Java first evaluates the expressions on either side of the `|` operator. Then, if at least one of them is `true`, the whole expression is `true`. Otherwise, the expression is `false`.

In most cases, you should use the conditional Or operator (`||`) instead of the regular Or operator (`|`), like this:

```
if ((salesTotal < 1000.0) || (salesClass == 3))
    commissionRate = 0.0;
```

Like the conditional And operator (`&&`), the conditional Or operator stops evaluating as soon as it knows what the outcome is. For example, suppose the sales total is $500. Then, there's no need to evaluate the second expression. Because the first expression evaluates to `true` and only one of the expressions needs to be `true`, Java can skip the second expression altogether. Of course, if the sales total is $5,000, the second expression must still be evaluated.

As with the And operators, you should use the regular Or operator only if your program depends on some side effect of the second expression, such as work done by a method call.

Using the ^ operator

The `^` operator performs what in the world of logic is known as an *exclusive or*, commonly abbreviated as *xor*. It returns `true` if one and only one of the two subexpressions is `true`. If both expressions are `true` or if both expressions are `false`, the `^` operator returns `false`.

Most programmers don't bother with the `^` operator because it's pretty confusing. My feelings won't be hurt if you skip this section.

Put another way, the `^` operator returns `true` if the two subexpressions have different results. If they both have the same result, it returns `false`.

As an example, suppose you're writing software that controls your model railroad set and you want to find out if two switches are set in a dangerous position that might allow a collision. If the switches were represented by simple integer variables named `switch1` and `switch2` and 1 meant the track was switched to the left and 2 meant the track was switched to the right, you could easily test them like this:

```
if ( switch1 == switch2 )
    System.out.println("Trouble! The switches are the same");
else
    System.out.println("OK, the switches are different.");
```

But what if, for some reason, one of the switches is represented by an int variable where 1 means the switch is left and any other value means the switch is right, but the other is an int variable where –1 means the switch is left and any other value means the switch is right. (Who knows, maybe the switches were made by different manufacturers.) You could use a compound condition like this:

```
if ( ((switch1==1)&&(switch2==-1)) ||
     ((switch1!=1)&&(switch2!=-1)))
    System.out.println("Trouble! The switches are the same");
else
    System.out.println("OK, the switches are different.");
```

But a xor operator could do the job with a simpler expression:

```
if ( (switch1==1)^(switch2==-1))
    System.out.println("OK, the switches are different.");
else
    System.out.println("Trouble! The switches are the same");
```

Frankly, the ^ operator is probably one you should avoid using. In fact, most of the Java books on my bookshelf (and believe me, I have a lot of them) don't even mention this operator except in its other, more useful application as a bitwise operator (see Bonus Chapter 2 on this book's Web site for information about bitwise operators). That's probably because many applications don't use it as a logic operator, and the applications that it is suitable for can also be solved with the more traditional And and Or operators.

Combining logical operators

You can combine simple boolean expressions to create more complicated expressions. For example:

```
if ((salesTotal<1000.0)||((salesTotal<5000.0)&&
    (salesClass==1))||((salestotal < 10000.0)&&
    (salesClass == 2)))
  CommissionRate = 0.0;
```

Can you tell what the expression in this if statement does? It sets the commission to zero if any one of these three conditions is true:

✦ The sales total is less than $1,000.

✦ The sales total is less than $5,000, and the sales class is 1.

✦ The sales total is less than $10,000, and the sales class is 2.

In many cases, you can clarify how an expression works just by indenting its pieces differently and spacing out its subexpressions. For example, this version of the previous if statement is a little easier to follow:

```
if (        (salesTotal < 1000.0)
    ||  ( (salesTotal < 5000.0) && (salesClass == 1) )
    ||  ( (salestotal < 10000.0) && (salesClass == 2) )
   )
     commissionRate = 0.0;
```

However, figuring out exactly what this if statement does is still tough. In many cases the better thing to do is to skip the complicated expression and code separate if statements:

```
if (salesTotal < 1000.0)
    commissionRate = 0.0;
if ( (salesTotal < 5000.0) && (salesClass == 1) )
    commissionRate = 0.0;
if ( (salestotal < 10000.0) && (salesClass == 2) )
    commissionRate = 0.0;
```

Boolean expressions can get a little complicated when you use more than one logical operator, especially if you mix And and Or operators. For example, consider this expression:

```
if ( a==1 && b==2 || c==3 )
    System.out.println("It's true!");
else
    System.out.println("No it isn't!");
```

What do you suppose this if statement does if a is 5, b is 7, and c = 3? The answer is that the expression evaluates to true and "It's true!" is printed. That's because Java applies the operators from left to right. So the && operator is applied to a==1 (which is false) and b==2 (which is also false). Thus, the && operator returns false. Then the || operator is applied to that false result and the result of c==3, which is true. Thus, the entire expression returns true.

Wouldn't this expression have been more clear if you had used a set of parentheses to clarify what the expression does? For example:

```
if ( (a==1 && b==2) || c==3 )
    System.out.println("It's true!");
else
    System.out.println("No it isn't!");
```

Now you can clearly see that the && operator is evaluated first.

Using the Conditional Operator

Java has a special operator called the *conditional operator* that's designed to eliminate the need for `if` statements altogether in certain situations. It's a *ternary operator*, which means that it works with three operands. The general form for using the conditional operator is this:

```
boolean-expression ? expression-1 : expression-2
```

The boolean expression is evaluated first. If it evaluates to `true`, then *expression-1* is evaluated, and the result of this expression becomes the result of the whole expression. If the expression is `false`, *expression-2* is evaluated, and its results are used instead.

For example, suppose you want to assign a value of `0` to an integer variable named `salesTier` if total sales are less than $10,000 and a value of `1` if the sales are $10,000 or more. You could do that with this statement:

```
int tier = salesTotal > 10000.0 ? 1 : 0;
```

Although not required, a set of parentheses helps make this statement easier to follow:

```
int tier = (salesTotal > 10000.0) ? 1 : 0;
```

One common use for the conditional operator is when you're using concatenation to build a text string and you have a word that might need to be plural, based on the value of an integer variable. For example, suppose you want to create a string that says `"You have x apples"`, with the value of a variable named `appleCount` substituted for *x*. But if `apples` is `1`, the string should be `"You have 1 apple"`, not `"You have 1 apples"`.

The following statement does the trick:

```
String msg = "You have " + appleCount + " apple"
    + ((appleCount>1) ? "s." : ".");
```

When Java encounters the `?` operator, it evaluates the expression (`appleCount>1`). If `true`, it uses the first string (`s.`). If `false`, it uses the second string (`.`).

Comparing Strings

Comparing strings in Java takes a little extra care because the `==` operator doesn't really work the way it should. For example, suppose you want to know if a string variable named `answer` contains the value `"Yes"`. You might be tempted to code an `if` statement like this:

```
if (answer == "Yes")
    System.out.println("The answer is Yes.");
```

Unfortunately, that's not correct. The problem is that in Java, strings are reference types, not primitive types, and when you use the == operator with reference types, Java compares the references to the objects, not the objects themselves. As a result, the expression answer == "Yes" doesn't test whether the value of the string referenced by the answer variable is "Yes". Instead, it tests whether the answer string and the literal string "Yes" point to the same string object in memory. In many cases, they do. But sometimes they don't, and the results are difficult to predict.

The correct way to test a string for a given value is to use the equals method of the String class:

```
if (answer.equals("Yes"))
    System.out.println("The answer is Yes.");
```

This method actually compares the value of the string object referenced by the variable with the string you pass as a parameter and returns a boolean result to indicate whether the strings have the same value.

The String class has another method, equalsIgnoreCase, that's also useful for comparing strings. It compares strings but ignores case, which is especially useful when you're testing string values entered by users. For example, suppose you're writing a program that ends only when the user enters the word End. You could use the equals method to test the string:

```
if (input.equals("end"))
    // end the program
```

But then, the user would have to enter end exactly. If the user enters End or END, the program won't end. It's better to code the if statement like this:

```
if (input.equalsIgnoreCase("end"))
    // end the program
```

Then, the user could end the program by entering end, End, END, or even eNd.

You can find much more about working with strings in Book IV, Chapter 1. For now, just remember that to test for string equality in an if statement (or in one of the other control statements that's presented in the next chapter), you must use the equals or equalsIgnoreCase method instead of the == operator.

Chapter 5: Going Around in Circles (Or, Using Loops)

In This Chapter

- ✔ The thrill of `while` loops
- ✔ The rapture of infinite loops
- ✔ The splendor of `do` loops
- ✔ The joy of validating input
- ✔ The wonder of `for` loops
- ✔ The ecstasy of nested loops

So far, all the programs in this book have started, run quickly through their `main` method, and then ended. If Dorothy from *The Wizard of Oz* were using these programs, she'd probably say, "My, programs come and go quickly around here!"

In this chapter, you find out how to write programs that don't come and go so quickly. They hang around by using *loops,* which let them execute the same statements more than once.

Loops are the key to writing one of the most common types of programs: programs that get input from the user, do something with it, then get more input from the user and do something with that, and keep going this way until the user has had enough.

Or, put another way, loops are like the instructions on your shampoo: Lather. Rinse. *Repeat.*

Like `if` statements, loops rely on conditional expressions to tell them when to stop looping. Without conditional expressions, loops would go on forever, and your users would grow old watching them run. So, if you haven't yet read Book II, Chapter 4, I suggest you do so before continuing much further.

Your Basic while Loop

The most basic of all looping statements in Java is while. The while statement creates a type of loop that's called a *while loop,* which is simply a loop that executes continuously as long as some conditional expression evaluates to true. while loops are useful in all sorts of programming situations, so you use while loops a lot. (I tell you about other kinds of loops later in this chapter.)

The while statement

The basic format of the while statement is like this:

```
while (expression)
    statement
```

The while statement begins by evaluating the expression. If the expression is true, *statement* is executed. Then, the expression is evaluated again, and the whole process repeats. If the expression is false, *statement* is not executed, and the while loop ends.

Note that the statement part of the while loop can either be a single statement or a block of statements contained in a pair of braces. Loops that have just one statement aren't very useful, so nearly all the while loops you code use a block of statements. (Well, okay, sometimes loops with a single statement are useful. It isn't unheard of. Just not all that common.)

A counting loop

Here's a simple program that uses a while loop to print the even numbers from 2 through 20 on the console:

```java
public class EvenCounter
{
    public static void main(String[] args)
    {
        int number = 2;
        while (number <= 20)
        {
            System.out.print(number + " ");
            number += 2;
        }
        System.out.println();
    }
}
```

If you run this program, the following output is displayed in the console window:

```
2 4 6 8 10 12 14 16 18 20
```

The conditional expression in this program's `while` statement is `number <= 20`. That means the loop repeats as long as the value of `number` is less than or equal to `20`. The body of the loop consists of two statements. The first prints the value of `number` followed by a space to separate this number from the next one. Then, the second statement adds 2 to `number`.

Figure 5-1 shows a flowchart for this program. This flowchart can help you visualize the basic decision making process of a loop.

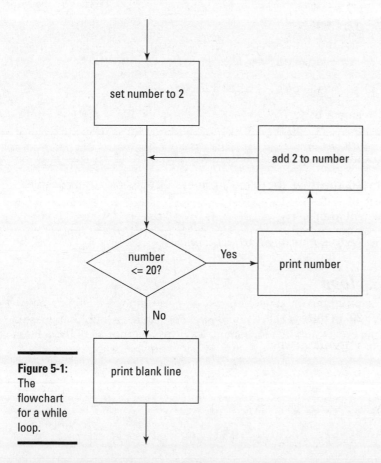

Figure 5-1:
The
flowchart
for a while
loop.

Breaking Out of a Loop

In many programs, you need to set up a loop that has some kind of escape clause. Java's escape clause is the `break` statement. When a `break` statement is executed in a `while` loop, the loop ends immediately. Any remaining statements in the loop are ignored, and the next statement executed is the statement that follows the loop.

For example, suppose you're afraid of the number 12. (I'm not doctor and I don't play one on TV, but I think the scientific name for this condition would be *duodecaphobia*.) You could modify the counting program shown in the previous section so that when it gets to the number 12, it panics and aborts the loop:

```
public class Duodecaphobia
{
    public static void main(String[] args)
    {
        int number = 2;
        while (number <= 20)
        {
            if (number == 12)
                break;
            System.out.print(number + " ");
            number += 2;
        }
        System.out.println();
    }
}
```

When you run this program, the following line is displayed on the console:

```
2 4 6 8 10
```

Whew! That was close. Almost got to 12 there.

Looping Forever

One common form of loop is called an *infinite loop*. That's a loop that goes on forever. You can create infinite loops many ways in Java (not all of them intentional), but the easiest is to just specify `true` for the `while` expression.

Here's an example:

```
public class CountForever
{
    public static void main(String[] args)
    {
        int number = 2;
        while (true)
        {
            System.out.print(number + " ");
            number += 2;
        }
    }
}
```

If you run this program, your console window quickly fills up with numbers and just keeps going. That's great if you like even numbers, but eventually you'll tire of this and want it to stop. You can stop an infinite loop three ways:

✦ Turn off your computer.

✦ Hit your computer with an ax or other heavy object.

✦ Close the console window.

The last one is probably the one you want to go with here.

Obviously, infinite loops are something you want to avoid in your programs. So whenever you use a `while` expression that's always `true`, be sure to throw in a `break` statement to give your loop some way to terminate. For example, you could use an infinite loop with a `break` statement in the duo-decaphobia program:

```
public class Duodecaphobia
{
    public static void main(String[] args)
    {
        int number = 2;
        while (true)
        {
            if (number == 12)
                break;
            System.out.print(number + " ");
            number += 2;
        }
        System.out.println();
    }
}
```

Here, the loop looks like it might go on forever, but the `break` statement panics out of the loop when it hits 12.

Letting the user decide when to quit

It turns out that infinite loops are also useful when you want to let the user be in charge of when to stop the loop. For example, suppose you don't know what numbers a user is afraid of, so you want to count numbers until the user says to stop. Here's a program that does that:

```
import java.util.Scanner;

public class NumberPhobia
{
    static Scanner sc = new Scanner(System.in);

    public static void main(String[] args)
```

```
    {
        int number = 2;
        String input;

        while (true)
        {
            System.out.println(number + " ");
            System.out.print("Do you want keep
counting?"
                + " (Y or N)");
            input = sc.next();
            if (input.equalsIgnoreCase("N"))
                break;
            number += 2;
        }
        System.out.println("\nWhew! That was
close.\n");
    }
}
```

Here's some typical console output from this program, for a user who has octophobia:

```
2
Do you want keep counting? (Y or N)y
4
Do you want keep counting? (Y or N)y
6
Do you want keep counting? (Y or N)n

Whew! That was close.
```

Another way to let the user decide

Another way to write a loop that a user can opt out of is to test the input string in the `while` condition. The only trick here is that you must first initialize the input string to the value that continues the loop. Otherwise, the loop doesn't execute at all! Here's a variation of the `NumberPhobia` program that uses this technique:

```
import java.util.Scanner;

public class NumberPhobia2
{
    static Scanner sc = new Scanner(System.in);

    public static void main(String[] args)
    {
        int number = 2;
        String input = "Y";
```

```
    while (input.equalsIgnoreCase("Y"))
    {
        System.out.println(number + " ");
        System.out.print("Do you want keep
counting?"
            + " (Y or N)");
        input = sc.next();
        number += 2;
    }
    System.out.println("\nWhew! That was close.");
}
}
```

This program works almost the same as the previous version, but with a subtle difference. In the first version, if the user says N after the program displays 6, the value of the number variable after the loop is 6. That's because the break statement bails out of the loop before adding 2 to number. But in this version, the value of number is 8.

Using the continue Statement

The break statement is rather harsh: It completely bails out of the loop. Sometimes that's what you need, but just as often, you don't really need to quit the loop; you just need to skip a particular iteration of the loop. For example, the Duodecaphobia program presented earlier in this chapter stops the loop when it gets to 12. What if you just want to skip the number 12, so you go straight from 10 to 14?

To do that, you can use the break statement's kinder, gentler relative, the continue statement. The continue statement sends control right back to the top of the loop, where the expression is immediately evaluated again. If the expression is still true, the loop's statement or block is executed again.

Here's a version of the Duodecaphobia program that uses a continue statement to skip the number 12 rather than stop counting altogether when it reaches 12:

```
public class Duodecaphobia2
{
    public static void main(String[] args)
    {
        int number = 0;
        while (number < 20)
        {
            number += 2;
            if (number == 12)
                continue;
            System.out.print(number + " ");
```

```
        }
        System.out.println();
    }
}
```

Run this program, and you get the following output in the console window:

```
2 4 6 8 10 14 16 18 20
```

Notice that I had to make several changes to this program to get it to work with a `continue` statement instead of a `break` statement. If I had just replaced the word `break` with `continue`, the program wouldn't have worked. That's because the statement that added 2 to the number came after the `break` statement in the original version. As a result, if you just replace the `break` statement with a `continue` statement, you end up with an infinite loop once you reach 12 because the statement that adds 2 to `number` never gets executed.

To make this program work with a `continue` statement, I rearranged the statements in the loop body so that the statement that adds 2 to `number` comes before the `continue` statement. That way, the only statement skipped by the `continue` statement is the one that prints `number` to the console.

Unfortunately, this change affected other statements in the program as well. Because 2 is added to `number` before `number` is printed, I had to change the initial value of `number` from 2 to 0, and I had to change the `while` expression from `number <= 20` to `number < 20`.

do-while Loops

A *do-while loop* (sometimes just called a *do loop*) is similar to a `while` loop, but with a critical difference: In a `do-while` loop, the condition that stops the loop isn't tested until after the statements in the loop have executed. The basic form of a `do-while` loop is this:

```
do
    statement
while (expression);
```

Note that the `while` keyword and the expression aren't coded until *after* the body of the loop. As with a `while` loop, the body for a `do-while` loop can be a single statement or a block of statements enclosed in braces.

Also, notice that the expression is followed by a semicolon. `do-while` is the only looping statement that ends with a semicolon.

Here's a version of the EvenCounter program that uses a `do-while` loop instead of a `while` loop:

```
public class EvenCounter2
{
    public static void main(String[] args)
    {
        int number = 2;
        do
        {
            System.out.print(number + " ");
            number += 2;
        } while (number <= 20);

        System.out.println();
    }
}
```

Here's the most important thing to remember about `do-while` loops: The statement or statements in the body of a `do-while` loop are *always* executed at least once. In contrast, the statement or statements in the body of a `while` loop are not executed at all if the `while` expression is `false` the first time it is evaluated.

Look at the flowchart in Figure 5-2 to see what I mean. You can see that execution starts at the top of the loop and flows through to the decision test after the loop's body has been executed once. Then, if the decision test is `true`, control flies back up to the top of the loop. Otherwise, it spills out the bottom of the flowchart.

Here are a few other things to be aware of concerning `do-while` loops:

✦ You often can skip initializing the variables that appear in the expression before the loop because the expression isn't evaluated until the statements in the loop body have been executed at least once.

✦ You can use `break` and `continue` statements in a `do-while` loop just as you can in a `while` loop.

✦ Some programmers like to place the brace that begins the loop body on the same line as the `do` statement and the `while` statement that ends the `do-while` loop on the same line as the brace that marks the end of the loop body. Whatever makes you happy is fine with me. Just remember that the compiler is agnostic when it comes to matters of indentation and spacing.

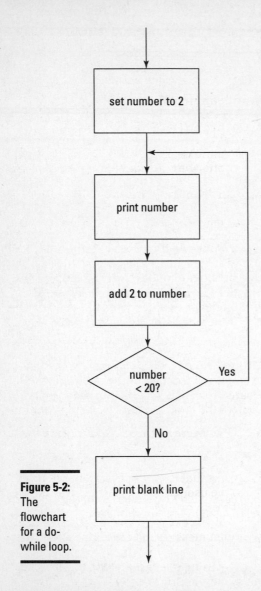

Figure 5-2: The flowchart for a do-while loop.

Validating Input from the User

do-while loops are especially useful for validating input by the user. For example, suppose you're writing a program that plays a betting game, and you want to get the amount of the user's bet from the console. The user can bet any dollar amount he wants (whole dollars only though), but can't bet more than he has in the bank, and he can't bet a negative amount or zero. Here's a program that uses a do-while loop to get this input from the user:

```
import java.util.Scanner;

public class GetABet
{

    static Scanner sc = new Scanner(System.in);

    public static void main(String[] args)
    {
        int bank = 1000;    // assume the user has $1,000
        int bet;            // the bet entered by the user

        System.out.println("You can bet between 1 and " +
            bank);
        do
        {
            System.out.print("Enter your bet: ");
            bet = sc.nextInt();
        } while ( (bet <= 0) || (bet > bank) );
        System.out.println("Your money's good here.");
    }
}
```

Here, the expression used by the do-while loop validates the data entered by the user, which means it checks the data against some set of criteria to make sure the data is acceptable.

The || operator performs an *or* test. It returns true if at least one of the expressions on either side of the operator is true. So if the bet is less than or equal to zero (bet <= 0), or if the bet is greater than the money in the bank (bet > bank), this expression returns true.

This type of validation testing only checks that if the user has entered a valid number, it is in an acceptable range. If the user enters something that isn't a valid number, such as the word Buttercup or Humperdink, the program chokes badly and spews forth a bunch of vile exception messages upon the console. You find out how to clean up that mess in Book II, Chapter 8.

(Actually, you can avoid this problem by using either a do loop or a while loop and the hasNextDouble method of the Scanner class that I describe in Book II, Chapter 2.)

If you want to display an error message when the user enters incorrect input, you have to use an if statement inside the loop, and this if statement must duplicate the expression that validates the input data. Thus, the expression that does the validation has to appear twice. For example:

```
import java.util.Scanner;

public class GetABet2
{

    static Scanner sc = new Scanner(System.in);

    public static void main(String[] args)
    {
        int bank = 1000;    // assume the user has $1,000
        int bet;            // the bet entered by the user

        System.out.println("You can bet between 1 and " +
            bank);
        do
        {
            System.out.print("Enter your bet: ");
            bet = sc.nextInt();
            if ( (bet <= 0) || (bet > bank) )
                System.out.println("What, are you
crazy?");
        } while ( (bet <= 0) || (bet > bank) );
        System.out.println("Your money's good here.");
    }
}
```

Here, the `if` statement displays the message `"What, are you crazy?"` if the user tries to enter an inappropriate bet.

You can avoid duplicating the expression that does the data validation in two ways. One is to add a boolean variable that's set in the body of the `do-while` loop if the data is invalid, as in this example:

```
import java.util.Scanner;

public class GetABet3
{

    static Scanner sc = new Scanner(System.in);

    public static void main(String[] args)
    {
        int bank = 1000;    // assume the user has $1,000
        int bet;            // the bet entered by the user
        boolean validBet;   // indicates if bet is valid

        System.out.println("You can bet between 1 and " +
            bank);
        do
        {
```

```
System.out.print("Enter your bet: ");
bet = sc.nextInt();
validBet = true;
if ( (bet <= 0) || (bet > bank) )
{
    validBet = false;
    System.out.println("What, are you
crazy?");
}
} while (!validBet);
System.out.println("Your money's good here.");
}
}
```

In this example, I use a boolean variable named validBet to indicate whether the user has entered a valid bet. After the user enters a bet, this variable is set to true before the if statement tests the validation criteria. Then, if the if statement finds that the bet is not valid, validBet is set to false.

The Famous for Loop

In addition to while and do-while loops, Java offers one more kind of loop: the *for loop*. You may have noticed that many of the loops presented so far in this minibook have involved counting. It turns out that counting loops are quite common in computer programs, so the people who design computer programming languages (they're called "computer programming language designers") long ago concocted a special kind of looping mechanism that's designed just for counting.

The basic principle behind a for loop is that the loop itself maintains a *counter variable* — that is, a variable whose value is increased each time the body of the loop is executed. For example, if you want a loop that counts from 1 to 10, you'd use a counter variable that starts with a value of 1 and is increased by 1 each time through the loop. Then, you'd use a test to end the loop when the counter variable reaches 10. The for loop lets you set this up all in one convenient statement.

People who majored in Computer Science call the counter variable an *iterator*. They do so because they think we don't know what it means. But we know perfectly well that the iterator is where you put your beer to keep it cold.

The formal format of the for loop

I would now like to inform you of the formal format for the for loop, so you know how to form it from now on. The for loop follows this basic format:

```
for (initialization-expression; test-expression; count-
    expression)
      statement;
```

The three expressions in the parentheses following the keyword `for` control how the `for` loop works. The following paragraphs explain what these three expressions do:

✦ The *initialization expression* is executed before the loop begins. Usually, you use this expression to initialize the counter variable. If you haven't declared the counter variable before the `for` statement, you can declare it here too.

✦ The *test expression* is evaluated each time the loop is executed to determine whether the loop should keep looping. Usually, this expression tests the counter variable to make sure it is still less than or equal to the value you want to count to. The loop keeps executing as long as this expression evaluates to `true`. When the test expression evaluates to `false`, the loop ends.

✦ The *count expression* is evaluated each time the loop executes. Its job is usually to increment the counter variable.

Figure 5-3 shows a flowchart to help you visualize how a `for` loop works.

Here's a simple `for` loop that displays the numbers 1 to 10 on the console:

```
public class CountToTen
{
    public static void main(String[] args)
    {
        for (int i = 1; i <= 10; i++)
            System.out.println(i);
    }
}
```

Run this program and here's what you see on the console:

```
1
2
3
4
5
6
7
8
9
10
```

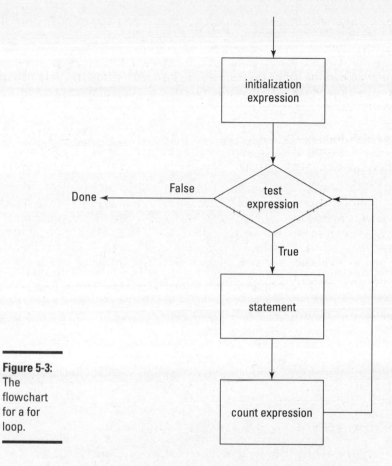

Figure 5-3:
The
flowchart
for a for
loop.

This `for` loop apart has the following pieces:

✦ The initialization expression is `int i = 1`. This expression declares a variable named `i` of type `int` and assigns it an initial value of `1`.

✦ The test expression is `i <= 10`. As a result, the loop continues to execute as long as `i` is less than or equal to `10`.

✦ The count expression is `i++`. As a result, each time the loop executes, the variable `i` is incremented.

✦ The body of the loop is the single statement `System.out.println(i)`. As a result, each time the loop executes, the value of the `i` variable is printed to the console.

I made up those terms I use to describe the three expressions in a `for` loop. Officially, Java calls them the *ForInit Expression*, the *Expression*, and the *ForUpdate Expression*. Don't you think my terms are more descriptive?

Scoping out the counter variable

If you declare the counter variable in the initialization statement, the scope of the counter variable is limited to the for statement itself. Thus, you can use the variable in the other expressions that appear within the parentheses and in the body of the loop, but you can't use it outside of the loop. For example, this code causes a compiler error:

```
public class CountToTenError
{
    public static void main(String[] args)
    {
        for (int i = 1; i <=10; i++)
            System.out.println(i);
        System.out.println("The final value of i is " + i);
    }
}
```

That's because the last statement in the main method refers to the variable i, which has gone out of scope because it was declared within the for loop.

However, you don't have to declare the counter variable in the for statement itself. Thus, the following program works:

```
public class CountToTenErrorFixed
{
    public static void main(String[] args)
    {
        int i;
        for (i = 1; i <=10; i++)
            System.out.println(i);
        System.out.println("The final value of i is " +
i);
    }
}
```

Note that because the i variable is declared before the for statement, the initialization expression doesn't name the variable's data type. When you run this program, the following appears in the console window:

```
1
2
3
4
5
6
7
8
9
10
The final value of i is 11
```

Counting even numbers

Earlier in this chapter, you saw a program that counts even numbers up to 20. You can do that with a `for` loop too. All you have to do is adjust the count expression. For example, here's a version of the CountEven program that uses a `for` loop:

```
public class ForEvenCounter
{
    public static void main(String[] args)
    {
        for (int number = 2; number <= 20; number += 2)
            System.out.print(number + " ");
        System.out.println();
    }
}
```

Run this program, and sure enough, the console window displays the following:

```
2 4 6 8 10 12 14 16 18 20
```

Counting backwards

No rule says `for` loops can count only forwards. To count backwards, you simply have to adjust the three `for` loop expressions. As usual, the initialization expression specifies the starting value for the counter variable. The test expression uses a greater-than test instead of a less-than test. And the count expression subtracts from the counter variable rather than adds to it.

For example:

```
public class CountDown
{
    public static void main(String[] args)
    {
        for (int count = 10; count >= 1; count--)
        {
            System.out.println(count);
        }
    }
}
```

Run this program, and you see this result in the console window:

```
10
9
8
7
6
5
```

```
4
3
2
1
```

TIP

For those of you who grew up like I did in the 1960s, watching NASA launches religiously, you'll appreciate this variation of the countdown program:

```java
public class LaunchControl
{
   public static void main(String[] args)
   {
      System.out.print("We are go for launch in T minus ");
      for (int count = 10; count >= 0; count--)
      {
         if (count == 8)
            System.out.println("Ignition sequence start!");
         else
            System.out.println(count + "...");
      }
      System.out.println("All engines running!");
      System.out.println("Liftoff! We have a liftoff!");
   }
}
```

When you run it, here's the output that's displayed:

```
We are go for launch in T minus 10...
9...
Ignition sequence start!
7...
6...
5...
4...
3...
2...
1...
0...
All engines running!
Liftoff! We have a liftoff!
```

Can't you hear the voice of Paul Haney, the famous "Voice of Mission Control" for NASA in the 1960s? If you can't, you're not nearly as nerdy as I am.

for loops without bodies

Some programmers get a kick out of writing code that is as terse as possible. I think *Seinfeld* did an episode about that . . . Jerry had a girlfriend who was a "terse-coder." He had to dump her because he couldn't understand her code.

Anyway, terse coders sometimes like to play with `for` statements in an effort to do away with the body of a `for` loop altogether. To do that, they take advantage of the fact that you can code any expression you want in the count expression part of a `for` statement, including method calls. For example, here's a program that prints the numbers 1 to 10 on the console using a `for` statement that has no body:

```
public class TerseCoder
{
    public static void main(String[] args)
    {
        for (int i = 1; i <=10; System.out.println(i++));
    }
}
```

Here, the count expression is a call to `System.out.println`. The parameter to the `println` method cleverly uses the increment operator so the variable is both printed and incremented in the same expression.

Stay away from terse coders! Seinfeld was right to dump her.

Ganging up your expressions

An obscure aspect of `for` loops is that the initialization and count expressions can actually be a list of expressions separated by commas. This can sometimes be useful if you need to keep track of two counter variables at the same time. For example, here's a program that counts from 1 to 10 and 10 to 1 at the same time, using two counter variables:

```
public class CountBothWays
{
    public static void main(String[] args)
    {
        int a, b;
        for (a = 1, b = 10; a <= 10; a++, b--)
            System.out.println(a + " " + b);
    }

}
```

If you run this program, here's what you see in the console window:

```
1  10
2  9
3  8
4  7
5  6
6  5
7  4
8  3
9  2
10  1
```

Keep in mind these rules when you use more than one expression for the initialization and counter expressions:

✦ In the initialization expression, you can't declare variables if you use more than one expression. That's why I declared the a and b variable before the for statement in the CountBothWays example.

✦ The expressions in an expression list can be assignment statements, increment or decrement statements (such as a++), method calls, or object creation statements that use the new keyword to create an object from a class. Other types of statements, such as if statements or loops, are not allowed.

✦ You can't list more than one expression in the test expression. However, you can use compound conditions created with boolean operators, so you don't need to use an expression list.

Here, just to prove I could do it, is a version of the LaunchController program that uses a bodiless for loop:

```
public class ExpressionGanging
{
    public static void main(String[] args)
    {
        System.out.print("We are go for launch in T minus
");
        for (int count = 10; count >= 0;
            System.out.println((count == 8) ?
                "Ignition sequence start!" :
                count + "..."),
            count--      );
        System.out.println("All engines running!");
        System.out.println("Liftoff! We have a
liftoff!");
    }
}
```

This program actually looks more complicated than it is. The count expression is a list of two expressions. First is a call to System.out.println that uses the ternary ?: operator to determine what to print. The ?: operator first evaluates the count variable to see if it equals 8. If so, the string "Ignition sequence start!" is sent to the println method. Otherwise, count + "..." is sent. The second expression simply increments the count variable.

I think you'll agree that coding the for statement like this example is way out of line. It's better to keep the expressions simple and do the real work in the loop's body.

Omitting expressions

Yet another oddity about `for` loops is that all three of the expressions are optional. If you omit one or more of the expressions, you just code the semicolon as a placeholder so the compiler knows.

Omitting the test expression or the iteration expression is not common, but omitting the initialization expression is common. For example, the variable you're incrementing in the `for` loop may already be declared and initialized before you get to the loop. In that case, you can omit the initialization expression, as in this example:

```
Scanner sc = new Scanner(System.in);
System.out.print("Where should I start? ");
int a = sc.nextInt();
for ( ; a >= 0; a--)
    System.out.println(a);
```

This `for` loop simply counts down from whatever number the user enters to zero.

If you omit the test expression, you'd better throw a `break` statement in the loop somewhere. Otherwise, you find yourself in an infinite loop.

You can also omit all three of the expressions if you want to, as in this example:

```
for(;;)
    System.out.println("Oops");
```

This program also results in an infinite loop. There's little reason to do this because `while(true)` has the same effect and is more obvious.

Breaking and continuing your for loops

You can use a break in a `for` loop just as you can in a `while` or `do-while` loop. For example, here I revisit the Duodecaphobia program from earlier in the chapter, this time with a `for` loop:

```
public class ForDuodecaphobia
{
    public static void main(String[] args)
    {
        for (int number = 2; number <=20; number += 2)
        {
            if (number == 12)
                break;
            System.out.print(number + " ");
        }
        System.out.println();
    }
}
```

As before, this version counts by 2s until it gets to 20. But when it hits 12, it panics and aborts the loop, so it never actually gets to 14, 16, 18, or 20. So the console output loops like this:

```
2 4 6 8 10
```

And here's a version that uses a `continue` statement to simply skip 12 rather than abort the loop:

```
public class ForDuodecaphobia2
{
    public static void main(String[] args)
    {
        for (int number = 2; number <=20; number += 2)
        {
            if (number == 12)
                continue;
            System.out.print(number + " ");
        }
        System.out.println();
    }
}
```

The console output from this version looks like this:

```
2 4 6 8 10 14 16 18 20
```

Nesting Your Loops

Loops can contain loops. The technical term for this is *Loop-de-Loop*. Just kidding. Actually, the technical term is *nested loop*. A nested loop is simply a loop that is completely contained inside another loop. The loop that's inside is called the *inner loop,* and the loop that's outside is called the *outer loop.*

A simple nested for loop

To demonstrate the basics of nesting, here's a simple little program that uses a pair of nested `for` loops:

```
public class NestedLoop
{
    public static void main(String[] args)
    {
        for(int x = 1; x < 10; x++)
        {
            for (int y = 1; y < 10; y++)
```

```
                System.out.print(x + "-" + y + "  ");
            System.out.println();
        }
    }
}
```

This program consists of two for loops. The outer loop uses x as its counter variable, and the inner loop uses y. For each execution of the outer loop, the inner loop executes 10 times and prints a line that shows the value of x and y for each pass through the inner loop. When the inner loop finishes, a call to System.out.println with no parameters starts a new line. Then, the outer loop cycles so the next line is printed.

When you run this program, the console displays this text:

```
1-1   1-2   1-3   1-4   1-5   1-6   1-7   1-8   1-9
2-1   2-2   2-3   2-4   2-5   2-6   2-7   2-8   2-9
3-1   3-2   3-3   3-4   3-5   3-6   3-7   3-8   3-9
4-1   4-2   4-3   4-4   4-5   4-6   4-7   4-8   4-9
5-1   5-2   5-3   5-4   5-5   5-6   5-7   5-8   5-9
6-1   6-2   6-3   6-4   6-5   6-6   6-7   6-8   6-9
7-1   7-2   7-3   7-4   7-5   7-6   7-7   7-8   7-9
8-1   8-2   8-3   8-4   8-5   8-6   8-7   8-8   8-9
9-1   9-2   9-3   9-4   9-5   9-6   9-7   9-8   9-9
```

A guessing game

Listing 5-1 shows a more complicated but realistic example of nesting. This program implements a simple guessing game in which the computer picks a number between 1 and 10 and you have to guess the number. After you guess, the computer tells you if you're right or wrong, and then asks if you want to play again. If you enter Y or y, the game starts over.

The nesting comes into play because the entire game is written in a while loop that repeats as long as you say you want to play another game. Then, within that loop, each time the game asks for input from the user, it uses a do-while loop to validate the user's entry. Thus, when the game asks the user to guess a number between 1 and 10, it keeps looping until the number entered by the user is in that range. And when the game asks the user whether he or she wants to play again, it loops until the user enters Y, y, N, or n.

Here's a sample of the console output displayed by this program:

```
Let's play a guessing game!

I'm thinking of a number between 1 and 10.
What do you think it is? 5
You're wrong! The number was 8
```

```
Play again? (Y or N)y

I'm thinking of a number between 1 and 10.
What do you think it is? 32
I said, between 1 and 10. Try again: 5
You're wrong! The number was 6

Play again? (Y or N)maybe

Play again? (Y or N)ok

Play again? (Y or N)y

I'm thinking of a number between 1 and 10.
What do you think it is? 5
You're right!

Play again? (Y or N)n
Thank you for playing.
```

LISTING 5-1: THE GUESSING GAME

```java
import java.util.Scanner;

public class GuessingGame
{

    static Scanner sc = new Scanner(System.in);

    public static void main(String[] args)
    {
        boolean keepPlaying = true;                              → 10

        System.out.println("Let's play a guessing game!");
        while (keepPlaying)                                      → 13
        {
            boolean validInput;                                 → 15
            int number, guess;
            String answer;

            // Pick a random number
            number = (int)(Math.random() * 10) + 1;             → 20

            // Get the guess
            System.out.println("\nI'm thinking of a number "
                + "between 1 and 10.");
            System.out.print("What do you think it is? ");
            do                                                  → 26
            {
                guess = sc.nextInt();
                validInput = true;
                if ( (guess < 1) || (guess > 10) )
                {
                    System.out.print("I said, between 1 and 10. "
```

```
            + "Try again: ");
            validInput = false;
        }
    } while (!validInput);                            → 36

    // Check the guess
    if (guess == number)                              → 39
        System.out.println("You're right!");
    else
        System.out.println("You're wrong!");

    // Play again?
    do                                                → 46
    {
        System.out.print("\nPlay again? (Y or N)");
        answer = sc.next();
        validInput = true;
        if (answer.equalsIgnoreCase("Y"))
            ;
        else if (answer.equalsIgnoreCase("N"))
            keepPlaying = false;
        else
            validInput = false;
    } while (!validInput);                            → 57
}                                                     → 58
System.out.println("\nThank you for playing!");       → 59
    }
}
```

The following paragraphs describe some of the key lines in this program:

→10 Defines a boolean variable named keepPlaying that's initialized to
true and changed to false when the user indicates he or she has
had enough of this silly game.

→13 Begins the main while loop for the game. The loop continues as long
as keepPlaying is true. This loop ends on line 58.

→15 Defines a boolean variable named validInput that's used to indicate whether the user's input is valid. The same variable is used for
both the entry of the user's guess and the Y or N string at the end of
each round.

→20 Picks a random number between 1 and 10. For more information,
refer to Book II, Chapter 3.

→26 Begins the do-while loop that gets a valid guess from the user. This
loop ends on line 36. The statements in this loop read the user's guess
from the console, and then test to make sure it is between 1 and 10. If
so, validInput is set to true. Otherwise, validInput is set to
false, an error message is displayed, and the loop repeats so the user
is forced to guess again. The loop continues as long as validInput is
false.

→**39** The `if` statement compares the user's guess with the computer's number. A message is displayed to indicate whether the user guessed right or wrong.

→**46** Begins the `do-while` loop that asks whether the user wants to play again. This loop ends on line 57. The statements in this loop read a string from the user. If the user enters `Y` or `y`, `validInput` is set to `true`. (`keepPlaying` is already `true`, so it is left alone.) If the user enters `N` or `n`, `validInput` is set to `true`, and `keepPlaying` is set to `false`. And if the user enters anything else, `validInput` is set to `false`. The loop continues as long as `validInput` is false.

→**59** This statement is executed after the program's main `while` loop finishes to thank the user for playing the game.

Chapter 6: Pulling a Switcheroo

In This Chapter

✔ **The trouble with big** else-if **statements**

✔ **Using the** switch **statement**

✔ **Creating case groups**

✔ **Using characters with case**

✔ **Falling through the cracks**

In Book II, Chapter 4, you find out about the workhorses of Java decision making: boolean expressions and the mighty if statement. In this chapter, you discover another Java tool for decision making: the switch statement. The switch statement is a pretty limited beast, but it excels at one particular type of decision making: choosing one of several actions based on a value stored in an integer variable. As it turns out, the need to do just that comes up a lot. So you want to keep the switch statement handy when such a need arises.

else-if Monstrosities

Many applications call for a simple logical selection of things to be done depending on some value that controls everything. As I describe in Book II, Chapter 4, such things are usually handled with big chains of else-if statements all strung together.

Unfortunately, these things can quickly get out of hand. else-if chains can end up looking like DNA double-helix structures, or those things that dribble down from the tops of the computer screens in *The Matrix*.

For example, Listing 6-1 shows a bit of a program that might be used to decode error codes in a Florida or Ohio voting machine.

LISTING 6-1: THE ELSE-IF VERSION OF THE VOTING MACHINE ERROR DECODER

```java
import java.util.Scanner;

public class VoterApp
{

  static Scanner sc = new Scanner(System.in);

  public static void main(String[] args)
  {

    System.out.println("Welcome to the voting machine "
      + "error code decoder.\n\n"
      + "If your voting machine generates "
      + "an error code,\n"
      + "you can use this program to determine "
      + "the exact\ncause of the error.\n");
    System.out.print("Enter the error code: ");
    int err = sc.nextInt();

    String msg;
    if (err==1)
      msg = "Voter marked more than one candidate.\n"
        + "Ballot rejected.";
    else if (err==2)
      msg = "Box checked and write-in candidate "
        + "entered.\nBallot rejected.";
    else if (err==3)
      msg = "Entire ballot was blank.\n"
        + "Ballot filled in according to secret plan.";
    else if (err==4)
      msg = "Nothing unusual about the ballot.\n"
        + "Voter randomly selected for tax audit.";
    else if (err==5)
      msg = "Voter filled in every box.\n"
        + "Ballot counted twice.";
    else if (err==6)
      msg = "Voter drooled in voting machine.\n"
        + "Beginning spin cycle.";
    else if (err==7)
      msg = "Voter lied to pollster after voting.\n"
        + "Voter's ballot changed "
        + "to match polling data.";
    else
      msg = "Voter filled out ballot correctly.\n"
        + "Ballot discarded anyway.";
    System.out.println(msg);
  }
}
```

Wow! And this program has to decipher just 7 different error codes. What if the machine had 500 different codes?

A Better Version of the Voter Machine Error Decoder Program

Fortunately, Java has a special statement that's designed just for the kind of task represented by the Voter Machine Error Decoder program: the `switch` statement. Specifically, the `switch` statement is sometimes useful when you need to select one of several alternatives based on the value of an integer or character type variable.

Listing 6-2 shows a version of the Voter Machine Error Decoder program that uses a `switch` statement instead of a big `else-if` structure. I think you'll agree that this version of the program is a bit easier to follow. The `switch` statement makes it clear that the messages are all selected based on the value of the `err` variable.

LISTING 6-2: THE SWITCH VERSION OF THE VOTING MACHINE ERROR DECODER

```java
import java.util.Scanner;

public class VoterApp2
{

  static Scanner sc = new Scanner(System.in);

  public static void main(String[] args)
  {

    System.out.println("Welcome to the voting machine "
      + "error code decoder.\n\n"
      + "If your voting machine generates "
      + "an error code,\n"
      + "you can use this program to determine "
      + "the exact\ncause of the error.\n");
    System.out.print("Enter the error code: ");
    int err = sc.nextInt();

    String msg;

    switch (err)
    {
      case 1:
        msg = "Voter marked more than one candidate.\n"
          + "Ballot rejected.";
        break;
      case 2:
        msg = "Box checked and write-in candidate "
        + "entered.\nBallot rejected.";
        break;
```

continued

LISTING 6-2 (CONTINUED)

```
        case 3:
          msg = "Entire ballot was blank.\n"
            + "Ballot filled in according to secret plan.";
          break;
        case 4:
          msg = "Nothing unusual about the ballot.\n"
            + "Voter randomly selected for tax audit.";
          break;
        case 5:
          msg = "Voter filled in every box.\n"
            + "Ballot counted twice.";
          break;
        case 6:
          msg = "Voter drooled in voting machine.\n"
            + "Beginning spin cycle.";
          break;
        case 7:
          msg = "Voter lied to pollster after voting.\n"
            + "Voter's ballot changed "
            + "to match polling data.";
          break;
        default:
          msg = "Voter filled out ballot correctly.\n"
            + "Ballot discarded anyway.";
          break;
      }
    System.out.println(msg);
  }
}
```

Using the switch Statement

The basic form of the switch statement is this:

```
switch (expression)
{
   case constant:
        statements;
        break;
 [ case constant-2:
        statements;
        break;  ] ...
 [ default:
        statements;
        break;  ] ...
}
```

The expression must evaluate to an int, short, byte, or char. It can't be a long or a floating-point type.

You can code as many case groups as you want or need. Each begins with the word `case` followed by a constant (usually a simple numeric literal) and a colon. Then, you code one or more statements that you want executed if the value of the `switch` expression equals the constant. The last line of each case group is a `break` statement, which causes the entire `switch` statement to end.

The `default` group, which is optional, is like a catch-all case group. Its statements are executed only if none of the previous case constants match the `switch` expression.

Note that the case groups are not true blocks marked with braces. Instead, each case group begins with the `case` keyword and ends with the `case` keyword that starts the next case group. However, all the case groups together are defined as a block marked with a set of braces.

The last statement in each case group usually is a `break` statement. A `break` statement causes control to skip to the end of the `switch` statement. If you omit the `break` statement, control falls through to the next case group. Accidentally leaving out `break` statements is the most common cause of trouble with the `switch` statement.

A Boring Business Example Complete with Flowchart

Okay, the Voter Machine Error Decoder was kind of fun. Now here's a more down-to-earth example. Suppose you need to set a commission rate based on a sales class represented by an integer that can be 1, 2, or 3, according to this table:

Class	Commission Rate
1	2%
2	3.5%
3	5%
Any other value	0%

You could do this with the following `switch` statement:

```
double commissionRate;
switch (salesClass)
{
    case 1:
        commissionRate = 0.02;
        break;
    case 2:
        commissionRate = 0.035;
        break;
```

```
case 3:
    commissionRate = 0.05;
    break;
default:
    commissionRate = 0.0;
    break;
}
```

Figure 6-1 shows a flowchart that describes the operation of this switch state-ment. As you can see, this flowchart is similar to the flowchart that was shown in Figure 4-3 in Book II, Chapter 4. That's because the operation of the switch statement is similar to the operation of a series of else-if statements.

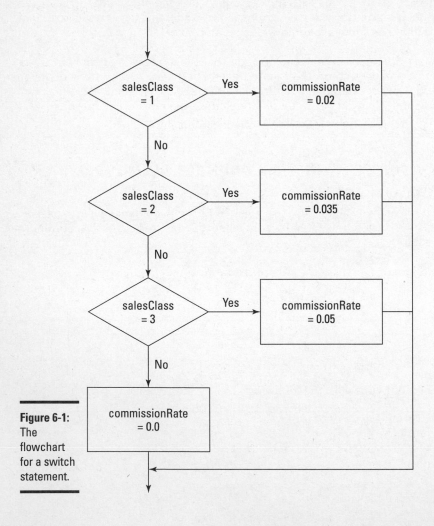

TIP

I like flowcharts because they remind me of my old days of computer programming, when we had to draw flowcharts for every program we wrote before we were allowed to write any code. The flowcharts didn't really help us write better programs, but they were fun to draw.

Putting if Statements Inside switch Statements

You're free to include any type of statements you want in the case groups, including if statements. For example, suppose your commission structure depends on total sales as well as sales class, like this:

Class	*Sales < $10,000*	*Sales $10,000 and Above*
1	1%	2%
2	2.5%	3.5%
3	4%	5%
Any other value	0%	0%

Then, you can use the following switch statement:

```
double commissionRate;
switch (salesClass)
{
    case 1:
        if (salesTotal < 10000.0)
            commissionRate = 0.01;
        else
            commissionRate = 0.02;
        break;
    case 2:
        if (salesTotal < 10000.0)
            commissionRate = 0.025;
        else
            commissionRate = 0.035;
        break;
    case 3:
        if (salesTotal < 10000.0)
            commissionRate = 0.04;
        else
            commissionRate = 0.05;
        break;
    default:
        commissionRate = 0.0;
        break;
}
```

Here, each case group includes an `if` statement. If necessary, these `if` statements could be complex nested `if` statements.

Other than the `if` statements within the case groups, there's nothing else here to see, folks. Move along.

Creating Character Cases

Aside from having a nice alliterative title, this section shows how you can use a `char` variable rather than an integer in a `switch` statement. When you use a `char` type, providing two consecutive `case` constants for each case group is common, to allow for both lower- and uppercase letters. For example, suppose you need to set the commission rates based on character codes rather than integer values for the sales class, according to this table:

Class	Commission Rate
A or a	2%
B or b	3.5%
C or c	5%
Any other value	0%

Here's the `switch` statement to do the trick:

```
double commissionRate;
switch (salesClass)
{
    case 'A':
    case 'a':
        commissionRate = 0.02;
        break;
    case 'B':
    case 'b':
        commissionRate = 0.035;
        break;
    case 'C':
    case 'c':
        commissionRate = 0.05;
        break;
    default:
        commissionRate = 0.0;
        break;
}
```

The key to understanding this example is realizing that you don't have to code any statements at all for a case group, and that if you omit the `break` statement from a case group, control falls through to the next case group. Thus, the `case 'A'` group doesn't contain any statements, but it falls through to the `case 'a'` group.

You use apostrophes, not quotation marks, to create character literals.

Falling through the Cracks

Although the most common cause of problems with the `switch` statement is accidentally leaving out a `break` statement at the end of a case group, sometimes you need to do it on purpose. For example, many applications have features that are progressively added based on a control variable. For example, your local car wash might sell several packages with different services:

Package	Services
A	Wash, vacuum, and hand dry
B	Package A + Wax
C	Package B + Leather/Vinyl Treatment
D	Package C + Tire Treatment
E	Package D + New Car Scent

Listing 6-3 shows an application that displays all the products you get when you order a specific package. It works by testing the package codes in a `switch` statement in reverse order (starting with package E) and adding the products that come with each package to the `details` variable. None of the case groups except the last includes a `break` statement. As a result, control falls through each case group to the next group. Thus, once a case group has tested `true`, the rest of the case groups in the `switch` statement are executed.

LISTING 6-3: THE CAR WASH APPLICATION

```java
import java.util.Scanner;

public class CarWashApp
{
  static Scanner sc = new Scanner(System.in);

  public static void main(String[] args)
  {
```

continued

LISTING 6-3 (CONTINUED)

```
      System.out.println("The car wash application!n\n\n");
      System.out.print("Enter the package code: ");
      String s = sc.next();
      char p = s.charAt(0);

      String details = "";

      switch (p)
      {
        case 'E':
        case 'e':
          details += "\tNew Car Scent, plus...\n";
        case 'D':
        case 'd':
          details += "\tTire Treatment, plus...\n";
        case 'C':
        case 'c':
        details += "\tLeather/Vinyl Treatment, plus...\n";
        case 'B':
        case 'b':
          details += "\tWax, plus...\n";
        case 'A':
        case 'a':
          details += "\tWash, vacuum, and hand dry.\n";
          break;
        default:
          details = "That's not one of the codes.";
          break;
      }
      System.out.println("\nThat package includes:\n");
      System.out.println(details);
    }
}
```

Just between you and me, writing programs that depend on switch statements falling through the cracks like this example isn't really a good idea. Instead, consider placing the statements for each case group in separate methods, and then calling all the methods you need for each case group. Then, you can use a break statement at the end of each group to prevent falling through. Listing 6-4 shows a version of the car wash application that uses this technique to avoid fall-throughs in the switch statement. (Using simple fall throughs to treat upper- and lowercase characters the same isn't as confusing, so this program still uses that technique.)

LISTING 6-4: A VERSION OF THE CAR WASH PROGRAM THAT AVOIDS NASTY FALLS

```
import java.util.Scanner;

public class CarWashApp2
{
```

```java
static Scanner sc = new Scanner(System.in);

public static void main(String[] args)
{

   System.out.println("The car wash application!\n\n");
   System.out.print("Enter the package code: ");
   String s = sc.next();
   char p = s.charAt(0);

   String details = "";

   switch (p)
   {
     case 'E':
     case 'e':
       details = packageE() + packageD() + packageC()
         + packageB() + packageA();
       break;
     case 'D':
     case 'd':
       details = packageD() + packageC()
         + packageB() + packageA();
       break;
     case 'C':
     case 'c':
       details = packageC() + packageB() + packageA();
       break;
     case 'B':
     case 'b':
       details = packageB() + packageA();
       break;
     case 'A':
     case 'a':
       details = packageA();
       break;
     default:
       details = "That's not one of the codes.";
       break;
   }
   System.out.println("\nThat package includes:\n");
   System.out.println(details);
}

public static String packageA()
{
   return "\tWash, vacuum, and hand dry.\n";
}

public static String packageB()
{
   return "\tWax, plus...\n";
}
```

continued

Book II
Chapter 6

Pulling a
Switcheroo

LISTING 6-4 (CONTINUED)

```java
public static String packageC()
{
  return "\tLeather/Vinyl Treatment, plus...\n";
}

public static String packageD()
{
  return "\tTire Treatment, plus...\n";
}

public static String packageE()
{
  return "\tNew Car Scent, plus...\n";
}

}
```

Chapter 7: Adding Some Methods to Your Madness

In This Chapter

✓ Introducing static methods

✓ Some good reasons to use methods in your programs

✓ Creating methods that return values

✓ Creating methods that accept parameters

*I*n Java, a *method* is a block of statements that has a name and can be executed by *calling* (also called *invoking*) it from some other place in your program. You may not realize it, but you're already very experienced with using methods. For example, to print text to the console, you use the `println` or `print` methods. To get an integer from the user, you use the `nextInt` method. And to compare string values, you use either the `equals` method or the `equalsIgnoreCase` method. And the granddaddy of all methods, `main`, is the method that contains the statements that are executed when you run your program.

All the methods you've used so far (with the exception of `main`) have been methods that are defined by the Java API and that belong to a particular Java class. For example, the `nextInt` method belongs to the `Scanner` class, and the `equalsIgnoreCase` method belongs to the `String` class.

In contrast, the `main` method belongs to the class defined by your application. In this chapter, you find out how to create additional methods that are a part of your application's class. You can then call these methods from your `main` method. As you'll see, this method turns out to be very useful for all but the shortest Java programs.

The Joy of Methods

The use of methods can dramatically improve the quality of your programming life. For example, suppose the problem your program is supposed to solve is complicated and you need at least 1,000 Java statements to get 'er done. You could put all those 1,000 statements in the `main` method, but it would go on for pages and pages. It's better to break your program up into a few well-defined sections of code and place each of those sections in a separate method. Then, your `main` method can simply call the other methods in the right sequence.

Or, suppose your program needs to perform some calculation, such as how long to let the main rockets burn to make a mid-course correction on a moon-flight, and the program needs to perform this calculation in several different places. Without methods, you'd have to duplicate the statements that do this calculation. That's not only error prone, but makes your programs more difficult to test and debug. But if you put the calculation in a method, you can simply call the method whenever you need to perform the calculation. Thus, methods help you cut down on repetitive code.

Another good use for methods is to simplify the structure of your code that uses long loops. For example, suppose you have a `while` loop that has 500 statements in its body. That makes it pretty hard to track down the closing brace that marks the end of the body. By the time you find it, you probably will have forgotten what the `while` loop does. You can simplify this `while` loop by placing the code from its body in a separate method. Then, all the `while` loop has to do is call the new method.

At this point, the object-oriented programming zealots in the audience are starting to boo and hiss. A few of them have already left the auditorium. They're upset because I'm describing methods in traditional procedural-programming terms instead of modern object-oriented programming terms.

Well, phooey. They're right, but so what? I get to the object-oriented uses for methods in Book III. There, you find out that methods have a far greater purpose than simply breaking a long `main` method into smaller pieces. But even so, some of the most object-oriented programs I know use methods just to avoid repetitive code or to slice a large method into a couple of smaller ones. So there.

The Basics of Making Methods

All methods — including the `main` method — must begin with a *method declaration*. Here's the basic form for a method declaration, at least for the types of methods I talk about in this chapter:

```
public static return-type method-name (parameter-list)
{
        statements...
}
```

The following paragraphs describe method declarations piece-by-piece:

✦ **public:** This keyword indicates that the method's existence should be publicized to the world, and that any Java program that knows about your program (or, more accurately, the class defined for your Java program) should be able to use your method. That's not very meaningful for the types of programs you're dealing with at this point in the book, but it will become more meaningful later on. In Book III, you find out more about what `public` means, as well as some alternatives to `public` that are useful in various and sundry situations.

✦ **static:** This keyword declares that the method is a *static method,* which means that it can be called without first creating an instance of the class in which it's defined. The `main` method must always be static, and any other methods in the class that contains the `main` method should usually be static as well.

✦ ***return-type:*** After the word `static` comes the *return type,* which indicates whether the method returns a value when it is called and, if so, what type the value is. If the method doesn't return a value, specify `void`. (I talk more about methods that return values later in this chapter, in the section "Methods That Return Values.")

✦ ***method-name:*** Now comes the name of your method. The rules for making up method names are the same as the rules for creating variable names: You can use any combination of letters and numbers, but the name has to start with a letter. And, it can include the dollar sign (`$`) and underscore character (`_`). No other special characters are allowed.

When picking a name for your method, try to pick a name that's relatively short but descriptive. A method name such as `calculateTheTotal AmountOfTheInvoice` is a little long, but just `calc` is pretty ambiguous. Something along the lines of `calculateInvoiceTotal` seems more reasonable to me.

✦ ***parameter list:*** You can pass one or more values to a method by listing the values in parentheses following the method name. The parameter list in the method declaration lets Java know what types of parameters a method should expect to receive and provides names so that the statements in the method's body can access the parameters as local variables. You discover more about parameters in the section "Using Methods That Take Parameters" later in this chapter.

If the method doesn't accept parameters, you must still code the parentheses that surround the parameter list. You just leave the parentheses empty.

✦ **Method body:** The method body consists of one or more Java statements enclosed in a set of braces. Unlike Java statements such as `if`, `while`, and `for`, you still have to use the braces even if the body of your method consists of only one statement.

An example

Okay, all that was a little abstract. Now for a concrete example, I offer a version of the Hello, World! program in which the message is displayed not by the `main` method, but by a method named `sayHello` that's called by the `main` method:

```
public class HelloWorldMethod
{
```

```
public static void main(String[] args)
{
    sayHello();
}

public static void sayHello()
{
    System.out.println("Hello, World!");
}
}
```

This program is admittedly trivial, but it illustrates the basics of creating and using methods in Java. Here, the statement in the `main` method calls the `sayHello` method, which in turn displays a message on the console.

The order in which methods appear in your Java source file doesn't matter. The only rule is that all the methods must be declared within the body of the class — that is, between the first left brace and the last right brace. For example, here's a version of the HelloWorldMethod program in which I reversed the order of the methods:

```
public class HelloWorldMethod
{
    public static void sayHello()
    {
        System.out.println("Hello, World!");
    }

    public static void main(String[] args)
    {
        sayHello();
    }

}
```

This version of the program works exactly like the previous version.

Another example

Okay, the last example was kind of dumb. No one in his (or her) right mind would create a method that has just one line of code, and then call it from another method that also has just one line of code. The Hello, World! program is too trivial to illustrate anything remotely realistic.

For example, a program in Book II, Chapter 5 plays a guessing game. Most of this program's `main` method is a large `while` loop that repeats the game as long as the user wants to keep playing. This loop has 41 statements in its body. That's not so bad, but what if the game were 100 times more complicated, so that the `while` loop needed 4,100 statements to play a single cycle of the game? Do you really want a `while` loop that has 4,100 statements in its body? I should think not.

Listing 7-1 shows how you can simplify this game a bit just by placing the body of the main `while` loop into a separate method. I called this method `playARound`, because its job is to play onc round of the guessing game. Now, instead of actually playing a round of the game, the `main` method of this program delegates that task to the `playARound` method.

LISTING 7-1: A VERSION OF THE GUESSING GAME PROGRAM THAT USES A PLAYAROUND METHOD

```java
import java.util.Scanner;

public class GuessingGameMethod
{

    static Scanner sc = new Scanner(System.in);
    static boolean keepPlaying = true;                          → 7

    public static void main(String[] args)
    {
        System.out.println("Let's play a guessing game!");
        while (keepPlaying)                                     → 12
        {
            playARound();                                      → 14
        }
        System.out.println("\nThank you for playing!");
    }

    public static void playARound()                            → 19
    {
        boolean validInput;
        int number, guess;
        String answer;

        // Pick a random number
        number = (int)(Math.random() * 10) + 1;
        System.out.println("\nI'm thinking of a number "
            + "between 1 and 10.");

        // Get the guess
        System.out.print("What do you think it is? ");
        do
        {
            guess = sc.nextInt();
            validInput = true;
            if ( (guess < 1) || (guess > 10) )
            {
                System.out.print("I said, between 1
                    and 10. " + "Try again: ");
                validInput = false;
            }
        } while (!validInput);

        // Check the guess
        if (guess == number)
            System.out.println("You're right!");
```

Book II
Chapter 7

Adding Some
Methods to Your
Madness

continued

LISTING 7-1 (CONTINUED)

```
        else
            System.out.println("You're wrong!"
                + " The number was " + number);

    // Play again?
    do
    {
        System.out.print("\nPlay again? (Y or N)");
        answer = sc.next();
        validInput = true;
        if (answer.equalsIgnoreCase("Y"))
            ;
        else if (answer.equalsIgnoreCase("N"))
            keepPlaying = false;                         → 60
        else
            validInput = false;
    } while (!validInput);
    }
}
```

Here are a few important details to notice about this method:

→ **7** Because the `main` method (in line 12) and the `playARound` method (in line 60) must both access the `keepPlaying` variable, I declared it as a class variable rather than as a local variable in the `main` method.

Class variables must be `static` if you intend to access them from static methods.

→**14** The body of the `while` loop in the `main` method is just one line: a call to the `playARound` method. Thus, each time the loop repeats, the program plays one round of the game with the user.

→**19** The declaration for the `playARound` method marks the method as `static` so that the static `main` method can call it.

The body of the `playARound` method is identical to the body of the `while` loop that was originally used in the single-method version of this program shown in Book II, Chapter 5. If you want a refresher on how this code works, I politely refer you to that chapter.

Methods That Return Values

Methods that just do work without returning any data are useful only in limited situations. The real utility of methods comes when they can perform some mundane task such as a calculation, and then return the value of that calculation to the calling method so the calling method can do something with the value. You find out how to do that in the following sections.

Declaring the method's return type

To create a method that returns a value, you simply indicate the type of the value returned by the method on the method declaration in place of the `void` keyword. For example, here's a method declaration that creates a method that returns an `int` value:

```
public static int getRandomNumber()
```

Here, the `getRandomNumber` method calculates a random number, and then returns the number to the caller.

The return type of a method can be any of Java's primitive return types (described in Book II, Chapter 2):

int	long	float	char
short	byte	double	boolean

Or, the return type can be a reference type, including a class defined by the API such as `String` or a class you create yourself.

Using the return statement to return the value

When you specify a return type other than `void` in a method declaration, the body of the method must include a `return` statement that specifies the value to be returned. The `return` statement has this form:

```
return expression;
```

The expression must evaluate to a value that's the same type as the type listed in the method declaration. In other words, if the method returns an `int`, the expression in the `return` statement must evaluate to an `int`.

For example, here's a program that uses a method that determines a random number between 1 and 10:

```
public class RandomNumber
{
    public static void main(String[] args)
    {
        int number = getRandomNumber();
        System.out.println("The number is " + number);
    }

    public static int getRandomNumber()
    {
        int num = (int)(Math.random() * 10) + 1;
        return num;
    }
}
```

In this program, the `getRandomNumber` method uses the `Math.random` method to calculate a random number from 1 to 10. (For more information about the `Math.random` method, see Book II, Chapter 3.) The `return` statement returns the random number that was calculated.

Because the `return` statement can specify an expression as well as a simple variable, I could just as easily have written the `getRandomNumber` method like this:

```
public static int getRandomNumber()
{
    return (int)(Math.random() * 10) + 1;
}
```

Here, the `return` statement includes the expression that calculates the random number.

Using a method that returns a type

You can use a method that returns a value in an assignment statement, like this:

```
int number = getRandomNumber();
```

Here, the `getRandomNumber` method is called, and the value it returns is assigned to the variable `number`.

You can also use methods that return values in expressions. For example:

```
number = getRandomNumber() * 10;
```

Here, the value returned by the `getRandomNumber` method is multiplied by 10, and the result is assigned to `number`.

You gotta have a proper return statement

If a method declares a return type other than void, it *must* use a `return` statement to return a value. The compiler doesn't let you get away with a method that doesn't have a correct `return` statement.

Things can sometimes get complicated if your `return` statements are inside `if` statements. Sometimes, the compiler can get fooled and refuse to compile your program. To explain this, I offer the following tale of multiple attempts to solve what should be a simple programming problem:

Suppose you want to create a random number method that returns random numbers between 1 and 20, but never returns 12 (because you have the condition known as duodecaphobia, which as Lucy from *Peanuts* would tell you is the fear of the number 12). Your first thought is to just ignore the 12s, like this:

```
public static int getRandomNumber()
{
    int num = (int)(Math.random() * 20) + 1;
    if (num != 12)
        return num;
}
```

However, the compiler isn't fooled by your trickery here. It knows that if the number is 12, the `return` statement won't get executed. So it issues the message `missing return statement` and refuses to compile your program.

Your next thought is to simply substitute 11 whenever 12 comes up:

```
public static int getRandomNumber()
{
    int num = (int)(Math.random() * 20) + 1;
    if (num != 12)
        return num;
    else
        return 11;
}
```

However, later that day you realize this solution isn't a good one because the number isn't really random anymore. One of the requirements of a good random number generator is that any number should be as likely as any other number to come up next. But because you're changing all 12s to 11s, you've made 11 twice as likely to come up as any other number.

To fix this error, you decide to put the random number generator in a loop that ends only when the random number is not 12:

```
public static int getRandomNumber()
{
    int num;
    do
    {
        num = (int)(Math.random() * 20) + 1;
        if (num != 12)
            return num;
    } while (num == 12);
}
```

But now the compiler refuses to compile the method again. It turns out that the compiler is smart, but not real smart. It doesn't catch the fact that the condition in the `do-while` loop is the opposite of the condition in the `if` statement, meaning that the only way out of this loop is through the `return` statement in the `if` statement. So the compiler whines `missing return statement` again.

After thinking about it a while, you come up with this solution:

```
public static int getRandomNumber()
{
    int num;
    while (true)
    {
        num = (int)(Math.random() * 20) + 1;
        if (num != 12)
            return num;
    }
}
```

Now everyone's happy. The compiler knows the only way out of the loop is through the `return` statement, your doudecaphobic user doesn't have to worry about seeing the number 12, and you know that the random number isn't twice as likely to be 11 as any other number. Life is good, and you can move on to the next topic.

Another version of the guessing game program

To illustrate the benefits of using methods that return values, Listing 7-2 presents another version of the guessing game program that uses four methods in addition to `main`:

✦ **playARound**: This method plays one round of the guessing game. It doesn't return a value.

✦ **getRandomNumber:** Returns a random number between 1 and 10.

✦ **getGuess:** Gets the user's guess, makes sure it is between 1 and 10, and returns the guess if it's within the acceptable range.

✦ **askForAnotherRound:** This method asks the user to play another round and returns a boolean value to indicate whether or not the user wants to continue playing.

LISTING 7-2: ANOTHER VERSION OF THE GUESSING GAME PROGRAM

```
import java.util.Scanner;

public class GuessingGameMethod2
{

    static Scanner sc = new Scanner(System.in);

    public static void main(String[] args)
    {
        System.out.println("Let's play a guessing game!");
        do                                                      → 11
        {
            playARound();                                       → 13
        } while (askForAnotherRound());                         → 14
```

```
      System.out.println("\nThank you for playing!");
   }

   public static void playARound()                              → 18
   {
      boolean validInput;
      int number, guess;
      String answer;

      // Pick a random number
      number = getRandomNumber();                               → 25

      // Get the guess
      System.out.println("\nI'm thinking of a number "
            + "between 1 and 10.");
      System.out.print("What do you think it is? ");
      guess = getGuess();                                       → 31

      // Check the guess
      if (guess == number)
         System.out.println("You're right!");
      else
         System.out.println("You're wrong!"
               + " The number was " + number);
   }

   public static int getRandomNumber()                          → 41
   {
      return (int)(Math.random() * 10) + 1;                     → 43
   }

   public static int getGuess()                                 → 46
   {
      while (true)                                              → 48
      {
         int guess = sc.nextInt();
         if ( (guess < 1) || (guess > 10) )
         {
            System.out.print("I said, between 1 and
                  10. " + "Try again: ");
         }
         else
            return guess;                                       → 57
      }

   }
   public static boolean askForAnotherRound()                   → 61
   {
      while (true)                                              → 63
      {
         String answer;
         System.out.print("\nPlay again? (Y or N) ");
         answer = sc.next();
         if (answer.equalsIgnoreCase("Y"))
            return true;                                        → 69
         else if (answer.equalsIgnoreCase("N"))
            return false;                                       → 71
      }
   }
}
```

The following paragraphs point out the key lines of this program:

→**11** The start of the do loop in the main method. Each cycle of this do loop plays one round of the game. The do loop continues until the user indicates that he or she wants to stop playing.

→**13** Calls the playARound method to play one round of the game.

→**14** Calls the askForAnotherRound method to determine whether the user wants to play another round. The boolean return value from this method is used as the expression for the do loop. Thus, the do loop repeats if the askForAnotherRound method returns true.

→**18** The start of the playARound method.

→**25** This line calls the getRandomNumber method to get a random number between 1 and 10. The value returned by this method is stored in the number variable.

→**31** This line calls the getGuess method to get the user's guess. This method returns a number between 1 and 10, which is stored in the guess variable.

→**41** The start of the getRandomNumber method, which indicates that this method returns an int value.

→**43** The return statement for the getRandomNumber method. The random number is calculated using the Math.random method, and the result of this calculation is returned as the value of the getRandomNumber method.

→**46** The start of the getGuess method, which indicates that this method returns an int value.

→**48** The getGuess method uses a while loop, which exits only when the user enters a number between 1 and 10.

→**57** The return statement for the getGuess method. Note that this return statement is in the else part of an if statement that checks if the number is less than 1 or greater than 10. If the number is outside of the acceptable range, the return statement isn't executed. Instead, the program displays an error message, and the while loop repeats.

→**61** The start of the askForAnotherRound method, which returns a boolean value.

→**63** The askForAnotherRound method uses a while loop that exits only when the user enters a valid Y or N response.

→**69** The askForAnotherRound method returns true if the user enters Y or y.

→**71** The askForAnotherRound method returns false if the user enters N or n.

Using Methods That Take Parameters

A *parameter* is a value that you can pass to a method. The method can then use the parameter as if it were a local variable initialized with the value of the variable passed to it by the calling method.

For example, the guessing game application that was shown in Listing 7-2 has a method named getRandomNumber that returns a random number between 1 and 10:

```
public static int getRandomNumber()
{
    return (int)(Math.random() * 10) + 1;
}
```

This method is useful, but it would be even more useful if you could tell it the range of numbers you want the random number to fall in. For example, it would be nice if you could call it like this to get a random number between 1 and 10:

```
int number = getRandomNumber(1, 10);
```

Then, if your program needs to roll dice, you could call the same method:

```
int number = getRandomNumber(1, 6);
```

Or, to pick a random card from a deck of 52 cards, you could call it like this:

```
int number = getRandomNumber(1, 52);
```

And you wouldn't have to start with 1, either. To get a random number between 50 and 100, you'd call it like this:

```
int number = getRandomNumber(50, 100);
```

In the following sections, you write methods that accept parameters.

Declaring parameters

A method that accepts parameters must list the parameters in the method declaration. The parameters are listed in a *parameter list* that's in the parentheses that follow the method name. For each parameter used by the method, you list the parameter type followed by the parameter name. If you need more than one parameter, you separate them with commas.

For example, here's a version of the getRandomNumber method that accepts parameters:

```
public static int getRandomNumber(int min, int max)
{
```

```
        return (int)(Math.random()
            * (max - min + 1)) + min;
}
```

Here, the method uses two parameters, both of type `int`, named `min` and `max`. Then, within the body of the method, these parameters can be used as if they were local variables.

The names you use for parameters can be the same as the names you use for the variables you pass to the method when you call it, but they don't have to be. For example, you could call the `getRandomNumber` method like this:

```
int min = 1;
int max = 10;
int number = getRandomNumber(min, max);
```

Or, you could call it like this:

```
int low = 1;
int high = 10;
int number = getRandomNumber(low, high);
```

Or, you can dispense with the variables altogether and just pass literal values to the method:

```
int number = getRandomNumber(1, 10);
```

You can also specify expressions as the parameter values:

```
int min = 1;
int max = 10;
int number = getRandomNumber(min * 10, max * 10);
```

Here, `number` is assigned a value between 10 and 100.

Scoping out parameters

The scope of a parameter is the method for which the parameter is declared. As a result, a parameter can have the same name as local variables used in other methods without causing any conflict. For example, consider this program:

```
public class ParameterScope
{
    public static void main(String[] args)
    {
        int min = 1;
        int max = 10;
        int number = getRandomNumber(min, max);
        System.out.println(number);
```

```
    }

    public static int getRandomNumber(int min, int max)
    {
        return (int)(Math.random()
            * (max - min + 1)) + min;
    }
}
```

Here, the `main` method declares variables named `min` and `max`, and the `getRandomNumber` method uses `min` and `max` for its parameter names. This doesn't cause any conflict, because in each case the scope is limited to a single method.

Understanding pass-by-value

When Java passes a variable to a method via a parameter, the method itself receives a copy of the variable's value, not the variable itself. This copy is called a *pass-by-value*, and it has an important consequence: If a method changes the value it receives as a parameter, that change is *not* reflected in the original variable that was passed to the method. The following program can help clear this up:

```
public class ChangeParameters
{
    public static void main(String[] args)
    {
        int number = 1;
        tryToChangeNumber(number);
        System.out.println(number);

    }

    public static void tryToChangeNumber(int i)
    {
        i = 2;
    }
}
```

Here, a variable named `number` is set to 1, and then passed to the method named `tryToChangeNumber`. This method receives the variable as a parameter named `i`, and then sets the value of `i` to 2. Meanwhile, back in the `main` method, `println` is used to print the value of `number` after the `tryToChangeNumber` method returns.

Because `tryToChangeNumber` only gets a copy of `number` and not the `number` variable itself, this program displays the following on the console (drumroll please...): 1.

The key point is this: Even though the `tryToChangeNumber` method changes the value of its parameter, that change has no effect on the original variable that was passed to the method.

Yet another example of the guessing game program

To show off the benefits of methods that accept parameters, Listing 7-3 shows one more version of the guessing game program. This version uses the following methods in addition to `main`:

- ✦ **playARound:** This method plays one round of the guessing game. It doesn't return a value, but it accepts two arguments: `min` and `max`, which indicate the minimum and maximum values for the number to be guessed.

- ✦ **getRandomNumber:** Returns a random number between `min` and `max` values passed as parameters.

- ✦ **getGuess:** This method also accepts two parameters, `min` and `max`, to limit the range within which the user must guess.

- ✦ **askForAnotherRound:** This method asks the user to play another round and returns a boolean value to indicate whether or not the user wants to continue playing. It accepts a `String` value as a parameter; this string is displayed on the console to prompt the user for a reply.

LISTING 7-3: ANOTHER VERSION OF THE GUESSING GAME PROGRAM

```java
import java.util.Scanner;

public class GuessingGameMethod3
{

    static Scanner sc = new Scanner(System.in);

    public static void main(String[] args)
    {
        System.out.println("Let's play a guessing game!");
        do
        {
            playARound(1, getRandomNumber(7, 12));               → 13
        } while (askForAnotherRound("Try again?"));
        System.out.println("\nThank you for playing!");
    }

    public static void playARound(int min, int max)
    {
        boolean validInput;
        int number, guess;
        String answer;

        // Pick a random number
        number = getRandomNumber(min, max);                      → 25

        // Get the guess
        System.out.println("\nI'm thinking of a number "
            + "between " + min + " and " + max + ".");           → 29
```

```
            System.out.print("What do you think it is? ");
            guess = getGuess(min, max);                              → 31

            // Check the guess
            if (guess == number)
                System.out.println("You're right!");
            else
                System.out.println("You're wrong!"
                    + " The number was " + number);
    }
    public static int getRandomNumber(int min, int max)             → 41
    {
        return (int)(Math.random()                                  → 43
            * (max - min + 1)) + min;
    }

    public static int getGuess(int min, int max)                    → 47
    {
        while (true)
        {
            int guess = sc.nextInt();
            if ( (guess < min) || (guess > max) )                   → 52
            {
                System.out.print("I said, between "
                    + min + " and " + max
                    + ". Try again: ");
            }
            else
                return guess;                                       → 59
        }

    }
    public static boolean askForAnotherRound(String prompt)         → 63
    {
        while (true)
        {
            String answer;
            System.out.print("\n" + prompt + " (Y or N) ");
            answer = sc.next();
            if (answer.equalsIgnoreCase("Y"))
                return true;
            else if (answer.equalsIgnoreCase("N"))
                return false;
        }
    }
}
```

Book II
Chapter 7

Adding Some
Methods to Your
Madness

The following paragraphs point out the key lines of this program:

→**13** Calls the `playARound` method to play one round of the game. The values for `min` and `max` are passed as literals. To add a small amount of variety to the game, the `getRandomNumber` method is called here to set the value for the `max` to a random number from 7 to 12.

→**25** The call to the `getRandomNumber` method passes the values of `min` and `max` as parameters to set the range for the random numbers.

→**29** The message that announces to the user that the computer has chosen a random number uses the `min` and `max` parameters to indicate the range.

→**31** The call to the `getGuess` method now passes the range of acceptable guesses.

→**41** The declaration for the `getRandomNumber` method specifies the `min` and `max` parameters.

→**43** The calculation for the random number is complicated a bit by the fact that `min` might not be 1.

→**47** The declaration for the `getGuess` method accepts the `min` and `max` parameters.

→**52** The `if` statement in the `getGuess` method uses the `min` and `max` values to validate the user's input.

→**59** The `return` statement for the `getGuess` method. Note that this `return` statement is in the `else` part of an `if` statement that checks if the number is less than 1 or greater than 10. If the number is outside of the acceptable range, the `return` statement isn't executed. Instead, the program displays an error message, and the `while` loop repeats.

→**63** The `askForAnotherRound` method accepts a string variable to use as a prompt.

Chapter 8: Handling Exceptions

In This Chapter

✔ What to do when bad things happen to good programs

✔ All about exceptions

✔ Using `try`, `catch`, and `finally`

✔ Preventing exceptions from happening in the first place

This chapter is about what happens when Java encounters an error situation that it can't deal with. Over the years, computer programming languages have devised many different ways to deal with these types of errors. The earliest programming languages dealt with them rudely, by abruptly terminating the program and printing out the entire contents of the computer's memory in hexadecimal. This output was called a *dump*.

Later programming languages tried various ways to keep the program running when serious errors occurred. In some languages, the statements that could potentially cause an error had extra elements added to them that would provide feedback about errors. For example, a statement that read data from a disk file might return an error code if an I/O error occurred. Still other languages let you create a special error processing section of the program, to which control would be transferred if an error occurred.

Being an object-oriented programming language, Java handles errors by using special *exception objects* that are created when an error occurs. In addition, Java has a special statement called the `try` statement that you must use to deal with exception objects. In this chapter, you find all the gory details of working with exception objects and `try` statements.

Understanding Exceptions

An *exception* is an object that's created when an error occurs in a Java program and Java can't automatically fix the error. The exception object contains information about the type of error that occurred. However, the most important information — the cause of the error — is indicated by the name of the exception class used to create the exception. You don't usually have to do anything with an exception object other than figure out which one you have.

Each type of exception that can occur is represented by a different exception class. For example, here are some typical exceptions:

✦ **IllegalArgumentException:** You passed an incorrect argument to a method.

✦ **InputMismatchException:** The console input doesn't match the data type expected by a method of the `Scanner` class.

✦ **ArithmeticException:** You tried an illegal type of arithmetic operation, such as dividing an integer by zero.

✦ **IOException:** A method that performs I/O encountered an unrecoverable I/O error.

✦ **ClassNotFoundException:** A necessary class couldn't be found.

There are many other types of exceptions besides these. You find out about many of them in later chapters of this book.

You need to know a few other things about exceptions:

✦ When an error occurs and an exception object is created, Java is said to have *thrown an exception.* Java has a pretty good throwing arm, so the exception is always thrown right back to the statement that caused it to be created.

✦ The statement that caused the exception can *catch* the exception if it wants it. But it doesn't have to catch the exception if it doesn't want it. Instead, it can duck and let someone else catch the exception. That someone else is the statement that called the method that's currently executing.

✦ If everyone ducks and the exception is never caught by the program, the program ends abruptly and displays a nasty looking exception message on the console. More on that in the next section.

✦ Two basic types of exceptions in Java are checked exceptions and unchecked exceptions:

  • A *checked exception* is an exception that the compiler requires you to provide for it one way or another. If you don't, your program doesn't compile.

  • An *unchecked exception* is an exception that you can provide for, but you don't have to.

✦ So far in this book, I've avoided using any Java API methods that throw checked exceptions. However, I have used methods that can throw unchecked exceptions. For example, the `nextInt` method of the `Scanner` class throws an unchecked exception if the user enters something other than a valid integer value. For more information, read on.

Witnessing an exception

Submitted for your approval, a tale of a hastily written Java program, quickly put together to illustrate certain Java programming details while ignoring others. Out of sight, out of mind, as they say. Said program played a guessing game with the user, accepting numeric input via a class called Scanner. Yet this same program ignored the very real possibility that the user may enter strange and unexpected data, data that could hardly be considered numeric, at least not in the conventional sense. The time: Now. The place: Here. This program is about to cross over into . . . the Exception Zone.

The program I'm talking about here is, of course, the guessing game program that's appeared in several forms in recent chapters. (You can find the most recent version at the very end of Book II, Chapter 7.) This program includes a validation routine that prevents the user from making a guess that's not between 1 and 10. However, that validation routine assumes that the user has entered a valid integer number. If the user enters something other than an integer value, the `nextInt` method of the `Scanner` class fails badly.

Figure 8-1 shows an example of what the console looks like if the user enters text (such as `five`) instead of a number. The first line after the user enters the incorrect data says the program has encountered an exception named `InputMismatchException`. In short, this exception means that the data entered by the user couldn't be properly matched with the type of data that was expected by the `Scanner` class. That's because the `nextInt` method expected to find an integer, and instead it found the word `five`.

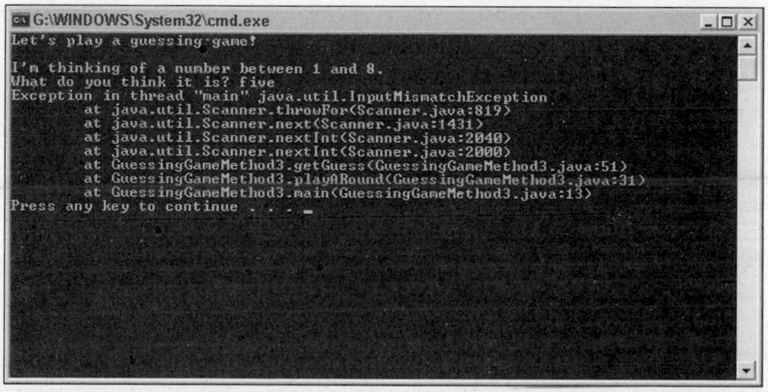

Figure 8-1:
This
program
has slipped
into The
Exception
Zone.

```
G:\WINDOWS\System32\cmd.exe                                    _ □ ×
Let's play a guessing game!

I'm thinking of a number between 1 and 8.
What do you think it is? five
Exception in thread "main" java.util.InputMismatchException
        at java.util.Scanner.throwFor(Scanner.java:819)
        at java.util.Scanner.next(Scanner.java:1431)
        at java.util.Scanner.nextInt(Scanner.java:2040)
        at java.util.Scanner.nextInt(Scanner.java:2000)
        at GuessingGameMethod3.getGuess(GuessingGameMethod3.java:51)
        at GuessingGameMethod3.playARound(GuessingGameMethod3.java:31)
        at GuessingGameMethod3.main(GuessingGameMethod3.java:13)
Press any key to continue . . . _
```

Finding the culprit

You can find the exact statement in your program that caused the exception to occur by examining the lines that are displayed right after the line that indicates which exception was encountered. These lines, called the *stack trace,* list the different methods that the exception passed through before your program was completely aborted. Usually, the first method listed is deep in the bowels of the Java API, and the last method listed is your application's `main` method. Somewhere in the middle, you find the switch from methods in the Java API to a method in your program. That's usually where you find the statement in your program that caused the error.

In Figure 8-1, the stack trace lines look like this:

```
at java.util.Scanner.throwFor(Scanner.java:819)
at java.util.Scanner.next(Scanner.java:1431)
at java.util.Scanner.nextInt(Scanner.java:2040)
at java.util.Scanner.nextInt(Scanner.java:2000)
at GuessingGameMethod3.getGuess(GuessingGameMethod3.java:51)
at GuessingGameMethod3.playARound(GuessingGameMethod3.java:31)
at GuessingGameMethod3.main(GuessingGameMethod3.java:13)
```

Each line lists not only a class and method name, but also the name of the source file that contains the class and the line number where the exception occurred. Thus, the first line in this stack trace indicates that the exception is handled in the `throwFor` method of the `Scanner` class at line 819 of the `Scanner.java` file. The next three lines also indicate methods in the `Scanner` class. The first line to mention the guessing game class (`GuessingGameMethod3`) is the fifth line. It shows that the exception happened at line 51 in the `GuessingGameMethod3.java` file. Sure enough, that's the line that calls the `nextInt` method of the `Scanner` class to get input from the user.

Catching Exceptions

Whenever you use a statement that might throw an exception, you should write special code to anticipate and catch the exception. That way, your program won't crash as shown in Figure 8-1 if the exception occurs.

You catch an exception by using a `try` statement, which has this general form:

```
try
{
    statements that can throw exceptions
}
catch (exception-type identifier)
{
    statements executed when exception is thrown
}
```

Here, you place the statements that might throw an exception within a *try block*. Then, you catch the exception with a *catch block*.

Here are a few things to note about `try` statements:

✦ You can code more than one `catch` block. That way, if the statements in the `try` block might throw more than one type of exception, you can catch each type of exception in a separate `catch` block.

✦ For scoping purposes, the `try` block is its own self-contained block, separate from the `catch` block. As a result, any variables you declare in the `try` block are not visible to the `catch` block. If you want them to be, declare them immediately before the `try` statement.

✦ You can also code a special block called a *finally block* after all the `catch` blocks. For more information about coding `finally` blocks, see the section "Using a finally Block" later in this chapter.

✦ The various exception classes in the Java API are defined in different packages. If you use an exception class that isn't defined in the standard `java.lang` package that's always available, you need to provide an `import` statement for the package that defines the exception class.

A simple example

To illustrate how to provide for an exception, here's a program that divides two numbers and uses a `try`/`catch` statement to catch an exception if the second number turns out to be zero:

```
public class DivideByZero
{
    public static void main(String[] args)
    {
        int a = 5;
        int b = 0;              // you know this won't work
        try
        {
            int c = a / b;     // but you try it anyway
        }
        catch (ArithmeticException c)
        {
            System.out.println("Oops, you can't divide by
                zero.");
        }
    }
}
```

Here, the division occurs within a `try` block, and a `catch` block handles `ArithmeticException`. `ArithmethicException` is defined by `java.lang`, so an `import` statement for it isn't necessary.

When you run this program, the following is displayed on the console:

```
Oops, you can't divide by zero.
```

There's nothing else to see here. The next section shows a more complicated example, though.

Another example

Listing 8-1 shows a simple example of a program that uses a method to get a valid integer from the user. If the user enters a value that isn't a valid integer, the catch block catches the error and forces the loop to repeat.

LISTING 8-1: GETTING A VALID INTEGER

```java
import java.util.*;

public class GetInteger
{
    static Scanner sc = new Scanner(System.in);

    public static void main(String[] args)
    {
        System.out.print("Enter an integer: ");
        int i = GetInteger();
        System.out.println("You entered " + i);
    }

    public static int GetInteger()
    {
        while (true)
        {
            try
            {
                return sc.nextInt();
            }
            catch (InputMismatchException e)
            {
                sc.next();
                System.out.print("That's not an integer. "
                    + "Try again: ");
            }
        }
    }
}
```

Here, the statement that gets the input from the user and returns it to the methods called is coded within the try block. If the user enters a valid integer, this statement is the only one in this method that gets executed.

However, if the user enters data that can't be converted to an integer, the `nextInt` method throws an `InputMismatchException`. Then, this exception is intercepted by the `catch` block, which disposes of the user's incorrect input by calling the `next` method as well as displays an error message. The `while` loop then repeats.

Here's what the console might look like for a typical execution of this program:

```
Enter an integer: three
That's not an integer. Try again: 3.001
That's not an integer. Try again: 3
You entered 3
```

Here are a few other things to note about this program:

✦ The `import` statement specifies `java.util.*` to import all the classes from the `java.util` package. That way, the `Input MismatchException` class is imported.

✦ The `next` method must be called in the `catch` block to dispose of the user's invalid input because the `nextInt` method leaves the input value in the `Scanner`'s input stream if an `InputMismatchException` is thrown. If you omit the statement that calls `next`, the `while` loop keeps reading it, throws an exception, and displays an error message in an infinite loop. If you don't believe me, look at Figure 8-2. I found this error out the hard way. (The only way to make it stop is to close the console window.)

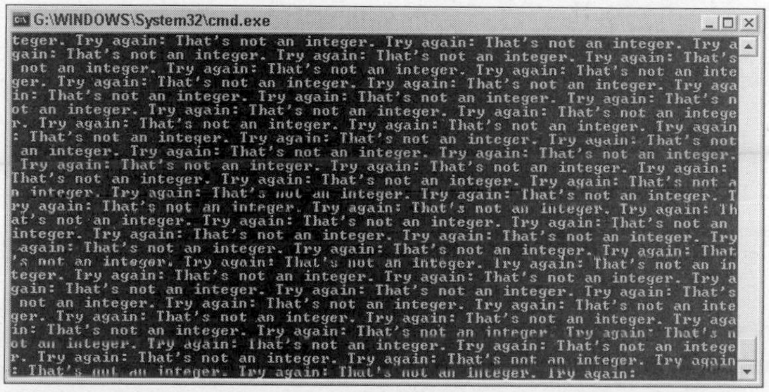

Figure 8-2:
Why you have to call next to discard the invalid input.

> G:\WINDOWS\System32\cmd.exe

Handling Exceptions with a Pre-emptive Strike

The `try` statement is a useful and necessary tool in any Java programmer's arsenal. However, the best way to handle exceptions is to prevent them from happening in the first place. That's not possible all the time, but in many cases it is. The key is to test your data before performing the operation that can lead to an exception and skipping or bypassing the operation of the data that is problematic. (One thing I really hate is problematic data.)

For example, you can usually avoid the ArithmethicException that results from dividing integer data by zero by checking the data before performing the division:

```
if (b != 0)
    c = a / b;
```

This eliminates the need for enclosing the division in a try block because you know the division by zero won't happen.

You can apply this same technique to input validation using the hasNextInt method of the Scanner class. This method checks the next input value to make sure it's a valid integer. (The Scanner class calls the next input value a *token,* but that won't be on the test.) You can do this technique in several ways, and I've been encouraging you to ponder the problem since Book II, Chapter 2. Now, the long awaited answer. Listing 8-2 shows a version of the GetInteger method that uses a while loop to avoid the exception.

LISTING 8-2: ANOTHER VERSION OF THE GETINTEGER METHOD

```java
import java.util.*;

public class GetInteger2
{
    static Scanner sc = new Scanner(System.in);

    public static void main(String[] args)
    {
        System.out.print("Enter an integer: ");
        int i = GetInteger();
        System.out.println("You entered " + i);
    }

    public static int GetInteger()
    {
        while (!sc.hasNextInt())
        {
            sc.nextLine();
            System.out.print("That's not an integer. "
                + "Try again: ");
        }
        return sc.nextInt();
    }
}
```

This is a clever little bit of programming, don't you think? The conditional expression in the `while` statement calls the `hasNextInt` method of the `Scanner` to see if the next value is an Integer. The `while` loop repeats as long as this call returns `false`, indicating that the next value is not a valid integer. The body of the loop calls `nextLine` to discard the bad data and displays an error message. The loop ends only when you know you have good data in the input stream, so the `return` statement calls `nextInt` to parse the data to an integer and return the resulting value.

Catching All Exceptions at Once

Java provides a catch-all exception class called `Exception` that all other types of exceptions are based on. (Don't worry about the details of what I mean by that. When you read Book III, Chapter 4, it will make more sense.)

If you don't want to be too specific in a `catch` block, you can specify `Exception` instead of a more specific exception class. For example:

```
try
{
    int c = a / b;
}
catch (Exception e)
{
    System.out.println("Oops, you can't divide by
        zero.");
}
```

In this example, the `catch` block specifies `Exception` rather than `ArithmeticException`.

If you have some code that might throw several different types of exceptions, and you want to provide specific processing for some but general processing for all the others, code the `try` statement:

```
try
{
    // statements that might throw several types of
    // exceptions
}
catch (InputMismatchException e)
{
    // statements that process InputMismatchException
}
catch (IOException e)
{
    // statements that process IOException
}
catch (Exception e)
```

```
{
        // statements that process all other exception types
}
```

In this example, imagine that the code in the `try` block might throw an `InputMismatchException`, an `IOException`, and perhaps some other type of unanticipated exception. Here, the three `catch` blocks provide for each of these possibilities.

When you code more than one `catch` block on a `try` statement, always list the more specific exceptions first. If you include a `catch` block to catch `Exception`, list it last.

Displaying the Exception Message

In most cases, the `catch block` of a `try` statement won't do anything at all with the exception object passed to it. However, you may occasionally want to display an error message; exception objects have a few interesting methods that can come in handy from time to time. These methods are listed in Table 8-1.

Table 8-1	Methods of the Exception Class
Method	*Description*
`String getMessage()`	A text message that describes the error.
`void printStackTrace()`	Prints the stack trace to the standard error stream.
`String toString()`	Returns a description of the exception. This description includes the name of the exception class followed by a colon and the `getMessage` message.

The following example shows how you might print the message for an exception in a `catch` block:

```
try
{
    int c = a / b;
}
catch (Exception e)
{
    System.out.println(e.getMessage());
}
```

This code displays the text `/ by zero` on the console if b has a value of zero. You can get even more interesting output with this line in the `catch` clause:

```
e.printStackTrace(System.out);
```

Using a finally Block

A `finally` block is a block that appears after all of the `catch` blocks for a statement. It's executed whether or not any exceptions are thrown by the `try` block or caught by any `catch` blocks. Its purpose is to let you clean up any mess that might be left behind by the exception, such as open files or database connections.

The basic framework for a `try` statement with a `finally` block is this:

```
try
{
    statements that can throw exceptions
}
catch (exception-type identifier)
{
    statements executed when exception is thrown
}
finally
{
    statements that are executed whether or not
    exceptions occur
}
```

Book II
Chapter 8

Handling
Exceptions

Listing 8-3 shows a contrived but helpful example that demonstrates how to use the `finally` clause. In this example, a method called `divideTheseNumbers` tries to divide the numbers twice. If the division fails the first time (due to a divide-by-zero exception), it tries the division again. Completely irrational, I know. But persistent, like a teenager.

LISTING 8-3: A PROGRAM THAT USES A finally CLAUSE

```
public class CrazyWithZeros
{
    public static void main(String[] args)
    {
        try
        {
            int answer = divideTheseNumbers(5, 0);          → 7
        }
        catch (Exception e)                                 → 9
        {
            System.out.println("Tried twice, "
                + "still didn't work!");
        }
    }

    public static int divideTheseNumbers(int a, int b)      → 16
        throws Exception
```

continued

LISTING 8-3 (CONTINUED)

```
{
    int c;
    try
    {
        c = a / b;                                              → 22
        System.out.println("It worked!");                       → 23
    }
    catch (Exception e)
    {
        System.out.println("Didn't work the first time.");      → 27
        c = a / b;                                              → 28
        System.out.println("It worked the second time!");       → 29
    }
    finally
    {
        System.out.println("Better clean up my mess.");         → 33
    }
    System.out.println("It worked after all.");                 → 35
    return c;                                                   → 36
}
}
```

Here's the console output for the program:

```
Didn't work the first time.
Better clean up my mess.
Tried twice, still didn't work!
```

The following paragraphs explain what's going on, step by step:

→ **7** The `main` method calls the `divideTheseNumbers` method, passing 5 and 0 as the parameters. You know already this method isn't going to work.

→ **9** The `catch` clause catches any exceptions thrown by line 7.

→**16** The `divideTheseNumbers` method declares that it throws `Exception`.

→**22** The first attempt to divide the numbers.

→**23** If the first attempt succeeds, this line is executed, and the message `"It worked!"` is printed. Alas, the division throws an exception, so this line never gets executed.

→**27** Instead, the `catch` clause catches the exception, and the message `"Didn't work the first time."` is displayed. That's the first line in the console output.

→**28** The `divideTheseNumbers` method stubbornly tries to divide the same two numbers again. This time, there's no `try` statement to catch the error.

→**29** However, because another exception is thrown for the second division, this line is never executed. Thus, you don't see the message `"It worked the second time!"` on the console. (If you do, you're in an episode of *The Twilight Zone*.)

→**33** This statement in the `finally` clause is always executed, no matter what happens. That's where the second line in the console output came from.

After the `finally` clause executes, the `ArithmeticException` is thrown back up to the calling method, where it is caught by line 9. That's where the last line of the console output came from.

→**35** If the division did work, this line would be executed after the `try` block ends, and you'd see the message `"It worked after all."` on the console.

→**36** Then, the `return` statement would return the result of the division.

Handling Checked Exceptions

Checked exceptions are exceptions that the designers of Java feel your programs absolutely must provide for, one way or another. Whenever you code a statement that might throw a checked exception, your program must do one of two things:

✦ Catch the exception by placing the statement within a `try` statement that has a `catch` block for the exception.

✦ Specify a `throws` clause on the method that contains the statement to indicate that your method doesn't want to handle the exception, so it's passing the exception up the line.

This is known as the *catch-or-throw* rule. In short, any method that includes a statement that might throw a checked exception must acknowledge that it knows the exception might be thrown. The method does this by either handling it directly, or passing the exception up to its caller.

To illustrate the use of checked exceptions, I have to use some classes with methods that throw them. Up to now, I've avoided introducing classes that throw checked exceptions. So the following illustrations use some classes you aren't yet familiar with. Don't worry about what those classes do or how they work. The point is to learn how to handle the checked exceptions they throw.

The catch-or-throw compiler error

Here's a program that uses a class called `FileInputStream`. To create an object from this class, you must pass the constructor a string that contains the path and name of a file that exists on your computer. If the file can't be found, the `FileInputStream` throws a `FileNotFoundException` that you must either catch or throw. This class is found in the `java.io` package, so any program that uses it must include an `import java.io` statement.

Consider the following program:

```
import java.io.*;

public class FileException1
{
    public static void main(String[] args)
    {
        openFile("C:\test.txt");
    }

    public static void openFile(String name)
    {
        FileInputStream f = new FileInputStream(name);
    }
}
```

This program won't compile. The compiler issues the following error message:

```
unreported exception java.io.FileNotFoundException;
    must be caught or declared to be thrown
```

This message simply means that you have to deal with the `FileNotFound Exception`.

Catching FileNotFoundException

One way to deal with the `FileNotFoundException` is to catch it using an ordinary `try` statement:

```
import java.io.*;

public class FileException2
{
    public static void main(String[] args)
    {
        openFile("C:\test.txt");
    }

    public static void openFile(String name)
    {
        try
        {
            FileInputStream f = new
FileInputStream(name);
        }
        catch (FileNotFoundException e)
        {
            System.out.println("File not found.");
```

```
        }
    }
}
```

In this example, the message "File not found." is displayed if the C:\test.txt file doesn't exist.

Throwing the FileNotFoundException

Suppose you don't want to deal with this error condition in the openFile method, but would rather just pass the exception up to the method that calls the openFile method?

To do that, you omit the try statement. Instead, you add a throws clause to the openFile method's declaration. That indicates that the openFile method knows that it contains a statement that might throw a FileNotFoundException, but that it doesn't want to deal with that exception here. Instead, the exception is passed up to the caller.

Book II
Chapter 8

Handling
Exceptions

Here's the openFile method with the throws clause added:

```
public static void openFile(String name)
    throws FileNotFoundException
{
    FileInputStream f = new FileInputStream(name);
}
```

As you can see, the throws clause simply lists the exception or exceptions that the method might throw. If more than one exception is on the list, separate them with commas:

```
public static void readFile(String name)
    throws FileNotFoundException, IOException
```

Adding a throws clause to the openFile method means that when the FileNotFoundException occurs, it is simply passed up to the method that called the openFile method. That means the calling method (in this illustration, main) must either catch or throw the exception. To catch the exception, the main method would have to be coded like this:

```
public static void main(String[] args)
{
    try
    {
        openFile("C:\test.txt");
    }
    catch (FileNotFoundException e)
    {
        System.out.println("File not found.");
    }
}
```

Then, if the file doesn't exist, the `catch` block catches the exception, and the error message is displayed.

Throwing an exception from main

If you don't want the program to handle the `FileNotFound` exception at all, you can add a `throws` clause to the `main` method, like this:

```
public static void main(String[] args)
    throws FileNotFoundException
{
    openFile("C:\test.txt");
}
```

Then, the program abruptly terminates with an exception message and stack trace if the exception occurs.

Swallowing exceptions

What if you don't want to do anything if a checked exception occurs? In other words, you want to simply ignore the exception? You can do that by catching the exception in the `catch` block of a `try` statement, but leaving the body of the `catch` block empty. For example:

```
public static void openFile(String name)
{
    try
    {
        FileInputStream f = new FileInputStream(name);
    }
    catch (FileNotFoundException e)
    {
    }
}
```

Here, the `FileNotFoundException` is caught and ignored. This is called *swallowing the exception*.

Swallowing an exception is considered to be a bad programming practice. Simply swallowing exceptions that you know you should handle when working on a complicated program is tempting. Because you plan on getting back to that exception handler after you iron out the basic functions of the program, a little exception swallowing doesn't seem like that bad of an idea. The problem is, inevitably, you'll never get back to the exception handler. So your program gets rushed into production with swallowed exceptions.

If you must swallow exceptions, at least write a message to the console indicating that the exception occurred. That way, you have a constant reminder that the program has some unfinished details yet to attend to.

Note that not all exception swallowing is bad. For example, suppose you want the openFile method to return a boolean value to indicate whether the file exists, rather than throw an exception. Then, you could code the method something like this:

```
public static boolean openFile(String name)
{
    boolean fileOpened = false;
    try
    {
        FileInputStream f = new FileInputStream(name);
        fileOpened = true;
    }
    catch (FileNotFoundException e)
    {
    }
    return fileOpened;
}
```

Here, the exception isn't really swallowed. Instead, its meaning is converted to a boolean result that's returned from the method. As a result, the error condition indicated by the FileNotFoundException isn't lost.

Throwing Your Own Exceptions

Although uncommon, you may want to write methods that throw exceptions all on their own. To do that, you use a throw statement. The throw statement has the following basic format:

```
throw new exception-class();
```

The exception-class can be Exception or a class that's derived from Exception. You find out how to create your own classes — including exception classes — in Book III. For now, I just focus on writing a method that throws a general Exception.

Here's a program that demonstrates the basic structure for a method that throws an exception:

```
public class MyException
{
    public static void main(String[] args)
    {
        try
        {
            doSomething(true);
        }
        catch (Exception e)
        {
```

```
            System.out.println("Exception!");
        }
    }

    public static void doSomething(boolean t) throws
        Exception
    {
        if (t)
            throw new Exception();
    }
}
```

Here, the `doSomething` method accepts a boolean value as a parameter. If this value is `true`, it throws an exception. Otherwise, it doesn't do anything.

Here are the essential points to glean from this admittedly trivial example:

✦ You throw an exception by executing a `throw` statement. The `throw` statement specifies the exception object to be thrown.

✦ If a method contains a `throw` statement, it must include a `throws` clause in its declaration.

✦ A method that calls a method that throws an exception must either catch or throw the exception.

✦ Yup, this example is pretty trivial. But it illustrates the essential points.

Book III

Object-Oriented Programming

The 5th Wave   By Rich Tennant

PROGENITORS TO THE JAVA PROGRAMMING LANGUAGE

Lava Developed in Hawaii, objects would suddenly erupt into a hot flowing stream of information.

Guava Objects "grew" on computers tree structure which users could convert to a data jam to be spread across the Web.

Jabba "The Hut" Named after the developer, objects tended to get lost in cyberspace.

Fava Objects were referred to as "beans", but would repeat themselves when overused.

Contents at a Glance

Chapter 1: Understanding Object-Oriented Programming

In This Chapter

✔ Looking at what object-oriented programming is

✔ Understanding objects and classes

✔ Investigating inheritance and interfaces

✔ Designing programs with objects

✔ Diagramming with UML

This chapter is a basic introduction to object-oriented programming. It introduces you to some of the basic concepts and terms you need to know as you learn about the specific details of how object-oriented programming works in Java.

If you're more of a hands-on type, you may want to just skip this chapter and go straight to Book III, Chapter 2, where you find out how to create your own classes in Java. Then, you can always return to this chapter later to learn about the basic concepts that drive object-oriented programming. Either way is okay by me. I get paid the same whether you read this chapter now or skip it and come back to it later.

What Is Object-Oriented Programming?

The term *object-oriented programming* means many different things. But at its heart, object-oriented programming is a type of computer programming based on the premise that all programs are essentially computer-based simulations of real-world objects or abstract concepts. For example:

✦ Flight simulator programs attempt to mimic the behavior of real airplanes. Some do an amazingly good job: military and commercial pilots train on them. In the 1960s, the Apollo astronauts used a computer-controlled simulator to practice for their moon landings.

✦ Many computer games are simulations of actual games humans play, such as baseball, Nascar racing, and chess. But even abstract games such as Pac Man or Final Fantasy 4 attempt to model the behavior of creatures and objects that *could* exist somewhere. Thus, those programs simulate a conceptual game — one that can't actually be played anywhere in the real world, but that can by simulated by a computer.

✦ Business programs can be thought of as simulations of business processes, such as order taking, customer service, shipping, and billing. For example, an invoice isn't just a piece of paper; it's a paper that represents a transaction that has occurred between a company and one of its customers. Thus, a computer-based invoice is really just a simulation of that transaction.

The notion of a programming language having a premise of this sort isn't new. Traditional programming languages such as C and its predecessors, including even COBOL, are based on the premise that computer programs are computerized implementations of procedures — the electronic equivalent of "Step 1: Insert Tab A into Slot B." The LISP programming language is based on the idea that all programming problems can be looked at as different ways of manipulating lists. And the ever popular database manipulation language SQL views programming problems as ways to manipulate mathematical sets.

Here are some additional thoughts about the notion of computer programs being simulations of real-world objects or abstract concepts:

✦ Sometimes the simulation is better than the real thing. Word processing programs started out as simulations of typewriters, but a modern word processing program is far superior to any typewriter.

✦ The idea that all computer programs are simulations of one type or another isn't a new one. In fact, the first object-oriented programming language (Simula) was developed in the 1960s. By 1967, this language had many of the features we now consider fundamental to object-oriented programming, including classes, objects, inheritance, and virtual methods.

✦ Come to think of it, manual business record keeping systems are simulations too. A file cabinet full of printed invoices doesn't hold actual orders. It holds written representations of those orders. A computer is a better simulation device than a file cabinet, but both are simulations.

Understanding Objects

All this talk of simulations is getting a little existential for me, so now I'm turning to the nature of the objects that make up object-oriented programming. Objects — both in the real world and in the world of programming — are entities that have certain basic characteristics. The following sections describe some of the more important of these characteristics: identity, type, state, and behavior.

Objects have identity

Every object in an object-oriented program has an *identity*. In other words, every occurrence of a particular type of object — called an *instance* — can be distinguished from every other occurrence of the same type of object, as well as from objects of other types.

In the real world, object identity is a pretty intuitive and obvious concept. Pick up two apples, and you know that although both of them are apples (that's the object type, described in the next section), you know they aren't the same apple. Each has a distinct identity. They're both roughly the same color, but not exactly. They're both roundish, but have minor variations in shape. Either one (or both) could have a worm inside.

Open a file cabinet that's full of invoices and you find page after page of papers that look almost identical to one another. However, each one has an invoice number printed somewhere near the top of the page. This number isn't what actually gives each of these invoices a unique identity, but it gives you an easy way to identify each individual invoice, just as your name gives others an easy way to identify you.

In object-oriented programming, each object has its own location in the computer's memory. Thus, two objects, even though they may be of the same type, have their own memory location. The address of the starting location for an object provides us with a way of distinguishing one object from another, because no two objects can occupy the same location in memory.

Here are a few other important thoughts about object identity in Java:

✦ Java pretty much keeps each object's identity to itself. In other words, there's no easy way to get the memory address of an object. Java figures that's none of your business, and rightfully so. If Java made that information readily available to you, you'd be tempted to tinker with it, which can cause all sorts of problems as any C or C++ programmer can tell you.

✦ Java objects have something called a *hash code,* which is an `int` value that's automatically generated for every object and *almost* represents the object's identity. In most cases, the hash code for an object is based on the object's memory address. But not always. Java doesn't guarantee that two distinct objects won't have the same hash code.

✦ When used with objects, the equality operator (`==`) actually tests the object identity of two variables or expressions. If they refer to the same object instance, the two variables or expressions are considered equal.

Objects have type

I remember studying *Naming of Parts*, a fine poem written by Henry Reed in 1942, back when I was an English major in college:

> *Today we have naming of parts. Yesterday,*
> *We had daily cleaning. And tomorrow morning,*
> *We shall have what to do after firing. But today,*
> *Today we have naming of parts. Japonica*
> *Glistens like coral in all of the neighboring gardens,*
>   *And today we have naming of parts.*

Sure, it's a fine anti-war poem and all that, but it's also a little instructive about object-oriented programming. After the first stanza, the poem goes on to name the parts of a rifle:

> *This is the lower sling swivel. And this*
> *Is the upper sling swivel, whose use you will see,*
> *When you are given your slings. And this is the piling swivel,*
> *Which in your case you have not got.*

Imagine a whole room of new soldiers taking apart their rifles, while the drill sergeant tells them "This is the lower sling swivel. And this is the upper sling swivel. . ." Each soldier's rifle has one of these parts — in object-oriented terms, an object of a particular type. The lower-sling swivels in each soldier's rifle are different objects, but all are of the type `LowerSlingSwivel`.

Like the drill sergeant in this poem, object-oriented programming lets you assign names to the different kind of objects in a program. In Java, types are defined by classes. So when you create an object from a type, you're saying that the object is of the type specified by the class. For example, the following statement creates an object of type `Invoice`:

```
Invoice i = new Invoice();
```

Then, the identity of this object (that is, its address in memory) is assigned to the variable `i`, which the compiler knows can hold references to objects of type `Invoice`.

Objects have state

Now switch gears to another literary genius:

> *One fish, two fish,*
> *Red fish, blue fish*

In object-oriented terms, Dr. Seuss here is enumerating a pair of objects of type `Fish`. The `Fish` type apparently has two attributes — call them `number` and `color`. These two objects have differing values for these attributes:

Attribute	Object 1	Object 2
Number	One	Two
Color	Red	Blue

The type of an object determines what attributes the object has. Thus, all objects of a particular type have the same attributes. However, they don't necessarily have the same values for those attributes. In this example, all `Fish` have attributes named `Number` and `Color`, but the two `Fish` objects have different values for these attributes.

The combination of the values for all the attributes of an object is called the object's *state*. Unlike its identity, an object's state can and usually does change over its lifetime. For example, some fish can change colors. The total sales for a customer changes each time the customer buys another product. The grade point average for a student changes each time a new class grade is recorded. And the address and phone number of an employee changes if the employee moves.

Here are a few more interesting details about object state:

✦ Some of the attributes of an object are publicly known, but others can be private. The private attributes may be vital to the internal operation of the object, but no one outside of the object knows they exist. They're like your private thoughts: They affect what you say and do, but nobody knows them but you.

✦ In Java, the state of an object is represented by class variables, which are called *fields*. A *public field* is a field that's declared with the `public` keyword so the variable can be visible to the outside world.

Objects have behavior

Another characteristic of objects is that they have *behavior,* which means they can do things. Like state, the specific behavior of an object depends on its type. But unlike state, the behavior isn't different for each instance of a type. For example, suppose all the students in a classroom have calculators of the same type. Ask them all to pull out the calculators and add two numbers — any two numbers of their choosing. All the calculators display a different number, but they all add the same. In other words, they all have a different state, but the same behavior.

Another way to say that objects have behavior is to say they provide services that can be used by other objects. You've already seen plenty examples of objects that provide services to other objects. For example, objects created from the `NumberFormat` class provide formatting services that turn numeric values into nicely formatted strings like $32.95.

In Java, the behavior of an object is provided by its methods. Thus, the `format` method of the `NumberFormat` class is what provides the formatting behavior for `NumberFormat` objects.

Here are a few other notable points about object behavior:

✦ The *interface* of a class is the set of methods and fields that the class makes public so other objects can access them.

✦ Exactly how an object does what it does can and should be hidden within the object. Someone who uses the object needs to know what the object does, but doesn't need to know how it works. If you later find a better way for the object to do its job, you can swap in the new improved version without anyone knowing the difference.

The Life Cycle of an Object

As you work with objects in Java, understanding how objects are born, live their lives, and die is important. This topic is called the *life cycle* of an object, and it goes something like this:

✦ Before an object can be created from a class, the class must be *loaded*. To do that, the Java runtime locates the class on disk (in a `.class` file) and reads it into memory. Then, Java looks for any *static initializers* that initialize static fields — fields that don't belong to any particular instance of the class, but rather belong to the class itself and are shared by all objects created from the class.

A class is loaded the first time you create an object from the class or the first time you access a static field or method of the class. For example, when you run the `main` method of a class, the class is initialized because the `main` method is static.

✦ An object is created from a class when you use the `new` keyword. To initialize the class, Java allocates memory for the object and sets up a reference to the object so the Java runtime can keep track of it. Then, Java calls the class *constructor,* which is like a method but is called only once, when the object is created. The constructor is responsible for doing any processing required to initialize the object, such as initializing variables, opening files or databases, and so on.

✦ The object lives its life, providing access to its public methods and fields to whoever wants and needs them.

✦ When it's time for the object to die, the object is removed from memory and Java drops its internal reference to it. You don't have to destroy objects yourself. A special part of the Java runtime called the *garbage collector* takes care of destroying all objects when they are no longer in use.

Working with Related Classes

So far, most of the classes you've seen in this book have created objects that stand on their own, each being a little island unto itself. However, the real power of object-oriented programming lies in its ability to create classes that describe objects that are closely related to each other.

For example, baseballs are similar to softballs. Both are specific types of balls. They both have a diameter and a weight. And both can be thrown, caught, or hit. However, they have different characteristics that cause them to behave differently when thrown, caught, or hit.

If you're creating a program that simulated the way baseballs and softballs work, you need a way to represent these two types of balls. One option is to create separate classes to represent each type of ball. These classes are similar, so you can just copy most of the code from one class to the other.

Another option is to use a single class to represent both types of balls. Then, you pass a parameter to the constructor to indicate whether an instance of the class behaves like a baseball or like a softball.

However, Java has two object-oriented programming features that are designed specifically to handle classes that are related like this: inheritance and interfaces. I briefly describe these features in the following sections.

Inheritance

Inheritance is an object-oriented programming technique that lets you use one class as the basis for another. The existing class is called the *base class, superclass,* or *parent class,* and the new class that's derived from it is called the *derived class, subclass,* or *child class.*

When you create a subclass, the subclass is automatically given all the methods and fields defined by its superclass. You can use these methods and fields as is, or you can override them to alter their behavior. In addition, you can add additional methods and fields that define data and behavior that's unique to the subclass.

You could use inheritance to solve the baseball/softball problem from the previous section by creating a class named `Ball` that provides the basic features of all types of balls, and then using it as the base class for separate classes named `BaseBall` and `SoftBall`. Then, these classes could override the methods that need to behave differently for each type of ball.

One way to think of inheritance is as a way to implement *is-a-type-of* relationships. For example, a softball is a type of ball, as is a baseball. Thus, inheritance is an appropriate way to implement these related classes. For more information about inheritance, see Book III, Chapter 4.

Interfaces

An *interface* is a set of methods and fields that a class must provide to *implement* the interface. The interface itself is simply a set of public method and field declarations that are given a name. Note that the interface itself doesn't provide any code that implements those methods. Instead, it just provides the declarations. Then, a class that *implements* the interface provides an implementation for each of the methods the interface defines.

You could use an interface to solve the baseball/softball problem by creating an interface named `Ball` that specifies all the methods and fields that a ball should have. Then, you could create the `SoftBall` and `BaseBall` classes so that they both implement the `Ball` interface.

Interfaces are closely related to inheritance, but have two key differences:

✦ The interface itself doesn't provide code that implements any of its methods. An interface is just a set of method and field signatures. In contrast, a base class can provide the implementation for some or all of its methods.

✦ A class can have only one base class. However, a class can implement as many interfaces as necessary.

You find out about interfaces in Book III, Chapter 5.

Designing a Program with Objects

An object-oriented program usually isn't just a single object. Instead, it's a group of objects that work together to get a job done. The most important part of developing an object-oriented program is designing the classes that are used to create the program's objects. The basic idea is to break a large problem down into a set of classes that are each manageable in size and complexity. Then, you write the Java code that implements those classes.

So, the task of designing an object-oriented application boils down to deciding what classes the application requires and what the public interface to each of those classes are. If you plan your classes well, implementing the application is easy. But if you poorly plan your classes, you'll have a hard time getting your application to work.

One common way to design object-oriented applications is to divide the application into several distinct *layers* or *tiers* that provide distinct types of functions. The most common is a three-layered approach, as shown in Figure 1-1. Here, the objects of an application are split up into three basic layers:

✦ **Presentation:** The objects in this layer handle all the direct interaction with users. For example, the HTML pages in a Web application go in this layer, as do the Swing page and frame classes in a GUI-based application (I cover Swing in Book VI).

✦ **Logic:** The objects in this layer represent the core objects of the application. For a typical business-type application, this layer includes objects that represent business entities such as customer, products, orders, suppliers, and the like. This layer is sometimes called the *business rules layer* because the objects in this layer are responsible for carrying out the rules that govern the application.

✦ **Database:** The objects in this layer handle all the details of interacting with whatever form of data storage is used by the application. For example, if the data is stored in a SQL database, the objects in this layer handle all of the SQL.

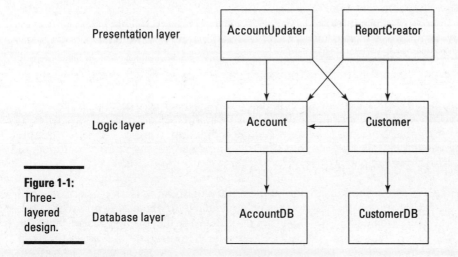

Presentation layer

Logic layer

Figure 1-1:
Three-
layered
design.

Database layer

Diagramming Classes with UML

Since the very beginning of computer programming, programmers have loved to create diagrams of their programs. Originally, they drew flowcharts that graphically represented a program's procedural logic.

Flowcharts were good at diagramming procedures, but they were way too detailed. When the Structured Programming craze hit in the 1970s and programmers started thinking about the overall structure of their programs, they switched from flowcharts to *structure charts,* which illustrated the organizational relationships among the modules of a program or system.

Now that object-oriented programming is the thing, programmers draw *class diagrams* to illustrate the relationships among the classes that make up an application. For example, the simple class diagram shown in Figure 1-2 shows a class diagram for a simple system that has four classes. The rectangles represent the classes themselves, and the arrows represent the relationships among the classes.

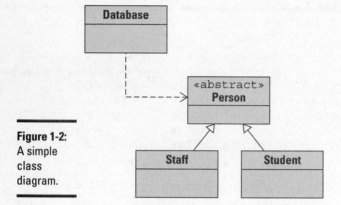

Figure 1-2:
A simple class diagram.

You can draw class diagrams in many ways. To add some consistency to their diagrams, most programmers use a standard called *UML,* which stands for *Unified Modeling Language.* The class diagram in Figure 1-2 is an example of a simple UML diagram, but UML diagrams can get much more complicated than this example.

The following sections describe the details of creating UML class diagrams. Note that these sections don't even come close to explaining all the features of UML. I include just the basics of creating UML class diagrams so that you can make some sense of UML diagrams when you see them, and so that you know how to draw simple class diagrams to help you design the class structure for your applications. If you're interested in digging deeper into UML, check out *UML 2 For Dummies* by Michael Jesse Chonoles and James A. Schardt (Wiley).

Drawing classes

The basic element in a class diagram is a class. In UML, each class is drawn as a rectangle. At the minimum, the rectangle must include the class name. However, you can subdivide the rectangle into two or three compartments that can contain additional information about the class, as shown in Figure 1-3.

```
         CustomerDB
    +connectionString
    +connectionStatus

    +getCustomer
    +updateCustomer
    +deleteCustomer
    +addCustomer
    +getCustomerList
```

Figure 1-3:
A class.

The middle compartment of a class lists the class variables, while the bottom compartment lists the class methods. The name of each variable or method can be preceded by a *visibility indicator,* which can be one of the symbols listed in Table 1-1. In actual practice, omiting the visibility indicator and listing only those fields or methods that have public visibility is common.

Table 1-1	Visibility Indicators for Class Variables and Methods
Indicator	*Description*
+	Public
–	Private
#	Protected

If you want, you can include type information for variables as well as for methods and parameters. The type of a variable is indicated by following the variable name with a colon and the type:

```
connectionString: String
```

A method's return type is indicated in the same way:

```
getCustomer(): Customer
```

Parameters are listed within the parentheses, and both the name and type are listed. For example:

```
getCustomer(custno: int): Customer
```

Note: Omitting the type and parameter information from UML diagrams is common.

TIP

Interfaces are drawn pretty much the same as classes, but the class name is preceded by the word *interface*:

```
«interface»
 ProductDB
```

Note: The word *interface* is enclosed within a set of double-left and double-right arrows. These arrows aren't just two less-than or greater-than symbols typed in a row; they're a special symbol. Fortunately, this symbol is a standard part of the ASCII character set. You can access them in Microsoft Word via the Insert Symbol command.

Drawing arrows

Besides rectangles to represent classes, class diagrams also include arrows to represent relationships among classes. UML uses a variety of different types of arrows, as I describe in the following paragraphs.

A solid line with a hollow closed arrow at one end represents inheritance:

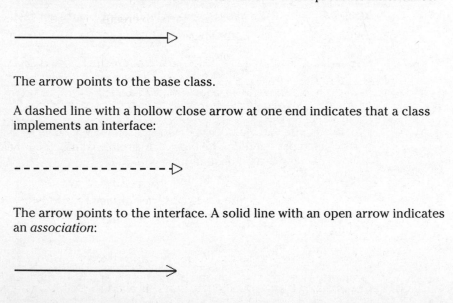

The arrow points to the base class.

A dashed line with a hollow close arrow at one end indicates that a class implements an interface:

The arrow points to the interface. A solid line with an open arrow indicates an *association*:

An association simply indicates that two classes work together. It may be that one of the classes creates objects of the other class, or that one class requires an object of the other class to perform its work. Or, perhaps instances of one class contain instances of the other class.

You can add a name to an association arrow to indicate its purpose. For example, if an association arrow indicates that instances of one class create objects of another class, you can place the word Creates next to the arrow.

Chapter 2: Making Your Own Classes

In This Chapter

✔ Creating your own class

✔ Looking at the pieces of a class declaration

✔ Finding out about class fields

✔ Constructing constructors

✔ Adding methods to your classes

✔ Using the `this` keyword

*O*kay, class, it's time to learn how to create your own classes.

In this chapter, you discover the basics of creating classes in Java. All Java programs are classes, so you've already seen many examples of classes. For example, you've seen class headers such as `public class GuessingGame` and static methods such as `public static void main`. Now, in this chapter, I show you how to create programs that have more than one class.

Declaring a Class

All classes must be defined by a *class declaration* that provides the name for the class and the body of the class. Here's the most basic form of a class declaration:

```
[public] class ClassName {class-body}
```

The `public` keyword indicates that this class is available for use by other classes. Although it is optional, you usually include it on your class declarations. After all, the main reason you write class declarations is so that other classes can create objects from the class. Find out more about using the `public` keyword in the section "Where classes go" later in this chapter.

In later chapters of this book, you find out about some additional elements that can go in a class declaration. The format I'm describing here is just the basic format, which you use to create basic classes.

Picking class names

The *ClassName* is an identifier that provides a name for your class. You can use any identifier you want to name a class, but the following three guidelines can simplify your life:

✦ **Begin the class name with a capital letter.** If the class name consists of more than one word, capitalize each word. For example, `Ball`, `RetailCustomer`, and `GuessingGame`.

✦ **Whenever possible, use nouns for your class names.** Classes create objects, and nouns are the words you use to identify objects. Thus, most class names should be nouns.

✦ **Avoid using the name of a Java API class.** No rule says you have to, but if you create a class that has the same name as a Java API class, you have to use fully qualified names (like `java.util.Scanner`) to tell your class and the API class with the same name apart.

There are literally thousands of Java API classes, so avoiding them all is pretty hard. But at the least, you should avoid commonly used Java class names as well as any API classes your application is likely to use. For example, creating a class named `String` or `Math` is just asking for trouble.

What goes in the class body

The *class body* of a class is everything that goes within the braces at the end of the class declaration. The `public class ClassName` part of a class declaration takes just one line, but the body of the class declaration may take hundreds of lines. Or thousands if you get carried away.

The class body can contain the following elements:

✦ **Fields:** Variable declarations define the public or private fields of a class.

✦ **Methods:** Method declarations define the methods of a class.

✦ **Constructors:** A *constructor* is a block of code that's similar to a method but is run to initialize an object when an instance is created. A constructor must have the same name as the class itself and, although it resembles a method, it doesn't have a return type.

✦ **Initializers:** These are stand-alone blocks of code that are run only once, when the class is initialized. There are actually two types, called *static initializers* and *instance initializers*. Although you won't use them often, I talk about instance initializers later in this chapter, in the section "Using Initializers." For information about static initializers, refer to Book III, Chapter 3.

✦ **Other classes and interfaces:** A class can include another class, which is then called an *inner class* or a *nested class*. Classes can also contain interfaces. For more information about inner classes, see Book III, Chapter 7. And for information about interfaces, refer to Book III, Chapter 5.

Unlike some programming languages, the order in which items appear in the class body doesn't matter. Still, being consistent about the order in which you place things in your classes is a good idea. That way you know where to find them. I usually code all the fields together at the start of the class, followed by constructors and then methods. If the class includes initializers, I place them near the fields they initialize. And if the class includes inner classes, I usually place them after the methods that use them.

Some programmers like to place the fields at the end of the class rather than at the beginning. Whatever brings you happiness is fine with me.

The fields, methods, classes, and interfaces contained within a class are called the *members* of the class. Constructors and initializers aren't considered to be members, for reasons that are too technical to explain just yet. (You can find the explanation in Book III, Chapter 3.)

Where classes go

A public class must be written in a source file that has the same name as the class, with the extension `java`. For example, a public class named `Greeter` must be placed in a file named `Greeter.java`.

As a result, you can't place two public classes in the same file. For example, the following source file (named `DiceGame.java`) won't compile:

```
public class DiceGame
{
    public static void main(String[] args)
    {
        Dice d = new Dice();
        d.roll();
    }
}

public class Dice
{
    public void roll()
    {
        // code that rolls the dice goes here
    }
}
```

The compiler coughs up a message indicating that Dice is a public class and must be declared in a file named Dice.java.

This problem has two solutions. The first is to remove the public keyword from the Dice class:

```
public class DiceGame
{
    public static void main(String[] args)
    {
        Dice d = new Dice();
        d.roll();
    }
}

class Dice
{
    public void roll()
    {
        // code that rolls the dice goes here
    }
}
```

The compiler gladly accepts this program.

This is not the same thing as an inner class. An inner class is a class that's defined within the body of another class, and is available only from within that class. For more information about inner classes, see Book III, Chapter 7.

When you code more than one class in a single source file, Java still creates a separate class file for each class. Thus, when you compile the DiceGame.java file, the Java compiler creates two class files, named DiceGame.class and Dice.class.

Removing the public keyword from a class is acceptable for relatively small programs. But its limitation is that the Dice class is available only to the classes defined within the DiceGame.java file. If you want the Dice class to be more widely available, opt for the second solution: Place it — with the public keyword — in a separate file named Dice.java.

If you're going to create an application that has several public classes, create a separate folder for the application. Then, save all the class files for the application to this folder. If your class files are together in the same folder, the Java compiler can find them. If you place them in separate folders, you may need to adjust your ClassPath environment variable to help the compiler find the classes.

Working with Members

The *members* of a class are the fields and methods defined in the class body. (Technically, classes and interfaces defined within a class are members too. But I don't discussed them in this chapter, so you can ignore them for now.)

The following sections describe the basics of working with fields and methods in your classes.

Fields

A *field* is a variable that's defined in the body of a class, outside of any of the class' methods. Fields, which are also called *class variables,* are available to all the methods of a class. In addition, if the field specifies the `public` keyword, the field is visible outside of the class. If you don't want the field to be visible outside of the class, use the `private` keyword instead.

Fields are defined the same as any other Java variable, but can have a modifier that specifies whether the field is public or private. Here are some examples of public field declarations:

```
public int trajectory = 0;
public String name;
public Player player;
```

To create a private field, specify `private` instead of public:

```
private int x-position = 0;
private int y-position = 0;
private String error-message = "";
```

Fields can also be declared as `final`:

```
public final int MAX_SCORE = 1000;
```

The value of a `final` field can't be changed once it has been initialized. *Note:* Spelling `final` field names with all capital letters is customary (but not required).

Methods

You define methods for a class using the same techniques that I describe in Book II, Chapter 7. To declare a method that's available to users of your class, add the `public` keyword to the method declaration:

```
public boolean isActive()
{
    return this.isActive;
}
```

To create a private method that can be used within the class but isn't visible outside of the class, use the `private` keyword:

```
private void calculateLunarTrajectory()
{
    // code to get the calculated lunar trajectory
}
```

Understanding visibility

In the preceding sections, I mention that both fields and methods can use the `public` or `private` keywords to indicate whether or not the field or method can be accessed from outside of the class. This is called the *visibility* of the field or method.

The combination of all the members that have `public` access is sometimes called the *public interface* of your class. These members are the only means that other objects have to communicate with objects created from your class. As a result, carefully consider which public fields and methods your class declares.

The term *expose* is sometimes used to refer to the creation of public fields and methods. For example, if a class has a public method named `isActive`, you could say that the class exposes the `isActive` method. That simply means that the method is available to other classes.

You can use private fields and methods within a class but not from other classes. They're used to provide implementation details that may be crucial to the operation of your class, but that shouldn't be exposed to the outside world. Private fields and methods are sometimes called *internal members,* because they're available only from within the class.

Getters and Setters

One of the basic goals of object-oriented programming is to hide the implementation details of a class inside the class while carefully controlling what aspects of the class are exposed to the outside world. As a general rule, you should avoid creating public fields. Instead, you can make all your fields private. Then, you can selectively grant access to the data those fields contain by adding special methods called *accessors* to the class.

There are two types of accessors: A *get accessor* (also called a *getter*) is a method that retrieves a field value, while a *set accessor* (*setter*) is a method that sets a field value. These methods are usually named `getFieldName` and `setFieldName,` respectively. For example, if the field is named `count`, the getter and setter methods are named `getCount` and `setCount`.

Here's a class that uses a private field named `Health` to indicate the health of a player in a game program:

```
public class Player
{
    private int health;

    public int getHealth()
    {
        return health;
    }

    public void setHealth(int h)
    {
        health = h;
    }
}
```

Here, the `health` field itself is declared as private, so it can't be accessed directly. Instead, it can be accessed only through the methods `getHealth` and `setHealth`.

Creating classes with accessors rather than simple public fields have several benefits:

✦ You can create a read-only property by providing a get accessor but not a set accessor. Then, other classes can retrieve the property value, but can't change it.

✦ Instead of storing the property value in a private field, you can calculate it each time the get accessor method is called. For example, suppose you have a class named `Order` that includes fields named `unitPrice` and `quantityOrdered`. This class might also contain a `getOrderTotal` method that looks like this:

```
public double getOrderTotal()
{
    return unitPrice * quantityOrdered;
}
```

Here, instead of returning the value of a class field, the get accessor calculates the value to be returned.

✦ You can protect the class from bad data by validating data in a property set accessor and either ignoring invalid data or throwing an exception if invalid data is passed to the method. For example, suppose you have a set accessor for an `int` property named `Health` whose value can be from 0 to 100. Here's a set accessor that prevents the `Health` property from being set to an incorrect value:

```
public void setHealth(int h)
{
    if (h < 0)
        health = 0;
    else if (h > 100)
        health = 100;
    else
        health = h;
}
```

Here, if the setHealth method is called with a value less than zero, the health is set to zero. Likewise, if the value is greater than 100, the health is set to 100.

For a little added insight on the use of accessors, see the sidebar "The Accessor Pattern."

The Accessor Pattern

The use of accessors as described in the section "Getters and Setters" in this chapter is an example of a design pattern that's commonly used by Java programmers. The *Accessor pattern* is designed to provide a consistent way to set or retrieve the value of class fields without having to expose the fields themselves to the outside world.

Most Java programmers quickly learn that one of the basic guidelines of object-oriented programming is to avoid public fields. Unfortunately, they often respond to this guideline by making all fields private, and then providing get and set accessors for every field whether they need them or not. So they write classes that look like this:

```
Public class MyClass
{
    private int fieldX;
    private int fieldY;
    public int getX() { return x; }
    public void setX(int xValue) { this.x = xValue; }
    public int getY() { return y; }
    public void setY(int yValue) { this.y = yValue; }
}
```

Why not just make fieldX and fieldY public fields and skip the accessors?

To be honest, you may as well. The point of making your fields private is so that you can carefully control access to them. If you blindly create accessors for all your fields, you may as well just make the fields public.

Instead, carefully consider which fields really should be accessible to the outside world, and provide accessors only for those fields that really need them.

Overloading Methods

A Java class can contain two or more methods with the same name, provided those methods accept different parameters. This is called *overloading* and is one of the keys to building flexibility into your classes. With overloading, you can anticipate different ways someone might want to invoke an object's functions, and then provide overloaded methods for each alternative.

The term *overloading* is accurate, but a little unfortunate. Normally, when you say something is overloaded, there's a problem. For example, I once saw a picture of a Volkswagen Jetta loaded down with 3,000 pounds of lumber. (You can find the picture courtesy of Snopes.com, the Urban Legend Reference Page Web site, at www.snopes.com/photos/lumber.asp.) That's a classic example of overloading. You don't have to worry about Java collapsing under the weight of overloaded methods.

You're already familiar with several classes that have overloaded methods, though you may not realize it. For example, the PrintWriter class (which you access via System.out) defines ten different versions of the println method that allow you to print different types of data. The following lines show the method declaration for each of these overloads:

```
void println()
void println(boolean x)
void println(char x)
void println(char[] x)
void println(double x)
void println(float x)
void println(int x)
void println(long x)
void println(Object x)
void println(String x)
```

The basic rule when creating overloaded methods is that every method must have a unique signature. A method's *signature* is the combination of its name and the number and types of parameters it accepts. Thus, each of the println methods has a different signature because although each has the same name, each accepts a different parameter type.

Two things that are *not* a part of a method's signature are

✦ **The method's return type:** You can't code two methods with the same name and parameters but with different return types.

✦ **The names of the parameters:** All that matters to the method signature are the types of the parameters and the order in which they appear. Thus, the following two methods have the same signature:

```
double someMethodOfMine(double x, boolean y)
double someMethodOfMine(double param1, boolean
    param2)
```

Creating Constructors

A *constructor* is a block of code that's called when an instance of an object is created. In many ways, a constructor is similar to a method, but with a few differences:

✦ A constructor doesn't have a return type.

✦ The name of the constructor must be the same as the name of the class.

✦ Unlike methods, constructors are not considered to be members of a class. (That's only important when it comes to inheritance, which is covered in Book III, Chapter 4.)

✦ A constructor is called when a new instance of an object is created. In fact, it's the new keyword that calls the constructor. After creating the object, you can't call the constructor again.

Here's the basic format for coding a constructor:

```
public ClassName (parameter-list) [throws exception...]
{
    statements...
}
```

The public keyword indicates that other classes can access the constructor. That's usually what you want, although in the next chapter you see why you might want to create a private constructor. ClassName must be the same as the name of the class that contains the constructor. And you code the parameter list the same as you code it for a method.

Notice also that a constructor can throw exceptions if it encounters situations it can't recover from. For more information about throwing exceptions, refer to Book II, Chapter 8.

Basic constructors

Probably the most common reason for coding a constructor is to provide initial values for class fields when you create the object. For example, suppose you have a class named Actor that has fields named firstName and lastName. You can create a constructor for the Actor class:

```
public Actor(String first, String last)
{
    firstName = first;
    lastName = last;
}
```

Then, you create an instance of the `Actor` class by calling this constructor:

```
Actor a = new Actor("Arnold", "Schwarzenegger");
```

A new `Actor` object for Arnold Schwarzenegger is created.

Like methods, constructors can be overloaded. In other words, you can provide more than one constructor for a class, provided each constructor has a unique signature. For example, here's another constructor for the `Actor` class:

```
public Actor(String first, String last, boolean good)
{
    firstName = first;
    lastName = last;
    goodActor = good;
}
```

This constructor lets you create an `Actor` object with additional information besides the actor's name:

```
Actor a = new Actor("Arnold", "Schwarzenegger", false);
```

Default constructors

I grew up on *Dragnet*. I can still hear Joe Friday reading some thug his rights: "You have the right to an attorney during questioning. If you desire an attorney and cannot afford one, an attorney will be appointed to you free of charge."

Java constructors are like that. Every class has a right to a constructor. If you don't provide a constructor, Java appoints one for you, free of charge. This free constructor is called the *default constructor*. It doesn't accept any parameters and it doesn't do anything, but it does allow your class to be instantiated.

Thus, the following two classes are identical:

```
public Class1
{
    public Class1() { }
}

public Class1 { }
```

In the first example, the class explicitly declares a constructor that doesn't accept any parameters and has no statements in its body. In the second example, Java creates a default constructor that works just like the constructor shown in the first example.

The default constructor is *not* created if you declare any constructors for the class. As a result, if you declare a constructor that accepts parameters and still want to have an empty constructor (with no parameters and no body), you must explicitly declare an empty constructor for the class.

An example might clear this point up. The following code does *not* compile:

```
public class BadActorApp
{
    public static void main(String[] args)
    {
        Actor a = new Actor();    // error: won't compile
    }
}

class Actor
{
    private String lastName;
    private String firstName;
    private boolean goodActor;

    public Actor(String last, String first)
    {
        lastName = last;
        firstName = first;
    }

    public Actor(String last, String first, boolean good)
    {
        lastName = last;
        firstName = first;
        goodActor = good;
    }
}
```

This program won't compile because it doesn't explicitly provide a default constructor for the `Actor` class, and because it does provide other constructors, the default constructor isn't automatically generated.

Calling other constructors

A constructor can call another constructor of the same class by using the special keyword `this` as a method call. This technique is commonly used when you have several constructors that build on each other.

For example, consider this class:

```
public class Actor
{
    private String lastName;
```

```
    private String firstName;
    private boolean goodActor;

    public Actor(String last, String first)
    {
        lastName = last;
        firstName = first;
    }

    public Actor(String last, String first, boolean good)
    {
        this(last, first);
        goodActor = good;
    }
}
```

Here, the second constructor calls the first constructor to set the `lastName` and `firstName` fields. Then, it sets the `goodActor` field.

You have a few restrictions on how to use the `this` keyword as a constructor call:

✦ You can call another constructor only in the very first statement of a constructor. Thus, the following won't compile:

```
public Actor(String last, String first, boolean good)
{
    goodActor = good;
    this(last, first);        // error: won't compile
}
```

If you try to compile a class with this constructor, you get a message saying `call to this must be first statement in constructor`.

✦ Each constructor can call only one other constructor. However, you can chain constructors together. For example, if a class has three constructors, the first constructor can call the second one, which in turn calls the third one.

✦ You can't create loops where constructors call each other. For example, here's a class that won't compile:

```
class CrazyClass
{
    private String firstString;
    private String secondString;

    public CrazyClass(String first, String second)
    {
        this(first);
        secondString = second;
    }
```

```
public CrazyClass(String first)
{
    this(first, "DEFAULT");  // error: won't
    // compile
}
}
```

The first constructor starts by calling the second constructor, which calls the first constructor. The compiler complains that this error is a `recursive constructor invocation` and politely refuses to compile the class.

If you don't explicitly call a constructor in the first line of a constructor, Java inserts code that automatically calls the default constructor of the base class — that is, the class that this class inherits. This little detail doesn't become too important until you get into inheritance, which is covered in Book III, Chapter 4. So you can just conveniently ignore it for now.

More Uses for this

As I describe in the previous section, you can use the `this` keyword in a constructor to call another constructor for the current class. You can also use `this` in the body of a class constructor or method to refer to the current object — that is, the class instance for which the constructor or method has been called.

The `this` keyword is usually used to qualify references to instance variables of the current object. For example:

```
public Actor(String last, String first)
{
    this.lastName = last;
    this.firstName = first;
}
```

Here, `this` isn't really necessary because the compiler can tell that `lastName` and `firstName` refer to class variables. However, suppose you use `lastName` and `firstName` as the parameter names for the constructor:

```
public Actor(String lastName, String firstName)
{
    this.lastName = lastName;
    this.firstName = firstName;
}
```

Here, the `this` keywords are required to distinguish between the parameters named `lastName` and `firstName` and the instance variables with the same names.

You can also use `this` in a method body. For example:

```
public String getFullName()
{
    Return this.firstName + " " + this.lastName;
}
```

Because this example has no ambiguity, `this` isn't really required. However, many programmers like to use `this` even when it isn't necessary because it makes it clear that you're referring to an instance variable.

Sometimes, you use the `this` keyword all by itself to pass a reference to the current object as a method parameter. For example, you can print the current object to the console by using the following statement:

```
System.out.println(this);
```

The `println` method calls the object's `toString` method to get a string representation of the object, and then prints it to the console. By default, `toString` prints the name of the class that the object was created from and the object's hash code. If you want the `println` method to print something more meaningful, provide a `toString` method of your own for the class.

Using Initializers

An *initializer* (sometimes called an *initializer block*) is a lonely block of code that's placed outside of any method, constructor, or other block of code. Initializers are executed whenever an instance of a class is created, regardless of which constructor is used to create the instance.

Initializer blocks are similar to variable initializers used to initialize variables. The difference is that with an initializer block, you can code more than one statement. For example, here's a class that gets the value for a class field from the user when the class is initialized:

```
class PrimeClass
{
    private Scanner sc = new Scanner(System.in);

    public int x;

    {
        System.out.print(
            "Enter the starting value for x: ");
        x = sc.nextInt();
    }

}
```

You can almost always achieve the same effect using other coding techniques that are usually more direct. For example, you could prompt the user for the value in the constructor. Or, you could call a method in the field initializer, like this:

```
class PrimeClass
{
    private Scanner sc = new Scanner(System.in);

    public int x = getX();

    private int getX()
    {
        System.out.print("Enter the starting value for
            x: ");
        return sc.nextInt();
    }
}
```

Either way, the effect is the same.

Here are a few other tidbits of information concerning initializers:

✦ If a class contains more than one initializer, the initializers are executed in the order in which they appear in the program.

✦ Initializers are executed before any class constructors.

✦ A special kind of initializer block called a *static initializer* lets you initialize static fields. For more information, refer to the next chapter.

✦ Initializers are sometimes used with anonymous classes, as I describe in Book III, Chapter 6.

Chapter 3: Working with Statics

In This Chapter

✔ Adding static fields to a class

✔ Creating static methods

✔ Creating classes that can be instantiated

✔ Using static initializers

A *static method* is a method that isn't associated with an instance of a class. (Unless you jumped straight to this chapter, you already knew that.) Instead, the method belongs to the class itself. As a result, you can call the method without first creating a class instance. In this chapter, you find out everything you need to know about creating and using static fields and methods.

Understanding Static Fields and Methods

According to my handy Webster's dictionary, the word *static* has several different meanings. Most of them relate to the idea of being stationary or unchanging. For example, a *static display* is a display that doesn't move. *Static electricity* is an electrical charge that doesn't flow. A *static design* is a design that doesn't change.

The term *static* as used by Java doesn't mean unchanging. For example, you can create a static field, and then assign values to it as a program executes. Thus, the value of the static field can change.

To further confuse things, the word *static* can also mean interference, as in radio static that prevents you from hearing music clearly on the radio. But in Java, the term *static* doesn't have anything to do with interference or bad reception.

So what does the term *static* mean in Java? It's used to describe a special type of field or method that isn't associated with a particular instance of a class. Instead, static fields and methods are associated with the class itself. That means you don't have to create an instance of the class to access a static field or methods. Instead, you access a static field or method by specifying the class name, not a variable that references an object.

Static fields and methods have many common uses. Here are but a few:

✦ **To provide constants or other values that aren't related to class instances.** For example, a `Billing` class might have a constant named `SALES_TAX_RATE` that provides the state sales tax rate.

✦ **To keep a count of how many instances of a class have been created.** For example, a `Ball` class used in a game might have a static field that counts how many balls currently exist. This count doesn't belong to any one instance of the `Ball` class.

✦ **In a business application, to keep track of a reference or serial number that's assigned to each new object instance.** For example, an `Invoice` class might maintain a static field that holds the invoice number that is assigned to the next `Invoice` object created from the class.

✦ **To provide an alternative way to create instances of the class.** An excellent example of this is the `NumberFormat` class, which has static methods such as `getCurrencyInstance` and `getNumberInstance` that return object instances to format numbers in specific ways. One reason you might want to use this technique is to create classes that can have only one object instance. This is called a *singleton class*, and is described more in the sidebar "The Singleton Pattern," which appears later in this chapter.

✦ **To provide utility functions that aren't associated with an object at all.** A good example in the Java API library is the `Math` class, which provides a bunch of static methods to do math calculations. An example you might code yourself would be a `DataValidation` class with static methods that validate input data or a database class with static methods that perform database operations.

Working with Static Fields

A *static field* is a field that's declared with the `static` keyword, like this:

```
private static int ballCount;
```

Note that the position of the `static` and visibility keywords (`private` and `public`, as well as `protected`, which I describe in the next chapter) are interchangeable. As a result, the following statement works as well:

```
static private int ballCount;
```

As a convention, most programmers tend to put the visibility keyword first.

Note that you can't use the `static` keyword within a class method. Thus, the following code won't compile:

```
static private void someMethod()
{
    static int x;
}
```

In other words, fields can be static, but local variables can't.

You can provide an initial value for a static field:

```
private static String district = "Northwest";
```

Static fields are created and initialized when the class is first loaded. That happens when a static member of the class is referred to or when an instance of the class is created, whichever comes first.

Another way to initialize a static field is to use a *static initializer,* which I cover later in this chapter, in the section "Using Static Initializers."

Using Static Methods

A *static method* is a method declared with the `static` keyword. Like static fields, static methods are associated with the class itself, not with any particular object created from the class. As a result, you don't have to create an object from a class before you can use static methods defined by the class.

The best-known static method is `main`, which is called by the Java runtime to start an application. The `main` method must be static, which means that applications are by default run in a static context.

One of the basic rules of working with static methods is that you can't access a non-static method or field from a static method. That's because the static method doesn't have an instance of the class to use to reference instance methods or fields. For example, the following code won't compile:

```
public class TestClass
{
    private int x = 5;          // an instance field

    public static void main(String[] args)
    {
        int y = x;              // error: won't compile
    }
}
```

Here, the `main` method is static, so it can't access the instance variable `x`.

Note: However, you *can* access static methods and fields from an instance method. For example, the following code works fine:

```
public class Invoice
{
    private static double taxRate = 0.75;

    private double salesTotal;

    public double getTax()
    {
        return salesTotal * taxRate;
    }
}
```

Here, the instance method named `salesTotal` has no trouble accessing the static field `taxRate`.

Counting Instances

One common use for static variables is to keep track of how many instances of a class have been created. To illustrate how you can do this, consider the program in Listing 3-1. This program includes two classes. The `CountTest` class is a simple class that keeps track of how many times its constructor has been called. Then, the `CountTestApp` class uses a `for` loop to create ten instances of the class, displaying the number of instances that have been created after creating each instance.

Note that the instance count in this application is reset to zero each time the application is run. As a result, it doesn't keep track of how many instances of the `CountTest` class have ever been created, only how many have been created during a particular execution of the program.

LISTING 3-1: THE COUNTTEST APPLICATION

```
public class CountTestApp                                    → 1
{
    public static void main(String[] args)
    {
        printCount();
        for (int i = 0; i < 10; i++)
        {
            CountTest c1 = new CountTest();                  → 8
            printCount();                                    → 9
        }
    }
```

```
        private static void printCount()
        {
            System.out.println("There are now "      → 15
                + CountTest.getInstanceCount()
                + " instances of the CountTest class.");
        }
    }

class CountTest                                      → 21
    {
        private static int instanceCount = 0;        → 23

        public CountTest()                           → 25
        {
            instanceCount++;
        }

        public static int getInstanceCount()         → 29
        {
            return instanceCount;
        }
    }
```

The following paragraphs describe some of the highlights of this program:

**Book III
Chapter 3**

Working with Statics

→ **1** The start of the `CountTestApp` class, which tests the `CountTest` class.

→ **8** Creates an instance of the `CountTest` class. Because this code is contained in a `for` loop, a total of 10 instances are created.

→ **9** Calls the `printCount` methods, which prints the number of `CountTest` objects that have been created so far.

→**15** This line prints a message indicating how many `CountTest` objects have been created so far. It calls the static `getInstanceCount` method of the `CountTest` class to get the instance count.

→**21** The start of the `CountTest` class.

→**23** The static `instanceCount` variable, which stores the instance count.

→**25** The constructor for the `CountTest` class. Notice that the `instanceCount` variable is incremented within the constructor. That way, each time a new instance of the class is created, the instance count is incremented.

→**29** The static `getInstanceCount` method, which simply returns the value of the static `instanceCount` field.

The Singleton Pattern

A *singleton* is a class that you can use to create only one instance. When you try to create an instance, the class first checks to see if an instance already exists. If so, the existing instance is used. If not, a new instance is created.

You can't achieve this effect by using Java constructors, because a class instance has already been created by the time the constructor is executed. (That's why you can use the `this` keyword from within a constructor.) As a result, the normal way to implement a singleton class is to declare all the constructors for the class as private. That way, the constructors aren't available to other classes. Then, you provide a static method that returns an instance. This method either creates a new instance or returns an existing instance.

Here's a barebones example of a singleton class:

```
class SingletonClass
{
    private static SingletonClass instance;

    private SingletonClass()
    {
    }

    public static SingletonClass getInstance()
    {
        if (instance == null)
            instance = new SingletonClass();
        return instance;
    }
}
```

Here, the `SingletonClass` contains a `private` instance variable that maintains a reference to an instance of the class. Then, a default constructor is declared with private visibility to prevent the constructor from being used outside of the class. Finally, the static `getInstance` method calls the constructor to create an instance if the `instance` variable is null. Then, it returns the instance to the caller.

Here's a bit of code that calls the `getInstance` method twice, and then compares the resulting objects:

```
SingletonClass s1 = SingletonClass.getInstance();
SingletonClass s2 = SingletonClass.getInstance();
if (s1 == s2)
    System.out.println("The objects are the same");
else
    System.out.println("The objects are not the same");
```

When this code is run, the first call to `getInstance` creates a new instance of the `SingletonClass` class. The second call to `getInstance` simply returns a reference to the instance that was created in the first call. As a result, the comparison in the `if` statement is true, and the first message is printed to the console.

Preventing Instances

Sometimes, you want to create a class that can't be instantiated at all. Then, the class consists entirely of static fields and methods. A good example in the Java API is the `Math` class. Its methods provide utility-type functions that aren't really associated with a particular object. You may occasionally find the need to create similar classes yourself. For example, you might create a class with static methods for validating input data. Or, you might create a database access class that has static methods to retrieve data from a database. You don't need to create instances of either of these classes.

You can use a simple trick to prevent anyone from instantiating a class. To create a class instance, you have to have at least one public constructor. If you don't provide a constructor in your class, Java automatically inserts a default constructor, which happens to be public.

All you have to do to prevent a class instance from being created, then, is to provide a single private constructor, like this:

```
public class Validation
{
    private Validation() {}       // prevents instances

    // static methods and fields go here
}
```

Now, because the constructor is private, the class can't be instantiated.

Incidentally, the `Math` class uses this technique to prevent you from creating instances from it. Here's an actual snippet of code from the `Math` class:

```
public final class Math {

    /**
     * Don't let anyone instantiate this class.
     */
    private Math() {}
```

I figure if this trick is good enough for the folks who wrote the `Math` class, it's good enough for me.

Using Static Initializers

In the last chapter, you discover *initializer blocks* that you can use to initialize instance variables. Initializer blocks aren't executed until an instance of a class is created, so you can't count on them to initialize static fields. After all, you might access a static field before you create an instance of a class.

Java provides a feature called a *static initializer* that's designed specifically to let you initialize static fields. The general form of a static initializer is this:

```
static
{
    statements...
}
```

As you can see, a static initializer is similar to an initializer block, but begins with the word `static`. Like an initializer block, you code static initializers in the class body but outside of any other block, such as the body of a method or constructor.

The first time you access a static member such as a static field or a static method, any static initializers in the class are executed provided you haven't already created an instance of the class. That's because the static initializers are also executed the first time you create an instance. In that case, the static initializers are executed *before* the constructor is executed.

If a class has more than one static initializer, they're executed in the order in which they appear in the program.

Here's an example of a class that contains a static initializer:

```
class StaticInit
{
    public static int x;

    static
    {
        x = 32;
    }

// other class members such as constructors and
// methods go here...
}
```

This example is pretty trivial. In fact, you can achieve the same effect just by assigning the value 32 to the variable when it is declared. However, suppose you had to perform a complicated calculation to determine the value of x, or suppose its value comes from a database? In that case, a static initializer can be very useful.

Chapter 4: Using Subclasses and Inheritance

In This Chapter

- ✔ Explaining inheritance
- ✔ Creating subclasses
- ✔ Using protected access
- ✔ Creating final classes
- ✔ Demystifying polymorphism
- ✔ Creating custom exception classes

As you find out in Book III, Chapter 1, a Java class can be based on another class. Then, the class becomes like a child to the parent class: It inherits all the characteristics of the parent class, good and bad. All the fields and methods of the parent class are passed on to the child class. The child class can use these fields or methods as is, or it can override them to provide its own versions. In addition, the child class can add fields or methods of its own.

In this chapter, you discover how this magic works, along with the basics of creating and using Java classes that inherit other classes. You also find out a few fancy tricks that help you get the most out of inheritance.

Introducing Inheritance

The word *inheritance* conjures up several different non-computer meanings:

- ✦ Children inherit certain characteristics from the parents. For example, two of my three children have red hair. Hopefully, they won't be half bald by the time they're 30.

- ✦ Children can also inherit behavior from their parents. As they say, the apple doesn't fall far from the tree.

- ✦ When someone dies, their heirs get their stuff. Some of it is good stuff, but some of it may not be. My kids are going to have a great time rummaging through my garage deciding who gets what.

✦ You can inherit rights as well as possessions. For example, you may be a citizen of a country by virtue of being born to parents who are citizens of that country.

In Java, *inheritance* refers to a feature of object-oriented programming that lets you create classes that are derived from other classes. A class that's based on another class is said to *inherit* the other class. The class that is inherited is called the *parent class,* the *base class*, or the *superclass.* The class that does the inheriting is called the *child class,* the *derived class,* or the *subclass.*

The terms *subclass* and *superclass* seem to be the preferred term among Java gurus. So if you want to look like you know what you're talking about, use these terms. Also, be aware that the term *subclass* can be used as a verb. For example, when you create a subclass that inherits a base class, you are *sub-classing* the base class.

You need to know a few important things about inheritance:

✦ A derived class automatically takes on all the behavior and attributes of its base class. Thus, if you need to create several different classes to describe types that aren't identical but have many features in common, you can create a base class that defines all the common features. Then, you can create several derived classes that inherit the common features.

✦ A derived class can add features to the base class it inherits by defining its own methods and fields. This is one way a derived class distinguishes itself from its base class.

✦ A derived class can also change the behavior provided by the base class. For example, a base class may provide that all classes derived from it have a method named `play`, but each class is free to provide its own implementation of the `play` method. In this case, all classes that extend the base class provide their own implementation of the `play` method.

✦ Inheritance is best used to implement *is-a-type-of* relationships. For example: Solitaire is a type of game; a truck is a type of vehicle; an invoice is a type of transaction. In each case, a particular kind of object is a specific type of a more general category of objects.

The following sections provide some examples that help illustrate these points.

Plains, trains, and automobiles

Inheritance is often explained in terms of real-world objects such as cars and motorcycles, birds and reptiles, or other familiar real-world objects. For example, consider various types of vehicles. Cars and motorcycles are two distinct types of vehicles. If you're writing software that represented vehicles, you could start by creating a class called Vehicle that would describe the features that arc common to all types of vehicles, such as wheels, a driver, the ability to carry passengers, and the ability to perform actions such as driving, stopping, turning, or crashing.

A motorcycle is a type of vehicle that further refines the Vehicle class. The Motorcycle class would inherit the Vehicle class, so it would have wheels, a driver, possibly passengers, and the ability to drive, stop, turn, or crash. In addition, it would have features that differentiate it from other types of vehicles. For example, it has two wheels and uses handle bars for steering control.

A car is also a type of vehicle. The Car class would inherit the Vehicle class, so it too would have wheels, a driver, possibly some passengers, and the ability to drive, stop, turn, or crash. Plus it would have some features of its own, such as having four wheels and a steering wheel, seat belts and air bags, and an optional automatic transmission.

Playing games

Because you'll unlikely ever actually write a program that simulates cars, motorcycles, or other vehicles, take a look at a more common example: games. Suppose you want to develop a series of board games such as Life, Sorry, or Monopoly. Most board games have certain features in common:

✦ They have a playing board that has locations that players can occupy.

✦ They have players that are represented by objects.

✦ The game is played by each player taking a turn, one after the other. Once the game starts, it keeps going until someone wins. (If you don't believe me, ask the kids who tried to stop a game of Jumanji before someone won.)

Each specific type of game has these basic characteristics, but adds features of its own. For example, Life adds features such as money, insurance policies, spouses and children, and a fancy spinner in the middle of the board. Sorry has cards you draw to determine each move and safety zones within which other players can't attack you. And Monopoly has Chance and Community Chest cards, properties, houses, hotels, and money.

If you were designing classes for these games, you might create a generic BoardGame class that defines the basic features common to all board games, and then use it as the base class for classes that represent specific board games, such as LifeGame, SorryGame, and MonopolyGame.

A businesslike example

If vehicles or games don't make it clear, here's an example from the world of business. Suppose you're designing a payroll system and you're working on the classes that represent the employees. You realize that the payroll basically includes two types of employees: salaried employees and hourly employees. So you decide to create two classes, sensibly named SalariedEmployee and HourlyEmployee.

You quickly discover that most of the work done by these two classes is identical. Both types of employees have names, addresses, Social Security numbers, totals for how much they've been paid for the year and how much tax has been withheld, and so on.

However, they have important differences. The most obvious is that the salaried employees have an annual salary and the hourly employees have an hourly pay rate. But there are other differences as well. For example, hourly employees have a schedule that changes week to week. And salaried employees may have a benefit plan that isn't offered to hourly employees.

So, you decide to create three classes instead of just two. A class named Employee handles all the features that are common to both types of employees. Then, this class is the base class for the SalariedEmployee and HourlyEmployee classes. These classes provide the additional features that distinguish salaried employees from hourly employees.

Inheritance hierarchies

One of the most important aspects of inheritance is that a class that's derived from a base class can in turn be used as the base class for another derived class. Thus, you can use inheritance to form a hierarchy of classes.

For example, you've already seen how an Employee class can be used as a base class to create two types of subclasses: a SalariedEmployee class for salaried employees and an HourlyEmployee class for hourly employees. Suppose that salaried employees fall into two categories: management and sales. Then, you could use the SalariedEmployee class as the base class for two more classes, named Manager and SalesPerson.

Thus, a Manager is a type of SalariedEmployee. And because a SalariedEmployee is a type of Employee, a Manager is also a type of Employee.

All classes ultimately derive from a Java class named Object. Any class that doesn't specifically state what class it is derived from is assumed to derive from the Object class. This class provides some of the basic features that are common to all Java classes, such as the toString method. For more information, see Book III, Chapter 5.

Creating Subclasses

The basic procedure for creating a subclass is simple. You just use the `extends` keyword on the declaration for the subclass. The basic format of a class declaration for a class that inherits a base class is this:

```
public class ClassName extends BaseClass
{
    // class body goes here
}
```

For example, suppose you have a class named `Ball` that defines a basic ball, and you want to create a subclass named `BouncingBall` that adds the ability to bounce.

```
public class BouncingBall extends Ball
{
    // methods and fields that add the ability to bounce
    // to a basic Ball object:

    public void bounce()
    {
        // the bounce method
    }
}
```

DESIGN PATTERN

The Delegation Pattern

Inheritance is one of the great features of object-oriented programming languages, such as Java. However, it isn't the answer to every programming problem. And, quite frankly, many Java programmers use it too much. In many cases, simply including an instance of one class in another class rather than using inheritance is easier. This technique is sometimes called the *Delegation Design pattern*.

For example, suppose you need to create a class named `EmployeeCollection` that represents a group of employees. One way to create this class would be to extend one of the collection classes supplied by the Java API, such as the `ArrayList` class. Then, your `EmployeeCollection` class would be a specialized version of the `ArrayList` class,

and would have all the methods that are available to the `ArrayList` class.

However, a simpler alternative would be to declare a class field of type `ArrayList` within your `EmployeeCollection` class. Then, you could provide methods that use this `ArrayList` object to add or retrieve employees from the collection.

Why is this technique called the *delegation*? Because rather than write code that implements the functions of the collection, you *delegate* that task to an `ArrayList` object, because `ArrayList` objects already know how to perform these functions. (For more information about the `ArrayList` class, see Book IV, Chapter 3.)

Here, I'm creating a class named `BouncingBall` that extends the `Ball` class. (*Extends* is Java's word for *inherits*.)

The subclass automatically has all the methods and fields of the class it extends. Thus, if the `Ball` class has fields named `size` and `weight`, the `BouncingBall` class has those fields too. Likewise, if the `Ball` class has a method named `throw`, the `BouncingBall` class gets that method too.

You need to know some important details to use inheritance properly:

+ A subclass inherits all the members from its base class. However, constructors are *not* considered to be members. As a result, a subclass does *not* inherit constructors from its base class.

+ The visibility (`public` or `private`) of any members inherited from the base class is the same in the subclass. That means that you can't access methods or fields that are declared in the base class as `private` from the subclass.

+ You can *override* a method by declaring a new member with the same signature in the subclass. For more information, see the next section.

+ A special type of visibility is called `protected` that hides fields and methods from other classes but makes them available to subclasses. For more information, see "Protecting Your Members" later in this chapter.

+ You can also add additional methods or fields, `private` or `protected`, to a subclass. For example, the `BouncingBall` class shown previously in this section adds a public method named `bounce`.

Overriding Methods

If a subclass declares a method that has the same signature as a public method of the base class, the subclass version of the method *overrides* the base class version of the method. This technique lets you modify the behavior of a base class to suit the needs of the subclass.

For example, suppose you have a base class named `Game` that has a method named `play`. The base class, which doesn't represent any particular game, implements this method:

```
public class Game
{
    public void play()
    {
    }
}
```

Then, you declare a class named Chess that extends the Game class, but provides an implementation for the play method:

```
public class Chess extends Game
{
    public void play()
    {
        System.out.println("I give up. You win.");
    }
}
```

Here, when you call the play method of a Chess object, the game announces that it gives up. (I was going to provide a complete implementation of an actual chess game program for this example, but it would have made this chapter about 600 pages long. So I opted for the simpler version here.)

Note that to override a method, three conditions have to be met:

✦ The class must extend the class that defines the method you want to override.

✦ The method must be declared in the base class with public access. You can't override a private method.

✦ The method in the subclass must have the same signature as the method in the base class. In other words, the name of the method and the parameter types must be the same.

Protecting Your Members

You're already familiar with the public and private keywords, used to indicate whether class members are visible outside of the class or not. When you inherit a class, all the public members of the superclass are available to the subclass, but the private members aren't. They do become a part of the derived class, but you can't access them directly in the derived class.

Java provides a third visibility option that's useful when you create subclasses: protected. A member with protected visibility is available to subclasses, but not to other classes. For example, consider this example:

```
public class Ball
{
    private double weight;

    protected double getWeight()
    {
        return this.weight;
    }
}
```

```
        protected void setWeight(double weight)
        {
            this.weight = weight;
        }
    }

    public class BaseBall extends Ball
    {
        public BaseBall()
        {
            setWeight(5.125);
        }
    }
```

Here, the getWeight and setWeight methods are declared with protect access, which means they're visible in the subclass BaseBall. However, these methods aren't visible to classes that don't extend Ball.

Using this and super in Your Subclasses

You already know about the this keyword: It provides a way to refer to the current object instance. It's often used to distinguish between a local variable or a parameter and a class field with the same name. For example:

```
    public class Ball
    {
        private int velocity;

        public void setVelocity(int velocity)
        {
            this.velocity = velocity;
        }
    }
```

Here, the this keyword indicates that the velocity variable referred to on the left side of the assignment statement is the class field named velocity, not the parameter with the same name.

But what if you need to refer to a field or method that belongs to a base class? To do that, you use the super keyword. It works similar to this, but refers to the instance of the base class rather than the instance of the current class.

For example, consider these two classes:

```
    public class Ball
    {
        public void hit()
```

```
    {
        System.out.println("You hit it a mile!");
    }
}

class BaseBall extends Ball
{
    public void hit()
    {
        System.out.println("You tore the cover off! ");
        super.hit();
    }
}
```

Here, the `hit` method in the `BaseBall` class calls the `hit` method of its base class object. Thus, if you call the `hit` method of a `BaseBall` object, the following two lines are displayed on the console:

```
You tore the cover off!
You hit it a mile!
```

You can also use the `super` keyword in the constructor of a subclass to explicitly call a constructor of the superclass. For more information, see the next section.

Inheritance and Constructors

When you create an instance of a subclass, Java automatically calls the default constructor of the base class before it executes the subclass constructor. For example, consider the following classes:

```
public class Ball
{
    public Ball()
    {
        System.out.println(
            "Hello from the Ball constructor");
    }
}

public class BaseBall extends Ball
{
    public BaseBall()
    {
        System.out.println(
            "Hello from the BaseBall constructor");
    }
}
```

If you create an instance of the `BaseBall` class, the following two lines are displayed on the console:

```
Hello from the Ball constructor
Hello from the BaseBall constructor
```

If you want, you can explicitly call a base class constructor from a subclass by using the `super` keyword. Because Java automatically calls the default constructor for you, the only reason to do this is to call a constructor of the base class that uses a parameter. For example, here's a version of the `Ball` and `BaseBall` classes in which the `BaseBall` constructor calls a `Ball` constructor that uses a parameter:

```
public class Ball
{
    private double weight;

    public Ball(double weight)
    {
        this.weight = weight;
    }
}

public class BaseBall extends Ball
{
    public BaseBall()
    {
        super(5.125);
    }
}
```

Here, the `BaseBall` constructor calls the `Ball` constructor to supply a default weight for the ball.

You need to obey a few rules and regulations when working with superclass constructors:

✦ If you use `super` to call the superclass constructor, you must do so in the very first statement in the constructor.

✦ If you don't explicitly call `super`, the compiler inserts a call to the default constructor of the base class. In that case, the base class must have a default constructor. If the base class doesn't have a default constructor, the compiler refuses to compile the program.

✦ If the superclass is itself a subclass, the constructor for its superclass is called in the same way. This continues all the way up the inheritance hierarchy, until you get to the `Object` class, which has no superclass.

Using final

Java has a `final` keyword that serves three purposes. When you use `final` with a variable, it creates a constant whose value can't be changed once it has been initialized. Constants are covered in Book II, Chapter 2, so I won't describe this use of the `final` keyword more here. The other two uses of the `final` keyword are to create final methods and final classes. I describe these two uses of `final` in the following sections.

Final methods

A *final method* is a method that can't be overridden by a subclass. To create a final method, you simply add the keyword `final` to the method declaration. For example:

```
public class SpaceShip
{
    public final int getVelocity()
    {
        return this.velocity;
    }
}
```

Here, the method `getVelocity` is declared as `final`. Thus, any class that uses the `SpaceShip` class as a base class can't override the `getVelocity` method. If it tries, the compiler issues an error message.

Here are some additional details about final methods:

✦ You might think that a subclass won't need to override a method, but there's no reason to be sure. Predicting how other people might use your class is difficult. As a result, you should usually avoid using final methods unless you have a compelling reason to.

✦ Final methods execute more efficiently than non-final methods. That's because the compiler knows at compile time that a call to a final method won't be overridden by some other method. The performance gain isn't huge, but for applications where performance is crucial, it can be noticeable.

✦ Private methods are automatically considered to be final. That's because you can't override a method you can't see.

Final classes

A *final class* is a class that can't be used as a base class. To declare a class as final, just add the `final` keyword to the class declaration:

```
public final class BaseBall
{
    // members for the BaseBall class go here
}
```

Then, no one can use the `BaseBall` class as the base class for another class.

When you declare a class to be final, all of its methods are considered to be final too. That makes sense when you think about it. Because you can't use a final class as the base class for another class, no class can possibly be in a position to override any of the methods in the final class. Thus, all the methods of a final class are final methods.

Casting Up and Down

An object of a derived type can be treated as if it were an object of its base type. For example, if the `BaseBall` class extends the `Ball` class, a `BaseBall` object can be treated as if it were a `Ball` object. This is called upcasting, and Java does it automatically, so you don't have to code a casting operator. Thus, the following code is legal:

```
Ball b = new BaseBall();
```

Here, an object of type `BaseBall` is created. Then, a reference to this object is assigned to the variable b, whose type is `Ball`, not `BaseBall`.

Now suppose you have a method in a ball game application named `hit` that's declared like this:

```
public void hit(Ball b)
```

In other words, this method accepts a `Ball` type as a parameter. When you call this method, you can pass it either a `Ball` object or a `BaseBall` object, because `BaseBall` is a subclass of `Ball`. So the following code works:

```
BaseBall b1 = new BaseBall();
hit(b1);
Ball b2 = b1;
hit(b2);
```

Automatic casting doesn't work the other way, however. Thus, you can't use a `Ball` object where a `BaseBall` object is called for. For example, suppose your program has a method declared like this:

```
public void toss(BaseBall b)
```

Then, the following code does *not* compile:

```
Ball b = new BaseBall();
toss(b);    // error: won't compile
```

However, you can explicitly cast the b variable to a BaseBall object, like this:

```
Ball b = new BaseBall();
toss((BaseBall) b);
```

Note that the second statement throws an exception of type ClassCast Exception if the object referenced by the b variable isn't a BaseBall object. So, the following code don't work:

```
Ball b = new SoftBall();
toss((BaseBall) b);         // error: b isn't a Softball
```

What if you want to call a method that's defined by a subclass from an object that's referenced by a variable of the superclass? For example, suppose the SoftBall class has a method named riseBall that isn't defined by the Ball class. How can you call it from a Ball variable? One way to do that is to create a variable of the subclass, and then use an assignment statement to cast the object:

```
Ball b = new SoftBall();
SoftBall s = (SoftBall)b;   // cast the Ball to a
   // SoftBall
s.riseBall();
```

But there's a better way: Java lets you cast the Ball object to a SoftBall and call the riseBall method in the same statement. All you need is an extra set of parentheses:

```
Ball b = new SoftBall();
((SoftBall) b).riseBall();
```

Here, the expression ((SoftBall) b) returns the object referenced by the b variable, cast as a SoftBall. You can then call any method of the SoftBall class using the dot operator. (This operator throws a ClassCastException if b is not a SoftBall object.)

As a general rule, you should declare method parameters with types as far up in the class hierarchy as possible. For example, rather than create separate toss methods that accept BaseBall and SoftBall objects, create a single toss method that accepts a Ball object. If necessary, the toss method can determine which type of ball it's throwing by using the instanceof operator, which is described in the next section.

**Book III
Chapter 4**

**Using Subclasses
and Inheritance**

Determining an Object's Type

As described in the previous section, a variable of one type can possibly hold a reference to an object of another type. For example, if `SalariedEmployee` is a subclass of the `Employee` class, the following statement is perfectly legal:

```
Employee emp = new SalariedEmployee();
```

Here, the type of the `emp` variable is `Employee`, but the object it refers to is a `SalariedEmployee`.

Suppose you have a method named `getEmployee` whose return type is `Employee`, but that actually returns either a `SalariedEmployee` or an `HourlyEmployee` object:

```
Employee emp = getEmployee();
```

In many cases, you don't need to worry about which type of employee this method returns. But sometimes you do. For example, suppose the `SalariedEmployee` class extends the `Employee` class by adding a method named `getFormattedSalary`, which returns the employee's salary formatted as currency. Similarly, the `HourlyEmployee` class extends the `Employee` class with a `getFormattedRate` method that returns the employee's hourly pay rate formatted as currency. Then, you'd need to know which type of employee a particular object is to know whether you should call the `getFormattedSalary` method or the `getFormattedRate` method to get the employee's pay.

To tell what type of object has been assigned to the `emp` variable, you can use the `instanceof` operator, which is designed specifically for this purpose. Here's the previous code rewritten with the `instanceof` operator:

```
Employee emp = getEmployee();
String msg;
if (emp instanceof SalariedEmployee)
{
    msg = "The employee's salary is ";
    msg += ((SalariedEmployee) emp).getFormattedSalary();
}
else
{
    msg = "The employee's hourly rate is ";
    msg += ((HourlyEmployee) emp).getFormattedRate();
}
System.out.println(msg);
```

Here, the `instanceof` operator is used in an `if` statement to determine the type of the object returned by the `getEmployee` method. Then, the emp can be cast without fear of `CastClassException`.

Poly What?

The term *polymorphism* refers to the ability of Java to use base class variables to refer to subclass objects, keep track of which subclass an object belongs to, and use overridden methods of the subclass even though the subclass isn't known when the program is compiled.

This sounds like a mouthful, but it's not that hard to understand when you see an example. Suppose you're developing an application that can play the venerable game of Tic-Tac-Toe. You start out by creating a class named `Player` that represents one of the players. This class has a public method named `move` that returns an `int` to indicate which square of the board the player wants to mark:

```
class Player
{
    public int move()
    {
        for (int i = 0; i < 9; i++)
        {
            System.out.println("\nThe basic player
                says:");
            System.out.println(
                "I'll take the first open square!");
            return firstOpenSquare();
        }
        return -1;
    }

    private int firstOpenSquare()
    {
        int square = 0;
        // code to find the first open square goes here
        return square;
    }
}
```

This basic version of the `Player` class uses a simple strategy to determine what its next move should be: It chooses the first open square on the board. This strategy stokes your ego by letting you think you can beat the computer every time. (To keep the illustration simple, I omitted the code that actually chooses the move.)

Now, you need to create a subclass of the `Player` class that uses a more intelligent method to choose its next move:

```
class BetterPlayer extends Player
{
    public int move()
    {
```

```
            System.out.println("\nThe better player says:");
            System.out.println(
                "I'm looking for a good move...");
            return findBestMove();
        }

        private int findBestMove()
        {
            int square;
            // code to find the best move goes here
            return square;
        }
    }
```

As you can see, this version of the Player class overrides the move method and uses a better algorithm to pick its move. (Again, to keep the illustration simple, I don't show the code that actually chooses the move.)

The next thing to do is write a short class that uses these two Player classes to actually play a game. This class contains a method named playTheGame that accepts two Player objects. It calls the move method of the first player, and then calls the move method of the second player:

```
public class TicTacToeApp
{
    public static void main(String[] args)
    {
        Player p1 = new Player();
        Player p2 = new BetterPlayer();
        playTheGame(p1, p2);
    }

    public static void playTheGame(Player p1, Player p2)
    {
        p1.move();
        p2.move();
    }
}
```

Notice that the playTheGame method doesn't know which of the two players is the basic player and which is the better player. It simply calls the move method for each Player object.

When you run this program, the following output is displayed on the console:

```
Basic player says:
I'll take the first open square!

Better player says:
I'm looking for a good move...
```

When the move method for p1 is called, the move method of the Player class is executed. But when the move method for p2 is called, the move method of the BetterPlayer class is called.

Java knows to call the move method of the BetterPlayer subclass because it uses a technique called *late binding*. Late binding simply means that when the compiler can't tell for sure what type of object a variable references, it doesn't hard-wire the method calls when the program is compiled. Instead, it waits until the program is executing to determine exactly which method to call.

Creating Custom Exceptions

The last topic I want to cover in this chapter is how to use inheritance to create your own custom exceptions. I covered most of the details of working with exceptions in Book II, Chapter 8. However, I hadn't explored inheritance, so I couldn't discuss custom exception classes in that chapter. So I promised that I'd get to it in this minibook. The following sections deliver on that long awaited promise.

The Throwable hierarchy

As you know, you use the try/catch statement to catch exceptions, and the throw statement to throw exceptions. Each type of exception that can be caught or thrown is represented by a different exception class. What you might not have realized is that those exception classes use a fairly complex inheritance chain, as shown in Figure 4-1.

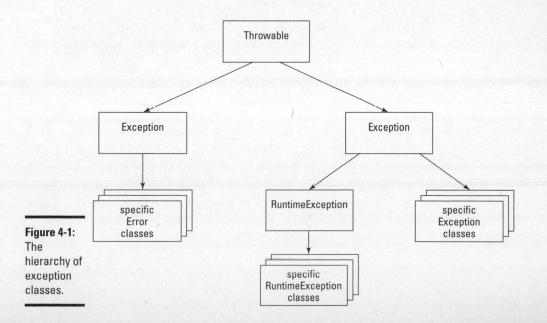

Figure 4-1: The hierarchy of exception classes.

The following paragraphs describe each of the classes in this hierarchy:

+ **Throwable:** The root of the exception hierarchy is the Throwable class. This class represents any object that can be thrown with a throw statement and caught with a catch clause.

+ **Error:** This subclass of Throwable represents serious error conditions that reasonable programs can't recover from. The subclasses of this class represent the specific types of errors that can occur. For example, if the Virtual Machine runs out of memory, a VirtualMachineError is thrown. You don't have to worry about catching these errors in your programs.

+ **Exception:** This subclass of Throwable represents an error condition that most programs should try to recover from. Thus, Exception is effectively the top of the hierarchy for the types of exceptions you catch with try/catch statements.

  With the exception (sorry) of RuntimeException, the subclasses of Exception represent specific types of checked exceptions that must be either caught or thrown. Note that some of these subclasses have subclasses of their own. For example, exception class named IOException has more than 25 subclasses representing different kinds of I/O exceptions that can occur.

+ **RuntimeException:** This subclass of Exception represents unchecked exceptions. You don't have to catch or throw unchecked exceptions, but you can if you want to. Subclasses of RuntimeException include NullPointerException and ArithmeticException.

If your application needs to throw a custom exception, you can create an exception class that inherits any of the classes in this hierarchy. Usually, however, you start with the Exception class to create a custom checked exception. The next section explains how to do that.

Creating an exception class

To create a custom exception class, you just define a class that extends one of the classes in the Java exception hierarchy. Usually, you extend Exception to create a custom checked exception.

For example, suppose you're developing a class that retrieves product data from a file or database, and you want methods that encounter I/O errors to throw a custom exception rather than the generic IOException that's provided in the Java API. You can do that by creating a class that extends the Exception class:

```
public class ProductDataException extends Exception
{
}
```

Unfortunately, constructors aren't considered to be class members, so they aren't inherited when you extend a class. As a result, the `ProductData` `Exception` has only a default constructor. The `Exception` class itself, and most other exception classes, have a constructor that lets you pass a String message that's stored with the exception and can be retrieved via the `getMessage` method. Thus, you want to add this constructor to your class. That means you want to add an explicit default constructor too. So the `ProductDataException` class now looks like this:

```
public class ProductDataException extends Exception
{
    public ProductDataException
    {
    }

    public ProductDataException(String message)
    {
        super(message);
    }
}
```

Although possible, adding additional fields or methods to a custom exception class is unusual.

Throwing a custom exception

As for any exception, you use a `throw` statement to throw a custom exception. You usually code this `throw` statement in the midst of a `catch` clause that catches some other more generic exception. For example, here's a method that retrieves product data from a file and throws a `ProductData` `Exception` if an `IOException` occurs:

```
public class ProductDDB
{
    public static Product getProduct(String code)
        throws ProductDataException
    {
        try
        {
            Product p;
            // code that gets the product from a file
            // and might throw an IOException
            p = new Product();
            return p;
        }
        catch (IOException e)
        {
            throw new ProductDataException(
                "An IO error occurred.");
        }
    }
}
```

Here's some code that calls the `getProduct` method and catches the exception:

```
try
{
    Product p = ProductDB.getProduct(productCode);
}
catch (ProductDataException e)
{
    System.out.println(e.getMessage());
}
```

Here, the message is simply displayed on the console if a `ProductData Exception` is thrown. In an actual program, you want to log the error, inform the user, and figure out how to gracefully continue the program even though this data exception has occurred.

Chapter 5: Using Abstract Classes and Interfaces

In This Chapter

✔ Abstract methods and classes

✔ Basic interfaces

✔ Using interfaces as types

✔ Adding constants to an interface

✔ Inheriting interfaces

✔ Working with callbacks

In this chapter, you find out how to use two similar but subtly distinct features: abstract classes and interfaces. Both let you declare the signatures of the methods and fields that a class implements separately from the class itself. Abstract classes accomplish this by way of inheritance. Interfaces do it without using inheritance, but the effect is similar.

Using Abstract Classes

Java lets you declare that a method or an entire class is *abstract,* which means that the method has no body. An abstract method is just a prototype for a method: a return type, a name, a list of parameters, and (optionally) a `throws` clause.

To create an abstract method, you specify the modifier `abstract` and replace the method body with a semicolon:

```
public abstract int hit(int batSpeed);
```

Here, the method named `hit` is declared as an abstract method that returns an `int` value and accepts an `int` parameter.

A class that contains at least one abstract method is called an *abstract class,* and must be declared with the `abstract` modifier on the class declaration. For example:

```
public abstract class Ball
{
    public abstract int hit(int batSpeed);
}
```

If you omit the `abstract` modifier from the class declaration, the Java compiler coughs up an error message to remind you that the class must be declared `abstract`.

An abstract class can't be instantiated. Thus, given the preceding declaration, the following line doesn't compile:

```
Ball b = new Ball();    // error: Ball is abstract
```

The Abstract Factory Pattern

One common use for abstract classes is to provide a way to obtain an instance of one of several subclasses when you don't know which subclass you need in advance. To do this, you can create an *Abstract Factory class* that has one or more methods that return subclasses of the abstract class.

For example, suppose you want to create a `Ball` object, but you want to let the user choose whether to create a `SoftBall` or a `BaseBall`. To use the Abstract Factory pattern, you create a class (I call it `BallFactory`) that has a method named `getBallInstance`. This method accepts a String parameter that's set to `"BaseBall"` if you want a `BaseBall` object or `"SoftBall"` if you want a `SoftBall` object.

Here's the factory class:

```
class BallFactoryInstance
{
    public static Ball getBall(String t)
    {
        if (s.equalsIgnoreCase("BaseBall"))
            return new BaseBall();
        if (s.equalsIgnoreCase("SoftBall"))
            return new SoftBall();
        return null;
    }
}
```

Then, assuming the String variable `userChoice` has been set according to the user's choice, you can create the selected type of ball object like this:

```
Ball b = BallFactory.getBallInstance(userChoice);
```

In an actual application, using an `enum` variable is better rather than a String variable to indicate the type of object to be returned.

The problem here isn't with declaring the variable b as a `Ball`. It's using the `new` keyword with the `Ball` class in an attempt to create a `Ball` object. Because `Ball` is an abstract class, you can use it to create an object instance.

You can create a subclass from an abstract class like this:

```
public class BaseBall extends Ball
{
    public int hit(int batSpeed)
    {
        // code that implements the hit method goes here
    }
}
```

When you subclass an abstract class, the subclass must provide an implementation for each abstract method in the abstract class. In other words, it must override each abstract method with a non-abstract method. (If it doesn't, the subclass is also abstract, so it too cannot be instantiated.)

Abstract classes are useful when you want to create a generic type that is used as the superclass for two or more subclasses, but the superclass itself doesn't represent an actual object. For example, if all employees are either salaried or hourly, creating an abstract `Employee` class makes sense, and then use it as the base class for the `SalariedEmployee` and `HourlyEmployee` subclasses.

Here are a few additional points to ponder concerning abstract classes:

✦ Not all the methods in an abstract class have to be abstract. A class can provide an implementation for some of its methods but not others. In fact, you can declare a class that doesn't have any abstract methods as abstract. In that case, the class can't be instantiated.

✦ A private method can't be abstract. That only makes sense, because a subclass can't override a private method, and abstract methods must be overridden.

✦ Although you can't create an instance of an abstract class, you can declare a variable using an abstract class as its type. Then, use the variable to refer to an instance of any of the subclasses of the abstract class.

✦ A class can't specify both `abstract` and `final`. That would cause one of those logical paradoxes that result in the complete annihilation of the entire universe. Well, hopefully the effect would be localized. But the point is that because an `abstract` class can only be used if you sub-class it, and a `final` class can't be subclassed, letting you specify both `abstract` and `final` for the same class doesn't make sense.

✦ Abstract classes are used extensively in the Java API. Many of the abstract classes have names that begin with `Abstract`, such as `AbstractBorder`, `AbstractCollection`, and `AbstractMap`. But most of the abstract classes don't. For example, the `InputStream` class (used by `System.in`) is abstract.

Using Interfaces

An *interface* is similar to an abstract class. However, it can only include abstract methods and final fields (constants), and it can't be used as a base class. Instead, a class *implements* an interface by providing an implementation for each method declared by the interface.

Interfaces have two advantages over inheritance:

✦ Interfaces are easier to work with than inheritance, because you don't have to worry about providing any implementation details in the interface.

✦ A class can extend only one other class, but it can implement as many interfaces as you need.

The following sections describe the details of creating and using interfaces.

Creating a basic interface

Here's a basic interface that defines a single method, named `Playable`, that includes a single method named `play`:

```
public interface Playable
{
    void play();
}
```

This interface declares that any class that implements the `Playable` interface must provide an implementation for a method named `play` that accepts no parameters and doesn't return a value.

This interface has a few interesting details:

✦ The interface itself is declared as `public` so that it can be used by other classes. Like a public class, a public interface must be declared in a file with the same name. Thus, this interface must be in a file named `Playable.java`.

✦ The name of the interface (`Playable`) is an adjective. Most interfaces are named using adjectives rather than nouns because they describe some additional capability or quality of the classes that implement the interface. Thus, classes that implement the `Playable` interface represent objects that can be played.

In case you haven't been to English class in a while, an *adjective* is a word that modifies a noun. You can convert many verbs to adjectives by adding –able to the end of the word. For example: *playable*, *readable*, *drivable*, and *stoppable*. This type of adjective is commonly used for interface names.

✦ Another common way to name interfaces is to combine an adjective with a noun to indicate that the interface adds some capability to a particular type of object. For example, you can call an interface that provides methods unique to card games `CardGame`. This interface might have methods such as `deal`, `shuffle`, and `getHand`.

✦ All the methods in an interface are assumed to be public and abstract. If you want, you can code the `public` and `abstract` keywords on interface methods. However, that's considered bad form, because it might indicate that you think the default is private and not abstract.

Implementing an interface

To implement an interface, a class must do two things:

✦ It must specify an `implements` clause on its class declaration.

✦ It must provide an implementation for every method declared by the interface.

For example, here's a class that implements the `Playable` interface:

```
public class TicTacToe implements Playable
{
    // additional fields and methods go here

    public void play()
    {
        // code that plays the game goes here
    }

    // additional fields and methods go here

}
```

Here, the declaration for the `TicTacToe` class specifies `implements` `Playable`. Then, the body of the class includes an implementation of the `play` method.

A class can implement more than one interface:

```
public class Hearts implements Playable, CardGame
{
    // must implement methods of the Playable
    // and CardGame interfaces
}
```

Here, the Hearts class implements two interfaces: Playable and CardGame.

A class can possibly inherit a superclass and implement one or more interfaces. For example:

```
public class Poker extends Game
     implements Playable, CardGame
{
     // inherits all members of the Game class
     // must implement methods of the Playable
     // and CardGame interfaces
}
```

Using an interface as a type

In Java, an interface is a kind of type, just like a class. As a result, you can use an interface as the type for a variable, parameter, or method return value.

Consider this snippet of code:

```
Playable game = getGame();
game.play();
```

Here, I assume that the getGame method returns an object that implements the Playable interface. This object is assigned to a variable of type Playable in the first statement. Then, the second statement calls the object's play method.

For another, slightly more complex example, suppose you have an interface named Dealable that defines a method named deal that accepts the number of cards to deal as a parameter:

```
public interface Dealable
{
     void deal(int cards);
}
```

Now, suppose you have a method called startGame that accepts two parameters: a Dealable object and a String that indicates what game to play. This method might look something like this:

```
private void startGame(Dealable deck, String game)
{
     if (game.equals("Poker"))
          deck.deal(5);
     else if (game.equals("Hearts"))
          deck.deal(13);
     else if (game.equals("Gin"))
          deck.deal(10);
}
```

Assuming you also have a class named `CardDeck` that implements the `Dealable` interface, you might use a statement like this example to start a game of Hearts:

```
Dealable d = new CardDeck();
startGame(d, "Hearts");
```

Notice that the variable d is declared as a `Dealable`. You could just as easily declare it as a `CardDeck`:

```
CardDeck d = new CardDeck();
startGame(d, "Hearts");
```

Because the `CardDeck` class implements the `Dealable` interface, it can be passed as a parameter to the `startGame` method.

More Things You Can Do with Interfaces

There's more to interfaces than just creating abstract methods. The following sections describe some additional interesting things you can do with interfaces. Read on. . . .

Adding fields to an interface

Besides abstract methods, an interface can also include final fields — that is, constants. Interface fields are used to provide constant values that are related to the interface. For example:

```
public interface GolfClub
{
    int DRIVER = 1;
    int SPOON = 2;
    int NIBLICK = 3;
    int MASHIE = 4;
}
```

Here, any class that implements the `GolfClub` interface has these four fields constants available.

Note that interface fields are automatically assumed to be `static`, `final`, and `public`. You can include these keywords when you create interface constants, but you don't have to.

Extending interfaces

You can extend interfaces by using the `extends` keyword. An interface that extends an existing interface is called a *subinterface,* and the interface being extended is called the *superinterface.*

When you use the `extends` keyword with interfaces, all the fields and methods of the superinterface are effectively copied into the subinterface. Thus, the subinterface consists of a combination of its fields and methods and the fields and methods of the subinterface.

Here's an example:

```
public interface ThrowableBall
{
    void throwBall();
    void catchBall();
}

public interface KickableBall
{
    void kickBall();
    void catchBall();
}

public interface PlayableBall
    extends ThrowableBall, KickableBall
{
    void dropBall();
}
```

Here, three interfaces are declared. The first, named `ThrowableBall`, defines two methods: `throwBall` and `catchBall`. The second, named `KickableBall`, also defines two methods: `kickBall` and `catchBall`. The third, named `PlayableBall`, extends `ThrowableBall` and `KickableBall`, and adds a method of its own, named `dropBall`.

Thus, any class that implements the `PlayableBall` interface must provide an implementation for four methods: `throwBall`, `catchBall`, `kickBall`, and `dropBall`. Note that because the `catchBall` methods defined by the `ThrowableBall` and `KickableBall` interfaces have the same signature, only one version of the `catchBall` method is included in the `PlayableBall` interface.

Using interfaces for callbacks

In the theater, a callback is when you show up for an initial audition, they like what they see, so they want you to come back so they can have another look.

In Java, a *callback* is sort of like that. It's a programming technique in which an object lets another object know that the second object should call one of the first object's methods whenever a certain event happens. The first object is called an *event listener*, because it waits patiently until the other object calls it. The second object is called the *event source,* because it's the source of events that result in calls to the listener.

The Marker Interface Pattern

A *marker interface* is an interface that doesn't have any members. Its sole purpose in life is to identify a class as belonging to a set of classes that possess some capability or have some characteristic in common.

The best-known example of a marker interface is the Java API `Cloneable` interface. It marks classes that can be cloned. The `Object` class, which all classes ultimately inherit, provides a method named `clone` that can be used to create a copy of the object. However, you're only allowed to call the `clone` method if the object implements the `Cloneable` interface. If you try to call `clone` for an object that doesn't implement `Cloneable`, `CloneNotSupported` `Exception` is thrown. (For more information

about the `clone` method, refer to Book III, Chapter 6.)

Here's the actual code for the `Cloneable` interface:

```
public interface Cloneable {
}
```

In some cases, you might find a use for marker interfaces in your own application. For example, if you're working on a series of classes for creating games, you might create a marker interface named `Winnable` to distinguish games that have a winner from games that you just play for enjoyment.

Okay, my theater analogy was a bit of a stretch. Callbacks in Java aren't really that much like callbacks when you're auditioning for a big part. A callback is more like when you need to get a hold of someone on the phone, and you call them when you know they aren't there and leave your phone number on their voicemail so they can call you back.

Callbacks are handled in Java using a set of interfaces designed for this purpose. The most common use of callbacks is in graphical applications built with Swing, where you create event listeners that handle user-interface events, such as mouse clicks.

You find out all about Swing in Book VI. For now, I look at callbacks using the `Timer` class, which is part of the `javax.Swing` package. This class implements a basic timer that generates events at regular intervals and lets you set up a listener object to handle these events. The listener object must implement the `ActionListener` interface, which defines a method named `actionPerformed` that's called for each timer event.

The `Timer` class constructor accepts two parameters:

✦ The first parameter is an `int` value that represents how often the timer events occur.

✦ The second parameter is an object that implements the `Action Listener` interface. This object's `actionPerformed` method is called when each timer event occurs.

The `ActionListener` interface is defined in the `java.awt.event` package. It includes the following code:

```
public interface ActionListener extends EventListener {

    /**
     * Invoked when an action occurs.
     */
    public void actionPerformed(ActionEvent e);

}
```

As you can see, the `ActionListener` interface consists of a single method named `actionPerformed`. It receives a parameter of type `ActionEvent`, but you don't make use of this parameter here. (But you do use the `Action Event` class in Book VI.)

The `Timer` class has about 20 methods, but I talk about only one of them here: `start`, which sets the timer in motion. This method doesn't require any parameters and doesn't return a value.

Listing 5-1 shows a program that uses the Timer class to alternately display the messages `Tick. . .` and `Tock. . .` on the console at one-second intervals. The `JOptionPane` class is used to display a dialog box; the program runs until the user clicks the OK button in this box. Figure 5-1 shows the Tick Tock program in action.

LISTING 5-1: THE TICK TOCK PROGRAM

```
import java.awt.event.*;                           → 1
import javax.swing.*;                              → 2

public class TickTock
{
    public static void main(String[] args)
    {
        // create a timer that calls the Ticker class
        // at one second intervals
        Timer t = new Timer(1000, new Ticker());   → 10
        t.start();                                 → 11

        // display a message box to prevent the
        // program from ending immediately
        JOptionPane.showMessageDialog(null,        → 15
            "Click OK to exit program");
```

```
        }
    }

class Ticker implements ActionListener                    → 20
{
    private boolean tick = true;                          → 22

    public void actionPerformed(ActionEvent event)        → 24
    {
        if (tick)
        {
            System.out.println("Tick...");                → 28
        }
        else
        {
            System.out.println("Tock...");                → 32
        }
        tick = !tick;                                     → 34
    }
}
```

Figure 5-1:
The Tick
Tock
application
in action.

The following paragraphs describe the important details of this program's operation:

→ **1** The `ActionListener` interface is part of the `java.awt.event` package, so this `import` statement is required.

→ **2** The `Timer` class is part of the `javax.swing` package, so this `import` statement is required.

→**10** This statement creates a new `Timer` object. The timer's interval is set to 1,000 milliseconds — which is equivalent to one second. A new instance of the `Ticker` class is passed as the second parameter. The timer calls this object's `actionPerformed` method at each timer tick — in other words, once per second.

→**11** This statement calls the `start` method to kick the timer into action.

→**15** The `JOptionPane` class is used to display a dialog box that tells the user to click the OK button to stop the application. You might think I included this dialog box to give the user a way to end the program. But in reality, I used it to give the timer some time to run. If you just end the `main` method after starting the timer, the application ends, which kills the timer. By using `JOptionPane` here, the application continues to run as long as the dialog box is displayed. (For more information about `JOptionPane`, see Book II, Chapter 2.)

→**20** The declaration of the `Ticker` class, which implements the `Action Listener` interface.

→**22** A private boolean class field that's used to keep track of whether the `Ticker` displays `Tick. . .` or `Tock. . .` Each time the `actionPerformed` method is called, this field is toggled.

→**24** The `actionPerformed` method, which is called at each timer interval.

→**28** Prints `Tick. . .` on the console if `tick` is true.

→**32** Prints `Tock. . .` on the console if `tick` is false.

→**34** Toggles the value of the `tick` variable. In other words, if `tick` is true, it's set to `false`. If `tick` is false, it's set to `true`.

Chapter 6: Using the Object and Class Classes

In This Chapter

✔ Using the `toString` method

✔ Implementing the `equals` method

✔ Trying out the `clone` method

✔ Understanding the `Class` class

1n this chapter, you find out how to use two classes of the Java API that are important to object-oriented programming:

✦ The `Object` class, which every other class inherits — including all the classes in the Java API and any class you create yourself

✦ The `Class` class, which is used to get information about an object's type

If I could, I'd plant a huge Technical Stuff icon on this entire chapter. All this stuff is a bit on the technical side, and many Java programmers get by for years without understanding or using it. Still, I recommend you read this chapter carefully. Even if it all doesn't sink in, it may help explain why some things in Java don't work quite the way you think they should, and the information in this chapter may someday help you program your way out of a difficult corner.

The Mother of All Classes: Object

`Object` is the mother of all classes. In Java, every class ultimately inherits the `Object` class. This class provides a set of methods that are available to every Java object.

Every object is an Object

Any class that doesn't have an `extends` clause implicitly inherits `Object`. Thus, you never have to code a class like this:

```
public class Product extends Object...
```

If a subclass has an `extends` clause that specifies a superclass other than `Object`, the class still inherits `Object`. That's because the inheritance hierarchy eventually gets to a superclass that doesn't have an `extends` clause, and that superclass inherits `Object` and passes it down to all its subclasses.

For example, suppose you have these classes:

```
public class Manager extends SalariedEmployee...

public class SalariedEmployee extends Employee...

public class Employee extends Person...

public class Person...
```

Here, the `Manager` class inherits the `Object` class indirectly because it inherits `SalariedEmployee`, which inherits `Employee`, which inherits `Person`, and `Person` inherits `Object`.

In Java, creating a class that doesn't inherit `Object` is not possible.

Using Object as a type

If you don't know or care about the type of an object referenced by a variable, you can specify its type as `Object`. For example, the following is perfectly legal:

```
Object emp = new Employee();
```

However, you can't do anything useful with the `emp` variable, because the compiler doesn't know it's an `Employee`. For example, if the `Employee` class has a method named `setLastName`, the following code doesn't work:

```
Object emp = new Employee();
emp.setLastName("Smith");      // error: won't compile
```

Because `emp` is an `Object`, not an `Employee`, the compiler doesn't know about the `setLastName` method.

Note that you could still cast the object to an `Employee`:

```
Object emp = new Employee();
((Employee)emp).setLastName("Smith");  // this works
```

But what's the point? You may as well make `emp` an `Employee` in the first place.

Declaring a variable, parameter, or return type as Object, however, in certain situations does make perfect sense. For example, the Java API provides a set of classes designed to maintain collections of objects. One of the most commonly used of these classes is the ArrayList class. It has a method named add that accepts an Object as a parameter. This method adds the specified object to the collection. Because the parameter type is Object, you can use the ArrayList class to create collections of any type of object. (For more information about the ArrayList class and other collection classes, see Book IV.)

Methods of the Object class

Table 6-1 lists all the methods of the Object class. Ordinarily, I wouldn't list all the methods of a class — I'd just list the ones that I think are most useful. However, because Object is such an important player in the game of object-oriented programming, I thought showing you all its capabilities is best, even though some of them are a bit obscure.

I warned you, this entire chapter should have a Technical Stuff icon.

Table 6-1	Methods of the Object Class
Method	*What It Does*
protected Object clone()	Returns a copy of this object.
boolean equals(Object obj)	Indicates whether this object is equal to the obj object.
protected void finalize()	Called by the garbage collector when the object is destroyed.
Class getClass()	Returns a Class object that represents this object's runtime class.
int hashCode()	Returns this object's hash code.
void notify()	Used with threaded applications to wake up a thread that's waiting on this object.
void notifyAll()	Used with threaded applications to wake up all threads that are waiting on this object.
String toString()	Returns a String representation of this object.
void wait()	Causes this object's thread to wait until another thread calls notify or notifyAll.
void wait(Long timeout)	A variation of the basic wait method.
void wait(Long timeout, int nanos)	Yet another variation of the wait method.

**Book III
Chapter 6**

Using the Object and Class Classes

Note: Almost half of these methods (notify, notifyAll, and the three wait methods) are related to threading. You find complete information about those five methods in Book V, Chapter 1. Here's the rundown on the remaining six methods:

✦ **clone:** This method is commonly used to make copies of objects, and overriding it in your own classes is not uncommon. I explain this method in detail later in this chapter, in the section "The clone Method."

✦ **equals:** This method is commonly used to compare objects. Any class that represents an object that can be compared with another object should override this method. Turn to the section "The equals Method" later in this chapter, for more info.

✦ **finalize:** This method is called when the garbage collector realizes that an object is no longer being used and can be discarded. The intent of this method was to allow you to create objects that clean up after themselves by closing open files and performing other clean-up tasks before being discarded. But because of the way the Java garbage collector works, there's no guarantee that the finalize method actually ever is called. As a result, this method isn't commonly used.

✦ **getClass:** This method is sometimes used in conjunction with the Class class, which I described later in this chapter in the section "The Class Class."

✦ **hashCode:** Every Java object has a *hash code,* which is an int representation of the class that's useful for certain operations. This method isn't terribly important until you start to work with hash tables, which is a pretty advanced technique best left to people with pocket protectors and tape holding their glasses together.

✦ **toString:** This method is one of the most commonly used methods in Java. I describe it in the section "The toString Method" later in this chapter.

Primitives aren't objects

I need to note that primitive types, such as int and double, are not objects. As a result, they do not inherit the Object class and don't have access to the methods listed in the previous section.

As a result, the following code won't work:

```
int x = 50;
String s = x.toString();   // error: won't compile
```

If you really want to convert an int to a string in this way, you can use a wrapper class such as Integer to create an object from the value, and then call its toString method:

```
String s = new Integer(x).toString();   // OK
```

Each of the wrapper classes also defines a static toString method you can use like this:

```
String s = Integer.toString(x);
```

Sometimes using the compiler shortcut that lets you use primitive types in string concatenation expressions is easier:

```
String s = "" + x;
```

Here, the int variable x is concatenated with an empty string.

The point of all this is that primitive types aren't objects, so they don't inherit anything from Object. If you want to treat a primitive value as an object, you can use the primitive type's wrapper class as I describe in Book II, Chapter 2.

The toString Method

The toString method returns a String representation of an object. By default, the toString method returns the name of the object's class plus its hash code. In the sections that follow, I show you how to use the toString method and how to override it in your own classes to create more useful strings.

Using toString

Here's a simple program that puts the toString method to work:

```
public class TestToString
{
    public static void main(String[] args)
    {
        Employee emp = new Employee("Martinez",
            "Anthony");
        System.out.println(emp.toString());
    }
}

class Employee
{
    private String lastName;
    private String firstName;

    public Employee(String lastName, String firstName)
    {
        this.lastName = lastName;
        this.firstName = firstName;
    }
}
```

Here, this code creates a new Employee object, and then the result of its toString method is printed to the console. When you run this program, the following line is printed on the console:

```
Employee@82ba41
```

Book III
Chapter 6

Using the Object and Class Classes

Note: The hash code — in this case, `82ba41` — may be different on your system.

It turns out that the explicit call to `toString` isn't really necessary in this example. I could have just as easily written the second line of the `main` method like this:

```
System.out.println(emp);
```

That's because the `println` method automatically calls the `toString` method of any object you pass it.

Overriding toString

The default implementation of `toString` isn't very useful in most situations. For example, you don't really learn much about an `Employee` object by seeing its hash code. Wouldn't it be better if the `toString` method returned some actual data from the object, such as the employee's name?

To do that, you must override the `toString` method in your classes. In fact, one of the basic guidelines of object-oriented programming in Java is to *always* override `toString`. Here's a simple program with an `Employee` class that overrides `toString`:

```
public class TestToString
{
    public static void main(String[] args)
    {
        Employee emp = new Employee("Martinez",
            "Anthony");
        System.out.println(emp.toString());
    }
}

class Employee
{
    private String lastName;
    private String firstName;

    public Employee(String lastName, String firstName)
    {
        this.lastName = lastName;
        this.firstName = firstName;
    }

    public String toString()
    {
        return "Employee["
            + this.firstName + " "
            + this.lastName + "]";
    }
}
```

When you run this program, the following line is displayed on the console:

```
Employee[Anthony Martinez]
```

Note that the output consists of the class name followed by some data from the object in brackets. This convention is common in Java programming.

The only problem with the preceding example is that the class name is hard-coded into the `toString` method. You can use the `getClass` method to retrieve the actual class name at runtime:

```java
public String toString()
{
    return this.getClass().getName() + "["
        + this.firstName + " "
        + this.lastName + "]";
}
```

Here, the `getClass` method returns a `Class` object that represents the class of the current object. Then, the `Class` object's `getName` method is used to get the actual class name. (You discover more about the `Class` object later in this chapter.)

The equals Method

Testing objects to see if they are equal is one of the basic tasks of any object-oriented programming language. Unfortunately, Java isn't very good at it. For example, consider this program:

```java
public class TestEquality1
{
    public static void main(String[] args)
    {
        Employee emp1 = new Employee(
            "Martinez", "Anthony");
        Employee emp2 = new Employee(
            "Martinez", "Anthony");
        if (emp1 == emp2)
            System.out.println(
                "These employees are the same.");
        else
            System.out.println(
                "These are different employees.");
    }
}

class Employee
{
    private String lastName;
```

```
    private String firstName;

    public Employee(String lastName, String firstName)
    {
        this.lastName = lastName;
        this.firstName = firstName;
    }
}
```

Here, the `main` method creates two `Employee` objects with identical data, and then compares them. Alas, the comparison returns `false`. Even though the `Employee` objects have identical data, they're not considered to be equal. That's because the equality operator (`==`) compares the object references, not the data contained by the objects. Thus, the comparison returns `true` only if both `emp1` and `emp2` refer to the same instance of the `Employee` class.

If you want to create objects that are considered to be equal if they contain identical data, you have to do two things:

1. Compare them with the `equals` method rather than the equality operator.

2. Override the `equals` method in your class to compare objects based on their data.

The following sections describe both of these steps.

Using equals

To test objects using the `equals` method rather than the equality operator, you simply rewrite the comparison expression like this:

```
if (emp1.equals(emp2))
    System.out.println("These employees are the same.");
else
    System.out.println("These are different
    employees.");
```

Here, the `equals` method of `emp1` is used to compare `emp1` with `emp2`.

By default, the `equals` operator returns the same result as the equality operator. So just replacing `==` with the `equals` method doesn't have any effect unless you also override the `equals` method, as explained in the next section.

Which object's `equals` method you use shouldn't matter. Thus, this `if` statement returns the same result:

```
if (emp2.equals(emp1))
    System.out.println("These employees are the same.");
else
    System.out.println("These are different employees.");
```

Note that I said it *shouldn't* matter. Whenever you override the `equals` method, you're supposed to make sure that comparisons work in both directions. However, sloppy programming sometimes results in `equals` methods where a equals b but b doesn't equal a. So be on your toes.

Overriding the equals method

You can override the `equals` method so that objects can be compared based on their values. At the surface, you might think this is easy to do. For example, you might be tempted to write the `equals` method for the `Employee` class like this:

```
// warning -- there are several errors in this code!
public boolean equals(Employee emp)
{
    if (this.getLastName().equals(emp.getLastName())
     && this.getFirstName().equals(emp.getFirstName())
    )
        return true;
    else
        return false;
}
```

The basic problem with this code — and the challenge of coding a good `equals` method — is that the parameter passed to the `equals` method must be an `Object`, not an `Employee`. That means that the `equals` method must be prepared to deal with anything that comes its way. For example, someone might try to compare an `Employee` object with a `Banana` object. Or with a null. The `equals` method must be prepared to deal with all possibilities.

Specifically, the Java API documentation says that whenever you override the `equals` method, you must ensure that the `equals` method meets five specific conditions. Here they are, quoted right out of the API documentation:

✦ It is *reflexive*. For any non-null reference value x, x.equals(x) should return `true`.

✦ It is *symmetric*. For any non-null reference values x and y, x.equals(y) should return `true` if and only if y.equals(x) returns `true`.

✦ It is *transitive*. For any non-null reference values x, y, and z, if x.equals(y) returns `true` and y.equals(z) returns `true`, then x.equals(z) should return `true`.

✦ It is *consistent*. For any non-null reference values x and y, multiple invocations of x.equals(y) consistently return `true` or consistently return `false`, provided no information used in equals comparisons on the objects is modified.

✦ For any non-null reference value x, x.equals(null) should return `false`.

Sound confusing? Fortunately, it's not as complicated as it seems at first. You can safely ignore the transitive rule, because if you get the other rules right, this one happens automatically. And the consistency rule basically means that you return consistent results. As long as you don't throw a call to `Math.random` into the comparison, that shouldn't be a problem.

Here's a general formula for creating a good `equals` method (assume the parameter is named `obj`):

1. **Test the reflexive rule.**

Use a statement like this:

```
if (this == obj)
    return true;
```

In other words, if someone is silly enough to see if an object is equal to itself, it returns `true`.

2. **Test the non-null rule.**

Use a statement like this:

```
if (this == null)
    return false;
```

Null isn't equal to anything.

3. **Test that `obj` is of the same type as `this`.**

You can use the `getClass` method to do that, like this:

```
if (this.getClass() != obj.getClass())
    return false;
```

The two objects can't possibly be the same if they aren't of the same type. (It may not be apparent at first, but this test is required to fulfill the symmetry rule — that if x equals y, then y must also equal x.)

4. **Cast `obj` to a variable of your class. Then, compare the fields you want to base the return value on and return the result.**

Here's an example:

```
Employee emp = (Employee) obj;
return this.lastName.equals(emp.getLastName())
    && this.firstname.equals(emp.getFirstName());
```

Notice that the field comparisons for the String values use the `equals` method rather than ==. This is because you can't trust == to compare strings. If you need to compare primitive types, you can use ==. But you should use `equals` to compare strings and any other reference types.

Putting it all together, Listing 6-1 shows a program that compares two `Employee` objects using a properly constructed `equals` method.

LISTING 6-1: COMPARING OBJECTS

```
public class TestEquality2
{
    public static void main(String[] args)
    {
        Employee emp1 = new Employee(                    → 5
            "Martinez", "Anthony");
        Employee emp2 = new Employee(                    → 7
            "Martinez", "Anthony");
        if (emp1.equals(emp2))                           → 9
            System.out.println(
                "These employees are the same.");
        else
            System.out.println(
                "These are different employees.");
    }
}

class Employee                                           → 18
{
    private String lastName;
    private String firstName;

    public Employee(String lastName, String firstName)
    {
        this.lastName = lastName;
        this.firstName = firstName;
    }

    public String getLastName()
    {
        return this.lastName;
    }

    public String getFirstName()
    {
        return this.firstName;
    }

    public boolean equals(Object obj)                    → 39
    {
        // an object must equal itself
        if (this == obj)                                 → 42
            return true;

        // no object equals null
        if (this == null)                                → 46
            return false;
```

Book III
Chapter 6

Using the Object
and Class Classes

continued

LISTING 6-1 (CONTINUED)

```
    // objects of different types are never equal
    if (this.getClass() != obj.getClass())              → 50
        return false;

    // cast to an Employee, then compare the fields
    Employee emp = (Employee) obj;                      → 54
    return this.lastName.equals(emp.getLastName())      → 55
        && this.firstName.equals(emp.getFirstName());
    }
}
```

Following are some noteworthy points in this listing:

→ **5** Creates an Employee object with the name Anthony Martinez.

→ **7** Creates another Employee object with the name Anthony Martinez.

→ **9** Compares the two Employee objects using the equals method.

→**18** The Employee class.

→**39** The overridden equals method.

→**42** Returns true if the same object instances are being compared. This meets the first equality test, that an object must always be equal to itself.

→**46** Returns false if the object being compared is null. This meets the last equality test, that nothing is equal to null.

→**50** Returns false if the object being compared isn't of the correct type. This helps ensure the symmetry test, that if x equals y, then y must equal x.

→**54** Having slid through the other tests, you can now assume that you're comparing two different Employee objects. So the next step is to cast the other object to an Employee.

→**55** Having cast the other object to an Employee, the two fields (lastName and firstName) are compared and the result of the compound comparison is returned.

The clone Method

Cloning refers to the process of making an exact duplicate of an object. Unfortunately, this process turns out to be a pretty difficult task in an object-oriented language such as Java. You'd think cloning would be as easy as this:

```
Employee emp1 = new Employee("Stewart", "Martha");
Employee emp2 = emp1;
```

However, this code doesn't make a copy of the Employee object at all. Instead, you now have two variables that refer to the same object, which usually isn't what you want. For example, suppose you execute these statements:

```
emp1.setLastName("Washington");
emp2.setLastName("Graham");
String lastName = emp1.getLastName();
```

After these statements execute, does lastName return Washington or Graham? The correct answer is Graham, because both emp1 and emp2 refer to the same Employee object.

In contrast, a *clone* is an altogether new object that has the same values as the original object. You can often manually create a clone using code like this:

```
Employee emp1 = new Employee("Stewart", "Martha");
Employee emp2 = new Employee();
emp2.setLastName(emp1.getLastName());
emp2.setFirstName(emp1.getFirstName());
emp2.setSalary(emp1.getSalary());
```

Here, a new Employee object is created and its fields are set to the same values as the original object.

Book III
Chapter 6

Using the Object
and Class Classes

Java provides a more elegant way to create object copies — the clone method, which is available to all classes because it's inherited from the Object class. However, as you discover in the following sections, the clone method can be difficult to create and use. For this reason, you want to implement it only for those classes that you think can really benefit from cloning.

Implementing the clone method

The clone method is defined by the Object class, so it's available to all Java classes. However, clone is declared with protected access in the Object class. As a result, the clone method for a given class is available only within that class. If you want other objects to be able to clone your object, you must override the clone method and give it public access.

Note that the clone method defined by the Object class returns an Object type. That makes perfect sense, because the Object class doesn't know the type of the class that you'll be overriding the clone method in. An inconvenient side-effect of this is that whenever you call the clone method for a class that overrides clone, you must cast the result to the desired object type.

Listing 6-2 gives a simple example of a program that clones Employee objects. In a nutshell, this program overrides the clone method for the Employee class. It creates an employee, and then clones it. Then, it changes the name of the original Employee object and prints out both objects to the console.

LISTING 6-2: A CLONING EXAMPLE

```
public class CloneTest
{
    public static void main(String[] args)
    {
        Employee emp1 = new Employee(                    → 5
            "Martinez", "Anthony");
        emp1.setSalary(40000.0);                         → 7
        Employee emp2 = (Employee)emp1.clone();          → 8
        emp1.setLastName("Smith");                       → 9
        System.out.println(emp1);                        → 10
        System.out.println(emp2);                        → 11
    }
}

class Employee                                           → 15
{
    private String lastName;
    private String firstName;
    private Double salary;

    public Employee(String lastName, String firstName)
    {
        this.lastName = lastName;
        this.firstName = firstName;
    }

    public String getLastName()
    {
        return this.lastName;
    }

    public void setLastName(String lastName)
    {
        this.lastName = lastName;
    }

    public String getFirstName()
    {
        return this.firstName;
    }

    public void setFirstName(String firstName)
```

```
    {
        this.firstName = firstName;
    }

    public Double getSalary()
    {
        return this.salary;
    }

    public void setSalary(Double salary)
    {
        this.salary = salary;
    }

    public Object clone()                          → 57
    {
        Employee emp;
        emp = new Employee(                        → 60
            this.lastName, this.firstName);
        emp.setSalary(this.salary);                → 62
        return emp;                                → 63
    }

    public String toString()
    {
        return this.getClass().getName() + "["
            + this.firstName + " "
            + this.lastName + ", "
            + this.salary + "]";
    }
}
```

When you run this program, the following lines appear on the console:

```
Employee[Anthony Smith, 40000.0]
Employee[Anthony Martinez, 40000.0]
```

As you can see, the name of the second `Employee` object was successfully changed without affecting the name of the first `Employee` object.

The following paragraphs draw your attention to some of the highlights of this program:

→ **5** Creates the first `Employee` object for an employee named Anthony Martinez.

→ **7** Sets Mr. Martinez' salary.

→ **8** Creates a clone of the `Employee` object for Mr. Martinez. Notice that the return value must be cast to an `Employee`. That's because the return value of the `clone` method is `Object`.

→ **9** Changes the last name for the second `Employee` object.

→**10** Prints the first `Employee` object.

→**11** Prints the second `Employee` object.

→**15** The `Employee` class. This class defines private fields to store the last name, first name, and salary, as well as getter and setter methods for each field.

→**57** This method overrides the `clone` method. Notice that its return type is `Object`, not `Employee`.

→**60** Creates a new `Employee` object using the last name and first name from the current object.

→**62** Sets the new employee's salary to the current object's salary.

→**63** Returns the cloned `Employee` object.

Using clone to create a shallow copy

In the previous example, the `clone` method manually creates a copy of the original object and returns it. In many cases, this is the easiest way to create a clone. However, what if your class has a hundred or more fields that need to be duplicated? Then, the chance of accidentally forgetting to copy one of the fields is high. And, if you later add a field to the class, you may forget to modify the `clone` method to include the new field.

Fortunately, you can solve this problem by using the `clone` method of the `Object` class directly in your own `clone` method. The `clone` method of the `Object` class can automatically create a copy of your object that contains duplicates of all the fields that are primitive types (such as `int` and `double`) as well as copies of immutable reference types — most notably, strings. So, if all the fields in your class are either primitives or strings, you can use the `clone` method provided by the `Object` class to clone your class.

This type of clone is known as a *shallow copy* for reasons I explain in the next section.

To call the `clone` method from your own `clone` method, just specify `super.clone()`. Before you can do that, however, you must do two things:

✦ Declare that the class supports the `Cloneable` interface. The `Cloneable` interface is a tagging interface that doesn't provide any methods. It simply marks a class as being appropriate for cloning.

✦ Enclose the call to `super.clone()` in a `try/catch` statement that catches the exception `CloneNotSupportedException`. This exception is thrown if you try to call `clone` on a class that doesn't implement the

`Cloneable` interface. Provided you implement `Cloneable`, this exception won't ever happen. But because `CloneNotSupportedException` is a checked exception, you must catch it.

Here's an example of an `Employee` class with a clone method that uses `super.clone()` to clone itself:

```
class Employee implements Cloneable
{
    // Fields and methods omitted...

    public Object clone()
    {
        Employee emp;
        try
        {
            emp = (Employee) super.clone();
        }
        catch (CloneNotSupportedException e)
        {
            return null;   // will never happen
        }
        return emp;
    }
}
```

Notice that this method doesn't have to be aware of any of the fields declared in the `Employee` class. However, this `clone` method works only for classes whose fields are all either primitive types or immutable objects such as strings.

Creating deep copies

It's not uncommon for some fields in a class to actually be other objects. For example, the `Employee` class might have a field of type `Address` that's used to store each employee's address:

```
class Employee
{
    public Address address;

    // other fields and methods omitted
}
```

If that's the case, the `super.clone()` method won't make a complete copy of the object. The clone won't get a clone of the address field. Instead, it has a reference to the same address object as the original.

To solve this problem, you must do a *deep copy* of the `Employee` object. A deep copy is a clone in which any subobjects within the main object are also cloned. To accomplish this feat, the `clone` method override first calls `super.clone()` to create a shallow copy of the object. Then, it calls the `clone` method of each of the subobjects contained by the main object to create clones of those objects. (Of course, for a deep copy to work, those objects must also support the `clone` methods.)

Listing 6-3 shows an example. Here, an `Employee` class contains a public field named `address`, which holds an instance of the `Address` class. As you can see, the `clone` method of the `Employee` class creates a shallow copy of the `Employee` object, and then sets the copy's `address` field to a clone of the original object's `address` field. To make this example work, the `Address` class also overrides the `clone` method. Its `clone` method calls `super.clone()` to create a shallow copy of the `Address` object.

LISTING 6-3: CREATING A DEEP COPY

```
public class CloneTest2
{
    public static void main(String[] args)
    {
        Employee emp1 = new Employee(                       → 5
            "Martinez", "Anthony");
        emp1.setSalary(40000.0);
        emp1.address = new Address(                         → 8
            "1300 N. First Street",
            "Fresno", "CA", "93702");
        Employee emp2 = (Employee)emp1.clone();             → 11

        System.out.println(                                 → 13
            "**** after cloning ****\n");
        printEmployee(emp1);
        printEmployee(emp2);

        emp2.setLastName("Smith");                          → 18
        emp2.address = new Address(                         → 19
            "2503 N. 6th Street",
            "Fresno", "CA", "93722");

        System.out.println(                                 → 23
            "**** after changing emp2 ****\n");
        printEmployee(emp1);
        printEmployee(emp2);

    }
```

```
      private static void printEmployee(Employee e)          → 30
      {
          System.out.println(e.getFirstName()
              + " " + e.getLastName());
          System.out.println(e.address.getAddress());
          System.out.println("Salary: " + e.getSalary());
          System.out.println();
      }
}

class Employee implements Cloneable                          → 40
{
      private String lastName;
      private String firstName;
      private Double salary;

      public Address address;                                → 46

      public Employee(String lastName, String firstName)
      {
          this.lastName = lastName;
          this.firstName = firstName;
          this.address = new Address();
      }

      public String getLastName()
      {
          return this.lastName;
      }

      public void setLastName(String lastName)
      {
          this.lastName = lastName;
      }

      public String getFirstName()
      {
          return this.firstName;
      }

      public void setFirstName(String firstName)
      {
          this.firstName = firstName;
      }

      public Double getSalary()
      {
          return this.salary;
      }
```

Book III
Chapter 6

Using the Object
and Class Classes

continued

LISTING 6-3 (CONTINUED)

```
public void setSalary(Double salary)
{
    this.salary = salary;
}

public Object clone()                                      → 85
{
    Employee emp;
    try
    {
        emp = (Employee) super.clone();                    → 90
        emp.address = (Address)address.clone();            → 91
    }
    catch (CloneNotSupportedException e)                   → 93
    {
        return null;    // will never happen
    }
    return emp;                                            → 97
}

public String toString()
{
    return this.getClass().getName() + "["
        + this.firstName + " "
        + this.lastName + ", "
        + this.salary + "]";
}
}

class Address implements Cloneable                         → 109
{
    private String street;
    private String city;
    private String state;
    private String zipCode;

    public Address()
    {
        this.street = "";
        this.city = "";
        this.state = "";
        this.zipCode = "";
    }

    public Address(String street, String city,
                String state, String zipCode)
    {
        this.street = street;
        this.city = city;
```

```
        this.state = state;
        this.zipCode = zipCode;
    }

    public Object clone()                                    → 133
    {
        try
        {
            return super.clone();                            → 137
        }
        catch (CloneNotSupportedException e)
        {
            return null;    // will never happen
        }
    }

    public String getAddress()
    {
        return this.street + "\n"
            + this.city + ", "
            + this.state + " "
            + this.zipCode;
    }
}
```

The main method in the CloneTest2 class creates an Employee object and sets its name, salary, and address. Then, it creates a clone of this object and prints the data contained in both objects. Next, it changes the last name and address of the second employee and prints the data again. Here's the output that's produced when this program is run:

```
**** after cloning ****

Anthony Martinez
1300 N. First Street
Fresno, CA 93702
Salary: 40000.0

Anthony Martinez
1300 N. First Street
Fresno, CA 93702
Salary: 40000.0

**** after changing emp2 ****

Anthony Martinez
1300 N. First Street
Fresno, CA 93702
Salary: 40000.0
```

```
Anthony Smith
2503 N. 6th Street
Fresno, CA 93722
Salary: 40000.0
```

As you can see, the two `Employee` objects have identical data after they are cloned. But they have different data after the fields for the second employee have been changed. Thus, you can safely change the data in one of the objects without affecting the other object.

The following paragraphs describe some of the highlights of this program:

→ **5** Creates an employee named Anthony Martinez.

→ **8** Sets the employee's address.

→ **11** Clones the employee.

→ **13** Prints the two `Employee` objects after cloning. They should have identical data.

→ **18** Changes the second employee's name.

→ **19** Changes the second employee's address.

→ **23** Prints the two `Employee` objects after changing the data for the second employee. The objects should now have different data.

→ **30** A utility method that prints the data for an `Employee` object.

→ **40** The `Employee` class. Notice that this class implements `Cloneable`.

→ **46** The `address` field, which holds an object of type `Address`.

→ **85** The `clone` method in the `Employee` class.

→ **90** Creates a shallow copy of the `Employee` object.

→ **91** Creates a shallow copy of the `Address` object and assigns it to the `address` field of the cloned `Employee` object.

→ **93** Catches `CloneNotSupportedException`, which won't ever happen because the class implements `Cloneable`. The compiler requires the `try/catch` statement here because `CloneNotSupportedException` is a checked exception.

→ **97** Returns the cloned `Employee` object.

→ **109** The `Address` class, which also implements `Cloneable`.

→ **133** The `clone` method of the `Address` class.

→ **137** Returns a shallow copy of the `Address` object.

The Class Class

Okay class, it's time for one last class before finishing this chapter: the `Class` class. This might get confusing, so put your thinking cap on. Every class used by a Java application is represented in memory by an object of type `Class`. For example, if your program uses `Employee` objects, there's also a `Class` object for the `Employee` class. This `Class` object has information not about specific employees, but about the `Employee` class itself.

You've already seen how you can get a `Class` object by using the `getClass` method. This method is defined by the `Object` class, so it's available to every object. For example:

```
Employee emp = new Employee();
Class c = emp.getClass();
```

Note that you have to initialize a variable with an object instance before you can call its `getClass` method. That's because the `getClass` method returns a `Class` object that corresponds to the type of object the variable refers to, not the type the variable is declared as.

For example, suppose an `HourlyEmployee` class extends the `Employee` class. Then consider these statements:

```
HourlyEmployee emp = new Employee();
Class c = emp.getClass();
```

Here, c refers to a `Class` object for the `HourlyEmployee` class, not the `Employee` class.

The `Class` class has more than 50 methods, but only two of them are worthy of your attention:

+ **getName():** Returns a String representing the name of the class

+ **getSuperclass():** Returns another `Class` object representing this `Class` object's superclass

If you're interested in the other capabilities of the `Class` class, you can always check it out in the Java API documentation.

One of the most common uses of the `getClass` method is to tell if two objects are of the same type by comparing their `Class` objects. This works because Java guarantees that the `Class` object has only one instance for each different class used by the application. So, even if your application instantiates 1,000 `Employee` objects, there is only one `Class` object for the `Employee` class.

As a result, the following code can determine if two objects are both objects of the same type:

```
Object o1 = new Employee();
Object o2 = new Employee();
if (o1.getClass() == o2.getClass())
    System.out.println("They're the same.");
else
    System.out.println("They are not the same.");
```

In this case, the type of both objects is Employee, so the comparison is true.

To find out if an object is of a particular type, use the object's getClass method to get the corresponding Class object. Then, use the getName method to get the class name, and use a string comparison to check the class name. For example:

```
if (emp.getClass().getName().equals("Employee"))
    System.out.println("This is an employee object.");
```

If all the strung-out method calls give you a headache, you can break it apart:

```
Class c = emp.getClass();
String s = c.getName();
if (s.equals("Employee"))
    System.out.println("This is an employee object.");
```

The result is the same.

Chapter 7: Using Inner Classes

In This Chapter

✔ Using inner classes

✔ Creating static inner classes

✔ Implementing anonymous classes

In this chapter, you find out how to use three advanced types of classes: inner classes, static inner classes, and anonymous inner classes. All three are useful in certain circumstances. In particular, inner classes and anonymous inner classes are commonly used with graphical applications created with Swing. For more information about Swing, refer to Book VI. In this chapter, I just concentrate on the mechanics of creating these types of classes.

Once again, this chapter could have a Technical Stuff icon pasted next to every other paragraph. The usefulness of some of the information I present in this chapter may seem questionable. But trust me, you need to know this stuff when you start writing Swing applications. If you want to skip this chapter for now, that's okay. You can always come back to it when you're learning Swing and you need to know how inner classes and anonymous inner classes work.

Declaring Inner Classes

An *inner class* is a class that's declared inside of another class. Thus, the basic structure for creating an inner class is as follows:

```
class outerClassName
{
    private class innerClassName
    {
        // body of inner class
    }
}
```

The class that contains the inner class is called an *outer class*. You can use a visibility modifier with the inner class to specify whether the class should be `public`, `protected`, or `private`. This visibility determines whether other classes can see the inner class.

Understanding inner classes

At the surface, an inner class is simply a class that's contained inside another class. However, there's more to it than that. Here are some key points about inner classes:

✦ An inner class automatically has access to all the fields and methods of the outer class — even private fields and methods. Thus, an inner class has more access to its outer class than a subclass has to its superclass. (A subclass can access public and protected members of its superclass, but not private members.)

✦ An inner class carries with it a reference to the current instance of the outer class that enables it to access instance data for the outer class.

✦ Because of the outer class instance reference, you can't create or refer to an inner class from a static method of the outer class. You can, however, create a *static inner class,* as I describe in the section "Using Static Inner Classes" later in this chapter.

✦ One of the main reasons for creating an inner class is to create a class that's only of interest to the outer class. As a result, you usually declare inner classes to be private so other classes can't access them.

✦ Occasionally, code in an inner class needs to refer to the instance of its outer class. To do that, you list the name of the outer class followed by the dot operator and `this`. For example, if the outer class is named `MyOuterClass`, you would use `MyOuterClass.this` to refer to the instance of the outer class.

An example

Book III, Chapter 5 introduces an application that uses the `Timer` class in the Swing package (`javax.swing.Timer`) that displays the lines `Tick...` and `Tock...` on the console at a one second interval. It uses a class named `Ticker` that implements the `ActionListener` interface to handle the `Timer` object's clock events.

In this chapter, you see a total of three different versions of this application. You may want to quickly review Book III, Chapter 5 if you're unclear on how this application uses the `Timer` class to display the `Tick...` and `Tock...` messages, or why the `JOptionPane` dialog box is required.

Listing 7-1 shows a version of this application that implements the `Ticker` class as an inner class.

LISTING 7-1: TICK TOCK WITH AN INNER CLASS

```java
import java.awt.event.*;
import javax.swing.*;

public class TickTockInner
{
    private String tickMessage = "Tick...";          → 6
    private String tockMessage = "Tock...";          → 7

    public static void main(String[] args)
    {
        TickTockInner t = new TickTockInner();       → 11
        t.go();                                      → 12
    }

    private void go()                                → 15
    {
        // create a timer that calls the Ticker class
        // at one second intervals
        Timer t = new Timer(1000, new Ticker());     → 19
        t.start();

        // display a message box to prevent the
        // program from ending immediately
        JOptionPane.showMessageDialog(null,          → 24
            "Click OK to exit program");
        System.exit(0);                              → 26
    }

    class Ticker implements ActionListener           → 29
    {
        private boolean tick = true;

        public void actionPerformed(ActionEvent event) → 33
        {
            if (tick)
            {
                System.out.println(tickMessage);     → 37
            }
            else
            {
                System.out.println(tockMessage);     → 41
            }
            tick = !tick;
        }
    }
}
```

The Observer Pattern

Event listeners in Java are part of a Java model called the Delegation Event Model. The Delegation Event Model is an implementation of a more general design pattern called the Observer pattern. This pattern is useful when you need to create objects that interact with each other when a change in the status of one of the objects occurs. The object whose changes are being monitored is called the *observable object*, and the object that monitors those changes is called the *observer object*. The observer object registers itself with the observable object, which then notifies the observer object when its status changes.

You discover more about how Java implements this pattern for event handling in Book VI. But if you're interested, you may want to investigate the `Observer` and `Observable` interfaces that are a part of the Java API. They provide a standard way to create simple implementations of the Observer pattern.

The following paragraphs describe some of the highlights of this program:

→ **6** The String variables named `tickMessage` and `tockMessage` (line 7) contain the messages to be printed on the console. Note that these variables are defined as fields of the outer class. As you'll see, the inner class `Ticker` is able to directly access these fields.

→ **11** Because an inner class can only be used by an instantiated object, you can't use it directly from the static `main` method. As a result, the `main` method in this program simply creates an instance of the application class (`TickTockInner`).

→ **12** This line executes the `go` method of the new instance of the `TickTockInner` class.

The technique used in lines 11 and 12 is a fairly common programming technique that lets an application quickly get out of a static context and into an object-oriented mode.

→ **15** The `go` method, called from line 12.

→ **19** This line creates an instance of the `Timer` class with the timer interval set to 1,000 milliseconds (1 second) and the `ActionListener` set to a new instance of the inner class named `Ticker`.

→ **24** Here, the `JOptionPane` class is used to display a dialog box. This dialog box is necessary to give the timer a chance to run. The application ends when the user clicks OK.

→ **26** This line calls the `exit` method of the `System` class, which immediately shuts down the Java Virtual Machine. This method call isn't strictly required here, but if you leave it out, the timer continues to run for a few seconds after you click OK before the JVM figures out that it should kill the timer.

→29 This line is the declaration for the inner class named `Ticker`. Note that this class implements the `ActionListener` interface.

→33 The `actionPerformed` method is called by the `Timer` object every 1,000 milliseconds.

→37 In this line and in line 41, the inner class directly accesses a field of the outer class.

Using Static Inner Classes

A *static inner class* is similar to an inner class, but doesn't require an instance of the outer class. Its basic form is the following:

```
class outerClassName
{
    private static class innerClassName
    {
        // body of inner class
    }
}
```

Like a static method, a static inner class can't access any non-static fields or methods in its outer class. It can, however, access static fields or methods.

Listing 7-2 shows a version of the Tick Tock application that uses a static inner class rather than a regular inner class.

Book III Chapter 7

Using Inner Classes

LISTING 7-2: TICK TOCK WITH A STATIC INNER CLASS

```
import java.awt.event.*;
import javax.swing.*;

public class TickTockStatic
{
    private static String tickMessage = "Tick...";      → 6
    private static String tockMessage = "Tock...";      → 7

    public static void main(String[] args)
    {
        TickTockStatic t = new TickTockStatic();
        t.go();
    }
```

continued

LISTING 7-2 (CONTINUED)

```
    private void go()
    {
        // create a timer that calls the Ticker class
        // at one second intervals
        Timer t = new Timer(1000, new Ticker());
        t.start();

        // display a message box to prevent the
        // program from ending immediately
        JOptionPane.showMessageDialog(null,
            "Click OK to exit program");
        System.exit(0);
    }

    static class Ticker implements ActionListener        → 29
    {
        private boolean tick = true;

        public void actionPerformed(ActionEvent event)
        {
            if (tick)
            {
                System.out.println(tickMessage);
            }
            else
            {
                System.out.println(tockMessage);
            }
            tick = !tick;
        }
    }
}
```

This version of the application and the Listing 7-1 version have only three differences:

→ **6** The `tickMessage` field is declared as static. This is necessary so that the static class can access it.

→ **7** The `tockMessage` field is also declared as static.

→**29** The `Ticker` class is declared as static.

Using Anonymous Inner Classes

Anonymous inner classes (usually just called *anonymous classes*) are probably the strangest feature of the Java programming language. The first time you see an anonymous class, you'll almost certainly think that someone made a mistake, and that the code can't possibly compile. But compile it does, and it even works. And once you get the hang of working with anonymous classes, you'll wonder how you got by without them.

An anonymous class is a class that's defined on the spot, right at the point where you want to instantiate it. Because you code the body of the class right where you need it, you don't have to give it a name. That's why it's called an *anonymous* class.

Creating an anonymous class

The basic form for declaring and instantiating an anonymous class is this:

```
new ClassOrInterface() { class-body }
```

As you can see, you specify the `new` keyword followed by the name of a class or interface that specifies the type of the object created from the anonymous class. This class or interface name is followed by parentheses, which may include a parameter list that's passed to the constructor of the anonymous class. Then, you code a class body enclosed in braces. This class body can include anything a regular class body can include: fields, methods, even other classes or interfaces.

Here's an example of a simple anonymous class:

```
public class AnonClass
{
    public static void main(String[] args)
    {
        Ball b = new Ball()
            {
                public void hit()
                {
                    System.out.println("You hit it!");
                }
            };
        b.hit();
    }

    interface Ball
    {
        void hit();
    }
}
```

In this example, I created an interface named `Ball` that has a single method named `hit`. Then, back in the `main` method, I declared a variable of type `Ball` and used an anonymous class to create an object. The body of the anonymous class consists of an implementation of the `hit` method that simply displays the message `You hit it!` on the console. After the anonymous class is instantiated and assigned to the `b` variable, the next statement calls the `hit` method.

When you run this program, the single line `You hit it!` is displayed on the console.

Here are some things to ponder when you work with anonymous classes:

✦ You can't create a constructor for an anonymous class. Because the anonymous class doesn't have a name, what would you call the constructor, anyway?

✦ If you list parameters in the parentheses following the class name, Java looks for a constructor in that class that matches the parameters you supply. If it finds one, that constructor is called with the parameters. If not, a compiler error is generated.

✦ You can't pass parameters if the anonymous class is based on an interface. That only makes sense, because interfaces don't have constructors so Java wouldn't have anything to pass the parameters to.

✦ An assignment statement can use an anonymous class as shown in this example. In that case, the anonymous class body is followed by a semicolon that marks the end of the assignment statement. Note that this semicolon is part of the assignment statement, not the anonymous class. (In the next section, you see an example of an anonymous class that's passed as a method parameter. In that example, the body isn't followed by a semicolon.)

✦ An anonymous class is a special type of inner class. So, like any inner class, it automatically has access to the fields and methods of its outer class.

✦ An anonymous class can't be static.

Tick Tock with an anonymous class

Listing 7-3 shows a more complex example of an anonymous class: a version of the Tick Tock application that uses an anonymous class as the action listener for the timer.

LISTING 7-3: TICK TOCK WITH AN ANONYMOUS CLASS

```java
import java.awt.event.*;
import javax.swing.*;

public class TickTockAnonymous
{
    private String tickMessage = "Tick...";
    private String tockMessage = "Tock...";
```

```
public static void main(String[] args)                 → 9
{
   TickTockAnonymous t = new TickTockAnonymous();
   t.go();
}

 private void go()
{
   // create a timer that calls the Ticker class
   // at one second intervals
   Timer t = new Timer(1000,                            → 19
      new ActionListener()                              → 20
      {                                                 → 21
          private boolean tick = true;

          public void actionPerformed(                  → 24
             ActionEvent event)
          {
             if (tick)
             {
                 System.out.println(tickMessage);
             }
             else
             {
                 System.out.println(tockMessage);
             }
             tick = !tick;
          }
      } );                                              → 37

   t.start();

   // display a message box to prevent the
   // program from ending immediately
   JOptionPane.showMessageDialog(null,
      "Click OK to exit program");
   System.exit(0);
}
}
```

By now, you've seen enough versions of this program that you should understand how it works. The following paragraphs explain how this version uses an anonymous class as the `ActionListener` parameter supplied to the `Timer` constructor:

→ **9** Anonymous classes won't work in a static context, so the `main` method creates an instance of the `TickTockAnonymous` class and executes the `go` method.

→ **19** In the `go` method, an instance of the `Timer` class is created.

→**20** The second parameter of the `TimerClass` constructor is an object that implements the `ActionListener` interface. This object is created here via an anonymous class. `ActionListener` is specified as the type for this class.

→**21** This left brace marks the beginning of the body of the anonymous class.

→**24** The `actionPerformed` method is called every 1,000 milliseconds by the timer. Note that this method can freely access fields defined in the outer class.

→**37** The right brace on this line marks the end of the body of the anonymous class. Then, the right parenthesis marks the end of the parameter list for the `Timer` constructor. The left parenthesis that's paired with this right parenthesis is on line 19. Finally, the semicolon marks the end of the assignment statement that started on line 19.

Chapter 8: Packaging and Documenting Your Classes

In This Chapter

✔ Creating packages for your classes

✔ Archiving your packages in JAR files

✔ Documenting your classes with JavaDocs

*N*ow that you know just about everything to know about creating classes, this chapter shows you what to do with the classes you create. Specifically, I show you how to organize your classes into neat packages. Packages enable you to keep your classes separate from classes in the Java API, allow you to reuse your classes in other applications, and even let you distribute your classes to others, assuming other people might be interested in your classes.

If that's the case, you probably won't want to just send those people all your separate class files. Instead, you want to bundle them into a single file called a JAR file. That's covered in this chapter too.

Finally, you find out how to use a feature called JavaDocs that lets you add documentation comments to your classes. With JavaDocs, you can build professional looking documentation pages automatically. Your friends will think you're a real Java guru when you post your JavaDoc pages to your Web site.

Working with Packages

A *package* is a group of classes that belong together. Without packages, the entire universe of Java classes would be a huge unorganized mess. Imagine the thousands of classes that are available in the Java API combined with millions of Java classes created by Java programmers throughout the world, all thrown into one big pot. Packages let you organize this pot into smaller, manageable collections of related classes.

Importing classes and packages

When you use `import` statements at the beginning of a Java source file, you make classes from the packages mentioned in the `import` statements available throughout the file. (I covered `import` statements in Book II, Chapter 1, but it doesn't hurt to repeat it here.)

An `import` statement can import all the classes in a package by using an asterisk wildcard:

```
import java.util.*;
```

Here, all the classes in the `java.util` package are imported.

Alternatively, you can import classes one at a time:

```
import java.util.ArrayList;
```

Here, just the `ArrayList` class is imported.

Note: You don't have to use an `import` statement to use a class from a package. But if you don't use an `import` statement, you must *fully qualify* any references to the class. For example, you can use the `ArrayList` class without importing `java.util`:

```
java.util.ArrayList = new java.util.ArrayList();
```

Because fully qualified names are a pain to always spell out, you should always use `import` statements to import the packages or individual classes your application uses.

You never have to explicitly import two packages:

✦ **java.lang:** This package contains classes that are so commonly used that the Java compiler makes them available to every program. Examples of the classes in this package are `String`, `Exception`, and the various wrapper classes, such as `Integer` and `Boolean`.

✦ **The default package:** This package contains classes that aren't specifically put in some other package. All the programs I show in this book up to this point rely on the default package.

For simple program development and experimentation, using the default package is acceptable. However, if you start work on a serious Java application, create a separate package for it and place all the application's classes there. You find out how to do that in the next section.

Creating your own packages

Creating your own packages to hold your classes is easy. Well, relatively easy anyway. You must go through a few steps:

1. **Pick a name for your package.**

You can use any name you wish, but I recommend you follow the established convention of using your Internet domain name (if you have one), only backwards. I own a domain called `LoweWriter.com`, so I use the name `com.lowewriter` for all my packages. (Using your domain name backwards ensures that your package names are unique.)

Notice that package names are all lowercase letters. That's not an absolute requirement, but it's a Java convention that you ought to stick to. If you start using capital letters in your package names, you'll be branded a rebel for sure.

You can add additional levels beyond the domain name if you want. For example, I put my utility classes in a package named `com.lowewriter.util`.

If you don't have a domain all to yourself, try using your e-mail address backwards. For example, if your e-mail address is `SomeBody@Some` `Company.com`, use `com.somecompany.somebody` for your package names. That way, they are still unique. (If you ever want to distribute your Java packages, though, you should register a domain name. Nothing says "Amateur" like a package name that starts with `com.aol`.)

2. **Choose a directory on your hard drive to be the root of your class library.**

   You need a place on your hard drive to store your classes. I suggest you create a directory such as `c:\javaclasses`.

   This folder becomes the *root directory* for your Java packages.

3. **Create subdirectories within the package root directory for your package name.**

   For example, for the package named `com.lowewriter.util`, create a directory named `com` in the `c:\javaclasses` directory (assuming that's the name of your root). Then, in the `com` directory, create a directory named `lowewriter`. Then, in `lowewriter`, create a directory named `util`. Thus, the complete path to the directory that contains the classes for the `com.lowewriter.util` package is `c:\javaclasses\` `com\lowewriter\util`.

4. **Add the root directory for your package to the ClassPath environment variable.**

   The exact procedure for doing this depends on your operating system. In Windows XP, you can set the ClassPath by double-clicking System from the Control Panel. Click the Advanced tab, and then click Environment Variables.

   Be careful not to disturb any directories already listed in the ClassPath. To add your root directory to the ClassPath, add a semicolon followed by the path to your root directory to the end of the ClassPath value. For example, suppose your ClassPath is already set to this:

   ```
   .;c:\util\classes
   ```

Then, you modify it to look like this:

```
.;c:\util\classes;c:\javaclasses
```

Here, I added `;c:\javaclasses` to the end of the ClassPath value.

5. **Save the files for any classes you want to be in a particular package in the directory for that package.**

   For example, save the files for a class that belongs to the `com.lowewriter.util` package in `c:\javaclasses\com\lowewriter\util`.

6. **Add a package statement to the beginning of each source file that belongs in a package.**

   The `package` statement simply provides the name for the package that any class in the file is placed in. For example:

   ```
   package com.lowewriter.util;
   ```

   The `package` statement must be the first non-comment statement in the file.

An example

Suppose you've developed a utility class named `Console` that has a bunch of handy static methods for getting user input from the console. For example, this class has a static method named `askYorN` that gets a Y or N from the user and returns a boolean value to indicate which value the user entered. You decide to make this class available in a package named `com.lowewriter.util` so you and other like-minded programmers can use it in their programs.

Here's the source file for the `Console` class:

```java
package com.lowewriter.util;

import java.util.Scanner;

public class Console
{
    static Scanner sc = new Scanner(System.in);

    public static boolean askYorN(String prompt)
    {
        while (true)
        {
            String answer;
            System.out.print("\n" + prompt + " (Y or N)
                ");
            answer = sc.next();
            if (answer.equalsIgnoreCase("Y"))
                return true;
```

```
        else if (answer.equalsIgnoreCase("N"))
            return false;
        }
    }
}
```

Okay, so far this class has just the one method (askYorN), but one of these days you'll add a bunch of other useful methods to it. In the meantime, you want to get it set up in a package so you can start using it right away.

So you create a directory named c:\javaclasses\com\lowewriter\util (as described in the preceding section) and save the source file to this directory. Then, you compile the program so the Console.class file is stored in that directory too. And you add c:\javaclasses to your ClassPath environment variable.

Now, you can use the following program to test that your package is alive and well:

```
import com.lowewriter.util.*;

public class PackageTest
{
    public static void main(String[] args)
    {
        while (Console.askYorN("Keep going?"))
        {
            System.out.println("D'oh!");
        }
    }
}
```

Here, the import statement imports all the classes in the com.lowewriter.util package. Then, the while loop in the main method repeatedly asks the user if he or she wants to keep going.

Putting Your Classes in a JAR File

A *JAR file* is a single file that can contain more than one class in a compressed format that the Java Runtime Environment can access quickly. (*JAR* stands for *Java archive*.) A JAR file can have just a few classes in it, or thousands. In fact, the entire Java API is stored in a single JAR file named rt.java. (The rt stands for *runtime*.) It's a pretty big file at over 35MB, but that's not bad considering that it contains more than 12,000 classes.

JAR files are created by the jar utility, which you find in the Java bin directory along with the other Java command line tools, such as java and javac. JAR files are similar in format to Zip files, a compressed format made popular by the PKZIP program. The main difference is that JAR files contain a special file, called the *manifest file,* that contains information about the files in the archive. This manifest is automatically created by the `jar` utility, but you can supply a manifest of your own to provide additional information about the archived files.

JAR files are the normal way to distribute finished Java applications. After finishing your application, you run the `jar` command from a command prompt to prepare the JAR file. Then, another user can copy the JAR file to his or her computer. The user can then run the application directly from the JAR file.

JAR files are also used to distribute class libraries. You can add a JAR file to the ClassPath environment variable. Then, the classes in the JAR file are automatically available to any Java program that imports the package that contains the classes.

jar command-line options

The `jar` command is an old-fashioned Unix-like command, complete with arcane command-line options that you have to get right if you expect to coax `jar` into doing something useful.

The basic format of the `jar` command is this:

```
jar options jar-file [manifest-file] class-files...
```

The options specify the basic action you want `jar` to perform and provide additional information about how you want the command to work. Table 8-1 lists the options.

Table 8-1	Options for the jar Command
Option	*Description*
c	Creates a new `jar` file.
u	Updates an existing `jar` file.
x	Extracts files from an existing `jar` file.
t	Lists the contents of a `jar` file.
f	Indicates that the `jar` file is specified as an argument. You almost always want to use this option.
v	Verbose output. This option tells the `jar` command to display extra information while it works.
0	Doesn't compress files when it adds them to the archive. This option isn't used much.

Option	Description
m	Specifies that a manifest file is provided. It's listed as the next argument following the `jar` file.
M	Specifies that a manifest file should not be added to the archive. This option is rarely used.

Note that you must specify at least the c, u, x, or t options to tell `jar` what action you want to perform.

Archiving a package

The most common use for the `jar` utility is to create an archive of an entire package. The procedure for doing that varies slightly depending on what operating system you're using. However, the `jar` command itself is the same regardless of your operating system. Here's the procedure for archiving a package on a PC running Windows XP:

1. **Open a command window.**

The easiest way to do that is to choose Start⇨Run, type cmd in the Open text box, and click OK.

2. **Use a `cd` command to navigate to your package root.**

For example, if your packages are stored in `c:\javaclasses`, use this command:

```
cd \javaclasses
```

3. **Use a `jar` command that specifies the options `cf`, the name of the jar file, and the path to the class files you want to archive.**

For example, to create an archive named `utils.jar` that contains all the class files in the `com.lowewriter.util` package, use this command:

```
jar cf utils.jar com\lowewriter\util\*.class
```

4. **To verify that the `jar` file was created correctly, use the `jar` command that specifies the options `tf` and the name of the jar file.**

For example, if the jar file is named `utils.jar`, use this command:

```
jar tf utils.jar
```

This lists the contents of the `jar` file so you can see what classes were added. Here's some typical output from this command:

```
META-INF/
META-INF/MANIFEST.MF
com/lowewriter/util/Console.class
com/lowewriter/util/Random.class
```

As you can see, the `utils.jar` file contains the two classes in my `com.lowewriter.util` package, `Console` and `Random`.

5. That's all!

You're done. You can leave the `jar` file where it is, or you can give it to your friends so they can use the classes it contains.

Adding a jar to your classpath

To use the classes in an archive, you must add the `jar` file to your ClassPath environment variable. I describe the procedure for modifying the ClassPath variable in Windows XP earlier in this chapter, in the section "Creating your own packages." So I won't repeat the details here.

To add an archive to the ClassPath variable, just add the complete path to the archive, making sure to separate it from any other paths already in the ClassPath with a semicolon. For example:

```
.;c:\javaclasses\utils.jar;c:\javaclasses
```

Here, I added the path `c:\javaclasses\utils.jar` to my ClassPath variable.

The first path in a ClassPath variable is always a single dot (`.`), which allows Java to find classes in the current directory.

Also, be aware that Java searches the various paths and archive files in the ClassPath variable in the order in which you list them. Thus, in the previous example, Java searches for classes first in the current directory, then in the `utils` archive, and finally in the `c:\javaclasses` directory.

Running a program directly from an archive

With just a little work, you can set up an archive so that a Java program can be run directly from it. All you have to do is create a *manifest file* before you create the archive. Then, when you run the `jar` utility to create the archive, you include the manifest file on the `jar` command line.

A manifest file is a simple text file that contains information about the files in the archive. Although it can contain many lines of information, it needs just one line to make an executable `jar` file:

```
Main-Class: ClassName
```

The *ClassName* is the fully qualified name of the class that contains the `main` method that is executed to start the application. It isn't required, but it's typical to use the extension `.mf` for manifest files.

For example, suppose you have an application whose main class is `GuessingGame`, and all the class files for the application are in the package com.lowewriter.game. First, create a manifest file named game.mf in the com\lowewriter\game directory. This file contains the following line:

```
Main-Class: com.lowewriter.game.GuessingGame
```

Then, run the jar command with the options cfm, the name of the archive to create, the name of the manifest file, and the path for the class files. For example:

```
jar cfm game.jar com\lowewriter\game\game.mf com\lowewriter\game\*.class
```

Now, you can run the application directly from a command prompt by using the java command with the -jar switch and the name of the archive file. For example:

```
java -jar game.jar
```

This command starts the JRE and executes the main method of the class specified by the manifest file in the game.jar archive file.

If your operating system is configured properly, you can also run the application by double-clicking an icon for the jar file.

Using JavaDoc to Document Your Classes

One last step remains before you can go public with your hot new class library or application: preparing the documentation for its classes. Fortunately, Java provides a tool called *JavaDoc* that can automatically create fancy HTML-based documentation based on comments in your source files. All you have to do is add a comment for each public class, field, and method, run the source files through the javadoc command and, *voila!* you have professional-looking Web-based documentation for your classes.

The following sections show you how to add JavaDoc comments to your source files, how to run the source files through the javadoc command, and how to view the resulting documentation pages.

Adding JavaDoc comments

The basic rule for creating JavaDoc comments is that they begin with /** and end with */. You can place JavaDoc comments in any of three different locations in a source file:

+ Immediately before the declaration of a public class
+ Immediately before the declaration of a public field
+ Immediately before the declaration of a public method or constructor

A JavaDoc comment can include text that describes the class, field, or method. Each subsequent line of a multi-line JavaDoc comment usually begins with an asterisk. JavaDoc ignores this asterisk and any white space between it and the first word on the line.

The text in a JavaDoc comment can include HTML markup if you want to apply fancy formatting. You should avoid using heading tags (<h1> and so on), because JavaDoc creates those and your heading tags just confuse things. But you can use tags for boldface and italics (<b> and <i>) or to format code examples (use the <pre> tag).

In addition, you can include special *doc tags* that provide specific information used by JavaDoc to format the documentation pages. Table 8-2 summarizes the most commonly used tags.

Table 8-2	Commonly Used JavaDoc Tags
Tag	*Explanation*
@author	Provides information about the author, typically the author's name, e-mail address, Web site information, and so on.
@version	The version number.
@since	Used to indicate the version with which this class, field, or method was added.
@param	Provides the name and description of a method or constructor parameter.
@return	Provides a description of a method's return value.
@throws	Indicates exceptions that are thrown by a method or constructor.
@deprecated	Indicates that the class, field, or method is deprecated and shouldn't be used.

To give you an idea of how JavaDoc comments are typically used, Listing 8-1 shows an Employee class with JavaDoc comments included.

LISTING 8-1: AN EMPLOYEE CLASS WITH JAVADOC COMMENTS

```
package com.lowewriter.payroll;

/** Represents an employee.
 * @author Doug Lowe
 * @author www.LoweWriter.com
 * @version 1.5
 * @since 1.0
 */
public class Employee
```

```
{
    private String lastName;
    private String firstName;
    private Double salary;

/** Represents the employee's address.
*/
    public Address address;

/** Creates an employee with the specified name.
 * @param lastName The employee's last name.
 * @param firstName The employee's first name.
*/
    public Employee(String lastName, String firstName)
    {
        this.lastName = lastName;
        this.firstName = firstName;
        this.address = new Address();
    }

/** Gets the employee's last name.
 * @return A string representing the employee's last
 *                   name.
*/
    public String getLastName()
    {
        return this.lastName;
    }

/** Sets the employee's last name.
 * @param lastName A String containing the employee's
 *                   last name.
 * @return No return value.
*/
    public void setLastName(String lastName)
    {
        this.lastName = lastName;
    }

/** Gets the employee's first name.
 * @return A string representing the employee's first
 *                   name.
*/
    public String getFirstName()
    {
        return this.firstName;
    }
```

Book III
Chapter 8

Packaging and
Documenting Your
Classes

continued

LISTING 8-1 (CONTINUED)

```
/** Sets the employee's first name.
 * @param firstName A String containing the employee's
 *                  first name.
 * @return No return value.
 */
    public void setFirstName(String firstName)
    {
        this.firstName = firstName;
    }

/** Gets the employee's salary.
 * @return A double representing the employee's salary.
 */
    public double getSalary()
    {
        return this.salary;
    }

/** Sets the employee's salary.
 * @param lastName A double containing the employee's
 *                  salary.
 * @return No return value.
 */
    public void setSalary(double salary)
    {
        this.salary = salary;
    }
}
```

Using the javadoc command

The `javadoc` command has a few dozen options you can set, making it a complicated command to use. However, you can ignore all these options to create a basic set of documentation pages. Just specify the complete path to all the Java files you want to create documentation for, like this:

```
javadoc com\lowewriter\payroll\*.java
```

The `javadoc` command creates the documentation pages in the current directory, so you may want to switch to the directory where you want the pages to reside first.

For more complete information about using this command, refer to the `javadoc` documentation at the Sun Web site. You can find it at:

```
java.sun.com/j2se/1.5.0/docs/guide/javadoc/index.html
```

Viewing JavaDoc pages

After you run the `javadoc` command, you can access the documentation pages by starting with the `index.html` page. To quickly display this page, just type `index.html` at the command prompt after you run the `javadoc` command. Or, you can start your browser, navigate to the directory where you created the documentation pages, and open the `index.html` page. Either way, Figure 8-1 shows an index page that lists two classes.

If you think this page looks familiar, that's because the documentation for the Java API was created using JavaDocs. So you should already know how to find your way around these pages.

To look at the documentation for a class, click the class name link. A page with complete documentation for the class comes up. For example, Figure 8-2 shows part of the documentation page for the `Employee` class. JavaDocs generated this page from the source file shown in Listing 8-1.

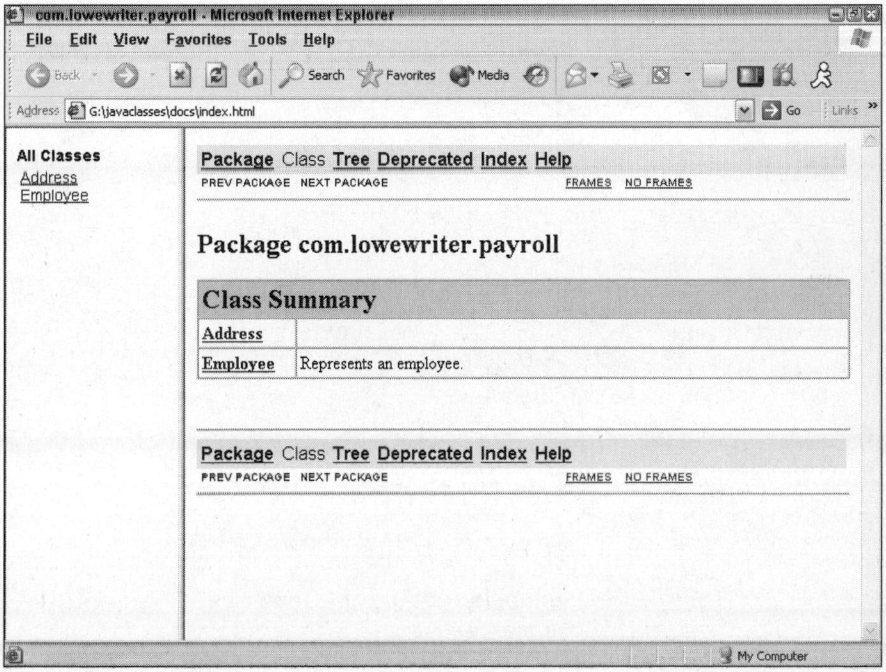

Figure 8-1:
A JavaDocs
index page.

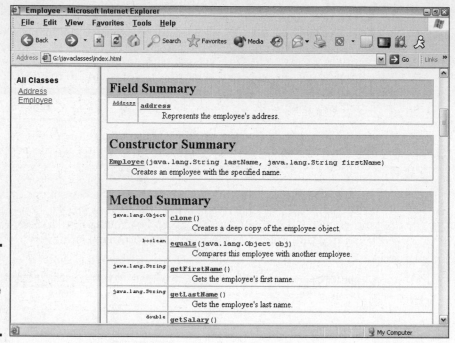

Figure 8-2:
Documen-
tation for the
Employee
class.

Book IV

Strings, Arrays, and Collections

The 5th Wave   By Rich Tennant

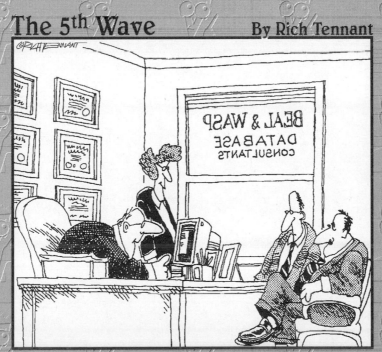

"Your database is beyond repair, but before I tell you our backup recommendation, let me ask you a question. How many index cards do you think will fit on the walls of your computer room?"

Contents at a Glance

Chapter 1: Working with Strings

In This Chapter

✔ Quickly reviewing what you already know about strings

✔ Examining string class methods

✔ Working with substrings

✔ Splitting up strings

✔ Using the `StringBuilder` **and** `StringBuffer` **classes**

✔ Using the `CharSequence` **interface**

S trings are one of the most common types of objects in Java. Throughout this book are various techniques for working with strings. You've seen how to create string variables, how to concatenate strings, and how to compare strings. But so far, I've only scratched the surface of what you can do with strings. In this chapter, I dive deeper into what Java can do with string.

I start with a brief review of what I covered so far about strings, so you don't have to go flipping back through the book to find basic information. Then, I look at the `String` class itself and some of the methods it provides for working with strings. Finally, you examine two almost identical classes named `StringBuilder` and `StringBuffer` that offer features not found in the basic `String` class.

Reviewing Strings

To save you the hassle of flipping back through this book, the following paragraphs summarize what is presented in earlier chapters about strings:

✦ Strings are reference types, not value types, such as `int` or `boolean`. As a result, a string variable holds a reference to an object created from the `String` class, not the value of the string itself.

✦ Even though strings aren't primitive types, the Java compiler has some features designed to let you work with strings almost as if they were. For example, Java lets you assign string literals to string variables, like this:

```
String line1 = "Oh what a beautiful morning!";
```

The Immutable Pattern

Many applications can benefit from classes that describe *immutable objects*. An immutable object is an object that, once created, can never be changed. The `String` class is the most commonly known example of an immutable object. After you create a `String` object, you can't change it.

As an example, suppose you're designing a game where the playing surface has fixed obstacles, such as trees. You can create the `Tree` class using the Immutable pattern. The constructor for the `Tree` class could accept parameters that define the size, type, and location of the tree. But once you create the tree, you can't move it.

Follow these three simple rules when creating an immutable object:

1. Provide one or more constructors that accept parameters to set the initial state of the object.

2. Do not allow any methods to modify any instance variables in the object. Set instance variables with constructors, and then leave them alone.

3. Any method that modifies the object should do so by creating a new object with the modified values. This method then returns the new object as its return value.

♦ Strings can include *escape sequences* that consist of a slash followed by another character. The most common escape sequences are \n for new line and \t for tab. If you want to include a slash in a string, you must use the escape sequence \\.

♦ Strings and characters are different. String literals are marked by quotation marks; character literals are marked by apostrophes. Thus, "a" is a string literal that happens to be one character long. In contrast, 'a' is a character literal.

♦ You can combine, or *concatenate,* strings by using the + operator, like this:

```
String line2 = line1 + "\nOh what a beautiful
    day!";
```

♦ You can also use the += operator with strings, like this:

```
line2 += = "\nI've got a beautiful feeling";
```

♦ When used in a concatenation expression, Java automatically converts primitive types to strings. Thus, Java allows the following:

```
int empCount = 50;
String msg = "Number of employees: " + empCount;
```

✦ The various primitive wrapper classes (such as `integer` and `double`) have `parse` methods that can convert string values to numeric types. For example:

```
String s = "50";
int i = Integer.parseInt(s);
```

✦ You can't compare strings using the equality operator (==). Instead, you should use the `equals` method. For example:

```
if (lastName.equals("Lowe"))
    System.out.println("This is me!");
```

✦ The `String` class also has an `equalsIgnoreCase` method that compares strings without considering case. For example:

```
if (lastName.equalsIgnoreCase("lowe"))
    System.out.println("This is me again!");
```

Using the String Class

The `String` class is the class used to create string objects. It has a whole gaggle of methods that are designed to let you find out information about the string that's represented by the `String` class. Table 1-1 lists the most useful of these methods.

Table 1-1	String Class Methods
Method	*Description*
`char charAt(int)`	Returns the character at the specified position in the string.
`int compareTo(String)`	Compares this string to another string based on alphabetical order. Returns −1 if this string comes before the other string, 0 if the strings are the same, and 1 if this string comes after the other string.
`int compareToIgnoreCase (String)`	Similar to `compareTo` but ignores case.
`boolean contains (CharSequence)`	Returns `true` if this string contains the parameter value. The parameter can be a `String`, `StringBuilder`, or `StringBuffer`.
`boolean endsWith(String)`	Returns `true` if this string ends with the parameter string.

(continued)

Book IV
Chapter 1

Working with Strings

Table 1-1 *(continued)*

Method	Description
`boolean equals(String)`	Returns `true` if this string has the same value as the parameter string.
`boolean equalsIgnoreCase (String)`	Similar to `equals` but ignores case.
`int indexOf(char)`	Returns the index of the first occurrence of the `char` parameter in this string. Returns -1 if the character isn't in the string.
`int indexOf(String)`	Returns the index of the first occurrence of the `String` parameter in this string. Returns -1 if the string isn't in this string.
`int indexOf (String, int start)`	Similar to `indexOf`, but starts the search at the specified position in the string.
`int lastIndexOf(char)`	Returns the index of the last occurrence of the `char` parameter in this string. Returns -1 if the character isn't in the string.
`int lastIndexOf(String)`	Returns the index of the last occurrence of the `String` parameter in this string. Returns -1 if the string isn't in this string.
`int lastIndexOf(String, int)`	Similar to `lastIndexOf`, but starts the search at the specified position in the string.
`int length()`	Returns the length of this string.
`String replace(char, char)`	Returns a new string that's based on the original string, but with every occurrence of the first parameter replaced by the second parameter.
`String replaceAll(String old, String new)`	Returns a new string that's based on the original string, but with every occurrence of the first string replaced by the second parameter. Note that the first parameter can be a regular expression.
`String replaceFirst(String old, String new)`	Returns a new string that's based on the original string, but with the first occurrence of the first string replaced by the second parameter. Note that the first parameter can be a regular expression.
`String[] split(String)`	Splits the string into an array of strings, using the string parameter as a pattern to determine where to split the strings.
`boolean startsWith(String)`	Returns `true` if this string starts with the parameter string.
`boolean startsWith (String, int)`	Returns `true` if this string contains the parameter string at the position indicated by the `int` parameter.

Method	Description
`String substring(int)`	Extracts a substring from this string beginning at the position indicated by the `int` parameter and continuing to the end of the string.
`String substring(int, int)`	Extracts a substring from this string beginning at the position indicated by the first parameter and ending at the position one character before the value of the second parameter.
`char[] toCharArray()`	Converts the string to an array of individual characters.
`String toLowerCase()`	Converts the string to lowercase.
`String toString()`	Returns the string as a `String`. (Pretty pointless if you ask me, but all classes must have a `toString` method.)
`String toUpperCase()`	Converts the string to uppercase.
`String trim()`	Returns a copy of the string but with all leading and trailing white space removed.
`String valueOf(primitiveType)`	Returns a string representation of any primitive type.

The most important thing to remember about the `String` class is that in spite of the fact that it has a bazillion methods, none of those methods lets you alter the string in any way. That's because a `String` object is *immutable,* which means it can't be changed.

Although you can't change a string after you create it, you can use methods of the `String` class to create new strings that are variations of the original string. The following sections describe some of the more interesting things you can do with these methods.

Finding the length of a string

One of the most basic string operations is determining the length of a string. You do that with the `length` method. For example:

```
String s = "A wonderful day for a neighbor.";
int len = s.length();
```

Here, `len` is assigned a value of 30 because the string `s` consists of 30 characters.

Getting the length of a string isn't usually very useful by itself. But the `length` method often plays an important role in other string manipulations, as you see throughout the following sections.

Making simple string modifications

Several of the methods of the String class return modified versions of the original string. For example, toLowerCase converts a string to all lower-case letters:

```
String s = "Umpa Lumpa";
s = s.toLowerCase();
```

Here, s is set to the string umpa lumpa. The toUpperCase method works the same, but converts strings to all uppercase letters.

The trim method removes white space characters (spaces, tabs, newlines, and so on) from the start and end of a word. For example:

```
String s = "   Umpa Lumpa   ";
s = s.trim();
```

Here, the spaces before and after Umpa Lumpa are removed. Thus, the resulting string is 10 characters long.

Bear in mind that because strings are immutable, these methods don't actu-ally change the String object. Instead, they create a new String with the modified value. A common mistake — especially for programmers who are new to Java but experienced with other languages — is to forget to assign the return value from one of these methods. For example, the following statement has no effect on s:

```
s.trim();
```

Here, the trim method trims the string, but then the program discards the result. The remedy is to assign the result of this expression back to s, like this:

```
s = s.trim();
```

Extracting characters from a string

You can use the charAt method to extract a character from a specific posi-tion in a string. When you do, keep in mind that the index number for the first character in a string is 0, not 1. Also, you should check the length of the string before extracting a character. If you specify an index value that's beyond the end of the string, the exception StringIndexOutOfBoundsException is thrown. (Fortunately, this is an unchecked exception, so you don't have to enclose the charAt method in a try/catch statement.)

Here's an example of a program that uses the `charAt` method to count the number of vowels in a string entered by the user:

```java
import java.util.Scanner;

public class CountVowels
{
    static Scanner sc = new Scanner(System.in);

    public static void main(String[] args)
    {
        System.out.print("Enter a string: ");
        String s = sc.nextLine();

        int vowelCount = 0;

        for (int i = 0; i < s.length(); i++)
        {
            char c = s.charAt(i);
            if (      (c == 'A')  ||  (c == 'a')
                 ||   (c == 'E')  ||  (c == 'e')
                 ||   (c == 'I')  ||  (c == 'i')
                 ||   (c == 'O')  ||  (c == 'o')
                 ||   (c == 'U')  ||  (c == 'u')  )
                vowelCount++;
        }
        System.out.println("That string contains "
            + vowelCount + " vowels.");
    }
}
```

Here, the `for` loop checks the length of the string to make sure the index variable `i` doesn't exceed the string length. Then, each character is extracted and checked with an `if` statement to see if it is a vowel. The condition expression in this `if` statement is a little complicated because it must check for five different vowels, both upper- and lowercase.

Extracting substrings from a string

The `substring` method lets you extract a portion of a string. This method has two forms. The first accepts a single integer parameter. It returns the substring that starts at the position indicated by this parameter and extending to the rest of the string. (Remember that string positions start with 0, not 1.) For example:

```java
String s = "Baseball";
String b = s.substring(4);        // "ball"
```

Here, `b` is assigned the string `ball`.

The second version of the substring method accepts two parameters to indicate the start and end of the substring you want to extract. Note that the substring actually ends at the character that's immediately before the position indicated by the second parameter. So to extract the characters at positions 2 through 5, specify 1 as the start position and 6 as the ending position. For example:

```
String s = "Baseball";
String b = s.substring(2, 6);     // "seba"
```

Here, b is assigned the string seba.

The following program uses substrings to replace all the vowels in a string entered by the user with asterisks:

```
import java.util.Scanner;

public class MarkVowels
{
    static Scanner sc = new Scanner(System.in);

    public static void main(String[] args)
    {
        System.out.print("Enter a string: ");
        String s = sc.nextLine();
        String originalString = s;

        int vowelCount = 0;

        for (int i = 0; i < s.length(); i++)
        {
            char c = s.charAt(i);
            if (    (c == 'A')  || (c == 'a')
                 || (c == 'E')  || (c == 'e')
                 || (c == 'I')  || (c == 'i')
                 || (c == 'O')  || (c == 'o')
                 || (c == 'U')  || (c == 'u')  )
            {
                String front = s.substring(0, i);
                String back = s.substring(i+1);
                s = front + "*" + back;
            }
        }
        System.out.println();
        System.out.println(originalString);
        System.out.println(s);
    }
}
```

This program uses a `for` loop and the `charAt` method to extract each character from the string. Then, if the character is a vowel, a string named `front` is created that consists of all the characters that appear before the vowel. A second string named `back` is then created with all the characters that appear after the vowel. Finally, the `s` string is replaced with a new string that's constructed from the `front` string, an asterisk, and the `back` string.

Here's some sample console output from this program so you can see how it works:

```
Enter a string: Where have all the vowels gone?

Where have all the vowels gone?
Wh*r* h*v* *ll th* v*w*ls g*n*?
```

Splitting up a string

The `split` command is especially useful for splitting a string into separate strings based on a delimiter character. For example, suppose you have a string with the parts of an address separated by colons, like this:

```
1500 N. Third Street:Fresno:CA:93722
```

With the `split` method, you can easily separate this string into four strings. In the process, the colons are discarded.

Unfortunately, the use of the `split` method requires that you use an array, and arrays are covered in the next chapter. I'm going to plow ahead with this section anyway on the chance that you already know a few basic things about arrays. If not, you can always come back to this section after you read the next chapter.

The `split` method carves a string into an array of strings separated by the delimiter character passed via a string parameter. Here's a routine that splits an address into separate strings, and then prints out all the strings:

```
String address =
    "1500 N. Third Street:Fresno:CA:93722";

String[] parts = address.split(":");

for (int i = 0; i < parts.length; i++)
    System.out.println(parts[i]);
```

If you run this code, the following lines are displayed on the console:

```
1500 N. Third Street
Fresno
CA
93722
```

Book IV
Chapter 1

Working with
Strings

The string passed to the `split` method is actually a special type of string used for pattern recognition, called a *regular expression*. You discover regular expressions in Book V. For now, here are a few regular expressions that might be useful when you use the `split` method:

Regular Expression	Explanation
\\t	A tab character
\\n	A newline character
\\|	A vertical bar
\\s	Any white space character
\\s+	One or more occurrences of any white space character

The last regular expression in this table, \\s+, is especially useful for breaking a string into separate words. For example, the following program accepts a string from the user, breaks it into separate words, and then displays the words on separate lines:

```java
import java.util.Scanner;

public class CountWords
{
    static Scanner sc = new Scanner(System.in);

    public static void main(String[] args)
    {
        System.out.print("Enter a string: ");
        String s = sc.nextLine();

        String[] word = s.split("\\s+");

        for (String w : word)
            System.out.println(w);
    }
}
```

Here's a sample of the console output for a typical execution of this program:

```
Enter a string: This string   has    several     words
This
string
has
several
words
```

Notice that some of the words in the string entered by the user are preceded by more than one space character. The \\s+ pattern used by the split method treats any consecutive white space character as a single delimiter when splitting the words.

Replacing parts of a string

You can use the replaceFirst or replaceAll methods to replace a part of a string that matches a pattern you supply with some other text. For example, here's the main method of a program that gets a line of text from the user, and then replaces all occurrences of the string cat with dog:

```
public static void main(String[] args)
{
    Scanner sc = new Scanner(System.in);
    System.out.print("Enter a string: ");
    String s = sc.nextLine();

    s = s.replaceAll("cat", "dog");

    System.out.println(s);
}
```

And here's the console for a typical execution of this program:

```
Enter a string: I love cats. Cats are the best.
I love dogs. Cats are the best.
```

As with the split methods, the first parameter of replace methods can be a regular expression that provides a complex matching string. For more information, see Book V.

Once again, don't forget that strings are immutable. As a result, the replace methods don't actually modify the String object itself. Instead, they return a new String object with the modified value.

Using the StringBuilder and StringBuffer Classes

The String class is powerful, but it's not very efficient for programs that require heavy-duty string manipulation. Because String objects are immutable, any method of the String class that modifies the string in any way must create a new String object and copy the modified contents of the original string object to the new string. That's not so bad if it happens only occasionally, but it can be inefficient in programs that do it a lot.

Even string concatenation is inherently inefficient. For example, consider these statements:

```
int count = 5;
String msg = "There are ";
String msg += count;
String msg += " apples in the basket.";
```

These four statements actually create five `String` objects:

✦ **"There are "**: Created for the literal in the second statement. The `msg` variable is assigned a reference to this string.

✦ **"5"**: Created to hold the result of `count.toString()`. The `toString` method is implicitly called by the third statement so `count` is concatenated with `msg`.

✦ **"There are 5"**: Created as a result of the concatenation in the third statement. A reference to this object is assigned to `msg`.

✦ **"apples in the basket."**: Created to hold the literal in the fourth statement.

✦ **"There are 5 apples in the basket."**: Created to hold the result of the concatenation in the fourth statement. A reference to this object is assigned to `msg`.

For programs that do only occasional string concatenation and simple string manipulations, these inefficiencies aren't a big deal. For programs that do extensive string manipulation, however, Java offers two alternatives to the `String` class: the `StringBuilder` and `StringBuffer` classes.

The `StringBuilder` and `StringBuffer` classes are mirror images of each other. Both have the same methods and perform the same string manipulations. The only difference is that the `StringBuffer` class is safe to use in applications that work with multiple threads. `StringBuilder` is not safe for threaded applications, but is more efficient than `StringBuffer`. As a result, you should use the `StringBuilder` class unless your application uses threads. (Find out how to work with threads in Book V.)

Note: The `StringBuilder` class was introduced in Java version 1.5. If you're using an older Java compiler, you have to use `StringBuffer` instead.

Creating a StringBuilder object

You can't assign string literals directly to a `StringBuilder` object as you can with a `String` object. However, the `StringBuilder` class has a constructor that accepts a `String` as a parameter. So, to create a `StringBuilder` object, you use a statement such as this:

```
StringBuilder sb = new StringBuilder("Today is the
    day!");
```

Internally, a `StringBuilder` object maintains a fixed area of memory where it stores a string value. This area of memory is called the *buffer*. The string held in this buffer doesn't have to use the entire buffer. As a result, a `StringBuilder` object has both a *length* and a *capacity*. The length represents the current length of the string maintained by the `StringBuilder`, and the *capacity* represents the size of the buffer itself. Note that the length can't exceed the capacity.

When you create a `StringBuilder` object, the capacity is initially set to the length of the string plus 16. The `StringBuilder` class automatically increases its capacity whenever necessary, so you don't have to worry about exceeding the capacity.

Using StringBuilder methods

Table 1-2 lists the most useful methods of the `StringBuilder` class. Note that the `StringBuffer` class uses the same methods. So if you have to use `StringBuffer` instead of `StringBuilder`, just change the class name and use the same methods.

Table 1-2	StringBuilder Methods
Method	*Description*
`append(primitiveType)`	Appends the string representation of the primitive type to the end of the string.
`append(Object)`	Calls the object's `toString` method and appends the result to the end of the string.
`append(CharSequence)`	Appends the string to the end of the `StringBuilder`'s string value. The parameter can be a `String`, `StringBuilder`, or `StringBuffer`.
`int capacity()`	Returns the capacity of this `StringBuilder`.
`char charAt(int)`	Returns the character at the specified position in the string.
`delete(int, int)`	Deletes characters starting with the first `int` and ending with the character before the second `int`.
`deleteCharAt(int)`	Deletes the character at the specified position.
`ensureCapacity(int)`	Ensures the capacity of `String-Builder` is at least equal to the `int` value. The capacity is increased if necessary.
`int indexOf(String)`	Returns the index of the first occurrence of the specified string. If the string doesn't appear, returns −1.

(continued)

Table 1-2 *(continued)*

Method	Description
int indexOf(String, int)	Returns the index of the first occurrence of the specified string, starting the search at the specified index position. If the string doesn't appear, returns −1.
insert(int, *primitiveType*)	Inserts the string representation of the primitive type at the point specified by the int argument.
insert(int, Object)	Calls the toString method of the Object parameter, and then inserts the resulting string at the point specified by the int argument.
insert(int, CharSequence)	Inserts the string at the point specified by the int argument. The second parameter can be a String, StringBuilder, or StringBuffer.
int lastIndexOf(String)	Returns the index of the last occurrence of the specified string. If the string doesn't appear, returns −1.
int lastIndexOf(String, int)	Returns the index of the last occurrence of the specified string, starting the search at the specified index position. If the string doesn't appear, returns −1.
int length()	Returns the length of this string.
replace(int, int, String)	Replaces the substring indicated by the first two parameters with the string provided by the third parameter.
reverse()	Reverses the order of characters.
setCharAt(int, char)	Sets the character at the specified position to the specified character.
setLength(int)	Sets the length of the string. If less than the current length, the string is truncated. If greater than the current length, new characters are hexadecimal zeros.
String substring(int)	Extracts a substring beginning at the position indicated by the int parameter and continuing to the end of the string.
String substring(int, int)	Extracts a substring beginning at the position indicated by the first parameter and ending at the position one character before the value of the second parameter.
String toString()	Returns the current value as a String.
String trimToSize()	Reduces the capacity of the StringBuffer to match the size of the string.

A StringBuilder example

To illustrate how the `StringBuilder` class works, here's a `StringBuilder` version of the MarkVowel program from earlier in this chapter:

```
import java.util.Scanner;

public class StringBuilderApp
{
    static Scanner sc = new Scanner(System.in);

    public static void main(String[] args)
    {
        System.out.print("Enter a string: ");
        String s = sc.nextLine();

        StringBuilder sb = new StringBuilder(s);

        int vowelCount = 0;

        for (int i = 0; i < s.length(); i++)
        {
            char c = s.charAt(i);
            if (    (c == 'A')  ||  (c == 'a')
                 || (c == 'E')  ||  (c == 'e')
                 || (c == 'I')  ||  (c == 'i')
                 || (c == 'O')  ||  (c == 'o')
                 || (c == 'U')  ||  (c == 'u')  )
            {
                sb.setCharAt(i, '*');
            }
        }
        System.out.println();
        System.out.println(s);
        System.out.println(sb.toString());
    }
}
```

This program uses the `setCharAt` method to directly replace any vowels it finds with asterisks. That's much more efficient that concatenating substrings the way the `String` version of this program worked.

Using the CharSequence Interface

The Java API includes a useful interface called `CharSequence`. All three of the classes in this chapter (`String`, `StringBuilder`, and `StringBuffer`) implement this interface. This method exists primarily to let you use `String`, `StringBuilder`, and `StringBuffer` interchangeably.

Toward that end, several of the methods of the `String`, `StringBuilder`, and `StringBuffer` classes use `CharSequence` as a parameter type. For those methods, you can pass a `String`, `StringBuilder`, or `StringBuffer` object. Note that a string literal is treated as a `String` object, so you can use a string literal anywhere a `CharSequence` is called for.

In case you're interested, the `CharSequence` interface defines four methods:

✦ **`char charAt(int)`:** Returns the character at the specified position.

✦ **`int length()`:** Returns the length of the sequence.

✦ **`subSequence(int start, int end)`:** Returns the substring indicated by the start and end parameters.

✦ **`toString()`:** Returns a `String` representation of the sequence.

If you're inclined to use `CharSequence` as a parameter type for a method so the method works with a `String`, `StringBuilder`, or `StringBuffer` object, be advised that you can use only these four methods.

Chapter 2: Using Arrays

In This Chapter

✔ Working with basic one-dimensional arrays

✔ Using array initializers to set the initial values of an array

✔ Using `for` loops with arrays

✔ Working with two-dimensional arrays

✔ Using the `Arrays` class

1 could use a raise. . . .

Oh, *arrays*. Sorry.

Arrays are an important aspect of any programming language, and Java is no exception. In this chapter, you discover just about everything you need to know about using arrays. I cover run-of-the-mill one-dimensional arrays, multi-dimensional arrays, and two classes that are used to work with arrays, named `Array` and `Arrays`.

Understanding Arrays

An *array* is a set of variables that are referenced using a single variable name combined with an index number. Each item of an array is called an *element*. All the elements in an array must be of the same type. Thus, the array itself has a type that specifies what kind of elements it can contain. For example, an `int` array can contain `int` values, and a `String` array can contain strings.

The index number is written after the variable name and enclosed in brackets. So, if the variable name is x, you could access a specific element with an expression like `x[5]`.

You might think `x[5]` would refer to the fifth element in the array. But index numbers start with zero for the first element, so `x[5]` actually refers to the sixth element. This little detail is one of the chief causes of problems when working with arrays — especially if you cut your array-programming teeth in a language in which arrays are indexed from 1 instead of 0. So get used to counting from 0 instead of 1.

The real power of arrays comes from the simple fact that you can use a variable or even a complete expression as an array index. So, for example, instead of coding x[5] to refer to a specific array element, you can code x[i] to refer to the element indicated by the index variable i. You see plenty of examples of index variables throughout this chapter.

Here are a few additional tidbits of array information to ponder before you get into the details of creating and using arrays:

✦ An array is itself an object. You can refer to the array object as a whole rather than a specific element of the array by using the array's variable name without an index. Thus, if x[5] refers to an element of an array, then x refers to the array itself.

✦ An array has a fixed length that's set when the array is created. This length determines the number of elements that can be stored in the array. The maximum index value you can use with any array is one less than the array's length. Thus, if you create an array of 10 elements, you can use index values from 0 to 9.

✦ You can't change the length of an array after you create the array.

✦ You can access the length of an array by using the length field of the array variable. For example, x.length returns the length of the array x.

Creating Arrays

Before you can create an array, you must first declare a variable that refers to the array. This variable declaration should indicate the type of elements that are stored by the array followed by a set of empty brackets, like this:

```
String[] names;
```

Here, a variable named names is declared. Its type is an array of String objects.

Just to make sure you're confused as much as possible, Java also lets you put the brackets on the variable name rather than the type. For example, the following two statements both create arrays of int elements:

```
int[] array1;   // an array of int elements
int array2[];   // another array of int elements
```

Both of these statements have exactly the same effect. Most Java programmers prefer to put the brackets on the type rather than the variable name.

By itself, that statement doesn't create an array. It merely declares a variable that can refer to an array. You can actually create the array in two ways:

✦ Use the `new` keyword followed by the array type, this time with the brackets filled in to indicate how many elements the array can hold. For example:

```
String[] names;
names = new String[10];
```

Here, an array of `String` objects that can hold 10 strings is created. Each of the strings in this array are initialized to an empty string.

✦ Like any other variable, you can combine the declaration and the creation into one statement:

```
String[] names = new String[10];
```

Here, the array variable is declared and an array is created in one statement.

 If you don't know how many elements the array needs at compile time, you can use a variable or an expression for the array length. For example, here's a routine from a method that stores player names in an array of strings. It starts by asking the user how many players are on the team. Then, it creates an array of the correct size:

```
System.out.print("How many players? ");
int count = sc.nextInt();          // sc is a Scanner
String[] players = new String[count];
```

Initializing an Array

One way to initialize the values in an array is to simply assign them one by one:

```
String[] days = new Array[7];
Days[0] = "Sunday";
Days[1] = "Monday";
Days[2] = "Tuesday";
Days[3] = "Wednesday";
Days[4] = "Thursday";
Days[5] = "Friday";
Days[6] = "Saturday";
```

Java has a shorthand way to create an array and initialize it with constant values:

```
String[] days = { "Sunday", "Monday", "Tuesday",
                  "Wednesday", "Thursday",
                  "Friday", "Saturday" };
```

Here, each element to be assigned to the array is listed in an *array initializer*. Here's an example of an array initializer for an `int` array:

```
int[] primes = { 2, 3, 5, 7, 11, 13, 17 };
```

Note: The length of an array created with an initializer is determined by the number of values listed in the initializer.

An alternative way to code an initializer is like this:

```
int[] primes = new int[] { 2, 3, 5, 7, 11, 13, 17 };
```

To use this type of initializer, you use the new keyword followed by the array type and a set of empty brackets. Then, you code the initializer.

Using for Loops with Arrays

One of the most common ways to process an array is with a `for` loop. In fact, `for` loops were invented specifically to deal with arrays. For example, here's a `for` loop that creates an array of 100 random numbers, with values from 1 to 100:

```
int[] numbers = new int[100];
for (int i = 0; i < 100; i++)
    numbers[i] = (int)(Math.random() * 100) + 1;
```

And here's a loop that fills an array of player names with strings entered by the user:

```
String[] players = new String[count];
for (int i = 0; i < count; i++)
{
    System.out.print("Enter player name: ");
    players[i] = sc.nextLine();      // sc is a Scanner
}
```

For this example, assume count is an `int` variable that holds the number of players to enter.

You can also use a `for` loop to print the contents of an array. For example:

```
for (int i = 0; i < count; i++)
    System.out.println(players[i]);
```

Here, the elements of a `String` array named `players` are printed to the console.

The previous example assumes that the length of the array was stored in a variable before the loop was executed. If you don't have the array length handy, you can get it from the array's `length` property:

```
for (int i = 0; i < players.length; i++)
    System.out.println(players[i]);
```

Solving Homework Problems with Arrays

Every once in awhile, an array and a `for` loop or two can help you solve your kids' homework problems for them. For example, I once helped my daughter solve a tough homework assignment for a seventh grade math class. The problem was stated something like this:

> Bobo (these problems always had a character named Bobo in them) visits the local high school on a Saturday and finds that all the school's 1,000 lockers are neatly closed. So he starts at one end of the school and opens them all. Then, he goes back to the start and closes every other locker (lockers 2, 4, 6, and so on). Then, he goes back to the start and hits every third locker: If it's open, he closes it. If it's closed, he opens it. Then he hits every fourth locker, every fifth locker, and so on. He keeps doing this all weekend long, walking the hallways opening and closing lockers 1,000 times. Then he gets bored and goes home. How many of the school's 1,000 lockers are left open, and which ones are they?

Sheesh!

This problem presented a challenge, and being the computer nerd father that I am, I figured this was the time to teach my daughter about `for` loops and arrays. So I wrote a little program that set up an array of 1,000 booleans. Each represented a locker: `true` meant open, `false` meant closed. Then I wrote a pair of nested `for` loops to do the calculation.

My first attempt told me that 10,000 of the 1,000 lockers were opened, so I figured I had made a mistake somewhere. And while I was looking at it, I realized that the lockers were numbered 1 to 1,000, but the elements in my array were numbered 0 to 999, and that was part of what led to the confusion that caused my first answer to be ridiculous.

So I decided to create the array with 1,001 elements and ignore the first one. That way the indexes corresponded nicely to the locker numbers.

After a few hours of work, I came up with the program in Listing 2-1.

```
public class BoboAndTheLockers
{
    public static void main(String[] args)
    {
        // true = open; false = closed
        boolean[] lockers = new boolean[1001];          → 6

        // close all the lockers
        for (int i = 1; i <= 1000; i++)                 → 9
            lockers[i] = false;

        for (int skip = 1; skip <= 1000; skip++)        → 12
        {
            System.out.println("Bobo is changing every "
                + skip + " lockers.");
            for (int locker = skip; locker < 1000;      → 16
                    locker += skip)
                lockers[locker] = !lockers[locker];     → 18
        }

        System.out.println("Bobo is bored"
            + " now so he's going home.");

        // count and list the open lockers
        String list = "";
        int openCount = 0;
        for (int i = 1; i <= 1000; i++)                 → 27
            if (lockers[i])
            {
                openCount++;
                list += i + " ";
            }

        System.out.println("Bobo left " + openCount
            + " lockers open.");
        System.out.println("The open lockers are: "
            + list);
    }
}
```

Here are the highlights of how this program works:

→ **6** This line sets up an array of booleans with 1,001 elements. I created one more element than I needed so I could ignore element zero.

→ **9** This `for` loop closes all the lockers. This step isn't really necessary, because booleans initialize to `false`. But being explicit about initialization is good.

→**12** Every iteration of this loop represents one complete trip through the hallways opening and closing lockers. The `skip` variable represents how many lockers Bobo skips on each trip. First he does every locker, then every second locker, and then every third locker. So this loop simply counts from 1 to 1,000.

→**16** Every iteration of this loop represents one stop at a locker on a trip through the hallways. This third expression in the `for` statement (on the next line) adds the `skip` variable to the `index` variable so that Bobo can access every *nth* locker on each trip through the hallways.

→**18** This statement uses the not operator (`!`) to reverse the setting of each locker. Thus, if the locker is open (`true`), it's set to closed (`false`). And vice versa.

→**27** Yet another `for` loop spins through all the lockers and counts the ones that are open. It also adds the locker number for each open locker to the end of a string so all the open lockers can be printed.

This program produces more than 1,000 lines of output. But only the last few lines are important. Here they are:

```
Bobo is bored now so he's going home.
Bobo left 31 lockers open.
The open lockers are: 1 4 9 16 25 36 49 64 81 100 121
    144 169 196 225 256 289 324 361 400 441 484 529 576
    625 676 729 784 841 900 961
```

So there's the answer: 31 lockers are left open. I got an A. (I mean, my daughter got an A.)

By the way, did you notice that the lockers that were left open were the ones whose numbers are perfect squares? Or that 31 is the largest number whose square is less than 1,000? I didn't either, until my daughter told me after school the next day.

Using the Enhanced for Loop

Java 1.5 introduces a new type of `for` loop called an *enhanced for loop* that's designed to simplify loops that process arrays and collections (which I cover in the next chapter). When used with an array, the enhanced `for` loop has this format:

```
for (type identifier : array)
{
    statements...
}
```

The *type* identifies the type of the elements in the array, and the *identifier* provides a name for a local variable that is used to access each element. And *array* names the array you want to process.

Here's an example:

```
String[] days = { "Sunday", "Monday", "Tuesday",
                  "Wednesday", "Thursday",
                  "Friday", "Saturday" };
for (String day : days)
{
    System.out.println(day);
}
```

This loop prints the following lines to the console:

```
Sunday
Monday
Tuesday
Wednesday
Thursday
Friday
Saturday
```

In other words, it prints each of the strings in the array on a separate line.

The enhanced `for` loop is a new feature for Java 1.5, so you can't use it if you're working with an earlier version. (That's one of many reasons you should upgrade as soon as you can.)

Using Arrays with Methods

You can write methods that accept arrays as parameters and return arrays as return values. You just use an empty set of brackets to indicate that the parameter type or return type is an array.

For example, here's a static method that creates and returns a `String` array with the names of the days of the week:

```
public static String[] getDaysOfWeek()
{
    String[] days = { "Sunday", "Monday", "Tuesday",
                      "Wednesday", "Thursday",
                      "Friday", "Saturday" };
    return days;
}
```

And here's a static method that prints the contents of any `String` array to the console, one string per line:

```
public static void printStringArray(String[] strings)
{
    for (String s : strings)
        System.out.println(s);
}
```

Finally, here are two lines of code that call these methods:

```
String[] days = getDaysOfWeek();
printStringArray(days);
```

The first statement declares a `String` array, and then calls `getDaysOfWeek` to create the array. The second statement passes the array to the `printStringArray` method as a parameter.

Using Two-Dimensional Arrays

The elements of an array can be any type of object you want, including another array. This is called a *two-dimensional array* or, sometimes, an *array of array*.

Two-dimensional arrays are often used to track data in a column and row format, much the way a spreadsheet works. For example, suppose you're working on a program that tracks five years worth of sales (2001 through 2005) for a company, with the data broken down for each of four sales territories (North, South, East, and West). You could create 20 separate variables, with names such as `sales2001North`, `sales2001South`, `sales2001East`, and so on. But that gets a little tedious.

Alternatively, you could create an array with 20 elements, like this:

```
double[] sales = new sales[20];
```

But then, how would you organize the data in this array so you know the year and sales region for each element?

With a two-dimensional array, you can create an array with an element for each year. Each of those elements, in turn, is another array with an element for each region.

Thinking of a two-dimensional array as a table or spreadsheet is common, like this:

	North	South	East	West
2001	23,853	22,838	36,483	31,352
2002	25,483	22,943	38,274	33,294
2003	24,872	23,049	39,002	36,888
2004	28,492	23,784	42,374	39,573
2005	31,932	23,732	42,943	41,734

Here, each row of the spreadsheet represents a year of sales, and each column represents one of the four sales regions.

Creating a two-dimensional array

To declare a two-dimensional array for this sales data, you simply list two sets of empty brackets, like this:

```
double sales[][];
```

Here, `sales` is a two-dimensional array of type `double`. Or, to put it another way, `sales` is an array of `double` arrays.

To actually create the array, you use the `new` keyword and provide lengths for each set of brackets. For example:

```
sales = new double[5][4];
```

Here, the first dimension specifies that the `sales` array has five elements. This array represents the rows in the table. The second dimension specifies that each of those elements has an array of type `double` with four elements. This array represents the columns in the table.

 A key point to grasp here is that one instance is of the first array, but a separate instance of the second array for each element is in the first array. Thus, this statement actually creates five `double` arrays with four elements each. Those five arrays are then used as the elements for the first array.

Note that as with a one-dimensional array, you can declare and create a two-dimensional array in one statement, like this:

```
double[][] sales = new double[5][4];
```

Here, the `sales` array is declared and created all in one statement.

Accessing two-dimensional array elements

To access the elements of a two-dimensional array, you use two indexes. For example, this statement sets the 2001 sales for the North region:

```
sales[0][0] = 23853.0;
```

As you might imagine, accessing the data in a two-dimensional array by hard-coding each index value can get tedious. So for loops are usually used instead. For example, the following bit of code uses a for loop to print the contents of the sales array to the console, separated by tabs. Each year is printed on a separate line, with the year at the beginning of the line. In addition, a line of headings for the sales regions is printed before the sales data. Here's the code:

```
NumberFormat cf = NumberFormat.getCurrencyInstance();
System.out.println("\tNorth\t\tSouth\t\tEast\t\tWest");
int year = 2001;
for (int y = 0; y < 5; y++)
{
    System.out.print(year + "\t");
    for (int region = 0; region < 4; j++)
    {
        System.out.print(cf.format(sales[y][region]));
        System.out.print("\t");
    }
    year++;
System.out.println();
```

Assuming the sales array has already been initialized, this code produces the following output on the console:

	North	South	East	West
2001	$23,853.00	$22,838.00	$36,483.00	$31,352.00
2002	$25,483.00	$22,943.00	$38,274.00	$33,294.00
2003	$24,872.00	$23,049.00	$39,002.00	$36,888.00
2004	$28,492.00	$23,784.00	$42,374.00	$39,573.00
2005	$31,932.00	$23,732.00	$42,943.00	$41,734.00

The order in which you nest the for loops that access each index in a two-dimensional array is crucial! The previous example lists the sales for each year on a separate line, with the sales regions arranged in columns. For example, you can print a listing with the sales for each region on a separate line, with the years arranged in columns by reversing the order in which the for loops that index the arrays are nested:

```
for (int region = 0; region < 4; region++)
{
    for (int y = 0; y < 5; y++)
```

```
    {
        System.out.print(cf.format(sales[y][region]));
        System.out.print("    ");
    }
    System.out.println();
}
```

Here, the outer loop indexes the region, and the inner loop indexes the year.

```
$23,853.00   $25,483.00   $24,872.00   $28,492.00   $31,932.00
$22,838.00   $22,943.00   $23,049.00   $23,784.00   $23,732.00
$36,483.00   $38,274.00   $39,002.00   $42,374.00   $42,943.00
$31,352.00   $33,294.00   $36,888.00   $39,573.00   $41,734.00
```

Initializing a two-dimensional array

The technique for initializing arrays by coding the array element values in curly braces works for two-dimensional arrays too. You just have to remember that each element of the main array is actually another array. So, you have to nest the array initializers.

Here's an example that initializes the sales array:

```
double[][] sales =
    { {23853.0, 22838.0, 36483.0, 31352.0},     // 2001
      {25483.0, 22943.0, 38274.0, 33294.0},     // 2002
      {24872.0, 23049.0, 39002.0, 36888.0},     // 2003
      {28492.0, 23784.0, 42374.0, 39573.0},     // 2004
      {31932.0, 23732.0, 42943.0, 41734.0} };   // 2005
```

Here, I added a comment to the end of each line to show the year the line initializes. Notice that the left brace for the entire initializer is at the beginning of the second line, and the right brace that closes the entire initializer is at the end of the last line. Then, the initializer for each year is contained in its own set of braces.

Using jagged arrays

When you create an array with an expression such as new int[5][3], you're specifying that each element of the main array is actually an array of type int with three elements. However, Java lets you create two-dimensional arrays in which the length of each element of the main array is different. This is sometimes called a *jagged array,* because the array doesn't form a nice rectangle. Instead, its edges are jagged.

For example, suppose you need to keep track of four teams, each consisting of two or three people. The teams are as follows:

Team	Members
A	Henry Blake, Johnny Mulcahy
B	Benjamin Pierce, John McIntyre, Jonathan Tuttle
C	Margaret Houlihan, Frank Burns
D	Max Klinger, Radar O'Reilly, Igor Straminsky

The following code creates a jagged array for these teams:

```
String[][] teams
    = { {"Henry Blake", "Johnny Mulcahy"},
        {"Benjamin Pierce", "John McIntyre",
            "Jonathan Tuttle"},
        {"Margaret Houlihan", "Frank Burns"},
        {"Max Klinger", "Radar O'Reilly",
            "Igor Straminsky"} };
```

Here, each nested array initializer indicates the number of strings for each subarray. For example, the first subarray has two strings, the second has three strings, and so on.

You can use nested `for` loops to access the individual elements in a jagged array. For each element of the main array, you can use the `length` property to determine how many entries are in that element's subarray. For example:

```
for (int i = 0; i < teams.length; i++)
{
    for (int j = 0; j < teams[i].length; j++)
        System.out.println(teams[i][j]);
    System.out.println();
}
```

Notice that the length of each subarray is determined with the expression `teams[i].length`. This `for` loop prints one name on each line, with a blank line between teams, like this:

```
John McIntyre
Jonathan Tuttle

Margaret Houlihan
Frank Burns

Max Klinger
Radar O'Reilly
Igor Straminsky

Henry Blake
Johnny Mulcahy
```

```
Benjamin Pierce
John McIntyre
Jonathan Tuttle
```

If you don't want to fuss with keeping track of the indexes yourself, you can use an enhanced `for` loop and let Java take care of the indexes. For example:

```
for (String[] team : teams)
{
    for (String player : team)
        System.out.println(player);
    System.out.println();
}
```

Here, the first enhanced `for` statement specifies that the type for the `team` variable is `String[]`. As a result, each cycle of this loop sets `team` to one of the subarrays in the main `teams` array. Then, the second enhanced `for` loop accesses the individual strings in each subarray.

Going beyond two dimensions

Java doesn't limit you to just two-dimensional arrays. Arrays can be nested within arrays to as many levels as your program needs. To declare an array with more than two dimensions, you just specify as many sets of empty brackets as you need. For example:

```
int[][][] threeD = new int[3][3][3];
```

Here, a three-dimensional array is created, with each dimension having three elements. You can think of this array as a cube. Each element requires three indexes to access.

You can access an element in a multi-dimensional array by specifying as many indexes as the array needs. For example:

```
threeD[0][1][2] = 100;
```

This statement sets element 2 in column 1 of row 0 to `100`.

You can nest initializers as deep as necessary, too. For example:

```
int[][][] threeD =
    { { {1,   2,  3}, { 4,  5,  6}, { 7,  8,  9} },
      { {10, 11, 12}, {13, 14, 15}, {16, 17, 18} },
      { {19, 20, 21}, {22, 23, 24}, {25, 26, 27} } };
```

Here, a three-dimensional array is initialized with the numbers 1 through 27.

You can also use multiple nested `if` statements to process an array with three or more dimensions. For example, here's another way to initialize a three-dimensional array with the numbers 1 to 27:

```
int[][][] threeD2 = new int[3][3][3];
int value = 1;
for (int i = 0; i < 3; i++)
    for (int j = 0; j < 3; j++)
        for (int k = 0; k < 3; k++)
            threeD2[i][j][k] = value++;
```

A Fun but Complicated Example: A Chess Board

Okay, so much for the business examples. Here's an example that's more fun, at least if you think chess is fun. The program in Listing 2-2 uses a two-dimensional array to represent a chessboard. Its sole purpose is to figure out the possible moves for a knight (that's the horse for those of you in Rio Linda) given its starting position. The user is asked to enter a starting position (such as f1) and the program responds by displaying the possible squares. Then, the program prints out a crude but recognizable representation of the board with the knight's position indicated with an X and his possible moves indicated with question marks.

In case you're not familiar with chess, it's played on a board that's 8 x 8, with alternating light and dark squares. The normal way to identify each square is to use a letter and a number, where the letter represents the column (called a *file*) and the number represents the row (called a *rank*), as shown in Figure 2-1. The knight has an interesting movement pattern: He moves two squares in one direction, then makes a 90-degree turn and moves one square to the left or right. The possible moves for the knight given a starting position of e4 are shaded dark. As you can see, this knight has eight possible moves: c3, c5, d6, f6, g5, g3, f2, and d2.

Here's a sample of what the console looks like if you enter e4 for the knight's position:

```
Welcome to the Knight Move calculator.

Enter knight's position: e4

The knight is at square e4
From here the knight can move to:
c5
d6
f6
g5
```

```
g3
f2
d2
c3
 -   -   -   -   -   -   -   -
 -   -   -   -   -   -   -   -
 -   -   -   ?   -   ?   -   -
 -   -   ?   -   -   -   ?   -
 -   -   -   -   X   -   -   -
 -   -   ?   -   -   -   ?   -
 -   -   -   ?   -   ?   -   -
 -   -   -   -   -   -   -   -

Do it again? (Y or N) n
```

As you can see, the program indicates that the knight's legal moves from e4 are c5, d6, f6, g5, g3, f2, d2, and c3. And the graphic representation of the board indicates where the knight is and where he can go.

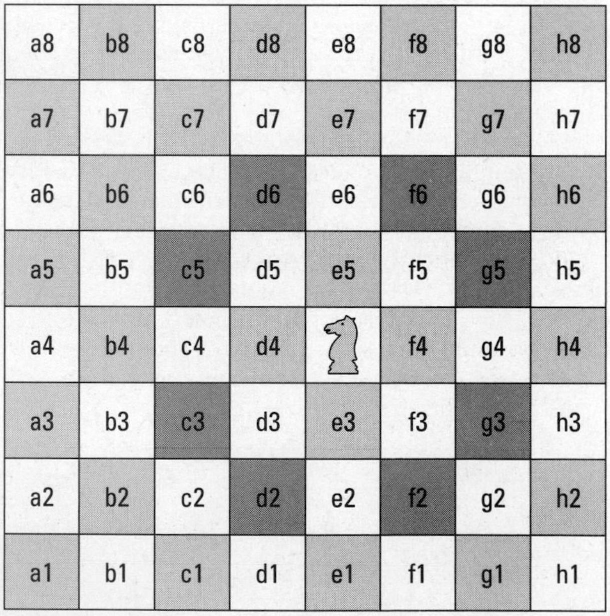

Figure 2-1:
A classic
chessboard.

LISTING 2-2: PLAYING CHESS IN A *FOR DUMMIES* BOOK?

```java
import java.util.Scanner;

public class KnightMoves
{
    static Scanner sc = new Scanner(System.in);

    // the following static array represents the 8
    // possible moves a knight can make
    // this is an 8 x 2 array
    static int[][] moves = { {-2, +1},                          → 10
                             {-1, +2},
                             {+1, +2},
                             {+2, +1},
                             {+2, -1},
                             {+1, -2},
                             {-1, -2},
                             {-2, -1} };

    public static void main(String[] args)
    {

        System.out.println("Welcome to the "
            + "Knight Move calculator.\n");
        do
        {
            showKnightMoves();                                  → 26
        }
        while (getYorN("Do it again?"));
    }

    public static void showKnightMoves()                        → 31
    {
        // The first dimension is the file (a, b, c, etc.)
        // The second dimension is the rank (1, 2, 3, etc.)
        // Thus, board[3][4] is square d5.
        // A value of 0 means the square is empty
        // 1 means the knight is in the square
        // 2 means the knight could move to the square
        int[][] board = new int[8][8];                          → 39

        String kSquare; // the knight's position as a square
        Pos kPos;       // the knight's position as a Pos

        // get the knight's initial position
        do                                                      → 45
        {
            System.out.print("Enter knight's position: ");
            kSquare = sc.nextLine();
            kPos = convertSquareToPos(kSquare);
        } while (kPos == null);

        board[kPos.x][kPos.y] = 1;                              → 52
        System.out.println("\nThe knight is at square "
            + convertPosToSquare(kPos));
```

Book IV
Chapter 2

Using Arrays

continued

LISTING 2-2 (CONTINUED)

```
System.out.println(
    "From here the knight can move to:");

for (int move = 0; move < moves.length; move ++)
{
    int x, y;
    x = moves[move][0];  // the x for this move
    y = moves[move][1];  // the y for this move
    Pos p = calculateNewPos(kPos, x, y);
    if (p != null)
    {
        System.out.println(convertPosToSquare(p));
        board[p.x][p.y] = 2;
    }
}

printBoard(board);

}


// this method converts squares such as a1 or d5 to
// x, y coordinates such as [0][0] or [3][4]
public static Pos convertSquareToPos(String square)
{
    int x = -1;
    int y = -1;
    char rank, file;

    file = square.charAt(0);
    if (file == 'a') x = 0;
    if (file == 'b') x = 1;
    if (file == 'c') x = 2;
    if (file == 'd') x = 3;
    if (file == 'e') x = 4;
    if (file == 'f') x = 5;
    if (file == 'g') x = 6;
    if (file == 'h') x = 7;

    rank = square.charAt(1);
    if (rank == '1') y = 0;
    if (rank == '2') y = 1;
    if (rank == '3') y = 2;
    if (rank == '4') y = 3;
    if (rank == '5') y = 4;
    if (rank == '6') y = 5;
    if (rank == '7') y = 6;
    if (rank == '8') y = 7;

    if (x == -1 || y == -1)
    {
        return null;
    }
    else
        return new Pos(x, y);
}
```

➜ 59

➜ 72

➜ 78

```
// this method converts x, y coordinates such as
// [0][0] or [3][4] to squares such as a1 or d5.
public static String convertPosToSquare(Pos p)                → 114
{
    String file = "";

    if (p.x == 0) file = "a";
    if (p.x == 1) file = "b";
    if (p.x == 2) file = "c";
    if (p.x == 3) file = "d";
    if (p.x == 4) file = "e";
    if (p.x == 5) file = "f";
    if (p.x == 6) file = "g";
    if (p.x == 7) file = "h";

    return file + (p.y + 1);
}


// this method calculates a new Pos given a
// starting Pos, an x move, and a y move
// it returns null if the resulting move would
// be off the board.
public static Pos calculateNewPos(Pos p, int x, int y)        → 134
{
    // rule out legal moves
    if (p.x + x < 0)
        return null;
    if (p.x + x > 7)
        return null;
    if (p.y + y < 0)
        return null;
    if (p.y + y > 7)
        return null;

    // return new position
    return new Pos(p.x + x, p.y + y);
}

public static void printBoard(int[][] b)                      → 150
{
    for (int y = 7; y >= 0; y--)
    {
        for (int x = 0; x < 8; x++)
        {
            if (b[x][y] == 1)
                System.out.print(" X ");
            else if (b[x][y] == 2)
                System.out.print(" ? ");
            else
                System.out.print(" - ");
        }
        System.out.println();
    }
}

public static boolean getYorN(String prompt)                  → 167
```

continued

LISTING 2-2 (CONTINUED)

```
    {
        while (true)
        {
            String answer;
            System.out.print("\n" + prompt + " (Y or N) ");
            answer = sc.nextLine();
            if (answer.equalsIgnoreCase("Y"))
                return true;
            else if (answer.equalsIgnoreCase("N"))
                return false;
        }
    }
}

// this class represents x, y coordinates on the board
class Pos
{
    public int x;
    public int y;

    public Pos(int x, int y)
    {
        this.x = x;
        this.y = y;
    }
}
```

→ 183

You have to put your thinking cap on to follow your way through this program. It's a bit on the complicated side. The following paragraphs can help clear up the more complicated lines:

→**10** This line declares a two-dimensional array that's used to store the possible moves for a knight in terms of x and y. For example, the knight's move of two squares left and one square up is represented as {-2, 1}. There are a total of eight possible moves, and each move has two values (x and y). So, this two-dimensional array has eight rows and two columns.

→**26** The code that gets the user's starting position for the knight and does all the calculations is complicated enough that I didn't want to include it in the main method, so I put it in a separate method named showNightMoves. That way, the do loop in the main method is kept simple. It just keeps going until the user enters N when getYorN is called.

→**31** The showNightMoves method begins here.

→**39** The board array represents the chessboard as a two-dimensional array with eight rows for the ranks and eight columns for the files. This array holds int values. A value of zero indicates that the square is empty. The square where the knight resides gets a 1, and any square the knight can move to gets a 2.

→ **45** This do loop prompts the user for a valid square to plant the knight in. The loop includes a call to the method convertSquareToPos, which converts the user's entry (such as e4) to a Pos object. (The Pos class is defined later in the program; it represents a board position as an x, y pair.) This method returns null if the user enters an incorrect square, such as a9 or x4. So to get the user to enter a valid square, the loop just repeats if the converSquareToPos returns null.

→ **52** The board position entered by the user is set to 1 to indicate the position of the knight.

→ **59** A for loop is used to test all the possible moves for the knight to see if they're valid from the knight's current position using the moves array that was created way back in line 10. In the body of this loop, the calculateNewPos method is called. This method accepts a board position and an x and y value to indicate where the knight can be moved. If the resulting move is legal, it returns a new Pos object that indicates the position the move leads to. If the move is not legal (that is, it takes the knight off the board), the calculateNewPos method returns null.

Assuming calculateNewPos returns a non-null value, the body of this loop then prints the square (it calls convertPosTosquare to convert the Pos object to a string, such as c3). Then, it marks the board position represented by the move with a 2 to indicate that the knight can move to this square.

→ **72** After all the moves are calculated, the printBoard method is called to print the board array.

→ **78** This is the convertSquareToPos method. It uses a pair of brute-force if statements to convert a string such as a1 or e4 to a Pos object representing the same position. I could probably have made this method a little more elegant by converting the first letter in the string to a Char and then subtracting the offset of the letter a to convert the value to a proper integer. But I think the brute-force method is clearer, and only a few more lines of code.

Note that if the user enters an incorrect square (such as a9 or x2), null is returned.

→**114** This is the convertPosToSquare method, which does the opposite of the convertSquareToPos method. It accepts a Pos argument and returns a string that corresponds to the position. It uses a series of brute-force if statements to determine the letter that corresponds to the file, but does a simple addition to calculate the rank. (The Pos object uses array indexes for the y position, which start with zero. So 1 is added to get the rank numbers, which start with 1.)

→**134** The calculateNewPos method accepts a starting position, an x offset, and a y offset. It returns a new position if the move is legal;

otherwise, it returns `null`. To find illegal moves, it adds the `x` and `y` offsets to the starting `x` and `y` position and checks to see if the result is less than zero or greater than 7. If the move is legal, it creates a new `Pos` object whose position is calculated by adding the `x` and `y` offsets to the `x` and `y` values of the starting position.

→**150** The `printBoard` method uses a nested `for` loop to print the board. The outer loop prints each rank. Notice that it indexes the array backwards, starting with 7 and going down to 0. That's necessary so that the first rank is printed at the bottom of the console output. An inner `for` loop is used to print the squares for each rank. In this loop, an `if` statement checks the value of the `board` array element that corresponds to the square to determine whether it prints an X, a question mark, or a hyphen.

→**167** The `getYorN` method simply displays a prompt on-screen and asks the user to enter Y or N. It returns `true` if the user enters Y, `false` if the user enters N. If the user enters anything else, this method prompts the user again.

→**183** The `Pos` class simply defines two public fields, `x` and `y`, to keep track of board positions. It also defines a constructor that accepts the `x` and `y` positions as parameters.

Using the Arrays Class

The final topic for this chapter is the `Arrays` class, which provides a collection of `static` methods that are useful for working with arrays. The `Arrays` class is in the `java.util` package, so you have to use an `import` statement for the `java.util.Arrays` class or the entire `java.util.*` package to use this class. Table 2-1 lists the most commonly used methods of the `Arrays` class.

Table 2-1	Handy Methods of the Arrays Class
Method	*Description*
`static int binarySearch` `(array, key)`	Searches for the specified key value in an array. The return value is the index of the element that matches the key. Returns −1 if the key couldn't be found. The array and the key must be of the same type and can be any primitive type or an object.
`boolean deepEquals(array1,` `array2)`	Returns `true` if the two arrays have the same element values. This method works for arrays of two or more dimensions.
`boolean equals(array1,` `array2)`	Returns `true` if the two arrays have the same element values. This method only checks equality for one-dimensional arrays.

Method	Description
`static void fill(array, value)`	Fills the array with the specified value. The value and array must be of the same type and can be any primitive type or an object.
`static void fill(array, from, to, value)`	Fills the elements indicated by the *from* and *to* int parameters with the specified value. The value and array must be of the same type and can be any primitive type or an object.
`static void sort(array)`	Sorts the array into ascending sequence.
`static void sort(array, from, to)`	Sorts the specified elements of the array into ascending sequence.
`static String toString(array)`	Formats the array values in a string. Each element value is enclosed in brackets, and the element values are separated from each other with commas.

Filling an array

The `fill` method can be handy if you want to pre-fill an array with values other than the default values for the array type. For example, here's a routine that creates an array of integers and initializes each element to 100:

```
int[] startValues = new int[10];
Arrays.fill(startValues, 100);
```

Although you can code a complicated expression as the second parameter, the `fill` method only evaluates this expression once. Then, it assigns the result of this expression to each element in the array.

For example, you might think you could fill an array of 1,000 integers with random numbers from 1 to 100 like this:

```
int[] ran = new int[1000]
Arrays.fill(ran, (int)(Math.random() * 100) + 1);
```

Unfortunately, this won't work. What happens is that the expression is evaluated once to get a random number. Then, all 1,000 elements in the array are set to that random number.

Sorting an array

The `sort` method is a quick way to sort an array into sequence. For example, these statements create an array with 100 random numbers, and then sort the array into sequence so the random numbers are in order:

```
int[] lotto = new int[6];
```

```
for (int i = 0; i < 6; i++)
    lotto[i] = (int)(Math.random() * 100) + 1;
Arrays.sort(lotto);
```

Searching an array

The `binarySearch` method is an efficient way to locate an item in an array by its value. For example, suppose you want to find out if your lucky number is in the `lotto` array created in the previous example. You could just use a `for` loop, like this:

```
int lucky = 13;
int foundAt = -1;
for (int i = 0; i < lotto.length; i++)
    if (lotto[i] == lucky)
        foundAt = i;
if (foundAt > -1)
    System.out.println("My number came up!");
else
    System.out.println("I'm not lucky today.");
```

Here, the `for` loop compares each element in the array with my lucky number. This works fine for small arrays, but what if the array had 1,000,000 elements instead of 6? In that case, it would take a while to look at each element. If the array is sorted into sequence, the `binarySearch` method can find your lucky number more efficiently and with less code:

```
int lucky = 13;
int foundAt = Arrays.binarySearch(lotto, lucky);
if (foundAt > -1)
    System.out.println("My number came up!");
else
    System.out.println("I'm not lucky today.");
```

The `binarySearch` method uses a technique similar to the strategy for guessing a number. If I say I'm thinking of a number between 1 and 100, you don't start guessing the numbers in sequence starting with 1. Instead, you guess 50. If I tell you that 50 is low, you guess 75. Then, if I tell you 75 is high, you guess halfway between 50 and 75. And so on until you find the number. The `binarySearch` method uses a similar technique, but it only works if the array is sorted first.

Comparing arrays

If you use the equality operator (==) to compare array variables, the array variables are considered equal only if both variables point to the exact same array instance. To compare two arrays element by element, you should use the `Arrays.equal` method instead. For example:

```
if (Arrays.equal(array1, array2))
    System.out.println("The arrays are equal!");
```

Here, the two arrays `array1` and `array2` are compared element by element. If both arrays have the same number of elements and each element has the same value, the `equals` method returns `true`. If any of the elements are not equal, or if one array has more elements than the other, the `equals` method returns `false`.

If the array has more than one dimension, you can use the `deepEquals` method instead. It compares any subarrays element by element to determine if the two arrays are identical.

Converting arrays to strings

The `toString` method of the `Arrays` class is handy if you want to quickly dump the contents of an array to the console to see what it contains. This method returns a string that shows the array's elements enclosed in brackets, with the elements separated by commas.

For example, here's a routine that creates an array, fills it with random numbers, and then uses the `toString` method to print the array elements:

```
int[] lotto = new int[6];
for (int i = 0; i < 6; i++)
    lotto[i] = (int)(Math.random() * 100) + 1;
System.out.println(Arrays.toString(lotto));
```

Here's a sample of the console output created by this code:

```
[4, 90, 65, 84, 99, 81]
```

Note that the `toString` method works only for one-dimensional arrays. To print the contents of a two-dimensional array with the `toString` method, use a `for` loop to call the `toString` method for each subarray.

Chapter 3: Using the ArrayList Class

In This Chapter

✔ Introducing the `ArrayList` **class**

✔ Creating an array list

✔ Adding elements to an array list

✔ Deleting or modifying elements from an array list

✔ A gentle introduction to generics

Some people love to collect things. My wife collects lots of things. Salt and pepper shakers, nutcrackers, bears, shot glasses, and tin signs to name but a few.

If I were writing a program to keep track of one of her collections, an array would be a poor choice for storing the data. That's because on any given day, she may come home with a new item she found at an estate sale or an auction. So if she had 87 tin signs before, and I had created an array big enough to hold all 87 signs, I'd have to change the array declaration to hold 88 signs.

Java's *collection classes* are designed to simplify the programming for applications that have to keep track of groups of objects. These classes are very powerful and surprisingly easy to use — at least the basics, anyway. The more advanced features of collection classes take some serious programming to get right, but for most applications, a few simple methods are all you need to use collection classes.

Unfortunately, Java's collection classes are organized according to a pretty complicated inheritance hierarchy that can be very confusing for beginners. Most of the Java books I have on my shelf start by explaining this inheritance scheme and showing how each of the various collection classes fits into this scheme, and why.

I'm not going to do that, because I think it's very confusing for a newcomer to collections to have to wade through a class hierarchy that doesn't make sense until you know some of the details of how the basic classes work. So instead, I just show you how to use two of the best of these classes. In this chapter, you find out how to use the `ArrayList` class. Then, in the next chapter, you find out how to use its first cousin, the `LinkedList`. Once you know how to use these two classes, you shouldn't have any trouble learning how to use the other collection classes from the API documentation.

Java 1.5 introduced a major new language feature called *generics* that is specifically aimed at making collections easier to work with. Because generics are an integral part of how collections work in Java 1.5, I incorporate the generics feature into this chapter from the very start. I point out the differences for using `ArrayList` without generics along the way, just in case you're using an older version of Java or are working with programs that were written before Java 1.5 became available. For a complete explanation of how the generics feature works, you can refer to Book IV, Chapter 5.

The ArrayList Class

An *array list* is the most basic type of Java collection. You can think of an array list as an array on steroids. It's similar to an array, but avoids many of the most common problems of working with arrays. Specifically:

✦ **An array list automatically resizes itself whenever necessary.** If you create an array with 100 elements, then fill it up and need to add a 101st element, you're out of luck. The best you can do is create a new array with 101 elements, copy the 100 elements from the old array to the new one, and then put the new data in the 101st element. With an array list, there's never a limit to how many elements you can create. You can keep adding elements as long as you want.

✦ **An array list lets you insert elements into the middle of the collection.** With an array, inserting elements is pretty hard to do. Suppose you have an array that can hold 100 elements, but only the first 50 have data. If you need to insert a new element after the 25th item, you must first make a copy of elements 26 through 50 to make room for the new element. With an array list, you just say you want to insert the new element after the 25th item and the array list takes care of shuffling things around.

✦ **An array list lets you delete items.** If you delete an item from an array, the deleted element becomes null but the empty slot that was occupied by the item stays in the array. When you delete an item from an array list, any subsequent items in the array are automatically moved forward one position to fill in the spot that was occupied by the deleted item.

✦ **The `ArrayList` class actually uses an array internally to store the data you add to the array list.** The `ArrayList` class takes care of managing the size of this array. When you add an item to the array list and the underlying array is full, the `ArrayList` class automatically creates a new array with a larger capacity and copies the existing items to the new array before it adds the new item.

The `ArrayList` class has several constructors and a ton of methods. For your reference, Table 3-1 lists the constructors and methods of the `ArrayList` class.

Table 3-1	The ArrayList Class
Constructor	*Explanation*
`ArrayList()`	Creates an array list with an initial capacity of 10 elements.
`ArrayList(int capacity)`	Creates an array list with the specified initial capacity.
`ArrayList(Collection c)`	Creates an array list and copies all the elements from the specified collection into the new array list.
Method	*Explanation*
`add(Object element)`	Adds the specified object to the array list. If you specified a type when you created the array list, the object must be of the correct type.
`add(int index, Object element)`	Adds the specified object to the array list at the specified index position. If you specified a type when you created the array list, the object must be of the correct type.
`addAll(Collection c)`	Adds all of the elements of the specified collection to this array list.
`addAll(int index, Collection c)`	Adds all the elements of the specified collection to this array list at the specified index position.
`clear()`	Deletes all elements from the array list.
`clone()`	Returns a shallow copy of the array list. The elements contained in the copy are the same object instances as the elements in the original.
`contains(Object elem)`	Returns a boolean that indicates whether or not the specified object is in the array list.
`containsAll(Collection c)`	Returns a boolean that indicates whether or not this array list contains all the objects that are in the specified collection.
`ensureCapacity(int minCapacity)`	Increases the array list's capacity to the specified value. (If the capacity is already greater than the specified value, this method does nothing.)
`get(int index)`	Returns the object at the specified position in the list.

**Book IV
Chapter 3**

**Using the
ArrayList Class**

(continued)

Table 3-1 *(continued)*

Method	Explanation
indexOf(Object *elem*)	Returns the index position of the first occurrence of the specified object in the array list. If the object isn't in the list, returns −1.
isEmpty()	Returns a boolean value that indicates whether or not the array list is empty.
iterator()	Returns an iterator for the array list.
lastIndexOf(Object *elem*)	Returns the index position of the last occurrence of the specified object in the array list. If the object isn't in the list, returns −1.
remove(int *index*)	Removes the object at the specified index. Returns the element that was removed.
remove(Object *elem*)	Removes an object from the list. Note that more than one element refers to the object; this method removes only one of them. Returns a boolean that indicates whether or not the object was in the list.
remove(int *fromIndex*, int *toIndex*)	Removes all objects whose index values are between the values specified. Note that the elements at the *fromIndex* and *toIndex* positions are not themselves removed.
removeAll(Collection *c*)	Removes all the objects in the specified collection from this array list.
retainAll(Collection *c*)	Removes all the objects that are not in the specified collection from this array list.
set(int *index*, Object *elem*)	Sets the specified element to the specified object. The element that was previously at that position is returned as the method's return value.
size()	Returns the number of elements in the list.
toArray()	Returns the elements of the array list as an array of objects (Object[]).
toArray(type[] *array*)	Returns the elements of the array list as an array whose type is the same as the array passed via the parameter.

The rest of this chapter shows you how to use these constructors and methods to work with ArrayList objects.

Creating an ArrayList Object

To create an array list, you first declare an `ArrayList` variable, and then call the `ArrayList` constructor to instantiate an array list object and assign it to the variable. You can do this on separate lines:

```
ArrayList signs;
signs = new ArrayList();
```

or, you can do it on a single line:

```
ArrayList signs = new ArrayList();
```

Here are a few things to note about creating array lists:

+ The `ArrayList` class is in the `java.util` package, so your program must import either `java.util.ArrayList` or `java.util.*`.

+ Unlike an array, you don't have to specify a capacity for an array list. However, you can if you want. Here's a statement that creates an array list with an initial capacity of 100:

    ```
    ArrayList signs = new ArrayList(100);
    ```

    If you don't specify a capacity for the array list, the initial capacity is set to 10. Providing at least a rough estimate of how many elements each array list can hold when you create it is a good idea.

+ The capacity of an array list is not a fixed limit. The `ArrayList` class automatically increases the list's capacity whenever necessary.

+ If you're using Java 1.5, you can also specify the type of elements the array list is allowed to contain. For example, this statement creates an array list that holds `String` objects:

    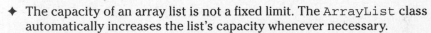
    ```
    ArrayList<String> signs = new ArrayList<String>();
    ```

    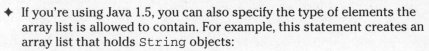
    The advantage of specifying a type when you declare an array list is that the compiler complains if you then try to add an object of the wrong type to the list. (This feature is called *generics* because it lets the Java API designers create generic collection classes that can be used to store any type of object. For more information, refer to Book IV, Chapter 5.)

+ The `ArrayList` class also has a constructor that lets you specify another collection object (typically another array list) whose items are copied into the new array list. This provides an easy way to make a copy of an array list, but you can also use it to convert any other type of collection to an array list.

Book IV
Chapter 3

Using the ArrayList Class

Adding Elements

After you create an array list, you can use the add method to add objects to the array list. For example, here's code that adds strings to an array list:

```
signs.add("Drink Pepsi");
signs.add("No minors allowed");
signs.add("Say Pepsi, Please");
signs.add("7-Up: You Like It, It Likes You");
signs.add("Dr. Pepper 10, 2, 4");
```

If you specified a type when you created the array list, the objects you add via the add method must be of the correct type.

You can insert an object at a specific position in the list by listing the position in the add method. For example, consider these statements:

```
ArrayList<String> nums = new ArrayList<String>();
nums.add("One");
nums.add("Two");
nums.add("Three");
nums.add("Four");
nums.add(2, "Two and a half");
```

After these statements execute, the nums array list contains the following strings:

```
One
Two
Two and a half
Three
Four
```

Here are some important points to keep in mind when you add elements to array lists:

+ If an array list is already at its capacity when you add an element, the array list automatically expands its capacity. Although this capacity is flexible, it's also inefficient. So, whenever possible, you should anticipate how many elements you're adding to an array list and set the list's initial capacity accordingly. (You can also change the capacity at any time by calling the ensureCapacity method.)

+ Like arrays, array lists are indexed starting with zero. Keep this in mind when you use the version of the add method that accepts an index number.

+ The add method that inserts elements at a specific index position throws the unchecked exception IndexOutOfBoundsException if an object isn't already at the index position you specify.

Accessing Elements

To access a specific element in an array list, you can use the `get` method. It specifies the index value of the element you want to retrieve. For example, here's a `for` loop that prints all the strings in an array list:

```
for (int i = 0; i < nums.size(); i++)
    System.out.println(nums.get(i));
```

Here, the `size` method is used to set the limit of the `for` loop's index variable.

The easiest way to access all the elements in an array list is by using an enhanced `for` statement. It lets you retrieve the elements without bothering with indexes or the `get` method. For example:

```
for (String s : nums)
    System.out.println(s);
```

Here, each `String` element in the `nums` array list is printed to the console.

If you need to know the index number of a particular object in an array list and you have a reference to the object, you can use the `indexOf` method. For example, here's an enhanced `for` loop that prints the index number of each string along with the string:

```
for (String s : nums)
{
    int i = nums.indexOf(s);
    System.out.println("Item " + i + ": " + s);
}
```

Depending on the contents of the array list, the output from this loop looks something like this:

```
Item 0: One
Item 1: Two
Item 2: Three
Item 3: Four
```

Printing an ArrayList

The `toString` method of the `ArrayList` class (as well as other collection classes) is designed to make it easy to quickly print out the contents of the list. It returns the contents of the array list enclosed in a set of brackets, with each element value separated by commas. The `toString` method of each element is called to obtain the element value.

Book IV
Chapter 3

Using the ArrayList Class

For example, consider these statements:

```
ArrayList<String> nums = new ArrayList<String>();
nums.add("One");
nums.add("Two");
nums.add("Three");
nums.add("Four");
System.out.println(nums);
```

When you run these statements, the following is displayed on the console:

```
[One, Two, Three, Four]
```

Although this output isn't very useful for actual applications, it's convenient for testing purposes or for debugging problems in programs that use array lists.

Using an Iterator

Another way to access all the elements in an array list (or any other collection type) is to use an iterator. An *iterator* is a special type of object whose sole purpose in life is to let you step through the elements of a collection.

The enhanced `for` statement introduced with Java 1.5 is designed to simplify programs that use iterators. As a result, if you're using Java 1.5, you can use the enhanced `for` statement instead of iterators. Still, you'll probably encounter existing programs that use iterators, so you need to know how they work.

An iterator object implements the `Iterator` interface, which is defined as part of the `java.util` package. As a result, to use an iterator, you must import either `java.util.Iterator` or `java.util.*`. The `Iterator` interface defines just three methods, as listed in Table 3-2. These methods are all you need to access each element of a collection. (Actually, you only need the `hasNext` and `next` methods. The `remove` method is gravy.)

Table 3-2	The Iterator Interface
Method	*Explanation*
`hasNext()`	Returns `true` if the collection has at least one element that hasn't yet been retrieved.
`next()`	Returns the next element in the collection.
`remove()`	Removes the most recently retrieved element.

The Iterator Pattern

Java's iterators follow a commonly known design pattern called the *Iterator pattern*. The Iterator pattern is useful whenever you need to provide sequential access to a collection of objects. The Iterator pattern relies on interfaces so the code that's using the iterator doesn't have to know what actual class is being iterated. As long as the class implements the iterator interface, it can be iterated.

The Iterator interface itself defines the methods used for sequential access. The common pattern is for this interface to provide at least two methods:

✔ **hasNext:** Returns a boolean value that indicates whether another item is available.

✔ **next:** Returns the next item.

Java also defines a third method for its Iterator interface: remove, which removes the most recently retrieved object.

In addition to the Iterator interface, the collection class itself needs a way to get an iterator object. It does so via the iterator method, which simply returns an iterator object for the collection. The iterator method is defined by the Iterable interface. Thus, any object that implements Iterable has an iterator method that provides an iterator for the object.

To use an iterator, you first call the array list's iterator method to get the iterator. Then, you use the iterator's hasNext and next methods to retrieve each item in the collection. The normal way to do that is with a while loop. For example:

```
ArrayList<String> nums = new ArrayList<String>();
nums.add("One");
nums.add("Two");
nums.add("Three");
nums.add("Four");

String s;
Iterator e = nums.iterator();
while (e.hasNext())
{
    s = (String)e.next();
    System.out.println(s);
}
```

Here, the first five statements create an array list and add four strings to it. Next, the `iterator` method is called to get an iterator for the `nums` array list. The `hasNext` method is called in the `while` statement, and the `next` method is called to get the element to be printed.

Note that the object returned by the `next` method must be cast to a `String`. That's because the `Iterator` interface has no knowledge of the type of objects stored in the collection. As a result, it simply returns an `Object`. You must then cast this object to the correct type before you can use it.

Updating Elements

You can use the `set` method to replace an existing object with another object. For example:

```
ArrayList<String> nums = new ArrayList<String>();
nums.clear();
nums.add("One");
nums.add("Two");
nums.add("Three");
System.out.println(nums);
nums.set(0, "Uno");
nums.set(1, "Dos");
nums.set(2, "Tres");
System.out.println(nums);
```

Here, an array list is created with three strings, and the contents of the array list is printed to the console. Then, each of the three strings is replaced by another string, and the contents is printed again. When you run this code, the following is printed on the console:

```
[One, Two, Three]
[Uno, Dos, Tres]
```

Because array lists contain references to objects, not the objects themselves, any changes you make to an object in an array list are automatically reflected in the list. As a result, you often don't have to use the `set` method.

For example:

```
ArrayList<Employee> emps = new ArrayList<Employee>();

// add employees to array list
emps.add(new Employee("Addams", "Gomez"));
emps.add(new Employee("Taylor", "Andy"));
emps.add(new Employee("Kirk", "James"));
```

```
// print array list
System.out.println(emps);

// change one of the employee's names
Employee e = emps.get(1);
e.changeName("Petrie", "Robert");

// print the array list again
System.out.println(emps);
```

It uses the `Employee` class whose constructor accepts an employee's last and first name to create a new employee object, as well as a `changeName` method that also accepts a last and first name. In addition, the `Employee` class overrides the `toString` method to return the employee's first and last name.

The `main` method begins by creating an `ArrayList` object and adding three employees. Then, it prints out the contents of the array list. Next, it retrieves the employee with index number 1 and changes that employee's name. Finally, it prints the contents of the array list again.

Here's what this code produces on the console:

```
[Gomez Addams, Andy Taylor, James Kirk]
[Gomez Addams, Robert Petrie, James Kirk]
```

Notice that the second employee's name was changed, even though the program doesn't use the `set` method to replace the changed `Employee` object in the collection. That's because the array list merely stores references to the `Employee` objects.

Deleting Elements

The `ArrayList` class provides several methods that let you remove elements from the collection. To remove all the elements, use the `clear` method, like this:

```
emps.clear();
```

To remove a specific element, use the `remove` method. It lets you remove an element based on the index number, like this:

```
emps.remove(0);
```

Here, the first element in the array list is removed.

Alternatively, you can pass the actual object you want removed. This is useful if you don't know the index of the object you want to remove, but you happen to have a reference to the actual object. For example:

```
ArrayList<Employee> emps = new ArrayList<Employee>();

// create employee objects
Employee emp1 = new Employee("Addams", "Gomez");
Employee emp2 = new Employee("Taylor", "Andy");
Employee emp3 = new Employee("Kirk", "James");

// add employee objects to array list
emps.add(emp1);
emps.add(emp2);
emps.add(emp3);

// print the array list
System.out.println(emps);

// remove one of the employees
emps.remove(emp2);

// print the array list again
System.out.println(emps);
```

Here's what this code produces on the console:

```
[Gomez Addams, Andy Taylor, James Kirk]
[Gomez Addams, James Kirk]
```

As you can see, Andy Taylor was removed from the list without knowing his index position.

Here are a few important details to keep in mind:

✦ The `clear` and `remove` methods don't actually delete objects. They simply remove the references to the objects from the array list. Like any other object, the objects in a collection are deleted automatically by the garbage collector, and then only if the objects are no longer being referenced by the program.

✦ You can remove more than one element at once by using the `removeRange` method. On it, you specify the starting and ending index numbers. (Note that this method removes all elements between the elements you specify, but the elements you specify aren't themselves removed. For example, `removeRange(5, 8)` removes elements 6 and 7. Elements 5 and 8 aren't removed.)

✦ You can also use the `removeAll` method to remove all the objects in one collection from another collection. And a similar method, `retainAll`, removes all the objects that are *not* in another collection.

Chapter 4: Using the LinkedList Class

The `ArrayList` class, which I cover in the previous chapter, is a collection class that's based on an array. Arrays have their strengths and their weaknesses. The strength of an array is that it's very efficient — at least until you fill it up or try to reorganize it by inserting or deleting elements. Then, it suddenly becomes very inefficient.

Over the years, computer scientists have developed various alternatives to arrays that are more efficient for certain types of access. One of the oldest of these is the *linked list*. A linked list is less efficient than an array for tasks such as directly accessing an element based on its index number. However, linked lists run circles around arrays when you need to insert or delete items in the middle of the list.

In this chapter, you find out how to use Java's `LinkedList` class, which provides a collection that's based on a linked list rather than an array. You'll find that although the `LinkedList` class provides many of the same features as the `ArrayList` class, it also has some tricks of its own.

The LinkedList Class

A *linked list* is a collection in which every object in the list maintains with it a pointer to the next object in the list and the previous object in the list. No array is involved at all in a linked list. Instead, the list is managed entirely by these pointers.

Don't worry — you don't have to do any of this pointer management yourself. It's all taken care of for you by the `LinkedList` class.

This arrangement has some compelling advantages over arrays:

✦ Because the `ArrayList` class uses an array to store list data, the `ArrayList` class frequently has to reallocate its array when you add items to the list. Not so with the `LinkedList` class. Linked lists don't have any size issues. You can keep adding items to a linked list until your computer runs out of memory.

✦ Like the `ArrayList` class, the `LinkedList` class lets you insert items into the middle of the list. However, with the `ArrayList` class, this is a pretty inefficient operation. It has to copy all the items past the insertion point one slot over to free up a slot for the item you're inserting. Not so with the `LinkedList` class. To insert an item in the middle of a linked list, all you have to do is change the pointers in the previous and the next objects.

✦ With an array list, removing items from the list is pretty inefficient. The `ArrayList` class has to copy every item after the deleted item one slot closer to the front of the array to fill in the gap left by the deleted item. Not so with the `LinkedList` class. To remove an item from a linked list, all that's necessary is to update the pointers in the items that were before and after the item to be removed.

For example, if you want to remove the third item from a list that has 10,000 items in it, the `ArrayList` class has to copy 9,997 items. In contrast, the `LinkedList` class does it by updating just two of the items. By the time the `ArrayList` class is done, the `LinkedList` class has had time to mow the lawn, read a book, and go to Disneyland.

✦ Linked lists are especially well suited for creating two common types of lists:

   • **Stacks:** A stack is a list in which items can only be added to and retrieved from the front of the list.

   • **Queues:** A queue is a list in which items are always added to the back of the list and always retrieved from the front.

Arrays are terribly inefficient for the sort of processing required by stacks and queues. (You see examples of how to use linked lists to create stacks and queues in Book IV, Chapter 5.)

✦ The `ArrayList` class actually uses an array internally to store the data you add to the array list. The `ArrayList` class takes care of managing the size of this array. When you add an item to the array list and the underlying array is full, the `ArrayList` class automatically creates a new array with a larger capacity and copies the existing items to the new array before it adds the new item.

There's no such thing as a free lunch, however. The flexibility of a linked list comes at a cost: Linked lists require more memory than an array, and are slower than arrays when it comes to simple sequential access.

Like the ArrayList class, the LinkedList class has several constructors and a ton of methods. For your reference, Table 4-1 lists the constructors and methods of the LinkedList class.

As you look over these methods, you'll find several methods that seem to do the same thing. These similar methods usually have a subtle difference. For example, the getFirst and peek methods both return the first element from the list without removing the element. The only difference is what happens if the list is empty. In that case, getFirst throws an exception, but peek returns null.

But in some cases, the methods are identical. For example, the remove and removeFirst methods are identical. In fact, if you're crazy enough to look at the source code for the LinkedList class, you'll find that the remove method consists of a single line: a call to the removeFirst method.

Table 4-1	The LinkedList Class
Constructor	*Explanation*
LinkedList()	Creates an empty linked list.
LinkedList(Collection *c*)	Creates a linked list and copies all the elements from the specified collection into the new linked list.
Method	*Explanation*
add(Object *element*)	Adds the specified object to the end of the linked list. If you specified a type when you created the linked list, the object must be of the correct type.
add(int *index*, Object *element*)	Adds the specified object to the linked list at the specified index position. If you specified a type when you created the linked list, the object must be of the correct type.
addAll(Collection *c*)	Adds all of the elements of the specified collection to this linked list.
addAll(int *index*, Collection *c*)	Adds all the elements of the specified collection to this linked list at the specified index position.
addFirst(Object *element*)	Inserts the specified object at the beginning of the list. If you specified a type when you created the linked list, the object must be of the correct type.

(continued)

Table 1-1 *(continued)*

Method	Explanation
addLast(Object *element*)	Adds the specified object to the end of the list. This method performs the same function as the add method. If you specified a type when you created the linked list, the object must be of the correct type.
clear()	Deletes all elements from the linked list.
clone()	Returns a copy of the linked list. The elements contained in the copy are the same object instances as the elements in the original.
contains(Object *elem*)	Returns a boolean that indicates whether or not the specified object is in the linked list.
containsAll(Collection *c*)	Returns a boolean that indicates whether or not this linked list contains all the objects that are in the specified collection.
element()	Retrieves the first element from the list. (The element is not removed.)
get(int *index*)	Returns the object at the specified position in the list.
getFirst()	Returns the first element in the list. If the list is empty, throws NoSuchElementException.
getLast()	Returns the last element in the list. If the list is empty, throws NoSuchElementException.
indexOf(Object *elem*)	Returns the index position of the first occurrence of the specified object in the list. If the object isn't in the list, returns −1.
isEmpty()	Returns a boolean value that indicates whether or not the linked list is empty.
iterator()	Returns an iterator for the linked list.
lastIndexOf(Object *elem*)	Returns the index position of the last occurrence of the specified object in the linked list. If the object isn't in the list, returns −1.
offer(Object *elem*)	Adds the specified object to the end of the list. This method returns a boolean value, which is always true.
peek()	Returns (but does not remove) the first element in the list. If the list is empty, returns null.
remove()	Retrieves the first element and removes it from the list. Returns the element that was retrieved. If the list is empty, throws NoSuchElement Exception.
remove(int *index*)	Removes the object at the specified index. Returns the element that was removed.

Method	Explanation
remove(Object *elem*)	Removes an object from the list. Note that if more than one element refers to the object, this method removes only one of them. Returns a boolean that indicates whether or not the object was in the list.
removeAll(Collection *c*)	Removes all the objects in the specified collection from this linked list.
removeFirst()	Retrieves the first element and removes it from the list. Returns the element that was retrieved. If the list is empty, throws NoSuchElement Exception.
removeLast()	Retrieves the last element and removes it from the list. Returns the element that was retrieved. If the list is empty, throws NoSuchElement Exception.
retainAll(Collection *c*)	Removes all the objects that are not in the specified collection from this linked list.
set(int *index*, Object *elem*)	Sets the specified element to the specified object. The element that was previously at that position is returned as the method's return value.
size()	Returns the number of elements in the list.
toArray()	Returns the elements of the linked list as an array of objects (Object[]).
toArray(type[] *array*)	Returns the elements of the linked list as an array whose type is the same as the array passed via the parameter.

Creating a LinkedList

Like any other kind of object, creating a linked list is a two-step affair. First, you declare a LinkedList variable, and then you call one of the LinkedList constructors to create the object. For example:

```
LinkedList officers = new LinkedList();
```

Here, a linked list is created and assigned to the variable officers.

If you're using Java 1.5 (and you should be), you can specify a type when you declare the linked list. For example, here's a statement that creates a linked list that holds strings:

```
LinkedList<String> officers = new LinkedList<String>();
```

Then, you can only add String objects to this list. If you try to add any other type of object, the compiler balks. (Base runners advance.)

Adding Items to a LinkedList

The LinkedList class has many different ways to add items to the list. The most basic is the add method, which works pretty much the same way it works for the ArrayList class. Here's an example:

```
LinkedList<String> officers = new LinkedList<String>();
officers.add("Blake");
officers.add("Burns");
officers.add("Houlihan");
officers.add("Pierce");
officers.add("McIntyre");
for (String s : officers)
    System.out.println(s);
```

The add method adds these items to the end of the list. So the resulting output is this:

```
Blake
Burns
Houlihan
Pierce
McIntyre
```

The addLast method works the same. However, the addFirst method adds items to the front of the list. Consider these statements:

```
LinkedList<String> officers = new LinkedList<String>();
officers.addFirst("Blake");
officers.addFirst("Burns");
officers.addFirst("Houlihan");
officers.addFirst("Pierce");
officers.addFirst("McIntyre");
for (String s : officers)
    System.out.println(s);
```

Here, the resulting output shows the officers in reverse order:

```
McIntyre
Pierce
Houlihan
Burns
Blake
```

To insert an object into a specific position into the list, specify the index in the add method. For example:

```
LinkedList<String> officers = new LinkedList<String>();
officers.add("Blake");
officers.add("Burns");
officers.add("Houlihan");
officers.add("Pierce");
officers.add("McIntyre");
officers.add(2, "Tuttle");
for (String s : officers)
    System.out.println(s);
```

The console output from these statements is this:

```
Blake
Burns
Tuttle
Houlihan
Pierce
McIntyre
```

Here are some other thoughts to consider when you ponder how to add elements to linked lists:

+ If you specified a type for the list when you created it, the items you add must be of the correct type. The compiler kvetches if they aren't.

+ Like arrays and everything else in Java, linked lists are indexed starting with zero.

+ If you specify an index that doesn't exist, the add method throws IndexOutOfBoundsException. This is an unchecked exception, so you don't have to handle it.

+ LinkedList also has a weird method named offer. It adds an item to the end of the list and has a return type of boolean. However, it always returns true. The offer method is defined by the Queue interface, which LinkedList implements. Some classes that implement Queue can refuse to accept an object added to the list via offer. In that case, the offer method returns false. But because a linked list never runs out of room, the offer method always returns true to indicate that the object offered to the list was accepted.

+ In case you're not a *M*A*S*H* fan, Tuttle was a fictitious officer that Hawkeye and B.J. made up in one episode so they could collect his paychecks and donate the money to the local orphanage. Unfortunately, the ruse got out of hand. When Tuttle won a medal and a general wanted to present it in person, they arranged for Tuttle to die in an unfortunate helicopter accident.

Retrieving Items from a LinkedList

As with the `ArrayList` class, you can use the `get` method to retrieve an item based on its index. If you pass it an invalid index number, the `get` method throws the unchecked `IndexOutOfBoundsException`.

You can also use an enhanced `for` loop to retrieve all the items in the linked list. The examples in the preceding section use this enhanced `for` loop to print the contents of the `officers` linked list:

```
for (String s : officers)
    System.out.println(s);
```

If you want, you can also use the `iterator` method to get an iterator that can access the list. For more information about iterators, refer to Book IV, Chapter 3.

The `LinkedList` class also has a variety of other methods that retrieve items from the list. Some of these methods remove the items as they are retrieved. Some throw exceptions if the list is empty, and others return `null`.

Six methods retrieve the first item in the list:

✦ **getFirst:** Retrieves the first item from the list. This method doesn't delete the item. If the list is empty, `NoSuchElement-Exception` is thrown.

✦ **element:** Identical to the `getFirst` method. This strangely named method exists because it's defined by the `Queue` interface, and the `LinkedList` class implements `Queue`.

✦ **peek:** Similar to `getFirst`, but doesn't throw an exception if the list is empty. Instead, it just returns `null`. (The `Queue` interface also defines this method.)

✦ **remove:** Similar to `getFirst`, but also removes the item from the list. If the list is empty, it throws `NoSuchElementException`.

✦ **removeFirst:** Identical to `remove`. If the list is empty, it throws `NoSuchElementException`.

✦ **poll:** Similar to `removeFirst`, but returns `null` if the list is empty. (Yet another method that the `Queue` interface defines.)

Two methods also retrieve the last item in the list:

✦ **getLast:** Retrieves the last item from the list. This method does not delete the item. If the list is empty, `NoSuchElement-Exception` is thrown.

✦ **removeLast:** Similar to `getLast`, but also removes the item. If the list is empty, it throws `NoSuchElementException`.

Isn't it strange that six methods get the first item but only two get the last? Seems to me there should be methods named `lastElement`, `peekLast`, and `pollLast` that would mirror the `element`, `peek`, and `poll` methods. But they didn't ask me.

Updating LinkedList Items

As with the `ArrayList` class, you can use the `set` method to replace an object in a linked list with another object. For example, in that *M*A*S*H* episode where Hawkeye and B.J. made up Captain Tuttle, they quickly found a replacement for him when he died in that unfortunate helicopter accident. Here's how Java implements that episode:

```
LinkedList<String> officers = new LinkedList<String>();

// add the original officers
officers.add("Blake");
officers.add("Burns");
officers.add("Tuttle");
officers.add("Houlihan");
officers.add("Pierce");
officers.add("McIntyre");
System.out.println(officers);

// replace Tuttle with Murdock
officers.set(2, "Murdock");
System.out.println("\nTuttle is replaced:");
System.out.println(officers);
```

The output from this code looks like this:

```
[Blake, Burns, Tuttle, Houlihan, Pierce, McIntyre]

Tuttle is replaced:
[Blake, Burns, Murdock, Houlihan, Pierce, McIntyre]
```

 As with an `ArrayList`, any changes you make to an object retrieved from a linked list are automatically reflected in the list. That's because the list contains references to objects, not the objects themselves. For more information about this issue, refer to Book IV, Chapter 3.

Removing LinkedList Items

You've already seen that several of the methods that retrieve items from a linked list also remove the items. In particular, the `remove`, `removeFirst`, and `poll` methods remove the first item from the list, and the `removeLast` method removes the last item.

You can also remove any arbitrary item by specifying either its index number or a reference to the object you want to remove on the remove method. For example, to remove item 3, use a statement like this:

```
officers.remove(3);
```

And if you have a reference to the item you want to remove, use the remove method like this:

```
officers.remove(tuttle);
```

To remove all the items from the list, use the clear method:

```
officers.clear();        // Goodbye, Farewell, and Amen.
```

Chapter 5: Creating Generic Collection Classes

In This Chapter

↙ Discovering why the generics feature was invented

↙ Using generics in your own classes

↙ Working with wildcards in a generic class

↙ Examining a pair of classes that demonstrate generics

In the previous two chapters, you've seen how you can specify the type for an `ArrayList` or a `LinkedList` so the compiler can prevent you from accidentally adding the wrong type of data to the collection. The `ArrayList` and `LinkedList` classes are able to do this because they take advantage of a new feature of Java 1.5 called *generics*.

In this chapter, I show you how the generics feature works and how to put it to use in your own classes. Specifically, you see examples of two classes that use the `LinkedList` class to implement a specific kind of collection. The first is a *stack,* a collection in which items are always added to the front of the list and retrieved from the front of the list. The second is a *queue,* a collection in which items are added to the end of the list and retrieved from the front.

This is one of those chapters where the entire chapter gets a Technical Stuff icon. Frankly, generics is on the leading edge of object-oriented programming. You can get by without knowing any of the information in this chapter, so feel free to skip it if you're on your way to something more interesting. However, this chapter is worth looking at even if you just want to get an idea of how the `ArrayList` and `LinkedList` classes use the new generics feature. And, you might find that someday you want to create your own generic classes. Your friends will surely think you're a genius.

To be sure, I won't be covering all the intricacies of programming with generics. If your next job happens to be writing Java class libraries for Sun, you'll need to know a lot more about generics than this chapter covers. I focus just on the basics of writing simple generic classes.

Why Generics?

Before Java 1.5, collection classes could hold any type of object. For example, the add method for the ArrayList class had this declaration:

```
public boolean add(Object o)
{
    // code to implement the add method
}
```

Thus, you can pass any type of object to the add method, and the array list gladly accepts it.

When you retrieved an item from a collection, you had to cast it to the correct object type before you could do anything with it. For example, if you had an array list named empList with Employee objects, you'd use a statement like this one to get the first Employee from the list:

```
Employee e = (Employee)empList.get(0);
```

The trouble is, what if the first item in the list isn't an Employee? Because the add method accepts any type of object, there was no way to guarantee that only certain types of objects could be added to the collection.

That's why generics were invented. Now, you can declare the ArrayList like this:

```
ArrayList<Employee> empList = new ArrayList<Employee>();
```

Here, empList is declared as an ArrayList that can hold only Employee types. Now, the add method has a declaration that is the equivalent of this:

```
public boolean add(Employee o)
{
    // code to implement the add method
}
```

Thus, you can only add Employee objects to the list. And the get method has a declaration that's equivalent to this:

```
public Employee get(int index)
{
    // code to implement the get method
}
```

Thus, the get method returns Employee objects. You don't have to cast the result to an Employee because the compiler already knows the object is an Employee.

Creating a Generic Class

Generics let you create classes that can be used for any type specified by the programmer at compile time. To accomplish that, the Java designers introduced a new feature to the language, called *formal type parameters*. To create a class that uses a formal type parameter, you list the type parameter after the class name in angle brackets. The type parameter has a name — Sun recommends you use single uppercase letters for type parameter names — that you can then use throughout the class anywhere you otherwise use a type.

For example, here's a simplified version of the class declaration for the ArrayList class:

```
public class ArrayList<E>
```

I left out the extends and implements clauses to focus on the formal type parameter: <E>. The E parameter specifies the type of the elements that are stored in the list. Sun recommends the type parameter name E (for Element) for any parameter that specifies element types in a collection.

So, consider this statement:

```
ArrayList<Employee> empList;
```

Here, the E parameter is Employee, which simply means that the element type for this instance of the ArrayList class is Employee.

Now, take a look at the declaration for the add method for the ArrayList class:

```
public boolean add(E o)
{
    // body of method omitted (thank you)
}
```

Where you normally expect to see a parameter type, you see the letter E. Thus, this method declaration specifies that the type for the o parameter is the type specified for the formal type parameter E. If E is Employee, that means the add method only accepts Employee objects.

So far, so good. Now take a look at how you can use a formal type parameter as a return type. Here's the declaration for the get method:

```
public E get(int index)
{
    // body of method omitted (you're welcome)
}
```

Here, E is specified as the return type. That means that if E is Employee, this method returns Employee objects.

One final technique you need to know before moving on: You can use the formal type parameter within your class to create objects of any other class that accepts formal type parameters. For example, the `clone` method of the `ArrayList` class is written like this:

```
public Object clone()
{
    try
    {
        ArrayList<E> v = (ArrayList<E>) super.clone();
        v.elementData = (E[])new Object[size];
        System.arraycopy(elementData, 0, v.elementData,
        0, size);
        v.modCount = 0;
        return v;
    }
    catch (CloneNotSupportedException e)
    {
        // this shouldn't happen since we're Cloneable
        throw new InternalError();
    }
}
```

You don't need to look much at the details in this method; just notice that the first statement in the `try` block declares an `ArrayList` of type `<E>`. In other words, the `ArrayList` class uses its own formal type parameter to create another array list object of the same type. If you think about it, that makes perfect sense. After all, that's what the `clone` method does: creates another array list just like this one.

The key benefit of generics is that this typing happens at compile time. Thus, after you specify the value of a formal type parameter, the compiler knows how to do the type checking implied by the parameter. That's how it knows not to let you add `String` objects to an `Employee` collection.

A Generic Stack Class

Now that you've seen the basics of creating generic classes, in this section you look at a simple generic class that implements a stack. A *stack* is a simple type of collection that lets you add objects to the top of the collection and remove them from the top. I name this `Stack` class in this section `GenStack` and it has five methods:

✦ **push:** This method adds an object to the top of the stack.

✦ **pop:** This method retrieves the top item from the stack. The item is removed from the stack in the process. If the stack is empty, this method returns `null`.

✦ **peek:** This method lets you peek at the top item on the stack. In other words, it returns the top item without removing it. If the stack is empty, it returns null.

✦ **hasItems:** This method returns a boolean value of true if the stack has at least one item in it.

✦ **size:** This method returns an int value that indicates how many items are in the stack.

The GenStack class uses a LinkedList to implement the stack. For the most part, this class simply exposes the various methods of the LinkedList class using names that are more appropriate for a stack. The complete code for the GenStack class is shown in Listing 5-1.

LISTING 5-1: THE GENSTACK CLASS

```java
import java.util.*;

public class GenStack<E>                                         → 3
{
    private LinkedList<E> list = new LinkedList<E>();   → 5

    public void push(E item)                                     → 7
    {
        list.addFirst(item);
    }

    public E pop()                                               → 12
    {
        return list.poll();
    }

    public E peek()                                              → 17
    {
        return list.peek();
    }

    public boolean hasItems()                                    → 22
    {
        return !list.isEmpty();
    }

    public int size()                                            → 27
    {
        return list.size();
    }
}
```

The following paragraphs highlight the important details in this class:

→ **3** The class declaration specifies the formal type parameter `<E>`. Thus, users of this class can specify the type for the stack's elements.

→ **5** This class uses a private `LinkedList` object list to keep the items stored in the stack. The `LinkedList` is declared with the same type as the `GenStack` class itself. Thus, if the `E` type parameter is `Employee`, the type for this `LinkedList` is `Employee`.

→ **7** The `push` method accepts a parameter of type `E`. It uses the linked list's `addFirst` method to add the item to the beginning of the list.

→**12** The `pop` method returns a value of type `E`. It uses the linked list's `poll` method, which removes and returns the first element in the linked list. If the list is empty, the `poll` method — and therefore the `pop` method — returns `null`.

→**17** The `peek` method also returns a value of type `E`. It simply returns the result of the linked list's `peek` method.

→**22** The `hasItems` method returns the opposite of the linked list's `isEmpty` method.

→**27** The `size` method simply returns the result of the linked list's `size` method.

So that's all there is to it. The following program gives the `GenStack` class a little workout to make sure it functions properly:

```java
public class GenStackTest
{
    public static void main(String[] args)
    {
        GenStack<String> gs = new GenStack<String>();

        System.out.println(
            "Pushing four items onto the stack.");
        gs.push("One");
        gs.push("Two");
        gs.push("Three");
        gs.push("Four");

        System.out.println("There are "
            + gs.size() + " items in the stack.\n");

        System.out.println("The top item is: " +
            gs.peek() + "\n");
```

```
System.out.println("There are still "
    + gs.size() + " items in the stack.\n");

System.out.println("Popping everything:");
while (gs.hasItems())
    System.out.println(gs.pop());

System.out.println("There are now "
    + gs.size() + " items in the stack.\n");

System.out.println("The top item is: " +
    gs.peek() + "\n");

    }
}
```

This program creates a GenStack object that can hold String objects. It then pushes four strings onto the stack and prints the number of items in the stack. Next, it uses the peek method to print the top item and again prints the number of items in the stack, just to make sure the peek method doesn't accidentally remove the item. Next, it uses a while loop to pop each item off the stack and print it. Then it once again prints the number of items (which should now be zero), and it peeks at the top item (which should be null).

Here's the output that results when you run this program:

```
Pushing four items onto the stack.
There are 4 items in the stack.

The top item is: Four

There are still 4 items in the stack.

Popping everything:
Four
Three
Two
One
There are now 0 items in the stack.

The top item is: null
```

Notice that when the program pops the items off the stack, they come out in reverse order in which they were pushed on to the stack. That's normal behavior for stacks. In fact, stacks are sometimes called *Last-In, First-Out* lists, or *LIFO* lists, for this very reason.

Using Wildcard Type Parameters

Suppose you have a method that's declared like this:

```
public void addItems(ArrayList<Object> list)
{
    // body of method not shown
}
```

Thought question: Does the following statement compile?

```
addItems(new ArrayList<String>());
```

Answer: Nope.

That's surprising because `String` is a subtype of `Object`. So you'd think that a parameter that says it accepts an `ArrayList` of objects accepts an `ArrayList` of strings.

Unfortunately, inheritance doesn't work quite that way when it comes to formal type parameters. Instead, you have to use another feature of generics, called *wildcards*.

In short, if you want to create a method that accepts any type of `ArrayList`, you have to code the method like this:

```
public void addItems(ArrayList<?> list)
```

Here, the question mark indicates that you can code any kind of type here.

That's almost as good as inheritance, but what if you want to actually limit the parameter to collections of a specific superclass? For example, suppose you're working on a payroll system that has an `Employee` superclass with two subclasses named `HourlyEmployee` and `SalariedEmployee`, and you want this method to accept an `ArrayList` of `Employee` objects, `HourlyEmployee` objects, or `SalariedEmployee` objects?

In that case, you can add an `extends` clause to the wildcard, like this:

```
public void addItems(ArrayList<? extends Employee> list)
```

Then, you can call the `addItems` method with an `ArrayList` of type `Employee`, `HourlyEmployee`, or `SalariedEmployee`.

Now, before you call it a day, take this example one step further. Suppose this `addItems` method appears in a generic class that uses a formal type parameter `<E>` to specify the type of elements the class accepts, and you want the `addItems` method to accept an `ArrayList` of type E or any of its subclasses. To do that, you'd declare the `addItems` method like this:

```
public void addItems(ArrayList<? extends E> list)
```

Here, the wildcard type parameter `<? extends E>` simply means that the `ArrayList` can be of type E or any type that extends E.

A Generic Queue Class

Now that you've seen how to use wildcards in a generic class, this section presents a generic class that implements a queue. A *queue* is another type of collection that lets you add objects to the end of the collection and remove them from the top. Queues are commonly used in all sort of applications, from data processing applications to sophisticated networking systems.

This queue class is named `GenQueue` and has the following methods:

✦ **enqueue:** This method adds an object to the end of the queue.

✦ **dequeue:** This method retrieves the first item from the queue. The item is removed from the queue in the process. If the queue is empty, this method returns `null`.

✦ **hasItems:** This method returns a boolean value of `true` if the queue has at least one item in it.

✦ **size:** This method returns an `int` value that indicates how many items are in the stack.

✦ **addItems:** This method accepts another `GenQueue` object as a parameter. All the items in that queue are added to this queue. In the process, all the items from the queue passed to the method are removed. The `GenQueue` parameter must be of the same type as this queue or a subtype of this queue's type.

The `GenQueue` class uses a `LinkedList` to implement its queue. The complete code for the `GenQueue` class is shown in Listing 5-2.

LISTING 5-2: THE GENQUEUE CLASS

```
import java.util.*;

public class GenQueue<E>                                          → 3
{
    private LinkedList<E> list = new LinkedList<E>();   → 5

    public void enqueue(E item)                                   → 7
    {
        list.addLast(item);
    }

    public E dequeue()                                            → 12
    {
        return list.poll();
    }

    public boolean hasItems()                                     → 17
    {
        return !list.isEmpty();
    }

    public int size()                                             → 22
    {
        return list.size();
    }

    public void addItems(GenQueue<? extends E> q)      → 27
    {
        while (q.hasItems())
            list.addLast(q.dequeue());
    }
}
```

The following paragraphs point out the highlights of this class:

→ **3** The class declaration specifies the formal type parameter <E>. Thus, users of this class can specify the type for the elements of the queue.

→ **5** Like the GenStack class, this class uses a private LinkedList object list to keep its items.

→ **7** The enqueue method accepts a parameter of type E. It uses the linked list's addLast method to add the item to the end of the queue.

→**12** The dequeue method returns a value of type E. Like the pop method of the GenStack class, this method uses the linked list's poll method to return the first item in the list.

→**17** The hasItems method returns the opposite of the linked list's isEmpty method.

→**22** The size method returns the result of the linked list's size method.

→**27** The addItems method accepts a parameter that must be another GenQueue object whose element type is either the same type as this GenQueue object's elements or a subtype of this GenQueue object's element type. This method uses a while loop to remove all the items from the q parameter and add them to this queue.

The following program exercises the GenQueue class:

```
public class GenQueueTest
{
    public static void main(String[] args)
    {
        GenQueue<Employee> empList;
        empList = new GenQueue<Employee>();

        GenQueue<HourlyEmployee> hList;
        hList = new GenQueue<HourlyEmployee>();
        hList.enqueue(new HourlyEmployee(
            "Trump", "Donald"));
        hList.enqueue(new HourlyEmployee(
            "Gates", "Bill"));
        hList.enqueue(new HourlyEmployee(
            "Forbes", "Steve"));

        empList.addItems(hList);

        while (empList.hasItems())
        {
            Employee emp = empList.dequeue();
            System.out.println(emp. emp.getFirstName()
                + " " + emp. emp.getLastName());
        }
    }
}

class Employee
{
    public String lastName;
    public String firstName;

    public Employee() {}
```

```
    public Employee(String last, String first)
    {
        this.lastName = last;
        this.firstName = first;
    }

    public String toString()
    {
        return firstName + " " + lastName;
    }
}

class HourlyEmployee extends Employee
{
    public double hourlyRate;

    public HourlyEmployee(String last, String first)
        {
            super(last, first);
        }
}
```

This program begins by creating a GenQueue object that can hold Employee objects. This queue is assigned to a variable named empList.

Next, the program creates another GenQueue object. This one can hold HourlyEmployee objects (HourlyEmployee is a subclass of Employee) and is assigned to a variable named hList.

Then, three rookie employees are created and added to the hList queue. The addItems method of the empList queue is then called to transfer these employees from the hList queue to the empList queue. Because HourlyEmployee is a subclass of Employee, the addItems method of the empList queue accepts hList as a parameter.

Finally, a while loop is used to print the employees that are now in the empList queue.

When this program is run, the following is printed on the console:

```
Donald Trump
Bill Gates
Steve Forbes
```

Thus, the addItems method successfully transferred the employees from the hlist queue, which held HourlyEmployee objects, to the empList queue, which holds Employee objects.

Book V

Programming Techniques

The 5th Wave   By Rich Tennant

©RICH TENNANT

Well heck, Justin—that's darn impressive! What else can that little programmable robot of yours do? How about sewing up and dressing that incision?

Contents at a Glance

Chapter 1: Programming Threads

In This Chapter

- ✔ Examining threads
- ✔ Creating threads from the `Thread` **class**
- ✔ Implementing the `Runnable` **interface**
- ✔ Creating threads that cooperate
- ✔ Interrupting threads

Remember the guy from the old *Ed Sullivan Show* who used to spin plates? Somehow he managed to keep all those plates spinning, running from pole to pole to give each plate a little nudge — just enough to keep it going.

In Java, *threads* are the equivalent of the spinning plate guy. Threads let you divide the work of an application up into separate pieces, which then all run simultaneously. The result is a faster and more efficient program, but along with the increased speed comes more difficult programming and debugging.

Truthfully, the subtleties of threaded programming is a topic for Computer Science majors. But the basics of working with threads aren't all that difficult to learn. In this chapter, I focus on those basics and leave the advanced techniques for the grad students.

The main application I use to illustrate threading in this chapter simulates the countdown clock for the space shuttle. Working with threads isn't really rocket science, but threading is used to solve difficult programming problems. You invariably find yourself trying to get two or more separate pieces of code to coordinate their activities, and that's not as easy as you might think at first guess. As a result, I can't possibly talk about threading without getting into some challenging mental exercises. So be prepared to spend some mental energy figuring out how it works.

The listings in this chapter as well as throughout the book are available at www.dummies.com/go/javaaiofd.

Understanding Threads

A *thread* is a single sequence of executable code within a larger program. All the programs shown so far in this book have used just one thread — the *main thread* that starts automatically when you run the program. However, Java lets you create programs that start additional threads to perform specific tasks.

You're probably already familiar with programs that use threads to perform several tasks at once. Here are some common examples:

✦ Web browsers can download files while still letting you view Web pages. When you download a file in a Web browser, the browser starts a separate thread to handle the download.

✦ E-mail programs don't make you wait for all your messages to download before you can read the first message. Instead, these programs use separate threads to display and download messages.

✦ Word processors can print long documents in the background while you continue to work. These programs start a separate thread to handle print jobs.

✦ Word processors also check your spelling as you type. Depending on how the word processor is written, it may run the spell check in a separate thread.

✦ Game programs commonly use several threads to handle different parts of the game to improve the overall responsiveness of the game.

✦ All GUI-based programs use at least two threads — one thread to run the application's main logic, and another thread to monitor mouse and keyboard events. You find out about creating GUI programs in Java in Book VI.

✦ Indeed, the Java Virtual Machine itself uses threading for some of its housekeeping chores. For example, the garbage collector runs as a separate thread so it can constantly monitor the state of the VM's memory and decide when it needs to remove objects that are no longer being used to create some free memory.

Creating a Thread

Suppose you're developing software for NASA, and you're in charge of the program that controls the final 31 seconds of the countdown for the space shuttle. Your software has to coordinate several key events that occur when the clock reaches certain points. In particular:

✦ **T-minus 16 seconds:** Flood launch pad. This releases 350,000 gallons of water onto the launch pad, which helps protect the shuttle systems during launch. (I'm not making this part up.)

✦ **T-minus 6 seconds:** Start the main engines. In the real space shuttle, the three engines are not started all at the same time. Instead, engine 1 is started at T-minus 6.6 seconds, engine 2 is started 120 milliseconds later at T-minus 6.48 seconds, and engine 3 120 milliseconds after that at T-minus 6.36 seconds. I fudge in my program and start all three engines at T-minus 6 seconds.

✦ **T-minus 0:** Lift off! The solid rocket boosters are lit, the clamps are released, and the shuttle flies into space.

For this program, I don't actually start any rocket engines or release huge amounts of water. Instead, I just display messages on the console to simulate these events. But I do create four separate threads to make everything work. One thread manages the countdown clock. The other three threads fire off their respective events at T-minus 16 seconds (flood the pad), T-minus 6 seconds (fire the engines), and T-minus 0 (launch).

For the first attempt at this program, I just get the countdown clock up and running. The countdown clock is represented by a class named `CountDown Clock`. All this class does is count down from 20 to 0 at one second intervals, displaying messages such as `T minus 20` on the console as it counts. This version of the program doesn't do much of anything, but it does demonstrate how to get a thread going. But first, I need to have a look at the `Thread` class.

Understanding the Thread class

The `Thread` class lets you create an object that can be run as a thread in a multi-threaded Java application. The `Thread` class has quite a few constructors and methods, but for most applications you only need to use the ones listed in Table 1-1. (Note that this table is here to give you an overview of the `Thread` class and to serve as a reference. Don't worry about the details of each constructor and method just yet. By the end of this chapter, I explain each of the constructors and methods.)

Table 1-1	Constructors and Methods of the Thread Class
Constructor	*Explanation*
`Thread()`	The basic `Thread` constructor without parameters. This constructor simply creates an instance of the `Thread` class.
`Thread(String name)`	Creates a `Thread` object and assigns the specified name to the thread.
`Thread(Runnable target)`	A more advanced constructor that lets you turn any object that implements an API interface called `Runnable` into a thread. You see how this constructor is used later in this chapter.
`Thread(Runnable target, String name)`	Creates a thread from any object that implements `Runnable` and assigns the specified name to the thread.

(continued)

Table 1-1 *(continued)*

Constructor	Explanation
`static int activeCount()`	Returns the number of active threads.
`static int enumerate(Thread[] t)`	Fills the specified array with a copy of each active thread. The return value is the number of threads added to the array.
`String getName()`	Returns the name of the thread.
`int getPriority()`	Returns the thread's priority.
`void interrupt()`	Interrupts this thread.
`boolean isInterrupted()`	Checks to see if the thread has been interrupted.
`void setPriority(int priority)`	Sets the thread's priority.
`void setName(String name)`	Sets the thread's name.
`static void Sleep (int milliseconds)`	Causes the currently executing thread to sleep for the specified number of milliseconds.
`void run()`	This method is called when the thread is started. Place the code that you want the thread to execute inside this method.
`void start()`	Starts the thread.
`static void yield()`	Causes the currently executing thread to yield to other threads that are waiting to execute.

Extending the Thread class

The easiest way to create a thread is to write a class that extends the `Thread` class. Then, all you have to do to start a thread is create an instance of your thread class and call its `start` method.

For example, Listing 1-1 is a version of the `CountDownClock` class that extends the `Thread` class.

LISTING 1-1: THE COUNTDOWNCLOCK CLASS (VERSION 1)

```
public class CountDownClock extends Thread        → 1
{
    public void run()                             → 3
    {
        for (int t = 20; t >= 0; t--)             → 5
        {
            System.out.println("T minus " + t);
            try
```

```
        {
            Thread.sleep(1000);                    → 10
        }
        catch (InterruptedException e)
        {}
    }
  }
}
```

Here are a few key points to notice in this class:

> **→ 1** The `CountDownClock` class extends the `Thread` class. `Thread` is
> defined in the `java.language` package, so you don't have to pro-
> vide an `import` statement to use it.

> **→ 3** The `CountDownClock` class has a single method, named `run`. This
> method is called by Java when the clock thread has been started. All
> the processing done by the thread must either be in the `run` method
> or in some other method called by the `run` method.

> **→ 5** The `run` method includes a `for` loop that counts down from 20 to 0.

> **→10** The `CountDownClock` class uses the `sleep` method to pause for
> one second. Because the `sleep` method throws `Interrupted`
> `Exception`, a `try/catch` statement handles this exception. If the
> exception is caught, it is simply ignored.

At some point in its execution, the `run` method must either call `sleep` or
`yield` to give other threads a chance to execute.

Creating and starting a thread

After you define a class that defines a `Thread` object, you can create and
start the thread. For example, here's the main class for the first version of
the countdown application:

```
public class CountDownApp
{
    public static void main(String[] args)
    {
        Thread clock = new CountDownClock();
        clock.start();
    }
}
```

Here, a variable of type `Thread` is declared, and an instance of the `Count`
`DownClock` is created and assigned to it. This creates a thread object, but
the thread doesn't begin executing until you call its `start` method.

When you run this program, the thread starts counting down in one second increments, displaying messages such as the following on the console:

```
T-minus 20
T-minus 19
T-minus 18
```

And so on, all the way to zero. So far, so good.

Implementing the Runnable Interface

For the threads that trigger specific countdown events such as flooding the launchpad, starting the events, or lifting off, I create another class called `LaunchEvent`. This class uses another technique for creating and starting threads, one that requires a few more lines of code but is more flexible.

The problem with creating a class that extends the `Thread` class is that a class can have one superclass. What if you'd rather have your thread object extend some other class? In that case, you can create a class that implements the `Runnable` interface rather than extends the `Thread` class. The `Runnable` interface marks an object that can be run as a thread. It has only one method, `run`, that contains the code that's executed in the thread. (The `Thread` class itself implements `Runnable`, which is why the `Thread` class has a `run` method.)

Using the Runnable interface

To use the `Runnable` interface to create and start a thread, you have to do the following:

1. **Create a class that implements `Runnable`.**

2. **Provide a `run` method in the `Runnable` class.**

3. **Create an instance of the `Thread` class and pass your `Runnable` object to its constructor as a parameter.**

 A `Thread` object is created that can run your `Runnable` class.

4. **Call the `Thread` object's `start` method.**

 The `run` method of your `Runnable` object is called, which executes in a separate thread.

The first two of these steps are easy. The trick is in the third and fourth steps, because you can complete them several ways. Here's one way, assuming that your `Runnable` class is named `RunnableClass`:

```
RunnableClass rc = new RunnableClass();
Thread t = new Thread(rc);
t.start();
```

Java programmers like to be as concise as possible, so you often see this compressed to something more like this:

```
Thread t = new Thread(new RunnableClass());
t.start();
```

or even just this:

```
new Thread(new RunnableClass()).start();
```

This single-line version works provided you don't need to access the thread object later in the program.

Creating a class that implements Runnable

To sequence the launch events for the NASA application, I create a `Runnable` object named `LaunchEvent`. The constructor for this class accepts two parameters: the countdown time at which the event fires, and the message that is displayed when the time arrives. Then, the `run` method for this class uses `Thread.sleep` to wait until the desired time arrives. Then, it displays the message.

Listing 1-2 shows the code for this class.

LISTING 1-2: THE LAUNCHEVENT CLASS (VERSION 1)

```
public class LaunchEvent implements Runnable      → 1
{
    private int start;
    private String message;

    public LaunchEvent(int start, String message)   → 6
    {
        this.start = start;
        this.message = message;
    }

    public void run()
    {
        try
        {
            Thread.sleep(20000 - (start * 1000));    → 16
        }
        catch (InterruptedException e)
        {}
        System.out.println(message);                 → 20
    }
}
```

The following paragraphs draw your attention to the listing's key lines:

→ **1** This class implements the `Runnable` interface.

→ **6** The constructor accepts two parameters: an integer representing the start time (in seconds) and a string message that's displayed when the time arrives. The constructor simply stores these parameter values in private fields.

→**16** In the `run` method, the `Thread.sleep` method is called to put the thread to sleep until the desired countdown time arrives. This length of time the thread should sleep is calculated by the expression `20000 - (start * 1000)`. The countdown clock starts at 20 seconds, which is 20,000 milliseconds. This expression simply subtracts the number of milliseconds that corresponds to the desired start time from 20,000. Thus, if the desired start time is 6 seconds, the `sleep` method sleeps for 14,000 milliseconds — that is, 14 seconds.

→**20** When the thread wakes up, it displays the message passed via its constructor on the console.

Using the CountDownApp class

Now that you've seen the code for the `LaunchEvent` and `CountDown Clock` classes, Listing 1-3 shows the code for a `CountDownApp` class that uses these classes to launch a space shuttle.

LISTING 1-3: THE COUNTDOWNAPP CLASS (VERSION 1)

```
public class CountDownApp
{
    public static void main(String[] args)
    {
        Thread clock = new CountDownClock();           → 5

        Runnable flood, ignition, liftoff;             → 7
        flood = new LaunchEvent(16, "Flood the pad!");
        ignition = new LaunchEvent(6, "Start engines!");
        liftoff = new LaunchEvent(0, "Liftoff!");

        clock.start();                                 → 12

        new Thread(flood).start();                     → 14
        new Thread(ignition).start();
        new Thread(liftoff).start();
    }
}
```

The following paragraphs summarize how this program works:

→ **5** The `main` method starts by creating an instance of the `CountDown Clock` class and saving it in the `clock` variable.

→ **7** Next, it creates three `LaunchEvent` objects to flood the pad at 16 seconds, start the engines at 6 seconds, and lift off at 0 seconds. These objects are assigned to variables of type `Runnable` named `flood`, `ignition`, and `liftoff`.

→**12** The `clock` thread is started. The countdown starts ticking.

→**14** Finally, the program starts the three `LaunchEvent` objects as threads. It does this by creating a new instance of the `Thread` class, passing the `LaunchEvent` objects as parameters to the `Thread` constructor, and then calling the `start` method to start the thread.

Note that because this program doesn't need to do anything with these threads once they're started, it doesn't bother creating variables for them.

When you run this program, the following output is displayed on the console:

```
T minus 20
T minus 19
T minus 18
T minus 17
T minus 16
Flood the pad!
T minus 15
T minus 14
T minus 13
T minus 12
T minus 11
T minus 10
T minus 9
T minus 8
T minus 7
T minus 6
Start engines!
T minus 5
T minus 4
T minus 3
T minus 2
T minus 1
Liftoff!
T minus 0
```

As you can see, the `LaunchEvent` messages are interspersed with the `CountDownClock` messages. Thus, the launch events are triggered at the correct time.

TIP

You can improve the `main` method for this class by using an `ArrayList` to store the `Runnable` objects. Then, you can start all the `LaunchEvent` threads by using an enhanced `for` loop. Here's what the improved code looks like:

```
public static void main(String[] args)
{
    Thread clock = new CountDownClock();

    ArrayList<Runnable> events
        = new ArrayList<Runnable>();
    events.add(new LaunchEvent(16, "Flood the pad!"));
    events.add(new LaunchEvent(6, "Start engines!"));
    events.add(new LaunchEvent(0, "Liftoff!"));

    clock.start();

    for (Runnable e : events)
        new Thread(e).start();
}
```

The advantage of this technique is that you don't need to create a separate variable for each `LaunchEvent`.

Creating Threads That Work Together

Unfortunately, the countdown application presented in the previous section has a major deficiency. The `CountDownClock` and `LaunchEvent` threads depend strictly on timing to coordinate their activities. After these threads start, they run independently of one another. As a result, random variations in their timings can cause the thread behaviors to change.

For example, if you run the program several times in a row, you'll discover that sometimes the `Start engines!` message appears after the `T minus 6` message, and sometimes it appears *before* the `T minus 6` message. That might not be a big deal to you, but it would probably be disastrous for the astronauts on the shuttle.

What these classes really need is a way to communicate with each other. Listing 1-4 shows an improved version of the countdown application that incorporates several enhancements. The `CountDownClock` class in this version adds a new method named `getTime` that gets the current time in the countdown. Then, the `LaunchEvent` class checks the countdown time every 10 milliseconds and triggers the events only when the countdown clock actually says it's time. This version of the application runs consistently.

In addition, you want to enable the LaunchEvent class to monitor the status of the CountDownClock, but you don't want to couple the LaunchEvent and CountDownClock classes too closely together. For example, suppose you later develop a better countdown clock? If the LaunchEvent class knows what class is doing the counting, you have to recompile it if you use a different countdown class.

The solution is to use an interface as a buffer between the classes. This interface defines a method that gets the current status of the clock. Then, the CountDownClock class can implement this interface, and the LaunchEvent class can use any object that implements this interface to get the time.

LISTING 1-4: THE COUNT DOWN APPLICATION (VERSION 2)

```
import java.util.ArrayList;

// version 2.0 of the Countdown application
public class CountDownApp
{
    public static void main(String[] args)
    {
        CountDownClock clock = new CountDownClock(20);          → 8

        ArrayList<Runnable> events = new ArrayList<Runnable>();  → 10

        events.add(                                              → 12
            new LaunchEvent(16, "Flood the pad!", clock));
        events.add(
            new LaunchEvent(6, "Start engines!", clock));
        events.add(
            new LaunchEvent(0, "Liftoff!", clock));

        clock.start();                                           → 19

        for (Runnable e : events)                                → 21
            new Thread(e).start();
    }
}

interface TimeMonitor                                            → 26
{
    int getTime();
}

class CountDownClock extends Thread implements TimeMonitor       → 31
{
    private int t;                                               → 33

    public CountDownClock(int start)                             → 35
    {
        this.t = start;
    }
```

continued

LISTING 1-4 (CONTINUED)

```
    public void run()
    {
        for (; t >= 0; t--)                                          → 42
        {
            System.out.println("T minus " + t);
            try
            {
                Thread.sleep(1000);
            }
            catch (InterruptedException e)
            {}
        }
    }

    public int getTime()                                             → 54
    {
        return t;
    }
}

class LaunchEvent implements Runnable                                → 60
{
    private int start;
    private String message;
    TimeMonitor tm;                                                  → 64

    public LaunchEvent(int start, String message,
        TimeMonitor monitor)
    {
        this.start = start;
        this.message = message;
        this.tm = monitor;
    }

    public void run()
    {
        boolean eventDone = false;
        while (!eventDone)
        {
            try
            {
                Thread.sleep(10);                                    → 81
            }
            catch (InterruptedException e)
            {}
            if (tm.getTime() <= start)                               → 85
            {
                System.out.println(this.message);
                eventDone = true;
            }
        }
    }
}
```

The following paragraphs describe the high points of this version:

→ **8** As you see in line 35, the constructor for the `CountDownClock` class now accepts a parameter to specify the starting time for the countdown. As a result, this line specifies 20 as the starting time for the `CountDownClock` object.

→**10** An `ArrayList` of `LaunchEvent` objects is used to store each launch event.

→**12** The lines that create the `LaunchEvent` objects pass the `Count DownClock` object as a parameter to the `LaunchEvent` constructor. That way, the `LaunchEvent` objects can call the clock's `abort` method if necessary.

→**19** The clock is started!

→**21** An enhanced `for` loop starts threads to run the `LaunchEvent` objects.

→**26** The `TimeMonitor` interface defines just one method, named `getTime`. This method returns an integer that represents the number of seconds left on the countdown timer.

→**31** The `CountDownClock` class now implements the `TimeMonitor` interface.

→**33** A private field named `t` is used to store the current value of the countdown clock. That way, the current clock value can be accessed by the constructor, the `run` method, and the `getTime` method.

→**35** The constructor for the `CountDownClock` class accepts the starting time for the countdown as a parameter. Thus, this countdown clock doesn't have to start at 20 seconds. The value passed via this parameter is saved in the `t` field.

→**42** The `for` loop in the `run` method tests and decrements the `t` variable. But because this variable is already initialized, it doesn't have an initialization expression.

→**54** The `getTime()` method simply returns the value of the `t` variable.

→**60** The start of the `LaunchEvent` class.

→**64** A private field of type `TimeMonitor` is used to access the countdown clock. A reference to this object is passed to the `LaunchEvent` class via its constructor. The constructor simply stores that reference in this field.

→**81** The `while` loop includes a call to `Thread.sleep` that sleeps for just 10 milliseconds. Thus, this loop checks the countdown clock every 10 milliseconds to see if its time has arrived.

→**85** This statement calls the `getTime` method of the countdown clock to see if it's time to start the event. If so, a message is displayed, and `eventDone` is set to `true` to terminate the thread.

Synchronizing Methods

Whenever you work on a program that uses threads, you have to consider the nasty issue of *concurrency*. In particular, what if two threads try to access a method of an object at precisely the same time? Unless you program carefully, the result can be disastrous. A method that performs a simple calculation returns inaccurate results. In an online banking application, you might discover that some deposits are credited twice and some withdrawals aren't credited at all. In an online ordering system, one customer's order might get recorded in a different customer's account.

The key to handling concurrency issues is recognizing methods that update data and that might be called by more than one thread. Once you identify those methods, the solution is simple: You just add the `synchronized` keyword to the method declaration, like this:

```
public synchronized void someMethod()...
```

This tells Java to place a *lock* on the object so that no other methods can call any other synchronized methods for the object until this method finishes. In other words, it temporarily disables multithreading for the object.

The tough part is knowing which methods to synchronize. When I said that any method that updates data can be synchronized, I didn't just mean any method that updates a database. Any method that updates instance variables is at risk and needs to be synchronized. That's because when two or more threads run a method at the same time, the threads share a common copy of the method's instance variables.

Even methods that consist of just one line of code are at risk. For example, consider this method:

```
int sequenceNumber = 0;

public int getNextSequenceNumber()
{
    return sequenceNumber++;
}
```

You'd think that because this method has just one statement, some other thread could not interrupt it in the middle. Alas, that's not the case. This method must get the value of the `sequenceNumber` field, add 1 to it, save the updated value back to the `sequenceNumber` field, and return the value. In fact, this single Java statement compiles to 11 bytecode instructions. If the thread is preempted between any one of them by another thread calling the same method, the serial numbers get munged.

For safety's sake, why not just make all the methods synchronized? There are two reasons:

✦ It takes time to synchronize methods. Java has to acquire a *lock* on the object being synchronized, run the method, and then release the lock. But before it can do that, it has to check to make sure some other thread doesn't already have a lock on the object. All of this takes time.

✦ More importantly, synchronizing all your methods defeats the purpose of multithreading. So you should synchronize only those methods that require it.

The synchronized keyword doesn't block all access to an object. Other threads can still run unsynchronized methods of the object while the object is locked.

The Object class provides three methods that can let synchronized objects coordinate their activities. The wait method puts a thread in the waiting state until some other thread calls either the object's notify or (more commonly) notifyAll method. These methods are useful in situations where one thread has to wait for another thread to do something before it can proceed. The classic example is a banking system where one thread makes withdrawals and the other makes deposits. If a customer's account drops to zero, the thread that makes withdrawals can call wait. Then, the thread that makes deposits can call notifyAll. That way, each time a deposit is made, the withdrawal thread can recheck the customer's account balance to see if it now has enough money to make the withdrawal.

Threadus Interruptus

You can interrupt another thread by calling its interrupt method, provided you have a reference to the thread. For example:

```
t.interrupt();
```

Here, the thread referenced by the t variable is interrupted. Now, all the interrupted thread has to do is find out that it has been interrupted and respond accordingly. That's the topic of the following sections.

Finding out if you've been interrupted

As you've already seen, several methods of the Thread class, including sleep and yield, throw InterruptedException. Up until now, I told you to simply ignore this exception. And in many cases, that's appropriate. However, many (if not most) threads should respond to Interrupted Exception in one way or another. In most cases, the thread should terminate when it's interrupted.

Unfortunately, finding out if a thread has been interrupted isn't as easy as it sounds. `InterruptedException` is thrown when another thread calls the `interrupt` method on this thread while the thread is not executing. That's why the methods that can cause the thread to give up control to another thread throw this exception. That way, when the thread resumes execution, you know it was interrupted.

However, the `yield` and `sleep` methods aren't the only way for control to be wrested away from a thread. Sometimes, the thread scheduler just steps in and says, "You've had enough time, now it's someone else's turn to play." If that happens, and then some other thread calls your thread's `interrupt` method, `InterruptedException` isn't thrown. Instead, a special flag called the *interrupted flag* is set to indicate that the thread was interrupted. You can test the status of this flag by calling the static `interrupted` method.

Unfortunately, that means your threads have to check twice to see if they have been interrupted. The usual way to do that is to follow this form:

```
public void run()
{
    boolean done = false
    boolean abort = false;
    while(!done)
    {
        // do the thread's work here
        // set done to true when finished
        try
        {
            sleep(100);   // sleep a bit
        }
        catch(InterruptedException e)
        {
            abort = true;
        }
        if (Thread.interrupted())
            abort = true;
        if (abort)
            break;
    }
}
```

Here, the `abort` boolean variable is set to true if `InterruptedException` is thrown or if the interrupted flag is set. Then, if `abort` has been set to true, a `break` statement is executed to leave the `while` loop. Of course, this scheme has a million variations. But this one works in most situations.

Aborting the countdown

To illustrate how you can interrupt threads, Listing 1-5 shows yet another version of the countdown application. This version aborts the countdown if something goes wrong with any of the launch events.

To simplify the code a bit, I assume that things aren't going well at NASA, so every launch event results in a failure that indicates to abort the countdown. Thus, whenever the start time for a LaunchEvent arrives, the LaunchEvent class attempts to abort the countdown. It goes without saying that in a real launch control program, you wouldn't want to abort the launch unless something actually does go wrong.

LISTING 1-5: THE COUNTDOWN APPLICATION WITH ABORTS

```
import java.util.ArrayList;

public class CountDownApp                                          → 3
{
    public static void main(String[] args)
    {
        CountDownClock clock = new CountDownClock(20);

        ArrayList<Runnable> events = new ArrayList<Runnable>();
        events.add(
            new LaunchEvent(16, "Flood the pad!", clock));
        events.add(
            new LaunchEvent(6, "Start engines!", clock));
        events.add(
            new LaunchEvent(0, "Liftoff!", clock));

        clock.start();

        for (Runnable e : events)
            new Thread(e).start();
    }
}

interface TimeMonitor
{
    int getTime();
    void abortCountDown();                                         → 26
}

class CountDownClock extends Thread implements TimeMonitor
{
    private int t;
```

continued

LISTING 1-5 (CONTINUED)

```
    public CountDownClock(int start)
    {
        this.t = start;
    }

    public void run()
    {
        boolean aborted = false;                              → 40
        for (; t >= 0; t--)
        {
            System.out.println("T minus " + t);
            try
            {
                Thread.sleep(1000);
            }
            catch (InterruptedException e)
            {
                aborted = true;                               → 50
            }
            if (Thread.interrupted())
                aborted = true;                               → 53
            if (aborted)                                      → 54
            {
                System.out.println("Stopping the clock!");
                break;
            }
        }
    }

    public int getTime()
    {
        return t;
    }

    public synchronized void abortCountDown()                → 67
    {
        Thread[] threads = new Thread[Thread.activeCount()];  → 69
        Thread.enumerate(threads);                            → 70
        for(Thread t : threads)                               → 71
            t.interrupt();
    }
}

class LaunchEvent implements Runnable
{
    private int start;
    private String message;
    TimeMonitor tm;

    public LaunchEvent(int start, String message,
        TimeMonitor monitor)
    {
        this.start = start;
        this.message = message;
        this.tm = monitor;
    }
```

```
public void run()
{
    boolean eventDone = false;
    boolean aborted = false;                            → 92
    while (!eventDone)
    {
        try
        {
            Thread.sleep(10);
        }
        catch (InterruptedException e)
        {
            aborted = true;                             → 101
        }
        if (tm.getTime() <= start)
        {
            System.out.println(this.message);
            eventDone = true;
            System.out.println("ABORT!!!!");            → 107
            tm.abortCountDown();                        → 108
        }
        if (Thread.interrupted())
            aborted = true;                             → 111
        if (aborted)                                    → 112
        {
            System.out.println("Aborting " + message);
            break;
        }
    }
}
```

The following paragraphs point out the highlights of this program:

→ **3** The `CountDownApp` class itself hasn't changed. That's the beauty of object-oriented programming. Although I changed the implementations of the `CountDownClock` and `LaunchEvent` classes, I didn't change the public interfaces for these classes. As a result, no changes are needed in the `CountDownApp` class.

→**26** The `LaunchEvent` class needs a way to notify the `CountDownTimer` class that the countdown should be aborted. To do that, I added an `abortCountDown` method to the `TimeMonitor` interface.

→**40** The `run` method of the `CountDownClass` uses a boolean variable named `aborted` to indicate whether the thread has been interrupted. This variable is set to true in line 50 if `InterruptedException` is caught. It's also set to true in line 53 if `Thread.interrupted()` returns `true`.

→**54** If the `aborted` field has been set to true, it means the thread has been interrupted. So the message `Stopping the clock!` is displayed, and a `break` statement exits the loop. Thus, the thread is terminated.

→ **67** The `abortCountDown` method is synchronized. That's because any of the `LaunchEvent` objects can call it, and there's no guarantee that they won't all try to call it at the same time.

→ **69** The `abortCountDown` method starts by creating an array of `Thread` objects that's large enough to hold all the active threads. The number of active threads is provided by the `activeCount` method of the `Thread` class.

→ **70** The `abortCountDown` method then calls the `enumerate` method of the `Thread` class to copy all the active threads into this array. Note that this method is static, so you don't need a reference to any particular thread to use it. (The `activeCount` method used in line 69 is static too.)

→ **71** An enhanced `for` loop is used to call the `interrupt` method on all the active threads. That shuts down everything.

→ **92** Like the `CountDownClock` class, the `LaunchEvent` class uses a boolean variable to indicate whether the thread has been interrupted. This thread is set if `InterruptedException` is caught in line 101 or if `Thread.interrupted()` returns `true` in line 111. Then, it's tested in line 112. If it has been set to true, the thread prints a message indicating that the launch event has been aborted, and a `break` statement is used to exit the loop and, therefore, terminate the thread.

→**101** When the launch event's start time arrives, the `LaunchEvent` class displays the message `ABORT!` and calls the `abortCountDown` method. Thus, the countdown is aborted the first time any launch event occurs.

When you run this version of the countdown application, here's what appears on the console:

```
T minus 20
T minus 19
T minus 18
T minus 17
T minus 16
Flood the pad!
ABORT!!!!
Stopping the clock!
Aborting Flood the pad!
Aborting Start engines!
Aborting Liftoff!
```

Chapter 2: Network Programming

In This Chapter

✔ IP addresses, DNS names, and other fun stuff

✔ The `InetAddress` class

✔ The `Socket` class

✔ The `ServerSocket` class

✔ A simple client/server program

✔ A server program that uses threads

The term *network programming* can mean a lot of different things. Applets are a form of network programming, as are Java Server Pages and servlets. I cover these network programming features in detail in Book VII.

File and database programming can also be thought of as a form of network programming, as files and databases can be located on a server computer rather than on the computer where the application is run. Book VIII covers the networking aspects of file and database programming.

In this chapter, you discover how to use Java's *sockets interface*, which lets you set up input and output streams between programs on client and server computers. In fact, I show you how to create a simple server program that can be accessed over the Internet.

Along the way, you find out about the TCP/IP networking protocol, IP addresses and ports, and other useful networking topics.

Understanding Network Programming

Network programming usually involves two types of programs: client programs and server programs. A *server program* is a program that provides services to one or more users who run *client programs* to access those services. These client and server computers communicate with each other through well-established *protocols,* which dictate the nature of the communications between clients and servers.

Examples of client and server programs abound:

✦ The World Wide Web uses *Web servers* that provide services. The clients in the World Wide Web are Web browsers, such as Internet Explorer or Navigator. The protocol used to communicate between Web servers and browsers is called *HTTP*.

✦ E-mail is made possible by a protocol called the *Simple Mail Transfer Protocol*, or SMTP. The servers are mail servers, such as sendmail and Microsoft Exchange; the clients are e-mail programs, such as Microsoft Outlook.

✦ The Internet system that converts human-friendly addresses such as www.dummies.com to numeric IP addresses such as 208.215.179.139 is managed by a protocol called DNS, which stands for *Domain Name System*. Your own computer serves as a DNS client, requesting address lookup from DNS servers. For example, when you type www.dummies.com in your Web browser, the browser first asks a DNS server to get the correct IP address for the Web site.

I could go on and on.

IP addresses and ports

An *IP address* is a number that uniquely identifies every computer on an IP network. IP addresses are 32-bit binary numbers, which means that theoretically, a maximum of something in the neighborhood of 4 billion unique host addresses can exist throughout the Internet.

IP addresses are usually represented in a format known as *dotted-decimal notation*. In dotted-decimal notation, each group of eight bits, known as an *octet*, is represented by its decimal equivalent. For example:

```
192.168.136.28
```

You usually see IP addresses represented in this format.

Besides an IP address, you must also use a port to access data from a computer over the Internet. The various services that a server computer might provide are assigned well-known port numbers. For example, the port number for the Web protocol HTTP is 80. As a result, a computer that wants to access a Web server HTTP must do so over port 80.

Port numbers are often specified with a colon following an IP address. For example, the HTTP service on a server whose IP address is 192.168.10.133 is 192.168.10.133:80.

Literally thousands of established ports are in use. If you need to make up a port number for an application, pick a number that's greater than 49151. Those numbers are available for private use.

Host names, DNS, and URLs

A *host name* is a name that's associated with a particular IP address. Host names are created using a naming standard called DNS, which stands for *Domain Name System*. If it weren't for DNS, you'd buy books from 207.171. 166.48 instead of from `www.amazon.com`, you'd sell your used furniture at 66.135.192.87 instead of on `www.ebay.com`, and you'd search the Web at 216.239.57.99 instead of at `www.google.com`.

The Internet has an entire network of DNS server computers throughout the world that look up host names and provide the corresponding IP address. For example, when you enter `www.dummies.com` into the address bar of a Web browser, your browser consults a DNS server to find out the IP address for `www.dummies.com`. Then it displays the home page for that address.

Closely related to DNS is URL, which stands for *Uniform Resource Locator*. URL is a naming scheme that can uniquely identify any resource on the Internet. By *resource,* I usually mean *file*. Thus, URL turns the DNS naming system into a huge file system that lets you access any file that's available anywhere on the Internet. It does this by appending filepath information to the end of a host name, like this:

```
ftp.someserver.com/pub/myfile.txt
```

This URL refers to a file named `myfile.txt` in a directory named `pub` on a computer identified by the host name `ftp.someserver.com`. I won't deal with URLs in this chapter, but they play a big role in Web programming. So be prepared to revisit them in Book VII.

Every computer has a special host name and IP address that's used to identify itself to itself. This host name is `localhost`, and the IP address is `127.0.0.1`. This it's-all-about-me address is sometimes called the *loopback address*. `localhost` is an invaluable testing feature because it lets you test networking programs without requiring that you use separate computers. In other words, you can run a client and server program on the same computer by having them both use `localhost` to refer to each other.

Telnet

Telnet is a handy debugging tool that can let you check out network programs interactively. It comes free with just about every operating system, though it may or may not be installed automatically. So if you don't have it, you may have to retrieve it from your operating system disks.

Using telnet is easy. From a command prompt, just type `telnet` followed by name of the host (or its IP address) and the port number you want to connect to. For example:

```
telnet somecomputer.com 80
```

This command connects to port 80 of `somecomputer.com`.

To connect to a network server program running on the same computer you're running telnet on, just use `localhost` as the host name. For example, here's a command that connects to a server program using port 1234:

```
telnet localhost 1234
```

Once telnet fires up, anything you type is sent to the port, and anything received from the port is displayed in the telnet window.

You may have to configure telnet to echo characters you type so you can see what you're typing. Each telnet program has a different way to do this, so you have to consult the program's help to find out. (Try running `telnet -?` from the command prompt to get help.)

The `telnet` command is a command-based telnet client. Windows also comes with a Windows-based telnet client named Hyperterminal. You can run it by choosing Start⇨Programs⇨Accessories⇨Communications⇨ Hyperterminal.

Getting Information about Internet Hosts

One of the most useful Java API classes for network programming is the `InetAddress` class. In the following sections, you discover what this class does and how to use it in a simple program that displays the IP address used for any domain name.

The InetAddress class

As you know, an IP address is simply a number that corresponds to a particular host computer on the Internet. The designers of Java could have simply represented IP addresses as `long` numbers. But instead, they created a powerful class called `InetAddress` that represents an IP address.

The `InetAddress` includes a number of useful methods that let you create `InetAddress` objects from strings that represent IP addresses or host names or perform useful lookups to find out the IP address for a given host name or vice versa. Table 2-1 lists the most commonly used methods.

Table 2-1	Methods of the InetAddress Class
Method	*Description*
`byte[] getAddress()`	Returns the raw IP address as an array of bytes.
`static InetAddress[] getAllByName(String host)`	Returns an array of Internet addresses for the specified host name. This method performs a DNS query to get the addresses. Throws `UnknownHostException` if the specified host doesn't exist.
`static InetAddress getByName (String host)`	Returns the Internet address for the specified host name or IP address. This method performs a DNS query to get the address. Throws `UnknownHostException` If the specified host doesn't exist.
`String getCannonicalHostName()`	Returns the fully qualified host name for this IP address.
`String getHostAddress()`	Returns the IP address as a formatted string.
`String getHostName()`	Performs a reverse DNS lookup to get the host name for this IP address.
`boolean isReachable (int timeout)`	Determines if the IP address can be reached. The attempt fails if no response is reached before the timeout period (in milliseconds) elapses.
`String toString()`	Converts the IP address to a string. The result includes both the host name and the IP address.

Here are a few additional points about this class:

✦ This class doesn't have a constructor. Instead, the normal way to create it is to call one of its static methods, such as `getByName`.

✦ The `isReachable`, `getAllByName`, and `getByName` methods throw exceptions.

✦ Several of these methods perform DNS queries to determine their return values. These methods use the DNS server configured for your system to perform these queries.

✦ This class is part of the `java.net` package, so any program that uses it must import either `java.net.InetAddress` or `java.net.*`.

A program that looks up host names

Listing 2-1 presents a program that uses the `InetAddress` class to look up the IP addresses associated with any given host name. This program uses the `getAllByName` method of the `InetAddress` class to do this lookup. Here's a sample of what this handy little program can do:

```
Welcome to the IP lookup application.

Enter a host name: www.wiley.com
www.wiley.com/208.215.179.146

Look up another? (Y or N) y

Enter a host name: www.dummies.com
www.dummies.com/208.215.179.139

Look up another? (Y or N) y

Enter a host name: amazon.com
amazon.com/207.171.166.48
amazon.com/207.171.166.102
amazon.com/207.171.163.30
amazon.com/207.171.163.90

Look up another? (Y or N) n
```

The Façade Pattern

The `InetAddress` class is an example of a commonly used design pattern called the *Façade pattern*. In this pattern, you use a single class to hide the details of a complex object or set of related classes. The `InetAddress` class combines the representation of an IP address with a variety of tasks that are commonly associated with IP addresses, such as using DNS to get the IP address based on a host name. (An even better example of the facade pattern is the `URL` class, which provides a single class to access the complex features of URLs.)

The Façade pattern is commonly used in Java programming, especially in systems that need to incorporate access to complicated existing systems. For example, suppose you have a fully integrated order handling system already in place, and you want to provide a way for Web users to order directly from your company via this system. Unfortunately, the existing system is way too complicated for your customers to use directly — it's designed to be used by trained sales personnel, and provides access to many different sales features that your customers don't need and shouldn't be exposed to.

One way to do this is to create a facade for the ordering system. This facade includes an interface that provides just the classes and methods needed to implement your ordering system online, hiding as much of the complexity of the real ordering system as possible.

As you can see, this program prompts the user for a host name. It then looks up the IP address or addresses for the host name, displays the results, and asks the user if he or she wants to look up another host.

LISTING 2-1: THE HOSTLOOKUP APPLICATION

```java
import java.util.Scanner;
import java.net.*;                                              → 2

public class HostLookup
{
    static Scanner sc = new Scanner(System.in);

    public static void main(String[] args)
    {
        System.out.println(
            "Welcome to the IP lookup application.");
        String host;
        do                                                      → 11
        {
            System.out.print("\nEnter a host name: ");
            host = sc.nextLine();                               → 14
            try
            {
                InetAddress[] addresses                         → 17
                    = InetAddress.getAllByName(host);
                for (InetAddress ip : addresses)                → 19
                    System.out.println(ip.toString());          → 20
            }
            catch (UnknownHostException e)
            {
                System.out.println("Unknown host.");
            }
        } while (doAgain());                                    → 26
    }

    private static boolean doAgain()
    {
        System.out.println();
        String s;
        while (true)
        {
            System.out.print("Look up another? (Y or
                N) ");
            s = sc.nextLine();
            if (s.equalsIgnoreCase("Y"))
                return true;
            else if (s.equalsIgnoreCase("N"))
                return false;
        }
    }
}
```

The following paragraphs describe the key lines in this program:

→ **2** The InetAddress class lives in the java.net package, so an import statement is required to use it.

→**11** This do loop lets the user look up as many host names as he or she wants. The loop ends in line 26, which calls the doAgain method to ask the user if he or she wants to look up another host.

→**14** This line gets the host name the user wants to look up and saves it in the string variable host.

→**17** This statement creates an array variable named addresses whose type is InetAddress. In other words, this variable holds an array of Internet addresses. Then, it calls the static getAllByName method of the InetAddress class, passing the host name entered in line 14 as the parameter. This method performs a DNS lookup on the host name and returns an array that contains all the Internet addresses for the name.

→**19** An enhanced for loop is used to process each InetAddress object in the addresses array.

→**20** This line calls the toString method to convert an Internet address to a string. The string returned by the toString method includes both the host name and the IP address.

Creating Network Server Applications

One popular form of network programming is creating client and server programs that work together to perform specific tasks. These programs communicate with each other by sending information over the network. The format of this information is governed by a *protocol,* which is merely an agreement on the types of messages the clients and servers can send and receive.

A few hundred well-established protocols already exist for such things as sending e-mail and Web pages, looking up DNS names, sharing files, and so on. However, for specialized networking applications, you may find yourself developing your own protocol to coordinate your clients and servers.

Each protocol usually has a unique port assigned to it. For example, port 80 is reserved for the HTTP protocol used to exchange Web pages, and port 25 is used for the SMTP protocol used to exchange e-mail messages. If you end up creating your own protocol, you need to pick a port that doesn't conflict with any of the known ports or with any ports that the users of your application may already be using for other purposes.

Client and server computers establish a connection on a port by means of a special object called a *socket.* In the following sections, I talk about two Java classes that are designed to work with sockets. Then, you see an example of a simple server program and a client that's designed to work with the server.

In this section, I look at two classes that are designed for communicating through sockets. The first, Socket, represents a basic socket object. The second, ServerSocket, is used to help servers establish socket connections with clients.

The Socket class

The Socket class represents a socket connection between two programs. Although the programs can be running on the same computer, they don't have to be. In fact, any two computers that are connected to the Internet can communicate with each other via a socket. Table 2-2 lists the most commonly used constructors and methods of this class.

Table 2-2	Constructors and Methods of the Socket Class
Constructor	*Description*
Socket()	Creates an unconnected socket.
Socket(InetAddress address, int port)	Creates a socket and connects it to the specified address and port.
Socket(String host, int port)	Creates a socket and connects it to the specified host and port.
Method	*Description*
void Close()	Closes the socket.
void connect(InetSocketAddress endpoint)	Connects the socket to the specified address.
InetAddress getInetAddress()	Gets the address to which the socket is connected.
InputStream getInputStream()	Gets an input stream that can be used to receive data sent through this socket.
OutputStream getOutputstream()	Gets an output stream that can be used to send data through this socket.
int getPort()	Gets the port to which this socket is connected.
boolean isBound()	Indicates whether or not the socket is bound to a port.
boolean isClosed()	Indicates whether or not the socket is closed.

Here are a few important details about the Socket class:

✦ Although the Socket class has constructors that let you connect to a specific address, the normal way to create a socket is to use the attach method of the ServerSocket class.

✦ The `InputStream` object returned by the `getInputStream` method can be passed to a constructor of the `Scanner` class. Then, you can use the resulting `Scanner` object to retrieve data from the socket.

✦ The `getOutputStream` method returns an object of the `Output Stream` class. This is the same class used by `System.out`. As a result, you can use the familiar `print` and `println` methods to send data to the socket.

✦ All the constructors and methods of this class except the default constructor and the `getInetAddress`, `getPort`, `isBound`, and `isClosed` methods throw exceptions. As a result, you need to enclose calls to these methods in a `try/catch` statement.

The ServerSocket class

A *server socket* is a socket that lets clients connect with your application. When a client connects, the server socket creates a `Socket` object, which the application can then use to communicate with the client. Table 2-3 lists the most commonly used constructors and methods of this class.

Table 2-3	Constructors and Methods of the ServerSocket Class
Constructor	*Description*
`ServerSocket()`	Creates a server socket that isn't bound to any port.
`ServerSocket(int port)`	Creates a server socket and binds it to the specified port. The server socket then listens for connection attempts on this port.
Method	*Description*
`Socket attach()`	Listens for connection attempts via the port this socket is bound to. The thread that calls this method waits until a connection is made. Then, this method returns, passing a `Socket` object that can be used to communicate with the client.
`void bind(InetSocketAddress endpoint)`	Binds this server socket to the specified address.
`void close()`	Closes the server socket.
`InetAddress getInetAddress()`	Gets the address to which the server socket is connected.
`boolean isBound()`	Indicates whether or not the server socket is bound to a port.
`boolean isClosed()`	Indicates whether or not the server socket is closed.

Here are some important points to remember about the `ServerSocket` class:

✦ When you call the `attach` method, the thread is suspended until a connection is made.

✦ The second constructor and the `attach`, `bind`, and `close` methods throw exceptions. As a result, you need to enclose calls to these methods in a `try/catch` statement.

Introducing BART

In this section, I create a simple network server program that provides clients with a randomly selected quote from a well known television program called the *Shrimpsons*. It seems that a certain young boy on this program, whose name shall remain unknown, frequently has to write sentences on the blackboard as punishment. The sentences that he has been known to write have some minor amusement value.

I call the server the BartServer, and the protocol used to communicate with the BartServer BART, short for *Blackboard Assignment Retrieval Transaction*, because it allows you to randomly retrieve blackboard assignments. The protocol itself is simple:

1. When you connect to the BartServer, it displays a greeting line and a line of instructions.

2. If you send the command `get`, the BartServer replies by sending you a randomly selected sentence from one of the young man's blackboard assignments.

3. If you send the command `bye`, the BartServer disconnects you.

4. If you send anything else, the BartServer replies "Huh?"

The BartServer communicates over port 1234. Once you get the BartServer up and running on your computer, you can test it out by running the `telnet` command from a command prompt. Type the command `telnet local host 1234`, and you're greeted with a message indicating that you have successfully connected. Here's a typical telnet session with the BartServer:

```
Welcome to BartServer 1.0
Enter GET to get a quote or BYE to exit.
get
I will not waste chalk.
get
I will not instigate a revolution.
get
I will not conduct my own fire drills.
gte
Huh?
bye
So long, suckers!

Connection to host lost.
```

Don't forget, it's the *Shrimp*-sons. We don't want to get sued, now, do we?

The BartQuote class

Before you roll up your sleeves and look at the network programming required to implement the BartServer, take a look first at the supporting class, named `BartQuote`. This class has a single method named `getQuote` that returns one of 20 randomly selected blackboard sentences. The code for this class is shown in Listing 2-2.

Note that the sentences are hard-coded into this program. That's not the way you'd do it if you really wanted to use the BartServer. Instead, you'd put the sentences in a file and read the file each time you start up the server. I don't cover File I/O until Book VIII, though, and I don't want to introduce any code here you couldn't follow, because the network programming in the rest of this chapter is complicated enough. Don't have a cow, man.

LISTING 2-2: THE BARTQUOTE CLASS

```java
import java.util.ArrayList;

public class BartQuote
{
    ArrayList<String> q = new ArrayList<String>();          → 5

    public BartQuote()                                       → 7
    {
        q.add("I will not waste chalk.");
        q.add("I will not skateboard in the halls.");
        q.add("I will not burp in class.");
        q.add("I will not instigate a revolution.");
        q.add("It's potato, not potatoe.");
        q.add("I will not encourage others to fly.");
        q.add("Tar is not a plaything.");
        q.add("I will not sell school property.");
        q.add("I will not get very far with this attitude.");
        q.add("I will not sell land in Florida.");
        q.add("I will not grease the monkey bars.");
        q.add("I will not hide behind the Fifth Amendment.");
        q.add("I am not a dentist.");
        q.add("I will finish what I sta");
        q.add("Hamsters cannot fly.");
        q.add("I will not aim for the head.");
        q.add("I will not expose the ignorance "
            + "of the faculty.");
        q.add("I will not conduct my own fire drills.");
        q.add("I will not fake seizures.");
        q.add("This punishment is not boring "
            + "and meaningless.");
    }
    public String getQuote()                                 → 33
    {
```

```
        int i = (int)(Math.random() * q.size());
        return q.get(i);
    }
}
```

Here are the key points of this class:

→ **5** The sentences are kept in an `ArrayList` object named q. If you haven't read about the `ArrayList` class, run (don't walk) to Book IV, Chapter 3.

→ **7** The `BartQuote` constructor uses the `add` method of the `ArrayList` class to add 20 sentences to the array list.

→**33** The `getQuote` method returns a sentence randomly selected from the array list. `Math.random` is used to calculate the random number. (For more information about `Math.random`, refer to Book II, Chapter 3.)

The BartServer program

The BartServer program is the program you run on a server computer to provide randomly selected blackboard sentences for clients that want them. This program is shown in Listing 2-3.

LISTING 2-3: THE BARTSERVER PROGRAM

```
import java.net.*;                                          → 1
import java.util.*;
import java.io.*;

public class BartServer
{
    public static void main(String[] args)
    {
        int port = 1234;                                    → 9

        BartQuote bart = new BartQuote();                   → 11

        try
        {
            System.out.println("BartServer 1.0");
            System.out.println("Listening on port " + port);
            ServerSocket ss;                                → 17
            ss = new ServerSocket(port);
            Socket s;                                       → 20
            s = ss.accept();

            String client;
            client = s.getInetAddress().toString();         → 24
            System.out.println("Connected to " + client);

            Scanner in;
            in = new Scanner(s.getInputStream());           → 28
```

continued

LISTING 2-3 (CONTINUED)

```
            PrintWriter out;
            out = new PrintWriter(s.getOutputStream(),
                true);                                          → 31

            out.println("Welcome to BartServer 1.0");           → 33
            out.println("Enter GET to get a quote "
                + "or BYE to exit.");

            while (true)                                        → 37
            {
                String input = in.nextLine();                   → 39
                if (input.equalsIgnoreCase("bye"))
                    break;
                else if (input.equalsIgnoreCase("get"))
                {
                    out.println(bart.getQuote());
                    System.out.println("Serving " + client);
                }
                else
                    out.println("Huh?");
            }
            out.println("So long, suckers!");
            s.close();                                          → 51
            System.out.println(
                "Closed connection to " + client);
        }
        catch (Exception e)                                     → 55
        {
            e.printStackTrace();
        }
    }
}
```

The following paragraphs walk you through the key parts of this program:

→ **1** This program begins with an `import` statement to import the `java.net` package. Notice also that the `java.io` package is imported. Later in this program, you'll see that this program uses the `PrintWriter` class. You're already familiar with this class — `System.out` is a `PrintWriter` object.

→ **9** The `port` variable stores the port that the server communicates on. This is hard-coded with the value `1234`, but you could just as easily ask the user to enter the port number or read it from a configuration file.

→ **11** This line creates a new instance of the `BartQuote` class and assigns it to a variable named `bart`.

→ **17** This line and the next line declare a `ServerSocket` variable and create a new `ServerSocket` object using the `port` variable. As a result, this `ServerSocket` object can be used to establish client connections on port 1234.

→**20** This line declares a `Socket` variable. Then the next line uses the `accept` method of the `ServerSocket` object to wait for a client to connect to port 1234. When a client connects, a `Socket` object is created and assigned to the variable `s`.

→**24** This statement uses the `getInetAddress` method of the `Socket` object to get an `InetAddress` object that represents the client's IP address. Then, it uses the `InetAddress` object's `toString` method to create a string that shows the client's address. This string is saved to the `client` variable.

→**28** The BartServer program uses a `Scanner` object to read data sent from the client over the socket. In this line, it uses the socket's `getInputStream` method to get a standard input stream for the socket. Then, it uses this input stream as a parameter to the `Scanner` constructor, which in turn creates a `Scanner` object that works over the socket's input stream. You can then use the `Scanner` object referenced by the `in` variable to get commands sent to the server from clients.

→**31** Next, you do a similar thing to get a `PrintWriter` object that can send data to a client through the socket. The `getOutputStream` method gets a standard output stream, which is then used as a parameter to the `PrintWriter` constructor. This `PrintWriter` is then assigned to a variable named `out`.

→**33** These lines send the greeting messages to the client.

→**37** The `while` loop processes commands from the client until the `bye` command is entered. That way, the client can request as many blackboard sentences as it wants.

→**39** The `Scanner` object is used to get a line of input from the client. The client input is then checked with nested `if` statements. If the client sent `bye`, the `break` statement breaks the `while` loop. If the client sent `get`, the `getQuote` method of the `BartQuote` object is called to get a random quote. Then, the quote is sent to the client via a `println` command. If the user enters anything else, the server sends back `Huh?`.

→**51** When the loop ends, the program displays a farewell message and closes the socket connection.

→**55** Most of the `Socket` class methods throw an exception if something goes wrong with the socket connection. That's why most of the statements for the `main` method are contained in a `try` block. If an exception is thrown, `e.printStackTrace` is called to print detailed information about the exception on the console.

You may have noticed that the BartServer program displays various status messages in its console window as it runs. For example, when a client connects, it displays a message showing the IP address of the client. And when a client requests a quote, a message is displayed on the console. Here's a typi-cal console screen for BartServer where a client connected, requested three quotes, and then disconnected:

```
BartServer 1.0
Listening on port 1234
Connected to /127.0.0.1
Serving /127.0.0.1
Serving /127.0.0.1
Serving /127.0.0.1
Closed connection to /127.0.0.1
```

This program is pretty simple as network server programs go. Still, it illus-trates the basic techniques of network server programming. Many server programs consist mostly of a big `while` loop that gets input from the client, inspects the input to see what the client wants to do, does what the client asks, and then sends some output back to the client.

The BartClient program

The preceding section shows you how to connect to the BartServer program with telnet to interact with the server. Now, this section presents a client program that communicates with a BartServer server. This program starts by asking the user for a host name. Then, it connects to the BartServer at that host, requests a quote, and displays that result on the computer's con-sole 20 times (as if the console were a blackboard).

Figure 2-1 shows a typical execution of this program. Here, I entered `localhost` as the BartServer host. `localhost` is useful for testing clients and servers together on the same computer system. The Java code for this program is shown in Listing 2-4.

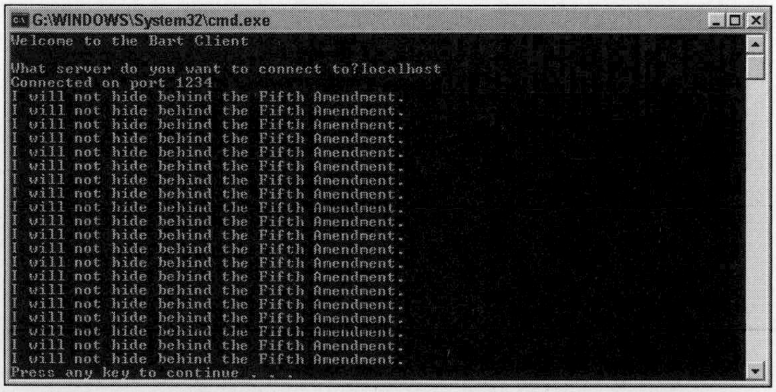

![Screenshot of the BartClient program running in a Windows command prompt window titled G:\WINDOWS\System32\cmd.exe. It shows "Welcome to the Bart Client", "What server do you want to connect to?localhost", "Connected on port 1234", and many repeated lines of "I will not hide behind the Fifth Amendment." followed by "Press any key to continue . . ."]

Figure 2-1:
Running the
BartClient
program.

LISTING 2-4: THE BARTCLIENT PROGRAM

```java
import java.net.*;
import java.util.*;
import java.io.*;

public class BartClient
{
    public static void main(String[] args)
    {
        int port = 1234;

        System.out.println("Welcome to the Bart Client\n");

        Socket s = getSocket(port);                              → 13

        try
        {
            System.out.println("Connected on port " + port);

            Scanner in =
                new Scanner(s.getInputStream());                → 20
            PrintWriter out;
            out = new PrintWriter(s.getOutputStream(),
                true);                                          → 23

            // discard the welcome message
            in.nextLine();                                      → 26

            // discard the exit instructions
            in.nextLine();                                      → 29

            // get a quote
            out.println("get");                                 → 32
            String quote = in.nextLine();                       → 33

            // disconnect from the server
            out.println("bye");                                 → 36
            s.close();                                          → 37

            // write the quote on the chalkboard
            for (int i = 0; i < 20; i++)                        → 41
                System.out.println(quote);
        }
        catch (Exception e)
        {
            e.printStackTrace();                                → 46
        }
    }

    private static Socket getSocket(int port)                   → 50
    {
        Socket s;
        String host;
        InetAddress ip;

        Scanner sc = new Scanner(System.in);
```

continued

LISTING 2-4 (CONTINUED)

```
    while (true)
    {
        System.out.print(
            "What server do you want to connect to?");
        host = sc.nextLine();                              → 62
        try
        {
            ip = InetAddress.getByName(host);              → 65
            s = new Socket(ip, port);                      → 66
            return s;                                      → 67
        }
        catch (UnknownHostException e)                     → 69
        {
            System.out.println("The host is unknown.");
        }
        catch (IOException e)
        {
            System.out.println("Network error.");
        }
    }
    }
}
```

Here's an explanation of the more confusing aspects of this program:

→13 Connecting to a server is a complicated enough procedure that I placed it in a separate method named getSocket. This method prompts the user for a host name and doesn't return until the user enters one that the program can connect to. The port number is passed as a parameter, and the return value is a Socket object that's connected to the server. (The nitty-gritty details about how this method works start with line 50.)

→20 This statement gets a Scanner object that can be used to read data from the client via the socket's input stream.

→23 This statement gets a PrintWriter object that can be used to send data to the client via the socket's output stream.

→26 Once connected, the server sends a welcome message. This message is helpful to users connected via telnet, but it isn't very useful to a client program such as this one. So this statement simply uses the Scanner object to read the line from the input stream and discards it.

Because the welcome message includes the version number for the server, the program could read the line and check it to make sure you're connected to a current version of the server. I don't think there will be much demand for additional features in BartServer, though, so you don't have to worry about version checking.

→29 The server also sends a line of helpful instructions that you need to read from the stream and discard.

→**32** This line sends the word `get` to the server. That's how the client program asks the server to send back a randomly selected sentence.

→**33** After sending the `get` request, the client reads the next line of data from the socket input stream. Note that if delays occur because the network is slow, the `nextLine` method simply waits until the line has been sent.

→**36** Having got what it came for (a blackboard sentence), the client program sends a `bye` command to the server. The server sends back a rude farewell message, but the client program isn't interested in it, so it doesn't even bother to read it.

→**37** The connection to the server is closed.

→**41** Now that the client program has its blackboard sentence writing assignment, it uses a `for` loop to write it on the board 20 times.

→**46** Any of the `socket I/O` statements can throw exceptions. They are all caught here as a generic exception, and the diagnostic information is sent to the console so you can debug any problems that might arise.

→**50** The `getSocket` method accepts a port number as a parameter and returns a socket that's connected via the specified port. This method doesn't give up until the user enters the name of a host the program can connect to.

→**62** The host name is read from the console.

→**65** The static `getByName` method of the `InetAddress` class is called to get an IP address for the host name entered by the user. Note that if the user enters a host name that doesn't exist, `UnknownHost Exception` is thrown. This exception is caught in line 69.

→**66** Now that you have an IP address, this line tries to create a `Socket` object using the specified address and port. This method throws `IOException` if it isn't able to connect to the IP address and port.

→**67** If you make it to this line, you can assume the socket has been created and you're connected. So the `return` statement passes the socket back to the caller, in line 13.

BartServer 2.0

The BartServer program that is presented in the previous section works fine, but it has one major deficiency: It handles connections for only one client. To make matters worse, it quits when that client disconnects. That's not much of a server.

So after much user feedback, I decided to release BartServer 2.0, with new and improved features. BartServer 2.0 uses threads to allow multiple clients to connect to the server at the same time. Each time a client connects, a thread is started to process any requests for that client. The main thread continues to run, waiting for other clients to connect. Figure 2-2 shows the multithreading features of BartServer 2.0 in action. Listing 2-5 shows the code for version 2.0 of BartServer.

LISTING 2-5   BARTSERVER 2.0

```java
import java.net.*;
import java.io.*;
import java.util.*;

public class BartServer2
{
    public static void main(String[] args)
    {
        int port = 1234;

        BartQuote bart = new BartQuote();

        try
        {
            System.out.println("BartServer 2.0");
            System.out.println("Listening on port " + port);
            ServerSocket ss = new ServerSocket(port);

            while (true)                                        → 19
            {
                Socket s = ss.accept();
                System.out.println(
                    "Connection established!");
                Thread t = new Thread(
                    new BartThread(s, bart));                   → 25
                t.start();
            }
        }
        catch (Exception e)
        {
            System.out.println("System exception!");
        }
    }
}

class BartThread implements Runnable                            → 36
{
    private Socket s;
    private BartQuote bart;

    public BartThread(Socket socket, BartQuote bart)            → 41
    {
        this.s = socket;
        this.bart = bart;
    }
```

```
public void run()                                       → 47
{
    String client = s.getInetAddress().toString();
    System.out.println("Connected to " + client);
    try
    {
        Scanner in = new Scanner(s.getInputStream());
        PrintWriter out;
        out = new PrintWriter(s.getOutputStream(),
            true);

        out.println("Welcome to the Bart Server");
        out.println("Enter BYE to exit.");

        while (true)
        {
            String input = in.nextLine();
            if (input.equalsIgnoreCase("bye"))
                break;
            else if (input.equalsIgnoreCase("get"))
            {
                out.println(bart.getQuote());
                System.out.println("Serving " + client);
            }
            else
                out.println("Huh?");
        }
        out.println("So long, suckers!");
        s.close();
    }
    catch (Exception e)
    {
        e.printStackTrace();
    }

    System.out.println("Closed connection to " + client);
}
}
```

Most of this code is the same as the code in version 1.0, so I just highlight the key changes:

→**19** A `while` loop is used to service connection requests through the `accept` method of the `ServerSocket` object.

→**25** Each time a new client connects, a thread is created using the `BartThread` class to create the thread's `Runnable` object. Then, this thread is started. In the meantime, the main thread stays in the `while` loop, waiting for other clients to connect.

If threading gives you a serious headache, you may want to turn back a chapter and review the information on programming with threads in Book V, Chapter 1.

→**36** The `BartThread` handles the processing required for each connected client. This class implements `Runnable`, which means it must define a `run` method. The `run` method is called each time a new thread is created.

→**41** The constructor for the `BartThread` class initializes the two class fields with values passed as parameters from the main thread. These parameters are the `Socket` object the client is connected to and a shared copy of the `BartQuote` object that was created by the main thread.

It isn't shown here, but the `getQuote` method of the `BartQuote` class used by this version of BartServer should be synchronized. That's because multiple threads access it. For more information, refer to Book V, Chapter 1.

→**47** The `run` method services the requests for a single client connected to the BartServer. Most of the code in this method was simply copied straight from the previous version, so you shouldn't have any trouble understanding how this method works.

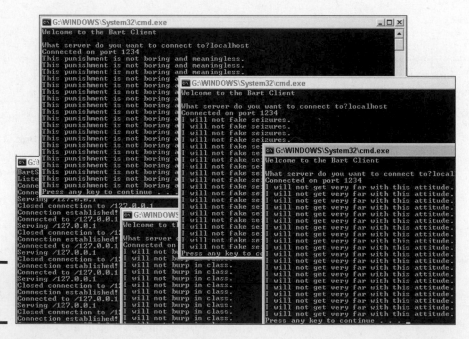

Figure 2-2: BartClients galore!

Chapter 3: Using Regular Expressions

In This Chapter

✔ Introducing regular expressions

✔ Trying out regular expressions with a helpful program

✔ Creating simple expressions that match patterns of characters

✔ Using regular expression features, such as custom classes, quantifiers, and groups

✔ Using regular expressions with the `String` class

✔ Using the `Pattern` and `Matcher` classes for more extensive regular expression work

Regular expressions are not expressions that have a lot of fiber in their diet. Instead, a *regular expression* is a special type of pattern matching string that can be very useful for programs that do string manipulation. Regular expression strings contain special pattern-matching characters in them that can be matched against another string to see if the other string fits the pattern. Regular expressions are very handy for doing complex data validation — for example, for making sure users enter properly formatted phone numbers, e-mail addresses, or Social Security numbers.

Regular expressions are also useful for many other purposes, including searching text files to see if they contain certain patterns (can you say, Google?), filtering e-mail based on its contents, or performing complicated search-and-replace functions.

In this chapter, you find out the basics of using regular expressions. I emphasize validation, and focus on comparing strings entered by users against patterns specified by regular expressions to see if they match up. For more complex uses for regular expressions, you have to turn to a more extensive regular expression reference.

Regular expressions are actually constructed using a simple but powerful mini-language, so they are like little programs unto themselves. Unfortunately, this mini-language is terse — *very* terse — to the point of sometimes being downright arcane. Much of it depends on single characters that are packed with meaning that's often obscure. So be warned — the syntax for regular expressions takes a little getting used to. But once you get your mind around the basics, you'll find that simple regular expressions aren't that tough to create and can be very useful.

Also, be aware that this chapter only covers a portion of all you can do with regular expressions. If you find that you need to use more complicated patterns, you can find plenty of helpful information on the Internet. Just search any search service for `regular expression`.

A regular expression is often called a *regex*. Most people pronounce that with a soft *g*, as if it were spelled *rejex*. And some pronounce it as if it were spelled *rejects*.

A Program for Experimenting with Regular Expressions

Before I get into the details of putting together regular expressions, Listing 3-1 presents a short program that can be a very useful tool while you're learning how to create regular expressions. This program lets you enter a regular expression. Then, you can enter a string, and the program tests it against the regular expression and lets you know whether or not the string matches the regex. The program then prompts you for another string to compare. You can keep entering strings to compare with the regex you've already entered. When you're done, just press the Enter key without entering a string. The program then asks if you want to enter another regular expression. If you answer Y, the whole process repeats. If you answer N, the program ends.

Here's a sample run of this program. For now, don't worry about the details of the regular expression string. Just note that it should match any three-letter word that begins with f, ends with r, and has an a, i, or o in the middle.

```
Welcome to the Regex Tester

Enter regex: f[aio]r
Enter string: for
Match.
Enter string: fir
Match.
Enter string: fur
Does not match.
Enter string: fod
Does not match.
Enter string:
Another? (Y or N) n
```

In this test, I entered the regular expression `f[aio]`. Then, I entered the string `for`. The program indicated that this string matched the expression and asked for another string. So I entered `fir`, which also matched. Then I entered `fur` and `fod`, which didn't match. I then entered a blank string, so the program asked if I wanted to test another regex. I entered `n`, so the program ended.

This program uses the `Pattern` and `Matcher` classes, which I don't explain until the end of the chapter. However, I suggest you use this program alongside this chapter. Regular expressions make a lot more sense if you actually try them out to see them in action. Plus, you can learn a lot by trying simple variations as you go. (You can always download the source code for this program from this book's Web site if you don't want to enter it yourself.)

In fact, I use portions of console output from this program throughout the rest of this chapter to illustrate regular expressions. There's no better way to see how regular expressions work than to see an expression and some samples of strings that match and don't match the expression.

LISTING 3-1: THE REGULAR EXPRESSION TEST PROGRAM

```
import java.util.regex.*;
import java.util.Scanner;

public final class Reg {

    static String r, s;
    static Pattern pattern;
    static Matcher matcher;
    static boolean match, validRegex, doneMatching;

    private static Scanner sc = new Scanner(System.in);

    public static void main(String[] args)
    {
        System.out.println("Welcome to the Regex Tester\n");
        do
        {
            do
            {
                System.out.print("\nEnter regex:  ");
                r = sc.nextLine();
                validRegex = true;
                try
                {
                    pattern = Pattern.compile(r);
                }
```

continued

LISTING 3-1 (CONTINUED)

```
            catch (Exception e)
            {
                System.out.println(e.getMessage());
                validRegex = false;
            }
        }while (!validRegex);

        doneMatching = false;
        while (!doneMatching)
        {
            System.out.print("Enter string: ");
            s = sc.nextLine();
            if (s.length() == 0)
                doneMatching = true;
            else
            {
                matcher = pattern.matcher(s);
                if (matcher.matches())
                    System.out.println("Match.");
                else
                    System.out.println(
                        "Does not match.");
            }
        }
    } while (askAgain());
}

private static boolean askAgain()
{
    System.out.print("Another? (Y or N) ");
    String reply = sc.nextLine();
    if (reply.equalsIgnoreCase("Y"))
        return true;
    return false;
}
}
```

Basic Character Matching

Most regular expressions simply match characters to see if a string complies to a simple pattern. For example, you can check a string to see if it matches the format for Social Security numbers (xxx-xx-xxxx), phone numbers [(xxx) xxx-xxxx], or more complicated patterns such as e-mail addresses. (Well actually, Social Security and phone numbers are more complicated than you might think too. More on that later.) In the following sections, you find out how to create regex patterns for basic character matching.

Matching single characters

The simplest regex patterns just match a string literal exactly. For cxample:

```
Enter regex:  abc
Enter string: abc
Match.
Enter string: abcd
Does not match.
```

Here, the pattern abc matches the string abc but not abcd.

Using predefined character classes

A *character class* represents a particular type of character rather than a specific character. Regex lets you use two types of character classes: predefined classes and custom classes. The predefined character classes are shown in Table 3-1.

Table 3-1	Character Classes
Regex	*Matches . . .*
.	Any character
\d	Any digit (0–9)
\D	Any non-digit (anything other than 0–9)
\s	Any white space character (spaces, tabs, newlines, returns, and backspaces)
\S	Any character other than a white space character
\w	Any word character (a–z, A–Z, 0–9, or an underscore)
\W	Any character other than a word character

The period is like a wildcard that matches any character. For example:

```
Enter regex:  c.t
Enter string: cat
Match.
Enter string: cot
Match.
Enter string: cart
Does not match.
```

Here, c.t matches any three-letter string that starts with c and ends with t. In this example, the first two strings (cat and cot) match, but the third string (cart) doesn't because it's more than three characters.

The \d class represents a digit and is often used in regex patterns used to validate input data. For example, here's a simple regex pattern that validates a U. S. Social Security number, which must be entered in the form XXX-XX-XXXX:

```
Enter regex:   \d\d\d-\d\d-\d\d\d\d
Enter string: 779-54-3994
Match.
Enter string: 550-403-004
Does not match.
```

Here, the regex pattern specifies that the string must contain three digits, a hyphen, two digits, another hyphen, and four digits.

Note that this regex pattern isn't really enough to validate real Social Security numbers, because the government places more restrictions on these numbers than just the pattern XXX-XX-XXXX. For example, no Social Security number can begin with 779. Thus, the number 779-54-3994 entered in the preceding example isn't really a valid Social Security number.

Note that the \d class has a counterpart: \D. The \D class matches any character that is *not* a digit. For example, here's a first attempt at a regex for validating droid names:

```
Enter regex:   \D\d-\D\d
Enter string: R2-D2
Match.
Enter string: C2-D0
Match.
Enter string: C-3PO
Does not match.
```

Here, the pattern matches strings that begin with a character that isn't a digit, followed by a character that is a digit, followed by a hyphen, followed by another non-digit character, and ending with a digit. Thus, R2-D2 and C3-P0 match. Unfortunately, this regex is far from perfect, as any *Star Wars* fan can tell you. That's because the proper spelling of the shiny gold protocol droid's name is C-3PO, not C3-P0. Typical.

The \s class matches white space characters including spaces, tabs, newlines, returns, and backspaces. This class is useful when you want to allow the user to separate parts of a string in various ways. For example:

```
Enter regex:   ...\s...
Enter string: abc def
Match.
Enter string: abc        def
Match.
```

Here, the pattern specifies that the string can be two groups of any three characters separated by one white space character. In the first string that's entered, the groups are separated by a space. In the second group, they're separated by a tab. The \s class also has a counterpart: \S. It matches any character that isn't a white space character.

TIP

If you want to limit white space characters to actual spaces, just use a space in the regex. For example:

```
Enter regex:  ... ...
Enter string: abc def
Match.
Enter string: abc        def
Does not match.
```

Here, the regex specifies two groups of any character separated by a space. The first input string matches this pattern, but the second does not because the groups are separated by a tab.

The last set of predefined classes are \w and \W. The \w class identifies any character that's normally used in words. That includes upper- and lowercase letters, digits, and the underscore. For example:

```
Enter regex:  \w\w\w\W\w\w\w
Enter string: abc def
Match.
Enter string: 123 456
Match.
Enter string: 123A456
Does not match.
```

Here, the pattern calls for two groups of word characters separated by a non-word character.

TECHNICAL STUFF

Isn't it strange that underscores are considered to be word characters? I don't know of too many words in the English language (or any other language, for that matter) that have underscores in them. I guess that's the computer-nerd origins of regular expressions showing through.

Using custom character classes

To create a *custom character class*, you simply list all the characters that you want included in the class within a set of brackets. For example:

```
Enter regex:  b[aeiou]t
Enter string: bat
Match.
```

```
Enter string: bet
Match.
Enter string: bit
Match.
Enter string: bot
Match.
Enter string: but
Match.
Enter string: bmt
Does not match.
```

Here, the pattern specifies that the string must start with the letter b, followed by a class that can include a, e, i, o, or u, followed by t. In other words, it accepts three letter words that begin with *b*, end with *t*, and have a vowel in the middle.

If you want to let the pattern include uppercase letters as well as lowercase letters, you have to list them both:

```
Enter regex:  b[aAeEiIoOuU]t
Enter string: bat
Match.
Enter string: BAT
Does not match.
Enter string: bAt
Match.
```

You can use as many custom groups on a line as you want. For example, here's one that defines classes for the first and last characters so they too can be upper- or lowercase:

```
Enter regex:  [bB][aAeEiIoOuU][tT]
Enter string: bat
Match.
Enter string: BAT
Match.
```

This pattern specifies three character classes. The first can be b or B, the second can be any upper- or lowercase vowel, and the third can be t or T.

Using ranges

Custom character classes can also specify *ranges* of letters and numbers. For example:

```
Enter regex:  [a-z][0-5]
Enter string: r2
Match.
Enter string: b9
Does not match.
```

Here, the string can be two characters long. The first must be a character from a through z, and the second must be from 0 through 5.

You can also use more than one range in a class, like this:

```
Enter regex:  [a-zA-Z][0-5]
Enter string: r2
Match.
Enter string: R2
Match.
```

Here, the first character can be lowercase a through z or uppercase A through Z.

You can use ranges to build a class that accepts only characters that appear in real words, as opposed to the \w class which allows underscores:

```
Enter regex:  [a-zA-Z0-9]
Enter string: a
Match.
Enter string: N
Match.
Enter string: 9
Match.
```

Using negation

Regular expressions can include classes that match any character *but* the ones listed for the class. To do that, you start the class with a caret, like this:

```
Enter regex:  [^cf]at
Enter string: bat
Match.
Enter string: cat
Does not match.
Enter string: fat
Does not match.
```

Here, the string must be a three-letter word that ends in at, but isn't fat or cat.

Matching multiple characters

The regex patterns described so far in this chapter require that each position in the input string always match a specific character class. For example, the pattern \d\W[a-z] requires a digit in the first position, a white space character in the second position, and one of the letters a through z in the third position. These are pretty rigid requirements.

To create more flexible patterns, you can use any of the *quantifiers* listed in Table 3-2. These quantifiers let you create patterns that match a variable number of characters at a certain position in the string.

Table 3-2	Quantifiers
Regex	*Matches the Preceding Element. . .*
?	Zero or one times
*	Zero or more times
+	One or more times
{n}	Exactly *n* times
{n, }	At least *n* times
{n, m}	At least *n* times but no more than *m* times

To use a quantifier, you code it immediately after the element you want it to apply to. For example, here's a version of the Social Security number pattern that uses quantifiers:

```
Enter regex:   \d{3}-\d{2}-\d{4}
Enter string: 779-48-9955
Match.
Enter string: 483-488-9944
Does not match.
```

Here, the pattern matches three digits, followed by a hyphen, followed by two digits, followed by another hyphen, followed by four digits.

Simply duplicating elements rather than using a quantifier is just as easy, if not easier. For example, \d\d is just as clear as \d{2}.

The ? quantifier lets you create an optional element that may or may not be present in the string. For example, suppose you want to allow the user to enter Social Security numbers without the hyphens. Then, you could use this pattern:

```
Enter regex:   \d{3}-?\d{2}-?\d{4}
Enter string: 779-48-9955
Match.
Enter string: 779489955
Match.
Enter string: 779-489955
Match.
Enter string: 77948995
Does not match.
```

The question marks indicate that the hyphens are optional. Notice that this pattern lets you include or omit either hyphen. The last string entered doesn't match because it has only eight digits, and the pattern requires nine.

Using escapes

In regular expressions, certain characters have special meaning. This leads to the question, what if you want to search for one of those special characters? In that case, you *escape* the character by preceding it with a backslash. For example:

```
Enter regex:   \(\d{3}\) \d{3}-\d{4}
Enter string: (559) 555-1234
Match.
Enter string: 559 555-1234
Does not match.
```

Here, \ (represents a left parenthesis, and \ ) represents a right parenthesis. Without the backslashes, the regular expression treats the parenthesis as a grouping element.

Here are a few additional points to ponder about escapes:

+ Strictly speaking, you need to use the backslash escape only for characters that have special meanings in regular expressions. However, I recommend you escape any punctuation character or symbol, just to be sure.

+ You can't escape alphabetic characters (letters). That's because a backslash followed by certain alphabetic characters represents a character, a class, or some other regex element.

+ To escape a backslash, code two slashes in a row. For example, the regex \d\d\\d\d accepts strings made up of two digits followed by a backslash and two more digits, such as 23\88 and 95\55.

Using parentheses to group characters

You can use parentheses to create groups of characters to apply other regex elements to. For example:

```
Enter regex:   (bla)+
Enter string: bla
Match.
Enter string: blabla
Match.
Enter string: blablabla
Match.
Enter string: bla bla bla
Does not match.
```

Here, the parentheses treat `bla` as a group, so the + quantifier applies to the entire sequence. Thus, this pattern looks for one or more occurrences of the sequence `bla`.

Here's an example that finds U.S. phone numbers that can have an optional area code:

```
Enter regex:   (\(\d{3}\)\s?)?\d{3}-\d{4}
Enter string: 555-1234
Match.
Enter string: (559) 555-1234
Match.
Enter string: (559)555-1239
Match.
```

This regex pattern is a little complicated, but if you examine it element by element, you should be able to figure it out. It starts with a group that indicates the optional area code: `(\(\d{3}\)\s?)?`. This group begins with the left parenthesis that marks the start of the group. The characters in the group consist of an escaped left parenthesis, three digits, an escaped right parenthesis, and an optional white space character. Then, a right parenthesis closes the group, and the question mark indicates that the entire group is optional. The rest of the regex pattern looks for three digits followed by a hyphen and four more digits.

When you mark a group of characters with parentheses, the text that matches that group is *captured* so you can use it later in the pattern. The groups that are captured are called *capture groups* and are numbered beginning with 1. You can then use a backslash followed by the capture group number to indicate that the text must match the text that was captured for the specified capture group.

For example, suppose that droids named following the pattern `\w\d-\w\d` must have the same digit in the second and fifth character. In other words, r2-d2 and b9-k9 are valid droid names, but r2-d4 and d3-r4 are not.

Here's an example that can validate that type of name:

```
Enter regex:   \w(\d)-\w\1
Enter string: r2-d2
Match.
Enter string: d3-r4
Does not match.
Enter string: b9-k9
Match.
```

Here, \1 refers to the first capture group. Thus, the last character in the string must be the same as the second character, which must be a digit.

Using the | symbol

The | symbol defines an or operation, which lets you create patterns that accept any of two or more variations. For example, here's an improvement to the pattern for validating droid names:

```
Enter regex:   (\w\d-\w\d)|(\w-\d\w\w)
Enter string: r2-d2
Match.
Enter string: c-3po
Match.
```

Here, the | character indicates that either the group on the left or the group on the right can be used to match the string. The group on the left matches a word character, a digit, a hyphen, a word character, and another digit. The group on the right matches a word character, a hyphen, a digit, and two word characters.

You may want to use an additional set of parentheses around the entire part of the pattern that the | applies to. Then, you can add additional pattern elements before or after the | groups. For example, what if you want to let a user enter the area code for a phone number with or without parentheses. Here's a regex pattern that does the trick:

```
Enter regex:   ((\d{3} )|(\(\d{3}\) ))?\d{3}-\d{4}
Enter string: (559) 555-1234
Match.
Enter string: 559 555-1234
Match.
Enter string: 555-1234
Match.
```

The first part of this pattern is a group that consists of two smaller groups separated by an | character. The first of these groups matches an area code without parentheses followed by a space, and the second matches an area code with parentheses followed by a space. So the outer group matches an area code with or without parentheses. This entire group is marked with a question mark as optional, and then the pattern continues with three digits, a hyphen, and four digits.

Using Regular Expressions in Java Programs

So far, this chapter has shown you the basics of creating regular expressions. Now, the following sections show you how to put them to use in Java programs.

The String problem

Before getting into the classes for working with regular expressions, I want to clue you in about a problem that Java has when dealing with strings that contain regular expressions. As you've seen throughout this chapter, regex patterns rely on the backslash character to mark different elements of a pattern. The bad news is that Java treats the backslash character in a string literal as an escape character. Thus, you can't just quote regular expressions in string literals, because Java steals the backslash characters before they get to the regular expression classes.

In most cases, the compiler simply complains that the string literal is not correct. For example, the following line won't compile:

```
String regex = "\w\d-\w\d";   // error: won't compile
```

The compiler sees the backslashes in the string and expects to find a valid Java escape sequence, not a regular expression.

Unfortunately, the solution to this problem is ugly: You have to double the backslashes wherever they occur. Java treats two backslashes in a row as an escaped backslash, and places a single backslash in the string. Thus, you have to code the statement shown in the previous paragraph like this:

```
String regex = "\\w\\d-\\w\\d";   // now it will
   compile
```

Here, each backslash I want in the regular expression is coded as a pair of backslashes in the string literal.

 If you're in doubt about whether you're coding your string literals right, just use System.out.println to print the resulting string. Then, you can check the console output to make sure you wrote the string literal right. For example, if I followed the previous statement with System.out.println (regex), the following output would appear on the console:

```
\w\d-\w\d
```

Thus, I know I coded the string literal for the regular expression correctly.

Using regular expressions with the String class

If all you want to do with a regular expression is check to see whether a string matches a pattern, you can use the `matches` method of the `String` class. This method accepts a regular expression as a parameter and returns a boolean that indicates whether or not the string matches the pattern.

For example, here's a static method that validates droid names:

```
private static boolean validDroidName(String droid)
{
    String regex = "(\\w\\d-\\w\\d)|(\\w-\\d\\w\\w)";
    return droid.matches(regex);
}
```

Here, the name of the droid is passed via a parameter, and the method returns a boolean that indicates whether the droid's name is valid. The method simply creates a regular expression from a string literal, and then uses the `matches` method of the `droid` string to match the pattern.

You can also use the `split` method to split a string into an array of `String` objects based on delimiters that match a regular expression. One common way to do that is to simply create a custom class of characters that can be used for delimiters. For example:

```
String s = "One:Two;Three|Four\tFive";
String regex = "[:;|\\t]";
String strings[] = s.split(regex);
for (String word : strings)
    System.out.println(word);
```

Here, a string is split into words marked by colons, semicolons, vertical bars, or tab characters. When you run this program, here's what's displayed on the console:

```
One
Two
Three
Four
Five
```

Using the Pattern and Matcher classes

The `matches` method is fine for occasional use of regular expressions. But if you want your program to do a lot of pattern matching, you should use the `Pattern` and `Matcher` classes instead. The `Pattern` class represents a regular expression that has been compiled into executable form (remember, regular expressions are like little programs). Then, you can use the compiled `Pattern` object to create a `Matcher` object, which you can then use to match strings.

The `Pattern` class itself is pretty simple. Although it has about ten methods, you usually use just these two:

✦ `static Pattern compile(String pattern)`: Compiles the specified pattern. This static method returns a `Pattern` object. It throws `PatternSyntaxExpression` if the pattern contains an error.

✦ `Matcher matcher(String input)`: Creates a `Matcher` object to match this pattern against the specified string.

First, you use the `compile` method to create a `Pattern` object. (`Pattern` is one of those weird classes that doesn't have constructors. Instead, it relies on the static `compile` method to create instances.) Because the `compile` method throws `PatternSyntaxException`, you must use a `try`/`catch` statement to catch this exception when you compile a pattern.

Once you have a `Pattern` instance, you then use the `matcher` method to create an instance of the `Matcher` class. This class has more than 30 methods that let you do all sorts of things with regular expressions that aren't covered in this chapter, such as finding multiple occurrences of a pattern in an input string or replacing text that matches a pattern with a replacement string. For purposes of this book, I'm concerned only with the `matches` method: `static boolean matches()` returns a boolean that indicates whether the entire string matches the pattern.

To illustrate how to use these methods, here's an enhanced version of the `validDroidName` method that creates a pattern for the droid validation regex and saves it in a static class field:

```
private static Pattern droidPattern;

private static boolean validDroidName(String droid)
{
    if (droidPattern == null)
    {
        String regex = "(\\w\\d-\\w\\d)|(\\w-
\\d\\w\\w)";
        droidPattern = Pattern.compile(regex);
    }
    Matcher m = droidPattern.matcher(droid);
    return m.matches();
}
```

Here, the private class field `droidPattern` saves the compiled pattern for validating droids. The `if` statement in the `validDroidName` method checks to see if the pattern has already been created. If not, the pattern is created by calling the static `compile` method of the `Pattern` class. Then, the `matcher` method is used to create a `Matcher` object for the string passed as a parameter, and the string is validated by calling the `matches` method of the `Matcher` object.

Chapter 4: Using Recursion

In This Chapter

✔ Introducing recursion

✔ Calculating factors with recursion

✔ Listing directories with recursion

✔ Sorting with recursion

*R*ecursion is a basic programming technique in which a method calls itself to solve some problem. A method that uses this technique is called *recursive*. Many programming problems can only be solved by recursion, and some problems that can be solved by other techniques are better solved by recursion.

I'm not sure, but I think the term *recursion* comes from the Latin *recurse, recurset, recursum,* which means to curse repeatedly. I do know that that's exactly what many programmers feel like when struggling with complex recursive programming problems.

It's true, sometimes the concept of recursion can get a little tricky. So many programmers steer clear, looking for other techniques to solve the problem at hand. And in many cases, a non-recursive solution is best. However, many problems just cry out for recursion.

The Classic Factorial Example

One of the classic problems for introducing recursion is calculating the factorial of an integer. The *factorial* of any given integer — I'll call it *n* so I sound mathematical — is the product of all the integers from 1 to *n*. Thus, the factorial of 5 is 120: 5 times 4 times 3 times 2 times 1.

The non-recursive solution

You don't have to use recursion to calculate factorials. Instead, you can use a simple `for` loop. For example, here's a method that accepts an `int` number and returns the number's factorial as a `long`:

```
private static long factorial(int n)
{
    long f = 1;
    for (int i = 1; i <=n; i++)
        f = f * i;
    return f;
}
```

This method just uses a `for` loop to count from 1 to the number, keeping track of the product as it goes. Here's a snippet of code that calls this method and displays the result:

```
int n = 5;
long fact;
fact = factorial(n);
System.out.println("The factorial of "+ n + " is "
    + fact + ".");
```

If you run this code, the following line is displayed on the console:

```
The factorial of 5 is 120.
```

Factorials get big fast. You should use a `long` rather than an `int` to calculate the result. And you should use the `NumberFormat` class to format the result. For example, if `int` is 20 instead of 5, the previous code prints this on the console:

```
The factorial of 20 is 2432902008176640000.
```

If you use the `NumberFormat` class to format the result, the console output is more readable:

```
The factorial of 20 is 2,432,902,008,176,640,000.
```

The recursive solution

The non-recursive solution to the factorial problem works, but it isn't much fun. The recursive solution is based on the notion that the factorial for any number *n* is equal to *n* times the factorial of *n* – 1, provided that *n* is greater than 1. If *n* is 1, the factorial of *n* is 1.

This definition of factorial is recursive because the definition includes the factorial method itself. It also includes the most important part of any recursive method: an *end condition*. The end condition indicates when the recursive method should stop calling itself. In this case, when *n* is 1, I just return 1. Without an end condition, the recursive method keeps calling itself forever.

Here's the recursive version of the factorial method:

```
private static long factorial(int n)
{
    if (n == 1)
        return 1;
    else
        return n * factorial(n-1);
}
```

This method returns exactly the same result as the version in the previous section, but it uses recursion to calculate the factorial.

One way to visualize how recursion works is to imagine that you have five friends, named Jordan, Jeremy, Jacob, Justin, and Bob. Your friends aren't very smart, but they're very much alike. In fact, they're clones of each other. Cloning isn't a perfect process yet, so these clones have limitations. Each can do only one multiplication and can ask one of its clones one question.

So you walk up to Joshua and say, "Joshua, what's the factorial of five?"

Jordan says, "I don't know, but I do know it's five times the factorial of four. Jeremy, what's the factorial of four?"

Jeremy says, "I don't know, but I do know it's four times the factorial of three. Jacob, what's the factorial of three?"

Jacob says, "I don't know, but I do know it's three times the factorial of two. Justin, what's the factorial of two?"

Justin says, "I don't know, but I do know it's two times the factorial of one. Hey, Bob! What's the factorial of one?"

Bob, being the most intelligent of the bunch on account of not having a J-name, replies, "Why, one of course." So he tells his answer to Justin.

Justin says, "Ah! Two times one is two." So he tells the answer to Jacob.

Jacob says, "Thanks. Three times two is six." Jacob tells his answer to Jeremy.

Jeremy says, "Dude! Four times six is 24." Jeremy tells his answer to Jordan.

Jordan says, "Very good! Five times 24 is 120." So he tells you the answer.

That's pretty much how recursion works.

Displaying Directories

Recursion lends itself well to applications that have to navigate through directory structures, such as a Windows or Unix file system. In a file system, a directory is a list of files and other directories. Each of those directories is itself a list of files and other directories, and so on. Directories can be snugly nestled inside of other directories and have no limit in number.

Listing 4-1 shows a program that uses a recursive method to list all the directories that are found starting from a given path. I use indentation to show the directory structure. For example, here's the console output for the directories I used to organize the documents for this book:

```
Welcome to the Directory Lister
Enter a path: C:\Java AIO

Listing directory tree of:
C:\Java AIO
   Apps
      Book 1
      Book 2
      Book 3
      Book 4
      Book 5
   Manuscript
      Book 1
      Book 2
      Book 3
      Book 4
      Book 5
      Front
   Plans
Another? (Y or N) n
```

Well, as you can see I haven't done Books VI through IX yet. By the time you read this chapter, there will be even more directories to list!

Don't enter c:\ unless you're prepared to wait a long time for the program to finish listing all of the directories on your hard drive.

The Directory Listing application is remarkably simple. Before I explain its details, though, I want to point out that this program uses the File class, which is part of the java.io package. The File class represents a single file or directory. You find out much more about this class in Book VIII. For now, you just need to know these five details:

✦ The constructor for this class accepts a directory path as a parameter and creates an object that represents the specified directory.

✦ You can use the `exists` method to find out if the directory specified by the path parameter exists.

✦ The `listFiles` method returns an array of `File` objects that represent every file and directory in the current `File` object.

✦ The `isDirectory` method returns a `boolean` that indicates whether or not the current `File` object is a directory. If this method returns `false`, you can assume the `File` object is a file.

✦ The `getName` method returns the name of the file.

LISTING 4-1: THE DIRECTORY LISTING APPLICATION

```
import java.io.File;                                    → 1
import java.util.Scanner;

public class DirList
{
    static Scanner sc = new Scanner(System.in);

    public static void main(String[] args)
    {
        System.out.print(
            "Welcome to the Directory Lister");
        do
        {
            System.out.print("\nEnter a path: ");
            String path = sc.nextLine();               → 15

            File dir = new File(path);                  → 17
            if (!dir.exists() || !dir.isDirectory())    → 18
                System.out.println(
                    "\nThat directory doesn't exist.");
            else
            {
                System.out.println(
                    "\nListing directory tree of:");
                System.out.println(dir.getPath());      → 25
                listDirectories(dir, "  ");             → 26
            }
        } while(askAgain());                            → 28
    }
```

continued

LISTING 4-1 (CONTINUED)

```
private static void listDirectories(            → 31
    File dir, String indent)
{
    File[] dirs = dir.listFiles();              → 34
    for (File f : dirs)                         → 35
    {
        if (f.isDirectory())                    → 37
        {
            System.out.println(
                indent + f.getName());          → 40
            listDirectories(f, indent + "  ");  → 41
        }
    }
}

private static boolean askAgain()
{
    System.out.print("Another? (Y or N) ");
    String reply = sc.nextLine();
    if (reply.equalsIgnoreCase("Y"))
        return true;
        return false;
}
}
```

The following paragraphs point out the highlights of how this program works:

→ **1** This import statement is required to use the File class.

→**15** A Scanner object is used to get the pathname from the user.

→**17** The pathname is passed to the File class constructor to create a new File object for the directory entered by the user.

→**18** The exists and isDirectory methods are called to make sure the path entered by the user exists and points to a directory rather than a file.

→**25** If the user entered a good path, the getPath method is called to display the name of the path represented by the File object. (I could just as easily have displayed the path variable here.)

→**26** The listDirectories method is called to list all the subdirectories in the directory specified by the user.

→**28** The user is asked if he or she wants to list another directory, and the loop repeats if the user enters Y.

→**31** This is the start of the `listDirectories` method. This method takes two parameters: a `File` object representing the directory to be listed and a `String` object that provides the spaces used to indent each line of the listing. When this method is first called from the `main` method, the indentation is set to two spaces by a string literal.

→**34** The `listFiles` method is called to get an array of all the `File` objects in this directory.

→**35** An enhanced `for` loop is used to process all the `File` objects in the array.

→**37** This `if` statement checks to see if a file is a directory rather than a file.

→**40** If the `File` object is a directory, the indentation string is printed, followed by the name of the directory as returned by the `getName` method.

→**41** Next, the `listDirectories` method is called recursively to list the contents of the `f` directory. However, two spaces are added to the indentation string so that any directories in the `f` directory are indented two spaces to the right of the current directory.

If you're having trouble understanding how the recursion in this program works, think of it this way: The `listDirectory` method lists all the sub-directories in a single directory. For each directory, this method does two things: (1) prints the directory's name, and (2) calls itself to print any sub-directories of that directory.

Previously, I mentioned that all recursive methods must have some type of condition test that causes the method to stop calling itself. In this program, the condition test may not be obvious. However, eventually the `listDirectories` method is passed a directory that doesn't have any subdirectories. When that happens, the recursion ends — at least for that branch of the directory tree.

Writing Your Own Sorting Routine

The world is full of Computer Science majors who don't know anything more about computers than you do. However, they once attended a class in which the instructor explained how sorting algorithms worked. They may have received a C in that class, but it was good enough to graduate.

Now, you have a chance to learn what you missed by not majoring in Computer Science. I'm going to show you how one of the most commonly used sorting techniques actually works. It's called *Quicksort,* and it's a very ingenious use of recursion. I even show you a simple Java implementation of it.

Quicksort is easily the most technical part of this entire book. If you never wanted to major in Computer Science, and if you don't even want to talk to people who did, you may want to just skip the rest of this chapter now.

For most of us, learning how sorting algorithms such as Quicksort work is merely an intellectual exercise. The Java API has sorting already built in — for example, check out the `Arrays.sort` method. Those sort routines are way better than any that you or I will ever write.

Understanding how Quicksort works

The Quicksort technique sorts an array of values by using recursion. Its basic steps are this:

1. **Pick an arbitrary value that lies within the range of values in the array.**

This value is called the *pivot point*. The most common way to choose the pivot point is to simply pick the first value in the array. Folks have written doctoral degrees on more sophisticated ways to pick a pivot point that results in faster sorting. I like to stick with using the first element in the array.

2. **Rearrange the values in the array so that all the values that are less than the pivot point are on the left side of the array and all the values that are greater than or equal to the pivot point are on the right side of the array.**

The pivot value indicates the boundary between the left side and the right side of the array. It probably won't be dead center, but that doesn't matter. This step is called *partitioning,* and the left and right sides of the arrays are called *partitions*.

3. **Now treat each of the two sections of the array as a separate array, and start over with Step 1 for that section.**

That's the recursive part of the algorithm.

The hardest part of the Quicksort algorithm is the partitioning step. This step must rearrange the partition so that all values that are smaller than the pivot point are on the left, and all elements that are larger than the pivot point are on the right. For example, suppose the array has these ten values:

```
38 17 58 22 69 31 88 28 86 12
```

Here, the pivot point is 38, and the task of the partitioning step is to rearrange the array to something like this:

```
17 12 22 28 31 38 88 69 86 58
```

Notice that the values are still out of order. However, the array has been divided around the value 38: All values that are less than 38 are to the left of 38, and all values that are greater than 38 are to the right of 38.

Now, you can divide the array into two partitions at the value 38 and repeat the process for each side. The pivot value itself goes with the left partition, so the left partition is this:

```
17 12 22 28 31 38
```

This time, the partitioning step picks 17 as the pivot point and rearranges the elements as follows:

```
12 17 22 28 31 38
```

As you can see, this portion of the array is now sorted. Unfortunately, Quicksort doesn't realize that at this point, so it takes a few more recursions to be sure. But that's the basic process.

The sort method

The actual code that drives a Quicksort routine is surprisingly simple:

```
public static void sort(int low, int high)
{
    if (low >= high)
        return;
    int p = partition(low, high);
    sort (low, p);
    sort (p+1, high);
}
```

This method sorts the portion of an array indicated by the low and high index values passed to it. Ignoring the `if` statement for now, the `sort` method works by calling a `partition` method. This method rearranges the array into two sections called *partitions* so that all the values in the left partition are smaller than all the values in the right partition. The `partition` method returns the index of the end of the left partition. Then, the `sort` method calls itself twice: once to sort the left partition, and then again to sort the right partition.

To get the `sort` started, you call it with zero as the low value and the array length and 1 as the high value. Thus, the `sort` method begins by sorting the entire array. Each time the `sort` method executes, it calls itself twice to sort smaller partitions of the array.

The `if` statement at the beginning of the `sort` method compares the low value with the high value. If the low value is equal to or greater than the high value, the partition has only one element (or perhaps no elements) and is therefore already sorted. In that case, the `sort` method simply returns without calling itself again. That's the condition that ends the recursion.

The partition method

The `sort` method itself is the simple part of the Quicksort technique. The hard part is the `partition` method. This method accepts two parameters: the low and high indexes that mark the portion of the array that should be sorted. The basic outline of the partition method goes something like this:

1. **Pick a pivot point.**

2. **Move all elements that are less than the pivot point to the left side of the partition.**

3. **Move all elements that are greater than the pivot point to the right side of the partition.**

4. **Return the index of the pivot point.**

The most commonly used technique for partitioning the array is to maintain two index variables, named `i` and `j`, that work from both ends of the array toward the center. First, `i` starts at the beginning of the array and moves forward until it encounters a value that's greater than the pivot value. Then, `j` starts at the opposite end of the array and moves backward until it finds a value that's less than the pivot point. At that point, the `partition` method has a value that's greater than the pivot point on the left side of the array and a value that's less than the pivot point on the right side of the array. So it swaps them.

Then, it repeats the cycle: `i` is incremented until it finds another value that's greater than the pivot value, `j` is decremented until it finds another value that's less than the pivot value, and the elements are swapped. This process repeats until `j` is less than `i`, which means the indexes have crossed and the partitioning is done.

Now put it together in some code:

```
public static int partition(int low, int high)
{
    int pivot = a[low];

    int i = low - 1;
    int j = high + 1;

    while (i < j)
    {
```

```
            for (i++; a[i] < pivot; i++);
            for (j--; a[j] > pivot; j--);
            if (i < j)
                swap(i, j);
        }
        return j;
    }
```

Note that in this code, the array being sorted is a static `int` array named a. The low and high ends of the partition to be partitioned are passed in as parameters, and the method starts by choosing the first element in the partition as the value for the pivot point. Next, it initializes the index variables i and j from the parameters. Notice that 1 is subtracted from the low value and 1 is added to the high value. The index variables take one step back from the array before the looping starts so they can get a good start.

The `while` loop is used to indicate when the partitioning is finished. It repeats as long as i is less than j. Once these index variables stop, the partitioning is done, and the value of j is returned to indicate the index point that divides the left partition from the right partition.

In the body of the `while` loop are two strange bodyless `for` loops. These for loops don't have a body because their only purpose is to move their index values until they find a value that's either less than or greater than the pivot value.

The first `for` loop increments the i index variable until it finds a value that's greater than the pivot point. Thus, this `for` loop finds the first value that might need to be moved to the other side of the array.

Next, the second `for` loop decrements the j index variable until it finds a value that's less than the pivot point. So this loop finds a value that may need to be swapped with the value found by the first `for` loop.

Finally, the `if` statement checks to see if the indexes have crossed. Assuming they haven't, a `swap` method is called to swap the elements. The `swap` method is mercifully simple:

```
public static void swap(int i, int j)
{
    int temp = a[i];
    a[i] = a[j];
    a[j] = temp;
}
```

This method moves the i element to a temporary variable, moves the j element to the i element, and then moves the temporary variable to the j element.

Putting it all together

Now that you've seen the basic steps necessary to create a Quicksort program, Listing 4-2 shows a program that gives these methods a workout. This program creates an array of 100 randomly selected numbers with values from 1 through 100. It prints the array, uses the sorting methods shown in the previous sections to sort the array, and then prints the sorted array. Here's a sample run:

```
Unsorted array:

65 51 38 47 93 87 50 36 77 58 22 92 46 60 49 90 28 39 27  8
66 76 40 99 90 35 34 30  7 41 45 34 41 17 36 63 52 65 50 77
 2 93 48  6 91 67 34 69 33 47 50 12 88 15 65 40 29 74 34 14
55 37 28 25 98 66 69 88 66 27 29 88 29 87  9 29 77 32  4 11
68 40 17 61 50 90 24  1 59 91 69  5 82 69 51 45 29 38 61 86


Sorted array:

 1  2  4  5  6  7  8  9 11 12 14 15 17 17 22 24 25 27 27 28
28 29 29 29 29 29 30 32 33 34 34 34 34 35 36 36 37 38 38 39
40 40 40 41 41 45 45 46 47 47 48 49 50 50 50 50 51 51 52 55
58 59 60 61 61 63 65 65 65 66 66 66 67 68 69 69 69 69 74 76
77 77 77 82 86 87 87 88 88 88 90 90 90 91 91 92 93 93 98 99
```

As you can see, the first array is in random order, but the second array is nicely sorted.

LISTING 4-2: A SORTING PROGRAM

```java
public class QuickSortApp
{
    public static void main(String[] args)
    {
        int LEN = 100;
        int[] unsorted = new int[LEN];
        for (int i = 0; i<LEN; i++)                          → 7
            unsorted[i] = (int)(Math.random() * 100) + 1;
        System.out.println("Unsorted array:");
        printArray(unsorted);                                → 10
        int[] sorted = sort(unsorted);                       → 11
        System.out.println("\n\nSorted array:");
        printArray(sorted);                                  → 13
    }

    private static void printArray(int[] array)              → 16
    {
        System.out.println();
        for (int i = 0; i < array.length; i++)
        {
```

```
        if (array[i] < 10)
            System.out.print(" ");
        System.out.print(array[i] + " ");
        if ((i+1) % 20 == 0)
            System.out.println();
    }
}

private static int[] a;                                → 29

public static int[] sort(int[] array)                  → 31
{
   a = array;
   sort(0, a.length - 1);
   return a;
}

public static void sort(int low, int high)             → 38
{
   if (low >= high)
      return;
   int p = partition(low, high);
   sort (low, p);
   sort (p+1, high);
}

public static int partition(int low, int high)         → 47
{
   int pivot = a[low];

   int i = low - 1;
   int j = high + 1;

   while (i < j)
   {
      for (i++; a[i] < pivot; i++);
      for (j--; a[j] > pivot; j--);
      if (i < j)
         swap(i, j);
   }
   return j;
}

public static void swap(int i, int j)                  → 64
{
   int temp = a[i];
   a[i] = a[j];
   a[j] = temp;
}
}
```

Most of the code in this program has already been explained, so I just point out a few of the highlights:

→ **7**   This `for` loop assigns 100 random values to the array.

→**10**   The `printArray` method is called to print the unsorted array.

→**11**   The `sort` method is called to sort the array.

→**13**   The `printArray` method is called again to print the sorted array.

→**16**   The `printArray` method uses a `for` loop to print array elements. Each element is separated by two spaces. However, an additional space is printed before each element if the element's value is less than `10`. That way, the values line up in columns. Also, the remainder operator (`%`) is used to call the `println` method every 20 elements. Thus, this method prints five lines with 20 values on each line. (The last few values in the array won't line up exactly if they happen to be 100, but that's okay.)

→**29**   A static variable named `a` is used to hold the array while it is being sorted.

→**31**   The `sort` method has two versions. The first accepts an `int` array as a parameter and returns an `int` array with the sorted values. This method sets the static `a` variable to the array passed via the parameters, calls the second version of the `sort` method to sort the entire array, and then returns the sorted array.

→**38**   This is the second sort method. It sorts the partition indicated by the parameters. The operation of this method is explained in detail in the section titled "The sort method."

→**47**   The `partition` method is also explained in detail in the previous section.

→**64**   The `swap` method simply exchanges the two indicated values.

Remember the cool XOR technique for exchanging two integer values without the need for a temporary variable? You can improve the performance of your sort ever so slightly by replacing the `swap` method with this code:

```
public static void swap(int i, int j)
{
    a[i] ^= a[j];
    a[j] ^= a[i];
    a[i] ^= a[j];
}
```

Book VI

Swing

FREELANCER NED WILLIS CONSULTS WITH A MEMBER OF HIS TECHNICAL STAFF

©RICHTENNANT

"...and that's pretty much all there is to converting a document to an HTML file."

Contents at a Glance

Chapter 1: Swinging into Swing

In This Chapter

- ✓ Examining some basic Swing concepts
- ✓ Fussing with frames
- ✓ Putting panels in your frames
- ✓ Looking at labels
- ✓ Beginning with buttons
- ✓ Leaping into layout

So far in this book, all the programs have been console-based, like something right out of the 1980s. Console-based Java programs have their place, especially when you're first learning about Java. But eventually, you'll want to create programs that work with a Graphical User Interface, also known as a GUI.

This chapter gets you started in that direction. You create simple GUI applications that display simple buttons and text labels. Along the way, you find out about two key classes: `JFrame` and `JPanel`, which provide the visual containers that hold buttons, labels, and other components I discuss in later chapters.

Some Important Swing Concepts You Need to Know

Learning Swing is one of the most complicated tasks of learning Java. Complicated enough, in fact, that I have to go over some conceptual information before I get into the nitty-gritty of writing GUI code. So put on your thinking cap for the next few sections.

Understanding what Swing does

Swing is a package that lets you create applications that use a flashy Graphical User Interface (or *GUI*) instead of a dull console interface. Figure 1-1 shows a typical window created with Swing. As you can see, this window includes a variety of user-interface components, including labels, text fields, drop-down lists, and buttons.

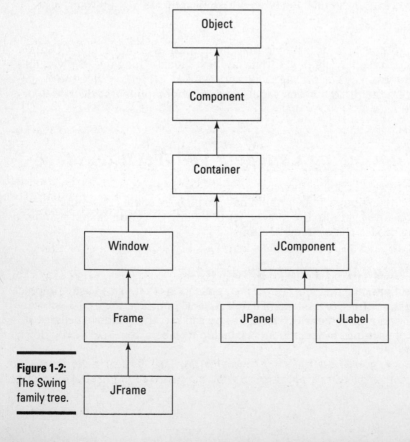

Figure 1-1:
A typical
Swing
window.

The Swing class hierarchy

The Swing API provides many different classes for creating various types of user interface elements. In this chapter, I look at three of those classes: JFrame, JPanel, and JLabel. However, these three classes are part of a larger collection of classes that are all related through inheritance, as shown in Figure 1-2. The Swing family tree splits at the Component class into one group of classes that are derived from the JComponent class, and another branch that descends from the Window class.

Figure 1-2:
The Swing
family tree.

The following paragraphs briefly describe each of the classes shown in this figure:

✦ **Object:** All classes ultimately derive from `Object`, so it's no surprise that this class is at the top of the tree.

✦ **Component:** The `Component` class represents an object that has a visual representation that can be shown on-screen and that can interact with users. This class defines some basic methods that are available to all Swing classes. For example, the `setVisible` method determines whether a component is visible or hidden. And the `setBounds` method sets the location and size of the component. This is an AWT class, not a Swing class.

✦ **Container:** The `Container` class builds on the basic visual capabilities of the `Component` class by adding the ability to hold other containers. This too is an AWT class rather than a Swing class. From this class, you get the `add` method, which lets you add components to a container. As you'll see, you use this method in almost all GUI programs.

✦ **Window:** This class defines a window, which is a specialized type of container object that has a border, a title bar, buttons that minimize, maximize, and close the window, and that can be repositioned and possibly even resized by the user.

✦ **Frame:** A *frame* is a type of `Window` that serves as the basis for Java GUI applications. `Frame` is an AWT class that has been improved upon by the `JFrame` class.

✦ **JFrame:** The Swing version of the older `Frame` class. Most of your Swing applications include at least one `JFrame` object.

✦ **JComponent:** The `JComponent` class is a Swing class that is the basis for all other Swing components except for frames.

✦ **JPanel:** This class creates *panels,* which are containers used to organize and control the layout of other components such as labels, buttons, text fields, and so on. In most Swing applications, one or more panels are added to a frame. Then, when the frame is displayed, the components that were added to its panels are made visible.

✦ **JLabel:** This class creates a label that displays a simple text value.

As you work with Swing, you'll find that some of the classes you use are defined in the `javax.swing` package. So you need to start every Swing application with this line:

```
import javax.swing.*;
```

In addition, you'll find that some Swing features use classes in the `java.awt` and `java.awt.event` packages. So you may need to import those packages as well.

I've Been Framed!

The top-level component for most Swing-based applications is called a *frame* and is defined by the JFrame class. By itself, a frame doesn't do much. But to do anything else in Swing, you must first create a frame. Figure 1-3 shows a frame that does nothing but display the message Hello, World! in its title bar.

Figure 1-3:
The frame
displayed by
the Hello,
World!
program.

The JFrame has about a bazillion methods, but only a few of them are useful in most programs. Table 1-1 lists the JFrame methods you use most, along with a couple of constructors.

Table 1-1	Useful JFrame Constructors and Methods
Constructor	*Description*
JFrame()	Creates a new frame with no title.
JFrame(String title)	Creates a new frame with the specified title.
Method	*Description*
void add(Component c)	Adds the specified component to the frame.
JMenuBar getJMenuBar()	Gets the menu for this frame.
void pack()	Adjusts the size of the frame to fit the components you've added to it.
void remove(Component c)	Removes the specified component from the frame.
void setDefaultCloseOperation	Sets the action taken when the user closes the frame. You should almost always specify JFrame.EXIT_ON_CLOSE.
void setIconImage (Icon image)	Sets the icon displayed when the frame is minimized.
void setLayout (LayoutManager layout)	Sets the layout manager used to control how components are arranged when the frame is displayed. The default is the BorderLayout manager.
void setLocation (int x, int y)	Sets the x and y position of the frame on-screen. The top-left corner of the screen is 0, 0.

Method	Description
void setLocationRelativeTo (Component c)	Centers the frame on-screen if the parameter is null.
void setResizeable (boolean value)	Sets whether or not the size of the frame can be changed by the user. The default setting is true (the frame can be resized).
void setSize(int width, int height)	Sets the size of the frame to the specified width and height.
void setJMenuBar(JMenuBar menu)	Sets the menu for this frame.

At the minimum, you want to set a title for a new frame, set the frame's size so it's large enough to see any components you add to it (by default, the frame is zero pixels wide and zero pixels high, so it isn't very useful), and call the setVisible method to make the frame visible. One way to do these three things is to create an instance of the JFrame class and set its properties using statements like this:

```
JFrame frame = new JFrame("This is the title");
frame.setSize(350, 260);
frame.setVisible(true);
```

However, creating a frame by declaring a class that extends the JFrame class is more common. Then, you call these methods in the constructor, as I describe in the next section.

By default, the user can change the size of a frame. If you want to fix the size of your frame so the user can't change it, just call setResizeable(false).

Hello, World! in Swing

To get you started with Swing, Listing 1-1 shows a Swing version of the classic Hello, World! program, using nothing but a frame. If you run this program, the frame shown in Figure 1-1 is displayed on-screen. As you can see, the frame's title bar contains the text "Hello, World!"

The purpose of this seemingly pointless little program is to illustrate one solution to the first problem you encounter when you work with Swing: The main method is a static method, but Swing frames are objects. So, you have to figure out how to get your program out of a static context. This program does that by creating the application as a class that extends JFrame. Then, the main method calls the class constructor, in effect creating an instance of itself. That's all the main method does; the real work of this application is done by the constructor.

LISTING 1-1: THE SWING VERSION OF THE HELLO, WORLD! PROGRAM

```
import javax.swing.*;                              → 1

public class HelloFrame extends JFrame             → 3
{
    public static void main(String[] args)         → 5
    {
        new HelloFrame();                          → 7
    }

    public HelloFrame()                            → 10
    {
        this.setSize(200,100);                     → 12
        this.setDefaultCloseOperation(             → 13
            JFrame.EXIT_ON_CLOSE);
        this.setTitle("Hello World!");             → 15
        this.setVisible(true);                     → 16
    }
}
```

The following paragraphs describe most of the features of this program:

→ **1** The program starts with an `import` statement that imports all the classes in the `javax.swing` package. Most of the Swing classes are defined in this package. However, you may have to import other classes as well, depending on what GUI features your program uses.

→ **3** The class for this application, named `JFrame`, extends a Swing class named `JFrame`. A class that extends `JFrame` is often called a *frame class*. The `JFrame` class defines a basic frame in which you can display GUI components, such as labels and text boxes. All Swing applications need at least one class that extends `JFrame`.

→ **5** Swing applications are still Java applications, and all Java applications need a static `main` method that starts the application. So the first method listed in this class is the `main` method.

→ **7** The first (and only) statement of the `main` method creates a new instance of the `HelloFrame` class. Unlike console applications, Swing applications can't run in a static context. As a result, the main purpose of the static `main` method in a Swing application is to create an instance of the application's frame class.

→ **10** When an instance of the `HelloFrame` class is created in line 7, the constructor that starts on this line is executed. The main job of the constructor for a frame class is to set the options for the frame and create any GUI components that are displayed in the frame.

→ **12** The first option that this constructor sets is the size of the frame. To do that, it calls the `setSize` method. The parameters specify that the frame should be 200 pixels wide and 100 pixels high. (A *pixel* is one of the little dots that makes up the image on a computer screen. *Pixel* is short for *picture element,* but that won't be on the test.)

→**13** The next option this constructor sets is what to do if the user closes the frame by clicking its Close button, which usually appears in the upper-right hand corner of the frame. By default, clicking the Close button hides the frame but doesn't terminate the application. As a result, the application's main thread (the one that's still running in a static context via the `main` method) keeps running for a while. Eventually, Java figures out that nothing's happening and shuts the application down. But the application exits more cleanly if you use the `setDefaultCloseOperation` to set the close operation to `JFrame.EXIT_ON_CLOSE`. That causes the program to terminate when the frame is closed.

→**15** The next statement uses the `setTitle` method to set the title of the frame.

→**16** The last statement in the constructor calls the `setVisible` method with a parameter value of `true`, which makes the frame visible on-screen. If you leave this statement out, the frame is created but the user never sees it.

That's all there is to this program. Granted, it's a little more complicated than the console-base Hello, World! program from Book I, Chapter 1. But not by much. Just to be sure its operation is clear, here's a recap of what happens when this program is run:

1. Java runs the static `main` method for the `HelloWorld` class.

2. The `main` method creates an instance of the `HelloWorld` class, which causes the constructor to be executed.

3. The constructor sets the frame size, the default close operation, and the title.

4. Now that the constructor is done, the program continues with the `main` method, where the `setVisible` method is called to display the frame.

Positioning the Frame On-Screen

The `JFrame` class provides two methods that let you specify the position of the frame on-screen. If you want to place the frame at some arbitrary location on-screen, use the `setLocation` method. For example, to put the frame at the top left corner of the screen, use this statement:

```
frame.setLocation(0,0);
```

If you want to center the frame on-screen, call the setLocationRelativeTo method and pass null as the parameter:

```
frame.setLocationRelativeTo(null);
```

This method is designed to let you position a frame relative to some other component that's already displayed. But if you pass null as the parameter, the method centers the frame on-screen.

If you want to position a window at some location other than the top left corner or dead center on-screen, you may need to know the width and height of the user's screen so you can calculate a location for your frame. To determine the size of the user's screen, you can use a class named Toolkit. The Toolkit class has a bunch of methods, but you need to know two of them here:

✦ **getDefaultToolkit:** A static method that creates a Toolkit object. You must use this method before you can use the getScreenSize method.

✦ **getScreenSize:** Returns the size of the screen as a Dimension object. The Dimension class has two public fields that represent the size of the screen: height and width. Both fields are of type int.

Suppose you want to position a frame so that its bottom-left corner is right at the center of the screen. The following code placed in the frame's constructor does the trick:

```
Toolkit tk = Toolkit.getDefaultToolkit();
Dimension d = tk.getScreenSize();
int x = d.width / 2;
int y = (d.height / 2) - this.getHeight();
this.setLocation(x, y);
```

This code first creates a Toolkit object and uses it to get the screen dimensions. It sets the x position to the horizontal center of the screen by dividing the screen width by 2. Then it sets the y position to the vertical center (the screen height divided by 2) less the width of the frame. That puts the *bottom* of the frame at the vertical midpoint.

Using the JPanel Class

A *panel* is a type of container that's designed to hold a group of components so they can be displayed on a frame. The normal way to display a group of controls such as text fields, labels, buttons, and other GUI widgets is to add those controls to a panel, and then add the panel to the frame. You can bypass the panel and add the controls directly to the frame if you want, but using a separate panel to hold the frames control is almost always a good idea.

Panels are defined by the `JPanel` class. Like the `JFrame` class, the `JPanel` class has a bevy of methods. Table 1-2 lists the most commonly used constructors and methods for the `JPanel` class.

Table 1-2	Interesting JPanel Constructors and Methods
Constructor	**Description**
`JPanel()`	Creates a new panel.
`JPanel(boolean isDoubleBuffered)`	Creates a new panel. If the parameter is `true`, the panel uses a technique called double-buffering, which results in better display for graphics applications. This constructor is usually used for game programs or other panels that display animations.
`JPanel(LayoutManager layout)`	Creates a new panel with the specified layout manager. The default layout manager is FlowLayout.
Method	**Description**
`void add(Component c)`	Adds the specified component to the panel.
`void remove (Component c)`	Removes the specified component from the panel.
`void setLayout (LayoutManager layout)`	Sets the layout manager used to control how components are arranged when the panel is displayed. The default is the FlowLayout manager.
`void setLocation(int x, int y)`	Sets the x and y position of the frame-screen. The top-left corner of the screen is 0, 0.
`void setSize(int width, int height)`	Sets the size of the frame to the specified width and height.
`void setToolTipText (String text)`	Sets the tooltip text that's displayed if the user rests the mouse over an empty part of the panel.

You can use several different techniques to create a panel and add it to a frame. One is to simply create a `JPanel` object and assign it to a variable in the `JFrame` constructor. You can then add components to the panel, and then add the panel to the frame. For example

```
// HelloFrame constructor
public HelloFrame()
{
    this.setSize(200,100);

    this.setDefaultCloseOperation(JFrame.EXIT_ON_CLOSE);
    this.setTitle("Hello, World!");

    JPanel panel = new JPanel();

    // code to add components to the panel goes here

    this.setVisible(true);
}
```

Another commonly used technique is to create a separate class for the panel. This class should extend JPanel. Then, you can add any components the panel needs in the constructor:

```
class HelloPanel extends JPanel
{
    public HelloPanel()
    {
        // code to add components to the panel goes here
    }
}
```

Then, in the frame class constructor, you create a new instance of the panel class and add it to the panel:

```
HelloPanel panel = new HelloPanel();
this.add(panel);
```

Or, just this statement does the trick:

```
this.add(new HelloPanel());
```

Using Labels

Now that you know how to create frames and panels, you can create a useful component to add to a panel: a label. A label is a component that simply displays text. Labels are used for a variety of purposes: to display captions for other controls such as text fields or combo boxes, to display informational messages, or to show the results of a calculation or a database lookup.

A label can also display an image, or it can display both an image and some text. And you have complete control over the appearance of the text: You can specify the font, size, whether the text is bold, italic, or underlined, what color the text is displayed as, and so on. In this chapter, I discuss how to work with basic labels. For more information about additional things you can do with labels, see Book IX, Chapters 1 and 2.

To create a label, you use the JLabel class. Table 1-3 shows its most commonly used constructors and methods.

Table 1-3	Tolerable JLabel Constructors and Methods
Constructor	*Description*
JLabel()	Creates a new label with no initial text.
JLabel(String text)	Creates a new label with the specified text.

Method	Description
`String getText()`	Returns the text displayed by the label.
`void setText(String text)`	Sets the text displayed by the label.
`void setToolTipText (String text)`	Sets the tooltip text that's displayed if the user rests the mouse over the label for a few moments.
`void setVisible (boolean value)`	Shows or hides the label.

When you create a label, you can pass the text you want it to display to the constructor, like this:

```
JLabel label1 = new JLabel("Hello, World!");
```

Or, you can create the label first, and then set its text later:

```
JLabel label1 = new JLabel();
label1.setText("Hello, World!");
```

A label won't be displayed until you add it to a panel that is, in turn, added to a frame. Here's an example of a constructor for a frame class that creates a panel, creates a label, adds the label to the panel, and adds the panel to the frame:

```
// HelloFrame constructor
public HelloFrame()
{
    this.setSize(200,100);

    this.setDefaultCloseOperation(JFrame.EXIT_ON_CLOSE);
    this.setTitle("Hello, World!");

    JPanel panel1 = new JPanel();
    JLabel label1 = new JLabel("Hello, World!")
    panel1.add(label1);
    this.add(panel1);

    this.setVisible(true);
}
```

Figure 1-4 shows what this frame looks like when the program is run.

Figure 1-4:
A frame with a panel, which has a label.

Creating Buttons

Next to labels, the Swing component you use most is the JButton component, which creates a button the user can click. Figure 1-5 shows a frame with a single button.

Figure 1-5:
A frame with a panel, which includes a button.

In the next chapter, you find out how to write the code that responds when the user clicks a button. Here, I just focus on how to create buttons and control their appearance. Table 1-4 lists the most commonly used constructors and methods that are available for the JButton class.

Table 1-4	Worthwhile JButton Constructors and Methods
Constructor	*Description*
JButton()	Creates a new button with no initial text.
JButton(String text)	Creates a new button with the specified text.
Method	*Description*
doClick()	Triggers an action event for the button as if the user clicked it. (I tell you why this is sometimes useful in the next chapter.)
String getText()	Returns the text displayed by the button.
void setBorderPainted (boolean value)	Shows or hides the button's border. The default setting is true (the border is shown).

Method	Description
void setContentAreaFilled (boolean value)	Specifies whether or not the button's background should be filled or left empty. The default setting is true (the background is filled in).
void setEnabled(boolean value)	Enables or disables the button. The default setting is true (enabled).
void setRolloverEnabled (boolean value)	Enables or disables the rollover effect, which causes the border to get thicker when the mouse moves over the button. The default setting is true (rollover effect enabled).
void setText(String text)	Sets the text displayed by the button.
void setToolTipText (String text)	Sets the tooltip text that's displayed if the user lets the mouse rest over the button.
void setVisible(boolean value)	Shows or hides the button. The default setting is true (the button is visible).

As you can see, the constructors of the JButton class are similar to the constructors for the JLabel class: You can either create an empty button or a button with text. For example, here's the code that creates the button shown in Figure 1-5:

```
JButton button1 = new JButton("Click me!");
```

If you don't provide the button text when you call the constructor, you can supply it later via the setText method, like this:

```
JButton button1 = new JButton();
button1.setText("Click me!");
```

You might not think you'd ever do that, but sometimes the meaning of a button changes depending on what the user is doing. For example, a program that lets a user add, change, or delete records in a file might set the text of a button to Add Record, Change Record, or Delete Record depending on what the user happens to be doing at the time. In a program like that, you may need to use the getText method to find out what text is currently displayed by a button.

Most of the other methods listed in Table 1-4 simply affect how a button looks. To disable a button so the user can't click it, call setEnabled(false). To remove the dark border from the edges of a button, call setBorderPainted (false). To remove the background from a button so all that's displayed is the text, call setContentAreaFilled(false). And to make a button disappear altogether, call setVisible(false).

A Word about the Layout of Components

Controlling the layout of components on a panel is one of the hardest things about using Swing. Hard enough, in fact, that I devote Book VI, Chapter 5 to it. Until then, you need to know a few key points:

✦ The layout of components on a panel (or frame) is controlled by a *layout manager,* which determines the final placement of each component. The layout manager takes the size of the component, the size of the panel, and the position of other nearby components into account when it makes its decisions.

✦ Swing provides seven different layout managers you can choose from. Each has is own way of deciding where each component goes.

✦ The default layout manager for panels is called `FlowLayout`. It places components one after another in a row, and starts a new row only when it gets to the end of the panel (or the frame that contains it).

✦ With `FlowLayout` (and with the other layout managers too), the layout changes if the user changes the size of the frame. The size of the frame makes a big difference in how `FlowLayout` arranges controls.

✦ You can always call the frame's `setResizeable(false)` method to prevent the user from resizing the frame.

✦ If you want to change the layout manager used for a panel, you call the panel's `setLayout` method.

✦ For many (if not most) Swing applications, you use more than one panel to display your components. Each panel can have a different layout manager. With this technique, you can create complex layouts with lots of components, all arranged just the way you want.

✦ If you need to, you can always turn off the layout manager altogether. To do that, you call the panel's `setLayout` method with `null` set as the parameter. Then, you use *absolute positioning,* which lets you set the x and y position and the size of each component by calling its `setBounds` method.

✦ This list could go on and on. For more information about controlling layout, refer to Book VI, Chapter 5.

Chapter 2: Handling Events

In This Chapter

- ✔ Understanding important event concepts
- ✔ Working with event handling classes and interfaces
- ✔ Responding to button clicks
- ✔ Using inner classes for event handling
- ✔ Providing an Exit button
- ✔ Dealing with the Close button

In the previous chapter, you find out how to create Swing frames that include panels, labels, and buttons. However, the frames don't do anything other than sit there. They look good, but they're completely unresponsive. Click them all you want, but they don't do anything. They're kind of like teenagers.

In this chapter, you get those buttons to do something. Specifically, you find out how to write code that's executed when a user clicks a button. The technique you use to do that is called *event listening,* and it's one of the most important aspects of writing Swing programs. It may seem a little complicated at first, but after you get the swing of it (sorry), event listening makes perfect sense.

Although event listening is used mostly to respond to button clicks, it can also be used to respond to other types of user interactions. For example, you can use event listening to write code that's executed when the user makes a selection from a combo box, moves the mouse over a label, or presses a key on the keyboard. The event-listening techniques in this chapter work for those events as well.

Examining Events

An *event* is an object that's generated when the user does something noteworthy with one of your user-interface components. For example, if the user clicks a button, drags the mouse over a label, or selects an item from a combo box, an event object is generated. This event object is then passed to a special method you create called an *event listener.* The event listener can examine the event object, determine exactly what type of event occurred, and respond accordingly. For example, if the user clicks a button, the event listener might write any data entered by the user via text fields to a file. If the user passes the mouse over a label, the event handler might change the text displayed by the label. And if the user selects an item from a combo box, the event handler might use the value that was selected to look up information in a database. The possibilities are endless!

There are several different types of event objects, represented by various classes that all inherit `AWTEvent`. Table 2-1 lists the most commonly used event classes. In addition, this table lists the *listener interface* that's used to create an object that can listen for the event and handle it when it is generated.

Note that these event classes are contained in the package `java.awt`. Strictly speaking, event handling is provided by AWT, not by Swing.

Table 2-1	Commonly Used Event Classes	
Event Class	**Listener Interface**	**Description**
`ActionEvent`	`ActionListener`	Created when the user performs an action with a button or other component. Usually, this means that the user has clicked the button. However, the user can also invoke a button action by tabbing to the button and pressing the Enter key.
`ItemEvent`	`ItemListener`	Created when the selected item in a list control, such as a combo box or list box, is changed.
`DocumentEvent`	`DocumentListener`	Created when the user changes the contents of a text component. such as a text field.
`WindowEvent`	`WindowListener`	Created when the status of the window (frame) changes.
`KeyEvent`	`KeyListener`	Created when the user presses a key on the keyboard. This event can be used to watch for specific keystrokes entered by the user.
`MouseEvent`	`MouseListener`	Created when the user does something interesting with the mouse, such as clicks one of the buttons, drags the mouse, or simply moves the mouse over another object.
`FocusEvent`	`FocusListener`	Created when a component receives or loses focus.

The events listed in Table 2-1 can be divided into two categories. The first three (`ActionEvent`, `ItemEvent`, and `DocumentEvent`) are called *semantic events* because they're related to user interactions that usually have some specific meaning. For example, when the user clicks a button, he or she is trying to do something specific. In contrast, the other events are called *low-level events*.

If you're cramming for the test, you absolutely need to know three important terms:

✦ **Event:** An object that's created when the user does something noteworthy with a component, such as clicking it.

✦ **Event Source:** The component that generated the event object. Usually, the event source is a button or other component the user can click, but any Swing component can be an event source.

✦ **Event Listener:** The object that listens for events and handles them when they occur. The event listener object must implement the interface appropriate for the event. These listener interfaces define the method or methods that the event source calls when the event occurs. Table 2-2 lists the methods that are defined by each of the interfaces that are listed in Table 2-1.

Table 2-2	Methods Defined by Event Listener Interfaces	
Listener Interface	*Method*	*Description*
`ActionListener (ActionEvent e)`	`void actionPerformed`	Called when an action event occurs.
`ItemListener`	`void itemStateChanged (ItemEvent e)`	Called when the selected item changes.
`DocumentListener`	`void changeUpdate (DocumentEvent e)`	Called when text is changed.
	`void insertUpdate (DocumentEvent e)`	Called when text is inserted.
	`void removeUpdate DocumentEvent e)`	Called when text is deleted.
`WindowListener`	`void windowActivated (WindowEvent e)`	Called when the window is activated.
	`void windowClosed (WindowEvent e)`	Called when the window has been closed.
	`void windowClosing (WindowEvent e)`	Called when the user attempts to close the window.
	`void windowDeactivated (WindowEvent e)`	Called when the window is deactivated.

(continued)

Table 2-2 *(continued)*

Listener Interface	Method	Description
	void windowDeiconified (WindowEvent e)	Called when the window is changed from icon to normal.
	void windowIconified (WindowEvent e)	Called when the window is minimized to an icon.
	void windowOpened (WindowEvent e)	Called when the window is opened.
KeyListener	void keyPressed (KeyEvent e)	Called when the user presses a key.
	void keyReleased (KeyEvent e)	Called when the user releases a key.
	void keyTyped (KeyEvent e)	Called when the user types a key.
MouseListener	void mouseClicked (MouseEvent e)	Called when the user clicks the mouse.
	void mouseEntered MouseEvent e)	Called when the mouse moves over a component.
	void mouseExited (MouseEvent e)	Called when the mouse leaves a component.
	void mousePressed (MouseEvent e)	Called when the user presses the mouse button.
	void mouseReleased (MouseEvent e)	Called when the user releases the mouse button.
FocusListener	void focusGained (FocusEvent e)	Called when the component gains focus.
FocusListener	void focusLost (FocusEvent e)	Called when the component looses focus.

Handling Events

Now that you know the basic objects that are used for event handling, you have to actually wire them up to create a program that responds to events.

To write Java code that responds to events, you have to do the following:

1. **Create a component that can generate events.**

You want to add buttons or other components that generate events to your frame so it displays components the user can interact with. (Strictly speaking, all Swing components can generate some events. Even a label generates a MouseEvent when the user moves the mouse over it. But a frame that consists of nothing but labels isn't very useful.)

Usually, you declare the variable that refers to the event source as a private class field, outside of the constructor for the frame or any other method. For example

```
private JButton button1;
```

Then, in the constructor for the frame class, you can create the button. For example, here's code that creates a panel, creates a button, adds it to a panel, and then adds the panel to the frame:

```
JPanel panel = new JPanel();
button1 = new JButton("Click me!");
panel.add(button1);
this.add(panel);
```

Note that this code appears in the constructor of the frame class, so this in the last line refers to the frame.

2. **Create a class that implements the listener interface for the event you want to handle.**

For example, to handle action events, you should create a class that implements the ActionListener interface. As you see later in this chapter, you can do that in at least four ways. But one of the easiest is to simply add implements ActionListener to the definition of the frame class. Thus, the frame class declaration looks something like this:

```
public class ClickMe
    extends JFrame implements ActionListener
```

Later in this chapter, I tell you about other ways to implement the event listener interface.

3. **Write the code for any methods defined by the listener.**

When you implement a listener interface, you must provide an implementation of each method defined by the interface. Most listener interfaces define just one method, corresponding to the type of event the interface listens for. For example, the ActionListener interface defines a method named actionPerformed. This method is called whenever an action event is created. Thus, the code you place inside the actionPerformed method is executed when an action event occurs.

For example, here's an actionPerformed method that responds to action events:

```
public void actionPerformed(ActionEvent e)
{
    if (e.getSource() == button1)
        button1.setText("You clicked!");
}
```

Here, this code changes the text displayed by button1 if the event source is button1.

4. Register the listener with the source.

The final step is to register the event listener with the event source. Every component that serves as an event source provides a method that lets you register event listeners to listen for the event. For `ActionEvent` sources, the method is `addActionListener`. Here's a modification to the frame constructor code that creates the `button1` button and registers the frame class as the action event listener:

```
JPanel panel = new JPanel();
button1 = new JButton("Click me!");
button1.addActionListener(this);
panel.add(button1);
this.add(panel);
```

Here, you can specify `this` as the event listener because the frame class itself implements `ActionListener`.

The ClickMe Program

To see how all these elements work together in a complete program, Figure 2-1 shows three incarnations of a frame created by a program called ClickMe. This program displays a frame that has a single button that initially says `Click Me!` When the user clicks the button, the button's text changes to `I've been clicked!` as shown in the second frame in the figure. Then, if the user clicks the button again, the text changes to `I've been clicked 2 times!` as shown in the third frame. Thereafter, the count increases each time the button is clicked. Listing 2-1 shows the complete code for this program.

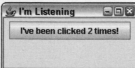

Figure 2-1:
The ClickMe
program in
action.

LISTING 2-1: THE CLICKME PROGRAM

```
import javax.swing.*;
import java.awt.event.*;                                          → 2

public class ClickMe
    extends JFrame implements ActionListener                      → 5
{
    public static void main(String [] args)                       → 7
    {
        new ClickMe();
    }

    private JButton button1;                                       → 12

    public ClickMe()                                               → 14
    {
        this.setSize(200,100);

        this.setDefaultCloseOperation(JFrame.EXIT_ON_CLOSE);
        this.setTitle("I'm Listening");

        JPanel panel1 = new JPanel();
        button1 = new JButton("Click Me!");                        → 21
        button1.addActionListener(this);                           → 22
        panel1.add(button1);
        this.add(panel1);

        this.setVisible(true);
    }

    private int clickCount = 0;                                    → 29

    public void actionPerformed(ActionEvent e)                     → 31
    {
        if (e.getSource() == button1)                              → 33
        {
            clickCount++;                                          → 35
            if (clickCount == 1)                                   → 36
                button1.setText("I've been clicked!");
            else
                button1.setText("I've been clicked "
                    + clickCount + " times!");
        }
    }
}
```

The following paragraphs point out some key lines of the program:

> → **2** The program must import the java.awt.event package, which defines the ActionEvent class and the ActionListener interfaces.

→ **5** The ClickMe class extends the JFrame class and implements ActionListener. That way, this class does double-duty: It defines the frame, and it listens for events generated by components added to the frame.

→ **7** The main method is required as usual. It simply creates an instance of the ClickMe class to get the frame started.

→**12** The button1 variable is defined as a private class field so both the ClickMe constructor and the actionPerformed method can access it.

→**14** The constructor does all the usual stuff that a constructor for a frame class does: It sets the frame size, default close operation, and title, and then it adds components to the frame. It ends by calling setVisible to make the frame visible on the screen.

→**21** This line creates a button and assigns it to the button1 field.

→**22** This line adds the current object as an action listener for the button1 button.

→**29** A field named clickCount is used to keep track of how many times the button has been clicked. This field is initialized to zero when the object is created.

→**31** The actionPerformed method must be coded because the ClickMe class implements the ActionListener interface. This method is called by the button1 object whenever the user clicks the button. The ActionEvent parameter is the event generated by the button click.

→**33** The getSource method of the ActionEvent parameter is called to determine the event source. In this program, this if statement isn't really required, because the program has only one event source. However, most Swing programs have more than one event source, so you need to test the event source in the event listener.

→**35** This statement increments the click count to indicate that the button has been clicked.

→**36** This if statement tests the value of the clickCount field and changes the text displayed by the button accordingly.

Using Inner Classes to Listen for Events

As explained in Book III, Chapter 7, an *inner class* is a class that's nested within another class. Inner classes are commonly used for event listeners. That way, the class that defines the frame doesn't also have to implement the event listener. Instead, it includes an inner class that handles the events.

Listing 2-2 shows a version of the ClickMe program that uses an inner class to handle the action event for the button.

LISTING 2-2: THE CLICKME2 PROGRAM WITH AN INNER CLASS

```java
import javax.swing.*;
import java.awt.event.*;

public class ClickMe2 extends JFrame                    → 4
{
   public static void main(String [] args)
   {
      new ClickMe2();
   }

   private JButton button1;                             → 11

   public ClickMe2()
   {
      this.setSize(200,100);
      this.setDefaultCloseOperation(
         JFrame.EXIT_ON_CLOSE);
      this.setTitle("I'm Listening");

      ClickListener cl = new ClickListener();           → 20

      JPanel panel1 = new JPanel();
      button1 = new JButton("Click Me!");
      button1.addActionListener(cl);                    → 24
      panel1.add(button1);
      this.add(panel1);

      this.setVisible(true);
   }

   private class ClickListener
      implements ActionListener                         → 32
   {
      private int clickCount = 0;                       → 34

      public void actionPerformed(ActionEvent e)
      {
         if (e.getSource() == button1)                  → 38
         {
            clickCount++;
            if (clickCount == 1)
               button1.setText("I've been clicked!");
            else
               button1.setText("I've been clicked "
                  + clickCount + " times!");
         }
      }
   }
}
```

This program works essentially the same as the program shown in Listing 2-1, so I won't review the basics. Instead, I just point out some highlights:

→ **4** The `ClickMe2` class still extends `JFrame`, but doesn't implement `ActionListener`.

→ **11** The button that serves as the event source must be referenced by a class field so the inner class can access it. This field can be private, because inner classes have access to private members of the class that contains them.

→ **20** This statement creates an instance of the `ClickListener` class (the inner class) and assigns it to the variable c1.

→ **24** This statement adds c1 as an action listener for the button. Note that because this frame has only one button, I could just as easily have omitted line 20 and coded line 24 like this:

```
button1.addActionListener(new ClickListener());
```

However, because most real-world applications have more than one event source, creating an instance of the listener class first, then reusing that object as the listener for each event source is common.

→ **32** The `ClickListener` class is declared as an inner class by placing its declaration completely within the `ClickMe2` class. The `ClickListener` class implements the `ActionListener` interface so it can handle action events.

→ **34** The `clickCount` variable is declared as a class field in the inner class.

→ **38** The `button1` variable is available to the inner class here because inner classes can access private members of the class that contains them.

Adding an Exit Button

In Book VI, Chapter 1, you find out how to create a frame that exits the application when the user clicks the frame's Exit button. To add an Exit button to your application, you must do three things:

1. **Create the Exit button and add it to the frame.**

Usually, you actually add the Exit button to a panel that is in turn added to the frame.

2. **Add an action event listener to the button.**

3. **Add code in the `actionPerformed` method of the action listener to quit the application when the user clicks the button.**

You normally do that by calling `System.exit(0)`.

In many applications, you don't want to just blindly terminate the application. Instead, you should make sure the user has saved his or her data before ending. If not, you can either save the data automatically or require the user to save the data before allowing the program to end.

Suppose you want to change the `ClickMe2` application that is shown in Listing 2-2 so that it has an Exit button, but the Exit button won't let the user quit unless he or she has clicked the ClickMe button at least once. First, you change Line 11 to declare an `exitButton` class field:

```
private JButton button1, exitButton;
```

Next, you add code to the constructor to create the button, register the event listener, and add the button to the panel:

```
exitButton = new JButton("Exit");
exitButton.addActionListener(cl);
panel1.add(exitButton);
```

Finally, you modify the `actionPerformed` method of the `ClickListener` class to handle the Exit button:

```
public void actionPerformed(ActionEvent e)
{
    if (e.getSource() == button1)
    {
        clickCount++;
        if (clickCount == 1)
            button1.setText("I've been clicked!");
        else
            button1.setText("I've been clicked "
                + clickCount + " times!");
    }
    else if (e.getSource() == exitButton)
    {
        if (clickCount > 0)
            System.exit(0);
        else
        {
    JOptionPane.showMessageDialog(ClickMe3.this,
                "You must click at least once!",
                "Not so fast, buddy",
                JOptionPane.ERROR_MESSAGE);
        }
    }
}
```

Here, an `if` statement is used to determine which button was clicked when the `actionPerformed` method is called. This step is necessary because the `ClickHandler` class is used to handle action events for both buttons. If the event source is the Exit button, another `if` statement checks to see if the `clickCount` variable is greater than zero. If it is, `System.exit(0)` is called to end the application. Otherwise, `JOptionPane` is used to display an error message, and the application is not ended.

Unfortunately, just adding this logic to the Exit button isn't enough, because the user can bypass your Exit button by clicking the frame's Close button. What you want is for the frame Close button to act exactly like the Exit button. To do that, you need to add a window event listener in addition to an action event listener, as I describe in the next section.

Catching the WindowClosing Event

Book VI, Chapter 1 shows you how to use the `setDefaultCloseOperation` method of the `JFrame` class to let the user quit the application by using the frame's Close button. However, if your application checks to see if data has been saved or other conditions have been met before allowing the user to exit, this approach won't work. In that case, you want to set up the Close button so it works the same as your Exit button.

To do that, you need to add a listener that listens for window events to the frame. When the user clicks the Close button, the frame generates a `window Closing` event which you can handle by registering a `WindowListener` with the frame itself. Then, in the `windowClosing` method of the `Window Listener`, you can just call the Exit button's `doClick` event. That triggers an action event for the Exit button as if the user clicked it. Thus, the Close button is handled in exactly the same way as the Exit button.

The first step to setting up a window listener is getting rid of the default behavior that automatically exits the application when the user clicks the Close button. To do that, you must change the constant you use in the `setDefaultCloseOperation` from `EXIT_ON_CLOSE` to `DO_NOTHING_ ON_CLOSE`, like this:

```
this.setDefaultCloseOperation(JFrame.DO_NOTHING_ON_
    CLOSE);
```

That way, the default action of the `JFrame` class is to completely ignore the Close button. Then, you can install a window listener to handle the Close button any way you want.

Next, you can set up the `WindowListener` to listen for window events. One way to do that is to create an inner class that implements the `Window Listener` interface. Unfortunately, the `WindowListener` interface has a lot of methods, and you must provide an implementation for each method even if you don't want to do anything for that method. Thus, your `Window Listener` looks something like this:

```
private class Closer implements WindowListener
{
```

```
public void windowClosing(WindowEvent e)
{
    exitButton.doClick();
}

public void windowActivated(WindowEvent e) {}
public void windowClosed(WindowEvent e) {}
public void windowDeactivated(WindowEvent e) {}
public void windowDeiconified(WindowEvent e) {}
public void windowIconified(WindowEvent e) {}
public void windowOpened(WindowEvent e) {}
}
```

Finally, you register the `WindowListener` with the frame by calling its `addWindowListener` method in the frame class constructor:

```
this.addWindowListener(new Closer());
```

If you find it annoying that you have to code all those dummy methods when you implement the `WindowListener` interface, you can use an *adapter class* instead. An adapter class is a class that implements an interface and provides dummy implementations for all the methods defined by the interface. Instead of implementing the interface, you extend the adapter class. Then, you only have to provide an implementation for the method or methods you're interested in.

Many of Java's event listener interfaces have corresponding adapter classes. They're listed in Table 2-3. Here's what the Closer class looks like if you extend `WindowAdapter` instead of implement `WindowListener`:

```
private class Closer extends WindowAdapter
{
    public void windowClosing(WindowEvent e)
    {
        exitButton.doClick();
    }
}
```

That saves some code. However, you can save even more code by skipping the `Closer` class altogether, and handling the window closing event with an anonymous inner class instead. Then, the statement in the frame constructor that registers the window event listener looks like this:

```
addWindowListener(new WindowAdapter()
    {
        public void windowClosing(WindowEvent e)
        {
            exitButton.doClick();
        }
    } );
```

Here, the window listener is created as an anonymous inner class that extends `WindowAdapter` and defines the `windowClosing` method.

Table 2-3	Adapter Classes for Event Listeners
Listener Interface	*Adapter Class*
WindowListener	WindowAdapter
KeyListener	KeyAdapter
MouseListener	MouseAdapter
FocusListener	FocusAdapter

An anonymous inner class is simply a class that has no name, that is used only once in the program, and is defined right at the spot where it's used. For a rundown of the weird syntax used to create an anonymous inner class, refer to Book III, Chapter 7.

The ClickMe Program Revisited

Now that you've mulled over the various techniques for creating an Exit button and handling the Close button, Listing 2-3 presents a third version of the ClickMe program that adds all these features so you can see how they work together. This version of the program adds an Exit button, but does not allow the user to quit until he or she has clicked the ClickMe button at least once. And it treats the Close button as if the user had clicked Exit.

LISTING 2-3: THE CLICKME APPLICATION WITH AN EXIT BUTTON

```
import javax.swing.*;
import java.awt.event.*;

public class ClickMe3 extends JFrame
{
    public static void main(String [] args)
    {
        new ClickMe3();
    }

    private JButton button1, exitButton;              → 11

    public ClickMe3()
    {
        this.setSize(275,100);
        this.setTitle("I'm Listening");
        this.setDefaultCloseOperation(              → 17
            JFrame.DO_NOTHING_ON_CLOSE);

        ClickListener cl = new ClickListener();
```

```
        JPanel panel1 = new JPanel();

        addWindowListener(new WindowAdapter()            → 24
        {
            public void windowClosing(WindowEvent e)
            {
                exitButton.doClick();                    → 28
            }
        } );

        button1 = new JButton("Click Me!");
        button1.addActionListener(cl);
        panel1.add(button1);

        exitButton = new JButton("Exit");                → 36
        exitButton.addActionListener(cl);
        panel1.add(exitButton);
        this.add(panel1);

        this.setVisible(true);
    }

    private class ClickListener implements
        ActionListener
    {
        private int clickCount = 0;

        public void actionPerformed(ActionEvent e)
        {
            if (e.getSource() == button1)
            {
                clickCount++;
                if (clickCount == 1)
                    button1.setText("I've been clicked!");
                else
                    button1.setText("I've been clicked "
                        + clickCount + " times!");
            }
            else if (e.getSource() == exitButton)        → 61
            {
                if (clickCount > 0)
                    System.exit(0);
                else
                {
                    JOptionPane.showMessageDialog(
                        ClickMe3.this,
                        "You must click at least once!",
                        "Not so fast, buddy",
                        JOptionPane.ERROR_MESSAGE);
                }
            }
        }
    }
}
```

The following paragraphs draw your attention to the key sections of this program:

→**11** The `exitButton` variable is declared along with the `button1` variable as a class field so it can be accessed from the inner classes.

→**17** The `setDefaultCloseOperation` method tells the `JFrame` class that no default action is taken if the user closes the window.

→**24** A window listener is installed on the frame to listen for window events. This listener is constructed from an anonymous inner class that extends the `WindowAdapter` class.

→**28** In the `windowClosing` method, the `doClick` method of the Exit button is called. That way, the Close button is handled exactly as if the user had clicked the Exit button.

→**36** This and the next two lines create the Exit button, register its action event listener, and add it to the panel.

→**61** In the `actionPerformed` method of the action listener class, this `if` statement checks to see if the action event came from the Exit button. If so, another `if` statement checks to see if the user has clicked the ClickMe button at least once. If so, the application exits. Otherwise, a message is displayed, and the program refuses to budge.

Chapter 3: Getting Input from the User

In This Chapter

✔ Text fields

✔ Text areas

✔ Scroll bars

✔ Check boxes

✔ Radio buttons

✔ Borders

✔ Sliders

In the first two chapters of Book VI, you find out how to use two basic Swing user interface components — labels and buttons — and how to handle events generated when the user clicks one of those buttons. If all you ever want to write are programs that display text when the user clicks a button, you can put the book down now. But if you want to write programs that actually do something worthwhile, you need to use other Swing components.

In this chapter, you find out how to use components that get information from the user. First, I cover two components that get text input from the user: text fields, which get a line of text, and text areas, which get multiple lines. Then, I move on to two components that get either/or information from the user: radio buttons and check boxes.

Along the way, I tell you about some features that let you decorate these controls to make them more functional. Specifically, I look at scroll bars, which are commonly used with text areas, and borders, which are used with radio buttons and check boxes.

Using Text Fields

A *text field* is a box that the user can type text in. You create text fields by using the JTextField class. Table 3-1 shows some of the more interesting and useful constructors and methods of this class.

Table 3-1	Handy JTextField Constructors and Methods
Constructor	*Description*
`JTextField()`	Creates a new text field.
`JTextField(int cols)`	Creates a new text field with the specified width.
`JTextField(String text, int cols)`	Creates a new text field with the specified width and initial text value.
Method	*Description*
`String getText()`	Gets the text value entered into the field.
`void requestFocus()`	Asks for the focus to be moved to this text field.
`void setColumns (int cols)`	Sets the size of the text field. (Better to do this in the constructor.)
`void setEditable (boolean value)`	If `false`, makes the field read-only.
`void setText(String text)`	Sets the field's text value.
`void setToolTipText (String text)`	Sets the tooltip text that's displayed if the user rests the mouse over the text field for a few moments.

When you create a text field by calling a constructor of the `JTextField` class, you can specify the width of the text field and an initial text value, as in these examples:

```
JTextField text1 = new JTextField(15);
JTextField text2 = new JTextField("Initial Value", 20);
```

The width is specified in columns, which is a vague and imprecise measurement that's roughly equal to the width of one character in the font that the text field uses. You have to experiment a bit to get the text fields the right size.

The usual way to work with text fields is to create them in the frame constructor, and then retrieve text entered by the user in the `actionPerformed` method of an action listener attached to one of the frame's buttons using code like this:

```
String lastName = textLastName.getText();
```

Here, the value entered by the user into the `textLastName` text field is assigned to the String variable `lastName`.

The following paragraphs describe a few additional details you need to know about using text fields:

✦ When you use a text field, you usually also want to place a label nearby to tell the user what type of text to enter into the field.

✦ You can create a read-only text field by calling the `setEditable` method with a value of `false`. The text field has a border around it like a regular text field, but the background is gray instead of white and the user can't change the text displayed by the control.

✦ In most programs, you want to make sure that the user enters acceptable data into text fields. This is especially true if the user is supposed to enter numeric data into the text fields, as I describe in the section "Using text fields for numeric entry," later in this chapter.

Looking at a sample program

Figure 3-1 shows the operation of a simple program that uses a text field to ask for the user's name. If the user enters a name, the program uses `JOptionPane` to say good morning to the user by displaying the middle message box shown in Figure 3-1. But if the user clicks the button without entering anything, the program displays the second `JOptionPane` message shown at the bottom.

Figure 3-1:
The Namer
application
in action.

The code for this program is shown in Listing 3-1.

LISTING 3-1: SAYING GOOD MORNING WITH A TEXT FIELD

```
import javax.swing.*;
import java.awt.event.*;

public class Namer extends JFrame                    → 4
{
    public static void main(String [] args)
    {
        new Namer();
    }
```

continued

LISTING 3-1 (CONTINUED)

```
private JButton buttonOK;
private JTextField textName;                              → 12

public Namer()
{
   this.setSize(325,100);
   this.setTitle("Who Are You?");
   this.setDefaultCloseOperation(
       JFrame.EXIT_ON_CLOSE);

   ButtonListener bl = new ButtonListener();

   JPanel panel1 = new JPanel();

   panel1.add(new JLabel("Enter your name: "));   → 25

   textName = new JTextField(15);                 → 27
   panel1.add(textName);

   buttonOK = new JButton("OK");
   buttonOK.addActionListener(bl);
   panel1.add(buttonOK);

   this.add(panel1);

   this.setVisible(true);
}

private class ButtonListener implements
    ActionListener
{
   public void actionPerformed(ActionEvent e)
   {
      if (e.getSource() == buttonOK)
      {
         String name = textName.getText();        → 46
         if (name.length() == 0)                  → 47
         {
             JOptionPane.showMessageDialog(
                Namer.this,
                "You didn't enter anything!",
                "Moron",
                JOptionPane.INFORMATION_MESSAGE);
         }
         else
         {
             JOptionPane.showMessageDialog(
                Namer.this,
                "Good morning " + name,
                "Salutations",
```

```
                    JOptionPane.INFORMATION_MESSAGE);
            }
            textName.requestFocus();                        →  63
        }
    }
}
```

This program isn't very complicated, so the following paragraphs just hit the highlights:

→ **4** The name of the frame class is `Namer`.

→**12** A class variable is used to store a reference to the text field so that both the constructor and the action listener can access it.

→**25** A label is created to tell the user what data to enter into the text field.

→**27** The text field is created with a length of 15 columns, and then added to the panel.

→**46** In the `actionPerformed` method of the action listener class, this statement retrieves the value entered by the user and stores it in a string variable.

→**47** This `if` statement checks to see if the user entered anything by examining the length of the string variable created in line 46. If the length is zero, `JOptionPane` is used to display an error message. Otherwise, `JOptionPane` is used to say good morning to the user.

→**63** The `requestFocus` method is called to move the focus back to the text field after the user clicks the button. If you don't do this, focus stays on the button and the user has to use the Tab key to move the focus to the text field.

Using text fields for numeric entry

You need to take special care if you're using a text field to get numeric data from the user. The `getText` method returns a string value. You can pass this value to one of the parse methods of the wrapper classes for the primitive numeric types. For example, to convert the value entered into a text box to an `int`, you use the `parseInt` method:

```
int count = Integer.parseInt(textCount.getText());
```

Here, the result of the `getText` method is used as the parameter to the `parseInt` method.

Table 3-2 lists the parse methods for the various wrapper classes. Note that each of these methods throws `NumberFormatException` if the string

can't be converted. As a result, you need to call the `parseInt` method in a
`try/catch` block to catch this exception.

Table 3-2	Methods that Convert Strings to Numbers
Wrapper Class	*Parse Method*
Integer	parseInt(String)
Short	parseShort(String)
Long	parseLong(String)
Byte	parseByte(String)
Float	parseByte(String)
Double	parseByte(String)

TIP

If your program uses more than one or two numeric entry text fields, consider creating separate methods to validate the user's input. For example,
here's a method that accepts a text field and a string that provides an error
message that's displayed if the data entered into the field can't be converted
to an `int`. The method returns a boolean that indicates whether the field
contains a valid integer:

```
private boolean isInt(JTextField f, String msg)
{
    try
    {
        Integer.parseInt(f.getText());
        return true;
    }
    catch (NumberFormatException e)
    {
        JOptionPane.showMessageDialog(f,
            "Entry Error", msg,
            JOptionPane.ERROR_MESSAGE);
        f.requestFocus();
        return false;
    }
}
```

Then, you can call this method whenever you need to check to see if a text
field has a valid integer. For example, here's the `actionPerformed` method
for a program that gets the value entered in a `textCount` text field and displays it in a `JOptionPane` message box if the value entered is a valid integer:

```
public void actionPerformed(ActionEvent e)
{
    if (e.getSource() == buttonOK)
    {
        if (isInt(textCount,
            "You must enter an integer."))
```

```
            {
                JOptionPane.showMessageDialog(Number.this,
                    "You entered "
                    +
        Integer.parseInt(textCount.getText()),
                    "Your Number",
                    JOptionPane.INFORMATION_MESSAGE);
            }
            textCount.requestFocus();
    }
}
```

Here, the `isInt` method is called to make sure the text entered by the user can be converted to an `int`. If so, the text is converted to an `int` and displayed in a message box. (In this example, the name of the outer class is `Number`, which is why the first parameter of the `showMessageDialog` method specifies `Number.this`.)

Creating a validation class

If you're feeling really ambitious, you can create a separate class to hold methods that do data validation. I suggest you make the methods static so you don't have to create an instance of the validation class to use its methods. And to avoid parsing the data twice, write the validation methods so they return two values: a boolean that indicates whether the data could be parsed, and a primitive that provides the parsed value.

Of course, a method can return only one value. The only way to coax a method into returning two values is to return an object that contains both of the values. And to do that, you have to create a class that defines the object. Here's an example of a class you could use as the return value of a method that validates integers:

```
public class IntValidationResult
{
    public boolean isValid;
    public int value;
}
```

And here's a class that provides a static method named `isInt` that validates integer data and returns an `IntValidationResult` object:

```
public class Validation
{
    public static IntValidationResult isInt(
        JTextField f, String msg)
    {
        IntValidationResult result =
            new IntValidationResult();
        try
```

```
            {
                result.value =
        Integer.parseInt(f.getText());
                result.isValid = true;
                return result;
            }
            catch (NumberFormatException e)
            {
                JOptionPane.showMessageDialog(f,
                    "Entry Error", msg
                    JOptionPane.ERROR_MESSAGE);
                f.requestFocus();
                result.isValid = false;
                result.value = 0;
                return result;
            }
        }
    }
```

Here's an `actionPerformed` method that uses the `isInt` method of this class to validate the `textCount` field:

```
public void actionPerformed(ActionEvent e)
{
    if (e.getSource() == buttonOK)
    {
        IntValidationResult ir;
        ir = Validation.isInt(textCount,
            "You must enter an integer.");
        if (ir.isValid)
        {
            JOptionPane.showMessageDialog(Number2.this,
                "You entered " + ir.value,
                "Your Number",
                JOptionPane.INFORMATION_MESSAGE);
        }
        textCount.requestFocus();
    }
}
```

Using Text Areas

A *text area* is similar to a text field, but lets the user enter more than one line of text. If the user enters more text into the text area than can be displayed at once, the text area can use a scroll bar to let the user scroll to see the entire text. Figure 3-2 shows a text area in action.

To create a text area like the one shown in Figure 3-2, you must actually use two classes. First, you use the `JTextArea` class to create the text area. But unfortunately, text areas by themselves don't have scroll bars. So you have to add the text area to a second component called a *scroll pane,* created by the JScrollPane class. Then, you add the scroll pane, not the text area, to a panel so it can be displayed.

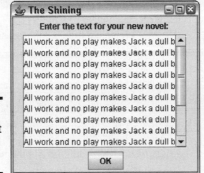

Figure 3-2:
A frame that uses a text area.

Creating a text area isn't as hard as it sounds. Here's the code I used to create the text area shown in Figure 3-2, which I then added to a panel:

```
textNovel = new JTextArea(10, 20);
JScrollPane scroll = new JScrollPane(textNovel,
    JScrollPane.VERTICAL_SCROLLBAR_ALWAYS,
    JScrollPane.HORIZONTAL_SCROLLBAR_NEVER);
panel1.add(scroll);
```

Here, the first statement creates a text area, giving it an initial size of 10 rows and 20 columns. Then, the second statement creates a scroll pane. Notice that the text area object is passed as a parameter to the constructor for the JScrollPane, along with constants that indicate whether the scroll pane should include vertical or horizontal scroll bars (or both). Finally, the third statement adds the scroll pane to the panel named panel1.

The following sections describe the constructors and methods of the JTextArea and JScrollPane classes in more detail.

The JTextArea class

Table 3-3 lists the most popular constructors and methods of the JTextArea class, which you use to create text areas. In most cases, you use the second constructor, which lets you set the number of rows and columns to display. The rows parameter governs the height of the text area, while the cols parameter sets the width.

Table 3-3	Clever JTextArea Constructors and Methods
Constructor	**Description**
JTextArea()	Creates a new text area.
JTextArea(int rows, int cols)	Creates a new text area large enough to display the specified number of rows and columns.
JTextArea(String text, int rows, int cols)	Creates a new text area with the specified initial text value, large enough to display the specified number of rows and columns.
Method	**Description**
void append(String text)	Adds the specified text to the end of the text area's text value.
int getLineCount()	Gets the number of lines currently in the text value.
String getText()	Gets the text value entered into the field.
void insert(String str, int pos)	Inserts the specified text at the specified position.
void requestFocus()	Asks for the focus to be moved to this text field.
void replaceRange(String str, int start, int end)	Replaces text indicated by the start and end position with the new specified text.
void setColumns(int cols)	Sets the width of the text area. (It's better to do this in the constructor.)
void setEditable(boolean value)	If false, makes the field read only.
void setLineWrap(boolean value)	If true, lines wrap if the text doesn't fit on one line.
void setText(String text)	Sets the field's text value.
void setToolTipText (String text)	Sets the tooltip text that's displayed if the user rests the mouse over the text field for a few moments.
void setWrapStyleWord()	If true, the text wraps at word boundaries.

To retrieve the text entered by the user into a text area, you use the getText method. For example, here's an actionPerformed method from an action listener that retrieves text from a text area:

```
public void actionPerformed(ActionEvent e)
{
    if (e.getSource() == buttonOK)
    {
        String text = textNovel.getText();
        if (text.contains("All work and no play"))
            JOptionPane.showMessageDialog(textNovel,
                "Can't you see I'm working?",
                "Going Crazy",
        JOptionPane.ERROR_MESSAGE);
    }
}
```

Here, a message box is displayed if the text contains the string `All work and no play`.

Notice that in addition to the `getText` method, the `JTextArea` class has methods that let you add text to the end of the text area's current value (`append`), insert text in the middle of the value (`insert`), and replace text (`replace`). You can use these methods to edit the value of the text area.

Two of the `JTextArea` methods are used to control how lines longer than the width of the text area are handled. If you call `setLineWrap` with a value of `true`, lines that are too long to display are automatically wrapped to the next line. And if you call `setWrapStyleWord` with a value of `true`, any lines that are wrapped split between words instead of in the middle of a word. You usually use these two methods together:

```
textItinerary = new JTextArea(10, 20);
textItinerary.setLineWrap(true);
textItinerary.setWrapStyleWord(true);
```

The JScrollPane class

Text areas aren't very useful without scroll bars. To create a text area with a scroll bar, you use the `JScrollPane` class, whose constructors and fields are listed in Table 3-4. Note that this table doesn't show any methods for the `JScrollPane` class. The `JScrollPane` class does have methods (plenty of them, in fact). But none of them are particularly useful for ordinary programming, so I didn't include any of them in the table.

Table 3-4	Essential JScrollPane Constructors and Fields
Constructor	**Description**
`JScrollPane((Component view)`	Creates a scroll pane for the specified component.
`JScrollPane(Component, int vert, int hor)`	Creates a scroll pane for the specified component with the specified policy for the vertical and horizontal scroll bars.
Field	**Description**
`VERTICAL_SCROLLBAR_ALWAYS`	Always adds a vertical scroll bar.
`VERTICAL_SCROLLBAR_AS_NEEDED`	Adds a vertical scroll bar if necessary.
`VERTICAL_SCROLLBAR_NEVER`	Never adds a vertical scroll bar.
`HORIZONTAL_SCROLLBAR_ALWAYS`	Always adds a horizontal scroll bar.
`HORIZONTAL_SCROLLBAR_AS_NEEDED`	Adds a horizontal scroll bar if necessary.
`HORIZONTAL_SCROLLBAR_NEVER`	Never adds a horizontal scroll bar.

**Book VI
Chapter 3**

**Getting Input from
the User**

The usual way to create a scroll pane is to use the second constructor. You use the first parameter of this constructor to specify the component you want to add scroll bars to. For example, to add scroll bars to a `textNovel` text area, you specify `textNovel` as the first parameter.

The second parameter tells the scroll pane whether or not to create a vertical scroll bar. The value you specify for this parameter should be one of the first three fields listed in Table 3-4. If you always want the scroll pane to show a vertical scroll bar, specify `VERTICAL_SCROLLBAR_ALWAYS`. If you want to see the vertical scroll bar only when the text area contains more lines that can be displayed at once, specify `VERTICAL_SCROLLBAR_AS_NEEDED`. Then, the vertical scroll bar is only shown when it's needed. Finally, if you never want to see a vertical scroll bar, specify `VERTICAL_SCROLLBAR_NEVER`.

The third parameter uses the three `HORIZONTAL_SCROLLBAR` constants to indicate whether the scroll pane includes a horizontal scroll bar always, never, or only when necessary.

Thus, the following code adds scroll bars to a text area. The vertical scroll bar is always shown, but the horizontal scroll bar is shown only when needed:

```
JScrollPane scroll = new JScrollPane(textNovel,
    JScrollPane.VERTICAL_SCROLLBAR_ALWAYS,
    JScrollPane.HORIZONTAL_SCROLLBAR_AS_NEEDED);
```

Use the `JScrollPane` class with other types of components besides text areas. As you see in the next chapter, scroll panes are often used with list controls as well.

Using Check Boxes

A *check box* is a control that the user can click to either check or uncheck. Check boxes are usually used to let the user specify Yes or No to an option. Figure 3-3 shows a frame with three check boxes.

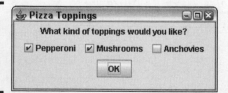

Figure 3-3:
A frame with three check boxes.

To create a check box, you use the `JCheckBox` class. Its favorite constructors and methods are shown in Table 3-5.

Table 3-5 **Notable JCheckBox Constructors and Methods**

Constructor	Description
JCheckBox()	Creates a new check box that is initially unchecked.
JCheckBox(String text)	Creates a new check box that displays the specified text.
JCheckBox(String text, boolean selected)	Creates a new check box with the specified text. The boolean parameter determines whether the check box is initially checked (true) or unchecked (false).

Method	Description
void addActionListener (ActionListener listener)	Adds an ActionListener to listen for action events.
void addItemListener (ItemListener listener)	Adds an ItemListener to listen for item events.
String getText()	Gets the text displayed by the check box.
Boolean isSelected()	Returns true if the check box is checked, false if the check box is not checked.
void setSelected(boolean value)	Checks the check box if the parameter is true; unchecks it if the parameter is false.
void setText(String text)	Sets the check box text.
void setToolTipText (String text)	Sets the tooltip text that's displayed if the user rests the mouse over the check box for a few moments.

As with any Swing component, if you want to refer to the component in both the frame class constructor and a listener, you have to declare class variables to refer to the check box components, like this:

```
JCheckBox pepperoni, mushrooms, anchovies;
```

Then, you can use statements like these in the frame constructor to create the check boxes and add them to a panel (in this case, panel1):

```
pepperoni = new JCheckBox("Pepperoni");
panel1.add(pepperoni);

mushrooms = new JCheckBox("Mushrooms");
panel1.add(mushrooms);

anchovies = new JCheckBox("Anchovies");
panel1.add(anchovies);
```

Notice that I didn't specify the initial state of these check boxes in the constructor. As a result, they're initially unchecked. If you want to create a check box that is initially checked, call the constructor like this:

```
Pepperoni = new JCheckBox("Pepperoni", true);
```

In an event listener, you can test the state of a check box by using the `isSelected` method, and you can set the state of a check box by calling its `setSelected` method. For example, here's an `actionPerformed` method that displays a message box and unchecks all three check boxes when the user clicks the OK button:

```
public void actionPerformed(ActionEvent e)
{
    if (e.getSource() == buttonOK)
    {
        String msg = "";
        if (pepperoni.isSelected())
            msg += "Pepperoni\n";
        if (mushrooms.isSelected())
            msg += "Mushrooms\n";
        if (anchovies.isSelected())
            msg += "Anchovies\n";
        if (msg.equals(""))
            msg = "You didn't order any toppings.";
        else
            msg = "You ordered these toppings:\n" +
msg;
        JOptionPane.showMessageDialog(buttonOK,
            msg, "Your Order",
            JOptionPane.INFORMATION_MESSAGE);
        pepperoni.setSelected(false);
        mushrooms.setSelected(false);
        anchovies.setSelected(false);
    }
}
```

Here, the name of each topping selected by the user is added to a text string. For example, if you select Pepperoni and Anchovies, the following message is displayed:

```
You ordered these toppings:
Pepperoni
Anchovies
```

If you want, you can add event listeners to check boxes to respond to events generated when the user clicks the check box. Check boxes support both action listeners and item listeners. The difference between them is subtle:

✦ An action event is generated whenever the user clicks a check box to change its state.

✦ An item event is generated whenever the state of the check box is changed, whether as a result of being clicked by the user or because the program called the `setSelected` method.

Suppose your restaurant has anchovies on the menu, but you refuse to actually make pizzas with anchovies on them. Here's an `actionPerformed` method from an action listener that displays a message if the user tries to check the Anchovies check box and unchecks the box:

```java
public void actionPerformed(ActionEvent e)
{
    if (e.getSource() == anchovies)
    {
        JOptionPane.showMessageDialog(anchovies,
            "We don't do anchovies here.",
            "Yuck!",
            JOptionPane.WARNING_MESSAGE);
        anchovies.setSelected(false);
    }
}
```

Book VI
Chapter 3

Getting Input from
the User

Only add a listener to a check box if you need to provide immediate feedback to the user when he or she checks or unchecks the box. In most applications, you wait until the user clicks a button to actually examine the state of any check boxes on the frame.

Using Radio Buttons

Radio buttons are similar to check boxes, but with a crucial difference: Radio buttons travel in groups, and a user can select only one radio button in each group at a time. When you click a radio button to select it, whatever radio button was previously selected is automatically deselected. Figure 3-4 shows a frame with three radio buttons.

Figure 3-4:
A frame
with three
radio
buttons.

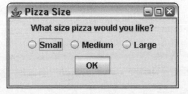

To work with radio buttons, you use two classes. First, you create the radio buttons themselves with the `JRadioButton` class, whose constructors and methods are shown in Table 3-6. Then, you create a group for the buttons with the ButtonGroup class. You must add the radio buttons themselves to a panel so they are displayed and to a button group so they're properly grouped with other buttons.

Table 3-6	Various JRadioButton Constructors and Methods
Constructor	*Description*
JRadioButton()	Creates a new radio button with no text.
JRadioButton(String text)	Creates a new radio button with the specified text.
Method	*Description*
void addActionListener (ActionListener listener)	Adds an ActionListener to listen for action events.
void addItemListener (ItemListener listener)	Adds an ItemListener to listen for item events.
String getText()	Gets the text displayed by the radio button.
Boolean isSelected()	Returns true if the radio button is selected, false if the radio button is not selected.
void setSelected(boolean value)	Selects the radio button if the parameter is true.
void setText(String text)	Sets the radio button text.
void setToolTipText (String text)	Sets the tooltip text that's displayed if the user rests the mouse over the radio button for a few moments.

The usual way to create a radio button is to declare a variable to refer to the button as a class variable so it can be accessed anywhere in the class. For example

```
JRadioButton small, medium, large;
```

Then, in the frame constructor, you call the JRadioButton constructor to create the radio button:

```
small = new JRadioButton("Small");
```

You can then add the radio button to a panel in the usual way.

To create a button group to group radio buttons that work together, just call the ButtonGroup class constructor:

```
ButtonGroup group1 = new ButtonGroup();
```

Then, call the add method of the ButtonGroup to add each radio button to the group:

```
group1.add(small);
group1.add(medium);
group1.add(large);
```

Note that button groups have nothing to do with how radio buttons appear on the frame. The buttons can appear anywhere on the frame, even in different panels. (I show you how to visually group radio buttons and other components by using borders in the next section, cleverly named "Using Borders.")

Where button groups really come in handy is when you have more than one set of radio buttons on a form. For example, suppose that in addition to choosing the size of the pizza, the user can also choose the style of crust — thin or thick. In that case, you use a total of five radio buttons and two button groups. The constructor code that creates the radio buttons might look something like this:

```
ButtonGroup size = new ButtonGroup();
ButtonGroup crust = new ButtonGroup();

small = new JRadioButton("Small");
medium = new JRadioButton("Medium");
large = new JRadioButton("Large");
size.add(small);
size.add(medium);
size.add(large);

thin = new JRadioButton("Thin Crust");
thick = new JRadioButton("Thick Crust");
crust.add(thin);
crust.add(thick);
```

(To keep this example simple, I omitted the statements that add the radio buttons to the panel.)

Strictly speaking, you don't have to create a button group if all the radio buttons on the frame are in the same group. In that case, Swing creates a default group and adds all the radio buttons to it. However, because it's only a few extra lines of code, I suggest you always create a button group even when you have only one group of radio buttons.

Using Borders

A *border* is a decorative element that visually groups components by drawing a line around them. Figure 3-5 shows a frame that shows some radio buttons and check boxes inside borders.

Figure 3-5:
A frame
with
borders.

You can apply a border to any object that inherits `JComponent`, but the usual technique is to apply the border to a panel and add any components you want to appear within the border to the panel. To create a border, you call one of the static methods listed in Table 3-7. Each of these methods creates a border with a slightly different visual style. You then apply the `Border` object to a panel by calling the panel's `setBorder` method.

The `BorderFactory` class is in the `javax.swing` package, but the `Border` interface that defines the resulting border objects is in `javax.swing.border`. Thus, you need to include this `import` statement at the beginning of the class — in addition to importing `javax.swing.*` — if you plan on using borders:

```
import javax.swing.border.*;
```

Table 3-7	BorderFactory Methods for Creating Borders
Method	*Description*
`Border createBevelBorder (int type)`	Creates a bevel border of the specified type. The type parameter can be `BevelBorder.LOWERED` or `BevelBorder.RAISED`.
`Border createEmptyBorder (int top, int left, int bottom, int right)`	Creates an empty border that occupies the space indicated by the parameters.
`Border createEtchedBorder()`	Creates an etched border.
`Border createLineBorder()`	Creates a line border.
`Border createLoweredBevelBorder()`	Creates a lowered bevel border.
`Border createRaisedBevelBorder()`	Creates a raised beveled border.
`Border createTitledBorder (String title)`	Creates a titled etched border.
`Border createTitledBorder (Border b, String title)`	Creates a titled border from the specified border.

The Factory Pattern

The `BorderFactory` class is an example of a very common design pattern called the *Factory pattern*. In short, when you use the Factory pattern, you don't use constructors to create objects. Instead, you use a *factory class* that has *factory methods* that create objects for you.

One benefit of the Factory pattern is that the users of the factory class don't need to know what type of object is actually created. For example, Swing actually defines several different classes for borders, all of which implement the `Border` interface. If you have to use constructors to create border objects, you have to know about all the border classes. By creating a `BorderFactory` class that returns `Border` objects, you only have to know about the `BorderFactory` class and its methods.

The designers of the Java API could have created a `Border` class (instead of an interface) that lets you specify what type of border to create via a parameter passed to the constructor. However, that approach had many problems. For starters, the `Border` class would be complicated because it would have to implement every type of border. But more importantly, adding a new type of border later on is difficult. With the Factory pattern, you can create a new border type easily by (1) creating a class that implements the `Border` interface for the new border, and (2) adding a method to the `BorderFactory` class to create the new border type.

**Book VI
Chapter 3**

Getting Input from the User

All the methods listed in Table 3-7 are static methods. As a result, you don't have to create an instance of the `BorderFactory` class to call these methods.

For example, here's a snippet of code that creates a panel, creates a titled border, and applies the border to the panel:

```
JPanel sizePanel = new JPanel();
Border b1 = BorderFactory.createTitledBorder("Size");
sizePanel.setBorder(b1);
```

Then, any components you add to `sizePanel` appears within this border.

The last method listed in Table 3-7 needs a little explanation. It simply adds a title to a border created by any of the other created methods of the `BorderFactory` class. For example, you can create a raised bevel border with the title `Options` like this:

```
Border b = BorderFactory.createRaisedBevelBorder();
b = BorderFactory.createTitledBorder(b, "Options");
```

Designing a Pizza-Ordering Program

To give you an idea of how borders work together with radio buttons and check boxes, Listing 3-2 presents the complete code for the program that created the frame that was shown in Figure 3-5. When the user clicks the OK button, this program displays a message box summarizing the user's order. For example, if the user orders a medium pizza with pepperoni and mushrooms, the following message is displayed:

```
You ordered a medium pizza with the following toppings:
Pepperoni
Mushrooms
```

If you order a pizza with no toppings, the message looks something like this:

```
You ordered a medium pizza with no toppings.
```

LISTING 3-2: THE PIZZA ORDER PROGRAM

```java
import javax.swing.*;
import java.awt.event.*;
import javax.swing.border.*;

public class Pizza extends JFrame
{
    public static void main(String [] args)
    {
        new Pizza();
    }

    private JButton buttonOK;                                        → 12
    private JRadioButton small, medium, large;
    private JCheckBox pepperoni, mushrooms, anchovies;

    public Pizza()
    {
        this.setSize(320,200);
        this.setTitle("Order Your Pizza");
        this.setDefaultCloseOperation(JFrame.EXIT_ON_CLOSE);

        ButtonListener bl = new ButtonListener();

        JPanel mainPanel = new JPanel();                             → 24

        JPanel sizePanel = new JPanel();                             → 26
        Border b1 =                                                  → 27
            BorderFactory.createTitledBorder("Size");
        sizePanel.setBorder(b1);                                     → 29

        ButtonGroup sizeGroup = new ButtonGroup();                   → 31

        small = new JRadioButton("Small");                           → 33
        small.setSelected(true);
```

```
        sizePanel.add(small);
        sizeGroup.add(small);

        medium = new JRadioButton("Medium");               → 38
        sizePanel.add(medium);
        sizeGroup.add(medium);

        large = new JRadioButton("Large");                 → 42
        sizePanel.add(large);
        sizeGroup.add(large);

        mainPanel.add(sizePanel);                          → 46

        JPanel topPanel = new JPanel();                    → 48
        Border b2 =
            BorderFactory.createTitledBorder("Toppings");
        topPanel.setBorder(b2);

        pepperoni = new JCheckBox("Pepperoni");            → 53
        topPanel.add(pepperoni);

        mushrooms = new JCheckBox("Mushrooms");
        topPanel.add(mushrooms);

        anchovies = new JCheckBox("Anchovies");
        topPanel.add(anchovies);

        mainPanel.add(topPanel);                           → 62

        buttonOK = new JButton("OK");                      → 64
        buttonOK.addActionListener(bl);
        mainPanel.add(buttonOK);

        this.add(mainPanel);                               → 68

        this.setVisible(true);
    }

    private class ButtonListener implements ActionListener
    {
        public void actionPerformed(ActionEvent e)
        {
            if (e.getSource() == buttonOK)
            {
                String tops = "";                          → 79
                if (pepperoni.isSelected())
                    tops += "Pepperoni\n";
                if (mushrooms.isSelected())
                    tops += "Mushrooms\n";
                if (anchovies.isSelected())
                    tops += "Anchovies\n";

                String msg = "You ordered a ";             → 87
                if (small.isSelected())
                    msg += "small pizza with ";
                if (medium.isSelected())
                    msg += "medium pizza with ";
                if (large.isSelected())
```

continued

LISTING 3-2 (CONTINUED)

```
              msg += "large pizza with ";

          if (tops.equals(""))                          → 95
              msg += "no toppings.";
          else
              msg += "the following toppings:\n"
                  + tops;
          JOptionPane.showMessageDialog(                 → 100
              buttonOK, msg, "Your Order",
              JOptionPane.INFORMATION_MESSAGE);

          pepperoni.setSelected(false);                  → 104
          mushrooms.setSelected(false);
          anchovies.setSelected(false);
          small.setSelected(true);
      }
  }
  }
}
```

I cover everything in this program in this chapter (or in previous chapters), so I just hit the highlights here:

→12 The components that are added to the frame are declared as class variables so both the constructor and the `actionPerformed` method of the action event listener can access them.

→24 This line creates `mainPanel`, the first of three panels that the program uses. This panel contains the other two panels, which use borders to visually group their components.

→26 This line creates `sizePanel`, the panel used to hold the radio buttons that let the user pick the pizza's size.

→27 The `BorderFactory` class is used to create a titled border with the word `Size` as its title.

→29 The titled border is attached to the size panel.

→31 A button group is created for the radio buttons.

→33 The Small radio button is created. Notice that this button's `set` `Selected` method is called. As a result, Small is the default size for a pizza order. Notice also that the radio button is added to both the `sizePanel` panel and the `size` button group.

→38 The Medium radio button is created and added to the panel and the button group.

→42 The Large radio button is created and added to the panel and the button group.

→ **46** The size panel is added to the main panel.

→ **48** A new panel named `topPanel` is created to hold the topping check boxes. Like the size panel, this panel is also given a titled border.

→ **53** The Pepperoni, Mushrooms, and Anchovies check boxes are created and added to the panel.

→ **62** The toppings panel is added to the main panel.

→ **64** The OK button is created and added directly to the main panel. Because this button isn't in a border, it doesn't need to be added to a separate panel like the radio buttons and check boxes do.

→ **68** The main panel is added to the frame. The frame is now complete and can be made visible.

→ **79** In the `actionPerformed` method of the action listener, a string named `tops` is constructed with the toppings that the user selected.

→ **87** Next, a string named `msg` is constructed with the pizza size. These lines build a string that says `You ordered a` *size* `pizza with`, where *size* is replaced by `small`, `medium`, or `large` depending on which radio button the user selected.

→ **95** This `if` statement finishes the `msg` string by adding `no toppings` if the user didn't pick any toppings, or the `tops` string if the user did pick toppings.

→**100** This line uses `JOptionPane` to show a message box that displays the user's order.

→**104** Finally, these lines reset the controls so the application is ready to accept a new order.

Using Sliders

As Figure 3-6 shows, a *slider* is a component that lets a user pick a value from a set range (say, from 0 to 50) by moving a knob. Sliders are a convenient way to get numeric input from the user when the input falls within a set range of values.

Figure 3-6:
A frame with a slider.

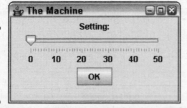

To create a slider control, you use the `JSlider` class. Table 3-8 shows its constructors and methods.

Table 3-8	**Selected JSlider Constructors and Methods**
Constructor	*Description*
`JSlider()`	Creates a new slider. The min and max values default to 0 and 100, and the initial value is set to 50.
`JSlider(int min, int max)`	Creates a new slider with the specified minimum and maximum values. The initial value is halfway between min and max.
`JSlider(int min, int max, int value)`	Creates a new slider with the specified minimum, maximum, and initial values.
`JSlider(int orientation, int min, int max, int value)`	Creates a new slider with the specified minimum, maximum, and initial values. The orientation can be either `JSlider.HORIZONTAL` or `JSlider.VERTICAL`.
Method	*Description*
`void addChangeListener (ChangeListener listener)`	Adds a `ChangeListener` to listen for change events.
`int getValue()`	Gets the value indicated by the current position of the knob.
`void setInvert(bolean value)`	If `true`, inverts the slider's direction so the max value is on the left and the min value is on the right.
`void setMajorTickSpacing (int value)`	Sets the interval for major tick marks. The marks aren't shown unless `setPaintTicks(true)` is called.
`void setMinimum(int value)`	Sets the minimum value.
`void setMaximum(int value)`	Sets the maximum value.
`void setMinorTickSpacing (int value)`	Sets the interval for minor tick marks. The marks aren't shown unless `setPaintTicks(true)` is called.
`setOrientation(int orientation)`	Sets the orientation. Allowed values are `JSlider.HORIZONTAL` and `JSlider.VERTICAL`.
`void setPaintLabels (boolean value)`	If `true`, tick labels are shown.
`void setSnapToTicks (boolean value)`	If `true`, the value returned by the `getValue` method is rounded to the nearest tick mark.
`void setToolTipText (String text)`	Sets the tooltip text that's displayed if the user rests the mouse over the slider for a few moments.

To create a barebones slider, just call the `JSlider` constructor. You can create a slider that ranges from 0 to 100 like this:

```
slider = new JSlider();
```

Here, the `slider` variable is declared as a class variable of type `JSlider`.

If you want to specify the minimum and maximum values, use this constructor:

```
slider = new JSlider(0, 50);
```

Here, the slider lets the user choose a value from 0 to 50. The initial position of the knob is 25, midway between the minimum and maximum values.

To set a different initial value, use this constructor:

```
slider = new JSlider(0, 0, 50);
```

Here, the slider ranges from 0 to 50, and the initial value is 0.

You usually want to add at least some adornments to the slider to make it more usable. The slider shown in Figure 3-6 has minimum and maximum tick marks with labels visible. Here's the code used to create it:

```
slider = new JSlider(0, 50, 0);
slider.setMajorTickSpacing(10);
slider.setMinorTickSpacing(1);
slider.setPaintTicks(true);
slider.setPaintLabels(true);
panel1.add(slider);
```

Note: Even if you set the major and minor tick spacing values, the tick marks won't display unless you call `setPaintTicks` with the parameter set to true. The `setPaintLabels` method shows the labels along with the tick marks. And the `setSnapToTicks` method rounds the value to the nearest tick mark.

To get the value of the slider, you use the `getValue` method. For example, here's the `actionPerformed` method for the action listener attached to the OK button in Figure 3-6:

```
public void actionPerformed(ActionEvent e)
{
    if (e.getSource() == buttonOK)
    {
        int level = slider.getValue();
        JOptionPane.showMessageDialog(slider,
            "Remember, this is for posterity.\n"
            + "Tell me...how do you feel?",
```

```
                        "Level " + level,
              JOptionPane.INFORMATION_MESSAGE);
      }
  }
```

Here, a message box is displayed when the user clicks the OK button. The current setting of the slider component is retrieved and stored in an int variable named level, which is then used to create the title for the message box.

You can also add an event listener that reacts whenever the user changes the value of the slider. To do that, you use the addChangeListener method. The parameter must be an object that implements the ChangeListener interface, which defines a single method named stateChanged. Here's an example of a class that can be used to react to slider changes:

```
private class SliderListener implements ChangeListener
{
    public void stateChanged(ChangeEvent e)
    {
        if (slider.getValue() == 50)
        {
            JOptionPane.showMessageDialog(slider,
                "No! Not 50!",
                "The Machine",
                JOptionPane.WARNING_MESSAGE);
        }
    }
}
```

To wire an instance of this class to the slider, use this method:

```
slider.addChangeListener(new SliderListener());
```

Then, the stateChanged method is called whenever the user moves the knob to another position. It checks the value of the slider and displays a message box if the user has advanced the slider all the way to 50.

Chapter 4: Choosing from a List

In This Chapter

✔ **Combo boxes**

✔ **Lists**

✔ **Spinners**

✔ **Trees**

A whole category of Swing components is designed to let the user choose one or more items from a list. This chapter presents four such controls. The first three — JList, JComboBox, and JSpinner — are straightforward. The fourth — JTree — is a bit more complicated, but worth the effort.

If you put a JTree control on a frame, your friends will surely think you're some kind of guru. They'll start pestering you with questions and asking for your help. As a result, use this component only if your application really needs it — and if you feel up to the technical challenge of figuring out how it works.

Using Combo Boxes

A *combo box* is a combination of a text field and a drop-down list from which the user can choose a value. If the text field portion of the control is editable, the user can enter a value into the field or edit a value retrieved from the drop-down list. However, making the text field uneditable is common. Then, the user must pick one of the values from the list. Figure 4-1 shows a frame with a simple combo box.

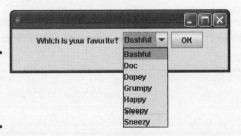

Figure 4-1:
A frame
with a
combo box.

You use the JComboBox class to create combo boxes. Table 4-1 lists the most frequently used constructors and methods of this class.

Table 4-1   **Common JComboBox Constructors and Methods**

Constructor	Description
JComboBox()	Creates an empty combo box.
JComboBox(Object[] items)	Creates a combo box and fills it with the values in the array.
JComboBox(Vector[] items)	Creates a combo box and fills it with the values in the vector.

Method	Description
void addActionListener (ActionListener listener)	Adds an action listener to the combo box.
void addItem(Object item)	Adds the item to the combo box.
void addItemListener (ItemListener listener)	Adds an item listener to the combo box.
Object getItemAt(int index)	Returns the item at the specified index.
int getItemCount()	Returns the number of items in the combo box.
int getSelectedIndex()	Returns the index of the selected item.
Object getSelectedItem()	Returns the selected item.
void insertItemAt(Object item, int index)	Inserts an item at a specified index.
Boolean isEditable()	Indicates whether or not the combo box's text field is editable.
void removeAllItems()	Removes all items from the combo box.
void removeItem(Object item)	Removes the specified item.
void removeItemAt(int index)	Removes the item at the specified index.
void setEditable(boolean value)	Specifies whether or not the combo box's text field is editable.
void setMaximumRowCount (int count)	Sets the number of rows displayed when the combo box list is dropped down.
void setSelectedIndex(int index)	Selects the item at specified index. Throws IllegalArgumentException if the index is less than zero or greater than the number of items in the combo box.
void setSelectedItem (Object item)	Selects the specified item. Throws IllegalArgumentException if the item is not in the combo box.

Creating combo boxes

Creating a combo box is easy. You have three constructors to choose from. The first creates an empty combo box:

```
JComboBox combo1 = new JComboBox();
```

Then, you can use the addItem to add items to the combo box:

```
combo1.addItem("Bashful");
combo1.addItem("Doc");
combo1.addItem("Dopey");
combo1.addItem("Grumpy");
combo1.addItem("Happy");
combo1.addItem("Sleepy");
combo1.addItem("Sneezy");
```

Alternatively, you can create a combo box and initialize its contents from an array. For example:

```
String[] theSeven = {"Bashful", "Doc", "Dopey", "Grumpy",
                     "Happy", "Sleepy", "Sneezy"};
JComboBox combo1 = new JComboBox(theSeven);
```

Or, if you have an existing Vector object with the data you want to display:

```
JComboBox combo1 = new JComboBox(vector1);
```

If the data you want to display is in an array list or other type of collection, use the toArray method to convert the collection to an array, and then pass the array to the JComboBox constructor:

```
JComboBox combo1 = new JComboBox(arraylist1.toArray());
```

Book VI
Chapter 4

Choosing from a List

You can add any kind of object you want to a combo box. The combo box calls the toString method of each item to determine the text to display in the drop-down list. For example, suppose you have an array of Employee objects. If you create a combo box from this array, the string returned by each employee's toString method is displayed in the combo box.

By default, the user is not allowed to edit the data in the text field portion of the combo box. If you want to allow the user to edit the text field, call setEditable(true). Then, the user can type a value that's not in the combo box.

To remove items from the combo box, use one of the remove methods. If you know the index position of the item you want to remove, call the removeItemAt method and pass the index number as a parameter. Otherwise, if you have the object you want to remove, call removeItem and pass the object.

To remove all the items in a combo box, call `removeAllItems`. For example, suppose you have a combo box named `custCombo` that's filled with `Customer` objects read from a file, and you need to periodically refresh this combo box to make sure it has all the current customers. Here's a method that does that:

```
private void fillCustomerCombo()
{
    ArrayList<Customer> customers = getCustomers();
    custCombo.removeAllItems();
    for (Customer c : customers)
        custCombo.addItem(c);
}
```

In this example, a method named `getCustomers` is called to get an `ArrayList` of customer objects from the file. Then, all the items currently in the combo box are deleted, and an enhanced `for` loop is used to add the customers to the combo box.

Getting items from a combo box

To get the item selected by the user, you use the `getSelectedItem` method. Unfortunately, this method returns an `Object` type, so you must cast the returned value to the appropriate type before you can use it. For example, here's the `actionPerformed` method from the event listener for the program that created the combo box frame that was shown in Figure 4-1:

```
public void actionPerformed(ActionEvent e)
{
    if (e.getSource() == buttonOK)
    {
        String s = (String)combo1.getSelectedItem();
        JOptionPane.showMessageDialog(combo1,
            "You picked " + s,
            "Your Favorite",
            JOptionPane.INFORMATION_MESSAGE);
    }
}
```

Here, the `getSelectedItem` method retrieves the selected item, casts it to a `String`, and saves it in a `String` variable named s. Then, a `JOptionPane` message box is shown to display the user's selection.

If you prefer, you can get the index of the selected item by calling the `getSelectedIndex` method. You might use this method if the combo box contains string values that correspond to objects stored in an array or a collection. Then, you can use the retrieved index value to get the actual object from the collection.

Handling combo box events

When the user selects an item from a combo box, an action event is generated. In most applications, you simply ignore this event. That's because you don't usually need to do anything immediately when the user selects an item. Instead, the selected item is processed when the user clicks a button.

If you want to provide immediate feedback when the user selects an item, you can handle the action event in the usual way: Create an `ActionListener` that handles the event in an `actionPerformed` method, and then call the `addActionListener` method of the combo box to add the action listener. The following action listener class displays a message box that says `My favorite too!` if the user picks Dopey:

```
private class ComboListener implements ActionListener
{
    public void actionPerformed(ActionEvent e)
    {
        if (e.getSource() == combo1)
        {
            String s =
    (String)combo1.getSelectedItem();
            if (s.equals("Dopey"))
                JOptionPane.showMessageDialog(combo1,
                    "He's my favorite too!",
                    "Good Choice",
        JOptionPane.INFORMATION_MESSAGE);
        }
    }
}
```

Combo boxes also generate item events when the user selects an item. In fact, the combo box generates *two* item events when the user selects an item, which can be a little confusing. The first event is generated when the previously selected item is deselected. Then, when the new item is selected, another item event is generated. In most cases, you handle combo box action events rather than item events.

Using Lists

A *list* is a powerful Swing component that displays lists of objects within a box. Depending on how the list is configured, the user can be allowed to select one item from the list or multiple list items. In addition, you have amazing control over how the items in the list are displayed, although this isn't always an advantage. Lists are almost always used in conjunction with scroll panes (covered in the previous chapter) to allow the user to scroll the contents of the list. Figure 4-2 shows a sample frame with a list component.

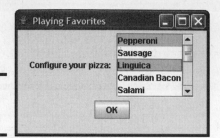

Figure 4-2:
A frame
with a list.

Lists and combo boxes have several important differences:

✦ A list doesn't have a text field the user can use to edit the selected item. Instead, the user must select items directly from the list.

✦ The list doesn't drop down. Instead, the list items are displayed in a box whose size you can specify.

✦ The list doesn't provide a scroll bar, so you almost always add the list component to a scroll pane so the user can scroll through the list.

✦ Lists allow you to select more than one item. By default, a list component lets you select any combination of items in the list. However, you can configure the list to allow the selection of a single range of adjacent values or just a single value.

To select multiple items in a list, hold down the Ctrl key and click the items you want to select. To select a range of items, click the first item, and then hold down the Shift key and click the last item.

✦ You can't directly change the values in a list after you create the list. If you want to create a list whose values you can change, you must take a few extra steps as I describe in the section "Changing list items" later in this chapter.

You use the JList class to create combo boxes. Table 4-2 lists the most frequently used constructors and methods of this class.

Table 4-2	Routine JList Constructors and Methods
Constructor	*Description*
JList()	Creates an empty list.
JList(ListModel list)	Creates a list that uses the specified list model.
JList(Object[] items)	Creates a list and fills it with the values in the array.
JList(Vector[] items)	Creates a list and fills it with the values in the vector.
void clearSelection()	Clears all selections.

Method	Description
`int getSelectedIndex()`	Returns the index of the first selected item, or -1 if no items are selected.
`int[] getSelectedIndexes()`	Returns an array with the index of each selected item. The array is empty if no items are selected.
`Object getSelectedValue()`	Returns the first selected item, or `null` if no items are selected.
`Object[] getSelected Values()`	Returns an array with all the selected items. The array is empty if no items are selected.
`boolean isSelectedIndex (int index)`	Returns `true` if the item at the specified index is selected.
`boolean isSelectionEmpty()`	Returns `true` if no items are selected.
`void setFixedCellHeight (int height)`	Sets the height of each row.
`void setFixedCellWidth (int width)`	Sets the width of each row.
`void setSelectedIndex(int index)`	Selects the item at the specified index.
`void setSelectedIndices (int[] indices)`	Selects the items at the indices specified in the array.
`void setSelectionMode (int mode)`	Sets the selection mode. Allowable values are: `ListSelectionModel.SINGLE_ SELECTION`, `ListSelectionModel. SINGLE_INTERVAL_SELECTION`, and `ListSelectionModel.MULTIPLE_ INTERVAL_SELECTION`.
`void setVisibleRowCount (int count)`	Sets the number of rows displayed by the list.

Creating a list

To create a list and specify its items, you pass an array to the `JList` constructor. Then, you call the `setVisibleRowCount` method to set the number of rows you want to be visible, add the list to a scroll pane, and add the scroll pane to a panel that you can later add to the frame. For example

```
String[] toppings = {"Pepperoni", "Sausage",
    "Linguica",
                    "Canadian Bacon", "Salami",
    "Tuna",
                    "Olives", "Mushrooms", "Tomatoes",
                    "Pineapple", "Kiwi", "Gummy
    Worms"};
list1 = new JList(toppings);
list1.setVisibleRowCount(5);
JScrollPane scroll = new JScrollPane(list1);
```

For more information about the JScrollPane class, including how to specify what scroll bars you want it to display, refer to Book VI, Chapter 3.

To control the type of selections the user can make, use the setSelection Mode method. You can pass this method one of three fields defined by the ListSelectionModel class:

+ **ListSelectionModel.SINGLE_SELECTION:** The user can select only one item at a time.

+ **ListSelectionModel.SINGLE_INTERVAL_SELECTION:** The user can select multiple items provided that they are all within a single range.

+ **ListSelectionModel.MULTIPLE_INTERVAL_SELECTION:** The user can select any combination of items.

For example, this statement restricts the list to a single selection:

```
list1.setSelectionMode(ListSelectionModel.SINGLE_SELECTION);
```

Note that the default is to allow any combination of multiple selections.

Getting items from a list

For a list that allows only a single selection, you can retrieve the selected item by calling the getSelectedValue method. You have to cast the value to the appropriate type before you use it. For example:

```
String topping = (String)list1.getSelectedValue();
```

If the list allows multiple selections, the getSelectedValue method returns just the first selected item. To get all the selections, you have to use the getSelectedValues method instead. This method returns an array of objects that includes each item selected by the user. When you retrieve these objects, you have to cast each one to the appropriate type — Java doesn't provide any way to cast the entire array.

For example, you can use the following actionPerformed method in an action listener for the list box shown in Figure 4-2:

```
public void actionPerformed(ActionEvent e)
{
    if (e.getSource() == buttonOK)
    {
        String s = (String)combo1.getSelectedItem();
        JOptionPane.showMessageDialog(combo1,
            "You picked " + s,
            "Your Favorite",
```

```
        JOptionPane.INFORMATION_MESSAGE);
    }
}
```

Here, the `getSelectedItem` method retrieves the selected item, casts it to a `String`, and saves it in a String variable named s. Then, a `JOptionPane` message box is shown to display the user's selection.

If you prefer, you can get the index of the selected item by calling the `getSelectedIndex` method. You might use this method if the combo box contains string values that correspond to objects stored in an array or a collection. Then, you can use the retrieved index value to get the actual object from the collection.

```
public void actionPerformed(ActionEvent e)
{
    if (e.getSource() == buttonOK)
    {
        Object[] toppings = list1.getSelectedValues();
        String msg =
            "You selected the following toppings:\n";
        for (Object topping : toppings)
            msg += (String)topping + "\n";
        JOptionPane.showMessageDialog(list1,
            msg,
            "Your Pizza",
            JOptionPane.INFORMATION_MESSAGE);
        list1.clearSelection();
    }
}
```

Here, the `getSelectedValues` method returns an array that contains the toppings selected by the user. Then, an enhanced `for` loop is used to build a string that lists each selected topping on a separate line. Then the `JOptionPane` class is used to display the `msg` string in a message box.

Changing list items

By default, the items in a `JList` component can't be changed after you create the list. If you want to create a list whose items can be changed, you must use another class named `DefaultListModel` to create an object called a *list model* that contains the items you want displayed in the `JList` component. Then, you pass the list model object to the `JList` constructor. The list model is responsible for managing the list that's displayed by the `JList` component. As a result, you can use the list model's methods to add or remove items. The `JList` component then automatically updates itself to reflect the list changes. Table 4-3 shows the most commonly used constructors and methods of the `DefaultListModel` class.

Table 4-3   Useful DefaultListModel Constructors and Methods

Constructor	Description
`DefaultListModel()`	Creates a new list model object.

Method	Description
`void add(Object element, int index)`	Adds an element at the specified position.
`void addElement(Object element))`	Adds an element to the end of the list.
`void clear()`	Removes all elements from the list.
`boolean Contains(Object element)`	Returns `true` if the specified element is in the list.
`Object firstElement()`	Returns the first element in the list.
`Object get(int index)`	Returns the element at the specified location.
`boolean isEmpty()`	Returns `true` if the list is empty.
`Object lastElement()`	Returns the last element in the list.
`void remove(int index)`	Removes the element from the specified position in the list.
`void removeElement(Object element)`	Removes the specified element from the list.
`int size()`	Returns the number of elements in the list.
`Object[] toArray()`	Returns an array containing each element in the list.

When you create the default data model, it's empty. But you can call the `add` or `addElement` methods to add elements to the list. For example:

```
String[] values = {"Pepperoni", "Sausage", "Linguica",
                    "Canadian Bacon", "Salami", "Tuna",
                    "Olives", "Mushrooms", "Tomatoes",
                    "Pineapple", "Kiwi", "Gummy Worms"};
DefaultListModel model = new DefaultListModel();
for (String value : values)
    model.addElement(value);
```

Here, the elements from the `values` array are added to the list model. Then, when you create the list control, pass the list model to the `JList` constructor:

```
list = new JList(model);
```

You can remove an element from the list model by calling the `remove` or `removeElement` methods. And to remove all the elements from the model, call the `clear` method.

Using Spinners

A *spinner* is a text field that has two little arrows next to it. The user can click one of these arrows to increase or decrease the value in the text field. Usually, the text field contains a number, so clicking one of the little arrows increments or decrements the number. However, you can also create a spinner that displays data taken from an array or a collection. Figure 4-3 shows a frame with three spinners arranged as a simple time picker.

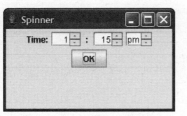

Figure 4-3:
A frame with three spinners.

To create a spinner control, you use the `JSpinner` class, whose constructors and methods are shown in Table 4-4. Note that the second constructor accepts an object of type `SpinnerModel` as a parameter. This table also shows constructors for two classes that implement the `SpinnerModel` interface.

Table 4-4	JSpinner and Related Classes
Constructor	*Description*
`JSpinner()`	Creates a default spinner. The default spinner lets the user choose an integer that has an initial value of zero and no minimum or maximum values.
`JSlider(SpinnerModel model)`	Creates a spinner using the specified `SpinnerModel` object.
Method	*Description*
`void addChangeListener (ChangeListener listener)`	Adds a `ChangeListener` to listen for change events.
`int getValue()`	Gets the value.
`void setToolTipText(String ext)`	Sets the tooltip text that's displayed if the user rests the mouse over the slider for a few moments.
Constructors for SpinnerModel Classes	*Description*
`SpinnerNumberModel(int init, int min, int max, int step)`	Creates a number spinner model that lets the user select integer values from `min` to `max` with an increment of `step`. The initial value is set to `init`.

(continued)

Table 4-4 *(continued)*

Constructors for SpinnerModel Classes	Description
`SpinnerNumberModel(double init, double min, double max, double step)`	Creates a number spinner model that lets the user select double values from `min` to `max` with an increment of `step`. The initial value is set to `init`.
`SpinnerListModel(Object[] values)`	Creates a list spinner model using the values from the specified array.
`SpinerListModel(List collection)`	Creates a list spinner model using the values from the specified collection. The collection must implement the `List` interface.

You can create a default spinner that lets the user select integer values like this:

```
JSpinner spinner = new JSpinner();
```

This spinner starts with a value of zero and increases or decreases the value by one each time the user clicks one of the spinner's arrows. You can retrieve the current value of the spinner at any time like this:

```
int value = spinner.getValue();
```

For most spinners, you want to use the second constructor, which requires that you first create an object that implements the `SpinnerModel` interface. Table 4-4 lists constructors for two classes that implement `Spinner`. The first, `SpinnerNumberModel`, creates numeric spinner controls that let you control the initial value, minimum and maximum values, and the step value that's added or subtracted each time the user clicks one of the arrows.

Here's how you can use the `SpinnerNumberModel` to create the first spinner in Figure 4-3, which accepts integers from 1 to 12, starting with 1:

```
JSpinner hours = new JSpinner(
    new SpinnerNumberModel(1, 1, 12, 1));
```

Here's the code for the second spinner in Figure 4-3, which lets the user pick numbers from 0 to 59:

```
JSpinner minutes = new JSpinner(
    new SpinnerNumberModel(0, 0, 59, 1));
```

You can also build a spinner control that selects values from a list by using the `SpinnerListModel` class. The constructor for this class accepts either an array or an object that implements the `List` interface. The `ArrayList` class implements this interface, which means you can use `SpinnerListModel` to create a spinner that selects items from an `ArrayList` object.

Here's the code for the third spinner in Figure 4-3, which lets the user choose am or pm:

```
String[] ampmString = {"am", "pm"};
ampm = new JSpinner(
    new SpinnerListModel(ampmString));
```

In this example, the `SpinnerListModel` uses an array of strings with two elements: am and pm.

Using Trees

A *tree* is a fancy Swing component that displays hierarchical data in outline form, which we computer nerds refer to as a tree. Trees are created from the `JTree` class.

The type of tree you're probably most familiar with is the directory structure of your disk drive. Figure 4-4 shows a Swing frame that has a tree control in it. In this example, I used a tree control to represent a few of my favorite TV shows along with shows that were spun off from them.

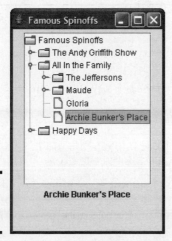

Figure 4-4:
A frame
with a tree.

Tree controls are probably the most difficult of all Swing controls to work with. To cover them completely, I'd have to devote a full chapter of 30 pages or more. In the few short pages that remain in this chapter, then, I'm just going to present the basics: how to create a tree component such as the one shown in Figure 4-4 and how to find out which element the user has selected.

Before I get into the mechanics of how to create a tree control, you need to know a few terms that describe the elements in the tree itself:

✦ **Node:** Each element in the tree is called a *node*. Nodes in a tree must be created from a class that implements the `TreeNode` interface. If you want, you can create your own class that implements `TreeNode`. For most purposes, however, you can use the `DefaultMutableTreeNode` class. (Unfortunately, you have to type that class name a lot when you work with tree controls.)

✦ **Root node:** The starting node for a tree. Every tree component must have one and only one root node. When you create a tree component, you pass the root node to the `JTree` constructor.

✦ **Child node:** The nodes that appear immediately below a given node are called that node's child nodes. A node can have more than one child.

✦ **Parent node:** The node immediately above a given node is called that node's parent. Every node except the root node must have one and only one parent.

✦ **Sibling nodes:** Nodes that are children of the same parent.

✦ **Leaf node:** A node that doesn't have any children. These nodes represent the end of a branch.

✦ **Path:** A node and all of its ancestors — that is, its parent, its parent's parent, and so on — all the way back to the root.

✦ **Expanded node:** A node whose children are visible.

✦ **Collapsed node:** A node whose children are hidden.

Building a tree

Before you can actually create a tree control, you must build the tree it displays. The easiest way to do that is to use the `DefaultMutableTreeNode` class, the details of which are shown in Table 4-5.

The `DefaultMutableTreeNode` class implements the `TreeNode` interface. As a result, you can use `DefaultMutableTreeNode` objects for any of the methods listed in this table that call for `TreeNode` objects.

Table 4-5	The DefaultMutableTreeNode Class
Constructor	*Description*
`DefaultMutableTreeNode()`	Creates an empty tree node.
`DefaultMutableTreeNode (Object userObject)`	Creates a tree node with the specified user object.

Method	Description
void add(TreeNode child)	Adds a child node.
TreeNode getFirstChild()	Gets the first of this node's children.
DefaultMutableTreeNode getNextSibling()	Gets the next sibling.
TreeNode getParent()	Gets this node's parent.
Object getUserObject()	Gets the user object for this node.

The DefaultMutableTreeNode class provides three basic characteristics for each node:

✦ The *user object,* which contains the data represented by the node. In my example, I use strings for the user objects. However, you can use objects of any type you wish for the user object. The tree control calls the user object's toString method to determine what text to display for each node. The easiest way to set the user object is to pass It via the DefaultMutableTreeNode constructor.

✦ The parent of this node, unless the node happens to be the root.

✦ Any children of this node, unless the node happens to be a leaf node. You create child nodes by calling the add method.

The DefaultMutableTreeNode class has many more methods for navigating the tree than the ones shown here. However, given a root node, you can use the getFirstChild and getNextSibling methods to "walk" the entire tree and access each node.

In this section, I build a tree that lists spin-off shows from three popular television shows of the past:

✦ *The Andy Griffith Show,* which had two spin-offs: *Gomer Pyle, U.S.M.C.* and *Mayberry R.F.D.*

✦ *All In the Family*, which directly spawned four spin-offs: *The Jeffersons, Maude, Gloria,* and *Archie Bunker's Place*. In addition, two of these spin-offs had spin-offs of their own, involving the maids: The Jeffersons' maid became the topic of a show called *Checking In*, and Maude's maid became the main character in *Good Times*.

✦ *Happy Days,* which spun off *Mork and Mindy, Laverne and Shirley,* and *Joanie Loves Chachi*.

You can take many different approaches to building trees, most of which involve some recursive programming. For more information about recursive programming, see Book V, Chapter 4. I'm going to avoid recursive programming in this section to keep things simple. However, that means you'll have to hard-code some of the details of the tree into the program. Most real programs that work with trees need some type of recursive programming to build the tree.

The first step when creating a tree is to declare a `DefaultMutableTreeNode` variable for each node that isn't a leaf node:

```
DefaultMutableTreeModel andy, archie, happy,
                        george, maude;
```

These can be local variables in the frame constructor because after you get the tree set up, you won't need these variables any more. You see why you don't need variables for the leaf nodes in a moment.

Next, I create the root node:

```
DefaultMutableTreeNode root =
  new DefaultMutableTreeNode("Famous Spinoffs");
```

Now, to simplify the task of creating all the other nodes, I create a helper method called `makeShow`:

```
private DefaultMutableTreeNode makeShow(String title,
    DefaultMutableTreeNode parent)
{
    DefaultMutableTreeNode show;
    show = new DefaultMutableTreeNode(title);
    parent.add(show);
    return show;
}
```

This method accepts a string and another node as parameters and returns a node whose user object is set to the string parameter. The returned node is also added to the parent node as a child. Thus, you can call this method to both create a new node and place the node in the tree.

Now I create some nodes. First, the nodes for *The Andy Griffith Show* and its spin-offs:

```
andy = makeShow("The Andy Griffith Show", root);
makeShow("Gomer Pyle, U.S.M.C.", andy);
makeShow("Mayberry R.F.D.", andy);
```

Here, `makeShow` is called to create a node for *The Andy Griffith Show*, with the root node specified as its parent. This node returned by this method is saved in the `andy` variable. Then, `makeShow` is called twice to create the spin-off shows, this time specifying `andy` as the parent node.

Because neither *Gomer Pyle* or *Mayberry R.F.D.* had spin-off shows, I don't need to pass these nodes as the parent parameter to the `makeShow` method. That's why I don't bother to create a variable to reference these nodes.

Next, I need to create nodes for *All In the Family* and its spin-offs:

```
archie = makeShow("All In the Family", root);
george = makeShow("The Jeffersons", archie);
makeShow("Checking In", george);
maude = makeShow("Maude", archie);
makeShow("Good Times", maude);
makeShow("Gloria", archie);
makeShow("Archie Bunker's Place", archie);
```

In this case, both *The Jeffersons* and *Maude* have child nodes of their own. As a result, variables are required for these two shows so they can be passed as the parent parameter to `makeShow` when I create the nodes for *Checking In* and *Good Times*.

Finally, here's the code that creates the nodes for *Happy Days* and its spin-offs:

```
happy = makeShow("Happy Days", root);
makeShow("Mork and Mindy", happy);
makeShow("Laverne and Shirley", happy);
makeShow("Joanie Loves Chachi", happy);
```

The complete tree is successfully created in memory, so I can get on with the task of creating a `JTree` component to show off the tree.

Creating a JTree component

You use the `JTree` class to create a tree component that displays the nodes of a tree. Table 4-6 shows the key constructors and methods of this class.

Table 4-6	Ordinary Constructors and Methods of the JTree Class
Constructor	**Description**
`void JTree()`	Creates an empty tree. Not very useful if you ask me.
`void JTree(TreeNode root)`	Creates a tree that displays the tree that starts at the specified node.
Method	**Description**
`void addTreeSelectionListener (TreeSelectionListener listener)`	Adds the specified listener to listen for tree selection events.
`Object getLastSelectedPathComponent()`	Gets the node that is currently selected.
`TreeSelectionModel getSelectionModel()`	Gets the selection model for the tree. See the text for what you can do with the `TreeSelectionModel` object.
`void setVisibleRowCount (int count)`	Sets the number of rows visible in the display.

The first step when creating a `JTree` component is to declare a `JTree` variable as a class instance variable so you can access the constructor and other methods:

```
JTree tree1;
```

Then, in the frame constructor, you call the `JTree` constructor to create the tree component, passing the root node of the tree you want it to display as a parameter:

```
tree1 = new JTree(root);
```

By default, the user is allowed to select multiple nodes from the tree. To restrict the user to a single selection, use this strange incantation:

```
tree1.getSelectionModel().setSelectionMode(
    TreeSelectionModel.SINGLE_TREE_SELECTION);
```

Here, the `getSelectionModel` method is called to get a `TreeSelection Model` object that determines how the user can select nodes in the tree. This class provides a method named `setSelectionMode` that lets you set the selection mode. To limit the tree to a single node selection, you must pass this method the `TreeSelectionModel.SINGLE_TREE_SELECTION` field. (I think they could have saved us all a lot of work by providing `setSingle TreeSelection` method for the `JTree` class, but nobody asked me.)

You can control the size of the tree component by calling the `setVisible RowCount` method. For example

```
tree1.setVisibleRowCount(12);
```

Here, the tree is just large enough to show 12 rows at a time.

Finally, you need to add the tree component to a scroll pane so the user can scroll the tree if it doesn't fit in the space provided. Then, you should add the scroll pane to a panel that is in turn added to the frame:

```
JScrollPane scroll = new JScrollPane(tree1);
panel1.add(scroll);
```

That's it! The tree component now appears as shown earlier in Figure 4-4.

Getting the selected node

The easiest way to determine the currently selected node in a tree control is to call the `getLastSelectedPathComponent` method. This method returns an object, so you want to cast it to the correct type. For example

```
Object o = tree1.getLastSelectedPathComponent();
DefaultMutableTreeNode show = (DefaultMutableTreeNode) o;
```

Here, the selected node is retrieved and stored in the `Object` variable o. Then, it's cast to a `DefaultMutableTreeNode` object.

You can use this method in an action event listener to retrieve the selected node when the user clicks a button. But what if your program needs to respond immediately when the user selects a node? For example, the frame shown in Figure 4-4 has a label beneath the list box. This label is updated with the title of the selected show whenever the user selects a show in the tree. To do that, you need to install a listener to listen for tree selection events.

To create a tree selection listener, you provide a class that implements the `TreeSelectionListener` interface. This interface provides a single method named `valueChanged`, which receives a `TreeSelectionEvent` object as a parameter. Here's a sample `TreeSelectionListener` class that simply sets the value of a label named `showName` to the value of the user object of the selected item:

```
private class TreeListener
    implements TreeSelectionListener
{
    public void valueChanged(TreeSelectionEvent e)
    {
        Object o = tree1.getLastSelectedPathComponent();
        DefaultMutableTreeNode show;
        show = (DefaultMutableTreeNode) o;
        String title = (String)show.getUserObject();
        showName.setText(title);
    }
}
```

Then, you can install an instance of this class to listen for tree selection events with this statement:

```
tree1.addTreeSelectionListener(new TreeListener());
```

The `JTree` class provides many other methods for retrieving the nodes that are selected. In addition, you can add listeners that listen for tree selection events that are generated when the user selects nodes. These events let you create applications that display data for the selected node immediately when the user selects a node. If you want to use these features, check out the API documentation for the `JTree` class.

Putting it all together

Whew! That was a lot of information to digest. To put it all together, Listing 4-1 shows the complete program that created the frame shown in Figure 4-4.

This program lets the user select a show from the tree. Then, the title of the selected show is displayed in the label beneath the tree.

LISTING 4-1: THE SPIN-OFF PROGRAM

```java
import javax.swing.*;
import java.awt.event.*;
import javax.swing.tree.*;
import javax.swing.event.*;

public class SpinOffs extends JFrame
{
    public static void main(String [] args)
    {
        new SpinOffs();
    }

    private JTree tree1;                                          → 13
    private DefaultTreeModel model;
    private JLabel showName;

    public SpinOffs()
    {
        this.setSize(225,325);
        this.setTitle("Famous Spinoffs");
        this.setDefaultCloseOperation(JFrame.EXIT_ON_CLOSE);

        JPanel panel1 = new JPanel();

        DefaultMutableTreeNode root, andy, archie,              → 25
                          happy, george, maude;

        root =                                                   → 28
            new DefaultMutableTreeNode("Famous Spin-offs");

        andy = makeShow("The Andy Griffith Show", root);         → 31
        makeShow("Gomer Pyle, U.S.M.C.", andy);
        makeShow("Mayberry R.F.D.", andy);

        archie = makeShow("All In the Family", root);            → 35
        george = makeShow("The Jeffersons", archie);
        makeShow("Checking In", george);
        maude = makeShow("Maude", archie);
        makeShow("Good Times", maude);
        makeShow("Gloria", archie);
        makeShow("Archie Bunker's Place", archie);

        happy = makeShow("Happy Days", root);                    → 43
        makeShow("Mork and Mindy", happy);
        makeShow("Laverne and Shirley", happy);
        makeShow("Joanie Loves Chachi", happy);

        tree1 = new JTree(root);                                 → 48
```

```
        tree1.getSelectionModel().setSelectionMode(               → 50
            TreeSelectionModel.SINGLE_TREE_SELECTION);
        tree1.setVisibleRowCount(12);
        tree1.addTreeSelectionListener(new TreeListener());

        JScrollPane scroll = new JScrollPane(tree1);              → 55
        panel1.add(scroll);

        showName = new JLabel();
        panel1.add(showName);
        this.add(panel1);
        this.setVisible(true);
    }

    private DefaultMutableTreeNode makeShow(                      → 64
        String title, DefaultMutableTreeNode parent)
    {
        DefaultMutableTreeNode show;
        show = new DefaultMutableTreeNode(title);
        parent.add(show);
        return show;
    }

    private class TreeListener                                    → 73
        implements TreeSelectionListener
    {
        public void valueChanged(TreeSelectionEvent e)
        {
            Object o = tree1.getLastSelectedPathComponent();
            DefaultMutableTreeNode show;
            show = (DefaultMutableTreeNode) o;
            String title = (String)show.getUserObject();
            showName.setText(title);
        }
    }
}
```

All the code in this program has been shown already in this chapter, so I just briefly point out the highlights here:

→**13** The tree and list models are defined as class instance variables.

→**25** DefaultMutableTreeNode variables are defined for the root node and each show that has spin-off shows.

→**28** The root node is created with the text Famous Spin-offs.

→**31** These lines create the nodes for *The Andy Griffith Show* and its spin-offs.

→**35** These lines create the nodes for *All In the Family* and its spin-offs.

→**43** These lines create the nodes for *Happy Days* and its spin-offs.

→**48** This line creates the `JTree` component, specifying `root` as the root node for the tree.

→**50** These lines configure the `JTree` component so it allows only a single selection, shows 12 rows at a time, and has a tree selection listener.

→**55** The `JTree` component is added to a scroll pane, which is then added to the frame.

→**64** The `makeShow` method creates a node from a string and adds the node to the node passed as the parent parameter.

→**73** The `TreeListener` class handles the `valueChanged` event to display the title of the selected show in the `showName` label.

Chapter 5: Using Layout Managers

In This Chapter

✔ **Flow layout**

✔ **Border layout**

✔ **Box layout**

✔ **Grid layout**

✔ **GridBag layout**

Controlling the layout of components on a frame is one of the most difficult aspects of working with Swing. In fact, it can be downright exasperating. Sometimes the components almost seem to have minds of their own. They get stubborn and refuse to budge. They line up on top of each other when you want them to be side by side. You make a slight change to a label or text field, and the whole frame seems to rearrange itself. At times you'll want to put your fist through the monitor.

 I recommend against putting your fist through your monitor. You'll make a mess, cut your hand, have to spend money on a new monitor, and when you get your computer working again, the components still don't line up the way you want them to be.

The problem isn't with the components, it's with the *layout managers* that are responsible for determining where each component appears in its frame or panel. In this chapter, you find out how to work with Swing's seven layout managers. This chapter takes the mystery out of Swing layout so you have complete control over where components are placed.

Introducing Layout Managers

Understanding layout managers is the key to creating Swing frames that are attractive and usable. Swing provides seven different layout managers for you to work with (five are described in the following list):

✦ **Flow:** This is the default layout manager for panels. It lays out components one after the other until it runs out of room. Then, it starts a new row of components.

✦ **Border:** This is the default layout manager for frames. It divides the container into five regions, called North, South, East, West, and Center.

When you add a component, you can specify which region you want to place the component in.

✦ **Box:** This layout manager arranges components into either a single row or a single column, depending on what alignment you specify when you create the layout manager.

✦ **Grid:** This layout manager is ideal when you want to create a grid of identically sized components.

✦ **GridBag:** This layout manager uses a more flexible grid than the Grid layout manager. With GridBag, each of the rows or columns can be a different size, a component can span two or more rows or columns, and you can tell the layout manager what to do if the component is smaller or larger than the space allotted for it.

Figure 5-1 shows frames arranged with each of these layout managers.

In addition to these five layout managers, Java provides a few additional ones. The Card layout manager lets you create tabbed layouts, but this manager has been largely replaced by other components that do the same thing more effectively. And the Spring layout manager uses a weird concept called *springs* to let you position components. This layout manager isn't intended to be hand-coded. Instead, it's designed to be used by code generators that create GUI code for you. Neither of these layout managers are covered in this book.

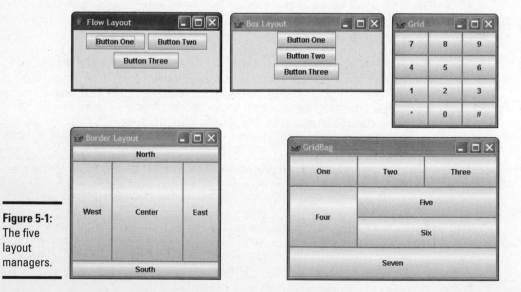

Figure 5-1: The five layout managers.

In many cases, the best approach to creating complex frame layouts is to use a combination of layout managers. For example, you might create a panel with buttons that appear at the bottom of the frame. This panel would use Flow layout. Then, you can add this panel to the South region of the frame, which uses Border layout by default.

To set the layout manager for a panel or frame, you use the `setLayout` method. For example, here's how you create a panel and set GridBag as its layout manager:

```
JPanel panel1 = new JPanel();
panel1.setLayout(new GridBagLayout());
```

If you want to use Flow layout with a panel or Border layout with a frame, you don't have to do anything because those are the defaults.

Using Flow Layout

Because Flow layout is the default layout manager for panels, you're already familiar with how it works. The components are laid out in a single row if possible. If a component doesn't fit on the current row, a new row is started.

By itself, the Flow layout manager isn't very useful. You'll probably use it mostly for small panels that consist of a few components, such as a row of buttons that is then added to a larger panel that uses one of the other layout managers.

Table 5-1 lists the constructors of the `FlowLayout` class, which you can use to create a new Flow layout manager.

Table 5-1	FlowLayout Constructors
Constructor	*Description*
`FlowLayout()`	Creates a Flow layout manager with centered alignment and no gaps.
`FlowLayout(int align)`	Creates a Flow layout manager with the specified alignment. The align parameter can be `FlowLayout.LEFT`, `FlowLayout.CENTER`, or `FlowLayout.RIGHT`.
`FlowLayout(int align, int hgap, int vgap)`	Creates a Flow layout manager with the specified alignment. The `int` parameters specify the size (in pixels) of gaps that are inserted between elements to space things out a bit.

By default, the rows are centered. You can specify left alignment for a panel like this:

```
JPanel panel1 = new JPanel();
panel1.setLayout(new FlowLayout(FlowLayout.LEFT));
```

To specify right alignment, use this statement instead:

```
panel1.setLayout(new FlowLayout(FlowLayout.RIGHT));
```

You can also specify gaps that are inserted between each component. For example

```
panel1.setLayout(new FlowLayout(FlowLayout.LEFT, 20, 15));
```

Here, the horizontal gap is set to 20, and the vertical gap is set to 15. Figure 5-2 shows a panel with six buttons created with these settings.

Figure 5-2:
Flow layout with left alignment and gaps.

Using Border Layout

The Border layout manager carves up a frame or panel into five regions: North, South, East, West, and Center, as shown in Figure 5-3. Then, when you add a component to the frame or panel, you can specify which of these regions the component goes in.

Border layout is the default for frames. To create a panel with Border layout, use one of the constructors of the `BorderLayout` class that's shown in Table 5-2. For example

```
JPanel panel1 = new JPanel();
panel1.setLayout(new BorderLayout());
```

North

West	Center	East

South

Figure 5-3:
How Border
layout
carves
things up.

Table 5-2	Border Layout Constructors and Fields
Constructor	**Description**
`BorderLayout()`	Creates a Border layout manager with no gaps.
`BorderLayout(int hgap, int vgap)`	Creates a Border layout manager with the specified horizontal and vertical gaps.
Field	**Description**
`NORTH`	The North region (at the top of the container).
`SOUTH`	The South region (at the bottom of the container).
`WEST`	The West region (at the left of the container).
`EAST`	The East region (at the right of the container).
`CENTER`	The Center region.

When you add a component to a panel or frame that uses the Border layout manager, you can specify the region to place the component in by using one of the `BorderLayout` fields, as in this example:

```
panel1.add(new JLabel("Welcome!"), BorderLayout.NORTH);
```

Here, the label is added to the North region.

Here are a few additional important points to know about Border layout:

✦ If you don't specify the region when you add a component, the component is placed in the center.

- ✦ When the Border layout manager determines the size of each region, it first determines the size for the regions on the edges — North, South, East, and West. Then, whatever space remains is given to the center.

- ✦ The Border layout manager automatically resizes the components in each region to completely fill up the region. If you don't want that to happen, place the components into separate panels that use Flow layout, and then add those panels to the Border layout regions.

- ✦ If you add two or more components to the same region of a Border layout panel or frame, the last one in wins the fight for space; the others aren't visible at all. To add more than one component to a region, you need to first add the components to a panel, and then add the panel to the Border layout region.

Using Box Layout

You can use the Box layout to create a panel that contains a single row or column of components. If the components are arranged in a single row, the box is called a *horizontal box*. If the components are stacked in a column, the box is a *vertical box*.

Although you can apply the Box layout directly to a panel, it's much more common to use the Box class, which is similar to a panel but defaults to Box layout rather than Flow layout. In addition, the Box class has several static methods that are useful for laying out components in the box. Table 5-3 lists the methods of this class.

Table 5-3	The Box and Dimension Classes
Box Methods	*Description*
`static Component createGlue()`	Creates a glue component. This component forces the components on any side of it as far away from each other as possible.
`static Box createHorizontalBox()`	Creates a horizontal box.
`static Component createHorizontalGlue()`	Creates a horizontal glue component. This component forces the components on either side of it as far away from each other as possible.
`static Component createHorizontalStrut (int width)`	Creates a horizontal strut component that places the specified amount of space between the components on either side of it.
`static createRigidArea (Dimension d)`	Creates an area with a fixed size.

Box Methods	Description
`static Box` `createVerticalBox()`	Creates a vertical box.
`static Component` `createVerticalGlue ()`	Creates a vertical glue component. This component forces the components above and below it as far away from each other as possible.

`static Component`
`createVerticalStrut(int`
`width)`
	Creates a vertical strut component that places the specified amount of space between the components above and below it.

Dimension Constructor	Description
`Dimension(int width, int` `height)`	Creates a new `Dimension` object with the specified width and height.

Here's an example that creates a horizontal box and adds three buttons to it:

```
Box box1 = Box.createHorizontalBox();
box1.add(new JButton("Accept"));
box1.add(new JButton("Cancel"));
box1.add(new JButton("Close"));
```

The real power of Box layouts is the use of struts, rigid area, and glue:

✦ A **strut** is a component that inserts a specified amount of space between components. You can create a strut by calling the `createHorizontalStrut` or `createVerticalStrut` methods, depending on which type of strut you want to create. For example, suppose you want the three buttons in the previous example to be separated by 20 pixels, and you want 20 pixels of blank space on either end of the box as well. This code does the trick:

```
Box box1 = Box.createHorizontalBox();

box1.add(Box.createHorizontalStrut(20));
box1.add(new JButton("Accept"));
box1.add(Box.createHorizontalStrut(20));
box1.add(new JButton("Cancel"));
box1.add(Box.createHorizontalStrut(20));
box1.add(new JButton("Close"));
box1.add(Box.createHorizontalStrut(20));
```

✦ A **rigid area** is like a strut, but spaces things out both horizontally and vertically. For example

```
box1.add(new JButton("Accept"));
box1.add(Box.createRigidArea(new Dimension(20,
    40)));
box1.add(new JButton("Cancel"));
```

Here, I used a rigid area that's 20 by 40 pixels to separate the Accept button from the Cancel button. One side effect of this rigid area is that it increases the height of the box itself to 40 pixels. Empty space is left above and below the buttons.

✦ **Glue** is similar to a strut, but it pushes components as far away from each other as possible within the bounds of the box itself. For example, this code uses glue to move the third button as far away from the first two buttons as possible based on the width of the box:

```
Box box1 = Box.createHorizontalBox();

box1.add(Box.createHorizontalStrut(20));
box1.add(new JButton("Accept"));
box1.add(Box.createRigidArea(new Dimension(20,
    40)));
box1.add(new JButton("Cancel"));

box1.add(Box.createHorizontalGlue());

box1.add(new JButton("Close"));
box1.add(Box.createHorizontalStrut(20));
```

Now, if you add this Box layout to the South region of a frame, the buttons appear as shown in Figure 5-4.

Figure 5-4:
Using Box
layout to
arrange
buttons.

Using Grid Layout

The Grid layout is designed for panels that need to have a set number of components all equally sized and arranged into a grid. You probably won't use it much, but if you need to create something that looks like a calculator or a phone, this is the layout manager you need. Table 5-4 lists the constructors of the GridLayout class, which you use to create a grid layout.

Table 5-4	The GridLayout Constructor
Constructor	*Description*
`GridLayout()`	Creates a grid layout that arranges components in a single row. This is equivalent to `GridLayout (1, 0)`.
`GridLayout(int rows, int columns)`	Creates a grid layout with the specified number of rows and columns. If one of the parameters is zero, the grid expands to fill as many rows or columns as necessary. (You can't specify zero for both parameters.)
`GridLayout(int rows, int columns, int hgap, int vgap)`	Creates a grid layout with the specified number of rows and columns with gaps of the specified size between the rows and columns.

To create a panel with Grid layout, you call the `GridLayout` constructor to specify the size of the grid. One of the parameters can be zero to allow the grid to expand to however many rows or columns are necessary to hold all the components you add to the panel.

For example, here's code that creates the Grid layout panel that resembles a phone and was shown earlier in Figure 5-1:

```
JPanel panel1 = new JPanel();
panel1.setLayout(new GridLayout(0,3));

panel1.add(new JButton("7"));
panel1.add(new JButton("8"));
panel1.add(new JButton("9"));
panel1.add(new JButton("4"));
panel1.add(new JButton("5"));
panel1.add(new JButton("6"));
panel1.add(new JButton("1"));
panel1.add(new JButton("2"));
panel1.add(new JButton("3"));
panel1.add(new JButton("*"));
panel1.add(new JButton("0"));
panel1.add(new JButton("#"));
```

As you add components to a panel with Grid layout, the components are dropped into the grid's cells row by row, working across each row from left to right. As each row is filled, a new row is started.

Using GridBag Layout

The GridBag layout manager is the layout manager you'll probably use most to lay out complicated panels. Like the Grid layout manager, GridBag lets you carve up a panel into a grid. However, the grid has the following special features:

✦ The rows and columns don't all have to be the same size. Instead, GridBag automatically adjusts the width of each column and the height of each row based on the components you add to the panel.

✦ You can specify which cell you want each component to go in. You can control each component's position on the panel.

✦ You can create components that span multiple rows or columns. For example, you can create a button that is two columns wide or a list box that is four rows high.

✦ You can tell GridBag to stretch a component to fill the entire space allotted to it if the component isn't already big enough to fill the entire area. You can specify that this stretching be done horizontally, vertically, or both.

✦ If a component doesn't fill its allotted area, you can tell the GridBag how you want the component positioned within the area. For example, components can be left or right aligned.

The following sections describe the ins and outs of working with GridBag layouts.

Sketching out a plan

The first step when preparing to create a GridBag panel is to draw a sketch of how you want the components on the panel to appear. Then, slice the panel into rows and columns and number the rows and columns starting with zero in the top left corner. Figure 5-5 shows such a sketch, prepared with my own hand.

After you have the panel sketched out, make a list of the components, their x and y coordinates on the grid, their alignment, and whether the component spans more than one row or column. For example

Component	x	y	Alignment	Spans
Label "Name"	0	0	right	
Label "Phone"	0	1	right	
Label "Address"	0	2	right	
Name text field	1	0	left	2
Phone text field	1	1	left	
Address text field	1	2	left	
Size box	0	3	left	
Style box	1	3	left	
Toppings box	2	3	left	
Button box	2	4	right	

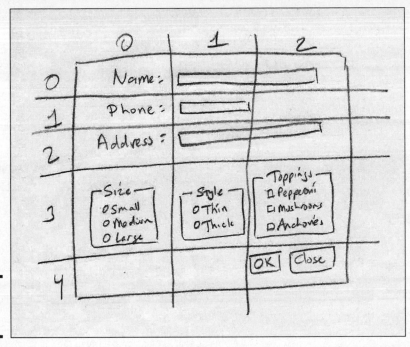

Figure 5-5:
Sketching
out a panel.

After you lay out the grid, you can write the code to add each component to its proper place.

Adding components to a GridBag

Before you can add components to a panel using the GridBag layout, you must first specify GridBag as the panel's layout manager. You do that by calling the `setLayout` method, passing a new `GridBagLayout` object as a parameter:

```
JPanel panel1 = new JPanel();
panel1.setLayout(new GridBagLayout());
```

When a panel uses the GridBag layout, the `add` method accepts two parameters: the component to add and a `GridBagConstraints` object that specifies where to place the component in the grid. The trick of using the GridBag layout is figuring out how to set the `GridBagConstraints` values to get each component to go where you want it to go. Table 5-5 lists the fields of the `GridBagConstraints` class.

Table 5-5	The GridBagContraints Class
Field	*Description*
`int gridx`	The x position of the component.
`int gridy`	The y position of the component.
`int gridwidth`	The number of columns spanned by the component. The default is 1.
`int gridheight`	The number of rows spanned by the component. The default is 1.
`double weightx`	A value that gives the grid layout a hint on how to apportion space for the component's width.
`double weighty`	A value that gives the grid layout a hint on how to apportion space for the component's height.
`Insets insets`	An `Insets` object that indicates how much space to use as padding around each component. The `Insets` class has a simple constructor: `Insets(int top, int left, int bottom, int right)`.
`int anchor`	A constant that indicates where to place the component if it doesn't fill the space. Values can be any of the following fields of the `Grid BagConstraints` class: `CENTER, NORTH, NORTHEAST, EAST, SOUTHEAST, SOUTH, SOUTHWEST, WEST,` and `NORTHWEST`.
`int fill`	A constant that indicates whether to stretch the object to fill available space. Values can be any of the following fields of the `GridBagConstraints` class: `NONE, HORIZONTAL, VERTICAL,` or `BOTH`.

A few of these fields need some extra explanation:

✦ The `weightx` and `weighty` fields give the GridBag layout manager a hint about how to adjust the size of the columns and rows. If you set one of these values to zero, the row or column remains fixed in size. A common technique is to set both of these parameters to `100`, and then adjust them if you think the layout could benefit from some tweaking.

✦ The `insets` field lets you provide some padding around components. You set this field to an `Insets` object. For example, assuming the `GridBagConstraints` object is named `gc`, this statement provides 5 pixels of space on each side of the component and sets the `insets` field like this:

```
gc.insets = new Insets(5, 5, 5, 5);
```

✦ By default, components are stretched to fill the cells of the grid. This is rarely what you want, so you usually want to set the `fill` field to change this behavior.

✦ You also want to set the `anchor` field to indicate where you want the component placed if it doesn't fill the cell or cells allotted to it.

Working with GridBagConstraints

To create a `GridBagConstraint` object, you call the `GridBagConstraint` constructor, and then set any of the fields that you want to vary from the default values. For example, here's code that creates a `GridBagConstraint` object to add the name text field that is shown earlier in Figure 5-5:

```
GridBagConstraints nameConstraints
    = new GridBagConstraints();
nameConstraints.gridx = 1;
nameConstraints.gridy = 0;
nameConstraints.gridwidth = 2;
nameConstraints.gridheight = 1;
nameConstraints.weightx = 100.0;
nameConstraints.weighty = 100.0;
nameConstraints.insets = new Insets(5, 5, 5, 5);
nameConstraints.anchor = GridBagConstraints.WEST;
nameConstraints.fill = GridBagConstraints.NONE;
```

Then, you can call the `add` method to add the name text field to the panel:

```
panel1.add(name, nameConstraints);
```

Obviously, this approach to controlling constraints is going to require a lot of coding. You have two common alternatives to creating a new constraint object for every component you add to the panel. The first is to create a single constraint object and reuse it for all the components in the panel. Then, you simply change the fields that need to be changed for each component. For example, here's code that adds all three text fields using a single constraint object:

```
GridBagConstraints gc = new GridBagConstraints();
gc.gridx = 0;
gc.gridy = 0;
gc.gridwidth = 1;
gc.gridheight = 1;
gc.weightx = 100.0;
gc.weighty = 100.0;
gc.insets = new Insets(5, 5, 5, 5);
gc.anchor = GridBagConstraints.WEST;
gc.fill = GridBagConstraints.NONE;

gc.gridy = 0;
gc.gridwidth = 2;
```

```
add(name, gc);
gc.gridy = 1;
gc.gridwidth = 1;
add(phone, gc);
gc.gridy = 2;
gc.gridwidth = 2;
add(address, gc);
```

Here, the first group of statements creates a `GridBagConstraints` object named `gc` and sets its values to the defaults that I want to apply to most of the components in the panel. Then, the second group of statements sets the `gridy` and `gridwidth` fields before adding each text field to the panel.

The second option is to create a helper method that you can call, passing just the values that vary for each component. For example, here's a method named `addItem` that adds a component and left aligns it within the specified cells:

```
private void addItem(JPanel p, JComponent c, int x, int y,
    int width, int height, int align)
{
    GridBagConstraints gc = new GridBagConstraints();
    gc.gridx = x;
    gc.gridy = y;
    gc.gridwidth = width;
    gc.gridheight = height;
    gc.weightx = 100.0;
    gc.weighty = 100.0;
    gc.insets = new Insets(5, 5, 5, 5);
    gc.anchor = align;
    gc.fill = GridBagConstraints.NONE;
    p.add(c, gc);
}
```

Then, you can call this method to add a component to the panel. You must pass the panel and the component, its x and y position, and its width and height. For example, here's how you add the name text field:

```
addItem(panel1, name, 0, 1, 2, 1,
    GridBagConstraints.WEST);
```

A GridBag layout example

Listing 5-1 shows the code for a program that displays the frame that I drew in Figure 5-5, and Figure 5-6 shows how this frame appears when the program is run. As you can see, the final appearance of this frame is pretty close to the way I sketched it out at McDonald's. I could probably fix a few minor variations with a little tweaking.

Figure 5-6:
The Pizza
Order
application
in action.

LISTING 5-1: THE PIZZA ORDER APPLICATION

```java
import javax.swing.*;
import java.awt.event.*;
import java.awt.*;

public class Pizza extends JFrame
{
    public static void main(String [] args)
    {
        new Pizza();
    }

    JTextField name, phone, address;
    JRadioButton small, medium, large, thick, thin;
    JCheckBox pepperoni, mushrooms, anchovies;
    JButton okButton, closeButton;

    public Pizza()
    {
        this.setTitle("Pizza Order");
        this.setDefaultCloseOperation(JFrame.EXIT_ON_CLOSE);

        JPanel panel1 = new JPanel();
        panel1.setLayout(new GridBagLayout());                    → 23

        addItem(panel1, new JLabel("Name:"),                      → 25
            0, 0, 1, 1, GridBagConstraints.EAST);
        addItem(panel1, new JLabel("Phone:"),
            0, 1, 1, 1, GridBagConstraints.EAST);
        addItem(panel1, new JLabel("Address:"),
            0, 2, 1, 1, GridBagConstraints.EAST);

        name = new JTextField(20);
        phone = new JTextField(10);
        address = new JTextField(20);

        addItem(panel1, name, 1, 0, 2, 1,                         → 36
            GridBagConstraints.WEST);
        addItem(panel1, phone, 1, 1, 1, 1,
```

continued

LISTING 5-1 (CONTINUED)

```
      GridBagConstraints.WEST);
addItem(panel1, address, 1, 2, 2, 1,
      GridBagConstraints.WEST);

Box sizeBox = Box.createVerticalBox();                        → 43
small = new JRadioButton("Small");
medium = new JRadioButton("Medium");
large = new JRadioButton("Large");
ButtonGroup sizeGroup = new ButtonGroup();
sizeGroup.add(small);
sizeGroup.add(medium);
sizeGroup.add(large);
sizeBox.add(small);
sizeBox.add(medium);
sizeBox.add(large);
sizeBox.setBorder(
      BorderFactory.createTitledBorder("Size"));
addItem(panel1, sizeBox, 0, 3, 1, 1,
      GridBagConstraints.NORTH);

Box styleBox = Box.createVerticalBox();                       → 59
thin = new JRadioButton("Thin");
thick = new JRadioButton("Thick");
ButtonGroup styleGroup = new ButtonGroup();
styleGroup.add(thin);
styleGroup.add(thick);
styleBox.add(thin);
styleBox.add(thick);
styleBox.setBorder(
      BorderFactory.createTitledBorder("Style"));
addItem(panel1, styleBox, 1, 3, 1, 1,
      GridBagConstraints.NORTH);

Box topBox = Box.createVerticalBox();                         → 72
pepperoni = new JCheckBox("Pepperoni");
mushrooms = new JCheckBox("Mushrooms");
anchovies = new JCheckBox("Anchovies");
ButtonGroup topGroup = new ButtonGroup();
topGroup.add(pepperoni);
topGroup.add(mushrooms);
topGroup.add(anchovies);
topBox.add(pepperoni);
topBox.add(mushrooms);
topBox.add(anchovies);
topBox.setBorder(
      BorderFactory.createTitledBorder("Toppings"));
addItem(panel1, topBox, 2, 3, 1, 1,
      GridBagConstraints.NORTH);

Box buttonBox = Box.createHorizontalBox();                    → 88
okButton = new JButton("OK");
closeButton = new JButton("Close");
buttonBox.add(okButton);
buttonBox.add(Box.createHorizontalStrut(20));
buttonBox.add(closeButton);
```

```
      addItem(panel1, buttonBox, 2, 4, 1, 1,
         GridBagConstraints.NORTH);

      this.add(panel1);
      this.pack();
      this.setVisible(true);
   }

   private void addItem(JPanel p, JComponent c,
      int x, int y, int width, int height, int align)
   {
      GridBagConstraints gc = new GridBagConstraints();
      gc.gridx = x;
      gc.gridy = y;
      gc.gridwidth = width;
      gc.gridheight = height;
      gc.weightx = 100.0;
      gc.weighty = 100.0;
      gc.insets = new Insets(5, 5, 5, 5);
      gc.anchor = align;
      gc.fill = GridBagConstraints.NONE;
      p.add(c, gc);
   }
}
```

Book VI
Chapter 5

Using Layout
Managers

Note that this application doesn't include any event listeners, so the buttons don't do anything other than demonstrate how to use the GridBag layout. The following paragraphs point out the highlights:

→**23** This line creates a GridBag layout manager for the panel.

→**25** These lines add the labels to the panel.

→**36** These lines add the text fields to the panel.

→**43** These lines use a vertical Box object to create the radio buttons that let the user select the size.

→**59** These lines use a vertical Box object to create the radio buttons that let the user select the crust style.

→**72** These lines use a vertical Box object to create the check boxes that let the user select check boxes.

→**88** These lines use a horizontal Box object to hold the OK and Close buttons.

Book VII

Web Programming

The 5th Wave   By Rich Tennant

"Well, this is festive- a miniature intranet amidst a swirl of Java applets."

Contents at a Glance

Chapter 1: Creating Applets

An *applet* is not a small piece of fruit. Rather, it's a Java application that's designed to run in a browser window on an Internet user's computer. When an Internet user visits a Web page that contains an applet, the Java applet class is downloaded to the user's computer and run there. The applet takes over a portion of the page and, within that space, can do anything it wants.

Applets are, at least in most cases, Swing applications. As a result, everything that's covered in Book VI applies to applets. In this chapter, you create applets that include Swing components. Then, you add an applet to a Web page so anyone who views the page can use it.

Understanding Applets

An applet is similar to a Swing application, with several crucial differences:

✦ Instead of extending the `JFrame` class, applets extend the `JApplet` class. Both `JFrame` and `JApplet` provide a "space" for your Swing application to operate in:

  • With `JFrame`, that space is a window that's managed by the host operating system's windowing system.

  • With `JApplet`, the space is a rectangular area of a Web page that's managed by a Web browser.

✦ Stand-alone Swing applications are started when the JVM calls the static `main` method. Thus, a Swing application typically starts by creating an instance of the class that extends `JFrame`. In contrast, the browser automatically creates an instance of the class that extends `JApplet` when the applet is started. As a result, applets don't have a static `main` method. Instead, a method named `init` is called to get the applet started. As a result, the `init` method is where you put the code that you'd put in the constructor for a class that extends `JFrame`.

✦ Stand-alone Swing methods need a way to let the user shut them down. Typically, Swing applications include an Exit button or an Exit menu command. Applets don't. An applet remains alive as long as the page that contains it is displayed.

✦ Applets aren't displayed in windows; they're displayed in a region of a Web page. As a result, you can't set the text for an applet's title bar, and you can't set the DefaultCloseOperation, because there's no Close button for the user to click. In addition, the user can't resize the applet.

✦ For security reasons, applets are prohibited from doing certain things. In particular, an applet is not allowed to do anything that affects the client computer's file system, including reading or writing files, or running programs on the client computer.

Other than these differences and restrictions, an applet works pretty much the same as a Swing application. In fact, the Swing components inside the applet look and behave *exactly* like they do in a stand-alone Swing application. Thus, applets let you create Swing applications and run them on any computer, anywhere in the world. Right?

Would that it were so. Unfortunately, the company that makes the world's most popular Web browser, whose name I won't mention but whose initials are MICROSOFT, hasn't played nice with Sun. Or maybe Sun hasn't played nice with Microsoft. Who knows. Either way, the result has been a mess when it comes to whether or not users' computers can run applets, and if they can, what version of Java they support. Users can download the Java plug-in from Sun, but the download is large, and most users either don't want to take the time, don't understand the process, or don't trust it.

As a result, applets aren't the best way to create Web-based applications that you expect to be used by the masses. The biggest sites on the Internet, such as eBay and Amazon, are *not* implemented with applets; instead, they're built using tools such as servlets and Java Server Pages as described in the other chapters of Book VII.

The JApplet Class

As I've already mentioned, an applet extends the JApplet class rather than the JFrame class. For the most part, the JApplet class works pretty much the same as the JFrame class. As a result, you can add panels and other components to it, create menus, doodle on it, and so on. Table 1-1 lists the most commonly used methods of the JApplet class.

Table 1-1	**Useful JApplet Constructors and Methods**
Constructor	*Description*
`JApplet()`	Creates a new applet. You don't usually need to call the `JApplet` constructor because it's called automatically when the browser loads the applet.
Method	*Description*
`void add (Component c)`	Adds the specified component to the applet.
`void destroy()`	Called by the browser to inform the applet that its memory is about to be reclaimed by the JVM. Most applets don't need to override this method.
`void init()`	Called by the browser to inform the applet that it has been loaded. This method takes the place of the `JFrame` constructor for a Swing application.
`void setLayout (LayoutManager layout)`	Sets the layout manager used to control how components are arranged when the applet is displayed. The default is the Border Layout manager.
`void setLocation (int x, int y)`	Sets the x and y position of the applet on-screen. The top left corner of the screen is 0, 0.
`void setLocationRelativeTo (Component c)`	Centers the applet on-screen if the parameter is `null`.
`void setSize(int width, int height)`	Sets the size of the applet to the specified width and height.
`void setJMenuBar (JMenuBar menu)`	Sets the menu for this applet.
`void start()`	Called by the browser to inform the applet to start its execution.
`void stop()`	Called by the browser when the applet temporarily leaves view. Override this method if you need to stop activities while the applet is hidden.

Looking At a Sample Applet

To see how a complete applet works, Listing 1-1 shows the complete code for an applet that lets the user order a pizza in one of three sizes (Small, Medium, and Large) with one of three toppings (Pepperoni, Mushrooms, and Anchovies). Figure 1-1 shows this applet in action on a Web page.

Figure 1-1:
The pizza
applet in
action.

LISTING 1-1: THE PIZZA ORDER APPLET

```java
import javax.swing.*;
import java.awt.event.*;
import javax.swing.border.*;

public class PizzaApplet extends JApplet                    → 5
{
    private JButton buttonOK;
    private JRadioButton small, medium, large;

    private JCheckBox pepperoni, mushrooms, anchovies;

    public void init()                                      → 12
    {
        this.setSize(320,200);                              → 14

        ButtonListener bl = new ButtonListener();

        JPanel mainPanel = new JPanel();

        JPanel sizePanel = new JPanel();
            Border b1 =
            BorderFactory.createTitledBorder("Size");
            sizePanel.setBorder(b1);

        ButtonGroup sizeGroup = new ButtonGroup();
```

```
small = new JRadioButton("Small");
small.setSelected(true);
sizePanel.add(small);
sizeGroup.add(small);

medium = new JRadioButton("Medium");
sizePanel.add(medium);
sizeGroup.add(medium);

large = new JRadioButton("Large");
sizePanel.add(large);
sizeGroup.add(large);

mainPanel.add(sizePanel);

JPanel topPanel = new JPanel();
Border b2 =
    BorderFactory.createTitledBorder("Toppings");
topPanel.setBorder(b2);

pepperoni = new JCheckBox("Pepperoni");
topPanel.add(pepperoni);

mushrooms = new JCheckBox("Mushrooms");
topPanel.add(mushrooms);

anchovies = new JCheckBox("Anchovies");
topPanel.add(anchovies);

mainPanel.add(topPanel);

buttonOK = new JButton("OK");
buttonOK.addActionListener(bl);
mainPanel.add(buttonOK);

this.add(mainPanel);

this.setVisible(true);
}

private class ButtonListener implements ActionListener
{
    public void actionPerformed(ActionEvent e)
    {
        if (e.getSource() == buttonOK)
        {
            String tops = "";
            if (pepperoni.isSelected())
                tops += "Pepperoni\n";
            if (mushrooms.isSelected())
                tops += "Mushrooms\n";
```

continued

LISTING 1-1 (CONTINUED)

```
        if (anchovies.isSelected())
            tops += "Anchovies\n";

        String msg = "You ordered a ";
        if (small.isSelected())
            msg += "small pizza with ";
        if (medium.isSelected())
            msg += "medium pizza with ";
        if (large.isSelected())
            msg += "large pizza with ";

        if (tops.equals(""))
            msg += "no toppings.";
        else
            msg += "the following toppings:\n"
                + tops;
        JOptionPane.showMessageDialog(buttonOK,
            msg, "Your Order",
            JOptionPane.INFORMATION_MESSAGE);

        pepperoni.setSelected(false);
        mushrooms.setSelected(false);
        anchovies.setSelected(false);
        small.setSelected(true);
    }
  }
 }
}
```

This is an applet version of a Swing program that is in Book VI, Chapter 3. For the details on how the Swing components work, you can refer to that chapter. Here, I just want to point out a few details that are specific to applets:

→ **5** The class extends JApplet instead of JFrame.

→**12** The init method is overridden, and the code that ordinarily is in the constructor for the JFrame class is placed in the init method.

→**14** The setSize method is called to set the size of the applet. Several methods that appeared in the Swing version of this program, however, are removed. In particular, the setTitle and setDefaultCloseAction methods are deleted, because those methods don't apply to applets. From the rest of this method, however, you can see that most of this code is exactly the same as it is for a stand-alone Swing application.

Creating an HTML Page for an Applet

To run an applet, you must create an HTML page that includes an APPLET tag that specifies the name of the applet and the size of the region you want to let the applet run inside. The APPLET tag also includes text that's displayed if the Web browser isn't capable of running the applet.

The basic form of the APPLET tag is this:

```
<APPLET code="classname" width=width height=height>
    Text to display if applet can't be loaded
</APPLET>
```

For example, here's the HTML file that I used to display the page shown in Figure 1-1:

```
<html>
  <head>
    <title>The Pizza Applet</title>
  </head>
  <body>
    <H1>Welcome to the Pizza Applet!</H1>
    <APPLET code="PizzaApplet" width="300" height="180">
    Sorry, your browser isn't able to run Java applets.
    </APPLET>
  </body>
</html>
```

Testing an Applet

Java comes with a special program called the *applet viewer* that lets you quickly run an applet after you compile it. Figure 1-2 shows the pizza applet displayed in the applet viewer.

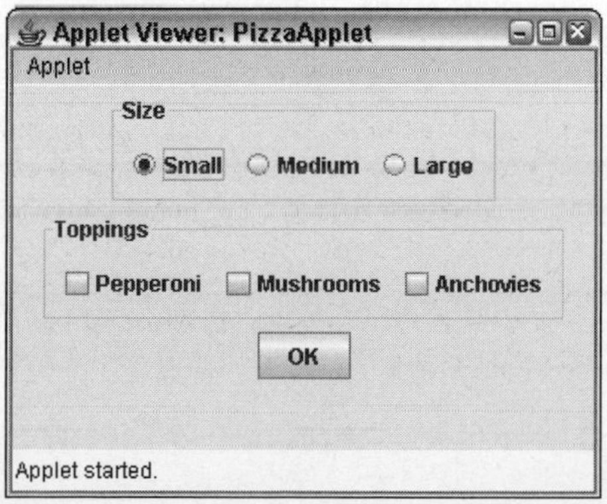

Figure 1-2:
The pizza applet displayed in the applet viewer.

If you're using TextPad, you can invoke the viewer by pressing Ctrl+3 after you compile the applet. From a command prompt, you must first create an HTML file as described in the previous section. Then, navigate to the directory that contains the HTML file and type this command:

```
appletviewer filename
```

For example, to display the pizza applet with an HTML file named PizzaApplet.html, use this command:

```
Appletviewer PizzaApplet.html
```

Chapter 2: Creating Servlets

In This Chapter

✓ Looking at servlets

✓ Downloading, installing, and configuring Tomcat

✓ Creating simple servlets

✓ Working with forms to get data from the user

Servlets are one of the most popular ways to develop Web applications today. Many of the best-known Web sites on the Internet are powered by servlets. In this chapter, I give you just the basics: what a servlet is, how to set up your computer so you can code and test servlets, and how to create a simple servlet. The next two chapters build on this chapter with additional Web programming techniques.

Understanding Servlets

Before you can understand what a servlet is and how it works, you need to understand the basics of how Web servers work. Web servers use a networking protocol called *HTTP* to send Web pages to users. (HTTP stands for *HyperText Transfer Protocol*, but that won't be on the test.) With HTTP, a client computer uses a URL to request a document that's located on the server computer. HTTP uses a *request/response model*, which means that client computers (Web users) send request messages to HTTP servers, which in turn send response messages back to the clients.

A basic HTTP interaction works something like this:

1. **Using a Web browser program running on a client computer, you specify the URL of a file that you want to access.**

In some cases, you actually type in the URL of the address. But most of the time, you click a link that specifies the URL.

2. **Your Web browser sends an HTTP request message to the server computer indicated by the URL.**

The request includes the name of the file that you want to retrieve.

3. **The server computer receives the file request, retrieves the requested file, and sends the file back to you in the form of an HTTP response message.**

4. The Web browser receives the file, interprets the HTML it contains, and displays the result on-screen.

The most important thing to note about normal Web interactions is that they are *static*. By that I mean that the contents of the file sent to the user is always the same. If the user requests the same file 20 times in a row, the same page displays 20 times.

In contrast, a *servlet* provides a way for the content to be dynamic. A servlet is simply a Java program that extends the `javax.servlet.Servlet` class. The `Servlet` class enables the program to run on a Web server in response to a user request, and output from the servlet is sent back to the Web user as an HTML page.

With servlets, Steps 1, 2, and 4 of the preceding procedure are the same. It's the fateful third step that sets servlets apart. If the URL specified by the user refers to a servlet rather than a file, Step 3 goes more like this:

3. The server computer receives the servlet request, locates the Java program indicated by the request, runs it, and returns the output from the program in the form of an HTTP response message.

In other words, instead of sending the contents of a file, the server sends the output generated by the servlet program. Typically, the servlet program generates some HTML that's displayed by the browser.

Servlets are designed to get their work done quickly, and then end. Each time a servlet runs, it processes one request from a browser, generates one page that's sent back to the browser, and then ends. The next time that user or any other user requests the same servlet, the servlet is run again.

Using Tomcat

Unfortunately, you can't just run servlet programs on any old computer. First, you have to install a special program called a *servlet engine* to turn your computer into a server that's capable of running servlets. The best-known servlet engine is called Tomcat, and it's available free from the Apache Software Foundation at `jakarta.apache.org/tomcat`.

Tomcat can also work as a basic Web server. In actual production environments, Tomcat is usually used in combination with a specialized Web server, such as Apache's HTTP Server.

Installing and configuring Tomcat

Installing Tomcat isn't rocket science, but it's not as easy as making toast. Here are the steps you can follow to set up Tomcat 5.5 on a Windows XP system:

1. **Download the Tomcat Zip file.**

You find the Zip file on the Apache Web site. Although Apache also offers an executable setup file for installing Tomcat, I suggest you download the Zip file instead.

2. **Extract the contents of the Zip file by right-clicking the file and choosing Extract All. Then, specify `c:\` as the location to extract the files to.**

I know you don't want to clutter up your root directory with a bunch of files, but the Tomcat Zip file contains a single folder named jakarta-tomcat-5.5.4 (the version number may vary), so only this one folder is created. After all the files are extracted, rename this folder to something a little easier to type. I suggest `c:\tomcat`.

3. **Create an environment variable named `JAVA_HOME` that points to the location of your JDK.**

To create an environment variable, open the Control Panel, double-click the System icon, click the Advanced Tab, and then click Environment Variables. Then, click New and create a variable named JAVA_HOME. The value of this variable needs to be the complete path to your JDK installation folder. For example: `c:\Program Files\Java\jdk1.5.0`.

A common mistake is to set this variable to the `bin` directory or to the directory for the JRE, not the JDK. If Tomcat doesn't start up later, double-check the JAVA_HOME directory.

4. **Copy the `servlet-api.jar` file to the `jre\lib\ext` folder in your JDK root.**

For example, if your JDF is installed in `c:\Program Files\Java\jdk1.5.0`, copy this file to `c:\Program Files\Java\jdk1.5.0\jre\lib\ext`. You find the `servlet-api.jar` file in `c:\tomcat\common\lib`, assuming you extracted the Tomcat files to `c:\tomcat`.

If you skip this step or copy the `servlet-api.jar` file to the wrong place, you can't compile your servlet programs. If you get compiler messages complaining that the `javax.servlet` package doesn't exist, double-check that you performed this step right.

5. **Edit the `context.xml` configuration file and add `reloadable="true"` to the `<context>` tag.**

The `context.xml` file is located in `c:\tomcat\conf`. The second line is initially this:

```
<Context>
```

Change it to:

```
<Context reloadable="true">
```

6. **Modify the `web.xml` file to enable the `invoker` servlet.**

Like `context.xml`, the `web.xml` file is located in `c:\tomcat\conf`. It contains two groups of lines that configure a Tomcat feature called the *invoker servlet* that you need to modify. These lines are initially commented out to disable the invoker servlet; all you have to do is remove the comment lines that appear before and after each group of lines.

The first group you want to de-comment looks like this:

```
<!--
    <servlet>
        <servlet-name>invoker</servlet-name>
        <servlet-class>

    org.apache.catalina.servlets.InvokerServlet
        </servlet-class>
        <init-param>
            <param-name>debug</param-name>
            <param-value>0</param-value>
        </init-param>
        <load-on-startup>2</load-on-startup>
    </servlet>
-->
```

Simply remove the first (`<!--`) and last (`-->`) of these lines.

The second group looks like this:

```
<!--
    <servlet-mapping>
        <servlet-name>invoker</servlet-name>
        <url-pattern>/servlet/*</url-pattern>
    </servlet-mapping>
-->
```

Once again, you must remove the first and last line so these lines aren't treated as comments.

You can quickly find these lines by searching for the word `invoker`.

7. **Create the `classes` directory.**

By default, Tomcat looks for the class files for your servlets in the directory `c:\tomcat\webapps\ROOT\WEB-INF\classes`. Unfortunately, the `classes` directory is missing. So you must navigate to `c:\tomcat\webapps\ROOT\WEB-INF` and create the `classes` directory. (Of course, the `c:tomcat` part of these paths varies if you installed Tomcat in some other location.)

Starting and stopping Tomcat

After you install and configure Tomcat, you can start it by opening a command window, changing to the c:\tomcat\bin directory, and typing startup. A batch file runs that starts Tomcat. When Tomcat starts, it opens up a second command window that displays various status messages. Figure 2-1 shows both of these windows in action.

```
Tomcat                                                          _|□|×|
Jan 24, 2005 8:13:19 PM org.apache.catalina.core.ApplicationContext log
INFO: ContextListener: contextInitialized()
Jan 24, 2005 8:13:19 PM org.apache.catalina.core.ApplicationContext log
INFO: SessionListener: contextInitialized()
Jan 24, 2005 8:13:19 PM org.apache.catalina.core.ApplicationContext log
INFO: ContextListener: contextInitialized()
Jan 24, 2005 8:13:19 PM org.apache.catalina.core.ApplicationContext log
INFO: SessionListener: contextInitialized()
Jan 24, 2005 8:13:20 PM org.apache.coyote.http11.Http11Protocol start
INFO: Starting Coyote HTTP/1.1 on http-8080
Jan 24, 2005 8:13:21 PM org.apache.jk.common.ChannelSocket init
INFO: JK2: ajp13 listening on /0.0.0.0:8009
Jan 24, 2005 8:13:21 PM org.apache.jk.server.JkMain start
INFO: Jk running ID=0 time=0/80 config=null
Jan 24, 2005 8:13:21 PM org.apache.catalina.startup.Catalina start
INFO: Server startup in 4817 ms
```

```
G:\WINDOWS\System32\cmd.exe                                    _|□|×|
G:\tomcat\bin>startup
Using CATALINA_BASE:   G:\tomcat
Using CATALINA_HOME:   G:\tomcat
Using CATALINA_TMPDIR: G:\tomcat\temp
Using JAVA_HOME:       G:\Program Files\Java\jdk1.5.0
G:\tomcat\bin>
```

Figure 2-1:
Starting up Tomcat.

You know that Tomcat has successfully started up when you see a line such as the following indicating how long the startup took:

```
INFO: Server startup in 2817 ms
```

If the Tomcat window appears for a few seconds, and then an exception message flies by quickly and the window closes, the most likely problem is that you already have a Web server running on your system and that server has already laid claim to the port Tomcat wants to use for HTTP communication. The solution to that problem is to edit the server.xml file in c:\tomcat\conf and look for this tag:

```
<Connector port="8080" ... />
```

Change the port number from 8080 to some other number, such as 18080. Later, when you display servlets in a browser window, you have to specify this number as the HTTP port number instead of 8080.

You don't need to shut down Tomcat once you start it up unless you make a change to one of its configuration files. If you do, you can shut down Tomcat by running the `shutdown` batch file from the `c:\tomcat\bin` directory. Then, you can run the `startup` batch file to get Tomcat going again.

Testing Tomcat

To find out if you have installed Tomcat correctly, you can try running the test servlets that are automatically installed when you install Tomcat. Open a browser window and type this address:

```
http://localhost:8080/servlets-examples/index.html
```

(If you changed the port number by editing the `server.xml` file, use the port number you specified instead of 8080.) The page shown in Figure 2-2 appears. If it doesn't, go to the earlier section "Installing and configuring Tomcat" and double-check that you did each step correctly.

Note: If you scroll down this page, you find links to a variety of sample servlets you can run along with links to each servlet's source code. By all means play around with these samples to get an idea of how servlets work and what you can do with them.

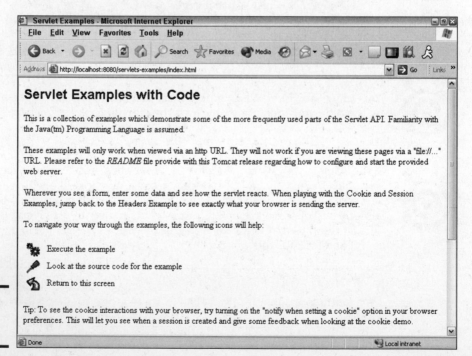

Figure 2-2:
Testing
Tomcat.

Creating a Simple Servlet

Okay, enough of the configuration stuff; now you can start writing some code. The following sections go over the basics of creating a simple Hello, World! type servlet.

Importing the servlet packages

Most servlets need access to at least three packages — `javax.servlet`, `javax.servlet.http`, and `java.io`. As a result, you usually start with these `import` statements:

```
import java.io.*;
import javax.servlet.*;
import javax.servlet.http.*;
```

Depending on what other processing your servlet does, you may need additional `import` statements.

Extending the HttpServlet class

To create a servlet, you write a class that extends the `HttpServlet` class. Table 2-1 lists six methods you can override in your servlet class.

Table 2-1		The HttpServlet Class
Method	*When Called*	*Signature*
doDelete	HTTP DELETE request	`public void doDelete(Http ServletRequest request, HttpServletResponse response) throws IOException, ServletException`
doGet	HTTP GET request	`public void doGet(HttpServlet Request request, HttpServlet Response response) throws IOException, ServletException`
doPost	HTTP POST request	`public void doPost(HttpServlet Request request, HttpServlet Response response) throws IOException, ServletException`
doPut	HTTP PUT request	`public void doPut(HttpServlet Request request, HttpServlet Response response) throws IOException, ServletException`
init()	First time servlet is run	`public void init() throws ServletException`
destroy()	Servlet is destroyed	`public void destroy()`

Most servlets override at least the doGet method. This method is called by the servlet engine when a user requests the servlet by typing its address into the browser's address bar or by clicking a link that leads to the servlet.

Two parameters are passed to the doGet method:

✦ An HttpServletRequest object that represents the incoming request from the user. You use the request parameter primarily to retrieve data entered by the user into form fields. You find out how to do that later in this chapter.

✦ An HttpServletResponse object that represents the response that is sent back to the user. You use the response parameter to compose the output that is sent back to the user. You find out how to do that in the next section.

Printing to a Web page

One of the main jobs of most servlets is writing HTML output that's sent back to the user's browser. To do that, you first call the getWriter method of the HttpServletResponse class. This returns a PrintWriter object that's connected to the response object. Thus, you can use the familiar print and println methods to write HTML text.

For example, here's a doGet method for a simple HelloWorld servlet:

```
public void doGet(HttpServletRequest request,
    HttpServletResponse response)
        throws IOException, ServletException
{
    PrintWriter out = response.getWriter();
    out.println("Hello, World!");
}
```

Here, the PrintWriter object returned by response.getWriter() is used to send a simple text string back to the browser. If you run this servlet, the browser displays the text Hello, World!.

Responding with HTML

In most cases, you don't want to send simple text back to the browser. Instead, you want to send formatted HTML. To do that, you must first tell the response object that the output is in HTML format. You can do that by calling the setContentType method, passing the string "text/html" as the parameter. Then, you can use the PrintWriter object to send HTML. For example, Listing 2-1 shows a basic HelloWorld servlet that sends an HTML response.

LISTING 2-1: THE HELLOWORLD SERVLET

```java
import java.io.*;
import javax.servlet.*;
import javax.servlet.http.*;
import java.util.*;

public class HelloWorld extends HttpServlet
{
    public void doGet(HttpServletRequest request,
        HttpServletResponse response)
            throws IOException, ServletException
    {
        response.setContentType("text/html");
        PrintWriter out = response.getWriter();
        out.println("<html>");
        out.println("<head>");
        out.println("<title>HelloWorld</title>");
        out.println("</head>");
        out.println("<body>");
        out.println("<h1>Hello, World!</h1>");
        out.println("</body>");
        out.println("</html>");
    }
}
```

Here, the following HTML is sent to the browser (I added indentation to show the HTML's structure):

```html
<html>
  <head>
    <title>HelloWorld</title>
  </head>
  <body>
    <h1>Hello, World!</h1>
  </body>
</html>
```

When run, the HelloWorld servlet produces the page shown in Figure 2-3.

 Obviously, you need a solid understanding of HTML to write servlets. If HTML is like a foreign language, you need to pick up a good HTML book, such as *HTML 4 For Dummies* by Ed Tittel and Natanya Pitts, before you go much further. For your reference, Table 2-2 summarizes all the HTML tags that I use in this book.

Book VII
Chapter 2

Creating Servlets

Figure 2-3:
The
HelloWorld
servlet
displayed in
a browser.

Table 2-2	Just Enough HTML to Get By
HTML tag	*Description*
`<html>`, `</html>`	Marks the start and end of an HTML document.
`<head>`, `</head>`	Marks the start and end of the head section of an HTML document.
`<title>`, `</title>`	A title element. The text between the start and end tags is shown in the title bar of the browser window.
`<body>`, `</body>`	Marks the start and end of the body section of an HTML document. The content of the document is provided between these tags.
`<h1>`, `</h1>`	The text between these tags is formatted as a level-1 heading.
`<h2>`, `</h2>`	The text between these tags is formatted as a level-2 heading.
`<h3>`, `</h3>`	The text between these tags is formatted as a level-3 heading.
`<form action="url"`, `method="method">`	Marks the start of a form. The `action` attribute specifies the name of the page, servlet, or JSP the form is posted to. The `method` attribute can be `GET` or `POST`; it indicates the type of HTTP request sent to the server.
`</form>`	Marks the end of a form.
`<input type="type"`, `name="name">`	Creates an input field. Specify `type="text"` to create a text field or `type="submit"` to create a Submit button. The `name` attribute provides the name you use in the program to retrieve data entered by the user.
` `	A non-breaking space.

Running a Servlet

So how exactly do you run a servlet? First, you must move the compiled class file into a directory that Tomcat can run the servlet from. For testing purposes, you can move the servlet's class file to `c:\tomcat\webapps\ROOT\WEB-INF\classes`. Then, type an address like this one in your browser's address bar:

```
http://localhost:8080/servlet/HelloWorld
```

You may also want to override the `doPost` method. This method is called if the user requests your servlet from a form. In many cases, you'll just call `doGet` from the `doPost` method, so that both get and post requests are processed in the same way.

As you know, the `doGet` method is called whenever the user enters the address of your servlet in the address bar or clicks a link that leads to your servlet. But many — if not most — servlets are associated with HTML forms, which provide fields the user can enter data into. The normal way to send form data from the browser to the server is with an HTTP POST request, not a GET request.

If you want a servlet to respond to POST requests, you can override the `doPost` method instead of, or in addition to, the `doGet` method. Other than the method name, `doPost` has the same signature as `doGet`. In fact, it's not uncommon to see servlets in which the `doPost` method simply calls `doGet`, so that both POST and GET requests are processed identically. To do that, code the `doPost` method like this:

```
public void doPost(HttpServletRequest request,
    HttpServletResponse response)
        throws IOException, ServletException
{
    doGet(request, response);
}
```

An Improved HelloWorld Servlet

The HelloWorld servlet that is shown earlier in Listing 2-1 isn't very interesting because it always sends the same text. Essentially, it is a static servlet, which pretty much defeats the purpose of using servlets in the first place. You could just as easily have provided a static HTML page.

Listing 2-2 shows the code for a more dynamic HelloWorld servlet. This version randomly displays one of six different greetings. It uses the `random` method of the `Math` class to pick a random number from 1 to 6, and then uses this number to decide which greeting to display. It also overrides the doPost method as well as the doGet method, so posts and gets are handled identically.

LISTING 2-2: THE HELLOSERVLET SERVLET

```java
import java.io.*;
import javax.servlet.*;
import javax.servlet.http.*;
import java.util.*;

public class HelloServlet extends HttpServlet
{
    public void doGet(HttpServletRequest request,
        HttpServletResponse response)
            throws IOException, ServletException
    {
        response.setContentType("text/html");
        PrintWriter out = response.getWriter();
        String msg = getGreeting();
        out.println("<html>");
        out.println("<head>");
        out.println("<title>HelloWorld Servlet</title>");
        out.println("</head>");
        out.println("<body>");
        out.println("<h1>");
        out.println(msg);
        out.println("</h1>");
        out.println("</body>");
        out.println("</html>");
    }
    public void doPost(HttpServletRequest request,
        HttpServletResponse response)
            throws IOException, ServletException
    {
        doGet(request, response);
    }

    private String getGreeting()
    {
        String msg = "";
        int rand = (int)(Math.random() * (6)) + 1;
        switch (rand)
        {
            case 1:
                return "Hello, World!";
            case 2:
                return "Greetings!";
            case 3:
                return "Felicitations!";
```

```
        case 4:
            return "Yo, Dude!";
        case 5:
            return "Whasssuuuup?";
        case 6:
            return "Hark!";
        }
        return null;
    }
}
```

Getting Input from the User

If a servlet is called by an HTTP GET or POST request that came from a form, you can call the `getParameter` method of the `request` object to get the values entered by the user into each form field. For example

```
String name = request.getParameter("name");
```

Here, the value entered into the form input field named `name` is retrieved and assigned to the `String` variable `name`.

Working with forms

As you can see, retrieving data entered by the user in a servlet is easy. The hard part is creating a form that the user can enter the data into. There are two basic approaches to doing that. One is to create the form using a separate HTML file. For example, Listing 2-3 shows an HTML file named `InputServlet.html` that displays the form shown in Figure 2-4.

LISTING 2-3: THE INPUTSERVLET.HTML FILE

```html
<html>
  <head>
    <title>Input Servlet</title>
  </head>
  <body>
    <form action="/servlet/InputServlet" method="post">
      Enter your name: 
      <input type="text" name="Name">
      <br><br>
      <input type="submit" value="Submit">
    </form>
  </body>
</html>
```

Figure 2-4:
A simple
input form.

The action attribute in the form tag of this form specifies that /servlet/ InputServlet is called when the form is submitted, and the method attribute indicates that the form is submitted via a POST rather than a GET request.

The form itself consists of an input text field named name and a Submit button. Nothing fancy; just enough to get some text from the user and send it to a servlet.

The InputServlet servlet

Listing 2-4 shows a servlet that can retrieve the data from the form shown in Listing 2-3.

LISTING 2-4: THE INPUTSERVLET SERVLET

```
import java.io.*;
import javax.servlet.*;
import javax.servlet.http.*;

public class InputServlet extends HttpServlet
{
    public void doGet(HttpServletRequest request,
        HttpServletResponse response)
            throws IOException, ServletException
    {
        String name = request.getParameter("Name");

        response.setContentType("text/html");
        PrintWriter out = response.getWriter();
        out.println("<html>");
        out.println("<head>");
        out.println("<title>Input Servlet</title>");
        out.println("</head>");
```

```
    out.println("<body>");
    out.println("<h1>");
    out.println("Hello " + name);
    out.println("</h1>");
    out.println("</body>");
    out.println("</html>");
    }

    public void doPost(HttpServletRequest request,
        HttpServletResponse response)
            throws IOException, ServletException
    {
        doGet(request, response);
    }
}
```

As you can see, this servlet really isn't that much different than the first HelloWorld servlet from Listing 2-1. The biggest difference is that it retrieves the value entered by the user into the name field and uses it in the HTML that's sent to the response PrintWriter object. For example, if the user enters Calvin Coolidge into the name input field, the following HTML is generated:

```
<html>
  <head>
    <title>HelloWorld</title>
  </head>
  <body>
    <h1>Hello Calvin Coolidge</h1>
  </body>
</html>
```

Thus, the message Hello Calvin Coolidge is displayed on the page.

Although real-life servlets do a lot more than just parrot back information entered by the user, most of them follow this surprisingly simple structure, with a few variations of course. For example, real-world servlets validate input data and display error messages if the user enters incorrect data or omits important data. And most real-world servlets retrieve or update data in files or databases. Even so, the basic structure is pretty much the same.

Using Classes in a Servlet

When you develop servlets, you often want to access other classes you've created, such as IO classes that retrieve data from files or databases, utility or helper classes that provide common functions such as data validation, and perhaps even classes that represent business objects such as customers or products. To do that, all you have to do is save the class files in the classes directory of the servlet's home directory that, for the purposes of this chapter, is `c:\tomcat\webapps\ROOT\WEB-INF\classes`.

To illustrate a servlet that uses several classes, Figure 2-5 shows the output from a servlet that lists movies read from a text file. This servlet uses three classes:

+ **Movie:** A class that represents an individual movie.

+ **MovieIO:** A class that has a static public method named `getMovies`. This method returns an `ArrayList` object that contains all the movies read from the file.

+ **ListFiles:** The main servlet class. It calls the `MovieIO.getMovies` class to get an `ArrayList` of movies, and then displays the movies on the page.

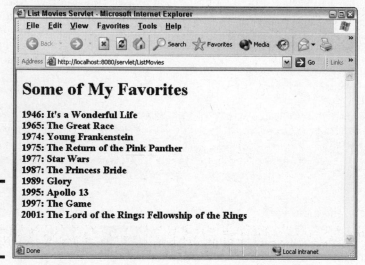

Figure 2-5:
The
ListMovies
servlet.

The code for the `Movie` class is shown in Listing 2-5. As you can see, this class doesn't have much: It defines three public fields (`title`, `year`, and `price`) and a constructor that lets you create a new `Movie` object and initialize the three fields. Note that the `price` field isn't used by this servlet.

LISTING 2-5: THE MOVIE CLASS

```
public class Movie
{
    public String title;
    public int year;
```

```
    public double price;

    public Movie(String title, int year, double price)
    {
        this.title = title;
        this.year = year;
        this.price = price;
    }
}
```

Listing 2-6 shows the `MovieIO` class. This class uses the file I/O features that are presented in Book VIII, Chapter 2 to read data from a text file. The text file uses tabs to separate the fields, and contains these lines:

```
It's a Wonderful Life⇨1946⇨14.95
The Great Race⇨1965⇨12.95
Young Frankenstein⇨1974⇨16.95
The Return of the Pink Panther⇨1975⇨11.95
Star Wars⇨1977⇨17.95
The Princess Bride⇨1987⇨16.95
Glory⇨1989⇨14.95
Apollo 13⇨1995⇨19.95
The Game⇨1997⇨14.95
The Lord of the Rings:The Fellowship of the Ring⇨
    2001⇨19.95
```

Here, the arrows represent tab characters in the file. I'm not going to go over the details of this class here, except to point out that `getMovies` is the only public method in the class, and It's static so you don't have to create an instance of the `MovieIO` class to use it. For the details on how this class works, refer to Book VIII, Chapter 2.

LISTING 2-6: THE MOVIEIO CLASS

```
import java.io.*;
import java.util.*;

public class MovieIO
{
    public static ArrayList<Movie> getMovies()
    {
        ArrayList<Movie> movies = new ArrayList<Movie>();
        BufferedReader in =
            getReader("c:\\data\\movies.txt");
        Movie movie = readMovie(in);
        while (movie != null)
        {
            movies.add(movie);
            movie = readMovie(in);
```

continued

LISTING 2-6 (CONTINUED)

```
        }
        return movies;
    }

    private static BufferedReader getReader(String name)
    {
        BufferedReader in = null;
        try
        {
            File file = new File(name);
            in = new BufferedReader(
                new FileReader(file) );
        }
        catch (FileNotFoundException e)
        {
            System.out.println("The file doesn't exist.");
            System.exit(0);
        }
        catch (IOException e)
        {
            System.out.println("I/O Error");
            System.exit(0);
        }
        return in;
    }

    private static Movie readMovie(BufferedReader in)
    {
        String title;
        int year;
        double price;
        String line = "";
        String[] data;

        try
        {
            line = in.readLine();
        }
        catch (IOException e)
        {
            System.out.println("I/O Error");
            System.exit(0);
        }

        if (line == null)
            return null;
        else
        {
            data = line.split("\t");
            title = data[0];
```

```
            year = Integer.parseInt(data[1]);
            price = Double.parseDouble(data[2]);
            return new Movie(title, year, price);
        }
    }
}
```

Listing 2-7 shows the code for the ListMovie servlet class.

LISTING 2-7: THE LISTMOVIE SERVLET CLASS

```
import java.io.*;
import javax.servlet.*;
import javax.servlet.http.*;
import java.util.*;

public class ListMovies extends HttpServlet
{
    public void doGet(HttpServletRequest request,            → 8
        HttpServletResponse response)
            throws IOException, ServletException
    {
        response.setContentType("text/html");
        PrintWriter out = response.getWriter();
        String msg = getMovieList();
        out.println("<html>");
        out.println("<head>");
        out.println("<title>List Movies Servlet</title>");
        out.println("</head>");
        out.println("<body>");
        out.println("<h1>Some of My Favorites</h1>");
        out.println("<h3>");
        out.println(msg);
        out.println("</h3>");
        out.println("</body>");
        out.println("</html>");
    }

    public void doPost(HttpServletRequest request,           → 28
        HttpServletResponse response)
            throws IOException, ServletException
    {
        doGet(request, response);
    }

    private String getMovieList()                            → 35
    {
        String msg = "";
        ArrayList<Movie> movies = MovieIO.getMovies();
```

Book VII
Chapter 2

Creating Servlets

continued

LISTING 2-7 (CONTINUED)

```
        for (Movie m : movies)
        {
            msg += m.year + ": ";
            msg += m.title + "<br>";
        }
        return msg;
    }
}
```

The following paragraphs describe what each of its methods do:

→ **8** The doGet method calls the getMovieList method to get a string that contains a list of all the movies separated by break tags. Then, it uses a series of out.println statements to write HTML that displays this list.

→**28** The doPost method simply calls the doGet method. That way, the servlet works whether it is invoked by a GET or POST request.

→**35** The getMovieList method calls the MovieIO.getMovies method to get an ArrayList that contains all the movies read from the file. Then, it uses an enhanced for loop to retrieve each Movie object. Each movie's year and title is added to the msg string, separated by <br> tags.

Chapter 3: Using Java Server Pages

In This Chapter

- ✔ Understanding how servlets work
- ✔ Using page directives
- ✔ Trying out expressions
- ✔ Putting scriptlets to work
- ✔ Devising declarations
- ✔ Comprehending classes

In the previous chapter, you discover how to create servlets that write HTML data directly to a page by using the `PrintWriter` object accessed through `response.out`. Although this technique works, it has one major drawback: You have to manually compose the HTML as a bunch of string literals. If the HTML has an error, you don't know about it until you run the servlet to see how it looks. And hand-crafting HTML in `out.println` statements certainly isn't the most efficient way to create attractive Web pages.

That's where *Java Server Pages,* usually called *JSP* for short, come in. A JSP is an HTML file that has Java servlet code embedded in it in special tags. When you run a JSP, all the HTML is automatically sent as part of the response, along with any HTML that's created by the Java code you embed in the JSP file. As a result, JSP spares you the chore of writing all those `out.println` statements.

In this chapter, you find out how to create basic Java Server Pages. Then, in the next chapter, I show you how to incorporate special Java classes called *JavaBeans* into your JSP pages.

Understanding Java Server Pages

A Java Server Page is an HTML document that's saved in a file with the extension `.jsp` instead of `.htm` or `.html`. Unlike servlet class files, you can store a JSP file in any directory that's available to the Web server.

The first time a user requests a JSP file, the JSP file is run through a translator program that converts the file into a Java servlet program and compiles it. All the HTML from the original JSP file is converted to `out.print` statements that send the HTML to the response, and the Java statements from the JSP file are incorporated into the servlet program. Then, the servlet program is executed and the results sent back to the browser.

Note that this translation occurs only once, the first time someone requests the JSP. After that, the servlet itself is run directly whenever a user requests the JSP.

Enough of the concept, now on to the code. When you create a JSP, you intermix special JSP elements with your normal HTML. You can include four types of JSP elements:

✦ **Directives:** A *directive* is an option setting that affects how the servlet is constructed from a JSP page. Directives let you do things such as specify what `import` statements the servlet requires, specify whether the servlet is thread-safe, and include other source files in the servlet.

✦ **Expressions:** An *expression* can be any Java expression. The expression is evaluated, converted to a string (if necessary) and the result is inserted into the document. Expressions assume the following form:

```
<%= expression %>
```

✦ **Scriptlets:** A *scriptlet* is a sequence of Java statements that are inserted directly into the servlet code generated for the JSP. You can do just about anything you want in a scriptlet, including `if` statements, looping, and calling other methods. You can even use `out.println` to add output to the page; the output is inserted in the page at the location where the scriptlet appears. Scriptlets have the following form:

```
<% statements %>
```

✦ **Declarations:** A *declaration* is Java code that is placed in the servlet class outside of any methods. You use declarations to create class variables or define methods that can be called by scriptlets or expressions. Declarations take on this form:

```
<%! statements %>
```

The remaining sections of this chapter show you how to create JSP pages that incorporate each of these elements.

Unfortunately, the current version of Tomcat (5.5.4) doesn't support the new features of Java 1.5 unless you jump through a bunch of extra configuration hoops. Because jumping through hoops can be dangerous, I avoid using Java 1.5 features in this chapter. Hopefully, the next version of Tomcat will work better with Java 1.5.

Using Page Directives

A *page directive* is a JSP element that sets options that determine how the JSP is converted to a servlet. The basic format of a page directive is this:

```
<%@ page attribute=value %>
```

The *attribute* can be any of the attributes listed in Table 3-1. (There are a few other attributes besides these, but they're rarely used.)

Table 3-1	Commonly Used Page Directive Attributes
Name	*Description*
import="package.class"	Adds an import statement to the servlet so you can use classes in other JSP elements without having to fully qualify them.
content-Type="MIME-type"	Lets you specify the type of document created by the servlet. The default is text/html. You rarely need to change this.
isThreadSafe="boolean"	If true, the servlet is assumed to be thread-safe. If false, implements SingleThreadModel is added to the servlet class declaration so that the thread runs in the single thread model. The default is true.
session="boolean"	If true, the servlet uses session management. The default is true.
buffer="size"	Specifies the size of the buffer used by the out variable. The default depends on the server, but is never smaller than 8K.
errorPage="URL"	Specifies the name of an error page that is displayed if this servlet throws an uncaught exception.
isErrorPage="boolean"	If true, this page is an error page for some other JSP page. The default is false.

**Book VII
Chapter 3**

**Using Java Server
Pages**

The page directive you use most is import, as it lets you import the packages for API classes so you can use them in expression, scriptlet, and declaration elements. For example, here's a page directive that imports the java.util package:

```
<%@ page import="java.util.*" %>
```

You can place page directives anywhere you want in a JSP document, but I suggest you place them at or near the top.

Using Expressions

A JSP *expression* is any Java expression that evaluates to a string. Actually, the expression doesn't have to evaluate directly. For example, here's how you can use the `java.util.Date` class to display the current date and time:

```
<%=new java.util.Date()%>
```

This expression creates a new instance of the `java.util.Date()` class, which represents the current date and time. The `toString()` method is implicitly called to convert this object to a string.

If you include a `page import` directive, you can omit the qualification on this expression. For example:

```
<%@ page import="java.util" %>
<%=new Date()%>
```

To do more interesting things with expressions, you can use *predefined variables,* which are also known as *implicit objects.* These are Java variables that are available to expressions, scriptlets, or declarations throughout a JSP page. Table 3-2 lists the JSP implicit objects you use most often.

Table 3-2	Implicit Objects
Name	*Description*
out	Used to write data to the response, equivalent to `response.getWriter()` in a servlet.
request	The request object, equivalent to the `request` parameter in the `doGet` or `doPost` method of a servlet.
response	The response object, equivalent to the `response` parameter in the `doGet` or `doPost` method of a servlet.
session	Used to manage sessions. Equivalent to `request.getSession()` in a servlet.

The implicit objects work the same as their corresponding objects do in servlets. For example, the `response` object is actually just the `response` parameter that's passed to the `doGet` or `doPost` method.

The implicit object you use most in expressions is the `request` object. In particular, you use its `getParameter` method to get values entered by the user in forms. For example, here's an expression that displays the value entered in an input field named `Name`:

```
<%= request.getParameter("Name")%>
```

The value of the Name field is inserted wherever this expression occurs in the JSP file. For example, here's a simple JSP named `InputJSP.jsp` that displays an input text box and a button. When the user clicks the button, whatever text he or she entered in the input field is displayed beneath the button:

```
<html>
  <head>
    <title>Input JSP</title>
  </head>
  <body>
    <form action="InputJSP.jsp" method="post">
      Enter some text: 
      <input type="text" name="Text">
      <br><br>
      <input type="submit" value="Submit">
    </form><br>
    <h3>You entered: 
    <%= request.getParameter("Text")%></h3>

  </body>
</html>
```

The HTML for this JSP defines a form that contains an input text field named `Text` and a Submit button. When the user clicks the Submit button, an HTTP POST request is sent to the server to request `InputJSP.jsp`. Any text entered by the user is sent along with the request. When the servlet is run, the text is retrieved by the expression `request.getParameter("Text")` and displayed beneath the button. Figure 3-1 shows this servlet in action.

**Book VII
Chapter 3**

**Using Java Server
Pages**

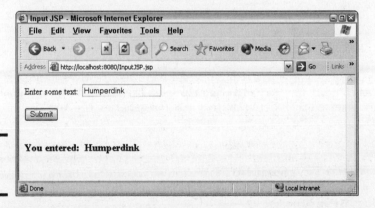

Figure 3-1:
InputJSP
in action.

Note: Expressions can also call methods that you add to the JSP with declaration elements. You see examples of how to do that later in this chapter, in the section "Using Declarations."

Using Scriptlets

A *scriptlet* is a statement or group of statements that's inserted directly into the servlet at the point where the `out.print` statements that create the surrounding HTML are generated. In short, scriptlets let you add your own code to the code that renders the page.

Scriptlets follow this basic form:

```
<% statements... %>
```

For example, here's a JSP named `DateJSP.jsp` that uses the `DateFormat` class to format the date and display it on the page:

```
<html>
   <%@ page import="java.text.*" %>
   <%@ page import="java.util.*" %>
   <head>
      <title>Date JSP</title>
   </head>
   <body>
      <h1>
         Today is
         <%
             DateFormat df = DateFormat.getDateInstance(
                 DateFormat.FULL);
             Date today = new Date();
             String msg = df.format(today);
             out.println(msg);
         %>
      </h1>
      <h1>Have a nice day!</h1>
   </body>
</html>
```

This JSP begins with a pair of `page import` directives to import the `java.text` and `java.util` packages. Then, the following Java statements are inserted right between the lines that generate the text `Today is` and `Have a nice day!`:

```
DateFormat df
    = DateFormat.getDateInstance(DateFormat.FULL);
Date today = new Date();
String msg = df.format(today);
out.println(msg);
```

These lines create a string variable named `msg`, and then use `out.println` to write the string to the response output. As a result, the formatted date is inserted between `<h1>Today is </h1>` and `<h1>Have a nice day! </h1>`. Figure 3-2 shows a page generated by this JSP.

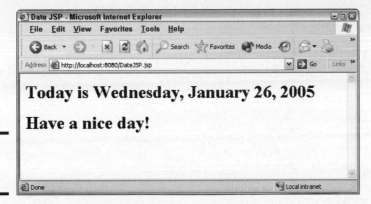

Today is Wednesday, January 26, 2005

Have a nice day!

Figure 3-2:
DateJSP
in action.

Note: Scriptlets don't have to add anything to the HTML output. In many cases, they perform functions such as writing information to a file. For example, suppose you have a JSP that gets data from a form that includes input text fields named `FirstName` and `LastName`. Suppose also that you have a class named `CustFile` with a static method named `writeCustomer` that accepts a first and last name as parameters and writes them to a file. Here's a scriptlet that gets the first and last names and calls the `writeCustomer` method to write the name to the customer file:

```
<% String firstName =
   request.getParameter("FirstName");
   String lastName = request.getParameter("LastName");
   CustFile.writeCustomer(firstName, lastName);
%>
```

If you want, you can get pretty tricky with scriptlets. No rule says you have to complete block statements such as `if` or `while` statements within a single scriptlet. If you leave a block open at the end of a scriptlet, any HTML that follows is generated by `out.print` statements that are included in the block. The only restriction is that you must eventually end the block with another scriptlet.

For example, here's a scriptlet named `LoopyJSP.jsp` that repeats a line 12 times on the page by including the line in the block of a `for` loop:

```
<html>
  <head>
    <title>Can't you see I'm trying to work here?</title>
  </head>
  <body>
    <% for (int i = 0; i < 12; i++)
       {
    %>
  All work and no play makes Jack a dull boy.<br>
    <%
       }
```

```
    %>
  </body>
</html>
```

If you run this scriptlet, the page appears as shown in Figure 3-3.

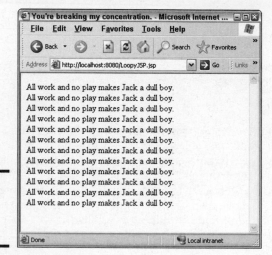

All work and no play makes Jack a dull boy.
All work and no play makes Jack a dull boy.
All work and no play makes Jack a dull boy.
All work and no play makes Jack a dull boy.
All work and no play makes Jack a dull boy.
All work and no play makes Jack a dull boy.
All work and no play makes Jack a dull boy.
All work and no play makes Jack a dull boy.
All work and no play makes Jack a dull boy.
All work and no play makes Jack a dull boy.
All work and no play makes Jack a dull boy.
All work and no play makes Jack a dull boy.

Figure 3-3:
LoopyJSP
.jsp doing
its thing.

Obviously, this sort of programming structure is prone to error. I suggest you avoid it whenever you can.

Using Declarations

A *declaration* is code that is included in the servlet but outside of any method. Declarations are used to create class variables or methods that can be used in expressions, scriptlets, or other declarations. Declarations follow this format:

```
<%! statements... %>
```

You can place declarations anywhere you want in a JSP.

Here's a servlet that declares a static class field named `count` that's incremented each time the page is displayed:

```
<html>
  <%@ page import="java.text.*" %>
  <%@ page import="java.util.*" %>

  <head>
    <title>Counter JSP</title>
  </head>
```

```
    <body>
      <h1>
        This JSP has been displayed <%= count++ %>
        time.</h1>
    </body>
</html>

<%!
private static int count = 1;
%>
```

In this servlet, the count variable is declared by the declaration element at the end of the JSP document:

```
<%!
private static int count = 1;
%>
```

Then, the expression in the body of the document displays and increments the count **variable:**

```
<%= count++ %>
```

When run, the JSP displays the number of times the page has been displayed since the server started.

Here's another example, this time declaring a method that's called in an expression:

```
<html>
  <%@ page import="java.text.*" %>
  <%@ page import="java.util.*" %>
  <head>
    <title>Date JSP</title>
  </head>
  <body>
    <h1>
      Today is <%= getDate() %></h1>
    <h1>Have a nice day!</h1>
  </body>
</html>

<%!
private String getDate()
{
    DateFormat df =
        DateFormat.getDateInstance(DateFormat.FULL);
    Date today = new Date();
    return df.format(today);
}
%>
```

The declaration at the end of this document declares a method that returns the current date as a string. Then, the expression `<%= getDate() %>` is used to insert the date into the document.

Using Classes

Most JSP applications are complicated enough that they need additional classes to keep their code manageable. For example, you want to create classes that handle the application's file or database I/O, and you may want to create classes to represent business objects such as `Products` or `Customers`.

Setting up Tomcat to work with classes can be a little tricky, but it's easy if you follow these simple guidelines:

✦ Contain all classes in packages. Choose a nice package name for your application, and then add a `package` statement to the beginning of each class file.

✦ Store the class files (not necessarily the source files) in the `WEB-INF\ classes\`*package*`\` directory beneath the directory the JSP pages are stored in. For example, if you're storing your JSP pages in `c:\tomcat\ webapps\ROOT\Movies` and the package name you're using is `movie`, save the class files in the following directory:

```
C:\tomcat\webapps\ROOT\Movies\WEB-INF\classes\movie
```

✦ If you prefer, you can save your class files in `c:\tomcat\shared\ classes\`*package*, where *package* is the name of your package. Then, the classes are available to any JSP or servlet.

✦ Any JSP that uses one of your classes has to include a page directive that imports the package. For example

```
<%@ page import="movie.*" %>
```

✦ Add the directory you saved the packages in to your ClassPath environment variable. Note that you want to add the directory that contains the packages, not the directory that contains the classes themselves. That's because the Java compiler uses the package name to find the package directory. So, if you put your classes in the `shared\classes` directory, you need to add `c:\tomcat\shared\classes` to your ClassPath.

To illustrate how a JSP can use classes, Figure 3-4 shows a JSP that lists the movies in the `movies.txt` file.

The JSP file that displayed this page is shown in Listing 3-1. The JSP file itself is stored in `c:\tomcat\webapps\ROOT`.

LISTING 3-1: LISTMOVIES.JSP

```
<!doctype html public "-//W3C//DTD HTML 4.0
Transitional//EN">
<%@ page import="movie.*" %>                              → 3
<%@ page import="java.util.*" %>
<html>
  <head>
    <title>List Movies: The Servlet</title>
  </head>
  <body>
    <h1>Some of My Favorites</h1>
    <h3>
      <%= getMovieList() %>                               → 12
    </h3>
  </body>
</html>

<%!
private String getMovieList()                             → 18
{
    String msg = "";
    ArrayList movies = MovieIO.getMovies();               → 21
    for (int i = 0; i < movies.size(); i++)               → 22
    {
        Movie m = (Movie)movies.get(i);                   → 24
        msg += m.year + ": ";
        msg += m.title + "<br>";
    }
    return msg;                                           → 28
}
%>
```

Following is an explanation of the key lines in this JSP:

→ 3   The JSP includes two page directives that import the `movie` and `java.util` packages.

→12   An expression is used to call the `getMovieList` method, which returns the list of movies to be displayed as a string.

→18   The `getMovieList` method is defined in a declaration.

→21   The `getMovies` method of the `MovieIO` class is called to retrieve an `ArrayList` that contains all the movies from the `movies.txt` file. Notice that I didn't specify a type for the `ArrayList` class. That's because Tomcat can't handle the syntax required for generic types without extra configuration work.

→**22** An old-fashioned `for` loop is used rather than an enhanced `for` loop to get the movies from the `ArrayList`. Again, this is to avoid using Java 1.5 features.

→**24** The `Movie` objects are retrieved from the `ArrayList` and the year and title is added to the `msg` string. Notice that the objects retrieved from the `ArrayList` must be cast to `Movie` objects.

→**28** The finished `msg` string is returned.

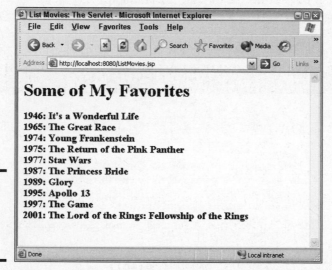

Figure 3-4:
The
ListMovies
JSP in
action.

Listing 3-2 shows the `Movie` class. There's nothing special to note here, other than the `package` statement that places the `Movie` class in the `movie` package. The class file that's compiled from this `.java` file is saved in `c:\tomcat\shared\classes\movie`.

LISTING 3-2: MOVIE.JAVA

```
package movie;

public class Movie
{
    public String title;
    public int year;
    public double price;

    public Movie(String title, int year, double price)
    {
```

```
        this.title = title;
        this.year = year;
        this.price = price;
    }
}
```

Finally, the `MovieIO` class is shown in Listing 3-3. This class reads the movies from a text file. For a detailed explanation of how this class works, jump forward to Book VIII, Chapter 2. Notice that this class, like the `Movie` class, includes a `package` statement that dumps the `MovieIO` class into the movie package. The class file compiled from this java file is saved in `c:\tomcat\shared\classes\movie`.

LISTING 3-3: MOVIEIO.JAVA

```
package movie;

import java.io.*;
import java.util.*;

public class MovieIO
{
    public static ArrayList<Movie> getMovies()
    {
        ArrayList<Movie> movies = new ArrayList<Movie>();
        BufferedReader in =
            getReader("g:\\data\\movies.txt");
        Movie movie = readMovie(in);
        while (movie != null)
        {
            movies.add(movie);
            movie = readMovie(in);
        }
        return movies;
    }

    private static BufferedReader getReader(String name)
    {
        BufferedReader in = null;
        try
        {
            File file = new File(name);
            in = new BufferedReader(
                new FileReader(file) );
        }
        catch (FileNotFoundException e)
        {
            System.out.println("The file doesn't exist.");
```

continued

LISTING 3-3 (CONTINUED)

```java
            System.exit(0);
        }
        catch (IOException e)
        {
            System.out.println("I/O Error");
            System.exit(0);
        }
        return in;
    }

    private static Movie readMovie(BufferedReader in)
    {
        String title;
        int year;
        double price;
        String line = "";
        String[] data;

        try
        {
            line = in.readLine();
        }
        catch (IOException e)
        {
            System.out.println("I/O Error");
            System.exit(0);
        }

        if (line == null)
            return null;
        else
        {
            data = line.split("\t");
            title = data[0];
            year = Integer.parseInt(data[1]);
            price = Double.parseDouble(data[2]);
            return new Movie(title, year, price);
        }
    }
}
```

Chapter 4: Using JavaBeans

In This Chapter

✔ **What is a JavaBean?**

✔ **Creating your own JavaBean classes**

✔ **Using JavaBeans in JSP pages**

✔ **Creating a simple shopping cart with session scope**

A *JavaBean* is a special type of Java class that you can use in several interesting ways to simplify program development. Some beans, such as Swing components, are designed to be visual components that you can use in a GUI editor to quickly build user interfaces. Other beans, known as *Enterprise JavaBeans*, are designed to run on special EJB servers and can run the data access and business logic for large Web applications.

In this chapter, I look at a more modest type of JavaBean that's designed to simplify the task of building Java Server Pages. In a nutshell, you can use the simple JavaBeans to build Java Server Pages without writing any Java code in the JSP itself. JavaBeans let you access Java classes by using special HTML-like tags in the JSP page.

What Is a JavaBean?

Simply put, a JavaBean is any Java class that conforms to the following rules:

✦ **It must have an empty constructor.** That is, a constructor that accepts no parameters. If the class doesn't have any constructors at all, it qualifies because the default constructor has no parameters. But if the class has at least one constructor that accepts one or more parameters, it must also have a constructor that has no parameters to qualify as a JavaBean.

✦ **It must have no `public` instance variables.** All the instance variables defined by the class must be either `private` or `protected`.

✦ **It must provide methods named `getProperty` and `setProperty` to get and set the value of any *properties* the class provides, except for boolean properties that use `isProperty` to get the property value.** The term *property* isn't really an official Java term. In a nutshell (or should it be, in a *beanpod*?), a property is any value of an object that can be retrieved by a `get` method (or an `is` method if the property is boolean) or set with a `set` method. For example, if a class has a property named `lastName`, it should use a method named `getLastName` to get the last name and `setLastName` to set the last name. Or, if the class has a `boolean` property named `taxable`, the method to set it is called `setTaxable`, and the method to retrieve it is `isTaxable`.

Note that a class doesn't have to have any properties to be a JavaBean, but if it does, the properties have to be accessed according to this naming pattern. Also, not all properties must have both a `get` and a `set` accessor. A *read-only property* can have just a `get` accessor, and a *write-only property* can have just a `set` accessor.

The property name is capitalized in the methods that access it, but the property name itself isn't. Thus, `setAddress` sets a property named `address`, not `Address`.

That's all there is to it. More advanced beans can also have other characteristics that allow them to have a visual interface so they can be used drag-and-drop style in an IDE. And some beans implement an interface that allows their state to be written to an output stream so they can be re-created later. But those features are optional; any class that meets the three criteria stated here is a bean and can be used as a bean in JSP pages.

You've already seen plenty of classes that have methods with names like `getCount` and `setStatus`. These names are part of a design pattern called the *Accessor pattern*, which is covered in Book III, Chapter 2. Thus, you've seen many examples of beans throughout this book, and you've probably written many bean classes yourself already.

Any class that conforms to this pattern is a bean. There's no `JavaBean` class you have to extend, nor is there a `Bean` interface you have to implement to be a bean. All a class has to do to be a bean is stick to the pattern.

Looking Over a Sample Bean

Listing 4-1 shows a sample JavaBean class named `Triangle` that calculates the Pythagorean Theorem, which calculates the long side of a right triangle if you know the length of the two short sides. This class defines three properties: `sideA` and `sideB` represent the two short sides of the triangle, and `sideC` represents the long side. The normal way to use this bean is to first use the `setSideA` and `setSideB` methods to set the `sideA` and `sideB` properties to the lengths of the short sides, and then use the `getSideC` method to get the length of the long side.

In case you can't remember way back to high school, the long side is equal to the square root of the first short side squared plus the second short side squared.

LISTING 4-1: THE TRIANGLE BEAN

```
package calculators;                                    → 1

public class Triangle
{
    private double sideA;                               → 5
    private double sideB;

    public Triangle()                                   → 8
    {
        this.sideA = 0.0;
        this.sideB = 0.0;
    }

    public String getSideA()                            → 14
    {
        return Double.toString(this.sideA);
    }

    public void setSideA(String value)                  → 19
    {
        try
        {
            this.sideA = Double.parseDouble(value);
        }
        catch (Exception e)
        {
            this.sideA = 0.0;
        }
    }

    public String getSideB()                            → 31
    {
        return Double.toString(this.sideB);
    }

    public void setSideB(String value)                  → 36
    {
        try
        {
            this.sideB = Double.parseDouble(value);
        }
        catch (Exception e)
        {
            this.sideB = 0.0;
```

Book VII
Chapter 4

Using JavaBeans

continued

LISTING 4-1 (CONTINUED)

```
        }
    }

    public String getSideC()                           → 48
    {
        if (sideA == 0.0 || sideB == 0.0)
            return "Please enter both sides.";
        else
        {
            Double sideC;
            sideC = Math.sqrt(
                (sideA * sideA) + (sideB * sideB));
            return Double.toString(sideC);
        }
    }
}
```

The following paragraphs point out the highlights of this bean class:

→ **1** As with most servlet classes, this bean is part of a package. In this case, the package is named `calculators`. (I'm assuming that if you need a bean to calculate the Pythagorean Theorem, you probably want other beans to calculate derivatives, prime numbers, Demlo numbers, and the like. You can put those beans in this package too.)

→ **5** This class uses a pair of instance variables to keep track of the two short sides. As per the rules for JavaBeans, these instance variables are declared as `private`.

→ **8** A constructor with no parameters is declared. (Strictly speaking, this constructor doesn't have to be explicitly coded here, because the default constructor does the trick, and the two instance variables are initialized to their default values of zero automatically.)

→**14** The `getSideA` method returns the value of the `sideA` property as a string.

→**19** The `setSideA` method lets you set the value of the `sideA` property with a string. This method uses a `try/catch` statement to catch the exceptions that are thrown if the string can't be parsed to a `double`. If the string is invalid, the `sideA` property is set to zero.

→**31** The `getSideB` method returns the value of the `sideB` property as a string.

→**36** The `setSideB` method sets the value of the `sideB` property from a string. Again, a `try/catch` statement catches any exceptions and sets the property to zero if the string can't be parsed to a `double`.

→**48** The `getSideC` method calculates the length of the long side, and then returns the result as a string. However, if either of the values is zero, the method assumes that the user hasn't entered any data, so it returns an error message instead. (That's a reasonable assumption, because none of the sides of a triangle can be zero.) Notice that there is no `setSideC` method. As a result, `sideC` is a read-only property.

TIP

For an interesting anecdote about the Pythagorean Theorem and *The Wizard of Oz*, refer to Book III, Chapter 2.

Using Beans with JSP Pages

To work with a bean in a JSP page, you add special tags to the page to create the bean, set its properties, and retrieve its properties. Table 4-1 lists these tags, and the following sections describe the details of using each one.

Table 4-1	JSP Tags for Working with Beans
Tag	*Description*
`<jsp:useBean id="name" class="package.class" />`	Establishes a reference to the bean and creates an instance if necessary. The name specified in the `id` attribute is used by the other tags to refer to the bean.
`<jsp:getProperty name="name" property="property" />`	Retrieves the specified property from the bean identified by the `name` attribute.
`<jsp:setProperty name="name" property="property" value="value" />`	Sets the specified property to the value specified in the `value` attribute.
`<jsp:setProperty name="name" property="property" param="parameter" />`	Sets the specified property to the value of the parameter specified in the `param` attribute. The `parameter` is usually the name of a form field.
`<jsp:setProperty name="name" property="* " />`	Sets all the properties defined by the bean to corresponding parameter values, provided a parameter with the correct name exists.

**Book VII
Chapter 4**

Using JavaBeans

Creating bean instances

To include a bean in a JSP page, you add a special `jsp:useBean` tag to the page. In its simplest form, this tag looks like this:

```
<jsp:useBean id="name" class="package.Class" />
```

The `id` attribute provides the name that you use elsewhere in the JSP to refer to the bean, and the `class` attribute provides the name of the class, qualified with the package name. For example, here's a `jsp:useBean` tag to use the `Triangle` bean:

```
<jsp:useBean id="triangle" class="calculators.Triangle"
   />
```

The `jsp:useBean` tag creates an instance of the bean by calling the empty constructor if an instance doesn't already exist. However, if the bean already exists, the existing instance is used instead.

Here are a few additional things you should know about the `jsp:useBean` tag:

✦ The `jsp:useBean` tag can appear anywhere in the JSP document, but it must appear before any other tag that refers to the bean.

✦ This and all bean tags are case sensitive, so be sure to code them exactly as shown. `<jsp:usebean.../>` won't work.

✦ If Tomcat complains that it can't find your bean when you run the JSP, double-check the package and class name — they're case sensitive too — and make sure the bean is stored in a directory under `WEB-INF\classes` that's named the same as the package. For example, store the `Triangle` bean's class file in `WEB-INF\classes\calculators`.

✦ The `jsp:useBean` element can have a body that contains `jsp:setProperty` tags that initialize property values. Then, the element is formed more like normal HTML, with proper start and end tags. For example:

```
<jsp:useBean id="t1" class="calculators.Triangle" >
 <jsp:setProperty name="t1" property="sideA"
   value="3.0" >
  <jsp:setProperty name="t1" property="sideB"
   value="3.0" >
</jsp:useBean>
```

Don't worry about the details of the `jsp:setProperty` tags just yet. Instead, just make a note that they're executed only if a new instance of the bean is actually created by the `jsp:useBean` tag. If an instance of the bean already exists, the `jsp:setProperty` tags are not executed.

✦ The `jspuseBean` tag also has a `scope` attribute, which I explain later in this chapter, in the section "Scoping Your Beans."

Getting property values

To get the value of a bean's property, you use the `jsp:getProperty` tag. The form of this tag is straightforward:

```
<jsp:getProperty name="name" property="property" />
```

For example, here's a tag that gets the `sideC` property from the `Triangle` bean created in the previous section:

```
<jsp:getProperty name="triangle" property="sideC" />
```

The `name` attribute must agree with the value you specify in the `id` attribute in the `jsp:useBean` tag that created the bean. And the `property` attribute is used to determine the name of the getter method — in this case, `getSideC`.

Remember to begin the property name with a lowercase letter. If you specify `property="SideC"`, you get an error message from the server when you run the page.

In most cases, you use `jsp:getProperty` to insert the value of a property into a page. However, you can also use it to specify the value of an attribute for some other tag in the JSP document. For example:

```
<input type="text" name="sideA"
        value="<jsp:getProperty name="triangle"
                      property="sideA" />" >
```

Here, the value of the `sideA` property is retrieved and used for the `value` attribute of an input field named `sideA`. As a result, when this input field is sent to the browser, its initial value is the value from the `Triangle` bean.

Be extra careful to match up the quotation marks and the open and close brackets for the tags. In this example, the entire `jsp:getProperty` tag is enclosed within the quotation marks that indicate the value of the input field's `value` attribute. The right bracket that appears at the very end closes the input element itself.

Setting property values

To set a property value, you can use one of several variations of the `jsp:setProperty` tag. If you want to set the property to a literal string, you write the tag like this:

```
<jsp:setProperty name="triangle"
                 property="sideA"
                 value="4.0" />
```

Here, the `name` attribute must match up to the `id` attribute from the `jsp:useBean` tag that created the bean, the `property` attribute is used to determine the name of the setter method (in this case, `setSideA`), and the `value` attribute provides the value to be set.

I put this tag on three lines only because it's too long to fit within the margins of this page on one line. In actual practice, most JSP developers string these tags out on a single line unless they get *really* long, which doesn't happen often.

Although this form of the `jsp:setProperty` tag is useful, the `param` form is more useful. It lets you set the property to the value entered by the user into a form field or passed to the JSP by way of a query string. For example, if your JSP contains a form that has an input field named `FirstSide`, you can assign that field's value to the `sideA` property like this:

```
<input type="text" name="FirstSide" >
<jsp:setProperty name="triangle"
                 property="sideA"
                 param="FirstSide" />
```

Here, if the user enters a value into the `FirstSide` field, that value is assigned to the bean's `sideA` property.

In the previous example, I purposely used a name other than `sideA` for the input field so you wouldn't be confused by the fact that the `property` and `param` attributes specify the same value. In actual practice, you usually give the input field the same name as the property it's associated with, like this:

```
<input type="text" name="sideA" >
<jsp:setProperty name="triangle"
                 property="sideA"
                 param="sideA" />
```

If your input fields have names that are identical to the property names, you can assign all of them to their corresponding properties with one tag, like this:

```
<jsp:setProperty name="triangle" property="*" />
```

Here, the asterisk (*) in the `property` attribute indicates that all properties that have names identical to form fields (or query string parameters) are automatically assigned. For forms that have a lot of fields, this form of the `jsp:setProperty` tag can save you a lot of coding.

A JSP page that uses a bean

So that you can see how these tags work together, Listing 4-2 shows a complete JSP page that uses the bean that was presented in Listing 4-1. This page displays two text input fields and a button. When the user enters the lengths of a triangle's two short sides in the fields and clicks the button, the page displays the `sideC` property of the bean to show the length of the third side. Figure 4-1 shows how this page appears when it is run.

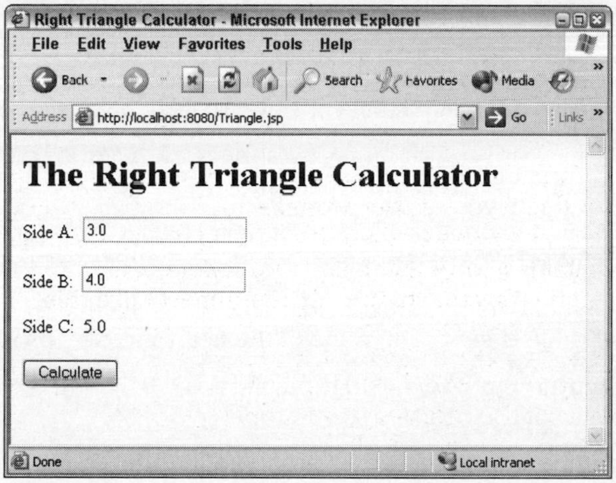

Book VII
Chapter 4

Using JavaBeans

Figure 4-1:
The
Triangle.jsp
page
displayed in
a browser.

LISTING 4-2: THE TRIANGLE.JSP PAGE

```
<html>
<jsp:useBean id="triangle"                              → 2
    class="calculators.Triangle" />
<jsp:setProperty name="triangle" property="*" />        → 4
  <head>
    <title>Right Triangle Calculator</title>
  </head>
  <body>
    <h1>The Right Triangle Calculator</h1>
    <form action="Triangle.jsp" method="post">          → 10
    Side A: 
    <input type="text" name="sideA"                     → 12
        value="<jsp:getProperty
                    name="triangle"
                    property="sideA" />" >
    <br><br>
    Side B: 
    <input type="text" name="sideB"                     → 18
        value="<jsp:getProperty
                    name="triangle"
                    property="sideB" />" >
    <br><br>
    Side C: 
    <jsp:getProperty name="triangle"                    → 24
        property="sideC" />
    <br><br>
    <input type="submit" value="Calculate" >            → 27
  </form>
  </body>
</html>
```

The following paragraphs explain the key lines in this JSP:

→ **2** The `jsp:useBean` tag creates an instance of the `calculators.Triangle` bean and names it `triangle`.

→ **4** The `jsp:setProperty` tag sets the `sideA` and `sideB` properties to the corresponding input fields named `sideA` and `sideB`.

→ **10** The `form` tag creates a form that posts back to the same JSP file using the HTTP POST method.

→ **12** The first of two input text fields. This one is named `sideA`, and its initial value is set to the value of the bean's `sideA` property.

→ **18** The second input text field is named `sideB`. Its initial value is set to the value of the bean's `sideB` property.

→ **24** This line is where the `sideC` property is retrieved, thus calculating the length of side C of the triangle based on the length of sides A and B. The result is simply inserted into the document.

→ **27** The Submit button submits the form so the `Triangle` bean can do its thing.

Scoping Your Beans

The *scope* of a JavaBean indicates how long the bean is kept alive. You specify the scope by using the `scope` attribute on the `jsp:useBean` tag. The `scope` attribute can have any of the four values listed in Table 4-2.

Table 4-2	Scope Settings
Scope	*Explanation*
page	The bean is associated with the current page. This means that every time the user requests the page, a new bean is created. Then, when the page is sent back to the browser, the bean is destroyed. Thus, each round trip to the server creates a new instance of the bean.
request	Similar to `page`, but the bean is available to other pages that are processed by the same request. This scope is useful for applications that use several different servlets or JSPs for a single request.
session	The bean is associated with a user's session. The first time the user requests a page from the application, a bean is created and associated with the user. Then, the same bean is used for other subsequent requests by the same user.
application	A single copy of the bean is used by all users of the application.

The default scope is `page`, which means that the bean is created and destroyed each time the user requests a new page. However, `session` scope can be very useful for Web applications that need to keep track of information about a user from one page to the next. The best known example of that is a shopping cart, in which a user can select items he or she wants to purchase. The contents of the shopping cart can be kept in a session bean.

A shopping cart application

Figure 4-2 shows a simple shopping cart application in which the user has the option to purchase three of my recent books by clicking one of the three buttons. When the user clicks a button, an item is added to the shopping cart. If the user has already added the book to the cart, the quantity is increased by one. In the figure, the user has clicked the button for *Networking All-in-One Desk Reference For Dummies* twice and *Networking For Dummies* once.

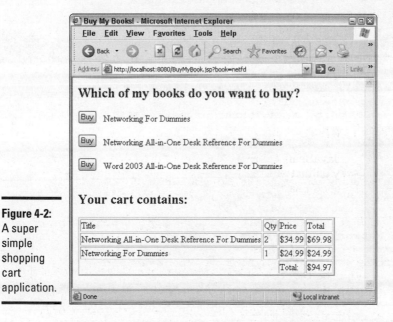

Figure 4-2:
A super
simple
shopping
cart
application.

The following paragraphs describe the key techniques that make this shopping cart work:

✦ The shopping cart itself is a JavaBean that has just two public methods: `setBook`, which adds a book to the shopping cart, and `getList`, which returns a string that shows the shopping cart items nicely formatted in an HTML table.

✦ The shopping cart class contains an inner class that represents a `Book` object. To keep the application simple, the `Book` class has the three titles hard-coded into it. In a real shopping cart program, you use a file or database instead of hard-coding these values.

✦ The list of products that appears at the top of the page is actually three separate forms, one for each product. Each of these forms specifies a parameter passed via a query string to the JSP on the server. The name of this parameter is `book`, and its value is the code of the book the user ordered. This parameter is bound to the `book` property of the shopping cart bean, so when the user clicks one of the buttons, the `setBook` method is called with the value passed via the `book` parameter. That's how the shopping cart knows which book the user ordered.

✦ Beneath the list of books, the JSP uses a `jsp:getProperty` tag to get the `list` property, which displays the shopping cart.

The shopping cart page

Listing 4-3 shows the JSP for the shopping cart page.

LISTING 4-3: BUYMYBOOK.JSP

```
<html>
<jsp:useBean id="cart" class="books.BookCart"           → 2
    scope="session"/>
<jsp:setProperty name="cart" property="*" />            → 4
  <head>
    <title>Buy My Books!</title>
  </head>
  <body>
    <h1>Which of my books do you want to buy?</h1>
    <form action="BuyMyBook.jsp?book=netfd"             → 10
        method="post">
      <input type="submit" value="Buy" >  
      Networking For Dummies<br><br>
    </form>
    <form action="BuyMyBook.jsp?book=netaio"            → 15
        method="post">
      <input type="submit" value="Buy" >  
      Networking All-in-One Desk Reference For Dummies
      <br><br>
    </form>
    <form action="BuyMyBook.jsp?book=wordaio"           → 21
        method="post">
      <input type="submit" value="Buy" >  
      Word 2003 All-In-One Desk Reference For Dummies
      <br><br>
    </form>
    <br><h2>Your cart contains:</h2>
    <jsp:getProperty name="cart" property="list" />     → 28
  </body>
</html>
```

The following paragraphs describe the JSP's most important lines:

→ **2** The `jsp:useBean` tag loads the `books.BookCart` JavaBean, specifying that it has session scope. Thus, the bean isn't deleted after each page is requested. Instead, the user works with the same bean instance for his or her entire session.

→ **4** The parameter properties are set. The first time the user displays the `BuyMyBook.jsp` page, there are no parameters, so this method doesn't do anything. But when the user clicks one of the three form buttons, a `book` parameter is added to the end of the URL that's posted to the server, so the cart's `setBook` method is called. This causes one copy of the selected book to be added to the cart.

→ **10** This is the form for the first book. Each book has its own form, with a Submit button labeled "Buy" and a book title. The `action` attribute specifies that when the Submit button is clicked, the form is posted to `BuyMyBook.jsp` with the `book` parameter set to `netfd`.

→ **15** The second book form. This one specifies `netaio` as the `book` parameter value.

→ **21** The form for the third book. This one specifies `wordaio` as the value of the `book` parameter.

→ **28** After the forms for each of the books, a `jsp:getProperty` tag calls the `getList` method of the bean. This returns a string that contains an HTML table that displays the current contents of the shopping cart.

The BookCart JavaBean

Now that you've seen the JSP for the shopping cart application, take a look at the Java code for the `BookCart` bean. It's shown in Listing 4-4.

LISTING 4-4: THE BOOKCART JAVABEAN

```
package books;                                              → 1

import java.util.ArrayList;
import java.text.NumberFormat;

public class BookCart
{
    private ArrayList<Book> cart;                           → 8

    private NumberFormat cf
        = NumberFormat.getCurrencyInstance();

    public BookCart()                                       → 13
    {
        cart = new ArrayList<Book>();
```

continued

LISTING 4-4 (CONTINUED)

```
    }

    public void setBook(String code)                          → 18
    {
        boolean found = false;
        for (Book b : cart)
            if (b.getCode().equals(code))
            {
                b.addQuantity(1);
                found = true;
            }
        if (!found)
            cart.add(new Book(code));
    }

    public String getList()                                    → 31
    {
        String list = "<table border=2>";
        list +="<tr><td>Title</td><td>Qty</td>"
            + "<td>Price</td><td>Total</td></tr>";
        double total = 0.0;
        for (Book b : cart)
        {
            list += "<tr><td>" + b.getTitle() + "</td>"
                + "<td>" + b.getQuantity()  + "</td>"
                + "<td>" + cf.format(b.getPrice()) + "</td>"
                + "<td>" + cf.format(b.getTotal()) + "</td>"
                + "</tr>";
            total += b.getTotal();
        }
        list +="<tr><td></td><td></td><td>Total:</td>"
            + "<td>" + cf.format(total) + "</td></tr>";
        list += "</table>";
        return list;
    }

    private class Book                                         → 52
    {
        private String code;                                   → 54
        private int quantity;

        public Book(String code)                               → 57
        {
            this.code = code;
            this.quantity = 1;
        }

        public String getCode()                                → 63
        {
            return this.code;
        }

        public String getTitle()                               → 68
        {
            if (code.equals("netfd"))
```

```
            return "Networking For Dummies";
        else if (code.equals("netaio"))
            return "Networking All-in-One Desk "
                + "Reference For Dummies";
        else if (code.equals("wordaio"))
            return "Word 2003 All-in-One Desk "
                + "Reference For Dummies";
        else
            return "Unknown book";
    }

    public double getPrice()                                → 82
    {
        if (code.equals("netfd"))
            return 24.99;
        else if (code.equals("netaio"))
            return 34.99;
        else if (code.equals("wordaio"))
            return 29.99;
        else
            return 0.0;
    }

    public int getQuantity()                                → 94
    {
        return this.quantity;
    }

    public void addQuantity(int qty)                        → 99
    {
        this.quantity += qty;
    }

    public double getTotal()                                → 104
    {
        return this.quantity * this.getPrice();
    }
    }
}
```

The following paragraphs describe the bean's high points:

→ **1** The BookCart class lives in the books package.

→ **8** The shopping cart itself is kept inside the BookCart bean as a private array list of Book items.

→**13** To be a JavaBean, you need a no-parameter constructor. This one simply initializes the cart array list.

→**18** The setBook method is called to add a book to the shopping cart. The book's code is passed as a parameter. This method first looks at all the books in the array list to see if the user has already added a book with this code. If so, that book's addQuantity method is called to increase the order quantity for that book by 1. If not, a new book with the specified code is created and added to the cart.

→ **31** This method builds a string that contains all the books in the cart presented as an HTML table. If you're not familiar with HTML tables, all you really need to know is that the `<tr>` and `</tr>` tags mark the start and end of each row, and the `<td>` and `</td>` tags mark the start and end of each cell within the row. The table includes one row for each book in the cart. Each row contains cells for the title, quantity, price, and total. If you compare the code in this method with the actual table shown in Figure 4-2, you can get an idea of the HTML that's actually created by this method.

Notice also that the loop that builds each table row keeps a running total for the entire shopping cart, which is displayed in a separate row at the bottom of the table. Also, a row of headings is displayed at the start of the table.

→ **52** The `Book` class is defined as an inner class so it can represent books in the array list.

→ **54** The `Book` class only stores two items of information for each book: the book code and the quantity, which represents the number of books ordered by the user. The other values are calculated by the methods that return them.

→ **57** The constructor accepts a book code and initializes the instance fields. Notice that the quantity is initialized to 1.

→ **63** The `getCode` method simply returns the `code` variable.

→ **68** The `getTitle` method returns one of three book titles depending on the code. If the code is not one of the three pre-defined codes, `Unknown book` is returned.

→ **82** Likewise, the `getPrice` method returns one of three prices depending on the code. If the code is not one of the three allowable codes, the book is free!

→ **94** The `getQuantity` method just returns the `quantity` variable.

→ **99** The `addQuantity` method adds a value to the `quantity` variable.

→**104** The `getTotal` method calculates the total by multiplying the price by the quantity.

Book VIII

Files and Databases

The 5th Wave   By Rich Tennant

@RICHTENNANT

"I couldn't get this 'job skills' program to work on my PC, so I replaced the mother-board, upgraded the BIOS and wrote a program that links it to my personal database. It told me I wasn't technically inclined and should pursue a career in sales."

Contents at a Glance

Chapter 1: Working with Files

In This Chapter

✔ Examining the `File` class

✔ Understanding command-line parameters

✔ Introducing the `JFileChooser` class

*I*n this chapter, you discover the ins and outs of working with files and directories. I don't show you how to read or write files, but you do find out how to find files on the disk, how to create, delete, or rename files, and how to work with directories. You find out how to use the Swing file chooser dialog box that lets you add filing capabilities to Swing applications. And finally, you find out how to retrieve parameters from the command line, a useful technique because command-line parameters are often used to pass file information to console programs.

Using the File Class

The `File` class is your key to processing files and directories. A `File` object represents a single file or directory. Note that the file or directory doesn't actually have to exist on disk. Instead, the `File` object represents a file that may or may not actually exist.

Java uses a single class to represent both files and directories because a directory is actually nothing more than a special type of file. I suppose the designers of Java could have created a separate `Directory` class to represent directories, but using one class to represent both has its advantages.

The `File` class is in the `java.io` package, so any program that uses it should import `java.io.File` or `java.io.*`.

Table 1-1 lists the main constructors and methods of the `File` class.

Table 1-1	The File Class
Constructor	*Description*
`File(String pathname)`	Creates a file with the specified pathname.
Field	*Description*
`String separator`	The character used to separate components of a pathname on this system; usually \ or /.
Method	*Description*
`boolean canRead()`	Determines whether the file can be read.
`boolean canWrite()`	Determines whether the file can be written.
`boolean createNewFile()`	Creates the file on disk if it doesn't already exist. Returns `true` if the file was created, `false` if the file already existed. Throws `IOException`.
`boolean delete()`	Deletes the file or directory. Returns `true` if the file was successfully deleted.
`boolean exists()`	Returns `true` if the file exists on disk, `false` if the file doesn't exist on disk.
`String getCanonicalPath()`	Returns the complete path to the file, including the drive letter if run on a Windows system. Throws `IOException`.
`String getName()`	Gets the name of this file.
`String getParent()`	Gets the name of the parent directory of this file or directory.
`File getParentFile()`	Gets a `File` object representing the parent directory of this file or directory.
`boolean isDirectory()`	Returns `true` if this `File` object is a directory, `false` if it is a file.
`boolean isFile()`	Returns `true` if this `File` object is a file, `false` if it is a directory.
`boolean isHidden()`	Returns `true` if this file or directory is marked by the operating system as hidden.
`long lastModified()`	Returns the time the file was last modified, expressed in milliseconds since 0:00:00 AM, January 1, 1970.
`long length()`	Returns the size of the file in bytes.
`String[] list()`	Returns an array of `String` objects with the name of each file and directory in this directory. Each string is a simple filename, not a complete path. If this `File` object is not a directory, returns `null`.
`File[] listFiles()`	Returns an array of `File` objects representing each file and directory in this directory. If this `File` object is not a directory, returns `null`.

Method	Description
`static File[] listRoots()`	Returns an array that contains a `File` object for the root directory of every file system available on the Java runtime. Unix systems usually have just one root, but Windows systems have a root for each drive.
`boolean mkdir()`	Creates a directory on disk from this `File` object. Returns `true` if the directory was successfully created.
`boolean mkdirs()`	Creates a directory on disk from this `File` object, including any parent directories that are listed in the directory path but don't already exist. Returns `true` if the directory was successfully created.
`boolean renameTo(File dest)`	Renames the `File` object to the specified destination `File` object. Returns `true` if the rename was successful.
`boolean setLastModified (long time)`	Sets the last modified time for the `File` object. Returns `true` if the time was successfully set.
`boolean setReadOnly()`	Marks the file as read-only. Returns `true` if the file was successfully marked.
`String toString()`	Returns the pathname for this file or directory as a string.

Creating a File object

To create a `File` object, you call the `File` constructor, passing a string representing the filename of the file as a parameter. For example:

```
File f = new File("hits.log");
```

Here, the file's name is `hits.log,` and it lives in the current directory, which is usually the directory from which the Java Virtual Machine was started.

If you don't want the file to live in the current directory, you can supply a complete pathname in the parameter string. However, you're now entering one of the few areas of Java that becomes system-dependent, because the way you write pathnames depends on the operating system you're using. For example, `c:\logs\hits.log` is a valid pathname for Windows systems, but not on Unix or Macintosh systems, which don't use drive letters and use forward slashes instead of backslashes to separate directories.

If you hard-code pathnames as string literals, remember that the backslash character is the escape character for Java strings. Thus, you must code two slashes to get one slash into the pathname. For example, you must code the path `c:\logs\hits.log` like this:

```
String path = "c:\\logs\\hits.log";
```

**Book VIII
Chapter 1**

Working with Files

Creating a file

Creating a `File` object doesn't create a file on disk. Instead, it creates an in-memory object that represents a file or directory that may or may not actually exist on disk. To find out if the file or directory exists, you can use the `exists` method. For example:

```
File f = new File(path);
if (!f.exists())
    System.out.println("The input file does not
        exist!");
```

Here, an error message is displayed on the console if the file doesn't exist.

To create a new file on disk, first create a `File` object with the filename you want to use. Then, use the `createNewFile` method, like this:

```
File f = new File(path);
if (f.createNewFile())
    System.out.println("File created.");
else
    System.out.println("File could not be created.");
```

Note that the `createNewFile` method returns a boolean that indicates whether or not the file was successfully created. If the file already exists, `createNewFile` returns `false`, so you don't have to use the `exists` method before you call `createNewFile`.

When you create a file with the `createNewFile` method, the file doesn't have anything in it. If you actually want the file to contain data, you can use the classes I describe in the next chapter to write information to the file.

Getting information about a file

Several of the methods of the `File` class simply return information about a file or directory. For example, you can find out if the `File` object represents a file or directory by calling its `isDirectory` or `isFile` method. Other methods let you find out if a file is read-only or hidden, or retrieve the file's age and when it was last modified.

You can get the name of the file represented by a `File` object in several popular ways:

✦ To get just the filename, use the `getName` method. This method returns a string that includes just the filename, not the complete path.

✦ To get the path that was specified to create the `File` object, (such as `\logs\hit.log`), use the `toString` method instead.

✦ To get the full path for a file — that is, the complete path including the drive letter (for Windows systems) and all the directories and subdirectories leading to the file — use the `getCannonicalPath` method. This method removes any system-dependent oddities such as relative paths, dots (which represent the current directory), and double-dots (which represent the parent directory) to get the file's actual path.

Getting the contents of a directory

A directory is a file that contains a list of other files or directories. Because a directory is just a special type of file, it is represented by an object of the `File` class. You can tell if a particular `File` object is a directory by calling its `isDirectory` method. If this method returns `true`, the `File` is a directory. You can then get an array of all the files contained in the directory by calling the `listFiles` method.

For example, the following code snippet lists the name of every file in a directory whose pathname is stored in the String variable path:

```
File dir = new File(path);
if (dir.isDirectory())
{
    File[] files = dir.listFiles();
    for (File f : files)
        System.out.println(f.getName());
}
```

The following snippet is a little more selective: It lists only files, not subdirectories, and it doesn't list hidden files:

```
File dir = new File(path);
if (dir.isDirectory())
{
    File[] files = dir.listFiles();
    for (File f : files)
    {
        if (f.isFile() && !f.isHidden())
            System.out.println(f.getName());
    }
}
```

Directory listings are especially well suited to recursive programming because each `File` object returned by the `listFiles` method may be another directory that itself has a list of files and directories. For an explanation of recursive programming along with an example that lists directories recursively, see Book V, Chapter 4.

Renaming files

You can rename a file by using the `renameTo` method. This method uses another `File` object as a parameter that specifies the file you want to rename the current file to. It returns a boolean value that indicates whether or not the file was successfully renamed.

For example, the following statements change the name of a file named `hits.log` to `savedhits.log`:

```
File f = new File("hits.log");
if (f.renameTo(new File("savedhits.log")))
    System.out.println("File renamed.");
else
    System.out.println("File not renamed.");
```

Depending on the capabilities of the operating system, the `renameTo` method can also move a file from one directory to another. For example, this code moves the file `hits.log` from the folder `logs` to the folder `savedlogs`:

```
File f = new File("logs\\hits.log");
if (f.renameTo(new File("savedlogs\\hits.log")))
    System.out.println("File moved.");
else
    System.out.println("File not moved.");
```

Always test the return value of the `renameTo` method to make sure the file was successfully renamed.

Deleting a file

To delete a file, create a `File` object for the file, and then call the `delete` method. For example:

```
File f = new File("hits.log");
if (f.delete())
    System.out.println("File deleted.");
else
    System.out.println("File not deleted.");
```

If the file is a directory, the directory must be empty to be deleted.

With some recursive programming, you can create a method that deletes a non-empty directory. The method looks something like this:

```
private static void deleteFile(File dir)
{
    File[] files = dir.listFiles();
    for (File f : files)
    {
```

```
        if (f.isDirectory())
            deleteFile(f);
        else
            f.delete();
        }
        dir.delete();
    }
```

Then, to delete a folder named `folder1` along with all its files and subdirectories, call the `deleteFile` method:

```
deleteFile(new File("folder1");
```

This feature is extremely dangerous to add to a program! Don't use it without first carefully testing it. If you accidentally delete all the files on your hard drive, don't blame me.

Using Command-Line Parameters

Ever since Book I, Chapter 1, I've used this construction in every Java program presented so far:

```
public static void main(String[] args)
```

It's high time you find out what the `args` parameter of the `main` method is used for. The `args` parameter is an array of strings that lets you access any command-line parameters that are specified by the user when he or she runs your program.

For example, suppose you run a Java program named Test from a command program like this:

```
C:\>java Test the quick brown fox
```

In this case, the Java program is passed four parameters: the, quick, brown, and fox. You can access these parameters via the `args` array.

Suppose the `main` method of the `Test` class is written like this:

```
public static void main(String[] args)
{
    for (String s : args)
        System.out.println(s);
}
```

Then, the program displays the following output on the console when run with the command shown a few paragraphs back:

```
the
quick
brown
fox
```

Command-line parameters are useful in Java programs that work with files as a way to pass pathnames to the program. For example, here's a program that lists all the files in a directory passed to the program as a parameter:

```
import java.io.*;

public class ListDirectory
{
    public static void main(String[] args)
    {
        String path = args[0];
        File dir = new File(path);
        if (dir.isDirectory())
        {
            File[] files = dir.listFiles();
            for (File f : files)
            {
                System.out.println(f.getName());
            }
        }
        else
            System.out.println("Not a directory.");
    }
}
```

Choosing Files in a Swing Application

For the most part, you don't want to mess around with command-line parameters in Swing applications. Instead, you want to use the JFileChooser class to let users pick the files they want to work with. This class lets you display Open and Save dialog boxes similar to the ones you've seen in other GUI applications with just a few lines of code.

For example, Figure 1-1 shows an Open dialog box created with just these two lines of code:

```
JFileChooser fc = new JFileChooser();
int result = fc.showOpenDialog(this);
```

This code appears in a frame class that extends the JFrame class, so the this keyword in the showOpenDialog call refers to the parent frame.

Figure 1-1:
An Open
dialog box
displayed
by the JFile
Chooser
class.

The result returned by the `showOpenDialog` method indicates whether the user chose to open a file or click Cancel. And the `JFileChooser` class provides a handy `getSelectedFile` method you can use to get a `File` object for the file selected by the user.

The important thing to remember about the `JFileChooser` class is that it doesn't actually open or save the file selected by the user. Instead, it just returns a `File` object for the file the user selects. Your program then has the task of opening or saving the file.

Of course, the `JFileChooser` class has many additional methods you can use to tailor its appearance and behavior just about any way imaginable. Table 1-2 lists the commonly used constructors and methods of this powerful class.

Table 1-2	The JFileChooser Class
Constructor	*Description*
`JFileChooser()`	Creates a file chooser that begins at the user's default directory. On Windows systems, this is usually My Documents.
`JFileChooser(File file)`	Creates a file chooser that begins at the location indicated by the file parameter.
`JFileChooser(String path)`	Creates a file chooser that begins at the location indicated by the path string.

(continued)

Table 1-2 *(continued)*

Method	Description
`void addChoosableFileFilter (FileFilter filter)`	Adds a file filter to the chooser.
`File getSelectedFile()`	Returns a `File` object for the file selected by the user.
`File[] getSelectedFiles()`	Returns an array of `File` objects for the files selected by the user if the file chooser allows multiple selections.
`void setAcceptAllFileFilterUsed (boolean value)`	If false, removes the All Files filter from the file chooser.
`void setApproveButtonText (String text)`	Sets the text for the Approve button.
`void setDialogTitle(String title)`	Sets the title displayed by the file chooser dialog box.
`void setFileHidingEnabled (boolean value)`	If true, hidden files are not shown.
`void setMultiSelectionEnabled (boolean value)`	If true, the user can select more than one file.
`int showDialog(Component parent, String text)`	Displays a custom dialog with the specified text for the Accept button. The return values are `JFileChooser.CANCEL_OPTION`, `APPROVE_OPTION`, and `ERROR_OPTION`.
`void setFileSelectionMode (int mode)`	Determines whether the user can select files, directories, or both. The parameter can be specified as `JFileChooser.FILES_ONLY`, `DIRECTORIES_ONLY`, or `FILES_AND_DIRECTORIES`.
`int showOpenDialog(Component parent)`	Displays an Open dialog box. The return values are the same as for the `showDialog` method.
`int showSaveDialog(Component parent)`	Displays a Save dialog box. The return values are the same as for the `showDialog` method.

Creating an Open dialog box

As you've just seen, you can create an Open dialog box with just a few lines of code. First, you call the `JFileChooser` constructor to create a `JFileChooser` instance. Then, you call the `showOpenDialog` method to display an Open dialog box.

If you don't pass a parameter to the constructor, the file chooser starts in the user's default directory, which on most systems is the operating system's current directory. If you want to start in some other directory, you have two options:

✦ You can create a `File` object for the directory, and then pass the `File` object to the constructor.

✦ You can just pass the pathname for the directory you want to start in to the constructor.

The `JFileChooser` class also includes methods that let you control the appearance of the chooser dialog box. For example, you can use the `setDialogTitle` method to set the title (the default is `Open`), and you can use the `setFileHidingEnabled` method to control whether or not hidden files are shown. If you want to allow the user to select more than one file, use the `setMultiSelectionEnabled` method.

A `setFileSelectionMode` method lets you specify whether users can select files, directories, or both. The options for this method need a little explanation:

✦ **`JFileChooser.FILES_ONLY`:** With this option, which is the default, the user can only choose files with the file chooser dialog box. The user can navigate through directories in the file chooser dialog box, but can't actually select a directory.

✦ **`JFileChooser.DIRECTORIES_ONLY`:** With this option, the user can select only directories, not files. One common use for this option is to let the user choose a default location for files used by your application without actually opening a file.

✦ **`JFileChooser.FILES_AND_DIRECTORIES`:** This option lets the user select either a file or a directory. For most applications, you want the user to pick either a file or a directory, but not both. So you probably won't use this option much.

In addition to an Open dialog box, you can also display a Save dialog box by calling the `showSaveDialog` method. A Save dialog box is similar to an Open dialog box, but has different default values for the title and the text shown on the Approve button. Otherwise, these dialog boxes work pretty much the same.

Getting the selected file

The file chooser dialog box is a *modal* dialog box, which means that after you call the `showOpenDialog` method, your application is tied up until the user closes the file chooser dialog box by clicking the Open or Cancel buttons.

You can find out which button the user clicked by inspecting the value returned by the showOpenDialog method:

✦ If the user clicked Open, this value is JFileChooser.APPROVE_OPTION.

✦ If the user clicked Cancel, the return value is JFileChooser.CANCEL_OPTION.

✦ If an I/O or other error occurs, the return value is JFileChooser.ERROR_OPTION.

Assuming the showOpenDialog method returns APPROVE_OPTION, you can then use the getSelectedFile method to get a File object for the file selected by the user. Then, you can use this File object elsewhere in the program to read or write data.

Putting it all together, then, here's a method that displays a file chooser dialog box and returns a File object for the file selected by the user. If the user cancels or an error occurs, null is returned:

```
private File getFile()
{
    JFileChooser fc = new JFileChooser();
    int result = fc.showOpenDialog(null);
    File file = null;
    if (result == JFileChooser.APPROVE_OPTION)
        file = fc.getSelectedFile();
    return file;
}
```

You can call this method from an action event handler when the user clicks a button, selects a menu command, or otherwise indicates that he or she wants to open a file.

Using file filters

The file chooser dialog box includes a Files of Type drop-down list *filter* that the user can choose to control what types of files are displayed by the chooser. By default, the only item available in this drop-down list is All Files, which doesn't filter the files at all. If you want to add another filter to this list, you must first create a class that extends the FileFilter abstract class. Then, you pass an instance of this class to the addChoosableFileFilter method.

Table 1-3 lists the methods of the FileFilter class. Fortunately, it has only two methods you need to implement. This class is in the javax.swing.filechooser package.

For some reason, the Java designers gave this class the same name as an interface that's in the `java.io` package, which is also frequently used in applications that work with files. As a result, you need to fully qualify this class when you extend it, like this:

```
class JavaFilter
    extends javax.swing.filechooser.FileFilter
```

Table 1-3	The FileFilter Class
Method	*Description*
`public boolean abstract accept(File f)`	You must implement this method to return `true` if you want the file displayed in the chooser, `false` if you don't want the file displayed.
`public String abstract getDescription()`	You must implement this method to return the description string that is displayed in the Files of Type drop-down list in the chooser dialog box.

The `getDescription` method simply returns the text displayed in the Files of Type drop-down list. You usually implement it with a single return statement that returns the description. For example:

```
public String getDescription()
{
    return "Java files (*.java)";
}
```

Here, the string `Java files (*.java)` is displayed in the Files of Type drop-down list.

The `accept` method does the work of a file filter. The file chooser calls this method for every file it displays. The file is passed as a parameter. The `accept` method returns a boolean that indicates whether or not the file is displayed.

The `accept` method can use any criteria it wants to decide which files to accept and which files to reject. Most filters do it based on the file extension part of the filename. Unfortunately, the `File` class doesn't have a method that returns the file extension. But you can get the name with the `getName` method, and then use the `matches` method with a regular expression to determine if the file is of the type you're looking for. For example, here's an `if` statement that determines whether the filename in the `name` variable is a java file:

```
if (name.matches(".*\\.java"))
```

Here, the regular expression matches strings that begin with any sequence of characters and end with `.java`. (For more information about regular expressions, refer to Book V, Chapter 3.)

Here's a complete file filter class that displays files with the extension .java:

```
private class javaFilter
    extends javax.swing.filechooser.FileFilter
{
    public boolean accept(File f)
    {
        if (f.isDirectory())
            return true;
        String name = f.getName();
        if (name.matches(".*\\.java"))
            return true;
        else
            return false;
    }

    public String getDescription()
    {
        return "Java files (*.java)";
    }
}
```

After you create a class that implements a file filter, you can add the file filter to the file chooser by calling the addChoosableFileFilter method, passing a new instance of the file filter class:

```
fc.setChoosableFileFilter(new JavaFilter());
```

If you want, you can remove the All Files filter by calling the method setAcceptAllFileFilterUsed, like this:

```
fc.setAcceptAllFileFilterUsed(false);
```

Then, only file filters you add to the file chooser appear in the Files of Type drop-down list.

Chapter 2: Using File Streams

1/O, I/O, it's off to work I go.

Or so goes the classic song, which pretty much sums up the whole purpose of computers. Without I/O, computers — and the programs that run on them — would be worthless.

Imagining any useful computer program that doesn't do some form of I/O is hard. Even the very first program presented in this book — the classic Hello, World! program — does I/O: It displays a simple message on-screen.

In this chapter, you find out about Java's most fundamental technique for getting data into and out of programs: streams. You've been working with streams all along in this book. When you use the `System.out.print` or `System.out.println` method to display text on the console, you're actually sending data to an output stream. And when you use a `Scanner` object to get data from `System.in`, you're reading data from an input stream.

In this chapter, you build on what you already know about stream I/O and see how it can be used to read and write data to disk files.

Understanding Streams

A *stream* is simply a flow of characters to and from a program. The other end of the stream can be anything that can accept or generate a stream of characters, including a console window, a printer, a file on a disk drive, or even another program.

Streams have no idea of the structure or meaning of your data; a stream is just a sequence of characters. In later chapters in Book VIII, you find out how to work with data at a higher level, by using databases and XML.

You can roughly divide the world of Java stream I/O into two camps:

✦ **Character streams:** *Character streams* read and write text characters that represent strings. You can connect a character stream to a text file to store text data on disk. Typically, text files use special characters called *delimiters* to separate elements of the file. For example:

  • A *comma-delimited file* uses commas to separate individual fields of data.

  • A *tab-delimited file* uses tabs to separate fields.

  You can usually display a text file in a text editor and make some sense of its contents.

✦ **Binary streams:** *Binary streams* read and write individual bytes that represent primitive data types. You can connect a binary stream to a *binary file* to store binary data on disk. The contents of a binary file makes perfect sense to the programs that read and write them. However, if you try to open a binary file in a text editor, the file's contents look like gibberish.

Conceptually, the trickiest part of understanding how streams work is getting your mind around all the different classes. Java has more than 60 classes for working with streams. Fortunately, you only need to know about a few of them for most file I/O applications. In the rest of this chapter, I tell you about the most important classes for working with character and binary streams.

All the classes in this chapter are in the `java.io` package. So programs that work with file streams include an `import java.io.*` statement.

Reading Character Streams

To read a text file through a character stream, you usually work with the following classes:

✦ **`File`:** The `File` class, which is covered in detail in the preceding chapter, represents a file on disk. In file I/O applications, the main purpose of the `File` class is to identify the file you want to read from or write to.

✦ **`FileReader`:** The `FileReader` class provides basic methods for reading data from a character stream that originates from a file. It provides methods that let you read data one character at a time. You won't usually work directly with this class. Instead, you create a `FileReader` object to connect your program to a file, and then pass that object to the constructor of the `BufferedReader` class, which provides more efficient access to the file. (This class extends the abstract class `Reader`, which is the base class for a variety of different classes that can read character data from a stream.)

✦ **BufferedReader:** This class "wraps" around the `FileReader` class to provide more efficient input. This class adds a *buffer* to the input stream that allows the input to be read from disk in large chunks rather than one byte at a time. This can result in a huge improvement in performance. The `BufferedReader` class lets you read data one character at a time or a line at a time. In most programs, you read data one line at a time, and then use Java's string-handling features to break the line into individual fields.

Table 2-1 lists the most important constructors and methods of these classes.

Table 2-1	The BufferedReader and FileReader Classes
Constructors	*Description*
`BufferedReader (Reader in)`	Creates a buffered reader from any object that extends the `Reader` class. Typically, you pass this constructor a `FileReader` object.
`FileReader(File file)`	Creates a file reader from the specified `File` object. Throws `FileNotFoundException` if the file doesn't exist or if it is a directory rather than a file.
`FileReader(String path)`	Creates a file reader from the specified pathname. Throws `FileNotFoundException` if the file doesn't exist or if it is a directory rather than a file.
Methods	*Description*
`void close()`	Closes the file. Throws `IOException`.
`int read()`	Reads a single character from the file and returns it as an integer. Returns −1 if the end of the file has been reached. Throws `IOException`.
`String readLine()`	Reads an entire line and returns it as a string. Returns `null` if the end of the file has been reached. Throws `IOException`.
`void skip(long num)`	Skips ahead the specified number of characters.

In the following sections, you find out how to read a file named `movies.txt` that contains one line for ten of my favorite movies. Each line of the file contains the title of the movie, a tab, the year the movie was released, another tab, and the price I paid for it at the video store. Here's the contents of the file:

```
It's a Wonderful Life⇨1946⇨14.95
The Great Race⇨1965⇨12.95
Young Frankenstein⇨1974⇨16.95
The Return of the Pink Panther⇨1975⇨11.95
Star Wars⇨1977⇨17.95
The Princess Bride⇨1987⇨16.95
Glory⇨1989⇨14.95
```

**Book VIII
Chapter 2**

Using File Streams

```
Apollo 13⇨1995⇨19.95
The Game⇨1997⇨14.95
The Lord of the Rings: The Fellowship of the Ring⇨
    2001⇨19.95
```

(In this list, the arrows represent tab characters.) Later in this chapter, I show you a program that writes data to this file.

If you create this file with a text editor, make sure your text editor correctly preserves the tabs.

Creating a BufferedReader

The normal way to connect a character stream to a file is to create a File object for the file using one of the techniques presented in the preceding chapter. Then, you can call the FileReader constructor to create a FileReader object and pass this object to the BufferedReader constructor to create a BufferedReader object. For example:

```
File f = new File("movies.txt");
BufferedReader in = new BufferedReader(
                new FileReader(f));
```

Here, a BufferedReader object is created to read the movies.txt file.

Reading from a character stream

To read a line from the file, you use the readLine method of the BufferedReader class. This method returns null when the end of the file is reached. As a result, testing the string returned by the readLine method in a while loop to process all the lines in the file is common.

For example, this code snippet reads each line from the file and prints it to the console:

```
String line = in.readLine();
while (line != null)
{
    System.out.println(line);
    line = in.readLine();
}
```

After you read a line of data from the file, you can use Java's string handling features to pull out the individual bits of data from the line. In particular, you can use the split method to separate the line into the individual strings that are separated by tabs. Then, you can use the appropriate parse methods (such as parseInt and parseDouble) to convert each string to its correct data type.

For example, here's a routine that converts a line read from the `movies.txt` file to the title (a string), year (an `int`), and price (a `double`):

```
String[] data = line.split("\t");
String title = data[0];
int year = Integer.parseInt(data[1]);
double price = Double.parseDouble(data[2]);
```

After the entire file is read, you can close the stream by calling the `close` method:

```
in.close();
```

Reading the movies.txt file

Listing 2-1 shows a complete, albeit simple, program that reads the `movies.txt` file and prints the contents of the file to the console.

LISTING 2-1: READING FROM A TEXT FILE

```
import java.io.*;                                        → 1
import java.text.NumberFormat;

public class ReadFile
{
    public static void main(String[] args)
    {
        NumberFormat cf = NumberFormat.getCurrencyInstance();

        BufferedReader in = getReader("movies.txt");     → 10

        Movie movie = readMovie(in);                     → 12
        while (movie != null)                            → 13
        {
            String msg = Integer.toString(movie.year);
            msg += ": " + movie.title;
            msg += " (" + cf.format(movie.price) + ")";
            System.out.println(msg);
            movie = readMovie(in);
        }
    }                                                    → 21

    private static BufferedReader getReader(String name) → 23
    {
        BufferedReader in = null;
        try
        {
            File file = new File(name);
            in = new BufferedReader(
                new FileReader(file) );
        }
        catch (FileNotFoundException e)
        {
```

continued

LISTING 2-1 (CONTINUED)

```
            System.out.println("The file doesn't exist.");
            System.exit(0);
        }
        catch (IOException e)
        {
            System.out.println("I/O Error");
            System.exit(0);
        }
        return in;
    }

    private static Movie readMovie(BufferedReader in)          → 45
    {
        String title;
        int year;
        double price;
        String line = "";
        String[] data;

        try
        {
            line = in.readLine();
        }
        catch (IOException e)
        {
            System.out.println("I/O Error");
            System.exit(0);
        }

        if (line == null)
            return null;
        else
        {
            data = line.split("\t");
            title = data[0];
            year = Integer.parseInt(data[1]);
            price = Double.parseDouble(data[2]);
            return new Movie(title, year, price);
        }
    }

    private static class Movie                                 → 75
    {
        public String title;
        public int year;
        public double price;

        public Movie(String title, int year, double price)
        {
            this.title = title;
            this.year = year;
            this.price = price;
        }
    }
}
```

If you run this program, the following output is displayed on the console:

```
1946: It's a Wonderful Life ($14.95)
1965: The Great Race ($12.95)
1974: Young Frankenstein ($16.95)
1975: The Return of the Pink Panther ($11.95)
1977: Star Wars ($17.95)
1987: The Princess Bride ($16.95)
1989: Glory ($14.95)
1995: Apollo 13 ($19.95)
1997: The Game ($14.95)
2001: The Lord of the Rings: The Fellowship of the Ring
     ($19.95)
```

Because I've already explained most of this code, the following paragraphs provide just a roadmap to this program:

→ **1** The program begins with import java.io.* to import all the Java I/O classes used by the program.

→**10** The program uses a method named getReader to create a BufferedReader object that can read the file. The name of the file is passed to this method as a parameter. Note that in a real program, you'd probably get this filename from the user via a JFileChooser dialog box or some other means. In any event, the BufferedReader object returned by the getReader method is saved in a variable named in.

→**12** Another method, named readMovie, is used to read each movie from the file. This method returns a Movie object — Movie is a private class that's defined later in the program. If the end of the file has been reached, this method returns null.

→**13** A while loop is used to process each movie. This loop simply builds a message string from the Movie object, displays it on the console, and then calls readMovie to read the next movie in the file.

→**21** The program ends without closing the file. That's okay, though, because the file is closed automatically when the program that opened it ends. If the program were to go on with other processing after it was finished with the file, you'd want to close the file first.

→**23** The getReader method creates a BufferedReader object for the filename passed as a parameter. If any exceptions are thrown while trying to create the BufferedReader, the program exits.

→**45** The readMovie method reads a line from the reader passed as a parameter, parses the data in the line, creates a Movie object from the data, and returns the Movie object. If the end of the file is reached, this method returns null. The statement that reads the line from the file is enclosed in a try/catch block that exits the program if an I/O error occurs.

→**75** The `Movie` class is a private inner class that defines the movie objects. To keep the class simple, it uses public fields and a single constructor that initializes the fields.

Writing Character Streams

The usual way to write data to a text file is to use the `PrintWriter` class, which as luck has it you're already familiar with: It's the same class that provides the `print` and `println` methods used to write console output. As a result, the only real trick to writing output to a text file is figuring out how to connect a print writer to a text file. To do that, you work with three classes:

✦ **`FileWriter`:** The `FileWriter` class connects to a `File` object but provides only rudimentary writing ability.

✦ **`BufferedWriter`:** This class connects to a `FileWriter` and provides output buffering. Without the buffer, data is written to disk one character at a time. This class lets the program accumulate data in a buffer and writes the data only when the buffer is filled up or when the program requests that the data be written.

✦ **`PrintWriter`:** This class connects to a `Writer`, which can be a `BufferedWriter`, a `FileWriter`, or any other object that extends the abstract `Writer` class. Most often, you connect this class to a `BufferedWriter`.

The `PrintWriter` class is the only one of these classes whose methods you usually use when you write data to a file. Table 2-2 lists the most important constructors and methods of this class.

Table 2-2	The PrintWriter, BufferedWriter, and FileWriter Classes
Constructors	*Description*
`PrintWriter(Writer out)`	Creates a print writer for the specified output writer.
`PrintWriter(Writer out, boolean flush)`	Creates a print writer for the specified output writer. If the second parameter is true, the buffer is automatically flushed whenever the `println` method is called.
`BufferedWriter(Writer out)`	Creates a buffered writer from the specified writer. Typically, you pass this constructor a `FileWriter` object.
`FileWriter(File file)`	Creates a file writer from the specified `File` object. Throws `IOException` if an error occurs.
`FileWriter(File file, boolean append)`	Creates a file writer from the specified `File` object. Throws `IOException` if an error occurs. If the second parameter is true, data is added to the end of the file if the file already exists.

Constructors	Description
`FileWriter(String path)`	Creates a file writer from the specified pathname. Throws `IOException` if an error occurs.
`FileWriter(String path, boolean append)`	Creates a file writer from the specified pathname. Throws `IOException` if an error occurs. If the second parameter is true, data is added to the end of the file if the file already exists.

PrintWriter Methods	Description
`void close()`	Closes the file.
`void flush()`	Writes the contents of the buffer to disk.
`int read()`	Reads a single character from the file and returns it as an integer. Returns -1 if the end of the file has been reached. Throws `IOException`.
`void print(value)`	Writes the value, which can be any primitive type or any object. If the value is an object, the object's `toString()` method is called.
`void println(value)`	Writes the value, which can be any primitive type or any object. If the value is an object, the object's `toString()` method is called. A line break is written following the value.

Connecting a PrintWriter to a text file

To connect a character stream to an output file, you first create a `File` object for the file as I describe in the preceding chapter. Then, you call the `PrintWriter` constructor to create a `PrintWriter` object you can use to write to the file. This constructor wraps around a `BufferedWriter` object, which in turn wraps around a `FileWriter` object like this:

```
File file = new File("movies.txt");
PrintWriter out =
    new PrintWriter(
        new BufferedWriter(
            new FileWriter(file) ) );
```

If you find this a little confusing, that's good! That makes me feel a little better, because I find it a little confusing too. The basic idea going on here is that each of the classes is adding a capability to the class it wraps. At the bottom is the `FileWriter` class, which has the ability to write characters to a file. The `BufferedWriter` class adds buffering to the mix, saving data in a buffer until it makes sense to write it all out to the file in one big spurt. And the `PrintWriter` class adds basic formatting capabilities, like adding line endings at the end of each line and converting primitive types to strings.

Both the `FileWriter` and the `PrintWriter` classes have an optional `boolean` parameter you can use to add extra capabilities to the file stream.

If you specify `true` in the `FileWriter` constructor, the file is *appended* if it exists. That simply means that any data in the file is retained; data you write to the file in your program is simply added on to the end of the file. Here's a `PrintWriter` constructor that appends data to its file:

```
File file = new File("movies.txt");
PrintWriter out =
    new PrintWriter(
        new BufferedWriter(
            new FileWriter(file, true )))// append mode
```

If you specify `false` instead of `true`, or if you leave this parameter out altogether, an existing file is deleted, and its data is lost.

The `boolean` parameter in the `PrintWriter` class has less dire consequences. It simply tells the `PrintWriter` class that it should tell the `BufferedWriter` class to flush its buffer whenever you use the `println` method to write a line of data. Although this option might decrease the efficiency of your program by a small amount, it also makes the program a little more reliable because it reduces the odds of losing data because your program or the whole computer crashes while unwritten data is in the buffer.

Unfortunately, the code for specifying this option looks a little goofy because of the way the constructors for the `BufferedWriter` and `FileWriter` classes are nested:

```
File file = new File("movies.txt");
PrintWriter out =
    new PrintWriter(
        new BufferedWriter(
            new FileWriter(file) ), true); ////mode flush
```

If all these nested constructors make your head spin, you can always construct each object separately and use variables to keep track of them. Here's an example that does that, and turns on append mode for the `FileWriter` and flush mode for the `PrintWriter`:

```
FileWriter fw = new FileWriter(file, true);
BufferedWriter bw = new BufferedWriter(fw);
PrintWriter out = new PrintWriter(bw, true);
```

If you find this coding technique easier to understand, by all means use it.

Writing to a character stream

After you successfully connect a character stream to a file, writing data to it is as easy as writing text to the console. You just use the `print` and `println` methods exactly as if you're writing to the console.

One minor complication is that if you're writing data to a text file in a delimited format, you have to include statements that write the delimiter characters to the file. For example, suppose the title and year for a movie you want to write to the text file are stored in String variables named `title` and `year`. This snippet of code writes these fields with a tab delimiter between them:

```
System.out.print(title);
System.out.print("\t");
System.out.println(year);
```

Here, the last item to be written is written with the `println` method rather than the `print` method. That ends the current line.

If you prefer to be a little more efficient, you can build a string representing the entire line, and then write the line all at once:

```
String line = title + "\t" + year;
System.out.println(line);
```

This way is a little more efficient than the previous version, but not as much as you'd think. In most cases, the `BufferedWriter` holds your text in a buffer until the `println` method is called anyway.

If you didn't specify the flush option when you created the `PrintWriter` object, you can still periodically force any data in the buffer to be written to disk by calling the `flush` method:

```
out.flush();
```

Also, when you're finished writing data to the file, you can close the file by calling the `close` method:

```
out.close();
```

Writing the movies.txt file

Listing 2-2 shows a complete program that writes lines to a text file. The data written is taken from an array that's hard-coded into the file, but you can easily imagine how to obtain the data from the user by prompting for console input or using text fields in a Swing application.

**Book VIII
Chapter 2**

Using File Streams

LISTING 2-2: WRITING TO A TEXT FILE

```
import java.io.*;

public class WriteFile
{
    public static void main(String[] args)                    → 5
```

continued

LISTING 2-2 (CONTINUED)

```java
    {
        Movie[] movies = getMovies();

        PrintWriter out = openWriter("movies.txt");
        for (Movie m : movies)
            writeMovie(m, out);
        out.close();
    }

    private static Movie[] getMovies()                        → 15
    {
        Movie[] movies = new Movie[10];

        movies[0] = new Movie("It's a Wonderful Life", 1946, 14.95);
        movies[1] = new Movie("The Great Race", 1965, 12.95);
        movies[2] = new Movie("Young Frankenstein", 1974, 16.95);
        movies[3] = new Movie("The Return of the Pink Panther", 1975,
            11.95);
        movies[4] = new Movie("Star Wars", 1977, 17.95);
        movies[5] = new Movie("The Princess Bride", 1987, 16.95);
        movies[6] = new Movie("Glory", 1989, 14.95);
        movies[7] = new Movie("Apollo 13", 1995, 19.95);
        movies[8] = new Movie("The Game", 1997, 14.95);
        movies[9] = new Movie("The Lord of the Rings: The Fellowship
            of the Ring", 2001, 19.95);

        return movies;
    }

    private static PrintWriter openWriter(String name)        → 40
    {
        try
        {
            File file = new File(name);
            PrintWriter out =
                new PrintWriter(
                    new BufferedWriter(
                        new FileWriter(file) ), true );
            return out;
        }
        catch (IOException e)
        {
            System.out.println("I/O Error");
            System.exit(0);
        }
        return null;
    }

    private static void writeMovie(Movie m,                   → 58
        PrintWriter out)
    {
        String line = m.title;
        line += "\t" + Integer.toString(m.year);
        line += "\t" + Double.toString(m.price);
        out.println(line);
```

```
    }

    private static class Movie                                    → 67
    {
        public String title;
        public int year;
        public double price;

        public Movie(String title, int year, double price)
        {
            this.title = title;
            this.year = year;
            this.price = price;
        }
    }
}
```

Because all the coding elements in this program have already been explained in this chapter, the following paragraphs just provide a roadmap to the major part of the program:

→ **5** The `main` method begins by calling a method named `getMovies`, which returns an array of `Movie` objects to be written to the file. (The `Movie` class is defined as an inner class later in the program.) Then, it calls `openWriter`, which creates a `PrintWriter` object the program can use to write data to the file. Next, it uses an enhanced `for` loop to call the `writeMovie` method for each movie in the array. This method accepts a `Movie` object that contains the movie to be written and a `PrintWriter` object to write the movie to. Finally, the `PrintWriter` is closed.

→ **15** The `getMovies` method returns an array of `Movie` objects that are written to a file. In a real-life program, you probably do something other than hard-code the movie information in this method. For example, you might prompt the user to enter the data or use a Swing frame to get the data.

→ **40** The `openWriter` method creates a `PrintWriter` object for the filename passed to it as a parameter. The `PrintWriter` uses a buffer that's flushed each time `println` is called.

→ **58** The `writeMovie` method accepts as parameters a `Movie` object to be written and the `PrintWriter` the movie should be written to. It creates a string that includes the title, a tab, the year, another tab, and the price. Then, it writes the string to the file.

→ **67** The `Movie` class is an inner class that defines a movie object. This class simply consists of three public fields (title, year, and price) and a constructor that initializes the fields.

Reading Binary Streams

Binary streams are a bit tougher to read than character streams, but not much. The biggest obstacle to pass when you're reading a binary stream is that you need to know exactly the type of each item that was written to the file. If any incorrect data is in the file, the program won't work. So you need to ensure the file contains the data your program expects it to contain.

To read a binary file, you usually work with the following classes:

✦ **File:** Once again, you use the `File` class to represent the file itself.

✦ **FileInputStream:** The `FileInputStream` is what connects the input stream to a file.

✦ **BufferedInputStream:** This class adds buffering to the basic `FileInputStream`, which improves the stream's efficiency and gives it a moist and chewy texture.

✦ **DataInputStream:** This is the class you actually work with to read data from the stream. The other `Stream` classes read a byte at a time. This class knows how to read basic data types, including primitive types and strings.

Table 2-3 lists the vital constructors and methods of these classes.

Table 2-3	The BufferedReader and FileReader Classes
Constructors	*Description*
`BufferedInputStream (InputStream in)`	Creates a buffered input stream from any object that extends the `InputStream` class. Typically, you pass this constructor a `FileInputStream` object.
`DataInputStream (InputStream in)`	Creates a data input stream from any object that extends the `InputStream` class. Typically, you pass this constructor a `BufferedInputStream` object.
`FileInputStream (File file)`	Creates a file input stream from the specified `File` object. Throws `FileNotFoundException` if the file doesn't exist or if it is a directory rather than a file.
`FileInputStream (String path)`	Creates a file input stream from the specified pathname. Throws `FileNotFoundException` if the file doesn't exist or if it is a directory rather than a file.
DataInputStream Methods	*Description*
`boolean readBoolean()`	Reads a `boolean` value from the input stream. Throws `EOFException` and `IOException`.
`byte readByte()`	Reads a `byte` value from the input stream. Throws `EOFException` and `IOException`.
`char readChar()`	Reads a `char` value from the input stream. Throws `EOFException` and `IOException`.

DataInputStream Methods	Description
`double readDouble()`	Reads a `double` value from the input stream. Throws `EOFException` and `IOException`.
`float readFloat()`	Reads a `float` value from the input stream. Throws `EOFException` and `IOException`.
`int readInt()`	Reads an `int` value from the input stream. Throws `EOFException` and `IOException`.
`long readLong()`	Reads a `long` value from the input stream. Throws `EOFException` and `IOException`.
`short readShort()`	Reads a `short` value from the input stream. Throws `EOFException` and `IOException`.
`String readUTF()`	Reads a string stored in UTF format from the input stream. Throws `EOFException`, `IOException`, and `UTFDataFormatException`.

The following sections present programs that read and write data in a binary file named `movies.dat` that contains information about movies. Each record in this file consists of a UTF string containing the movie's title, an `int` representing the year the movie was released, and a `double` representing the price I paid for the movie at my local discount video store. Although the format of this file is different than the `movies.txt` file shown earlier in this chapter, the file contains the same data. You can refer to the earlier section "Reading Character Streams" to see a listing of the movies in this file.

Creating a DataInputStream

To read data from a binary file, you want to connect a `DataInputStream` object to an input file. To do that, you use a `File` object to represent the file, a `FileInputStream` object that represents the file as an input stream, a `BufferedInputStream` object that adds buffering to the mix, and finally a `DataInputStream` object to provide the methods that read various data type. The constructor for such a beast looks like this:

```
File file = new File("movies.dat");
DataInputStream in = new DataInputStream(
      new BufferedInputStream(
        new FileInputStream(file) ) );
```

If all the nesting makes you nauseous, you can do it this way instead:

```
File file = new File("movies.dat");
FileInputStream fs = new FileInputStream(file);
BufferedInputStream bs = new BufferedInputStream(fs);
DataInputStream in = new DataInputStream(bs);
```

Either way, the effect is the same.

Reading from a data input stream

With binary files, you don't read an entire line into the program and parse it into individual fields. Instead, you use the various read methods of the `DataInputStream` class to read the fields one at a time. To do that, you have to know the exact sequence in which data values appear in the file.

For example, here's a code snippet that reads the information for a single movie and stores the data in variables:

```
String title = in.readUTF();
int year = in.readInt();
double price = in.readDouble();
```

Note that the read methods all throw `EOFException` if the end of the file is reached and `IOException` if an I/O error occurs. So you need to call these methods inside a `try/catch` block that catches these exceptions. The `readUTF` method also throws `UTFDataFormatException`, but that exception is a type of `IOException`, so you probably don't need to catch it separately.

The read methods are usually used in a `while` loop to read all the data from the file. When the end of the file is reached, `EOFException` is thrown. You can then catch this exception and stop the loop. One way to do that is to use a `boolean` variable to control the loop:

```
boolean eof = false;
while (!eof)
{
    try
    {
        String title = in.readUTF();
        int year = in.readInt();
        double price = in.readDouble();
        // do something with the data here
    }
    catch (EOFException e)
    {
        eof = true;
    }
    catch (IOException e)
    {
        System.out.println("An I/O error has
            occurred!");
        System.exit(0);
    }
}
```

Here, the `boolean` variable eof is set to `true` when `EOFException` is thrown, and the loop continues to execute as long as eof is `false`.

After you read a line of data from the file, you can use Java's string handling features to pull out the individual bits of data from the line. In particular, you can use the `split` method to separate the line into the individual strings that are separated by tabs. Then, you can use the appropriate parse methods to parse each string to its correct data type.

For example, here's a routine that converts a line read from the `movies.txt` file to the title (a string), year (an `int`), and price (a `double`):

```
String[] data = line.split("\t");
String title = data[0];
int year = Integer.parseInt(data[1]);
double price = Double.parseDouble(data[2]);
```

After the entire file has been read, you can close the stream by calling the `close` method:

```
in.close();
```

This method also throws `IOException`, so you want to place it inside a `try`/`catch` block.

Reading the movies.dat file

Now that you've seen the individual elements of reading data from a binary file, Listing 2-3 presents a complete program that uses these techniques. This program reads the `movies.dat` file, creates a `Movie` object for each title, year, and price value, and prints a line on the console for the movie. If you run this program, the output looks exactly like the output from the text file version presented earlier in this chapter, in the section "Reading the movies.txt file."

LISTING 2-3. READING FROM A BINARY FILE

```
import java.io.*;
import java.text.NumberFormat;

public class ReadBinaryFile
{
    public static void main(String[] args)                    → 6
    {
        NumberFormat cf = NumberFormat.getCurrencyInstance();

        DataInputStream in = getStream("movies.dat");

        boolean eof = false;
        while (!eof)
        {
            Movie movie = readMovie(in);
            if (movie == null)
```

Book VIII
Chapter 2

Using File Streams

continued

LISTING 2-3 (CONTINUED)

```
                eof = true;
            else
            {
                String msg = Integer.toString(movie.year);
                msg += ": " + movie.title;
                msg += " (" + cf.format(movie.price) + ")";
                System.out.println(msg);
            }
        }
        closeFile(in);
    }
    private static DataInputStream getStream(String name)          → 28
    {
        DataInputStream in = null;
        try
        {
            File file = new File(name);
            in = new DataInputStream(
                    new BufferedInputStream(
                        new FileInputStream(file) ) );
        }
        catch (FileNotFoundException e)
        {
            System.out.println("The file doesn't exist.");
            System.exit(0);
        }
        catch (IOException e)
        {
            System.out.println("I/O Error creating file.");
            System.exit(0);
        }
        return in;
    }

    private static Movie readMovie(DataInputStream in)             → 51
    {
        String title = "";
        int year = 0;;
        double price = 0.0;;

        try
        {
            title = in.readUTF();
            year = in.readInt();
            price = in.readDouble();
        }
        catch (EOFException e)
        {
            return null;
        }
        catch (IOException e)
        {
            System.out.println("I/O Error");
            System.exit(0);
        }
        return new Movie(title, year, price);
    }
}
```

```
private static void closeFile(DataInputStream in)          → 76
{
    try
    {
        in.close();
    }
    catch(IOException e)
    {
        System.out.println("I/O Error closing file.");
        System.out.println();
    }
}

private static class Movie                                 → 89
{
    public String title;
    public int year;
    public double price;

    public Movie(String title, int year, double price)
    {
        this.title = title;
        this.year = year;
        this.price = price;
    }
}
}
```

The following paragraphs describe what each method in this program does:

→ **6** The `main` method is intentionally kept simple so it can focus on controlling the flow of the program rather than doing the detail work of accessing the file. As a result, it calls a method named `getStream` to get a data input stream object to read the file. Then, it uses a `while` loop to call a method named `readMovie` to get a movie object. If the `Movie` object isn't `null`, the movie's data is then printed to the console. Finally, when the loop ends, a method named `closeFile` is called to close the file.

→**28** The `getStream` method creates a `DataInputStream` object for the filename passed as a parameter. If any exceptions are thrown, the program exits.

→**51** The `readMovie` method reads the data for a single movie and creates a `Movie` object. If the end of the file is reached, the method returns `null`.

→**76** The `closeFile` method closes the input stream.

→**89** As in the other programs in this chapter, the `Movie` class is defined as a private inner class.

Writing Binary Streams

To write data to a binary file, you use the following classes:

✦ **FileOutputStream:** The FileOutputStream class connects to a File object and creates an output stream that can write to the file. However, this output stream is limited in its capabilities: It can write only raw bytes to the file. In other words, it doesn't know how to write values such as ints, doubles, or strings.

✦ **BufferedOutputStream:** This class connects to a FileOutput Stream and adds output buffering.

✦ **DataOutputStream:** This class adds the ability to write primitive data types and strings to a stream.

Table 2-4 lists the essential constructors and methods of these classes.

Table 2-4	The DataOutputStream, BufferedOutputStream, and FileOutputStream Classes
Constructors	*Description*
DataOutputStream (OutputStream out)	Creates a data output stream for the specified output stream.
BufferedIOutputStream (OutputStream out)	Creates a buffered output stream for the specified stream. Typically, you pass this constructor a FileOutputStream object.
FileOutputStream (File file)	Creates a file writer from the file. Throws FileNotFoundException if an error occurs.
FileOutputStream(File file, boolean append)	Creates a file writer from the file. Throws FileNotFoundException if an error occurs. If the second parameter is true, data is added to the end of the file if the file already exists.
FileOutputStream (String path)	Creates a file writer from the specified pathname. Throws FileNotFoundException if an error occurs.
FileOutputStream(String path, boolean append)	Creates a file writer from the specified pathname. Throws FileNotFoundException if an error occurs. If the second parameter is true, data is added to the end of the file if the file already exists.
DataInputStream Methods	*Description*
void close()	Closes the file.
void flush()	Writes the contents of the buffer to disk.
int size()	Returns the number of bytes written to the file.
void writeBoolean (boolean value)	Writes a boolean value to the output stream. Throws IOException.

DataInputStream Methods	Description
`void writeByte(byte value)`	Writes a `byte` value to the output stream. Throws `IOException`.
`void writeChar(char value)`	Writes a `char` value to the output stream. Throws `IOException`.
`void writeDouble(double value)`	Writes a `double` value to the output stream. Throws `IOException`.
`void writeFloat(float value)`	Writes a `float` value to the output stream. Throws `IOException`.
`void writeInt(int value)`	Writes an `int` value to the output stream. Throws `IOException`.
`void writeLong(long value)`	Writes a `long` value to the output stream. Throws `IOException`.
`void writeShort(short value)`	Writes a `short` value to the output stream. Throws `IOException`.
`void writeUTF(String value)`	Writes a string stored in UTF format to the output stream. Throws `EOFException`, `IOException`, and `UTFDataFormatException`.

Creating a DataOutputStream

Creating a `DataOutputStream` object requires yet another one of those crazy nested constructor things:

```
File file = new File(name);
DataOutputStream out = new DataOutputStream(
        new BufferedOutputStream(
            new FileOutputStream(file) ) );
```

If you prefer, you can unravel the constructors like this:

```
File file = new File(name);
FileOutputStream fos = new FileOutputStream(file);
BufferedOutputStream bos = new
    BufferedOutputStream(fos);
DataOutputStream out = new DataOutputStream(bos);
```

The `FileOutputStream` class has an optional `boolean` parameter you can use to indicate that the file should be appended if it exists. To use this feature, call the constructors like this:

```
File file = new File(name);
DataOutputStream out = new DataOutputStream(
        new BufferedOutputStream(
            new FileOutputStream(file, true) ) );
```

If you specify `false` instead of `true` or leave the parameter out altogether, an existing file is deleted and its data is lost.

Writing to a binary stream

After you successfully connect a `DataOutputStream` to a file, writing data to it is simply a matter of calling the various write methods to write different data types to the file. For example, the following code writes the data for a `Movie` object to the file:

```
out.writeUTF(movie.title);
out.writeInt(movie.year);
out.writeDouble(movie.price);
```

Of course, these methods throw `IOException`. As a result, you have to enclose them in a `try/catch` block.

If you included the `BufferedOutputStream` class in the stream, it accumulates data in its buffer until it decides to write the data to disk. If you want, you can force the buffer to be written to disk by calling the `flush` method, like this:

```
out.flush();
```

Also, when you finish writing data to the file, close the file by calling the `close` method, like this:

```
out.close();
```

Both the `flush` and `close` methods also throw `IOException`, so you need a `try/catch` to catch the exception.

Writing the movies.dat file

Listing 2-4 presents a program that writes the `movies.dat` file from an array of `Movie` objects whose values are hard-coded into the program.

LISTING 2-4: WRITING TO A TEXT FILE

```
import java.io.*;

public class WriteBinaryFile
{
    public static void main(String[] args)                          → 5
    {
        Movie[] movies = getMovies();
        DataOutputStream out = openOutputStream("movies.dat");
        for (Movie m : movies)
            writeMovie(m, out);
        closeFile(out);
    }

    private static Movie[] getMovies()                              → 14
```

```
    {
        Movie[] movies = new Movie[10];

        movies[0] = new Movie("It's a Wonderful Life", 1946, 14.95);
        movies[1] = new Movie("The Great Race", 1965, 12.95);
        movies[2] = new Movie("Young Frankenstein", 1974, 16.95);
        movies[3] = new Movie("The Return of the Pink Panther", 1975,
            11.95);
        movies[4] = new Movie("Star Wars", 1977, 17.95);
        movies[5] = new Movie("The Princess Bride", 1987, 16.95);
        movies[6] = new Movie("Glory", 1989, 14.95);
        movies[7] = new Movie("Apollo 13", 1995, 19.95);
        movies[8] = new Movie("The Game", 1997, 14.95);
        movies[9] = new Movie("The Lord of the Rings: The Fellowship
            of the Ring", 2001, 19.95);
        return movies;
    }

    private static DataOutputStream
        openOutputStream(String name)                           → 39
    {
        DataOutputStream out = null;
        try
        {
            File file = new File(name);
            out = new DataOutputStream(
                    new BufferedOutputStream(
                        new FileOutputStream(file) ) );
            return out;
        }
        catch (IOException e)
        {
            System.out.println(
                "I/O Exception opening file.");
            System.exit(0);
        }
        return out;
    }

    private static void writeMovie(Movie m,                     → 59
        DataOutputStream out)
    {
        try
        {
            out.writeUTF(m.title);
            out.writeInt(m.year);
            out.writeDouble(m.price);
        }
        catch (IOException e)
        {
            System.out.println(
                "I/O Exception writing data.");
            System.exit(0);
        }
    }

    private static void closeFile(DataOutputStream out)         → 76
    {
```

Book VIII
Chapter 2

Using File Streams

continued

LISTING 2-4 (CONTINUED)

```
        try
        {
            out.close();
        }
        catch (IOException e)
        {
            System.out.println("I/O Exception closing file.");
            System.exit(0);
        }
    }

    private static class Movie                                    → 89
    {
        public String title;
        public int year;
        public double price;

        public Movie(String title, int year, double price)
        {
            this.title = title;
            this.year = year;
            this.price = price;
        }
    }
}
```

Because this chapter explains all the coding elements in this program, the following paragraphs just provide a roadmap to the major part of the program:

→ **5** The main method calls getMovies to get an array of Movie objects. Then, it calls openOutputStream to get an output stream to write data to the file. Then, an enhanced for loop calls writeMovie to write the movies to the file. Finally, it calls closeFile to close the file.

→**14** The getMovies method creates an array of movies to be written to the file.

→**39** The openOutputStream method creates a DataOutputStream object so the program can write data to the file.

→**59** The writeMovie method accepts two parameters: the movie to be written and the output stream to write the data to.

→**76** The closeFile method closes the file.

→**89** Once again, the Movie class is included as an inner class.

Chapter 3: Database for $100, Please

In This Chapter

✔ Understanding some basic database concepts

✔ Taking a quick look at SQL

✔ Creating tables

✔ Selecting data

✔ Joining data

✔ Updating and deleting data

SQL stands for Structured Query Language. SQL is the *lingua franca* (that's not a type of pasta — it's a type of tongue) of relational databases. SQL is the standard language used for creating and accessing relational databases and is the foundation of database processing in Java.

Note that Java doesn't provide any implementation of SQL itself. Instead, Java provides *JDBC* — Java DataBase Connectivity — that lets you formulate SQL statements, send them off to a database server, and process the results. But in order to use JDBC, you need to know some basic concepts of SQL databases and a least enough SQL to formulate some sensible SQL statements.

This chapter won't make you a database guru or a SQL expert. SQL is a complicated language that is the subject of many of its own books, including *SQL For Dummies* by Allen G. Taylor (Wiley). This chapter covers just enough SQL to get you going with JDBC. Also, this chapter doesn't cover JDBC. I decided to defer that until the next chapter so that if you already know SQL, you can skip this chapter altogether.

What Is a Relational Database?

The term *relational database* is one of the most used and abused buzzwords in all of computerdom. A relational database can be

✦ **A database in which data is stored in tables.** Relationships can be established between tables based on common information. For example, a table of customers and a table of invoices might both contain a customer number column. This column can serve as the basis for a relationship between the tables.

✦ **A database that is accessed via Structured Query Language (SQL).** SQL was originally invented by IBM back in the 1970s to provide a practical way to access data stored in relational databases.

✦ **Any database system developed since about 1980, with the exception of a few cutting-edge Object Oriented Databases.** Marketers quickly figured out that the way to sell database programs was to advertise them as relational. Thus, just about every database program ever made has claimed to be relational, whether it really is or not.

From a Java programmer's perspective, the second definition is the only one that matters. If you can use SQL to access the database, the database is relational.

What Is SQL, and How Do You Pronounce It?

SQL is a query language, which means it is designed to extract, organize, and update information in relational databases. Way back in the 1970s, when SQL was invented (SQL is old enough to be Java's grandfather), SQL was supposed to be an English-like query language that could be used by untrained end users to access and update relational database data without the need for programming. Of course, that didn't happen. SQL is nothing like English. It's way too complicated and esoteric for untrained end users to learn, but it has become the overwhelming favorite among programmers.

Ever since you first saw the letters SQL, you've probably been wondering how to pronounce it. If not, humor me. Two schools of thought exist on this subject:

✦ Spell out the letters: *Es – Que – El*.

✦ Pronounce it like the word *sequel*.

Either one does the job, but *sequel* makes you sound less like a database rookie.

SQL Statements

Unlike Java, SQL is *not* object oriented. Remember, SQL was invented during the Nixon administration. However, like Java, SQL does use statements to get work done. Table 3-1 lists the SQL statements you use most often.

Table 3-1	Common SQL Statements
SQL Statement	*Description*
Data Manipulation	
`select`	Retrieves data from one or more tables. This is the statement you use most often.
`insert`	Inserts one or more rows into a table.
`delete`	Deletes one or more rows from a table.
`update`	Updates existing rows in a table.
Data Definition	
`create`	Creates tables and other database objects.
`alter`	Changes the definitions of a table or other database object.
`drop`	Deletes a table or other database object.
`use`	Used in scripts to indicate what database subsequent statements apply to.

Note that unlike Java, statements in SQL are not case sensitive. Thus, you can write `select`, `Select`, or `SELECT`. You could even write `sElEcT` for kicks, if you want.

Creating a SQL Database

Before you can store data in a relational database, you must create the database. You don't normally do that from a Java program. Instead, you do it by writing a script file that contains the `Create` statements necessary to create the table, and then run the script through the database server's administration program. (Note that some database servers also let you define databases interactively. However, the script approach is preferred because you often need to delete and re-create a database while testing your applications.)

The scripts shown in this section (and in the rest of this chapter) are for version 4.1 of MySQL. MySQL is a free SQL database server you can download from www.mysql.com. MySQL includes a program called the MySQL Command Line Client that lets you enter SQL commands from a prompt and immediately see the results.

Script statements end with semicolons. That's about the only thing SQL scripts have in common with Java. Be aware, however, that the semicolon isn't required when you use SQL statements in a Java program. The semicolon is required only when you use SQL statements in a script or interactively from the MySQL Command Line Client program.

I don't have room in this book to go into a complete tutorial on writing scripts that create SQL databases. So instead, I present a sample script,

Listing 3-1, that creates a database named `movies` that's used in the rest of this chapter and in the next, and walk you through its most important lines.

LISTING 3-1: A DATABASE CREATION SCRIPT

```
drop database movies;                                           → 1
create database movies;                                         → 2
use movies;                                                     → 3
create table movie (                                            → 4
    id int not null auto_increment,                             → 5
    title varchar(50),                                          → 6
    year int,                                                   → 7
    price decimal(8,2),                                         → 8
    primary key(id)                                             → 9
);

insert into movie (title, year, price)                          → 12
    values ("It's a Wonderful Life", 1946, 14.95);
insert into movie (title, year, price)
    values ("The Great Race", 1965, 12.95);
insert into movie (title, year, price)
    values ("Young Frankenstein", 1974, 16.95);
insert into movie (title, year, price)
    values ("The Return of the Pink Panther", 1975, 11.95);
insert into movie (title, year, price)
    values ("Star Wars", 1977, 17.95);
insert into movie (title, year, price)
    values ("The Princess Bride", 1987, 16.95);
insert into movie (title, year, price)
    values ("Glory", 1989, 14.95);
insert into movie (title, year, price)
    values ("Apollo 13", 1995, 19.95);
insert into movie (title, year, price)
    values ("The Game", 1997, 14.95);
insert into movie (title, year, price)
    values ("The Lord of the Rings: The Fellowship of the Ring, 2001,
    19.95);
```

The following paragraphs describe the important lines of this script:

→ **1** It's common for a script that creates a database to begin with a `drop database` statement to delete any existing database with the same name. During testing, it's common to delete and re-create the database, so you want to include this statement in your scripts.

→ **2** This statement creates a new database named `movies`.

→ **3** The `use` statement indicates that the script statements that follow applies to the newly created `movies` database.

→ **4** This `create table` statement creates a table named `movie` with columns named `id`, `title`, `year`, and `price`. This statement also specifies that the primary key for the table is the `id` column.

→ **5** The id column's data type is int, which corresponds to Java's int type. This column also specifies not null, which means that it must have a value for every row, and it specifies auto increment, which means that the database server itself provides values for this column. Each time a new row is added to the table, the value for the id column is automatically incremented.

→ **6** The title column's data type is varchar, which is like a Java String.

→ **7** The year column's data type is int.

→ **8** The price column's data type is decimal. Java doesn't have a decimal type, so the values from this column are converted to double.

→ **9** The create table statement specifies that the id column is the table's primary key. A *primary key* is a column (or a combination of columns) that contains a unique value for each row in a table. Every table should have a primary key.

→**12** The insert statements add data to the database. Each of these ten statements adds a row to the movie table. The syntax of the insert statement is weird, because you first list all the columns that you want to insert data for, and then you list the actual data. For example, each of the insert statements inserts data for three columns: title, year, and price. The first insert statement (the one in line 12) inserts the values "It's a Wonderful Life", 1946, and 14.95.

To run this script in MySQL, start the MySQL Command Line Client from the Start menu. Then, use a source command that names the script. For example:

```
mysql> source c:\data\create.sql
```

Querying a Database

As the name Structured Query Language suggests, queries are what SQL is all about. A *query* is an operation that is performed against one or more SQL tables that extracts data from the tables and creates a *result set* containing the selected rows and columns. A crucial point to understand is that the result set is itself a table consisting of rows and columns. When you query a database from a Java program, the result set is returned to the program in an object created from the ResultSet class. This class has methods that let you extract the data from each column of each row in the result set.

Using your basic select

To query a database, you use the select statement. In the select statement, you list the table or tables from which you want to retrieve the data, the specific table columns you want to retrieve (you might not be interested in everything that's in the table), and other clauses that indicate which specific rows to retrieve, what order to present the rows in, and so on. Here's a simple `select` statement that lists all the movies in the `movie` table:

```
select title, year
    from movie
    order by year;
```

When you take this statement apart piece by piece, you get:

- `select title, year` names the columns you want included in the query result.

- `from movie` names the table you want the rows retrieved from.

- `order by year` indicates that the result is sorted into sequence by the `year` column so the oldest movie appears first.

In other words, this `select` statement retrieves the title and date for all the rows in the `movie` table and sorts them into `year` sequence. You can run this query by typing it directly into the MySQL Command Line Client. Here's what you get:

```
mysql> select title, year from movie order by year;
+-----------------------------------------------------+------+
| title                                               | year |
+-----------------------------------------------------+------+
| It's a Wonderful Life                               | 1946 |
| The Great Race                                      | 1965 |
| Young Frankenstein                                  | 1974 |
| The Return of the Pink Panther                      | 1975 |
| Star Wars                                           | 1977 |
| The Princess Bride                                  | 1987 |
| Glory                                               | 1989 |
| Apollo 13                                           | 1995 |
| The Game                                            | 1997 |
| The Lord of the Rings: The Fellowship of the Ring   | 2001 |
+-----------------------------------------------------+------+
10 rows in set (0.09 sec)
```

As you can see, the Command Line Client displays the rows returned by the `select` statement. This can be very handy when you're planning the `select` statements your program needs or when you're testing a program that updates a table and you want to make sure the updates are made correctly.

If you want the query to retrieve all the columns in each row, you can use an asterisk instead of naming the individual columns:

```
select * from movie order by year;
```

Use an asterisk in this manner in a program is not a good idea, however, because the columns that make up the table might change. If you use an asterisk, your program can't deal with changes to the table's structure.

Both examples so far include an order by clause. In a SQL database, the rows stored in a table are not assumed to be in any particular sequence. As a result, if you want to display the results of a query in sequence, you must include an order by in the select statement.

Narrowing down the query

Suppose you want to find information about one particular video title. To select certain rows from a table, use the where clause in a select statement. For example:

```
mysql> select title, year from movie
    ->      where year <= 1980
    ->      order by year;
+-------------------------------+------+
| title                         | year |
+-------------------------------+------+
| It's a Wonderful Life         | 1946 |
| The Great Race                | 1965 |
| Young Frankenstein            | 1974 |
| The Return of the Pink Panther| 1975 |
| Star Wars                     | 1977 |
+-------------------------------+------+
5 rows in set (0.00 sec)
```

Here, the select statement selects all the rows in which the year column is less than or equal to 1980. The results are ordered by the year column.

Excluding rows

Perhaps you want to retrieve all rows except those that match certain criteria. For example, here's a query that ignores movies made in the 1970s (which is probably a good idea):

```
mysql> select title, year from movie
    ->      where year < 1970 or year > 1979
    ->      order by year;
+------------------------------------------------------+------+
| title                                                | year |
+------------------------------------------------------+------+
| It's a Wonderful Life                                | 1946 |
| The Great Race                                       | 1965 |
| The Princess Bride                                   | 1987 |
| Glory                                                | 1989 |
| Apollo 13                                            | 1995 |
| The Game                                             | 1997 |
| The Lord of the Rings: The Fellowship of the Ring    | 2001 |
+------------------------------------------------------+------+
7 rows in set (0.41 sec)
```

Singleton selects

When you want to retrieve information for a specific row, mention the primary key column in the where clause, like this:

```
mysql> select title, year from movie where id = 7;
+-------+------+
| title | year |
+-------+------+
| Glory | 1989 |
+-------+------+
1 row in set (0.49 sec)
```

Here, the where clause selects the row whose id column equals 7. This type of select statement is called a *singleton select* because it retrieves only one row. Singleton selects are commonly used in Java programs to allow users to access or update a specific database row.

Sounds like

Suppose you want to retrieve information about a movie, but you can't quite remember the name. You know it has the word *princess* in it though. One of the more interesting variations of the where clause is to throw in the word like, which lets you search rows using wildcards. Here's an example in which the percent sign (%) is a wildcard character:

```
mysql> select title, year from movie
    ->       where title like "%princess%";
+--------------------+------+
| title              | year |
+--------------------+------+
| The Princess Bride | 1987 |
+--------------------+------+
1 row in set (0.00 sec)
```

Column functions

What if you want a count of the total number of movies in the movie table? Or a count of the number of movies that were made before 1970? To do that, you use a *column function*. SQL's column functions let you make calculations on columns. You can calculate the sum, average, largest or smallest value, or count the number of values for an entire column. Table 3-2 summarizes these functions. Note that these functions operate on the values returned in a result set, which isn't necessarily the entire table.

Table 3-2	Column Functions
Function	*Description*
sum(*column-name*)	Adds up the values in the column.
avg(*column-name*)	Calculates the average value for the column. Null values are not figured in the calculation.
min(*column-name*)	Determines the lowest value in the column.
max(*column-name*)	Determines the highest value in the column.

Function	Description
count(*column-name*)	Counts the number of rows that have data values for the column.
countDistinct (*column-name*)	Counts the number of distinct values for the column.
count(*)	Counts the number of rows in the result set.

To use one of these functions, specify the function rather than a column name in a select statement. For example, the following select statement calculates the number of rows in the table and the year of the oldest movie:

```
mysql> select count(*), min(year) from movie;
+----------+----------+
| count(*) | min(year) |
+----------+----------+
|       10 |     1946 |
+----------+----------+
1 row in set (0.00 sec)
```

As you can see, ten movies are in the table, and the oldest was made in 1946.

If the select statement includes a where clause, only the rows that match the criteria are included in the calculation. For example, this statement finds out how many movies in the table were made before 1970:

```
mysql> select count(*) from movie where year < 1970;
+----------+
| count(*) |
+----------+
|        2 |
+----------+
1 row in set (0.00 sec)
```

The result is only two.

Selecting from more than one table

In the real world, most select statements retrieve data from two or more tables. Suppose you want a list of all the movies you've currently loaned out to friends. To do that, you have to create another table in your database that lists your friends' names and the ids of any movie they've borrowed. Here's a create table statement that creates just such a table:

```
create table friend (
    lastname varchar(50),
    firstname varchar(50),
    movieid int
);
```

Now load it up with some data:

```
insert into friend (lastname, firstname, movieid)
    values ("Haskell", "Eddie", 3);
insert into friend (lastname, firstname, movieid)
    values ("Haskell", "Eddie", 5);
insert into friend (lastname, firstname, movieid)
    values ("Cleaver", "Wally", 9);
insert into friend (lastname, firstname, movieid)
    values ("Mondello", "Lumpy", 2);
insert into friend (lastname, firstname, movieid)
    values ("Cleaver", "Wally", 3);
```

With that out of the way, you can get to the business of using both the friend and movie tables in a single select statement. All you have to do is list both tables in the from clause, and then provide a condition in the where clause that correlates the tables. For example:

```
mysql> select lastname, firstname, title
    ->      from movie, friend
    ->      where movie.id = friend.movieid;
+----------+-----------+---------------------+
| lastname | firstname | title               |
+----------+-----------+---------------------+
| Haskell  | Eddie     | Young Frankenstein  |
| Haskell  | Eddie     | Star Wars           |
| Cleaver  | Wally     | The Game            |
| Mondello | Lumpy     | The Great Race      |
| Cleaver  | Wally     | Young Frankenstein  |
+----------+-----------+---------------------+
5 rows in set (0.00 sec)
```

Here, you can see which movies have been lent out and who has them. Notice that the id and movieid columns in the where clause are qualified with the name of the table the column belongs to.

Here's a select statement that lists all the movies Eddie Haskell has borrowed:

```
mysql> select title from movie, friend
    ->      where movie.id = friend.movieid
    ->      and lastname = "Haskell";
+--------------------+
| title              |
+--------------------+
| Young Frankenstein |
| Star Wars          |
+--------------------+
2 rows in set (0.00 sec)
```

That rat has two of your best movies! Notice in this example that you can refer to the friend table in the where clause even though you're not actually retrieving any of its columns. However, you must still mention both tables in the from clause.

Eliminating duplicates

If you want to know just the names of everyone who has a movie checked out, you can do a simple `select` from the `friend` table:

```
mysql> select lastname, firstname from friend;
+----------+-----------+
| lastname | firstname |
+----------+-----------+
| Haskell  | Eddie     |
| Haskell  | Eddie     |
| Cleaver  | Wally     |
| Mondello | Lumpy     |
| Cleaver  | Wally     |
+----------+-----------+
5 rows in set (0.00 sec)
```

However, this result set has a problem: Eddie Haskel and Wally Cleaver are listed twice. Wouldn't it be nice if you could eliminate the duplicate rows? Your wish is granted in the next paragraph.

You can eliminate duplicate rows by adding the `distinct` keyword in the `select` statement:

```
mysql> select distinct lastname, firstname from friend;
+----------+-----------+
| lastname | firstname |
+----------+-----------+
| Haskell  | Eddie     |
| Cleaver  | Wally     |
| Mondello | Lumpy     |
+----------+-----------+
3 rows in set (0.07 sec)
```

Notice that no duplicates appear; each distinct name appears only once in the result set.

Updating and Deleting Rows

You've already seen how to create databases, insert rows, and retrieve result sets. All that remains now is updating and deleting data in a table. For that, you use the `update` and `delete` statements, as described in the following sections. I explain the `delete` statement first, because it has a simpler syntax.

The delete statement

The basic syntax of the `delete` statement is:

```
delete from table-name where condition;
```

For example, here's a statement that deletes the movie whose id is 10:

```
mysql> delete from movie where id = 10;
Query OK, 1 row affected (0.44 sec)
```

Notice that the Command Line Client shows that this statement affected one line. You can confirm that the movie was deleted by following up with a select statement:

```
mysql> select * from movie;
+----+-------------------------------+------+-------+
| id | title                         | year | price |
+----+-------------------------------+------+-------+
|  1 | It's a Wonderful Life         | 1946 | 14.95 |
|  2 | The Great Race                | 1965 | 12.95 |
|  3 | Young Frankenstein            | 1974 | 16.95 |
|  4 | The Return of the Pink Panther| 1975 | 11.95 |
|  5 | Star Wars                     | 1977 | 17.95 |
|  6 | The Princess Bride            | 1987 | 16.95 |
|  7 | Glory                         | 1989 | 14.95 |
|  8 | Apollo 13                     | 1995 | 19.95 |
|  9 | The Game                      | 1997 | 14.95 |
+----+-------------------------------+------+-------+
9 rows in set (0.00 sec)
```

As you can see, movie 10 is gone.

If the where clause selects more than one row, all the selected rows are deleted. For example

```
mysql> delete from friend where lastname = "Haskell";
Query OK, 2 rows affected (0.45 sec)
```

A quick query of the friend table shows that both records for Eddie Haskell are deleted:

```
mysql> select * from friend;
+----------+-----------+---------+
| lastname | firstname | movieid |
+----------+-----------+---------+
| Cleaver  | Wally     |       9 |
| Mondello | Lumpy     |       2 |
| Cleaver  | Wally     |       3 |
+----------+-----------+---------+
3 rows in set (0.00 sec)
```

If you don't include a where clause, the entire table is deleted. For example, this statement deletes all the rows in the movie table:

```
mysql> delete from movie;
Query OK, 9 rows affected (0.44 sec)
```

A quick select of the movie table confirms that it is now empty:

```
mysql> select * from movie;
Empty set (0.00 sec)
```

Fortunately, you can now just run the `create.sql` script again to create the table.

The update statement

The `update` statement selects one or more rows from a table, and then modifies the value of one or more columns in the selected rows. Its syntax is this:

```
update table-name
    set expressions...
    where condition;
```

The `set` expressions resemble Java assignment statements. For example, here's a statement that changes the price of movie 8 to 18.95:

```
mysql> update movie set price = 18.95 where id = 8;
Query OK, 1 row affected (0.44 sec)
Rows matched: 1  Changed: 1  Warnings: 0
```

You can use a quick `select` statement to verify that the price was changed:

```
mysql> select id, price from movie;
+----+--------+
| id | price  |
+----+--------+
|  1 | 14.95  |
|  2 | 12.95  |
|  3 | 16.95  |
|  4 | 11.95  |
|  5 | 17.95  |
|  6 | 16.95  |
|  7 | 14.95  |
|  8 | 18.95  |
|  9 | 14.95  |
| 10 | 19.95  |
+----+--------+
10 rows in set (0.01 sec)
```

To update more than one column, use commas to separate the expressions. For example, here's a statement that changes Eddie Haskell's name in the `friend` table:

```
mysql> update friend set lastname = "Bully",
    ->        firstname = "Big"
    ->        where lastname = "Haskell";
Query OK, 2 rows affected (0.46 sec)
Rows matched: 2  Changed: 2  Warnings: 0
```

Again, a quick `select` shows that the rows are properly updated:

```
mysql> select firstname, lastname from friend;
+-----------+----------+
| firstname | lastname |
+-----------+----------+
| Big       | Bully    |
| Big       | Bully    |
| Wally     | Cleaver  |
| Lumpy     | Mondello |
| Wally     | Cleaver  |
+-----------+----------+
5 rows in set (0.00 sec)
```

One final trick with the `update` statement you should know about is that the `set` expressions can include calculations. For example, the following statement increases the price of all the movies by 10 percent:

```
mysql> update movie set price = price * 1.1;
Query OK, 10 rows affected (0.46 sec)
Rows matched: 10  Changed: 10  Warnings: 0
```

Here's a `select` statement to verify that this update worked:

```
mysql> select id, price from movie;
+----+-------+
| id | price |
+----+-------+
|  1 | 16.45 |
|  2 | 14.25 |
|  3 | 18.65 |
|  4 | 13.15 |
|  5 | 19.75 |
|  6 | 18.65 |
|  7 | 16.45 |
|  8 | 20.85 |
|  9 | 16.45 |
| 10 | 21.95 |
+----+-------+
10 rows in set (0.01 sec)
```

Chapter 4: Using JDBC to Connect to a Database

In This Chapter

✓ **Configuring JDBC drivers**

✓ **Creating a connection**

✓ **Executing SQL statements**

✓ **Retrieving result data**

✓ **Updating and deleting data**

*J*DBC — *Java Database Connectivity* — is a Java feature that lets you connect to almost any relational database system, execute SQL commands, and process the results all from within a Java program. In this chapter, you set up JDBC and use it to access data in a MySQL database.

If you aren't familiar with the basics of SQL, read the previous chapter before you tackle this chapter.

Setting Up a Driver

Before you can write a Java program to access a database via JDBC, you must first install a driver that links Java's database API classes to an actual database. Getting the driver set up right can be tricky, but once you get it working, accessing the database is easy.

The following sections describe two basic approaches to setting up a driver to connect to a database: ODBC or a database connector.

Setting up an ODBC data source

ODBC is a generic database connection standard that almost every database program available can speak to. It's inherently inefficient, but it is easy to set up and performs adequately for small applications and for testing purposes. If you're using Access files for your database, ODBC is the way to go.

Assuming you have created a database in Access that you want to access from a Java program, you can follow these steps to create an ODBC data source for the Access database:

1. **Open the Control Panel and double-click Administrative Tools**.

A window with icons for various administrative tools comes up.

2. **Double click Data Sources (ODBC).**

The ODBC Data Source Administrator dialog box opens, as shown in Figure 4-1.

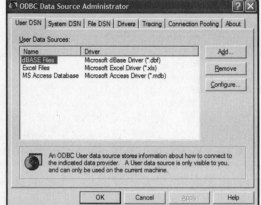

Figure 4-1:
The ODBC
Data Source
Administra-
tor dialog
box.

3. **Click the System DSN tab, and then click Add.**

A dialog box listing a bunch of ODBC drivers appears.

4. **Choose Microsoft Access Driver, and then click Finish.**

The Finish button is strangely named, but this is when the real configu-ration actually begins. The dialog box shown in Figure 4-2 now appears.

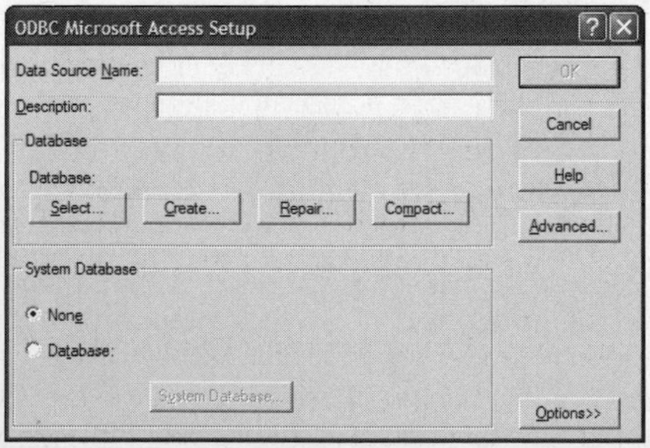

Figure 4-2:
Configuring
an Access
data source.

5. Type a name for the data source.

You use this name in your Java program to access the data source, so choose it wisely.

6. Click the Select button, and then choose the database you want to connect to and click OK.

A Select Database dialog box appears. From this dialog box, you can navigate to the folder that contains your Access data file to select it.

7. Click OK.

The data source is added to the list of configured ODBC data sources.

8. Click OK to dismiss the ODBC Data Source Administrator.

You're all done.

Setting up the MySQL JDBC connector

An alternative to using ODBC is to use a *database connector,* which is a driver provided by your database vendor. Database connectors are designed to work exclusively with a specific type of database. As a result, they're considerably more efficient and powerful than ODCB.

You have to obtain the JDBC connector for the database you're using from the company that makes the database server you're using. For example, you can get a JDBC connector for MySQL from the MySQL Web site at `www.mysql.com`. Along with the driver, you get detailed instructions on how to set it up. But the following procedure works for a simple testing environment:

1. Download the driver from `www.mysql.com/products/connector` and unzip it.

The driver you're looking for is called *MySQL Connector/J.* After you download it from MySQL's Web site, unzip the files to any folder you wish. I suggest one with a simple pathname, such as `c:\MySql`.

2. Add the driver's `.jar` file to your ClassPath variable.

To change the ClassPath, open Control Panel and double-click System. Then, click the Advanced tab, and then click Environment Variables. You can then click New to add a new environment variable. The ClassPath variable has to specify the complete path for the connector's `jar` file. For example, here's a sample ClassPath variable for a driver located in `c:\mysql`:

```
.;c:\mysql\mysql-connector-java-3.1.6-bin.jar
```

Notice that the ClassPath variable starts with a period and a semicolon. This ensures that Java can find classes that are in the current directory.

If the ClassPath variable already exists, just add the connector's `jar` file to the end of the existing text.

That's all you have to do. You can now connect to MySQL from a Java program.

Connecting to a Database

Before you can use JDBC to access a SQL database, you must first establish a connection to the database. The first step to establishing a connection involves *registering* the driver class so the class is available. To do that, you use the `forName` method of the `Class` class, specifying the package and class name of the driver. For example, to register the MySQL connector, use this statement:

```
Class.forName("com.mysql.jdbc.Driver");
```

To register the standard ODBC driver, use this statement instead:

```
Class.forName("sun.jdbc.odbc.JdbcOdbcDriver");
```

Note that the `forName` method throws `ClassNotFoundException`, so you have to enclose this statement in a `try/catch` block that catches `ClassNotFoundException`.

After you register the driver class, you can call the static `getConnection` method of the `DriverManager` class to open the connection. This method takes three `String` parameters: the database URL, the user name, and a password. Here's an example:

```
String url = "jdbc:mysql://localhost/Movies";
String user = "root";
String pw = "pw";
con = DriverManager.getConnection(url, user, pw);
```

The URL parameter has the following syntax:

```
jdbc:subprotocol:subname
```

where *subprotocol* is `mysql` for a MySQL database and `odbc` for an ODBC driver. The *subname* is the database name. For a MySQL database, this can be a complete URL, but for a database on your own computer, you just specify `//localhost/` plus the name of the database.

For ODBC, you use the name you used when you created the data source. For example

```
String url = "jdbc:odbc:Movies";
```

The user and password parameters must also be valid for the database server you're using. For testing purposes on a MySQL database, you can use `root` and the password you created when you installed MySQL. For ODBC, use `admin` with no password for testing.

Note that the `getConnection` method throws `SQLException`, so you need to enclose It in a `try`/`catch` block statement that catches this exception.

Putting it all together, here's a method that returns a `Connection` object that connects to the `movies` database in MySQL:

```
private static Connection getConnection()
{
    Connection con = null;
    try
    {
        Class.forName("com.mysql.jdbc.Driver");
        String url = "jdbc:mysql://localhost/Movies";
        String user = "root";
        String pw = "NuttMutt";
        con = DriverManager.getConnection(url, user, pw);
    }
    catch (ClassNotFoundException e)
    {
        System.out.println(e.getMessage());
        System.exit(0);
    }
    catch (SQLException e)
    {
        System.out.println(e.getMessage());
        System.exit(0);
    }
    return con;
}
```

You can find these classes — and the other classes for working with SQL databases — in the `java.sql` package. As a result, you have to include an `import` statement that specifies this package in any program that uses JDBC.

Querying a Database

After you establish a connection to a database, you can execute `select` statements to retrieve data. To do so, you have to use several classes and interfaces:

+ **Connection:** The `Connection` class has two methods you're likely to use. The `close` method closes the connection, and the `createStatement` method returns a `Statement` object, which you then use to execute statements.

✦ **Statement:** The Statement interface contains the methods necessary to send statements to the database for execution and return the results. In particular, you use the executeQuery method to execute a select statement or the executeUpdate method to execute an insert, update, or delete statement.

✦ **ResultSet:** The ResultSet interface represents rows returned from a query. It provides methods you can use to move from row to row and to get the data for a column.

Table 4-1 lists the methods of the Connection class and the Statement interface you use to execute queries. You find out about the many methods of the ResultSet interface later in this chapter, in the section "Navigating through the result set."

Table 4-1	Connection and Statement Methods
Connection Class Methods	**Description**
void close()	Closes the connection.
Statement createStatement()	Creates a Statement object that can execute a SQL statement on the database connected by the connection.
Statement createStatement (int type, int concur)	Creates a Statement object that can execute a SQL statement on the database connected by the connection.
Statement Interface Methods	**Description**
ResultSet executeQuery (String sql)	Executes the select statement contained in the string parameter and returns the result data as a ResultSet object.
ResultSet executeQuery (String sql)	Executes the select statement contained in the string parameter and returns the result data as a ResultSet object.
int executeUpdate (String sql)	Executes the insert, update, or delete statements contained in the string parameter and returns the result data as a ResultSet object.

The first parameter of the createStatement method specifies the type of result set that is created, and can be one of the following:

```
ResultSet.TYPE_FORWARD_ONLY
ResultSet.TYPE_SCROLL_INSENSITIVE
ResultSet.TYPE_SCROLL_SENSITIVE
```

The second parameter indicates whether the result set is read-only or updatable, and can be one of the following:

```
ResultSet.CONCUR_READ_ONLY
ResultSet.CONSUR_UPDATABLE
```

Executing a select statement

The following snippet executes a `select` statement and gets the result set:

```
Statement s = con.createStatement();
String select = "Select title, year, price "
    + "from movie order by year";
ResultSet rows = s.executeQuery(select);
```

Here, the result set is stored in the `rows` variable.

Navigating through the result set

The `ResultSet` object returned by the `executeQuery` statement contains all the rows that are retrieved by the `select` statement. You can only access one of those rows at a time. The result set maintains a pointer called a *cursor* to keep track of the current row. You can use the methods shown in Table 4-2 to move the cursor through a result set.

For example, the following snippet shows how you can structure code that processes each row in a result set:

```
while(rows.next())
{
    // process the current row
}
```

All you have to do is replace the comment with statements that retrieve data from the result set and process it, as described in the next section.

Table 4-2	Navigation Methods of the ResultSet Interface
Method	*Description*
`void close()`	Closes the result set.
`void last()`	Moves the cursor to the last row.
`int getRow()`	Gets the current row number.
`boolean next()`	Moves to the next row.

Getting data from a result set

Table 4-3 lists the methods of the `ResultSet` interface you can use to retrieve data from the current row. As you can see, each of these methods comes in two versions: One specifies the column by name, the other by index number. If you know the index number, using it to access the column values is more efficient than using the column names.

Here's a bit of code that gets the title, year, and price for the current row:

```
String title = row.getString("title");
int year = row.getInt("year");
double price = row.getDouble("price");
```

The following code does the same thing, assuming the columns appear in order:

```
String title = row.getString(1);
int year = row.getInt(2);
double price = row.getDouble(3);
```

Note that unlike almost every other index in Java, column indexes start with 1, not zero.

Table 4-3	Get Methods of the ResultSet Interface
Method	*Description*
`BigDecimal getBigDecimal(String columnName)`	Gets the value of the specified column as a `BigDecimal`.
`BigDecimal getBigDecimal(int columnIndex)`	Gets the value of the specified column as a `BigDecimal`.
`boolean getBoolean(String columnName)`	Gets the value of the specified column as a `boolean`.
`boolean getBoolean(int columnIndex)`	Gets the value of the specified column as a `boolean`.
`Date getDate(String columnName)`	Gets the value of the specified column as a `Date`.
`Date getDate(int columnIndex)`	Gets the value of the specified column as a `Date`.
`double getDouble(String columnName)`	Gets the value of the specified column as a `double`.
`double getDouble(int columnIndex)`	Gets the value of the specified column as a `double`.
`float getFloat(String columnName)`	Gets the value of the specified column as a `float`.
`float getFloat(int columnIndex)`	Gets the value of the specified column as a `float`.
`int getInt(String columnName)`	Gets the value of the specified column as a `int`.
`int getInt(int columnIndex)`	Gets the value of the specified column as a `int`.

Method	Description
`long getLong(String columnName)`	Gets the value of the specified column as a `long`.
`long getLong(int columnIndex)`	Gets the value of the specified column as a `long`.
`short getShort(String columnName)`	Gets the value of the specified column as a `short`.
`short getShort(int columnIndex)`	Gets the value of the specified column as a `short`.
`String getString(String columnName)`	Gets the value of the specified column as a `String`.
`String getString(int columnIndex)`	Gets the value of the specified column as a `String`.

Putting it all together: A program that reads from a database

Now that you've seen the various elements that make up a program that uses JDBC to query a database, Listing 4-1 shows a program that reads data from the `movies` database and lists it on the console. When you run this program, the following appears on the console:

```
1946: It's a Wonderful Life ($16.45)
1965: The Great Race ($14.25)
1974: Young Frankenstein ($18.65)
1975: The Return of the Pink Panther ($13.15)
1977: Star Wars ($19.75)
1987: The Princess Bride ($18.65)
1989: Glory ($16.45)
1995: Apollo 13 ($20.85)
1997: The Game ($16.45)
2001: The Lord of the Rings: The Fellowship of the Ring
    ($21.95)
```

LISTING 4-1: THE MOVIE LISTING PROGRAM

```java
import java.sql.*;
import java.text.NumberFormat;

public class ListMovies
{
    public static void main(String[] args)                    → 6
    {
        NumberFormat cf = NumberFormat.getCurrencyInstance();

        ResultSet movies = getMovies();
```

continued

LISTING 4-1 (CONTINUED)

```
        try
        {
            while (movies.next())
            {
                Movie m = getMovie(movies);
                String msg = Integer.toString(m.year);
                msg += ": " + m.title;
                msg += " (" + cf.format(m.price) + ")";
                System.out.println(msg);
            }
        }
        catch (SQLException e)
        {
            System.out.println(e.getMessage());
        }
    }

    private static ResultSet getMovies()                    → 28
    {
        Connection con = getConnection();
        try
        {
            Statement s = con.createStatement();
            String select = "Select title, year, price "
                + "from movie order by year";
            ResultSet rows;
            rows = s.executeQuery(select);
            return rows;
        }
        catch (SQLException e)
        {
            System.out.println(e.getMessage());
        }
        return null;
    }

    private static Connection getConnection()               → 46
    {
        Connection con = null;
        try
        {
            Class.forName("com.mysql.jdbc.Driver");
            String url = "jdbc:mysql://localhost/Movies";
            String user = "root";
            String pw = "NuttMutt";
            con = DriverManager.getConnection(url, user, pw);
        }
        catch (ClassNotFoundException e)
        {
            System.out.println(e.getMessage());
            System.exit(0);
        }
        catch (SQLException e)
        {
            System.out.println(e.getMessage());
```

```
            System.exit(0);
        }
        return con;
    }

    private static Movie getMovie(ResultSet movies)          → 70
    {
        try
        {
            String title = movies.getString("Title");
            int year = movies.getInt("Year");
            double price = movies.getDouble("Price");
            return new Movie(title, year, price);
        }
        catch (SQLException e)
        {
            System.out.println(e.getMessage());
        }
        return null;
    }

    private static class Movie                                → 86
    {
        public String title;
        public int year;
        public double price;

        public Movie(String title, int year, double price)
        {
            this.title = title;
            this.year = year;
            this.price = price;
        }
    }
}
```

The following paragraphs describe the basics of how this program works:

→ **6** The `main` method begins by calling the `getMovies` method to get a `ResultSet` object that contains the movies to be listed. Then, a `while` loop reads each row of the result set. The `getMovie` method is called to create a `Movie` object from the data in the current row. Then, an output string is created and sent to the console. The loop is contained in a `try/catch` statement because the `next` method may throw `SQLException`.

→**28** The `getMovies` method is responsible for getting a database connection, and then querying the database to get the movies. The first task is delegated to the `getConnection` method. Then, a `Statement` is created and executed with the following `select` statement:

```
select title, year, price from movie order by year
```

Then, the result set is returned to the `main` method.

→**46** The getConnection method creates a Connection object to the database. Note that the user id and password are hard-coded into this method. In a real application, you get this information from the user or from a configuration file.

→**70** The getMovie method extracts the title, year, and price from the current row and uses these values to create a Movie object.

→**86** The Movie class is created as an inner class. To keep this application simple, this class uses public fields and a single constructor that initializes the fields with the values passed as parameters.

Updating SQL Data

Besides executing select statements, you can also use a Statement object to execute insert, update, or delete statements as well. To do that, you call the executeUpdate method instead of the executeQuery method. This method returns an int value that indicates how many rows were updated. You can test the return value to determine whether the data was properly updated.

For example, here's a method that accepts a movie id, last name, and first name and inserts a row into the friend table:

```
private static void loanMovie(int id, String lastName,
    String firstName)
{
    Connection con = getConnection();
    try
    {
        Statement stmt = con.createStatement();
        String insert = "insert into friend "
            + "(lastname, firstname, movieid) "
            + "values ("
            + "\"" + lastName + "\", \""
            + firstName + "\", " +
            + id + ")";
        int i = stmt.executeUpdate(insert);
        if (i == 1)
            System.out.println("Loan recorded.");
        else
            System.out.println("Loan not recorded.");
    }
    catch (SQLException e)
    {
        System.out.println(e.getMessage());
        System.exit(0);
    }
}
```

The getConnection method called at the start of this method is the same getConnection method in Listing 4-1. After a connection is created, a Statement object is created, and an insert statement is constructed using the values passed via the parameters. For example, if you pass id 3, last name Haskell, and first name Eddie, the following insert statement is built:

```
Insert into friend (lastname, firstname, movieid)
    Values ("Haskell", "Eddie", 3)
```

Then, the executeUpdate method is called to execute the insert statement. An if statement is used to determine whether or not the row is inserted.

You can execute update or delete statements in the same manner.

While you're testing database code that executes SQL statements constructed from strings like this, throw in a System.out.println call to print the statement to the console. That way, you can verify that the statement is being created properly.

Using an Updatable RowSet Object

If you're using a newer JDBC driver (one that supports JDBC 2.0 or later), you have another option for updating data: with an updatable result set. With an updatable result set, you can change data in a result set row, add a row to the result set, or delete a row from the result set. When you do, the updates are automatically written back to the underlying database.

To create an updatable result set, you must specify the ResultSet. CONCUR_UPDATABLE field on the createStatement method when you create the Statement object, like this:

```
Statement stmt = con.createStatement(
    ResultSet.TYPE_SCROLL_SENSITIVE,
    ResultSet.TYPE_CONCUR_UPDATABLE);
```

The first parameter indicates that the result set is scrollable, which means you can move the cursor backwards as well as forwards through the result set. You can use the methods listed in Table 4-4 to scroll the result set. This parameter also indicates that the result set can be synchronized with the database so that any changes made by other users are reflected in the result set.

Table 4-4	Methods for Scrollable Result Sets
Method	*Description*
`boolean absolute (int row)`	Moves the cursor to the given row number in this `ResultSet` object.
`void afterLast()`	Moves the cursor to the end of this `ResultSet` object, just after the last row.
`void beforeFirst()`	Moves the cursor to the front of this `ResultSet` object, just before the first row.
`boolean first()`	Moves the cursor to the first row in this `ResultSet` object.
`boolean last()`	Moves the cursor to the last row in this `ResultSet` object.
`boolean next()`	Moves the cursor down one row from its current position.
`boolean previous()`	Moves the cursor to the previous row in this `ResultSet` object.
`boolean relative (int rows)`	Moves the cursor a relative number of rows, either positive or negative.

The second parameter indicates that the result set is updatable, and any changes you make to the result set are automatically written back to the database. You can use any of the methods listed in Table 4-5 to update the result set, and thus update the underlying database.

Table 4-5	Methods for Updatable Result Sets
Method	*Description*
`void cancelRowUpdates()`	Cancels the updates made to the current row in this `ResultSet` object.
`void deleteRow()`	Deletes the current row from this `ResultSet` object and from the underlying database.
`void insertRow()`	Inserts the contents of the insert row into this `ResultSet` object and into the database.
`void moveToCurrentRow()`	Moves the cursor to the remembered cursor position, usually the current row.
`void moveToInsertRow()`	Moves the cursor to the insert row.
`void refreshRow()`	Refreshes the current row with its most recent value in the database.
`void updateRow()`	Updates the underlying database with the new contents of the current row of this `ResultSet` object.

Deleting a row

To delete a row from a result set, use one of the navigation methods in Table 4-4 to move to the row you want to delete, and then use the `deleteRow` method to delete the row. For example, here's code that deletes the third row in the result set:

```
try
{
    rs.absolute(3);
    rs.deleteRow();
}
catch (SQLException e)
{
    System.out.println(e.getMessage());
    System.exit(0);
}
```

Updating the value of a row column

To update the value of a row column, navigate to the row you want to update, and then use one of the updater methods listed in Table 4-6 to change one or more column values. Finally, call updateRow to apply the changes.

For example:

```
try
{
    rs.absolute(6);
    rs.updateInt("year", 1975);
    rs.updateRow();
}
catch (SQLException e)
{
    System.out.println(e.getMessage());
    System.exit(0);
}
```

Here, the year column of the sixth row in the result set is changed to 1975.

Table 4-6	Update Methods of the ResultSet Interface
Update by Column Name	**Update by Column Index**
void updateBigDecimal (String columnName, BigDecimal value)	void updateBigDecimal(int columnIndex, BigDecimal value)
void updateBoolean (String columnName, boolean value)	void updateBoolean(int columnIndex, boolean value)
void updateDate(String columnName, Date value)	void updateDate(int columnIndex, Date value)

(continued)

Table 4-6 *(continued)*

Update by Column Name	Update by Column Index
void updateDouble (String columnName, double value)	void updateDouble(int columnIndex, double value)
void updateFloat(String columnName, float value)	void updateFloat(int columnIndex, float value)
void updateInt(String columnName, int value)	void updateInt(int columnIndex, int value)
void updateLong(String columnName, long value)	void updateLong(int columnIndex, long value)
void updateShort(String columnName, short value)	void updateShort(int columnIndex, short value)
void updateString(String columnName, String value)	void updateString(int columnIndex, String value)

Inserting a row

To insert a row, you use a special row in the result set called the *insert row*. First, you call the `moveToInsertRow` method to move the cursor to the insert row. Then, you use update methods to set the value for each column in the insert row. You then call the `insertRow` method to copy the insert row into the result set, which in turn writes a new row to the database. And finally, you call `moveToCurrentRow` to move back to the previous position in the result set.

Here's an example:

```
try
{
    rs.moveToInsertRow();
    rs.updateString("title",
        "Monty Python and the Holy Grail");
    rs.updateInt("year", 1975);
    rs.updateDouble("price", 13.95);
    rs.insertRow();
    rs.moveToCurrentRow();
}
catch (SQLException e)
{
    System.out.println(e.getMessage());
    System.exit(0);
}
```

Chapter 5: Working with XML

In This Chapter

✔ Understanding XML

✔ Defining structure with DTD

✔ Looking at DOM and SAX

✔ Reading a document into memory

✔ Navigating a document

✔ Getting attribute and element values

In this chapter, you find out how to work with XML — the best thing to happen to computing since the invention of the vacuum tubes, at least according to some over-enthusiastic prognosticators.

This chapter focuses on the basics of reading an XML document into memory and extracting data from it. With the background in this chapter, you shouldn't have much trouble studying the API documentation on your own to learn more about XML programming.

What Exactly Is XML, Anyway?

XML is the latest and greatest fad in computing. Most computer industry pundits agree that XML will completely change the way you work with computers. Here are just some of the ways XML will revolutionize the world of computers:

✦ Unlock all the vast warehouses of data that's locked up in the vaults of corporate mainframe computers.

✦ Enable every electronic device on the planet from the most complex supercomputers to desktop computers to cellphones to wrist watches to communicate with one another.

✦ Allow every computer program ever written to exchange data with every other computer program ever written.

✦ Probably cure cancer and solve the budget deficit, too.

Yawn.

So what is XML, really? Simply put, XML is a way to store and exchange information in a standardized way that's easy to create, retrieve, and exchange between different types of computer systems or programs.

When XML is stored in a file, the file is usually given the extension xml.

Tags

Like HTML, XML uses tags to mark the data. For example, here's a bit of XML that describes a book:

```
<Book>
  <Title>Java All-In-One Desk Reference For
  Dummies</Title>
  <Author>Lowe</Author>
</Book>
```

This chunk of XML defines an *element* called Book, which contains information for a single book. The Book element, in turn, contains two subordinate elements: Title and Author.

Notice how each element begins with a tag that lists the element's name. This tag is called the *start tag*. The element ends with an element that repeats the element name, preceded by a slash (an *end* tag).

Everything that appears between the start tag and the end tag is the element's *content*. An element's content can consist of text data, or it can consist of one or more additional elements. In that case, the additional elements nested within an element are called *child elements,* and the element that contains them is called the *parent element*.

The highest level element in an XML document is called the *root element*. A properly formed XML document consists of a single root element, which can contain elements nested within it. For example, suppose you want to create an XML document with information about two movies. The XML document might look something like this:

```
<Movies>
  <Movie>
    <Title>It's a Wonderful Life</Title>
    <Year>1946</Year>
    <Price>14.95</Price>
  </Movie>
  <Movie>
    <Title>The Great Race</Title>
    <Year>1965</Year>
    <Price>12.95</Price>
  </Movie>
</Movies>
```

Here, the root element named Movies contains two Movie elements, each of which contains a Title, Year, and Price element.

Although XML superficially resembles HTML, you find two key differences between XML and HTML:

✦ The tags used in HTML indicate the format of data that displays. In contrast, tags in an XML document indicate the meaning of the data. For example, HTML has tags such as `<B>` and `<I>` that indicate data is bold or italic. In contrast, an XML document that holds information about books may have tags such as `<Title>` and `<Author>` that provide the title and author of the book.

✦ The tags used in an HTML document are set in stone. In contrast, you can make up any tags you want to use in an XML document. If you're creating an XML document about cars, you may use tags such as `<Make>`, `<Model>`, and `<Year>`. But if you're creating an XML document about classes taught at a university, you may use tags such as `<Course>`, `<Title>`, `<Instructor>`, `<Room>`, and `<Schedule>`.

Attributes

Instead of using child elements, you can use attributes to provide data for an element. An *attribute* is a name and value pair that's written inside of the start tag for an element. For example, here's a `Movie` element that uses an attribute instead of a child element to record the year:

```
<Movie year="1946">
    <Title>It's a Wonderful Life</Title>
    <Price>14.95</Price>
</Movie>
```

Whether you use attributes or child elements is largely a matter of personal preference. Many XML purists say that you should avoid attributes, or use them only for identifying data such as identification numbers or codes. Others say to use attributes freely. In my experience, a few attributes here and there don't hurt, but I avoid them for the most part.

The movies.xml file

For your reference, Listing 5-1 shows the `movies.xml` file that the programs that appear later in this chapter use.

LISTING 5-1: THE MOVIES.XML FILE

```
<Movies>
    <Movie year="1946">
        <Title>It's a Wonderful Life</Title>
        <Price>14.95</Price>
    </Movie>
```

continued

LISTING 5-1 (CONTINUED)

```
<Movie year="1965">
  <Title>The Great Race</Title>
  <Price>12.95</Price>
</Movie>
<Movie year="1974">
  <Title>Young Frankenstein</Title>
  <Price>16.95</Price>
</Movie>
<Movie year="1975">
  <Title>The Return of the Pink Panther</Title>
  <Price>11.95</Price>
</Movie>
<Movie year="1977">
  <Title>Star Wars</Title>
  <Price>17.95</Price>
</Movie>
<Movie year="1987">
  <Title>The Princess Bride</Title>
  <Price>16.95</Price>
</Movie>
<Movie year="1989">
  <Title>Glory</Title>
  <Price>14.95</Price>
</Movie>
<Movie year="1995">
  <Title>Apollo 13</Title>
  <Price>19.95</Price>
</Movie>
<Movie year="1997">
  <Title>The Game</Title>
  <Price>14.95</Price>
</Movie>
<Movie year="2001">
  <Title>The Fellowship of the Ring</Title>
  <Price>19.95</Price>
</Movie>
</Movies>
```

Using a DTD

An XML document can have a DTD, which spells out exactly what elements can appear in an XML document and in what order the elements can appear. DTD stands for *Document Type Definition,* but that won't be on the test.

For example, a DTD for an XML document about movies may specify that each Movie element must have a Title and Price subelements and an attribute named `year`. It can also specify that the root element is named `Movies` and consists of any number of `Movie` elements.

The main purpose of the DTD is to spell out the structure of an XML document so that users of the document know how to interpret it. But another equally important use of the DTD is to *validate* the document to make sure it doesn't have any structural errors. For example, if you create a Movies XML document that has two titles for a movie, you can use the DTD to detect the error.

You can store the DTD for an XML document in the same file as the XML data, but more often you store the DTD in a separate file. That way, you can use a DTD to govern the format of several XML documents of the same type. To indicate the name of the file that contains the DTD, you add a `<!DOCTYPE>` tag to the XML document. For example:

```
<!DOCTYPE Movies SYSTEM "movies.dtd">
```

Here, the XML file is identified as a `Movies` document, whose DTD you can find in the file `movies.dtd`. Add this tag near the beginning of the `movies.xml` file, right after the `<?xml>` tag.

Listing 5-2 shows a DTD file for the `movies.xml` file that was shown in Listing 5-1.

LISTING 5-2: A DTD FILE FOR THE MOVIES.XML FILE

```
<?xml version="1.0" encoding="UTF-8"?>
<!ELEMENT Movies (Movie*)>
<!ELEMENT Movie (Title, Price)>
<!ATTLIST Movie year CDATA #REQUIRED>
<!ELEMENT Title (#PCDATA)>
<!ELEMENT Price (#PCDATA)>
```

Each of the `ELEMENT` tags in a DTD defines a type of element that can appear in the document and indicates what can appear as the content for that element type. The general form of the `ELEMENT` tag is this:

```
<!ELEMENT element (content)>
```

Use the rules listed in Table 5-1 to express the content.

For example, the first `ELEMENT` tag in the DTD I showed in Listing 5-2 says that a `Movies` element consists of zero or more `Movie` elements. The second `ELEMENT` tag says that a `Movie` element consists of a `Title` element followed by a `Price` element. The third and fourth `ELEMENT` tags say that the `Title` and `Price` elements consist of text data.

Table 5-1	**Specifying Element Content**
Content	*Description*
`element*`	The specified element can occur zero or more times.
`element+`	The specified element can occur 1 or more times.
`element?`	The specified element can occur 0 or 1 times.
`element1|element2`	Either element1 or element2 can appear.
`element1, element2`	Element1 followed by element2.
`#PCDATA`	Text data.
`ANY`	Any child elements are allowed.
`EMPTY`	No child elements of any type are allowed.

If this notation looks vaguely familiar, it's because it is derived from regular expressions.

The `ATTLIST` tag provides the name of each attribute. Its general form is this:

```
<!ATTLIST element attribute type default-value>
```

Here's a breakdown of this tag:

+ *element* names the element whose tag the attribute can appear in.

+ *attribute* provides the name of the attribute.

+ *type* specifies what can appear as the attribute's value. The *type* can be any of the items listed in Table 5-2.

+ *default* provides a default value and indicates whether the attribute is required or optional. *default* can be any of the items listed in Table 5-3.

Table 5-2	**Attribute Types**
Element	*The Attribute Value . . .*
`CDATA`	Can be any character string.
`(string1|string2...)`	Can be one of the listed strings.
`NMTOKEN`	Must be a name token, which is a string made up of letters and numbers.
`NMTOKENS`	Must be one or more name tokens separated by white space.
`ID`	Is a name token that must be unique. In other words, no other element in the document can have the same value for this attribute.

Element	The Attribute Value . . .
IDREF	Must be the same as an ID value used elsewhere in the document.
IDREFS	Is a list of IDREF values separated by white space.

Table 5-3	Attribute Defaults
Default	*Optional or Required?*
#REQUIRED	Required.
#IMPLIED	Optional.
value	Optional. This value is used if the attribute is omitted.
#FIXED *value*	Optional. However, if included, it must be this value, and if omitted, this value is used by default.

For example, here's the ATTLIST tag declaration from `movies.dtd`:

```
<!ATTLIST Movie year CDATA #REQUIRED>
```

This declaration indicates that the attribute goes with the Movie element, is named year, can be any kind of data, and is required.

Here's an ATTLIST tag that specifies a list of possible values along with a default:

```
<!ATTLIST Movie genre (SciFi|Action|Comedy|Drama)
    Comedy>
```

This form of the ATTLIST tag lets you create an attribute that's similar to an enumeration, with a list of acceptable values.

Processing XML in Two Ways

In general, you can process XML documents in a Java program with two approaches. These two approaches are referred to as DOM and SAX:

* **DOM:** *DOM* stands for *Document Object Model.* The basic idea of DOM is that you read an entire XML document from a file into memory, where the document is stored as a collection of objects that are structured as a tree. You can then process the elements of the tree (called *nodes*) however you wish. If you change any of the nodes, you can write the document back to a file.

✦ **SAX:** *SAX* stands for *Simple API for XML*. SAX is a read-only technique for processing XML that lets you read the elements of an XML document from a file and react to them as they come. Because SAX doesn't require that you store an entire XML document in memory at one time, it's often used for very large XML documents.

In this chapter, I cover the basics of using DOM to retrieve information from an XML document. DOM represents an XML document in memory as a tree of `Node` objects. For example, Figure 5-1 shows a simplified DOM tree for an XML document that has two `Movie` elements. Notice that the root element (`Movies`) is a node, each `Movie` element is a node, and each `Title` and `Price` element is a node. In addition, text values are stored as child nodes of the elements they belong to. Thus, the `Title` and `Price` elements each have a child node that contains the text for these elements.

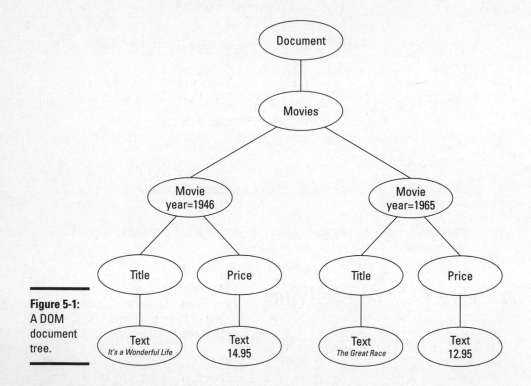

Figure 5-1:
A DOM
document
tree.

Reading a DOM Document

Before you can process a DOM document, you have to read the document into memory from an XML file. You'd think that would be a fairly straightforward proposition, but unfortunately it involves some pretty strange incantations. Rather than go through all the classes and methods you have to use, I just look at the finished code for a complete method that accepts a `String` that contains a filename as a parameter and returns a document object as its return value. Along the way, you find out what each class and method does.

Here's the code:

```
private static Document getDocument(String name)
{
    try
    {
        DocumentBuilderFactory factory =
            DocumentBuilderFactory.newInstance();
        factory.setIgnoringComments(true);

        factory.setIgnoringElementContentWhitespace(true);
        factory.setValidating(true);
        DocumentBuilder builder =
            factory.newDocumentBuilder();
        return builder.parse(new InputSource(name));
    }
    catch (Exception e)
    {
        System.out.println(e.getMessage());
    }
    return null;
}
```

Creating a document builder factory

The first statement of the preceding example calls the `newInstance` method of the `DocumentBuilderFactory` class to create a new `DocumentBuilderFactory` object. The job of the document builder factory is to create document builder objects that are able to read XML input and create DOM documents in memory.

Why not just call the `DocumentBuilderFactory` constructor? It turns out that `DocumentBuilderFactory` is an abstract class, so it doesn't have a constructor. `newInstance` is a static method that determines which class to create an instance of based on the way your system is configured.

Configuring the document builder factory

After you get a document builder factory, you can configure it so it reads the document the way you want. The next three statements configure three options that are applied to document builders created by this factory object:

```
factory.setIgnoringComments(true);
factory.setIgnoringElementContentWhitespace(true);
factory.setValidating(true);
```

Here's a closer look at these statements:

✦ **The `setIgnoringComments` method tells the document builder to not create nodes for comments in the XML file.** Most XML files don't contain comments, but if they do, they're not part of the data represented by the document, so they can be safely ignored. Setting this option causes them to be ignored automatically. (If you don't set this option, a node is created for each comment in the document. And because you can't predict when or where comments appear, your program has to check every node it processes to make sure it isn't a comment.)

✦ **The `setIgnoringElementContentWhitespace` method causes the document builder to ignore any white space that isn't part of a text value.** If you don't include this option, the DOM document includes nodes that represent white space. The only thing these white space nodes are good for is making the DOM document harder to process, so you should always set this option.

✦ **The `setValidating` method tells the document builder to validate the input XML if it specifies a DTD.** Validating the input can also dramatically simplify your program, because you know that the DOM document conforms to the requirements of the DTD. For example, if you're processing the `movies.xml` file shown earlier in Listing 5-1, you know for certain that the first child of a `Movie` element is a `Title` element and the second child is a `Price` element. Without the validation, all you know is that the first child of a `Movie` element *should be* a `Title` element, but you have to check it to make sure.

Creating a document builder and the document

After you set the options, you can call the `newDocumentBuilder` method to create a document builder:

```
DocumentBuilder builder =
    factory.newDocumentBuilder();
```

Here, the document builder is referenced by a variable named `builder`.

Finally, you can create the DOM document by calling the `parse` method of the document builder. This method accepts an `InputSource` object as a parameter. Fortunately, the `InputSource` class has a constructor that takes a filename parameter and returns an input source linked to the file. So you can create the input source, parse the XML file, create a DOM document, and return the DOM document to the caller all in one statement:

```
return builder.parse(new InputSource(name));
```

Note that several of these methods throw exceptions. In particular, `newDocumentBuilder` throws `ParserConfigurationException` and `parse` throws `IOException` and `SAXException`. To keep this example simple, I caught all exceptions in one `catch` clause and printed the exceptions message to the console.

Using the getDocument method

By adding the `getDocument` method, you can create a DOM document from a file with a single statement, like this:

```
Document doc = getDocument("movies.xml");
```

Here, the `movies.xml` file is read and a DOM document is created and assigned to the `doc` variable.

Also, note that you must provide three `import` statements to use the `getDocument` method:

```
import javax.xml.parsers.*;
import org.w3c.dom.*;
import org.xml.sax.*;
```

`DocumentBuilder` and `DocumentBuilderFactory` are in the `javax.xml.parsers` package, `Document` is in `org.w3c.dom`, and `InputSource` is in `org.xml.sax`.

Remember how I said I wouldn't use SAX in this chapter? I lied. The `parse` method of the `DocumentBuilder` class uses SAX to read the XML file while it builds the DOM object.

Reading DOM Nodes

After you have a DOM document in memory, you can easily retrieve data from the document's nodes. The DOM API is based on interfaces rather than classes, so each node of the DOM document is represented by an object that implements one or more DOM interfaces. The following paragraphs give you an overview of the interfaces you need to work with:

✦ **Document:** The entire document is represented by an object that implements the Document interface. The method you use most from this interface is getDocumentElement, which returns an Element object that represents the document's root node. After you have the root node, you can then navigate to other nodes in the document to get the information you're looking for.

✦ **Node:** The Node interface represents a node in the DOM document. This interface provides methods that are common to all nodes. Table 5-4 lists the most useful of these methods. This table also lists some of the fields' values that the getNodeType method can return.

✦ **Element:** The Element interface represents nodes that correspond to elements in the XML document. Element extends Node, so any object that implements Element is also a Node. Table 5-5 lists some of the more useful methods of this interface.

✦ **Text:** The text content of an element is not contained in the element itself, but in a Text node that's stored as a child of the element. The Text interface has a few interesting methods you may want to look up, but for most applications, you just use the getNodeValue method inherited from the Node interface to retrieve the text stored by a text node.

✦ **NodeList:** A NodeList is a collection of nodes that's returned by methods such as the getChildNodes method of the Node interface or the getElementsByTagName of the Element interface. NodeList has just two methods: item(int i), which returns the node at the specified index, and getLength(), which returns the number of items in the list. (Like *almost* every other index in Java, the first node is index 0, not 1.)

Table 5-4	The Node Interface
Method	*Description*
NodeList getChildNodes()	Gets a NodeList object that contains all of this node's child nodes.
Node getFirstChild()	Gets the first child of this node.
Node getLastChild()	Gets the last child of this node.
int getNodeType()	Gets an int that indicates the type of the node. The value can be one of the fields listed later in this table.
String getNodeValue()	Gets the value of this node, if the node has a value.
Node getNextSibling()	Gets the next sibling node.
Node getPrevSibling()	Gets the previous sibling node.
boolean hasChildNodes()	Determines whether the node has any child nodes.
Field	*Description*
ATTRIBUTE_NODE	The node is an attribute node.
CDATA_SECTION_NODE	The node contains content data.

Field	Description
COMMENT_NODE	The node is a comment.
DOCUMENT_NODE	The node is a document node.
ELEMENT_NODE	The node is an element node.
TEXT_NODE	The node is a text node.

Table 5-5	The Element Interface
Method	*Description*
String getAttribute (String name)	Gets the value of the specified attribute.
NodeList getElementsBy TagName(String name)	Gets a NodeList object that contains all of the element nodes that are contained within this element and have the specified name.
boolean hasAttribute (String name)	Determines whether the element has the specified attribute.

Processing elements

Assuming you use a DTD to validate the XML file when you build the document, you can usually navigate your way around the document to pick up information you need without resorting to NodeList objects. For example, here's a routine that simply counts all the Movie elements in the movies.xml file (shown earlier in Listing 5-1) after it's been parsed into a Document object named doc:

```
int count = 0;
Element root = doc.getDocumentElement();
Node movie = root.getFirstChild();
while (movie != null)
{
    count++;
    movie = movie.getNextSibling();
}
System.out.println("There are " + count + " movies.");
```

This method first calls the getFirstChild method to get the first child of the root element. Then, it uses each child element's getNextSibling method to get the next element that's also a child of the root element.

If you run a program that contains these lines, the following line appears on the console:

```
There are 10 movies.
```

This program doesn't do anything with the `Movie` elements other than count them, but you soon see how to extract data from the `Movie` elements.

An alternative way to process all the elements in the `movies.xml` file is to use the `getChildNodes` method to return a `NodeList` object that contains all the elements. You can then use a `for` loop to access each element individually. For example, here's a snippet of code that lists the name of each element:

```
Element root = doc.getDocumentElement();
NodeList movies = root.getChildNodes();
for (int i = 0; i < movies.getLength(); i++)
{
    Node movie = movies.item(i);
    System.out.println(movie.getNodeName());
}
```

Here, the `item` method is used in the `for` loop to retrieve each `Movie` element. If you run a program that contains these lines, ten lines with the word `Movie` are displayed in the console window.

Getting attribute values

To get the value of an element's attribute, call the `getAttribute` method and pass the name of the attribute as the parameter. This returns the string value of the attribute. You can then convert this value to another type if necessary. Note that the value may include some white space, so you should run the value through the `trim` method to get rid of any superfluous white space.

Here's an example that gets the `year` attribute from each movie in the `movies.xml` file and determines the year of the oldest movie in the collection:

```
Element root = doc.getDocumentElement();
Element movie = (Element)root.getFirstChild();
int oldest = 9999;
while (movie != null)
{
    String s = movie.getAttribute("year");
    int year = Integer.parseInt(s);
    if (year < oldest)
        oldest = year;
    movie = (Element)movie.getNextSibling();
}
System.out.println("The oldest movie in the file "
    + "is from " + oldest + ".");
```

The `year` attribute is extracted with these two lines of code:

```
String s = movie.getAttribute("year");
int year = Integer.parseInt(s);
```

The first line gets the string value of the `year` attribute, and the second line converts it to an `int`.

Notice the extra casting that's done in this method. It's necessary because the `movie` variable has to be an `Element` type so you can call the `getAttribute` method. However, the `getNextSibling` method returns a `Node`, not an `Element`. As a result, the compiler doesn't let you assign the node to the `movie` variable unless you first cast it to an `Element`.

Getting child element values

You might be surprised to learn that the text content of an element is not stored with the element. Instead, it's stored in a child node of type `Text`. For example, consider the following XML:

```
<Title>The Princess Bride</Title>
```

This element results in two nodes in the XML document: an `Element` node named `Title`, and a `Text` node that contains the text `The Princess Bride`.

Thus, if you have a `Title` element in hand, you must first get the `Text` element before you can get the text content. For example

```
Node textElement = titleElement.getFirstChild();
String title = textElement.getNodeValue();
```

If you prefer to write your code a little more tersely, you can do it in a single statement like this:

```
String title =
    titleElement.getFirstChild().getNodeValue();
```

If you find this incantation a little tedious and you're doing a lot of it in your program, write yourself a little helper method. For example

```
private static String getTextValue(Node n)
{
    return n.getFirstChild().getNodeValue();
}
```

Then, you can get the text content for an element by calling the `getTextValue` method, like this:

```
String title = getTextValue(titleElement);
```

After you get the text content, you can parse it to a numeric type if you need to.

Putting It All Together: A Program That Lists Movies

Now that you've seen the various interfaces and classes you use to get data from an XML file, Listing 5-3 shows a complete program that reads the `movies.xml` file (shown earlier in Listing 5-1) and lists the title, year, and price of each movie on the console. When you run this program, the following appears on the console:

```
1946: It's a Wonderful Life ($14.95)
1965: The Great Race ($12.95)
1974: Young Frankenstein ($16.95)
1975: The Return of the Pink Panther ($11.95)
1977: Star Wars ($17.95)
1987: The Princess Bride ($16.95)
1989: Glory ($14.95)
1995: Apollo 13 ($19.95)
1997: The Game ($14.95)
2001: The Lord of the Rings:The Fellowship of the Ring
   ($19.95)
```

LISTING 5-3: READING AN XML DOCUMENT

```java
import java.io.*;                                            → 1
import javax.xml.parsers.*;
import org.xml.sax.*;
import org.w3c.dom.*;
import java.text.*;

public class ListMoviesXML
{
    private static NumberFormat cf =
        NumberFormat.getCurrencyInstance();

    public static void main(String[] args)                  → 12
    {
        Document doc = getDocument("movies.xml");

        Element root = doc.getDocumentElement();

        Element movieElement = (Element)root.getFirstChild();
        Movie m;
        while (movieElement != null)
        {
            m = getMovie(movieElement);
            String msg = Integer.toString(m.year);
            msg += ": " + m.title;
            msg += " (" + cf.format(m.price) + ")";
            System.out.println(msg);
            movieElement =
                (Element)movieElement.getNextSibling();
        }
    }
}
```

```
private static Document getDocument(String name)                    → 33
{
    try
    {
        DocumentBuilderFactory factory =
            DocumentBuilderFactory.newInstance();
        factory.setIgnoringComments(true);
        factory.setIgnoringElementContentWhitespace(true);
        factory.setValidating(true);
        DocumentBuilder builder =
            factory.newDocumentBuilder();
        return builder.parse(new InputSource(name));
    }
    catch (Exception e)
    {
        System.out.println(e.getMessage());
    }
    return null;
}

private static Movie getMovie(Element e)                            → 53
{
    // get the year attribute
    String yearString = e.getAttribute("year");
    int year = Integer.parseInt(yearString);

    // get the Title element
    Element tElement = (Element)e.getFirstChild();
    String title = getTextValue(tElement).trim();

    // get the Price element
    Element pElement =
        (Element)tElement.getNextSibling();
    String pString = getTextValue(pElement).trim();
    double price = Double.parseDouble(pString);

    return new Movie(title, year, price);
}

private static String getTextValue(Node n)                          → 72
{
    return n.getFirstChild().getNodeValue();
}

private static class Movie                                          → 77
{
    public String title;
    public int year;
    public double price;

    public Movie(String title, int year, double price)
    {
        this.title = title;
        this.year = year;
        this.price = price;
    }
}
}
```

Because all the code in this program is elsewhere in this chapter, the following paragraphs just provide a simple description of what each method in this program does:

→ **1** Wow, that's a lot of packages to import. Too bad Java's designers couldn't have put all of these XML classes in one big package.

→ **12** The `main` method starts by calling the `getDocument` method to get a `Document` object from the file `movies.xml`. Then, it gets the root element and uses a `while` loop to spin through all the child elements, which you know to be `Movie` elements because the document was validated when it was parsed. As each `Movie` element is processed, it is passed to the `getMovie` method, which extracts the `year` attribute and the `title` and `price` elements and returns a `Movie` object. Then, the movie is printed on the console.

→ **33** The `getDocument` method accepts a filename as a parameter and returns a `Document` object. Before it creates the `DocumentBuilder` object, it sets the configuration options so that comments and white space are ignored and the XML file is validated.

→ **53** The `getMovie` method is passed an `Element` object that represents a `Movie` element. It extracts the `year` attribute, gets the text value of the `title` element, and parses the text value of the `price` element to a `double`. It then uses these values to create a new `Movie` object, which is then returned to the caller.

→ **72** The `getTextValue` method is simply a little helper method that gets the text content from a node. This method assumes that the node has a child node that contains the text value, so you shouldn't call this method unless you know that to be the case. (Because the XML document was validated, you do.)

→ **77** The `Movie` class is a private inner class that represents a single movie. It uses public fields to hold the title, year, and price, and provides a simple constructor that initializes these fields.

Book IX

Fun and Games

The 5th Wave   By Rich Tennant

"This time, just for fun, let's see what you'd look like with bat ears and squash for a nose."

Contents at a Glance

Chapter 1: Fun with Fonts and Colors

In This Chapter

ↈ Setting the font of a text control

ↈ Getting a list of available fonts

ↈ Playing with colors

ↈ Using system colors

ↈ Setting foreground and background colors

In this chapter, I look at ways of dressing up the text that appears in Swing controls. In particular, I show you how to change the font that text is displayed in — including bold, italic, and size — as well as how to change the color of your text.

Most of the examples work with labels, but the methods you call to set the font and color are available to all Swing components because they're defined by the `Component` class, which all Swing components inherit.

Also, the information about fonts and colors that I present in this chapter also applies to graphics created with the methods of the `Graphics2D` class in Book IX, Chapter 3.

Working with Fonts

In Java, a font is represented by the `Font` class. Each `Font` object has three basic characteristics: the font name, a style identifier (plain, bold, italic, or bold and italic), and a point size.

Although the `Font` class has a ton of methods, you probably won't use them unless you're writing a desktop publishing program in Java. Instead, you can get by with the basic constructor, which has this form:

```
Font(String name, int style, int size)
```

For example, this statement creates a `Font` object for a font named Papyrus:

```
Font("Papyrus", Font.PLAIN, 14)
```

Here, the font style is plain, and the size is 14-point.

 Realizing that the `Font` class constructor doesn't really create a font is important. Instead, it creates a `Font` object that represents a font that's already installed on your computer. Creating a `Font` object with the name "Comic Strip" doesn't actually create a font named `Circus Clowns` unless that font is already installed on the computer.

Using font names

The `name` parameter specifies the name of the installed font you want to use. For example, if you specify `Times New Roman`, the Times New Roman font is used.

Coding string literals for specific fonts is usually not a good idea, because you have no way to guarantee that every computer has the exact font you specify. You can get around that problem in two ways:

✦ Let the user configure the fonts by picking from a list of available fonts. Check out the later section, "Getting a list of all available fonts."

✦ Use one of several *logical font names* that Java provides in an attempt to let you specify fonts generically. Table 1-1 lists the logical font names. You don't get much choice when you use logical font names, but at least you can choose between a basic serif font, sans-serif font, and mono-spaced font. And you can use the `Dialog` and `Dialog Input` fonts to set the font used in dialog boxes.

Table 1-1	Logical Font Names
Logical font	*Description*
Serif	A basic serif font. Times New Roman on Windows, usually Times Roman on other systems.
SansSerif	A sans-serif font. Arial on Windows, usually Helvetica on non-Windows systems.
Monospaced	A monospaced font. Courier New on Windows, usually Courier on non-Windows systems.
Dialog	The font used to display text in system dialog boxes.
DialogInput	The font used for text input in system dialog boxes.

Using font styles

Fonts can have one of four styles: plain, bold, italic, and bold-italic. To set the font style, you use the following three constants as the second parameter to the `Font` class constructor:

```
Font.BOLD
Font.ITALIC
Font.PLAIN
```

For example, here's how you create a `Font` object for 24-point JSL Ancient Bold:

```
Font("JSL Ancient", Font.BOLD, 24)
```

You may have noticed that bold-italic has no constant. To create a bold-italic font, you combine the `Font.BOLD` and `Font.ITALIC` constants with a `|` operator, like this:

```
Font("Garamond", Font.BOLD | Font.ITALIC, 12)
```

Here, the `Font` object is Garamond, bold and italic, and 12-point.

Setting a component's font

To set the font used to display a component, just call the component's `setFont` method and pass it a `Font` object. For example:

```
JLabel textLabel = new JLabel("Arghh, Matey");
Font f = new Font("JSL Ancient", Font.PLAIN, 16);
textLabel.setFont(f);
```

Here, the font of the label named `textLabel` is set to 16-point JSL Ancient. (JSL Ancient is one of my personal favorites; it's used in the Pirates of the Caribbean ride at Disneyland.)

If the font is used for only one component, you can just create the component right in the `setFont` method call:

```
textLabel.setFont(new Font("JSL Ancient", Font.PLAIN, 16));
```

If you want a component to inherit the font used by the container that holds it (such as a panel), call the component's `setFont` method with the parameter set to `null`. For example, here's code that sets the font for a pair of buttons in a panel named `panel1` to JSL Ancient:

```
JPanel panel1 = new JPanel();
panel1.setFont(new Font("JSL Ancient", Font.PLAIN, 16));

JButton b1 = new JButton("Jolly");
b1.setFont(null);
panel1.add(b1);
```

```
JButton b2 = new JButton("Roger");
b2.setFont(null);
panel1.add(b2);
```

In this example, both buttons have their fonts set to `null`, so they both pick up the font of their parent `panel1`.

Getting a list of all available fonts

If you want to let the user pick a font, you want to get a list of all the available fonts on the system so you can put the font names in a combo box. To do that, you first have to get an object called a `GraphicsEnvironment` that represents the graphics environment the program is running in. The `GraphicsEnvironment` class has a static method named `getLocalGraphicsEnvironment` that does this for you:

```
GraphicsEnvironment g;
g = GraphicsEnvironment.getLocalGraphicsEnvironment();
```

Note that the `GraphicsEnvironment` class is in the `java.awt` package, so you need to provide an `import` statement to import that package.

After you have a `GraphicsEnvironment` object, you can call its `getAvailableFontFamilyNames` method, which returns an array of strings containing all the font names that are available on the system. For example:

```
String[] fonts;
fonts = g.getAvailableFontFamilyNames();
```

You can then use this array in the constructor of a combo box, like this:

```
JComboBox fontComboBox = new JComboBox(fonts);
```

Then, you can create a font from the name selected by the user with code similar to this:

```
String name = (String) fontComboBox.getSelectedItem();
Font f = new Font(name, Font.PLAIN, 12);
```

A program that plays with fonts

So that you can see how these elements work together, Listing 1-1 presents a simple program that lets the user choose a font, style, and size for the sample text that's displayed. Figure 1-1 shows this program in action. Whenever the user chooses a font or size from one of the combo boxes or checks or unchecks one of the check boxes, the font used to display the text at the top of the form is changed accordingly.

Figure 1-1:
The Fonts
program in
action.

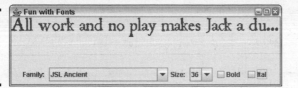

LISTING 1-1: A PROGRAM THAT PLAYS WITH FONTS

```java
import javax.swing.*;
import java.awt.event.*;
import java.awt.*;

public class Fonts extends JFrame
{
    public static void main(String [] args)
    {
        new Fonts();
    }

    private JLabel sampleText;                              → 12

    private JComboBox fontComboBox;                         → 14
    private JComboBox sizeComboBox;
    private JCheckBox boldCheck, italCheck;

    private String[] fonts;                                 → 18

    public Fonts()
    {
        this.setSize(500,150);
        this.setTitle("Fun with Fonts ");
        this.setDefaultCloseOperation(JFrame.EXIT_ON_CLOSE);

        FontListener fl = new FontListener();               → 26

        sampleText = new JLabel(
            "All work and no play makes Jack a dull boy");
        this.add(sampleText, BorderLayout.NORTH);           → 30

        GraphicsEnvironment g;                              → 32
        g = GraphicsEnvironment
                .getLocalGraphicsEnvironment();
        fonts = g.getAvailableFontFamilyNames();

        JPanel controlPanel = new JPanel();                 → 37

        fontComboBox = new JComboBox(fonts);                → 39
        fontComboBox.addActionListener(fl);
        controlPanel.add(new JLabel("Family: "));
        controlPanel.add(fontComboBox);

        Integer[] sizes = {7, 8, 9, 10, 11, 12,             → 44
                        14, 18, 20, 22, 24, 36};
```

continued

LISTING 1-1 (CONTINUED)

```
        sizeComboBox = new JComboBox(sizes);
        sizeComboBox.setSelectedIndex(5);
        sizeComboBox.addActionListener(fl);
        controlPanel.add(new JLabel("Size: "));
        controlPanel.add(sizeComboBox);

        boldCheck = new JCheckBox("Bold");                      → 52
        boldCheck.addActionListener(fl);
        controlPanel.add(boldCheck);

        italCheck = new JCheckBox("Ital");                      → 56
        italCheck.addActionListener(fl);
        controlPanel.add(italCheck);

        this.add(controlPanel, BorderLayout.SOUTH);             → 60
        fl.updateText();

        this.setVisible(true);
    }

    private class FontListener implements ActionListener
    {
        public void actionPerformed(ActionEvent e)
        {
            updateText();                                       → 70
        }

        public void updateText()                                → 73
        {
            String name
                = (String) fontComboBox.getSelectedItem();

            Integer size
                = (Integer)sizeComboBox.getSelectedItem();

            int style;
            if (   boldCheck.isSelected()
                && italCheck.isSelected())
                style = Font.BOLD | Font.ITALIC;
            else if (boldCheck.isSelected())
                style = Font.BOLD;
            else if (italCheck.isSelected())
                style = Font.ITALIC;
            else
                style = Font.PLAIN;

            Font f = new Font(name, style,
                size.intValue());
            sampleText.setFont(f);
        }
    }
}
```

The following paragraphs hit the high points of this program:

→**12** The label whose font is changed when the user makes a selection.

→**14** The controls that the user works with to pick the font, size, and style.

→**18** The `fonts` variable is an array of strings that is used to hold the name of each font available on the system.

→**26** The `fl` variable holds a reference to the action listener object that handles action events for both combo boxes and both check boxes.

→**30** The label that contains the sample text is added to the North region of the frame.

→**32** These lines get the `GraphicsEnvironment` object, and then use it to populate the `fonts` array with the names of the fonts available on the system.

→**37** A panel is used to hold the two combo box and two check box controls.

→**39** These lines create the font combo box and add it to the panel.

→**44** These lines create the size combo box and add it to the panel. The combo box is filled from an array of integers that lists commonly used point sizes. If you want, you could call `setEditable(true)` to make this combo box editable. Then, the user could type any desired font size into the combo box. To keep the application simple, I did not make the combo box editable.

→**52** These lines create the bold check box and add it to the panel.

→**56** These lines create the italic check box and add it to the panel.

→**60** The panel is added to the South region of the frame. Then, the next line calls the action listener's `updateText` method, which applies the currently selected font, style, and size to the label. (If you don't call this method here, the label is initially displayed with the default font, not with the font indicated by the initial value of the font combo box.)

→**70** The `actionPerformed` method of the action listener class simply calls `updateText`.

→**73** The `updateText` method changes the font of the `sampleText` label to the font selected by the user. First, it gets the name selected in the font combo box. Next, it gets the size selected by the user in the size combo box. Because combo boxes return objects, the selected item is cast to an `Integer`. Next, the settings of the two check boxes are evaluated to determine how to set the `style` variable. Finally, a new `Font` object is created and assigned to the `sampleText` label.

Working with Color

In Java, a particular color is represented by an instance of the Color class. Every color is a unique combination of three different constituent colors: red, green, and blue. Each constituent is represented by an integer that ranges from 0 to 255, with zero meaning the constituent color is completely absent and 255 meaning the color is completely saturated with the constituent color.

In the following sections, you discover how to use the Color class to create color objects. Then, you apply colors to Swing components. And finally, you use a handy Swing dialog box called the Color Chooser.

Creating colors

One way to create a Color object is to call the Color constructor, passing it the red, green, and blue values you want to use. For example:

```
Color c = new Color(255, 255, 0);
```

Here, a color with full red, full green, and no blue is created. This results in bright yellow.

If all three constituent colors are zero, the resulting color is black. If all three are 255, the result is white. And if all three values are the same, somewhere between 0 and 255, the result is a shade of gray.

Because color numbers can be confusing to work with and hard to remember, the Color class provides several static constants that give you pre-defined colors. Table 1-2 lists these constants. For example, here's a statement that creates a Color object that represents the color red:

```
Color c = Color.RED;
```

Table 1-2	Constants Defined by the Color Class		
BLACK	GRAY	MAGENTA	RED
BLUE	GREEN	ORANGE	WHITE
CYAN	LIGHT_GRAY	PINK	YELLOW
DARK_GRAY			

Colors also have a characteristic called *alpha,* which indicates the transparency of the color. By default, alpha is set to 255, meaning that the color is not transparent. If you want to set a different alpha value, you can call a second `Color` constructor that accepts the alpha value as a fourth parameter. For example:

```
Color c = new Color(255, 0, 0, 128);
```

Here, the color is semitransparent.

The following paragraphs describe a few additional details worth knowing about the `Color` class:

✦ `Color` objects are immutable; there are no `set` methods that let you change a color.

✦ You can get the red, green, blue, and alpha values by using the `getRed`, `getGreen`, `getBlue`, and `getAlpha` methods.

✦ You can use the `brighter` method to create a color that is brighter than the current color. Likewise, the `darker` method returns a color object that's a little darker than the current color. These methods work by increasing the red, green, and blue values but keeping them in proportion to one another.

✦ If you call the `Color` constructor with a parameter that's less than zero or greater than 255, `IllegalArgumentException` is thrown. As a result, you need to check the parameter values before calling the constructor.

✦ The `Color` class provides an alternative constructor that lets you set the constituent colors using `float` values between 0.0 and 1.0.

✦ The `Color` class is in the `java.awt` package, so you need an `import` statement that specifies either `java.awt.Color` or `java.awt.*`.

Using system colors

You can use the `SystemColor` class to get colors that correspond to the colors configured by the underlying operating system for various GUI elements, such as menu text or the desktop background. Note that the `SystemColor` class extends the `Color` class, so you can use `SystemColor` objects with the `setForeground` and `setBackground` methods or with any other methods that call for `Color` objects.

The `SystemColor` class has a bevy of static methods that return `SystemColor` objects for the colors used by different parts of the system's GUI interface, as listed in Table 1-3. For example, here's a statement that sets the background color of a button to the color used as the background for tooltips:

```
button1.setBackground(SystemColor.info);
```

Table 1-3	SystemColor Methods
Field	*Description*
`static SystemColor activeCaption`	Background color of the active window's title bar.
`static SystemColor activeCaptionBorder`	Border color of the active window's title bar.
`static SystemColor activeCaptionText`	Text color of the active window's title bar.
`static SystemColor control`	Background color used for controls.
`static SystemColor controlText`	Text color used for controls.
`static SystemColor desktop`	Background color used for the desktop.
`static SystemColor inactiveCaption`	Background color used for the title bar of inactive windows.
`static SystemColor inactiveCaptionBorder`	Border color used for the title bar of inactive windows.
`static SystemColor inactiveCaptionText`	Text color used for the title bar of inactive windows.
`static SystemColor info`	Background color used for tooltips.
`static SystemColor infoText`	Text color used for tooltips.
`static SystemColor menu`	Background color used for menus.
`static SystemColor menuText`	Text color used for menus.
`static SystemColor textHighlight`	Background color used for highlighted text.
`static SystemColor textHighlightText`	Text color used for highlighted text.
`static SystemColor textInactiveText`	Text color used for inactive text.
`static SystemColor textText`	Text color used for text boxes and other text controls.
`static SystemColor extHighlight`	Background color used for highlighted text.
`static SystemColor window`	Background color used for windows.
`static SystemColor windowBorder`	Border color used for windows.
`static SystemColor windowText`	Text color used for windows.

Setting the color of Swing components

Every Swing component has two methods that let you set the colors used to draw the component: `setForeground` and `setBackground`. The `setForeground` method sets the color used to draw the component's text, and the `setBackground` method sets the color that fills in behind the text.

For example, here's code that sets the foreground color of a label to red:

```
JLabel errorMessage = new JLabel("Oops!");
errorMessage.setForeground(Color.RED);
```

As with fonts, you can force a component to use the color of its container by setting the color to `null`, like this:

```
textLabel.setForeground(null);
```

Then, if you add `textLabel` to a panel, the label uses the panel's foreground color.

Using a color chooser

The `JColorChooser` class creates a standardized dialog box that lets the user pick a color. This dialog box includes three tabs that let the user choose one of three methods to pick a color:

✦ The Swatches tab, shown in Figure 1-2, provides 279 different pre-defined color choices.

✦ The HSB tab lets the user select the color by specifying the hue (that is, the base color), saturation (the amount of the color), and brightness.

✦ The RGB tab lets the user specify the red, green, and blue values for the color.

All you need is one line of code to display a Color Chooser dialog box. Just call the static `showDialog` method, which takes three parameters:

✦ The parent component to use for the dialog box (`null` to center the dialog box on-screen)

✦ The text to display in the title bar

✦ The initial color

The `showDialog` method returns the color selected by the user, or `null` if the user cancels without selecting a color.

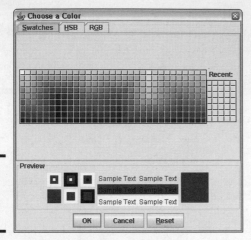

Figure 1-2:
A Color Chooser dialog box.

Here's an example:

```
Color c = JColorChooser.showDialog(null, "Choose a
    Color",
    sampleText.getForeground());
```

Just to prove how easy it is to use a color chooser, Listing 1-2 shows the complete code for a program that uses a color chooser. This program displays the frame shown in Figure 1-3; when the user clicks the Choose Color button, a color chooser just like the one in Figure 1-2 appears. Then, when the user selects a color and clicks OK, the color selected by the user is applied to the label.

Figure 1-3:
The Color Chooser program.

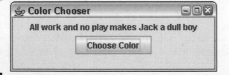

LISTING 1-2: A PROGRAM THAT USES A COLOR CHOOSER

```
import javax.swing.*;
import java.awt.event.*;
import java.awt.*;

public class ColorChooser extends JFrame
{
    public static void main(String [] args)
    {
        new ColorChooser();
```

```
    }

    private JLabel sampleText;                                      → 12
    private JButton chooseButton;

    public ColorChooser()
    {
        this.setSize(300,100);
        this.setTitle("Color Chooser");
        this.setDefaultCloseOperation(JFrame.EXIT_ON_CLOSE);

        JPanel panel1 = new JPanel();

        sampleText = new JLabel(
            "All work and no play makes Jack a dull boy");
        sampleText.setBackground(null);
        panel1.add(sampleText);

        chooseButton = new JButton("Choose Color");
        chooseButton.addActionListener(new ButtonListener());
        panel1.add(chooseButton);

        this.add(panel1);
        this.setVisible(true);
    }

    private class ButtonListener implements ActionListener
    {
        public void actionPerformed(ActionEvent e)
        {
            Color c = JColorChooser.showDialog(null,              → 40
                "Choose a Color",
                sampleText.getForeground());
            if (c != null)                                        → 43
                sampleText.setForeground(c);
        }
    }
}
```

Here are the key points to note as you peruse this program:

→**12** This label's color is set to the value chosen by the user.

→**40** In the `actionPerformed` method of the action listener attached to the button, this statement calls the static `showDialog` method of the `JColorChooser` class to display a Color Chooser dialog box. The color selected by the user is saved in the variable `c`.

→**43** If `c` is `null`, the user canceled out of the Color Chooser dialog box, so the label's foreground color is unchanged. Otherwise, the label's `setForeground` method is called to set the label's color to the color chosen by the user.

Chapter 2: Drawing Shapes

In This Chapter

↙ **Creating basic shapes such as lines, rectangles, and ellipses**

↙ **Setting the fill color and stroke thickness**

↙ **Creating shapes you can see through**

↙ **Creating gradient fills**

↙ **Rotating shapes**

↙ **Drawing text on-screen**

Were you one of those kids who, way back in school, passed away the boring hours of algebra class by doodling in the margins of the book? If so, you're in luck. Now that you're a grown up and you're learning Java programming, you don't have to doodle in the book. Instead, you can write programs that doodle on-screen.

This chapter is a gentle introduction to the fascinating world of drawing in Java. The designers of Java call this feature *Java 2D*. With Java2D, you can draw basic shapes such as lines, arcs, rectangles, ellipses, and so on. You can set the style used to draw the shape's outline, and you can fill the shape with a solid color, a gradient fill, or text that's created from an image. You can make your shapes solid or transparent, and you can rotate, clip, skew, and do all sorts of other unspeakable things to them.

Getting a Graphics Context

Before you can do any drawing with Java 2D, you have to get yourself an object called a *graphics context*. The best way to do that is to place all the code that does your drawing in the `paint` method of a component that's added to a frame or panel so it can be displayed. The paint `method` receives the graphics context for the component as a parameter.

The `paint` method is called by Swing whenever a component needs to be repainted for any reason. That happens when the component is first displayed, but it can happen again if the user minimizes the window that displays the component and then restores it, or if the user moves another window over it and then moves that window out of the way. In addition, you can cause the `paint` method to be called at any time by calling the component's `repaint` method. You should do this whenever something happens that affects the appearance of the component.

The graphics context object is created from a class called `Graphics2D`. However, just to be ornery, the `paint` method is passed an object of the `Graphics` class, from which `Graphics2D` is derived. As a result, the very first thing you need to do in your `paint` method is to cast the `Graphics` parameter to a `Graphics2` object, like this:

```
public void paint(Graphics g)
{
    Graphics2D g2 = (Graphics2D)g;

    // more to come...
}
```

The `Graphics2` class has a `setRenderingHint` method that lets you set a variety of *hints* that influence how your drawings are rendered to the component. Most of them are pretty esoteric, but one can give you dramatically better looking graphics: the antialiasing hint. To apply it, use this statement:

```
g2.setRenderingHint(
    RenderingHints.KEY_ANTIALIASING,
    RenderingHints.VALUE_ANTIALIAS_ON);
```

Drawing Shapes

To draw a shape, you must first create a `Shape` object that represents the shape you want to draw. Java 2D provides several different classes that implement the `Shape` interface. I have more to say about those classes later in this chapter, but to get started, I create a basic rectangle:

```
Shape rect = new Rectangle2D.Float(10, 20, 120, 150);
```

This statement creates a rectangle whose upper-left corner is at (10, 20), whose width is 120, and whose height is 150. Note that the upper-left corner of a component is (0, 0), so this rectangle appears in the upper-left part of the component's display area.

Never mind about the strange incantation `Rectangle2D.Float`. I explain that in the section "Creating Shapes" later in this chapter.

After you have a shape in hand, you can draw it by calling the `draw` method of the graphics context, like this:

```
g2.draw(rect);
```

This method draws an outline of the shape using the current color.

Here are some ways you can tweak a shape:

✦ **Change the color before you draw the shape:** Call the `setColor` method, like this:

```
g2.setColor(Color.RED);
```

Here, the color is changed to red.

✦ **Change the thickness of the line used to draw the shape:** Call `setStroke` and pass it a new instance of the `BasicStroke` class. For example:

```
g2.setStroke(new BasicStroke(4));
```

Here, the stroke thickness is set to 4.

✦ **Fill a shape with color:** Call the `fill` method. For example:

```
g2.fill(rect);
```

✦ **Create a shape with both an outline and a fill color:** Call both `draw` and `fill` and change the color in between. For example:

```
g2.setColor(Color.BLACK);
g2.draw(rect);
g2.setColor(Color.MAGENTA);
g2.fill(rect);
```

Here, the rectangle is drawn with a black outline, and then filled with magenta.

To give you an idea of how graphics programs are usually constructed, Listing 2-1 shows a simple program that displays an ellipse. Figure 2-1 shows the frame displayed by this program. It's not very exciting, but I promise things get more interesting by the end of this chapter.

I use the basic structure of this program throughout this chapter to illustrate how graphics programming works. In particular, whenever you see code examples that call methods on an object named `g2`, you can assume that code appears inside a `paint` method, such as the one shown in this listing.

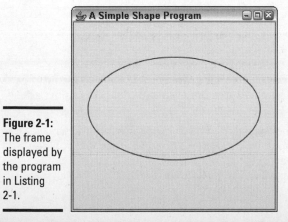

Figure 2-1:
The frame displayed by the program in Listing 2-1.

LISTING 2-1: THE SIMPLESHAPE PROGRAM

```
import javax.swing.*;                                          → 1
import java.awt.*;
import java.awt.geom.*;

public class SimpleShape extends JFrame                        → 5
{
    public static void main(String [] args)                    → 7
    {
        new SimpleShape();
    }

    public SimpleShape()                                       → 12
    {
        this.setSize(300, 300);
        this.setTitle("A Simple Shape Program");
        this.setDefaultCloseOperation(JFrame.EXIT_ON_CLOSE);

        this.add(new PaintSurface(), BorderLayout.CENTER);

        this.setVisible(true);
    }

    private class PaintSurface extends JComponent              → 23
    {
        public void paint(Graphics g)                          → 25
        {
            Graphics2D g2 = (Graphics2D)g;

            g2.setRenderingHint(                               → 29
                RenderingHints.KEY_ANTIALIASING,
                RenderingHints.VALUE_ANTIALIAS_ON);

            Shape s = new Ellipse2D.Float(                     → 33
                20, 50, 250, 150);
            g2.setPaint(Color.BLACK);
            g2.draw(s);
        }
    }
}
```

The following paragraphs hit the important points of this program:

→ **1** The program imports three packages: java.swing, java.awt, and java.geom. Most programs that draw graphics need at least these three classes, and some features may require that you import additional classes.

→ **5** The SimpleShape class extends JFrame. However, it works just as well as an applet by extending JApplet instead, provided you remove the constructor statements that call methods that aren't defined by JApplet (in particular, setTitle and setDefaultCloseOperation).

→ **7** The `main` method simply creates a new instance of the `SimpleShape` class to get things going.

→**12** The `SimpleShape` constructor does the normal frame housekeeping duties. Then, it adds an instance of the `PaintSurface` class to the frame just before making the frame visible.

→**23** The `PaintSurface` class extends `JComponent`.

→**25** The `paint` method is overridden here. It receives a single parameter of type `Graphics`, named g. Notice that the first thing this method does is cast the `Graphics` parameter to a `Graphics2D` variable. This parameter allows you to use features of the `Graphics2D` class that aren't available if the graphics context is treated as a `Graphics` object.

→**29** After casting the graphics context object, the program sets the rendering hint to use antialiasing. This results in much smoother output.

→**33** After setting the rendering hint, this program creates a shape (an ellipse), sets the painting color to black, and draws the shape on the component.

Creating Shapes

All the various shapes you can draw with Java 2D are created with classes that implement the `Shape` interface. Although the `Shape` interface has some interesting methods of its own, for now I focus on the various classes that implement the `Shape` interface, listed in Table 2-1.

Table 2-1	Classes That Represent Basic Shapes
Class Constructor	*Description*
`Arc2D.Float(float x, float y, float w, float h, float start, float extent, int type)`	Creates an arc, which is a segment of an ellipse defined by the first four parameters. `start` is the starting angle of the arc in degrees, `extent` is the angular extent of the arc, and `type` is the type of arc to draw. Type can be `OPEN`, `CHORD`, and `PIE`.
`Ellipse2D.Float(float x, float y, float w, float h)`	Creates an ellipse that fits within the rectangle whose top-left corner is at (x, y), whose width is w and whose height is h. To create a circle, specify the same value for w and h.
`Line2D.Float(float x1, float y1, float x2, float y2)`	Creates a line from $(x1, y1)$ to $(x2, y2)$.
`Line2D.Float(Point2D p1, Point2D p2)`	Creates a line from p1 to p2.

(continued)

Table 2-1 *(continued)*

Class Constructor	Description
Rectangle2D.Float(float x, float y, float w, float h)	Creates a rectangle whose top-left corner is at (x, y), whose width is w, and whose height is h.
RoundRectangle2D.Float (float x, float y, float w, float h, float arcw, float arch)	Creates a rounded rectangle whose top-left corner is at (x, y), whose width is w, and whose height is h. The arcw and arch parameters specify the width and height of the corner arcs.

One complication you'll immediately notice about using these classes is that the class names are weird. For example, the class for creating a rectangle is Rectangle2D.Float. Here's why: The Float class is actually an inner class of the Rectangle2D class, which is abstract. What's not shown in the table is that each of these classes also has an inner class named Double that lets you represent shapes with more precision. For most purposes, float precision is adequate, but you may need to use the Double classes if you're working on an application that requires high precision to represent shapes.

Figure 2-2 shows several of these shapes drawn in a frame. The code that created this figure is shown in Listing 2-2, later in the chapter. Before examining the code in detail, however, I describe how you use each of the constructors listed in Table 2-1 to create these shapes.

Creating lines

The most basic type of shape is a line, created with the Line2D.Float class. To create a line, you specify the x and y coordinates of the start and end of the line. For example:

```
Shape line1 = new Line2D.Float(0, 0, 100, 200);
```

Here, a line that goes from (0,0) to (100, 200) is created.

The Line2D.Float class has an alternate constructor that accepts Point2D objects for its parameters. Point2D is also an abstract class with inner classes named Float and Double, so you must use Point2D.Float or Point2D.Double to actually create a Point2D object. For example, here's the same line created using Point2D objects:

```
Point2D start = new Point2D.Float(0, 0);
Point2D end = new Point2D.Float (100, 200);
Shape line1 = new Line2D.Float(start, end);
```

The grid lines in Figure 2-2 were drawn by line shapes inside for loops, like this:

```
for (int i = 0; i < getSize().width; i += 10)
    g2.draw(new Line2D.Float(i, 0, i,
    getSize().height));
for (int i = 0; i < getSize().height; i += 10)
    g2.draw(new Line2D.Float(0, i, getSize().width, i));
```

The first `for` loop draws the vertical lines, and the second draws the horizontal lines.

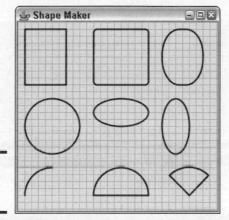

Figure 2-2:
A bunch of shapes.

Creating rectangles

A rectangle requires an (x, y) starting point and a width and height. For example, here's the code that creates the first rectangle shown in Figure 2-2:

```
Shape rect1 = new Rectangle2D.Float(10, 10, 60, 80);
```

Here, the rectangle starts at (10, 10). Its width is 60, and its height is 80.

Java2D also provides a RoundRectangle2D class that lets you create rectangles with rounded corners. The constructor for this class takes two additional parameters that specify the width and height of the arc used to draw the corners. For example, here's the rounded rectangle in the middle of the first row of shapes in Figure 2-2:

```
Shape round1 = new RoundRectangle2D.Float(
                    110, 10, 80, 80, 10, 10);
```

Here, the corners are rounded with an arc whose height and width are both 10.

You can create some interesting shapes by using unequal values for the arc's width and height. For example, here's the code for the third shape in the first row of Figure 2-2:

```
Shape round2 = new RoundRectangle2D.Float(210, 10, 60,
                      80, 50, 75);
```

Here, the arc's width is 50, and its height is 75.

Creating ellipses

An *ellipse* is a round shape that fits within a rectangular area. Thus, the constructor for the `Ellipse2D.Float` class is similar to the `Rectangle2D.Float` constructor. Here's an example that creates an ellipse where the bounding rectangle is a square:

```
Shape ellipse1 = new Ellipse2D.Float(10, 110, 80, 80);
```

Note that if the bounding rectangle happens to be a square, the ellipse is a circle. This one is the first shape in the second row in Figure 2-2. Here's the code for the second ellipse in the figure:

```
Shape ellipse2 = new Ellipse2D.Float(110, 110, 80, 40);
```

Here, the ellipse fits inside a rectangle whose width is 80 and height is 40. Thus, the ellipse is short and wide, kind of like me. If I ate a little less and exercised a little more, maybe I'd look more like the third ellipse, created with this code:

```
Shape ellipse3 = new Ellipse2D.Float(210, 110, 40, 80);
```

Creating arcs

Another useful type of shape is an *arc,* which is a segment of an ellipse. To create an arc, you supply the bounding rectangle that contains the ellipse. Here are the parameters you need to specify:

✦ The starting angle for the arc in degrees — 0 is due east, or 3 o'clock as they say in the movies.

✦ The *extent,* which is an angle that represents how much of the ellipse the arc spans. This too is specified in degrees. The important thing to know is that the arc travels counterclockwise from the starting point. So if you specify 0 as the starting point and 90 as the extent, the arc travels from 3 o'clock to 12 o'clock high.

✦ One of three arc types: `Arc2D.OPEN` indicates that you want to draw just the arc itself. `Arc2D.CHORD` means you want to draw the arc, and then connect the ends with a straight line to create a closed shape. `Arc2D.PIE` means you want to connect the ends with straight lines back to the center of the ellipse to create a shape that looks like a piece of pie.

Here's an example that creates the first arc shown in the figure:

```
Shape arc1 = new Arc2D.Float(10, 210, 80, 80, 90, 90,
                        Arc2D.OPEN);
```

The second arc is created with this statement:

```
Shape arc1 = new Arc2D.Float(110, 210, 80, 80, 0, 180,
                        Arc2D.CHORD);
```

And the third arc (the pie slice) is created by this statement:

```
Shape arc1 = new Arc2D.Float(210, 210, 45, 180, 45, 90,
                        Arc2D.PIE);
```

Looking at the ShapeMaker program

Now that you've seen how to create a variety of shapes, you're ready to take a glance at Listing 2-2, which draw the shapes that were shown earlier in Figure 2-2. This program relies on a very useful technique for any program that works with more than a few shapes. Instead of creating and drawing each shape separately in the `paint` method, the shapes are stored in an `ArrayList` object of type `Shape`. The shapes are created in the `PaintComponent` constructor, so the code that creates the shapes is executed only once. Then, in the `paint` method, an enhanced `for` loop is used to draw each shape in the `ArrayList`. This technique is especially handy for programs that let the user draw shapes. Each time the user draws a new shape, you just add the shape to the `ArrayList`. Then, whenever the `paint` method is called, all the shapes are drawn.

LISTING 2-2   THE SHAPEMAKER PROGRAM

```
import javax.swing.*;
import java.awt.event.*;
import java.awt.*;
import java.awt.geom.*;
import java.util.*;

public class ShapeMaker extends JFrame
{
    public static void main(String [] args)
    {
        new ShapeMaker();
    }

    public ShapeMaker()
    {
        this.setSize(300, 300);
        this.setTitle("Shape Maker");
        this.setDefaultCloseOperation(JFrame.EXIT_ON_CLOSE);
        this.add(new PaintSurface(), BorderLayout.CENTER);
```

continued

LISTING 2-2 (CONTINUED)

```
        this.setVisible(true);
    }

    private class PaintSurface extends JComponent
    {
        ArrayList<Shape> shapes = new ArrayList<Shape>();
        Point startDrag, endDrag;
        Shape found = null;

        public PaintSurface()
        {
            Shape s;

            // a rectangle
            s = new Rectangle2D.Float(10, 10, 60, 80);
            shapes.add(s);

            // a rounded rectangle
            s = new RoundRectangle2D.Float(110, 10, 80, 80,10, 10);
            shapes.add(s);

            // a rounded rectangle
            s = new RoundRectangle2D.Float(210, 10, 60, 80, 50, 75);
            shapes.add(s);

            // a circle
            s = new Ellipse2D.Float(10, 110, 80, 80);
            shapes.add(s);

            // an ellipse
            s = new Ellipse2D.Float(110, 110, 80, 40);
            shapes.add(s);

            // another ellipse
            s = new Ellipse2D.Float(210, 110, 40, 80);
            shapes.add(s);

            // an arc
            s = new Arc2D.Float(10, 210, 80, 80, 90, 90, Arc2D.OPEN);
            shapes.add(s);

            // another arc
            s = new Arc2D.Float(110, 210, 80, 80, 0, 180, Arc2D.CHORD);
            shapes.add(s);

            // another arc
            s = new Arc2D.Float(210, 210, 80, 80, 45, 90, Arc2D.PIE);
            shapes.add(s);
        }

        public void paint(Graphics g)
        {
```

```
        Graphics2D g2 = (Graphics2D)g;

        // turn on antialiasing
    g2.setRenderingHint(
        RenderingHints.KEY_ANTIALIASING,
        RenderingHints.VALUE_ANTIALIAS_ON);

        // draw background grid
    g2.setPaint(Color.LIGHT_GRAY);
    for (int i = 0; i < getSize().width; i += 10)
        g2.draw(new Line2D.Float(i, 0, i, getSize().height));
    for (int i = 0; i < getSize().height; i += 10)
        g2.draw(new Line2D.Float(0, i, getSize().width, i));

        // draw all the shapes in the array list
    g2.setColor(Color.BLACK);
    g2.setStroke(new BasicStroke(2));
    for (Shape s : shapes)
        g2.draw(s);
    }
    }
}
```

Filling Shapes

As explained earlier in the chapter, you can fill a shape with a solid color by first calling the setPaint method to set the fill color, and then calling the fill method to fill the shape. For example:

```
g2.setColor(Color.RED);
g2.fill(rect1);
```

Here, the fill color is set to red, and then the shape named rect1 is filled.

But there's more to filling than solid colors. In the following sections, you find out how to create fills that are partially transparent and fills that gradually fade from one color to another.

Drawing transparently

Java 2D lets you create transparent shapes by specifying a *compositing rule*. The compositing rule can do more than just set the transparency, but its other uses are more advanced than this short chapter allows. So rather than go into all the gory details, just accept my word that to set the transparency, you must use this odd incantation:

```
g2.setComposite(AlphaComposite.getInstance(
    AlphaComposite.SRC_OVER, 0.50F));
```

The key here is the `float` parameter value, which must be from 0.0 to 1.0. In this case, the transparency is set to `0.50F`, which means that the shapes are 50% transparent. As a result, whatever is under the shape when it is drawn partially shows through.

Using a gradient fill

Instead of using a solid color, you can specify a *gradient fill,* which blends two colors by using the `GradientPaint` class, whose constructors are shown in Table 2-2. A gradient fill is created from two color points. Imagine a line drawn between these two points. The gradient fill varies the color smoothly from the color that's set at the first point to the color set at the second point. Then, it extends the colors on this line at 90 degree angles to the line to fill an entire area.

Table 2-2	Constructors of the GradientPaint Class
Constructor	*Description*
`GradientPaint(float x1, floaty1, Color c1, float x2, float y2, Color c2)`	Creates a gradient in which the color at point `x1`, `y1` is `color1`, the color at point `x2`, `y2` is `color2`, and points in between are smoothly blended. All points beyond the `x1`, `y1` point have `color1`, and all points beyond the `x2`, `y2` point have `color2`.
`GradientPaint(Point2D p1, Color c1, Point2D p2 Color c2)`	Creates a gradient in which the color at point `p1` is `color1`, the color at point `p2` is `color2`, and points in between are smoothly blended. All points beyond `p1` have `color1`, and all points beyond `p2` have `color2`.
`GradientPaint(float x1, floaty1, Color c1, float x2, float y2, Color c2, boolean cyclic)`	Same as the first constructor, but if the `cyclic` parameter is true, the gradient pattern repeats infinitely beyond the two points.
`GradientPaint(Point2D p1, Color c1, Point2D p2 Color c2, boolean cyclic)`	Same as the second constructor, but if the `cyclic` parameter is true, the gradient pattern repeats infinitely beyond the two points.

Here's an example that sets a gradient fill that varies the color from magenta to yellow:

```
GradientPaint gp =
    new GradientPaint(0, 0, Color.MAGENTA,
                      0, 100, Color.YELLOW);
```

Here are some suggestions for choosing the location of the two color points:

◆ The points are relative to the top-left corner of the component, not to the shape you're filling. You usually want both points to lie at or near the edges of the shape you're drawing.

◆ The easiest way to keep the number straight is to create variables named x, y, width, and height, and use these variables to create both the shapes and the gradient fills.

◆ If you want to have the first color at the top and the second color at the bottom, use (x, y) for the first point and (x, y+height) as the second point.

◆ If you want to have the first color at the left and the second color at the right, use (x, y) for the first point and (x+width, y) as the second point.

◆ Each point is painted with the full color you specify. If you want a band of solid color on the edges of the object before the gradient begins, choose points that are somewhat inside the object. For example, use (10, 10) and (width-10, height-10).

◆ If you use the third or fourth constructors and specify true for the cyclic parameter, the gradient pattern repeats itself. Then, you want to pick points that are closer together so you can see the repetition within your object. For example, if the width of the object is 150, pick points such as (0, 0) and (0, 50) to see the cycle repeat three times within the object.

Table 2-3 shows four different examples of gradient fills created with the GradientPaint class. Each of the rectangles is 100 x 100. The table also shows the location of the points for each fill relative to x, y, width, and height. For each fill, the color for point 1 is black, and for point 2, white.

Table 2-3		Four Gradient Fill Examples	
Gradient Fill	*Name*	*Point 1 (Black)*	*Point 2 (White)*
	gp1	x, y	x, y + height
	gp2	x, y	x + width, y
	gp3	x, y+35	x, y + height + 35
	gp4	x+35, y+35	x+width-35, y+height-35

Here's the code that creates these four gradient fills:

```
GradientPaint gp1 = new GradientPaint(x, y,
    Color.BLACK,
    x, y + h, Color.WHITE);
GradientPaint gp2 = new GradientPaint(x, y,
    Color.BLACK,
    x + w, y, Color.WHITE);
GradientPaint gp3 = new GradientPaint(x, y+35,
    Color.BLACK, x, y+h-35, Color.WHITE, true);
GradientPaint gp4 = new GradientPaint(x+35, y+35,
    Color.BLACK, x+w-35, y+h-35, Color.WHITE, true);
```

Using this code as a starting point, you can devise many different variations to create your own fills.

Rotating and Translating

This section describes two methods of the `Graphics2D` class that modify how a shape is drawn:

+ The `translate` method moves the (0, 0) point from the top-left corner to any arbitrary point.

+ The `rotate` method rotates the component's coordinate system so that shapes are drawn at an angle.

Translate method

The translate method takes two parameters, namely the x and y coordinate of the point you want to designate as the center of the universe. For many graphics applications, translating to the center of the component is useful, so (0, 0) is in the middle of the component. Then, points with a negative x value appear to the left of center, and points with a negative y value appear above center. Here's a code snippet that does that regardless of the size of the component:

```
int cx = getSize().width / 2;       // center X;
int cy = getSize().height / 2;      // center Y;
g2.translate(cx, cy);
```

Rotate method

Rotation is a little more complicated. The `rotate` method itself is simple enough — it takes just a single parameter that rotates the coordinate system by the angle you specify. For example:

```
g2.rotate(angle);
```

The angle isn't measured in degrees. Instead, it's measured in *radians,* which if you'll remember back to your high-school math is the length of the arc subtended by the angle (assuming the radius is 1). Java's Math class has a handy toRadians method that automatically converts degrees to radians. So, to rotate the coordinate space by 45 degrees, you use this statement:

```
g2.rotate(Math.toRadians(45));
```

Note that the rotate method rotates the entire coordinate space for the component you're painting on, not just a single shape. As a result, to draw a shape rotated around its center, you first translate to the center of the shape you want to rotate, call the rotate method, and then draw the shape. The Graphics2D class provides a convenient version of the rotate method that does that for you automatically. It takes three parameters: the rotation angle and the x and y coordinates of the point around which you want to rotate. For example:

```
g2.rotate(Math.toRadians(45), 100, 150);
```

Here, the coordinate space is rotated 45 degrees around point 100, 150. (The translation is only temporary; the rotate method restores the previous translation after it does the rotation.)

Here's an example from a paint method that creates an ellipse, and then draws it several times at different rotations:

```
int x = 50;
int y = 75;
int width = 200;
int height = 100;
Shape r1 = new Ellipse2D.Float(x, y, width, height);
for (int angle = 0; angle <= 360; angle += 45)
{
    g2.rotate(Math.toRadians(angle),
        x + width/2, y + height/2);
    g2.setPaint(Color.YELLOW);
    g2.fill(r1);
    g2.setStroke(new BasicStroke(4));
    g2.setPaint(Color.BLACK);
    g2.draw(r1);
}
```

Here, the rotate method is called inside a for loop that varies the angle from 0 degrees through 360 degrees in 45 degree increments. Assuming the paint method has set antialiasing and 50% transparency and has drawn the line grids shown in the previous examples, Figure 2-3 shows how the shapes drawn by these statements appear.

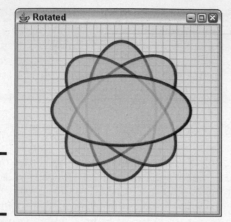

Figure 2-3:
Rotated
shapes.

Drawing Text

You can use the drawString method to draw the text contained in a string. This method accepts three parameters: the string to be drawn and the x and y coordinates of the lower-left corner of the first character to be drawn (technically speaking, the start of the *baseline* for the text). For example:

```
g2.drawString("This is some text!", 100, 50);
```

Here, the string "This is some text!" is drawn at point (100, 50).

The current stroke, color, translation, and rotation apply to the text that's drawn, as well as the current font that you specify via the setFont method. This method accepts a Font object, like this:

```
g2.setFont(new Font("Times New Roman", Font.PLAIN, 36));
```

Here, the font is set to 36-point Times New Roman. For more information about creating fonts, refer to Book IX, Chapter 1.

Letting the User Draw on a Component

In many applications, you need to let the user doodle directly on a panel. To do that, you need to create listeners that listen for mouse events such as clicks, drags, or just basic movement. Then, you need to coordinate those listeners with the paint method so that the mouse events generated by the user are translated into shapes that are drawn on the component. Table 2-4 lists the mouse events you need to listen for in programs that let the user draw shapes.

Table 2-4	Mouse Events and Listeners
MouseListener Methods	*Description*
`void mouseClicked(MouseEvent e)`	The user clicked a mouse button.
`void mouseEntered(MouseEvent e)`	The mouse entered a component.
`void mouseExited(MouseEvent e)`	The mouse exited a component.
`void mousePressed(MouseEvent e)`	The user pressed a mouse button.
`void mouseReleased(MouseEvent e)`	The user released a mouse button.
MouseMotionListener Methods	*Description*
`void mouseMoved(MouseEvent e)`	The user moved the mouse without pressing a button.
`void mouseDragged(MouseEvent e)`	The user moved the mouse while a button was pressed.
MouseEvent Methods	*Description*
`int getButton()`	Gets the mouse button that has been clicked, pressed, or released. The result can be BUTTON1, BUTTON2, BUTTON3, or NOBUTTON.
`int getClickCount()`	Gets the number of clicks to determine if the user has double- or triple-clicked.
`Point getPoint()`	Gets the mouse position as a `Point` object.
`int getX()`	Gets the x position.
`int getY()`	Gets the y position.

Note that both the `MouseListener` and `MouseMotionListener` interfaces have corresponding adapter classes named `MouseAdapter` and `MouseMotionAdapter`. If you use one or both of these adapter classes, you only have to override the methods for the events you want to respond to. (For more information about adapter classes and listeners, refer to Book VI, Chapter 2.)

To see how mouse events can be used to create programs that let the user draw on-screen, take a look at a simple program that lets the user draw rectangles. The basic technique used by the program goes something like this:

✦ When the user presses the mouse button, you make a note of the location to use as the starting point of the rectangle to be drawn.

✦ When mouse movement is detected, you make a note of the mouse location and call `repaint` to force the component to be repainted. Then, in the `paint` method, you draw a temporary rectangle from the original starting position to the current mouse position to give the user a visual clue while he or she is drawing the rectangle. This rectangle is drawn with a light gray line and isn't filled. Each time the user moves the mouse, this rectangle is redrawn according to the current mouse position. As a result, the rectangle appears to grow and shrink with the mouse movements.

✦ When the user releases the mouse button, you create a new `Rectangle2D.Float` object using the original starting location and the mouse location when the button was released. You then add the rectangle to an `ArrayList` of `Shape` objects and call `repaint` to force the component to be repainted. This causes all the rectangles in the `ArrayList` to be drawn in the order in which the user created them.

✦ Also when the user releases the mouse button, you clear the two mouse locations that were saved while the user was drawing the rectangle. That way, the `paint` method knows not to draw the temporary rectangle.

Here are a few other points to know about this program before I dive into the code:

✦ Rectangles created with the `Rectangle2D` class are always specified with the (x, y) coordinate of the top-left corner and a width and height. However, users don't always draw rectangles starting with the top-left corner. The user might press the mouse button to anchor the rectangle, and then draw the mouse up and to the left, so that the original position is the bottom-right corner instead of the top-left corner. To facilitate this, the program includes a helper method that creates a rectangle from any two arbitrary points that mark opposite corners. This method uses these points to determine the location of the top-left corner and the width and height.

✦ To make the rectangles visually interesting, the program uses an array of colors to fill each one with a different color. And each rectangle is filled with 50% transparency so rectangles beneath it are visible.

✦ The component surface also shows a grid drawn with `Line2D` shapes.

Figure 2-4 shows this program in action, after the user has drawn several rectangles. Listing 2-3 provides the complete code for the program.

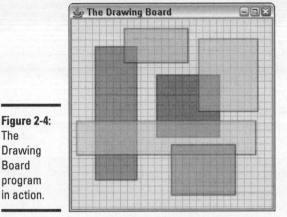

Figure 2-4:
The
Drawing
Board
program
in action.

LISTING 2-3: THE DRAWINGBOARD PROGRAM

```
import javax.swing.*;
import java.awt.event.*;
import java.awt.*;
import java.awt.geom.*;
import java.util.*;

public class DrawingBoard extends JFrame
{
    public static void main(String [] args)                    → 8
    {
        new DrawingBoard();
    }

    public DrawingBoard()                                      → 13
    {
        this.setSize(300, 300);
        this.setTitle("The Drawing Board");
        this.setDefaultCloseOperation(JFrame.EXIT_ON_CLOSE);
        this.add(new PaintSurface(), BorderLayout.CENTER);
        this.setVisible(true);
    }
    private class PaintSurface extends JComponent
    {
        ArrayList<Shape> shapes = new ArrayList<Shape>();      → 24
        Point startDrag, endDrag;

        public PaintSurface()
        {
            this.addMouseListener(new MouseAdapter()
              {
                public void mousePressed(MouseEvent e)         → 31
                {
                    startDrag = new Point(e.getX(), e.getY());
```

continued

LISTING 2-3 (CONTINUED)

```
            endDrag = startDrag;
            repaint();
        }

        public void mouseReleased(MouseEvent e)                → 38
        {
            Shape r = makeRectangle(
                        startDrag.x, startDrag.y,
                        e.getX(), e.getY());
            shapes.add(r);
            startDrag = null;
            endDrag = null;
            repaint();
        }
    } );

    this.addMouseMotionListener(new MouseMotionAdapter()
    {
        public void mouseDragged(MouseEvent e)                 → 52
        {
            endDrag = new Point(e.getX(), e.getY());
            repaint();
        }
    } );
}

public void paint(Graphics g)                                  → 59
{
    Graphics2D g2 = (Graphics2D)g;

    // turn on antialiasing
    g2.setRenderingHint(
        RenderingHints.KEY_ANTIALIASING,
        RenderingHints.VALUE_ANTIALIAS_ON);

    // draw background grid
    g2.setPaint(Color.LIGHT_GRAY);
    for (int i = 0; i < getSize().width; i += 10)
    {
        Shape line = new Line2D.Float(
            i, 0, i, getSize().height);
        g2.draw(line);
    }

    for (int i = 0; i < getSize().height; i += 10)
    {
        Shape line = new Line2D.Float(
            0, i, getSize().width, i);
        g2.draw(line);
    }

    // draw the shapes
    Color[] colors = {Color.RED, Color.BLUE,                   → 85
                      Color.PINK, Color.YELLOW,
                      Color.MAGENTA, Color.CYAN };
    int colorIndex = 0;
```

```
    g2.setStroke(new BasicStroke(2));                      → 90
    g2.setComposite(AlphaComposite.getInstance(
        AlphaComposite.SRC_OVER, 0.50f));

    for (Shape s : shapes)                                 → 94
    {
        g2.setPaint(Color.BLACK);
        g2.draw(s);
        g2.setPaint(colors[(colorIndex++)%6]);
        g2.fill(s);
    }

    // paint the temporary rectangle
    if (startDrag != null && endDrag != null)              → 103
    {
        g2.setPaint(Color.LIGHT_GRAY);
        Shape r = makeRectangle(
            startDrag.x, startDrag.y,
            endDrag.x, endDrag.y);
        g2.draw(r);
    }
}

private Rectangle2D.Float makeRectangle(                   → 113
    int x1, int y1, int x2, int y2)
{
    int x = Math.min(x1, x2);
    int y = Math.min(y1, y2);
    int width = Math.abs(x1 - x2);
    int height = Math.abs(y1 - y2);
    return new Rectangle2D.Float(
        x, y, width, height);
}
}
}
```

The following paragraphs provide a road map through this program:

→ **8** The main method creates an instance of the DrawingBoard class.

→**13** The constructor for the DrawingBoard class initializes the frame in the usual way, adding a new instance of a JComponent class named PaintSurface.

→**24** The PaintSurface class begins by defining three instance variables. The first, named shapes, is an ArrayList object that holds the shapes drawn by the user. The next two are Point objects that represent the start and end point for the rectangle currently being drawn by the user.

→**31** The PaintSurface constructor uses anonymous inner classes to create the mouse listeners. The mousePressed method is invoked when the user presses a mouse button. It sets the startDrag and endDrag variables to the current position of the mouse, and then calls repaint to force the component to be repainted.

→**38** The mouseReleased method is called when the user releases the mouse, indicating that a rectangle has been drawn. It calls the makeRectangle method to create a rectangle from the starting x and y values and the current x and y values. Then, it adds this rectangle to the shapes collection, clears the startDrag and endDrag points, and calls repaint to force the component to be repainted.

→**52** The mouseDragged method in the MouseMotionAdapter anonymous class is called when the mouse moves while the button is held down. This method simply sets the endDrag variable to the new mouse location and calls repaint to repaint the component.

→**59** The paint method is where the good stuff happens in this program. This begins by casting the Graphics object to a Graphics2D object, turning on antialiasing, and drawing the background grid. Then, it draws the shapes from the shapes collection.

→**85** To fill each rectangle with a different color, the program creates an array of Color objects that specifies six different colors. Then, it defines a variable named colorIndex to index the array. Each time a rectangle is drawn, this index is incremented.

→**90** The stroke thickness is set to 2, and the setComposite method is used to set the transparency to 50%.

→**94** An enhanced for loop is used to draw each rectangle. First, the color is set to black, and the rectangle is drawn. Then, the color is set, and the rectangle is filled. The modulo division operator (%) is used to constrain the index from 0 through 5, and the index is incremented so the next rectangle uses the next color in the array.

→**103** This if statement draws the temporary rectangle while the user is dragging the mouse. If either startDrag or endDrag is null, the rectangle isn't drawn.

→**113** makeRectangle is a helper method that creates a Rectangle2D. Float object given the points of two opposite corners. It sets the starting point to the smaller of the two x values and the smaller of the two y values, and sets the width and height to the absolute value of the difference between the two x values and the two y values.

Chapter 3: Using Images and Sound

In This Chapter

- ✔ Displaying images in Swing components
- ✔ Drawing images directly on a panel
- ✔ Scaling images
- ✔ Using a file chooser to pick an image
- ✔ Adding annoying sound effects and music to your programs

So far in this book, all of the Swing applications have been pretty boring. They've had plenty of labels, text fields, combo boxes, and the like, but no pictures!

This chapter remedies that. You find out how to incorporate graphic images (that is, pictures — not necessarily images of a graphic nature) into your Swing applications. And just to make things interesting, I show you how to throw in sound effects and music, too.

Java's support for images and sound is designed assuming that you're going to use them in applets that run over a slow Internet connection. As a result, they go to great lengths to accommodate large files that can take a long time to download. They included a special class called MediaTracker that's designed to let you monitor the progress of a long download so you can either display a progress bar or display the image or play the sound piece by piece as it arrives. Fortunately, they also included some shortcut methods that let you just load an image or sound file and use it without worrying about the MediaTracker details.

I'm a big believer in shortcuts, except on family vacations. I took a shortcut once on a family trip to see Mt. Lassen. It turned out the shortcut involved about five miles on a windy dirt road that took about an hour. We would have arrived half an hour sooner had we gone the long way. But trust me, this isn't that kind of shortcut. You really get there faster if you skip the MediaTracker details until the end.

Using Images

An *image* is a file that contains a picture. Java supports pictures in several different formats, including:

✦ **GIF:** Graphics Interchange Format, commonly used for small images such as those used for button icons and such.

✦ **JPEG:** An organization called the Joint Photographic Experts Group (hence the name *JPEG*) devised this format to store photographic images in a compressed form. JPEG is the preferred form for larger images.

✦ **PNG:** The Portable Network Graphics format, which was designed specifically for portability and network access. You'd think this would be the most common format for Java applications, because Java too was designed for portability and network access. But although Java does indeed support PNG, GIF and JPEG are the more popular choices.

Java does *not* directly support other common graphics file formats such as BMP (Windows bitmap), PCX (PC Paintbrush bitmap), or WMF (Windows Media Format). The easiest way to deal with this limitation is to simply convert your images to GIF, JPEG, or PNG. Programs that can do that conversion are readily available. If you insist on using images in those formats, you can get third-party packages that do it. Hop on the Internet and cruise to your favorite search service and look for "Java" and the format you want to support.

Using the ImageIcon Class

The easiest way to work with images is to use the `ImageIcon` class. This class lets you load an image from a file using a filename or URL. Then, you can display it by attaching it to a label or button component or painting it directly. The `ImageIcon` class shelters you from the details of using the `MediaTracker` class by automatically waiting for the entire image to load.

Icons are typically small images used to provide visual cues for what a button does. However, the `ImageIcon` class isn't just for small images. You can use it to display large images as well, as long as you're willing to hold up your program while the image loads. For Swing applications, that's not usually a problem. For applets, you may want to consider alternatives for large image files.

Table 3-1 lists the most important constructors and methods of the classes you use to work with `ImageIcon` objects. I describe these constructors and methods in the following sections.

Table 3-1	Classes for Working with ImageIcon Objects
ImageIcon Constructors and Methods	*Description*
ImageIcon(String filename)	Creates an ImageIcon object from the file indicated by the specified filename.
ImageIcon(URL url)	Creates an ImageIcon object from the file indicated by the specified URL.
Image getImage()	Gets the Image object associated with this ImageIcon.
JLabel and JButton Constructors	*Description*
JLabel(Icon image)	Creates a label with the specified image. (Note that ImageIcon implements the Icon interface.)
JButton(Icon image)	Creates a button with the specified image.
JButton(String text, Icon image)	Creates a button with the specified text and image.

Using ImageIcon in a Swing application

In a Swing application, you can load an image directly into an ImageIcon object by specifying the filename in the ImageIcon constructor, like this:

```
ImageIcon pic = new ImageIcon("HalfDome.jpg");
```

Here, an ImageIcon object is created from a file named HalfDome.jpg. This file must live in the same directory as the class file. However, you can just as easily provide a path in the String parameter, like this:

```
ImageIcon pic = new ImageIcon("c:\\HalfDome.jpg");
```

Here, the file is in the root directory of the C: drive. (Remember that you have to use two backslashes to get a single backslash in a Java string literal.)

You can then attach the image to a Swing component such as a label or button to display the image. Many Swing components can display icons directly, including JLabel, JButton, JCheckBox, and JRadioButton. If you simply want to display the image, use a JLabel component and specify the ImageIcon object in its constructor, like this:

```
JLabel picLabel = new JLabel(pic);
```

Here, a label is created from the previously created ImageIcon object named pic. Then, when you add this label to a panel or frame, the image is displayed.

Putting this all together, here's a complete application that displays the HalfDome.jpg image in a frame; Figure 3-1 shows the frame displayed when this program is run.

```
import javax.swing.*;

public class PictureApp extends JFrame
{
    public static void main(String [] args)
    {
        new PictureApp();
    }

    public PictureApp()
    {
        this.setTitle("Picture Application");
        this.setDefaultCloseOperation(
            JFrame.EXIT_ON_CLOSE);

        JPanel panel1 = new JPanel();

        ImageIcon pic = new ImageIcon("HalfDome.jpg");
        panel1.add(new JLabel(pic));

        this.add(panel1);
        this.pack();
        this.setVisible(true);
    }
}
```

Figure 3-1:
Displaying
an image in
a Swing
application.

Although this example shows how to display a large JPEG file, the ImageIcon class is also commonly used to attach smaller GIF images as icons for various types of buttons. To do that, you simply pass the ImageIcon object to the button constructor.

For example, the following code produces the button shown in the margin:

```
JButton openButton;
ImageIcon openIcon = new ImageIcon("OpenIcon.gif");
openButton = new JButton(openIcon);
```

You can also create buttons with both text and an icon. For example, I created the button shown in the margin with this code:

```
openButton = new JButton("Open", openIcon);
```

Using ImageIcon in an applet

If the program is an applet, use a URL instead of a filename to identify the image file. The only trick is figuring out how to get a URL for a file that lives in the same location as the applet itself. To do that, you can use this strange but functional incantation:

```
URL url = PictureApplet.class.getResource("HalfDome.
    jpg");
```

Here, you use the `class` property of the class that defines your applet (in this case, `PictureApplet`) to get its `Class` object, and then call the `getResource` method, which returns a `URL` object for the specified file. After you have the URL of the image file, you can create an `ImageIcon` from it like this:

```
pic = new ImageIcon(url);
```

Then, you can use the `ImageIcon` object in a label or button component, or you can use the `getImage` method to get the underlying `Image` object so you can paint it directly to the screen.

Using the Image Class

If you want to paint an image directly to a graphics context (for example, from the `paintComponent` method of a panel), you need to use the `Image` class to represent the image. You want to create the `Image` object in the panel constructor but paint it in the `paintComponent` method. As a result, you need to declare the variable that references the Image as an instance variable so you can refer to it from both the constructor and the `paintComponent` method. The declaration for the instance variable looks something like this:

```
Image img;
```

Table 3-2 lists the most important constructors and methods of the classes you use to work with `Image` objects. I describe these constructors and methods in the following sections.

Table 3-2	Classes for Working with Image Objects
Image *Class Methods and Fields*	*Description*
Image getScaledInstance (int x, int x, int hints)	Gets an Image object that has been scaled according to the x and y parameters. If either x or y is negative, the aspect ratio of the image is preserved. The hint parameter can be one of these fields: DEFAULT, SPEED, or SMOOTH.
int DEFAULT	The default scaling method.
int SPEED	A scaling method that favors speed over smoothness.
int SMOOTH	A scaling method that favors smoothness over speed.
Toolkit *Class Methods*	*Description*
static Toolkit getDefaultToolkit()	Gets a Toolkit object.
Image getImage(String filename)	Gets an Image object from the specified filename.
Graphics *Class Methods*	*Description*
void drawImage(Image img, int x, int y, ImageObserver observer)	Draws the specified image at the position indicated by the x and y parameters. The observer parameter specifies the object that listens for image update events.
void drawImage(Image img, int x, int y, int width, int height, ImageObserver observer)	Draws the specified image at the position indicated by the x and y parameters using the size specified by the width and height parameters. The observer parameter specifies the object that listens for image update events.

Creating an Image object

Image is an abstract class, so it doesn't have a handy constructor you can use to create an image from a file or URL. However, you can create an Image object from a file two fairly simple ways: with the ImageIcon class, as described in the previous section, or with the Toolkit class.

To create an image from an ImageIcon object, you first create an ImageIcon object as described in the previous section. Then, you can use the getImage method to extract the Image from the ImageIcon. For example:

```
ImageIcon picIcon = new ImageIcon("c:\\HalfDome.jpg");
Image picImage = picIcon.getImage();
```

You want to put this code in the panel constructor so it's executed only once.

The other way is to use the getImage method of the Toolkit class. First, you use the static getDefaultToolkit method to get a Toolkit object. Then, you call getImage to load an image from a file. For example:

```
Toolkit kit = Toolkit.getDefaultToolkit();
img = kit.getImage("HalfDome.jpg");
```

Again, this code goes in the panel constructor to avoid reloading the image every time it needs to be painted.

If you're just loading a single image and the image is small, either technique is suitable. If you're loading a lot of images, or if the image is large, the Toolkit technique is a better choice for two reasons. First, it avoids creating a bunch of unnecessary ImageIcon objects. And second, it doesn't tie up the application until the entire image is loaded.

Drawing an Image object

After you load an image and create an Image object, you can draw it by adding code in the paint method:

```
g.drawImage(img, 0, 0, this);
```

The drawImage method takes four parameters. The first three are easy enough to understand: They are the image to be painted and the x and y coordinates where you want the image to appear. The fourth parameter is an object that implements the ImageObserver interface. This interface includes a method called imageUpdate that's called whenever the status of the image has changed. For small images or for applications that load the image from a local file, this method is probably called only once, when the image has finished loading. However, if you load a large image over the Internet (for example, in an applet), the imageUpdate method is likely called several times as each chunk of the image is received.

Fortunately, it turns out that all Swing components including JPanel implement the ImageObserver interface, and their default implementation of the imageUpdate method is to simply call repaint. This method in turn calls the paint method, so the image is automatically drawn again.

Note that there's another form of the drawImage method that lets you set the size you want the image drawn. For example:

```
g.drawImage(img, 0, 0, 200, 200, this);
```

Here, the image is drawn in a 200 x 200 rectangle starting at the top-left corner of the panel.

Depending on the size of the original image, this may result in some distortion. For example, if the original image was 400 x 600, displaying it at 200 x 200 shows the image at half its original width but one third its original height, making everyone look short and fat. A better way to scale the image is to call the image's `getScaledInstance` method:

```
img = img.getScaledInstance(200, -1,
    Image.SCALE_DEFAULT);
```

The first two parameters of this method specify the desired width and height. If you set one of these parameters to a negative value, the `getScaledInstance` method calculates the appropriate value while preserving the original image's aspect ratio. The third parameter is a constant that indicates what scaling method to use. The three choices you use most are `SCALE_DEFAULT`, which uses the default method, `SCALE_SPEED`, which favors speed over smoothness, and `SCALE_SMOOTH`, which favors smoothness over speed.

An Image example

To show how the elements presented in the last two sections work together, Listing 3-1 shows a complete program that uses the `Image` class to display an image in a panel.

To add a little interest, this application uses a JFileChooser dialog box to let the user select the image to be displayed, as shown in Figure 3-2. The file chooser includes a filter so only JPEG, GIF, and PNG files are listed. For more information about the `JFileChooser` class, refer to Book VIII, Chapter 1.

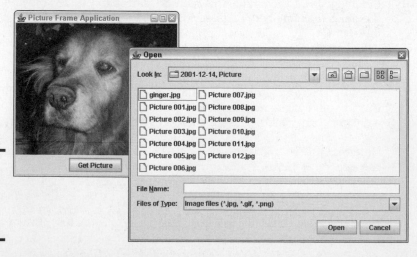

Figure 3-2:
The Picture Frame application in action.

LISTING 3-1: THE PICTURE FRAME APPLICATION

```java
import javax.swing.*;
import java.awt.event.*;
import java.awt.*;
import java.io.*;

public class PictureFrame extends JFrame
    implements ActionListener
{
    Image img;                                              → 9
    JButton getPictureButton;

    public static void main(String [] args)
    {
        new PictureFrame();
    }

    public PictureFrame()
    {
        this.setSize(300, 300);
        this.setTitle("Picture Frame Application");
        this.setDefaultCloseOperation(JFrame.EXIT_ON_CLOSE);

        JPanel picPanel = new PicturePanel();               → 23
        this.add(picPanel, BorderLayout.CENTER);

        JPanel buttonPanel = new JPanel();                  → 26
        getPictureButton = new JButton("Get Picture");
        getPictureButton.addActionListener(this);
        buttonPanel.add(getPictureButton);
        this.add(buttonPanel, BorderLayout.SOUTH);

        this.setVisible(true);
    }

    public void actionPerformed(ActionEvent e)              → 35
    {
        String file = getImageFile();
        if (file != null)
        {
            Toolkit kit = Toolkit.getDefaultToolkit();
            img = kit.getImage(file);
            img = img.getScaledInstance(
                300, -1, Image.SCALE_SMOOTH);
            this.repaint();
        }
    }

    private String getImageFile()                           → 48
    {
        JFileChooser fc = new JFileChooser();
        fc.setFileFilter(new ImageFilter());
        int result = fc.showOpenDialog(null);
        File file = null;
        if (result == JFileChooser.APPROVE_OPTION)
        {
```

continued

LISTING 3-1 (CONTINUED)

```
                file = fc.getSelectedFile();
                return file.getPath();
        }
        else
            return null;
    }

    private class PicturePanel extends JPanel            → 63
    {
        public void paint(Graphics g)
        {
            g.drawImage(img, 0, 0, this);
        }
    }

    private class ImageFilter                            → 71
        extends javax.swing.filechooser.FileFilter
    {
        public boolean accept(File f)
        {
            if (f.isDirectory())
                return true;
            String name = f.getName();
            if (name.matches(".*((.jpg)|(.gif)|(.png))"))
                return true;
            else
                return false;
        }

        public String getDescription()
        {
            return "Image files (*.jpg, *.gif, *.png)";
        }
    }
}
```

The following paragraphs hit the highlights of this program:

→ **9** The img variable is declared here so the class can access it.

→**23** In the frame class constructor, a new instance of the PicturePanel class is created and added to the center of the frame.

→**26** Next, a panel is created to hold the button the user clicks to open an image file. The button specifies this for the action listener, and the panel is added to the South region of the frame.

→**35** The actionPerformed method is invoked when the user clicks the Get Picture button. It calls the getImageFile method, which displays the file chooser and returns the filename of the file selected by the user. Then, assuming the filename returned is not null, the Toolkit class is used to load the image. The image is then scaled so it is 300 pixels wide while preserving the aspect ratio, and the frame is repainted.

→48 The `getImageFile` method creates and displays a file chooser dialog box that shows only `.jpg`, `.gif`, and `.png` files. If the user selected a file, the complete path of the file chosen by the user is returned. Otherwise, `null` is returned.

→63 The `PicturePanel` class defines the panel that displays the picture. It consists of just one method — `paint`, which uses the `drawImage` method to draw the image.

→71 The `ImageFilter` class is used to limit the file chooser display to just `.jpg`, `.gif`, and `.png` files. It uses the following regular expression to do so:

```
.*((.jpg)|(.gif)|(.png))
```

For more information about file filters, refer to Book VIII, Chapter 1. And for more information about regular expressions, turn to Book V, Chapter 3.

Playing Sounds and Making Music

Java provides built-in support for playing sound and music files. You can play sound and music files in a variety of formats, including wave files in several formats (WAV, AU, RMF, and AIFF as well as MIDI files). Wave files are usually used to add specific sound effects to your application, such as chimes, explosions, or drum rolls. Midi files let you play music while your application is running.

An audio file is represented by an object that implements the `AudioClip` interface, whose methods are listed in Table 3-3. As you can see, this interface is simple: You can play a sound once, play it in a loop, and stop playing the sound. Note that when you play or loop a sound, your program doesn't wait for the sound to finish playing. Instead, the sound is played in a separate thread so your program can continue with its other chores.

Table 3-3	The AudioClip Interface
Methods	*Description*
`void play()`	Plays the clip once.
`void loop()`	Plays the clip in a loop.
`void stop()`	Stops playing the clip.

Interestingly enough, the easiest way to create an `AudioClip` object is to use a static method of the `Applet` class called `newAudioClip`. This is a little confusing; because it's a static method, you can use it in non-applet programs as easily as applets. Go figure. Anyway, the `newAudioClip` method requires a URL, not a simple filename, so you must first figure out how to get a URL for the sound file you want to play.

Here's a snippet of code that creates an `AudioClip` from a file named `hit.wav` and plays it:

```
URL url = MyApp.class.getResource("hit.wav");
click = Applet.newAudioClip(url);
click.play();
```

The first line gets the `Class` object for the current class (assumed here to be `MyApp`), and then uses the `getResource` method to get a `URL` object for the specified file, which must be in the same directory as the `MyApp` class. Then, the `newAudioClip` method is called to create an `AudioClip` object. Finally, the `play` method is called to play it.

To make things a little more interesting, Listing 3-2 shows a program that plays the `hit.wav` sound every time you click the mouse in the program's frame. This program displays an empty frame that has a `MouseListener` installed. Then, each time the `mouseClicked` method is called, the sound is played.

LISTING 3-2: THE MOUSECLICKER PROGRAM

```
import javax.swing.*;
import java.awt.event.*;
import java.awt.*;
import java.applet.*;
import java.net.URL;

public class MouseClicker extends JFrame
{
    AudioClip click;

    public static void main(String [] args)
    {
        new MouseClicker();
    }

    public MouseClicker()
    {
        this.setSize(400, 400);
        this.setTitle("Mouse Clicker");
        this.addMouseListener(new Clicker());

        URL urlClick = MouseClicker.class.getResource("hit.wav");
```

```
        click = Applet.newAudioClip(urlClick);

        this.setVisible(true);
    }

    private class Clicker extends MouseAdapter
    {
        public void mouseClicked(MouseEvent e)
        {
            click.play();
        }
    }
}
```

Chapter 4: Animation and Game Programming

In This Chapter

✔ **Using threads to control animation**

✔ **Creating a bouncing ball**

✔ **Creating a whole room full of bouncing balls**

✔ **Devising a simple Pong-like game**

*B*ecause of its powerful drawing capabilities, Java lends itself especially well to creating game programs — especially games that are created as applets so they can be played over the Internet. Game programming is a huge subject, big enough for a whole shelf of books. In this chapter, I just scratch the surface of creating basic animations and playing simple games. Specifically, you find out how to get a ball bouncing in an applet, how to create a paddle to hit the ball, and how to find out when you missed.

In other words, welcome to the 1970s! You're going to create an applet that plays Pong!

This chapter combines features that are presented in several different chapters throughout this book. Specifically, you find information about drawing shapes in Book IX, Chapter 2. For information about working with threads, refer to Book V, Chapter 1. For information creating event listeners, see Book VI, Chapter 2. And for details about creating and running applets, see Book VII, Chapter 1.

Animating a Sprite

In animation and game programming, an object that moves around the screen is usually called a *sprite*. The sprite itself can be drawn by various means. If the sprite is a simple geometric shape such as a circle, you can just create an `Ellipse2D` object and use the `draw` or `fill` method to render it. More commonly, the sprite is represented by a small image. Then, you use the `drawImage` method to render the sprite.

In some cases, the sprite may have a series of images associated with it. For example, if the sprite is a little person who walks around in your game world, you might have several images representing him walking left and right, or in various stages of his little stride. Then, you can put these images in an array and use an index variable to keep track of which image to draw.

No matter what the sprite looks like, the basic technique for animating the sprite in Java is the same: Create a thread that periodically repaints the drawing component, and then calculate a new position for the sprite each time the component is repainted and draw the sprite in its new position.

For example, suppose you want to create a ball that travels across a component, starting at the left side of the component and traveling across to the right side. To do that, you have to do the following things:

✦ Create the component that the ball is drawn on. Usually, this component can just extend JComponent.

✦ Create a thread whose run method includes a loop. Inside the loop, call the sleep method to sleep for a small time interval (typically 10 or 20 milliseconds), then call the drawing component's repaint method. Simply creating the drawing component is easiest so it not only extends JComponent, but also implements Runnable. That way, you can create the run method as a member of the drawing component class.

✦ In the paint method, recalculate the position of each shape being animated, and then draw it.

✦ To get the animation going, create an instance of the drawing component and add it to a frame or applet. Then, pass this instance to the Thread class constructor to create a Thread object. And finally, call the Thread object's start method.

Sound simple enough? Listing 4-1 shows the first of several versions of an applet program that animates a moving ball. Figure 4-1 shows this applet in action when run in the applet viewer.

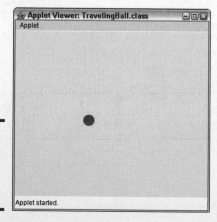

Figure 4-1:
The
BallRoom
applet in
action.

LISTING 4-1: THE BALLROOM APPLET

```java
import java.applet.*;
import java.awt.*;
import javax.swing.*;
import java.awt.geom.*;

public class BallRoom extends JApplet                    → 6
{
    private final int WIDTH = 350;
    private final int HEIGHT = 300;

    private PaintSurface canvas;

    public void init()                                   → 13
    {
        this.setSize(WIDTH, HEIGHT);
        canvas = new PaintSurface();
        this.add(canvas, BorderLayout.CENTER);
        Thread t = new AnimationThread(this);
        t.start();
    }
}

class AnimationThread extends Thread                     → 23
{
    JApplet c;

    public AnimationThread(JApplet c)                    → 27
    {
        this.c = c;
    }

    public void run()                                    → 32
    {
        while (true)
        {
            c.repaint();
            try
            {
                Thread.sleep(20);
            }
            catch (InterruptedException ex)
            {
                // swallow the exception
            }
        }
    }
}

class PaintSurface extends JComponent                    → 49
```

continued

LISTING 4-1 (CONTINUED)

```
{
    int x_pos = 0;        // the starting X position
    int y_pos = 150;      // the starting Y position
    int d = 20;           // the diameter of the ball

    public void paint(Graphics g)                          →55
    {
        Graphics2D g2 = (Graphics2D)g;
        g2.setRenderingHint(
            RenderingHints.KEY_ANTIALIASING,
            RenderingHints.VALUE_ANTIALIAS_ON);

        x_pos += 1;      // move ball right one pixel

        Shape ball = new Ellipse2D.Float(
            x_pos, y_pos, d, d);
        g2.setColor(Color.RED);
        g2.fill(ball);
    }
}
```

The following paragraphs describe the key portions of this program:

→ **6** The `BallRoom` class extends `JApplet` and defines two public static constants, named `WIDTH` and `HEIGHT`. These constants are used to set the size of the component the ball is animated within. It also defines a `PaintSurface` variable named `canvas` that is used as the canvas on which the animated ball is drawn.

→**13** The `init` method is called when the applet starts up. It sets the size of the applet, and then creates a new instance of the `PaintSurface` class on which the ball is animated and adds it to the applet. It then uses the `AnimationThread` class to create a thread, and then calls the thread's `start` method to start the animation.

→**23** The `AnimationThread` class defines the thread that's used to animate the ball.

→**27** The constructor for the `AnimationThread` class accepts a `JApplet` object as a parameter and stores it in the `c` variable so it can be used later.

→**32** The `run` method contains the code that controls the animation. As you can see, it consists of an infinite loop that calls the `repaint` method of the `JApplet` object that was passed to the constructor. Next, the `sleep` method is called to put the thread to sleep for 20 milliseconds. (Because the `sleep` method can throw `InterruptedException`, it must be called inside a `try`/`catch` statement. However, the `catch` clause simply ignores the exception.)

→**49** The `PaintSurface` class extends `JComponent`. The instance variables defined for this class define the characteristics of the ball that is animated: its x and y position on the component and the ball's diameter.

→**55** The `paint` method is called whenever the `PaintSurface` component needs to be redrawn. This method is triggered every 20 milliseconds by the `run` method of the `AnimationThread` class. The `paint` method begins by casting the graphics context to a `Graphics2D` object and setting antialiasing on. Then, it calculates a new position for the ball by adding 1 to the x position. It then creates a `Shape` object to represent the ball as an ellipse at the current `x_pos` and `y_pos` positions, using the width and height specified by the `d` variable. Finally, it sets the color and draws the ball by calling the `fill` method.

What about Double Buffering?

If you've looked into animation and game programming before, you may have heard of a technique called *double buffering* that's required to produce smooth, flicker-free animation. When you use double-buffering, you don't draw shapes directly to the component. Instead, you create an off-screen image object called a *buffer* and draw the shapes to it. Then, when all the shapes are drawn, you transfer the entire buffer image to the component.

Fortunately, any drawing you do on a Swing component is automatically double-buffered. Before Swing, you had to manually do double buffering by creating an `Image` object and creating a graphics context so you could write to the `Image`. But with Swing, you don't have to do anything special to use double-buffering.

If for some reason you want to turn double-buffering off — maybe just to see how much it improves the animation for your application — you can do so by calling the `setDoubleBuffered` method of the component you're drawing to, like this:

```
this.setDoubleBuffered(false);
```

Bouncing the Ball

The program shown in Listing 4-1 illustrates the basic framework for a program that animates sprites. However, the ball it animates isn't very interesting: It just flies across the screen in a straight line and disappears off the right edge, never to be seen again. To be more interesting, the ball should travel in different directions and bounce off the edges of the component so it stays visible.

The trick of animating the ball so it travels in other than horizontal (or vertical) lines and bounces off the walls is calculating the ball's new (x, y) position for each animation cycle. This problem has at least two basic approaches:

✦ The most realistic approach is to keep track of two variables for the ball: the angle it's traveling at and its speed. Then, you can use high-school trigonometry to calculate the new (x, y) position of the ball for each cycle. And if the ball hits one of the edges, you have to calculate the ball's new angle. You probably need some sines and cosines and maybe a square root or a logarithm or something. I'm not sure, I didn't do so good in math.

✦ The easier way is to store two variables — call them `x_speed` and `y_speed` — that represent the distance the ball travels horizontally and vertically for each animation cycle. This technique is much easier because it doesn't require any math more complicated than addition. For each animation cycle, just add `x_speed` to the x position and add `y_speed` to the y position. If the ball hits the left or right edge, negate `x_speed` to reverse the ball's horizontal direction, and if the ball hits the top or bottom edge, negate `y_speed` so the ball reverses its vertical direction. The result is a pretty convincing bounce off the wall.

To add the ability for the ball to bounce, you need to add some instance variables and modify the `paint` method a bit. The resulting `PaintSurface` class is shown in Listing 4-2.

LISTING 4-2: A BOUNCING VERSION OF THE PAINTSURFACE CLASS

```
class PaintSurface extends JComponent
{
    int x_pos = 0;                                          → 3
    int y_pos = 0;
    int x_speed = 1;
    int y_speed = 2;
    int d = 20;
    int width = BallRoom.WIDTH;
    int height = BallRoom.HEIGHT;

    public void paint(Graphics g)
    {
        Graphics2D g2 = (Graphics2D)g;
        g2.setRenderingHint(
            RenderingHints.KEY_ANTIALIASING,
            RenderingHints.VALUE_ANTIALIAS_ON);
        if (x_pos < 0 || x_pos > width - d)                 → 17
            x_speed = -x_speed;
        if (y_pos < 0 || y_pos > height - d)                → 19
            y_speed = -y_speed;
        x_pos += x_speed;                                   → 21
```

```
        y_pos += y_speed;

        Shape ball = new Ellipse2D.Float(              → 24
            x_pos, y_pos, d, d);
        g2.setColor(Color.RED);
        g2.fill(ball);
    }
}
```

The following paragraphs describe the key elements of this class:

→ **3** For this version of the PaintSurface class, the instance variables keep track of the ball's x and y position and speed as well as its diameter and the height and width of the drawing surface.

→**17** This if statement checks to see if the ball has hit the left wall (the x position is less than zero) or the right wall (the x position is greater than the width of the component less the diameter of the ball). If so, the x speed is reversed. (You must take the diameter of the ball into account on the right wall because the x position indicates the position of the *left* side of the ball, and you want the ball to bounce when its *right* side hits the right wall.)

→**19** This if statement applies the same logic to the y speed to see if the ball has hit the top or bottom wall.

→**21** After the x and y speed values are adjusted for bounces, the next two statements move the ball. If x_speed is a positive number, the ball moves right. If it's negative, the ball moves left. Similarly, if y_speed is positive, the ball moves down; if it's negative, the ball moves up.

→**24** These lines draw the ball at its new location.

Bouncing a Bunch of Balls

Most games require that you animate more than one sprite. For example, more than one ball may be on-screen at one time, or there might be other sprites besides balls. Thus, the paint method needs to have the ability to move and draw multiple sprites.

One way to do that is to create a class for the sprites to be animated, and then add instances of that class to an array list or other collection. Then, the paint method can use a loop to move and draw each sprite in the collection.

Creating a Ball class

To add the ability to animate more than one ball, start by adding a class that represents a single ball, as shown in Listing 4-3.

LISTING 4-3: A BALL CLASS

```
class Ball extends Ellipse2D.Float                                    → 1
{
    private int x_speed, y_speed;                                     → 3
    private int d;
    private int width = BallRoom.WIDTH;
    private int height = BallRoom.HEIGHT;

    public Ball(int diameter)                                         → 8
    {
        super((int)(Math.random() * (BallRoom.WIDTH - 20) + 1),
              (int)(Math.random() * (BallRoom.HEIGHT - 20) + 1),
              diameter, diameter);
        this.d = diameter;
        this.x_speed = (int)(Math.random() * 5 + 1);
        this.y_speed = (int)(Math.random() * 5 + 1);
    }

    public void move()                                                → 18
    {
        if (super.x < 0 || super.x > width - d)
            x_speed = -x_speed;
        if (super.y < 0 || super.y > height - d)
            y_speed = -y_speed;
        super.x += x_speed;
        super.y += y_speed;
    }
}
```

The following paragraphs point out the highlights of this program:

→ **1** Because a ball is essentially an ellipse with a few additional characteristics, this class extends the `Ellipse2D.Float` class. An advantage of implementing the `Ball` class this way is that you can pass a `Ball` object directly to the `draw` and `fill` methods to paint the ball.

→ **3** The `Ball` class defines five private instance variables, representing the x and y speeds, the diameter of the ball, and the width and height of the component the balls are animated within. Notice that the x and y positions of the ball have no instance variables. Because the `Ellipse2D.Float` class already keeps track of its x and y positions, you just use the `x` and `y` fields of the superclass when you need those values.

→ **8** The `Ball` class defines a single constructor that accepts the diameter of the ball to create as a parameter, but calculates the other values at random. As a result, you can call the `Ball` constructor several times to create several balls, and each ball has a different starting position and trajectory.

→**18** The `Ball` class also has a `move` method, which can be called to move the ball. This method first adjusts the ball's trajectory if it has hit one of the edges. Then, it simply adds the `x_speed` and `y_speed` values to the `x` and `y` fields of the superclass.

Animating random balls

With the `Ball` class in hand, Listing 4-4 shows a version of the `PaintComponent` class that creates an array list with 10 randomly placed balls, and then draws each one in the `paint` method.

LISTING 4-4: THE PAINTSURFACE CLASS FOR BOUNCING BALLS

```
class PaintSurface extends JComponent
{
    public ArrayList<Ball> balls = new ArrayList<Ball>();

    public PaintSurface()
    {
        for (int i = 0; i < 10; i++)
            balls.add(new Ball(20));
    }

    public void paint(Graphics g)
    {
        Graphics2D g2 = (Graphics2D)g;
        g2.setRenderingHint(
            RenderingHints.KEY_ANTIALIASING,
            RenderingHints.VALUE_ANTIALIAS_ON);
        g2.setColor(Color.RED);
        for (Ball ball : balls)
        {
            ball.move();
            g2.fill(ball);
        }
    }
}
```

This class starts by declaring an instance variable named `balls` that holds the balls to be animated. Then, in the constructor, it uses a `for` loop to create 10 balls and add them to the collection. And in the `paint` method, which is called once every 20 milliseconds, a `for` loop is used to call each ball's `move` method, and then pass the ball to the `fill` method to paint it on the component.

Figure 4-2 shows this program in action, with ten balls bouncing around randomly on-screen. If you feel daring, try changing the `for` statement in the `PaintComponent` constructor so it creates 100 balls instead of 10. The little applet window gets pretty crowded!

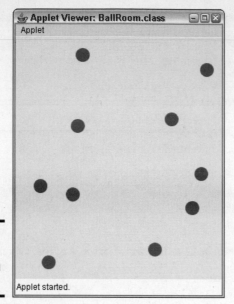

Figure 4-2:
A room full
of bouncing
balls!

Creating Collidable Balls

The balls created by the `Ball` class shown previously have one slightly unrealistic behavior: They're transparent to each other. If two balls happen to arrive at the same place at the same time, they simply pass right through each other without noticing.

If you want to create balls that bounce off each other as well as off the walls, all you have to do is make a modification to the `move` method of the `Ball` class. Just get a reference to the collection that contains all the other balls and check each ball to see if the current ball has hit any of the other balls. If so, adjust the trajectory of each ball accordingly.

Listing 4-5 shows a version of the `Ball` class in which the balls bounce off each other.

LISTING 4-5: A BALL CLASS THAT HANDLES COLLISIONS

```
class Ball extends Ellipse2D.Float
{
    public int x_speed, y_speed;
    private int d;
    private int width = BallRoom.WIDTH;
    private int height = BallRoom.HEIGHT;
    private ArrayList<Ball> balls;
```

```
public Ball(int diameter, ArrayList<Ball> balls)                        → 9
{
    super((int)(Math.random() * (BallRoom.WIDTH - 20) + 1),
          (int)(Math.random() * (BallRoom.HEIGHT - 20) + 1),
          diameter, diameter);
    this.d = diameter;
    this.x_speed = (int)(Math.random() * 5 + 1);
    this.y_speed = (int)(Math.random() * 5 + 1);
    this.balls = balls;
}

public void move()                                                      → 20
{
    // detect collision with other balls
    Rectangle2D r = new Rectangle2D.Float(
        super.x, super.y, d, d);
    for (Ball b : balls)
    {
        if (b != this &&                                                → 27
            b.intersects(r))
        {
            // on collision, the balls swap speeds                      → 30
            int tempx = x_speed;
            int tempy = y_speed;
            x_speed = b.x_speed;
            y_speed = b.y_speed;
            b.x_speed = tempx;
            b.y_speed = tempy;
            break;                                                      → 37
        }
    }
    if (super.x < 0)                                                    → 40
    {
        super.x = 0;
        x_speed = Math.abs(x_speed);
    }
    else if (super.x > width - d)
    {
        super.x = width - d;
        x_speed = -Math.abs(x_speed);
    }
    if (super.y < 0)
    {
        super.y = 0;
        y_speed = Math.abs(y_speed);
    }
    else if (super.y > height - d)
    {
        super.y = height - d;
        y_speed = -Math.abs(y_speed);
    }
    super.x += x_speed;
    super.y += y_speed;
}
}
```

The following lines describe the high points of this version of the `Ball` class:

→ **9**   The constructor accepts a reference to the array list that holds the balls. The `Ball` class needs this list so each ball can determine if it has struck any other balls. The reference to the array list is saved in an instance variable named `balls`.

→**20**   The `move` method begins by creating a rectangle from the current ball. You see how this is used in a moment. Then, it uses a `for` loop to check for a collision with each of the balls in the `balls` array list.

→**27**   For each ball, an `if` statement tests two conditions. First, it eliminates the current ball by checking `b != this`. If you allowed balls to collide with themselves, the balls wouldn't be in constant collision and wouldn't be able to move.

Next, the `if` statement checks to see if the current ball has collided with the other ball. It does that by calling `intersects`, a method defined by the `Shape` interface. This method accepts a rectangle object and returns `true` if the shape intersects any part of the specified rectangle. The rectangle object created before the `for` loop began is used as the parameter to this method. (Note that this isn't a perfect collision test; it sometimes treats near misses as collisions. But it's close enough.)

→**30**   If a collision is detected, the x and y speed values of the two balls are swapped. That means that not only do the balls bounce away from each other, but the slower ball picks up speed, and the faster ball slows down.

→**37**   A `break` statement is executed if a collision is detected. That's to prevent detecting collisions with more than one ball. Without this `break` statement, collisions that involve more than two balls usually result in pretty strange behavior. Try removing the `break` statement to see what happens. (Even with this `break` statement, the balls sometimes behave in unexpected ways. I think it's kind of fun to watch, but then again I'm pretty easily entertained.)

→**40**   The rest of this method is different from the previous version primarily because when you check for collisions with both the edges of the component and other balls, the ball always has a chance to collide with both the edge and another ball. Thus, the `if` statements that check for edge collisions force the x and y speed values to be appropriate negative or positive numbers.

Playing Games

The key to turning an animation program into a game program is adding user interaction, either via the mouse or keyboard. Either way, the technique is the same: You add event listeners to handle keyboard or mouse events.

Then, in the event listeners, you make appropriate changes to the game's sprites according to the user's actions.

For example, suppose you want to create a paddle that the user can move back and forth by dragging the mouse. To do that, just add a listener for mouse motion and save the mouse's x position in an instance variable that represents the top-left corner of the paddle. Here's code to do this as an anonymous inner class:

```
addMouseMotionListener(new MouseMotionAdapter()
{
    public void mouseMoved(MouseEvent e)
    {
        paddle_x = e.getX() - 30;
    }
} );
```

Place this code in the constructor for the component the animation is drawn on. Notice that I subtracted 30 from the x position. That's because the width of the paddle is 60, and you want the mouse position to be the center of the paddle, not the left edge.

Having stored the mouse position in an instance variable, you can use it to draw the paddle in the `paint` method. For example:

```
Shape paddle = new Rectangle2D.Float(
                      paddle_x, 360, 60, 8);
g2.setColor(Color.BLACK);
g2.fill(paddle);
```

Here, the paddle is drawn as a 60 x 8 black rectangle. When the user moves the mouse over the applet, the paddle moves along with the mouse.

To show how you can incorporate this technique into a program that plays a simple game, Listing 4-6 shows the complete code for a simple Pong-like game, where a ball bounces around and the user tries to hit it with the paddle. Each time the user hits the ball, he or she gets points based on how fast the ball is moving at the time. If the user misses the ball, 1,000 points are deducted, and the ball is replaced by a new ball with a random speed and trajectory.

To add a small amount of interest to this admittedly boring game, the player can put English on the ball by moving the mouse quickly at the moment it hits the ball. When the program detects this movement, the ball changes color and its x velocity is increased by 50%. Thus, the ball bounces off the paddle at a skewed angle and increases its speed. The player scores more points with each hit, but of course the ball is harder to hit when it's traveling faster.

Figure 4-3 shows this program in action. As you can see, I'm getting pretty good at it.

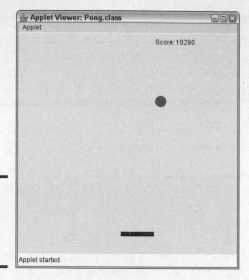

Figure 4-3:
The
NotPong
game in
action.

LISTING 4-6: THE NOTPONG PROGRAM

```java
import java.applet.*;
import java.awt.*;
import java.awt.event.*;
import javax.swing.*;
import java.awt.geom.*;

public class NotPong extends JApplet                              → 7
{
    public static final int WIDTH = 400;
    public static final int HEIGHT = 400;

    private PaintSurface canvas;

    public void init()                                            → 15
    {
        this.setSize(WIDTH, HEIGHT);
        canvas = new PaintSurface();
        this.add(canvas, BorderLayout.CENTER);
        Thread t = new AnimationThread(this);
        t.start();
    }
}

class AnimationThread extends Thread                              → 25
{
    JApplet c;

    public AnimationThread(JApplet c)
    {
        this.c = c;
    }
```

**Book IX
Chapter 4**

**Animation and
Game Programming**

```
    public void run()
    {
        while (true)
        {
            c.repaint();
            try
            {
                Thread.sleep(20);
            }
            catch (InterruptedException ex)
            {
                // swallow the exception
            }
        }
    }
}

class PaintSurface extends JComponent                       → 51
{
    int paddle_x = 0;                                       → 53
    int paddle_y = 360;

    int score = 0;                                          → 56
    float english = 1.0f;

    Ball ball;                                              → 59

    Color[] color = {Color.RED, Color.ORANGE,              → 61
                     Color.MAGENTA, Color.ORANGE,
                     Color.CYAN, Color.BLUE};
    int colorIndex;

    public PaintSurface()                                   → 66
    {
        addMouseMotionListener(new MouseMotionAdapter()
            {
                public void mouseMoved(MouseEvent e)
                {
                    if (e.getX() - 30 - paddle_x > 5)
                        english = 1.5f;
                    else if (e.getX() - 30 - paddle_x < -5)
                        english = -1.5f;
                    else
                        english = 1.0f;
                    paddle_x = e.getX() - 30;
                }
            } );
        ball = new Ball(20);
    }

    public void paint(Graphics g)                           → 84
    {
        Graphics2D g2 = (Graphics2D)g;
        g2.setRenderingHint(
            RenderingHints.KEY_ANTIALIASING,
            RenderingHints.VALUE_ANTIALIAS_ON);
```

continued

LISTING 4-6 (CONTINUED)

```
        Shape paddle = new Rectangle2D.Float(                     → 91
            paddle_x, paddle_y, 60, 8);

        g2.setColor(color[colorIndex % 6]);                       → 94

        if (ball.intersects(paddle_x, paddle_y, 60, 8)            → 96
            && ball.y_speed > 0)
        {
            ball.y_speed = -ball.y_speed;
            ball.x_speed = (int)(ball.x_speed * english);
            if (english != 1.0f)
                colorIndex++;
            score += Math.abs(ball.x_speed * 10);
        }

        if (ball.getY() + ball.getHeight()                        → 106
            >= NotPong.HEIGHT)
        {
            ball = new Ball(20);
            score -= 1000;
            colorIndex = 0;
        }
        ball.move();                                              → 113
        g2.fill(ball);

        g2.setColor(Color.BLACK);                                 → 116
        g2.fill(paddle);

        g2.drawString("Score: " + score, 250, 20);                → 119
    }
}

class Ball extends Ellipse2D.Float                                → 123
{
    public int x_speed, y_speed;
    private int d;
    private int width = NotPong.WIDTH;
    private int height = NotPong.HEIGHT;

    public Ball(int diameter)
    {
        super((int)(Math.random() * (NotPong.WIDTH - 20) + 1),
            0, diameter, diameter);
        this.d = diameter;
        this.x_speed = (int)(Math.random() * 5 + 5);
        this.y_speed = (int)(Math.random() * 5 + 5);
    }

    public void move()
    {
        if (super.x < 0 || super.x > width - d)
            x_speed = -x_speed;
        if (super.y < 0 || super.y > height - d)
```

```
        y_speed = -y_speed;
    super.x += x_speed;
    super.y += y_speed;
    }
}
```

The following paragraphs explain the gory details of how this program works:

→ **7** Like the other examples in this chapter, the `NotPong` class extends `JApplet`. However, you can get the program to run as a stand-alone Swing application with just a few minor changes.

→**15** The `init` method is called when the applet is started. It sets the size of the applet, creates a new `PaintSurface` object and adds it to the applet, and then creates and starts the thread that controls the animation.

→**25** The `AnimationThread` class in this program is the same as in the other programs in this chapter. In the `run` method, a `while` loop calls the `repaint` method to force the animation to update itself, and then sleeps for 20 milliseconds.

→**51** The `PaintSurface` class extends `JComponent`. It provides the surface on which the animations are drawn.

→**53** These instance variables define the initial position of the paddle.

→**56** These instance variables keep track of the score and the English applied to the ball. The English is initially set to 1.0, but as you see later it is changed to –1.5 or 1.5 if the user moves the paddle quickly as the ball is hit.

→**59** This instance variable represents the ball.

→**61** An array of `Color` objects and an index variable are used so the ball can be drawn with several different colors. Each time the user hits the ball with English applied, the index variable is incremented so the ball is drawn with a different color.

→**66** The constructor for the `PaintSurface` class adds a mouse motion listener that extends the `MouseMotionAdapter` class. In this anonymous class, the `mouseMoved` method simply updates the paddle's x position. After the listener is added, a new ball object is created.

→**84** The `paint` method is called each time the component is repainted, which happens approximately every 20 milliseconds because of the `repaint` method called by the loop in the thread's `run` method. This method begins by casting the graphics context object to `Graphics2D` and enabling antialiasing to eliminate flicker.

→**91** This statement creates the `Shape` object that represents the paddle.

→ **94** This statement sets the color used to draw the ball. Note that the remainder division operator is used to provide an index value that's always between 0 and 6.

→ **96** This `if` statement determines if the ball has struck the paddle. It does this by calling the `intersects` method of the ball (the `Ball` class inherits this method from its base class `Rectangle2D.Float`). (The second part of the `if` condition makes sure the ball is traveling downward when it hits. Thus, a hit isn't registered if the ball is traveling up. This happens on occasion, especially when the ball is moving fast.)

If the ball has hit the paddle, the y speed is reversed (to make the ball travel up instead of down), and the x speed is multiplied by the English amount. Then, if the English amount is other than 1.0, the color index variable is incremented. And finally, the player's score is increased by 10 times the ball's x speed. Thus, the user scores more if he or she hits a fast-moving ball.

→**106** This `if` statement checks to see if the ball has hit the south wall. If so, a new ball is created, the color index is reset to zero, and 1,000 points are deducted from the score.

→**113** These statements move the ball and draw it in its new position.

→**116** These statements draw the paddle after setting the color to black.

→**119** This statement draws the score near the top right of the playing area.

→**123** This class defines the ball. As it turns out, this class is nearly identical to the `Ball` class shown earlier in this chapter, in the section "Creating a Ball class." For an explanation of how it works, refer to that section.

Index

Symbols and Numerics

& (ampersand) for and operators, 154–155

* (asterisk)
in compound assignment operator (*=), 123, 124
for JavaDoc comments (/** and */), 347
as multiplication operator, 114, 118
as regular expression quantifier, 484
as SQL wildcard, 708
for traditional comments (/* and */), 75

@ (at sign) in doc tags, 348

\ (backslash)
in character classes, 479
in escape sequences, 95, 356, 485
escaping, 485
string problem with, 488

{ } (braces)
for blocks, 72–73
for body of class, 66
for body of method, 67
for do-while loops, 169
with if statements, 145

^ (caret)
for negation in regular expressions, 483
for xor operator (^), 156–157

: (colon) in IP addresses, 454

$ (dollar sign), avoiding in names, 74

. (dot)
in names, 74
in regular expressions, 479

= (equals sign)
as assignment operator, 78, 122–123
in compound assignment operators, 123–124, 356
with JSP expressions, 634
in relational operators, 142, 159–160

! (exclamation mark)
with JSP expressions, 634
in nonequality relational operator (!=), 142
as not operator, 153–154

> (greater-than sign)
for redirecting standard output, 106
in relational operators, 142

(hash sign) in class diagrams, 247

< (less-than sign) in relational operators, 142

- (minus sign)
in class diagrams, 247
in compound assignment operator (-=), 123
as decrement operator (−), 114, 118, 120–121
as subtraction operator, 114, 118

( ) (parentheses)
enclosing boolean expressions, 144
enclosing expression with not operator, 154
in regular expressions, 485–487

% (percent sign)
in compound assignment operator (%=), 123
with JSP elements, 634
as remainder operator, 114, 115, 116–117, 118
as SQL wildcard, 710

. (period). *See* . (dot)

+ (plus sign)
as addition operator, 114, 118
in class diagrams, 247
in compound assignment operator (+=), 123, 124, 356
as concatenation operator, 99, 356
as increment operator (++), 114, 118, 120–121
as regular expression quantifier, 484

? (question mark)
for conditional operator (?), 159
as regular expression quantifier, 484–485

; (semicolon)
ending SQL script statements, 705
ending statements, 71
ending variable declarations, 84

/ (slash)
in compound assignment operator (/=), 123
as division operator, 114, 116, 118
for end-of-line comments (//), 74
for JavaDoc comments (/** and */), 347
for traditional comments (/* and */), 75
three-layered design approach, 244–245

| (vertical bar)
for or operators (| and ||), 155–156, 171
in regular expressions, 487

F

BUSINESS, CAREERS & PERSONA[...]

0-7645-5307-0

0-7645-5331-3 *†

- Accou[...]ing For Dummies †
  0-7645-5314-3
- Business Plans Kit For Dummies †
  0-7645-5365-8
- Cover Letters For Dummies
  0-7645-5224-4
- Frugal Living For Dummies
  0-7645-5403-4
- Leadership For Dummies
  0-7645-5176-0
- Managing For Dummies
  0-7645-1771-6

- Marketing For Dummies
  0-7645-5600-2
- Personal Finance For Dummies *
  0-7645-2590-5
- Project Management For Dummies
  0-7645-5283-X
- Resumes For Dummies †
  0-7645-5471-9
- Selling For Dummies
  0-7645-5363-1
- Small Business Kit For Dummies *†
  0-7645-5093-4

HOME & BUSINESS COMPUTER BASICS

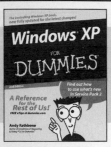

0-7645-4074-2

0-7645-3758-X

Also available:

- ACT! 6 For Dummies
  0-7645-2645-6
- iLife '04 All-in-One Desk Reference
  For Dummies
  0-7645-7347-0
- iPAQ For Dummies
  0-7645-6769-1
- Mac OS X Panther Timesaving
  Techniques For Dummies
  0-7645-5812-9
- Macs For Dummies
  0-7645-5656-8

- Microsoft Money 2004 For Dummies
  0-7645-4195-1
- Office 2003 All-in-One Desk Reference
  For Dummies
  0-7645-3883-7
- Outlook 2003 For Dummies
  0-7645-3759-8
- PCs For Dummies
  0-7645-4074-2
- TiVo For Dummies
  0-7645-6923-6
- Upgrading and Fixing PCs For Dummies
  0-7645-1665-5
- Windows XP Timesaving Techniques
  For Dummies
  0-7645-3748-2

FOOD, HOME, GARDEN, HOBBIES, MUSIC & PETS

0-7645-5295-3

0-7645-5232-5

Also available:

- Bass Guitar For Dummies
  0-7645-2487-9
- Diabetes Cookbook For Dummies
  0-7645-5230-9
- Gardening For Dummies *
  0-7645-5130-2
- Guitar For Dummies
  0-7645-5106-X
- Holiday Decorating For Dummies
  0-7645-2570-0
- Home Improvement All-in-One
  For Dummies
  0-7645-5680-0

- Knitting For Dummies
  0-7645-5395-X
- Piano For Dummies
  0-7645-5105-1
- Puppies For Dummies
  0-7645-5255-4
- Scrapbooking For Dummies
  0-7645-7208-3
- Senior Dogs For Dummies
  0-7645-5818-8
- Singing For Dummies
  0-7645-2475-5
- 30-Minute Meals For Dummies
  0-7645-2589-1

INTERNET & DIGITAL MEDIA

0-7645-1664-7

0-7645-6924-4

Also available:

- 2005 Online Shopping Directory
  For Dummies
  0-7645-7495-7
- CD & DVD Recording For Dummies
  0-7645-5956-7
- eBay For Dummies
  0-7645-5654-1
- Fighting Spam For Dummies
  0-7645-5965-6
- Genealogy Online For Dummies
  0-7645-5964-8
- Google For Dummies
  0-7645-4420-9

- Home Recording For Musicians
  For Dummies
  0-7645-1634-5
- The Internet For Dummies
  0-7645-4173-0
- iPod & iTunes For Dummies
  0-7645-7772-7
- Preventing Identity Theft For Dummies
  0-7645-7336-5
- Pro Tools All-in-One Desk Reference
  For Dummies
  0-7645-5714-9
- Roxio Easy Media Creator For Dummies
  0-7645-7131-1

* Separate Canadian edition also available

† Separate U.K. edition also available

SPORTS, FITNESS, PARENTING,

0-7645-5146-9

0-7645-5418-2

0-7645-5488-3
- Basketball For Dummies
0-7645-5248-1
- The Bible For Dummies
0-7645-5296-1
- Buddhism For Dummies
0-7645-5359-3
- Catholicism For Dummies
0-7645-5391-7
- Hockey For Dummies
0-7645-5228-7

...Jaism For Dummies
...645-5299-6
...rtial Arts For Dummies
0-7645-5358-5
- Pilates For Dummies
0-7645-5397-6
- Religion For Dummies
0-7645-5264-3
- Teaching Kids to Read For Dummies
0-7645-4043-2
- Weight Training For Dummies
0-7645-5168-X
- Yoga For Dummies
0-7645-5117-5

TRAVEL

0-7645-5438-7

0-7645-5453-0

Also available:
- Alaska For Dummies
0-7645-1761-9
- Arizona For Dummies
0-7645-6938-4
- Cancún and the Yucatán For Dummies
0-7645-2437-2
- Cruise Vacations For Dummies
0-7645-6941-4
- Europe For Dummies
0-7645-5456-5
- Ireland For Dummies
0-7645-5455-7

- Las Vegas For Dummies
0-7645-5448-4
- London For Dummies
0-7645-4277-X
- New York City For Dummies
0-7645-6945-7
- Paris For Dummies
0-7645-5494-8
- RV Vacations For Dummies
0-7645-5443-3
- Walt Disney World & Orlando For Dummies
0-7645-6943-0

GRAPHICS, DESIGN & WEB DEVELOPMENT

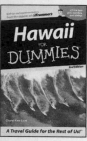

0-7645-4345-8

0-7645-5589-8

Also available:
- Adobe Acrobat 6 PDF For Dummies
0-7645-3760-1
- Building a Web Site For Dummies
0-7645-7144-3
- Dreamweaver MX 2004 For Dummies
0-7645-4342-3
- FrontPage 2003 For Dummies
0-7645-3882-9
- HTML 4 For Dummies
0-7645-1995-6
- Illustrator CS For Dummies
0-7645-4084-X

- Macromedia Flash MX 2004 For Dummies
0-7645-4358-X
- Photoshop 7 All-in-One Desk
Reference For Dummies
0-7645-1667-1
- Photoshop CS Timesaving Techniques
For Dummies
0-7645-6782-9
- PHP 5 For Dummies
0-7645-4166-8
- PowerPoint 2003 For Dummies
0-7645-3908-6
- QuarkXPress 6 For Dummies
0-7645-2593-X

NETWORKING, SECURITY, PROGRAMMING & DATABASES

0-7645-6852-3

0-7645-5784-X

Also available:
- A+ Certification For Dummies
0-7645-4187-0
- Access 2003 All-in-One Desk
Reference For Dummies
0-7645-3988-4
- Beginning Programming For Dummies
0-7645-4997-9
- C For Dummies
0-7645-7068-4
- Firewalls For Dummies
0-7645-4048-3
- Home Networking For Dummies
0-7645-42796

- Network Security For Dummies
0-7645-1679-5
- Networking For Dummies
0-7645-1677-9
- TCP/IP For Dummies
0-7645-1760-0
- VBA For Dummies
0-7645-3989-2
- Wireless All In-One Desk Reference
For Dummies
0-7645-7496-5
- Wireless Home Networking For Dummies
0-7645-3910-8